THE FOSSIL BOOK

A Record of Prehistoric Life

Diplodocus, *a plant-eating dinosaur 87 feet (26.5 m) long, has a slender neck and tail. This restoration of the reptile as it looked during life is based on skeletons found in northeastern Utah*

THE
FOSSIL BOOK
A Record of Prehistoric Life

CARROLL LANE FENTON
and MILDRED ADAMS FENTON

Revised and expanded by
Patricia Vickers Rich, Thomas Hewitt Rich,
and Mildred Adams Fenton

DOUBLEDAY
NEW YORK LONDON TORONTO SYDNEY AUCKLAND

Books by
CARROLL LANE FENTON *and* MILDRED ADAMS FENTON

THE FOSSIL BOOK
GIANTS OF GEOLOGY
THE ROCK BOOK
MOUNTAINS
ROCKS AND THEIR STORIES
THE LAND WE LIVE ON
OUR CHANGING WEATHER

Books by
CARROLL LANE FENTON

OUR AMAZING EARTH
OUR LIVING WORLD

PUBLISHED BY DOUBLEDAY
a division of Bantam Doubleday Dell Publishing Group, Inc.
666 Fifth Avenue, New York, New York 10103

DOUBLEDAY and the portrayal of an anchor with a dolphin are trademarks
of Doubleday, a division of Bantam Doubleday Dell Publishing Group, Inc.

Library of Congress Cataloging-in-Publication Data

Fenton, Carroll Lane, 1900–
    The fossil book.
    Includes index.
    1. Paleontology.   I. Fenton, Mildred Adams, 1899–
II. Rich, Patricia V.   III. Title.
QE711.F38   1987   560   86-16245

2   4   6   8   9   7   5   3
            BVG

Acknowledgments

This book surveys the realm of fossils from the earliest traces of Precambrian life to beasts and birds that lived only a few centuries ago. Only a brief mention of man is made. This is not because his story is unimportant, but because such a vast literature is available on our species that we have chosen to present a brief outline and a guide to where to find much more.

A survey as broad-ranging as this goes far beyond the firsthand knowledge of authors whose research has been limited to algae, early invertebrates, birds, and mammals. We have, therefore, drawn material from a wide array of technical articles and monographs as well as from textbooks and reference works, many of which are mentioned in Chapter XXXVII. We were also able to use a manuscript written by R. A. Carroll, which is an update of A. S. Romer's *Vertebrate Paleontology*. This was extremely valuable for the fish and early-tetrapod chapters. We are also greatly indebted, in the second edition, to a number of paleontologists who reviewed chapters in their areas of specialty: N. Archbold (brachiopods), R. Baird (birds), D. Blake (bryozoans), F. M. Carpenter (insects), H. V. Daly (insects), T. A. Darragh (bivalves), J. W. Durham and P. Jell (echinoderms), T. F. Flannery (mammals), D. Holloway (trilobites), S. R. A. Kelly (bivalves), J. Long (fishes), J. R. Macdonald (several areas), C. Mallett (foraminifera), J. McEwen-Mason (plants), R. E. Molnar (amphibians and reptiles), J. Pickett (sponges), P. A. Raven (plants), A. Ritchie (fishes), I. Stewart (graptolites), C. Tassell (gastropods, molluscs), T. Thulborn (reptiles), G. F. van Tets (birds), L. Werdelin (mammals), B. Wagstaff (plants), A. Warren (amphibians), J. Warren (Precambrian organisms), and M. Whitelaw (plants).

In the first edition of this book, E. Dorf (plants), K. E. Caster (all invertebrates), B. Schaeffer (fishes), E. H. Colbert (amphibians and reptiles), and G. L. Jepsen (birds and mammals) read and criticized manuscript. Mrs. Rachel Nichols, who later joined the staff of the *Bibliography of Fossil Vertebrates*, headed by C. L. Camp, guided C. L. and M. A. Fenton to many important books and papers in the Osborn Library of the American Museum of Natural History.

Most of the photographs of invertebrate fossils—and some vertebrates—

were made at the National Museum of Natural History (Washington, D.C.), where we were helped by R. S. Bassler, G. A. Cooper, C. L. Gazin, D. Dunkle, J. B. Reeside, and R. W. Brown. For the first edition, E. Yochelson provided a beautiful Permian snail with coloration preserved, and A. R. Palmar provided photographs and information about the remarkably preserved insects of the Mojave Desert. Specimens for photography were provided by S. Welles, R. A. Stirton, and R. W. Chaney, at the University of California (Berkeley), and E. Dorf and B. F. Howell, at Princeton University. H. A. Andrews (Washington University) provided negatives of sections through Pennsylvanian plants. F. M. Carpenter (Harvard University) lent negatives showing fossil insects and sent data on specimens. Color photographs of restorations (dioramas) in the Exhibit Museum of the University of Michigan were furnished by I. G. Reimann, the museum's director at the time of the first-edition publication.

For the second edition, many people have generously provided 35-mm. color slides or black-and-white prints of specimens or localities upon which they are working: D. Baird (Princeton University), F. M. Carpenter (Harvard University), M. Chow (Institute of Vertebrate Paleontology and Paleoanthropology, Beijing) M. Dawson (Carnegie Museum), Y. Hasagawa and K. Ono (National Science Museum of Japan), Q. B. Hendey (South African Museum), J. A. Jensen (Brigham Young University), Z. Kielan-Jaworowska (Polska Akademia Nauk, Zaklad Paleobiologii), M. Leakey (National Museum of Kenya), M. C. McKenna (American Museum of Natural History), C. Mourer (Université Claude Bernard, Lyon), G. M. Philip (University of Sydney), N. S. Pledge (South Australian Museum), D. E. Savage (University of California, Berkeley), B. Shelton (Cranbourne, Victoria), B. Sigé (University of Montpellier), I. Stewart and J. A. Warren (Monash University), and G. Viohl (Jura-Museum, Eichstätt). F. Coffa (Museum of Victoria) and S. Morton (Monash University) both provided excellent new photographic material for the second edition. B. Wilson, D. Anderson, and E. McClellan were all extremely helpful in providing access to Museum of Victoria specimens and archival material.

For the second edition, many others provided us with literature and illustrations that were important in developing our revisions, including especially R. A. Carroll, M. Chiba, E. H. Colbert, and E. M. Thompson.

Drawings of actual fossils were made from specimens, photographs, and published figures. Most of the drawings in both editions are original, but some are borrowed. The latter include figures of brachiopods from Volume VIII of *The Paleontology of New York,* and of echinoids from *Mesozoic and Cenozoic Echinodermata of the United States,* by W. B. Clark and M. W. Twitchell, published as Monograph 54 of the United States Geological Survey.

Restorations of invertebrates are based chiefly on the work of C. L. and M. A. Fenton. Those of vertebrates in the first edition embody the work of

Acknowledgments

Knight, Horsfall, Price, Germann, and other artists, and such paleontologists as Osborn, Matthew, Scott, Case, Williston, Merriam, Stock, Simpson, and Romer. Restorations of plants reveal our debt to Seward, Wieland, Goldring, and other authorities.

New charts in the second edition have been prepared mainly by D. Gelt (Monash University), and restorations and drawings have been made by P. Trusler (Blackburn, Victoria) and F. Knight (Canberra, A.C.T.). For the use of F. Knight's reconstructions from *Kadimakara: Extinct Vertebrates of Australia* we thank D. Stone and Pioneer Design Studio (Lilydale, Victoria) and the Museum of Victoria.

Much technical assistance in the form of typing, translation, and cross-checking of names and references has been provided by M. Leicester, P. Hermansen, P. Komarower, S. Sabatier, R. Sheehan, P. Coates, T. McConnell, and M. Whitelaw (all of Monash University). An Osborne microcomputer made production of manuscript decidedly quicker and easier.

The person to whom we all owe the greatest debt, however, is Professor Minchen Chow (Institute of Vertebrate Paleontology and Paleoanthropology, Beijing), who introduced Mildred Fenton to Tom and Pat Rich. That meeting allowed the idea of the second edition of *The Fossil Book* to blossom. Monash University and the Museum of Victoria also provided support throughout this project, which we greatly appreciate. And to Tom and Pat's young daughter, Leaellyn, we owe thanks for her patience throughout the three years required for the revision.

ABOUT ILLUSTRATIONS AND THEIR CAPTIONS

The illustrations in this book portray the progress of life upon our planet. They also enable readers to recognize and understand fossils they find or see in museums or in the field. For both purposes, the caption above or below each picture is as important as the drawing or photograph itself.

Captions like those in Chapter I require little comment. They tell what each fossil shows and may or may not give its age and the region in which it was found. Most of them mention size. Geologic and geographic data are included when the fossils are characteristic of certain formations or regions.

Most of the remaining captions are more concerned with detail and include the following information:

1. The name of the genus or species to which the specimen belongs.
2. Geologic age, such as Silurian or Late Ordovician. This is followed (in parentheses) by the name of the series, group, or formation in which the particular species is found, when any information is of importance. Thus, *Caryocrinites ornatus* is of Silurian age and is found in rocks of the Niagaran Group.
3. Geographic range. Some fossils have been found at only one place, such as Burgess Pass, British Columbia, or Florissant, in Colorado. Others are found at many places in extensive regions: New York, the Atlantic Coastal Plain, and so on. These regions are mentioned in captions unless precise localities are important.
4. Size. This is given when it seems helpful but omitted when size varies widely.

    Dimensions are given in both feet and inches and meters, centimeters, and millimeters. (A millimeter is about one twenty-fifth of an inch.) Some illustrations are merely marked "enlarged," but for others the scale of enlargement is given. A drawing marked × 4, for example, has dimensions four times those of the actual specimen.

Paleontologists may wonder why *Early, Middle,* and *Late* are used to subdivide periods, rather than *Lower, Middle,* and *Upper.* The reason is that we are more concerned with the history of life than with stratigraphy. In other words, we tell when a given organism dwelt upon earth, not where its remains are found in a sequence of beds of formations. Thus, a certain fossil may be found in *Lower* Devonian rocks, but it lived during *Early* Devonian times and is of *Early* Devonian age.

Contents

Contents

Color Plates

CHAPTER I

Tales Told by the Dead

As age goes in earth history, hills west of Rockford, Iowa, are young. Barely twelve thousand years have passed since the prairie of which they are part was laid bare by the melting of glacial ice. The hills themselves took shape still later under the wear of rain forming rills that ran to the nearby Shellrock River.

Though both rounded heights and depressions are young, the rocks beneath them are ancient. They began as plastic or limy mud that settled in a shallow sea some 270 million years ago. For a time, the seafloor was almost barren; later it teemed with seaweeds, corals, and other organisms. Diminutive clams plowed through the mud; snails crept over it; sea lilies waved to and fro above it. There were hordes of brachiopods, or lampshells, some lying free on the bottom, though others fastened themselves to it or to other shells. Distant relatives of the *Nautilus* swam or crawled about, sea urchins devoured scumlike plants, marine carrion, and animals called bryozoans built colonies that looked like corals. Fish swam lazily above them, some breathing with lungs instead of gills.

These creatures give a glimpse into the long story of life on our planet. That story has been one of change—change that led from jellylike blobs to great oaks and redwoods; from very simple creatures to snails, elephants, and dinosaurs. Such change produced the million or so species that are living today, as well as many more millions that are yet to be discovered or are extinct. Some of those extinct types vanished utterly, leaving only gaps —real missing links—as "evidence" of their existence. Others, like inhabitants of the ancient Iowa sea, died but became fossils. They enable us partly to reconstruct the story of life during past ages.

WHAT FOSSILS ARE

Here we pause for a definition. The word "fossil" means something dug up. But, in everyday language, fossils are generally prehistoric animals and plants that have been petrified, or "turned into stone." Cartoons and comic

1

strips have clothed some of them in flesh, producing herbivorous dinosaurs that served as steeds for Stone Age men who pursued hairy mammoths or fled from *Tyrannosaurus rex.*

These comic strips, though entertaining, have little connection with fact. At least 40 million years divided the "tyrant" dinosaur from the great long-necked herbivores, and the last dinosaur died 60 million years before mammoths ranged from Europe to South America, or before man learned to wield stone weapons. These varied creatures associate only when their bones are displayed in museums of natural history. Even there they generally stand in widely separated halls.

The concept of fossils as petrified remains of prehistoric organisms also is inadequate. It is true that countless fossils have been "turned into stone," but others are footprints, charred wood, tar-soaked bones, and frozen or dried flesh. These things also vary greatly in age, from some 3,500 million years for very ancient fossils to a few centuries for the latest moas (giant birds) of New Zealand. Though all are literally *prehistoric,* that term acquires much greater meaning than it had when prehistory was restricted to the half million years or so before man learned to write.

The everyday concept of fossils, therefore, fails; it lumps too much together, ignores too much, and tells far too little. We replace it with a definition that says that *fossils are remains or traces of organisms that lived during past geologic times and were buried in rocks that accumulated in the earth's outer portion, or crust.*

This covers the ground if we bear in mind two amplifications: First, the term "past geologic times" embraces all earth history from the earliest ages recorded in rocks to the epoch that immediately followed the last Ice Age—a

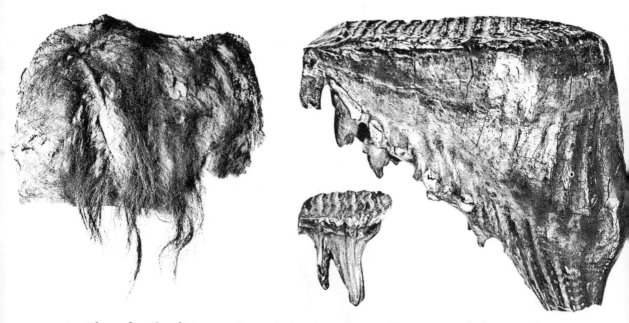

These fossils of **Mammuthus** primigenius, *the woolly mammoth, have undergone little change. At the right are adult and milk molars. At the left is some skin, with wool and hair. The skin was preserved in ground ice of Siberia*

range approaching 4,000 million years. Second, the word *rock* need not and often does not mean "stone." To the geologist, a rock can be any deposit that makes up part of the earth's outer portion, its so-called crust. In this sense, gravel beds and clay are rocks; so are the ground ice, or permafrost, of Siberia and Alaska, natural paraffin beds of Poland, and asphalt that oozes to the surface in southern California. Remains found in such deposits are fossils, quite as truly as any embedded in hard stone.

HOW FOSSILS HAVE BEEN PRESERVED

We have said that fossils range from footprints to frozen bodies; from petrified bones and shells to wood and desiccated skin. Suppose we now review the methods of preservation.

Freezing. The ideal fossil is one that has been kept in cold storage since death, undergoing a minimum of change. Such ideal remains are rare, however, and they never are very old. Among animals, they are restricted to hairy elephants and rhinoceroses, of the last great Ice Age that fell into pits or crevasses in ground ice and remained there for thousands of years. Such remains preserve bone, muscles, skin, and hair, as well as internal organs. Dried blood fills arteries and veins; partly digested food still lies in the stomach. The famous frozen mammoths of Siberia and Alaska are examples of such preservation. One from Alaska has been displayed, still safely frozen, in an American museum.

Drying, or Desiccation. Next in quality to frozen fossils are those that have been thoroughly dried. Such remains of camels, ground sloths, moas, marsupial wolves and a few other animals have been found in caves of the semiarid southwestern United States, South America, New Zealand, and Australia. Cave-dwelling sloths also are represented by their dried dung. Sloths of one Patagonian cavern were evidently penned in by ancient Indians, who apparently kept the animals until they were needed for food and then killed them.

Wax and Asphalt. Natural paraffin is almost as good a preservative as ice. In 1907 the head, forelegs, and a large part of the skin of a woolly rhinoceros were dug from a paraffin mine in eastern Poland. Asphalt, however, preserves only hard parts, such as bones, teeth, and the shells of insects. Vast numbers of these have been found in asphalt deposits of California, especially those now enclosed by Hancock Park, in Los Angeles. There an exhibit enables visitors to walk into a pit and examine fossil bones as they still lie in the tar. Another such tar seep has preserved countless Pleistocene vertebrates near Talara, in Peru.

Simple Burial. Plant remains and limy shells often lie for long periods without much change. Postglacial peat, for example, contains cones, stems, and pollen grains that accumulated in bogs. Buried forests of Norfolk, En-

External molds of shells in porous dolomite

Internal molds of clamshells in shale

The snail shell is crumbling, leaving only the internal mold

The coprolite is fossilized excrement

Underside of a sandstone slab showing internal molds of shells where they were attached to the sea bottom

Impression of a leaf in coarse sandstone

Impression of a fern-like leaf in a shale nodule, Mazon Creek, Illinois

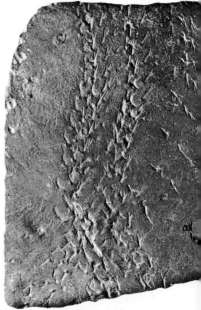

Tracks left by unknown xiphosurans, or horseshoe crabs

Fossils that are impressions or traces

gland, are famous for their logs, stumps, and masses of fern roots. Logs buried in German lignite about 40 million years old are discolored and slightly decayed, but the texture and grain of their wood show little alteration. Sand dollars, sea urchins, and mollusc shells whose ages range from a few thousand to at least 75 million years generally have lost their colors, but their hard, limy substance has suffered little change.

Carbonization. This is a process of incomplete decay which gets rid of volatile substances but leaves carbon behind. "Charred" plant remains of peat bogs reveal an early stage of carbonization; a more advanced one appears in the crumbly woods of many lignite deposits. At its extreme, carbonization reduces plants and animals to shiny black films that are finer than tissue paper. This process can preserve the shapes of leaves, as well as the fleshy parts of ancient aquatic reptiles, and internal organs of some marine invertebrates and fish.

Petrification. This process, which results in stony fossils, takes place in two, related ways. The simpler, termed *permineralization,* takes place when fat and other organic substances decay while water containing dissolved mineral matter soaks into every cavity and pore of hard—especially limy—structures. There the minerals are deposited, producing stony fossils that still contain a good deal of their original solid material. Most marine fossils were preserved in this way, as were the bones and teeth of vertebrates.

Replacement. This takes place when water dissolves original hard parts and replaces them with mineral matter. It may happen very slowly—so slowly that the new mineral matter duplicates microscopic structures of shell, coral, bone, or wood. Replacement also may take place with such speed that no trace of original structure remains. The difference may be seen by contrasting massively agatized and structureless wood with plant remains from so-called coal balls, which retain the detail of every microscopic cell. Many replaced bones and shells show equal detail, but others have lost all trace of their original structure.

Such replacement is primary; it takes place when organic remains first become petrified. Secondary replacement, on the other hand, destroys microscopic structure after it was preserved. This often happens when limy fossils are dissolved and replaced by such minerals as silica. On the other hand, many petrifactions formed of silica in the first place are among our best-preserved fossils.

Chemical Fossils. These "fossils" are organically derived compounds formed by living organisms that occur in some rocks. There are usually no visible traces of actual organisms. An example would be the carbon 12 enrichment encountered in sequences such as the Onverwacht Group of Precambrian age discussed in Chapter V.

Molds and Casts. Shells, stumps, and other remains often lie in sediment until it becomes firm. Later the dead objects decay or dissolve, leaving a cavity known as a natural mold. This may be collected and studied as it is,

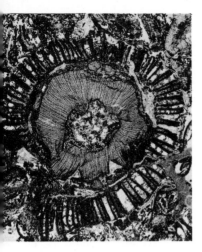

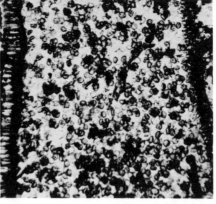

Spores in the cone of *Lepidocarpon,* a lycopod

Mycelia of a fungus that
grew in a fern stem, × 210

Cells in the stem of *Lyginopteris,*
a seed fern, enlarged

*Examples of the remarkably preserved plants found in coal balls. (Photographs by
Dr. Henry Andrews)*

or it may be filled with plaster of paris, wax, or some other compound. This
filling, which duplicates the shape and surface of the fossil, is termed a cast,
or squeeze.

Casts and internal molds also are produced by nature. The former develop
when grains of sand, clay, or finer materials fill natural molds, but internal
molds consist of material that fills such things as empty shells. Internal
molds (sometimes miscalled casts) of mussel and snail shells are common.
Natural molds of shells and trees are plentiful too, especially in beds of
sandstone. The finest of all molds, however, are fossil insects in northern
European amber. The amber began as resin that oozed from ancient trees,
often trapping insects. Since that time, the resin has hardened, and the insects have dried to almost nothing. In spite of this, their forms remain as
cavities showing heads, antennae, bodies, and legs. With a microscope, one
may examine scales on the wings or count bristles on the bodies of these
almost nonexistent creatures.

Another interesting, but rare, external mold is one of a rhinoceros, probably *Diceratherium,* in a basalt flow of the Columbia River Basalts near Blue
Lake, Washington. Evidently, sometime in the Late Oligocene or Early Miocene the rhinoceros died, and its bloated body floated in a shallow lake.
Lava flowed into the lake, and pillow lavas were formed. These lavas were
plastic enough to pack around the body and were cooled by the water so
they became rigid quickly. Thus, an impression of the animal's outsides was
formed, and some of its bones remained inside the mold after basalt solidified and the fleshy parts were wasted away.

Imprints.　These are little more than external molds of very thin objects,
such as leaves. They are found in rocks such as sandstone, shale, and layers
of tuff formed by volcanic ash. Vast numbers of plant imprints lie in strata of

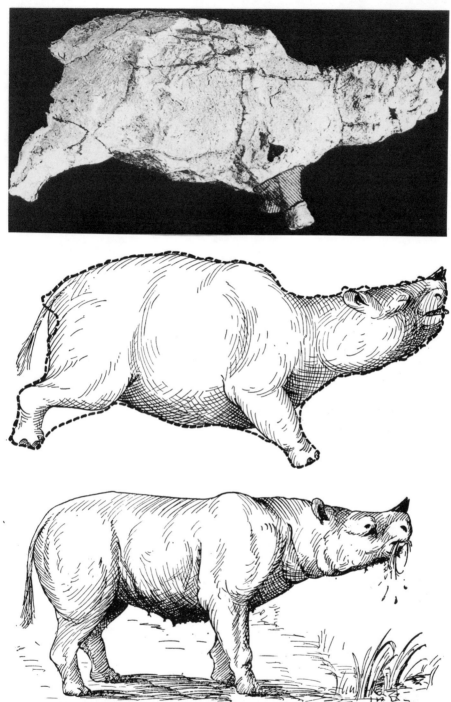

External mold of a rhinoceros, probably Diceratherium, *from a Late Oligocene or Early Miocene basalt flow in the Columbia River Basalts in Washington State. The top illustration is a cast made by applying plaster-soaked burlap (hessian) strips to the sides of a hollow mold and then removing them in sections. The middle illustration shows what the bloated carcass looked like before it was overcome by basalt. The bottom illustration shows the living* Diceratherium. *The specimen was first discovered because several bones of the rhinoceros were preserved inside the cavity. Only later was it realized that the cavity itself was an impression of the rhino's outsides. The total length of the head and body is about 94 inches (240 cm.). (Illustration provided by D. E. Savage, Department of Paleontology, University of California, Berkeley)*

A carbonized marine animal, showing internal organs. Middle Cambrian, British Columbia

This scallop shell still contains much of its original material

Carbonized leaves and bark in Pennsylvanian shale. Illinois

Permineralized corals that preserve both shape and structure

Wood completely replaced by silica still shows its original grain. Yuma County, Arizona

These silicified fossils preserve the shapes of corals but not their detailed structure

Details of grain, cell structure, and injury are preserved in this silicified wood from Lincoln County, Idaho

This coral from the "silex" beds at Tampa, Florida, is a hollow chalcedony geode. Only the shape of the coral remains

Fossils preserved in various ways

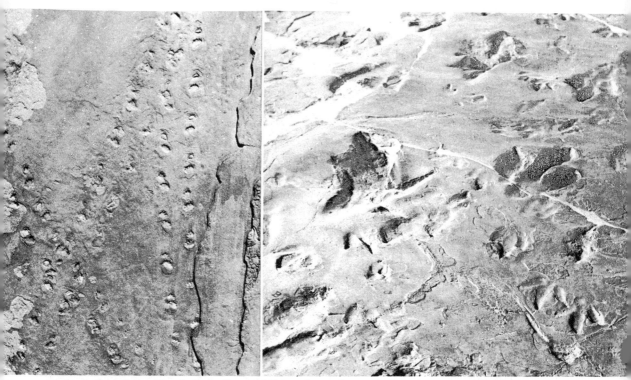

At the left are tracks of a small amphibian from the Permian Coconino Sandstone, of the Grand Canyon, Arizona. Footprints at the right were made by Triassic dinosaurs in what is now New Jersey

the Carboniferous (the age of coal), especially in Illinois. There the finest are enclosed in concretions, which must be split in order to reveal their fossils.

Tracks, Trails, and Burrows. These, even more than casts and molds, explain why we say that fossils are either remains or traces of ancient organisms. Some of the most famous fossil tracks are those left by dinosaurs that walked upon moist mudbanks or plastic swamp bottoms that later solidified. Other reptile tracks have also been found, as well as footprints of amphibians, birds, elephants, ground sloths, and even Stone Age people. A great variety of trails also were left by creeping and crawling invertebrates. Others burrowed in sand, mud, or soil, or bored into hard organisms. Many sponges, sea anemones, snails, and crabs are known from their burrows or borings, as well as from petrified remains. Structures called *Cruziana* seem to be filled pits that once may have held eggs laid by the trilobite *Olenellus;* and *Daemonelix,* the "devil's corkscrew," apparently was the home of a land-dwelling beaver whose bones are named *Steneofiber.* The animal dug a spiral hole 6 to 8 feet deep, followed by a tunnel that sloped upward, growing larger as it went. Freshets sometimes filled these odd burrows with sand, which now forms spectacular fossils in buttes and banks of western Nebraska.

Castings and Coprolites. Castings are remnants of indigestible meals swallowed by burrowing invertebrates. Lugworms, for example, swallow sand in order to eat small organisms. Once this food has been extracted, the sediment is regurgitated in the form of contorted castings. Ancient worms doubtless had similar habits, and fossil castings are common in some marine formations. Other castings may have been made by burrowing sea cucumbers, which now feed as if they were worms.

The term *coprolite* ("dung stone") is applied to feces preserved by petrifaction or as molds or casts. Some show grooves made by the spiral valve found in sharks' intestines; their origin is obvious. Others seem to be hardened droppings of amphibians, and others came from reptiles and mammals. Still others can only be attributed to unknown vertebrates.

Gastroliths, or Gizzard Stones.   Everyone who has seen a fowl being prepared for cooking knows that the birds swallow stones. They come to

This sandstone cast of skin on the chest of Anatosaurus, *a duck-billed dinosaur, shows thousands of small, bony plates (photograph from the American Museum of Natural History). Plates in the skin of* Placosaurus ("Glyptosaurus"), *an Oligocene lizard, are petrified, as are the jaws and teeth*

rest in the muscular stomach, or gizzard, where they help grind food to pieces as it is squeezed to and fro.

Many ancient reptiles and other backboned animals shared this habit of grinding food with gizzard stones. Called gastroliths, these stones may be recognized by their rounded edges and smooth—even polished—surfaces, *provided they are associated with vertebrate remains.* Those seven words are important, for pebbles may be rounded and smoothed by running water or windblown dust as well as by churning against each other in the stomach of a reptile. The surest proof, of course, is to find gastroliths among fossil bones in the place once occupied by a stomach. Lacking that, bones should lie near the pebbles, with no hint that the latter might have been polished by water or wind. Smoothed pebbles that merely lie in beds that may hold reptilian or bird remains should not be called gastroliths.

Gastroliths do not seem to be associated with any particular diet. The fish-eating plesiosaurs had them, but so, too, did herbivores like the large New Zealand birds, the moas, and so does the living chicken.

HOW MUCH DO FOSSILS TELL?

We now come to a critical question: How much do these varied types of fossils tell about life in the past?

Answers depend upon the fossils found in particular places, and upon the questioner. If the fossils are only trails or burrows in rocks such as sandstone, they may tell us what ancient creatures did, but reveal almost nothing about those organisms themselves. In New Jersey and southern New England, for example, footprints show that dinosaurs walked, ran, and rested on muddy sandbanks, but there are few petrified bones to tell what those ancient reptiles were like. Some of the oldest snail fossils are mere furrows made as the animals crawled in mud. Such traces are welcome when nothing else can be found, but they are disappointing to anyone who wants to know what these Early Cambrian snails looked like and the group to which they belonged.

Even the best and most plentiful fossils disappoint people who want to know as much about ancient faunas (animals) and floras (plants) as they might—but seldom do—learn about modern ones. Fossils are remains or traces that have been preserved; but most ancient organisms decayed, were eaten, or were weathered a short time after they died. Bones were crushed by carnivores and gnawed by rodents; logs and dead leaves rotted; shells were ground to bits by waves. Tracks and trails were washed away; beds of sand containing burrows were stirred up and reworked before they finally became stone. Only a small part of the things that actually lived, left traces, and then died, escaped these varied forces of destruction and finally became fossils. To restore life's past from such records, say some critics, is like trying to reconstruct a city from a few of its cemeteries.

This comparison holds a measure of truth, but it also is exaggerated. Though fossils do not record all the things that lived during past ages, they include a vast variety of organisms, many of which are well preserved and show the ways in which they lived. Such fossils do more than tell a general story; for many epochs and in many places they provide an amazing amount of detail.

This becomes clear when we reconsider the fossils found near Rockford, Iowa. There seaweeds are not much more than impressions; small floating and scumlike plants have vanished; so, we may confidently assume, have small animals without shells or similar hard parts. But other creatures, from one-celled protists to vertebrates, remain, and their hard parts were neither worn nor broken before fossilization. Their very excellence shows that most of them lie where they lived and died. Few were mixed and worn by waves and currents, or carried long distances before they came to rest and were buried in slowly settling mud.

As the restoration shows, these fossils present a general picture of sessile (attached) and crawling animal life, as well as a few swimmers—a general picture that is filled out by facts about structure and anatomy. Stony corals, for instance, contain complex systems of plates built by and as supports for the body. The halves of a brachiopod fall apart, revealing notches and teeth that held them together, scars to which muscles were fastened, and channels for watery blood. Some shells have bands and blotches of color, while broken ones show fibrous structure that could not be seen while the creatures were alive.

Many petrified fossils from elsewhere equal those from Iowa, but few show as much detail as those from Miocene concretions in the Mojave Desert. The specimens are prepared by dissolving the concretions from what are popularly known as "button beds." Finds include silicified spiders, insects, and fairy shrimps that once lived in or near a lake that resembled Soap Lake, in the Grand Coulee region of present-day Washington, or one of the ephemeral salt lakes in central Australia. Brood pouches of female fairy shrimps contain eggs; some insects still lie in their pupal cases; others died and were preserved in the act of emerging. Jointed antennae as well as spines on legs are seen on some specimens. Especially fine fossils preserved in calcium carbonate show muscles as well as tubes that took air through the insects' bodies.

Such fossils are surpassed only by rare insects and spiders whose soft parts, as well as shapes, are preserved in amber. One amber spider contains the abdominal organs and muscles of the legs; another shows the structures of cells in the abdominal wall. In one specimen, the individual threads of a spider's silk can be traced to separate spinning tubes.

Countless specimens that are inferior to these still provide information, which is often overlooked by critics who dwell on "imperfections in the fossil record." Thus, many petrified trees preserve what once were woody cell walls, as do stems, roots, and cones found in chert or limy coal balls. Palmlike cycads still bear organs that served the purpose of flowers, and plants that falsely resemble ferns contain seeds in pods at the tips of their leaves. Fossil spores are abundant in cannel coal, and some reveal nuclei that once were the centers of life in their gelatinous cells. Nuclei even contain chromosomes, those complex, though tiny, structures whose elements, called genes, control heredity. Cones, roots, and even seeds are common fossils, and flowers are not as rare as they once seemed to be. A cactus some 50 million years old bears both flowers and fruit. Carbonized marine invertebrates of vastly greater age show internal organs, as well as bristles, scales, and other external structures.

Fossil vertebrates are often called near-perfect if they contain all important bones and if most of their teeth remain in the jaws. But fish found in a suburb of Cleveland, Ohio, also possess carbonized flesh and fins, and so do some aquatic reptiles. Dinosaurs buried in fine-grained sandstone have impressions of skin around their bones. Frozen elephants preserve almost as many details as do those shot, but seldom studied, by hunters in Africa.

Muscles, Brains, and Senses. Even bones devoid of flesh may tell a great deal about soft anatomy. The key parts of any body are its muscles, for they both give it shape and, together with bones, determine its movements. Muscles, in turn, are fastened to bones, often leaving marks that indicate sizes, shapes, and functions of these varied organs.

Brains and nerves determine intelligence and behavior, and their principal features can be determined from cavities and channels in skulls. Thanks to them, we know the mental and sensory equipment of many fossil vertebrates, from jawless prefish to mammals. Thus, flying reptiles and birds saw well but smelled very poorly; both obviously hunted by sight, because the optic lobes of the brain that receive visual impulses are greatly enlarged. Early mammals, however, reversed this order and found their food by smell.

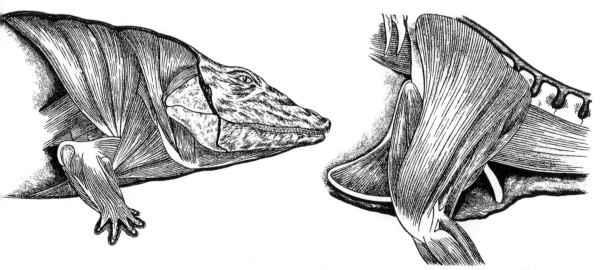

Muscles in the shoulder and head of the amphibian Eryops *(left) and the hip of a carnivorous dinosaur (right). Both are restored from marks left on the petrified bones by attachment of ligaments and tendons*

The largest dinosaurs had such small, weak brains that most of their actions were regulated by swellings, or ganglia, in the spinal cord. Some of the small, bipedal theropods, however, had enlarged brains (relative to body size), reminiscent of those of birds. Brain casts of dinosaurs and some fossil mammals sometimes show minute details of brain shape. Impressions preserved on the insides of skulls can give clues as to the behavior of animals, such as packing behavior in doglike carnivores.

Growth, Injury, and Disease.   Living things now change as they grow up and age, and that rule also holds for organisms of the past. Fossils 300 million to 500 million years old show that the jointed invertebrates called trilobites developed from minute oval larvae into adults as much as 30 inches (76 cm.) in length. Many molluscs and brachiopods changed shape and ornamentation from the time they first developed shells until they died. Dinosaur eggs contain bones of unhatched young, and small skeletons have been identified as the young of much larger species. Another example of growth in fossil animals is illustrated in mammals in which many bones have bony caps (epiphyses) on either end separated by soft cartilage. When the mammal reaches adulthood, the caps fuse to the main shaft of the bone, forming

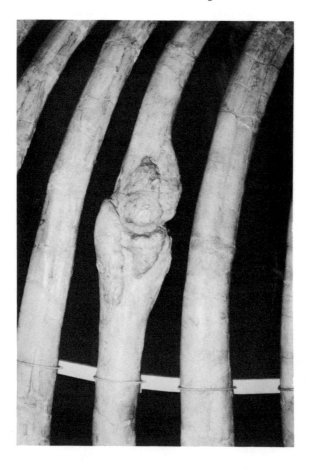

Rib of a titanothere, or brontothere, Brontotherium, from the Early Oligocene of North America. The rib was evidently broken and rehealed, forming a joint between the two fragments. Paleopathological studies on bones such as these can give some idea of what diseases or misfortunes occurred in the lives of animals now long extinct. (Photo by E. S. Gaffney of a specimen in the American Museum of Natural History, New York)

one solid bone. Different epiphyses fuse at different times, and archaeologists use this information to very accurately age the animals, including man, from their digs.

Some petrified logs bear scars made by fire, apparently while the trees were alive. Other fossil plants reveal pathologic burls, spot fungi, and insect galls. Tumors, rheumatic disorders, arthritis, and abscesses are shown by the bones of ancient vertebrates. Some skeletons are distorted by what seem to be muscular spasms that ended in death. Some fossil bones show that breakage and mending have occurred during the life of the animal.

Form and Function.   Much can be learned about the habits of an organism from the shape of its skeleton, be it an invertebrate or a vertebrate. Living clams that inhabit soft, unstable muddy surfaces generally have low-density shells that tend to be small and often covered with spines. All these specializations prevent the molluscs from sinking into the mud. Likewise, birds that are flightless, such as the dodo, of Mauritius, have reduced wing bones and lose the keel on the sternum, or breastbone. In birds like the penguin, which use their wings as paddles, the wing bones are flattened and are no longer hollow, but instead nearly solid and quite dense. These adaptations produce a streamlined structure that is heavy enough to allow the bird to operate below the ocean surface. There are countless, predictable specializations for herbivorous and carnivorous lifestyle, for cursorial (running), volant (flying), and fossorial (digging) habits. Plants have special adaptations for living in areas of high rainfall, such as drip points on leaves that help drain water off the plant rapidly. Such specializations certainly leave their characteristic marks on organisms, and the observant paleontologist can learn a great deal about the former habits of these fossils by studying such clues.

Activities and Instincts.   Enlarged areas in brains tell us that some animals hunted by sight though others relied on smell. Mastodons often waded into swamps so far that they mired in mud that still contains their bones. Large size and skeletal structure prove that ground sloths were terrestrial, though their modern relatives climb trees. A crab found in an ancient worm burrow lived there, just as its modern relatives dwell in burrows made by similar worms. Tusks of so-called giant pigs, or entelodonts, are deeply notched—a feature that became significant when someone discovered that the notches were worn by dirty roots that the animals dug for food.

The habits of invertebrates are sometimes shown by their shapes, sometimes by their relationships, and sometimes by the positions in which they are found. Ancient oysters, for instance, were attached to other shells or to rocks; belemnoids (Chapter XVIII) swam like the squids they resemble; some snails bored holes in other shells and devoured the animals inside. Other snails crawled to the tops of sea lilies (crinoids) and there fed upon waste materials from meals eaten by their hosts. The snails moved so little and clung so tightly that their shells grew to fit the plated sea-lily bodies. A few

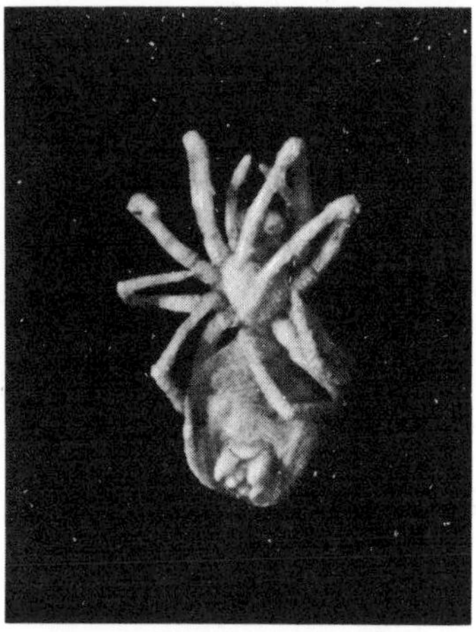

1

2

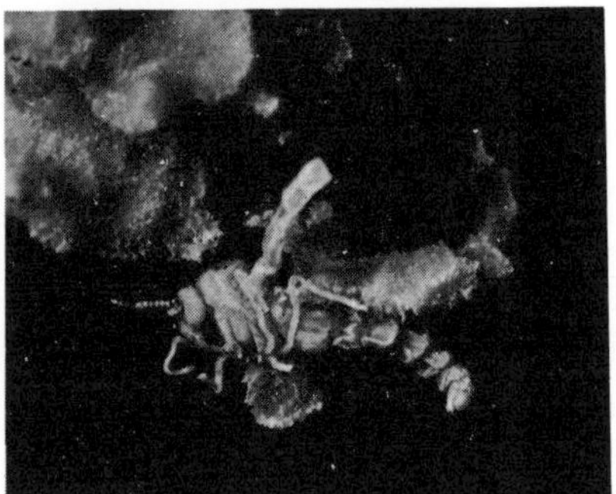

3

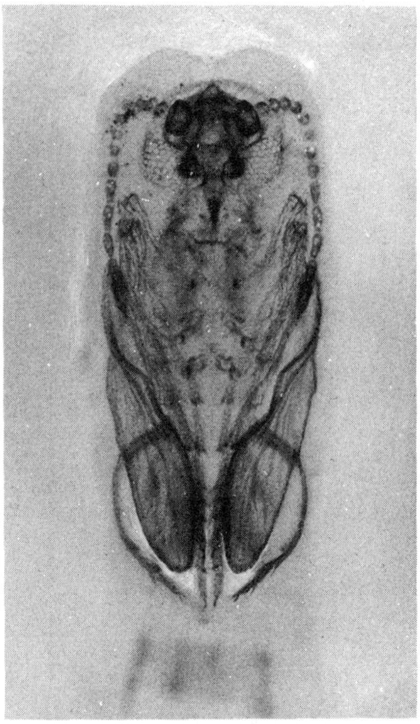

4

5

6

Miocene insects and a spider from the Mojave Desert.   1. Undersurface of a spider, × 20. 2. Undersurface of a leaf hopper, × 10. 3. An adult male midge, × 10. 4. Female of the same species of midge, still in her pupal case, × 50. 5. A larval water beetle, × 10. 6. A larval dragonfly, × 5. (Photographs by N. W. Shupe)

Fossil burrows, called Daemonelix, *in Miocene rocks of western Nebraska, and a restoration of a small rodent that apparently dug the spiral burrows, which are now filled with rock*

starfish adopted the same sort of life, but instead of growing to fit, they coiled tightly around their hosts' jointed arms.

Several modern snails bore holes into other molluscs, insert a rough, tongue-like structure containing rasping teeth (the radula), and devour flesh inside the shells of their victims. Bored fossils show that this method of feeding was practiced during ancient ages as remote as the Ordovician. Many fish and reptiles, on the other hand, swallow active victims whole. Fossil marine reptiles from Germany contain the undigested remains of such meals, and so do some American fish. In one, the predator seemingly choked to death, for its victim is only partly swallowed. Another, the 14-foot (4.2-m.) "bulldog tarpon" *(Portheus molossus)* swallowed a 5-foot 7-inch (1.7-m.) meal in one piece but died soon afterward. The victim's death struggles probably caused fatal internal injuries.

Some marine reptiles were swift, strong swimmers, and gastroliths sometimes show the range, though not the speed, of their travels. One mosasaur swallowed lumps of a special pink quartzite in western Iowa or Minnesota but died in Kansas, some 400 airline miles (more than 650 km.) away. Since the reptile did not travel by air, it doubtless roamed much farther than this minimum of four hundred miles.

Still more remarkable, as a record of behavior, is the devil's corkscrew, *Daemonelix,* with its helical shaft and upward slanting tunnel. Such a burrow demanded more than mere digging; it meant digging by an inherited pattern as precise as the one that leads a goldfinch or a robin to build its distinctive nest. Since we call nest building instinctive, this term may also be

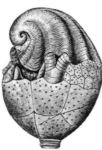

These brachiopod shells show marks left by muscles, blood vessels, and other organs, as well as the structure of the shells themselves

This snail clung to a crinoid so persistently that the shell grew to fit its resting-place

Here sand filled pits, preserving marks that match legs and spines of trilobites. The pits may have contained eggs

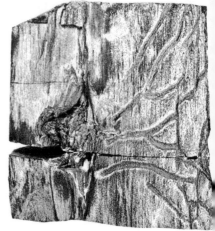

Larval beetles, called *Paleoscolythus*, gnawed tunnels in this ancient wood. Triassic, Petrified Forest, Arizona

Gastroliths, or "gizzard stones," of dinosaurs. One stone contains petrified corals. These helped to grind up food

These brachiopod shells were distorted after injury to their mantles

Snails bored through these brachiopod shells and ate the animals inside

Burrowlike trail of a snail, called *Scolicia (Olivellites),* in Pennsylvanian sandstone from west-central Texas. The actual snail shell is unknown. About × 0.25

Teeth of this fish, *Ichthyodectes,* show that it was a predaceous carnivore. Late Cretaceous (Niobrara chalk), western Kansas

Fossils that reveal habits of ancient animals

applied to the actions of that ancient beaver. By only a moderate stretching of terms, *Daemonelix* becomes a fossilized instinct about 15 million years old.

Taphonomy.   What happens to fossils from the time they die until they are deposited and buried, and then discovered by a fossil hunter, can also leave its mark on bones and shells. The study of such marks is taphonomy. The high representation of long, slender bones in cross-bedded sandstones can mean that the fossil sample accumulated in a stream that has selected for certain sizes and shapes of bones that have fallen into that stream environment. It does not mean that animals with long, slender bones were the only ones around at the time the stream was depositing bones. Many factors can determine the likelihood of a living organism becoming a fossil: its size, whether it has hard parts, the number of hard parts, whether it is young or old, whether it is colonial or solitary, where it lives, and what kind of habits it had.

Paleontologists studying this aspect of fossils need to carefully document the field situation, collect as large a sample as possible, and then carefully examine shapes, sizes, and numbers of fossils, as well as their surface textures and breakage, before meaningful results can be reached. Such studies are valuable, however, in understanding how fossil assemblages were formed. They can determine whether the fossils actually lived together (biocenose) in some past time or if they were associated with one another only after they had died (taphocenose).

It is very important, then, when a person is collecting fossils, to carefully document the field situation and to be sure to collect every scrap that is exposed. If such information is not collected from the beginning, then a great deal of knowledge about the fossils can be lost forever.

ENVIRONMENTS AND TEMPERATURES

Fossils also tell a great deal about their surroundings and the conditions under which they lived. Trees obviously grew on land, but seaweeds inhabited salt water. So, we may safely assume, did corals, oysters, and squidlike creatures, all of whose living relatives are found only in seas today.

More detailed information on such environmental factors as amount of light, kind of surface the animal or plant lived on, amount of sediment in the water, and how saline (salty) the water was can often be determined.

Reef-forming corals, for example, that contain certain kinds of algae are generally found in water less than 90 feet in depth, where light is available, and are usually restricted to within 30 degrees latitude of the equator. Corals are also restricted to relatively clear water, because they cannot feed if the water is muddy. They are also nearly restricted to normal marine conditions, with between thirty and forty parts of salt per thousand of water.

Plants and animals of a Late Devonian sea in what is now northern Iowa

ammonoid   stromatoporoid   lungfish   nautiloid

rugose corals,   snail   colonial   and   rugose   corals

bryozoans, and brachiopods   clams and brachiopods
                                    rugose corals and several brachiopods

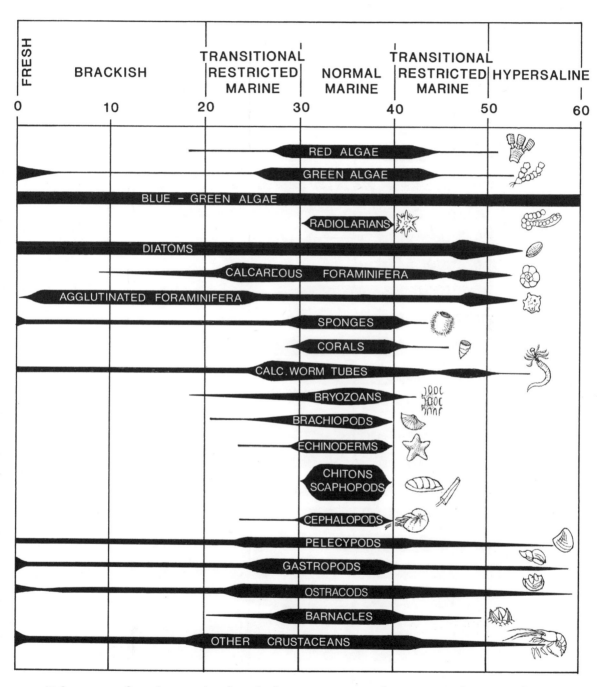

Tolerances of various animal and plant groups to salt concentrations, varying from freshwater to hypersaline. Some groups are restricted entirely to normal marine conditions. Knowing the tolerances of living animals, paleontologists can tell what kind of conditions may have prevailed in times past by analyzing the fossil composition. (Modified from a figure in R. L. Anstey and T. L. Chase, 1974. **Environments Through Time.** *Burgess Publishing Co., Minneapolis)*

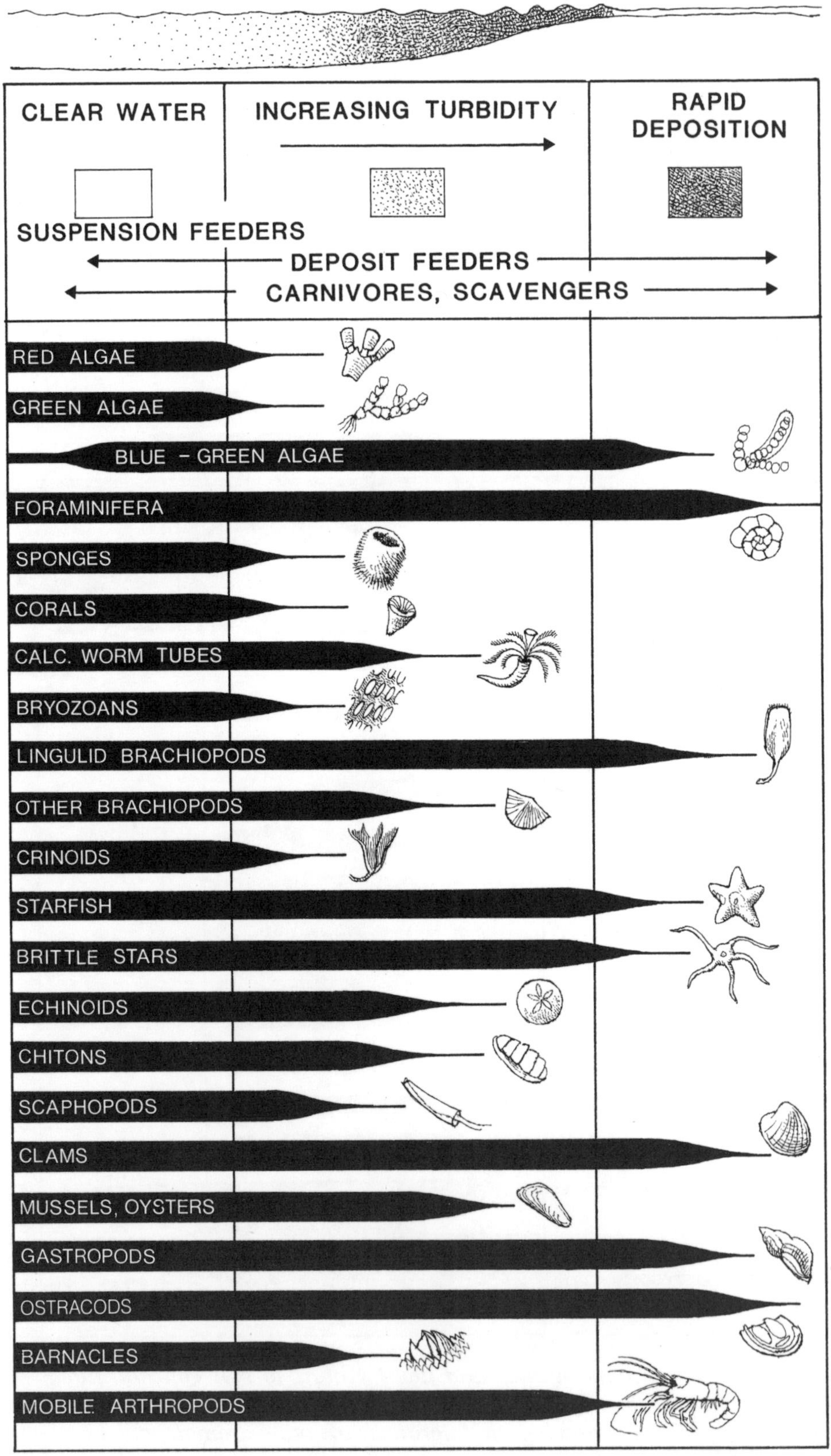

CLEAR WATER   INCREASING TURBIDITY →   RAPID DEPOSITION

SUSPENSION FEEDERS
← DEPOSIT FEEDERS →
← CARNIVORES, SCAVENGERS →

RED ALGAE
GREEN ALGAE
BLUE – GREEN ALGAE
FORAMINIFERA
SPONGES
CORALS
CALC. WORM TUBES
BRYOZOANS
LINGULID BRACHIOPODS
OTHER BRACHIOPODS
CRINOIDS
STARFISH
BRITTLE STARS
ECHINOIDS
CHITONS
SCAPHOPODS
CLAMS
MUSSELS, OYSTERS
GASTROPODS
OSTRACODS
BARNACLES
MOBILE ARTHROPODS

Tolerances of various plant and animal groups to amounts of suspended sediment in the water, from clear to turbid water. (Modified from Anstey and Chase)

Something of the surface upon which organisms lived can also be determined. For instance, if you study one species of benthonic (bottom-dwelling) marine clam living on substrates with an increasing mud content, you often will find a decrease in the mass and size and an increase in spinosity of individuals. All of these are adaptations to keep the animal from sinking in the mud. There is generally a decrease in the number of species (species diversity) as you move from sandy into muddy environments. Snails, mussels, and fish belonging to groups now found only in fresh water may be assigned to that environment. Animals such as horses and camels surely lived on dry land, while animals built like the hippopotamus made their homes in swamps.

Protists, plants, and animals also give clues to ancient climates. Palms, for example, tend to live in warm regions, though a few occur as far south as southern New Zealand today; spruces thrive where weather grows cold. Ferns require a great deal of moisture, but grasses and most cacti get along with much less. Reindeer are evidence of cold weather, and so are woolly mammoths, whose remains have been found in frozen ground.

Facts such as these have been refined until they provide remarkably exact pictures of ancient lands, waters, and climates. Not until 1950, however, did fossils provide data on temperature in actual degrees. In that year Dr. H. C. Urey analyzed a Jurassic belemnoid (Chapter XVIII) roughly 150 million years old. From the isotopes of oxygen in this fossil, Dr. Urey found that the animal hatched in the summer, lived almost four years, and died early in its fourth spring. During the animal's life, summer temperatures ranged between 20 and 21 degrees Celsius, or 68 to almost 70 degrees Fahrenheit. The highest winter average was 64 degrees Fahrenheit and the lowest 59.

Several people have applied Urey's method to fossils of other kinds and ages, with equally convincing results. One series of data shows how temperatures changed during the latter part of the Mesozoic, or era of reptiles; these changes may well be related to the rise and fall of Cretaceous dinosaurs. A general discussion of temperature measurements may be found in an article on "Ancient Temperatures," by Cesare Emiliani, in *Scientific American,* Volume 198, pages 54–63, for February 1958.

CHAPTER II

Rocks, Fossils, and Ages

We have said that fossils are remains or traces of once living things buried in rocks of the earth's crust. But we did not say that all such rocks contain fossils. Which do and which do not? How can we arrange them in order, and how—by means other than guessing—can we tell their ages?

ROCKS AND THEIR FOSSILS

Rocks, which vary greatly in hardness and composition, also differ in origin. Origins, in turn, determine our chances of finding fossils in them.

Igneous Rocks. The word *igneous* means "fiery"; though rocks of this class did not really burn, all once were intensely hot. They include lavas that came to the surface in eruptions, as well as related deposits that cooled and hardened underground. Most lavas were fluid when they came from cracks or volcanoes and flowed out upon the surface. Subterranean masses were much stiffer; they are termed *magma,* a Greek word for "dough," before cooling. Upon cooling they form granite and similar rocks, which lack the bubbles and traces of flowage that are characteristic of lava.

Igneous rocks that hardened underground contain no fossils, for nothing can live in great heat or far below the surface. Fossils are very rare in lavas, most of which destroyed all plants and animals over which they flowed. Exceptions are the rhinoceros described in Chapter I and tree trunks that left molds in rapidly cooling flows.

Lavas often are blown to pieces and shot into the air, where they cool rapidly. Falling to the ground, they form deposits called agglomerate if the fragments are coarse, and tuff if they are very fine. Both bridge the gap between igneous and sedimentary rocks, since their particles settle upon the earth's surface although they once were hot.

Agglomerate covers many fossil trees, some of which were dead logs at the time of burial. The most famous are in Yellowstone National Park, where as many as eighteen successive forests of redwoods, pines, sycamores, and

At the left are two petrified redwoods (Sequoia) *in tuff, a soft rock composed of volcanic ash. Pliocene, near Calistoga, California. At the right is a mold of a charred pine tree preserved in solidified lava of Recent age. Craters of the Moon National Monument, near Arco, Idaho*

oaks were buried under showers of volcanic rock. Hills west of Vantage, Washington, also contain petrified logs covered by agglomerate and lava flows.

Redwood logs, excellently preserved, are found in light-colored tuff a few miles from Calistoga, California. Ash mixed with mud settled in lakes near Florissant, Colorado, forming light gray shale. It contains enormous numbers of leaves, as well as eleven hundred species of butterflies, crickets, grasshoppers, flies, beetles, and other insects. The butterflies still preserve their original stripes and spots.

Trackways can sometimes be found in ashfalls, or tuff. A famous example is one in East Africa from Laetoli, dated at 3.5 million years. Thousands of tracks of antelope, lions, and even the relatives of modern man are preserved in detail.

Sedimentary Rocks and Their Fossils. Though fossils are exceptional in igneous rocks, they are the rule in sedimentary deposits.

Sediment literally means "something that settles"; sedimentary rocks consist of dust, sand, mud, and other materials that settled underwater or on

25

land. As they did so, they built up deposits called strata or beds, layers, and laminae, depending upon their thickness. Few sedimentary rocks were hot when they accumulated, and many consist largely of shells, corals, plants, and other remains. Coal is a well-known sedimentary rock that is made up almost wholly of plants.

Still, not all sedimentary rocks contain fossils. Most conglomerates, for instance, lack them, for organisms that lived among coarse sands and shifting pebbles were ground to pieces soon after they died. Fine-grained limestones may be equally barren, since they consist of material that once was dissolved in water. Shells and corals are rare in most marine sandstones— corals because they generally don't live amid sand, shells because they were destroyed by acids in beds of sand or by water seeping through the porous rock after it solidified. Where fossils do remain, they often are nothing more then external molds or remains with only coarse detail preserved. Still, in some cases, delicate structures, such as tiny reptile jaws, can be preserved in conglomerates, and exquisite sand dollars with minute detail can be found in ancient sandstones.

In contrast to these barren deposits are others in which fossils are abun-

Collecting fossil fish from freshwater shale of Triassic age at Princeton, New Jersey

dant or actually form most of the rock. The Iowa clay shale described in Chapter I contains so many remains that a collector who takes small ones with large may get ten thousand specimens in a day. Slabs of limestone from Missouri are covered with crinoids, while limy shales from the Cincinnati region and southeastern Indiana are crowded with shells. The chalk of England and northern France is little more than a mass of tiny shells through which larger ones are scattered. Other limestones consist of mollusc shells, corals, or the puzzling creatures called stromatoporoids, held together by matrix worn from similar remains. Reefs described in Chapter V consist almost entirely of unworn algal masses.

Even coarse sandstones may enclose bones of large dinosaurs, while fine-grained beds containing clay and mica often abound in tracks and burrows. Other fine-grained sandstones that settled on land are rich in fossil mammals. In the famous Middle Cenozoic Agate bone bed of Nebraska (Chapter XXXIII), fine sandstone merely fills spaces between closely packed skulls and other bones.

Metamorphic Rocks. These are typified by slate, true marble, and contorted crystalline rocks often called granite, though the proper terms are gneiss and schist. Some began as sediments; others were igneous. All have been changed by heat, by steam from buried magmas, or by pressure that bent and squeezed rocks into mountains. The process often went so far that we no longer can tell whether a given deposit began as magma, lava, or sediment.

Intensely metamorphosed rocks contain no fossils; any that may have been present were utterly destroyed. But stromatolites are abundant in some slightly changed marbles, and shells of various kinds have been found in slate, which is mildly metamorphosed shale. Such fossils were flattened and squeezed sidewise or stretched as the rocks were forced into mountain ranges. Though such remains can be recognized, their shapes may be quite different from those the creatures had when alive. Interestingly, the alterations in shape can sometimes be used by structural geologists to understand the direction and intensity of the forces that deformed the original rocks.

WHERE ARE FOSSILS FOUND?

We now are ready to answer the question of where and how fossils can be found. The first step, of course, is to rule out igneous and metamorphic formations, in which fossils are almost sure to be lacking. Then, unless the collector is interested in special problems such as stromatolites (Chapter V) or animals of ancient rocky shores, he eliminates formations and beds in which remains are likely to be rare and poor. This still leaves him a vast range of formations in which fossils are fairly common to abundant, and good to superb in quality.

About many of these deposits there is no question; experts have combed them again and again and have published reports describing their finds and the best localities for collecting. Other formations are judged to be promising because of their appearance, because they are related to known fossil-bearing deposits, or because specimens found in them appear on curio stands or in museums. Following such leads, the determined collector examines every exposure he can find until he either brings home an array of specimens or proves that they are not to be found.

Here the collector who deals with invertebrates has a great advantage over the one who seeks vertebrate fossils. Although a few beds are filled with teeth and bones, fossil vertebrates are much less common than shells or

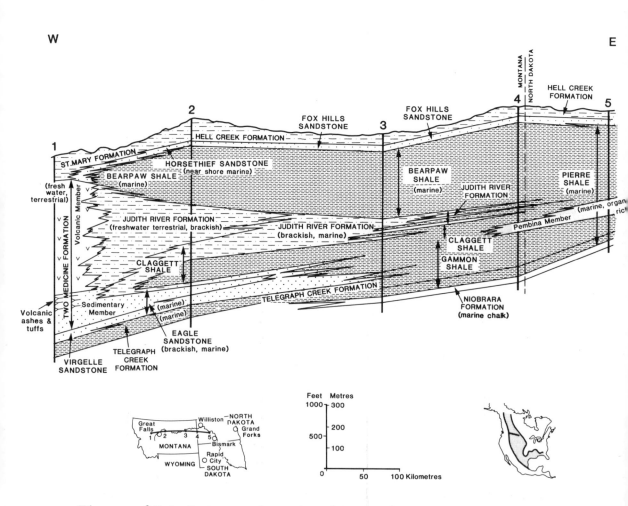

Diagram of Late Cretaceous formations from northern Montana (left) to South Dakota (right). Location of the section is shown by the line on the map. Shading shows the general extent of Late Cretaceous seas in the west and south of North America

corals and much harder to identify. Most snails, after all, can be recognized as snails, but a skull or even a skeleton may appear as little more than a light- or dark-colored bump on a rock. In the hands of an unskilled collector it also may be easily destroyed, though many invertebrates (by no means all!) are easily removed from the rocks in which they were fossilized.

FOSSILS AND FORMATIONS

Every collector soon notices that fossils of certain types are found in particular kinds of rocks. Marsh plants, for example, are most abundant in shales and sandstones between beds of coal. The colonial animals called graptolites (Chapter XXI) are generally found in dark, fine-grained shales that split into thin layers. Both reptile tracks and invertebrate trails characterize fine-grained sandstone, especially where it is interbedded with shale. Corals are found in limy shales and massive limestones, many of which are the remains of ancient reefs.

Records of Change. Equally obvious is the fact that fossils are similar throughout some series of strata, although they differ in others. These similarities and differences show what beds should be grouped together and what should be separated, while the fossils themselves may reveal the conditions under which rocks were deposited.

These related aspects of fossils may be observed along the course of the Two Medicine River in Pondera and Glacier counties, Montana. At first we find ledges of gray to buff sandstone whose beds bear traces of shifting currents and waves (cross-bedding), as well as impressions of shells related to some that now live near sandy seashores. Next come greenish-gray clays and soft sandstones with oyster shells and basket clams, which now are found in the brackish water of bays where rivers empty into the sea. Above these are clays and sandstones that contain freshwater mussels and snails, as well as plants and dinosaur bones. Some of the dinosaurs look as if they walked on dry land, but others were web-footed reptiles that probably swam in swampy rivers or lakes. Near its middle, the series is interrupted by a thin deposit containing seashells. Evidently the lowland was submerged under the sea but soon became land again.

These rocks are some 1,750 feet thick, and we follow them for miles. Then we come to dark gray, rather limy shale with petrified shells of molluscs whose nearest relatives now are marine. The shale is capped by more coarse sandstone with oysters, basket clams, and jingle shells, all relatives of molluscs that now inhabit brackish water.

Different fossils, thus, enable us to distinguish several separate units, though some of their strata are almost identical in appearance. We also trace a series of changes in physical conditions. Putting all these facts together in conventional form, we get a composite stratigraphic section, which should be read from bottom to top:

Horsethief Sandstone. Slabby to massive sandstone, brack-
    ish-water and marine   360 feet
Bearpaw Shale. Dark gray clay shale with marine fossils that
    in several areas grades into sandstones   490 feet
Two Medicine Formation. Gray to greenish clay and soft
    sandstone, with some red clay and nodular limestone.
    Terrestrial and freshwater, with one marine horizon   1,750 feet
Eagle Sandstone. Greenish-gray clay and sandstone with
    brackish-water fossils. To the north and west this be-
    comes part of the Two Medicine Formation   200 feet

The formations change from one place to another; witness the fact that the brackish-water Eagle Sandstone gives way to freshwater and terrestrial deposits which add a basal 200 feet to the Two Medicine Formation. Still greater changes appear if we travel southeastward toward the Black Hills of South Dakota. First the lower sandstones and the Two Medicine Formation vanish and the Bearpaw interfingers with a thick formation of shale called the Pierre (pronounced "peer"), which tells of a sea that changed very little while land and salt water repeatedly shifted in what is now western Montana and Alberta. At last, however, the sea shallowed, and sandstone was deposited. Though called the Fox Hills Sandstone, it once was continuous with the Horsethief Sandstone, which caps ridges near the Two Medicine River.

If we take the time—several geologists have done so—we can trace the formations in our section, making sure how they come to an end, intergrade, or overlie one another. We also can trace deposits at the bottom or top of the series to places where they lie upon or are covered by older and younger beds. By repeating this process several times, we expand our first section

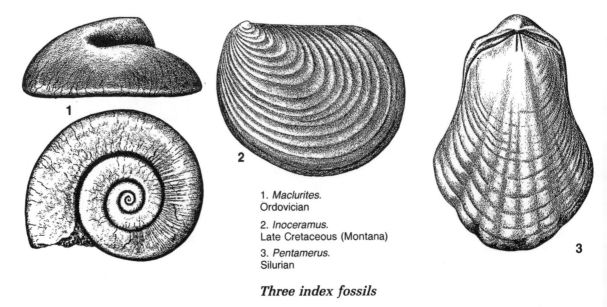

1. *Maclurites.*
Ordovician

2. *Inoceramus.*
Late Cretaceous (Montana)

3. *Pentamerus.*
Silurian

Three index fossils

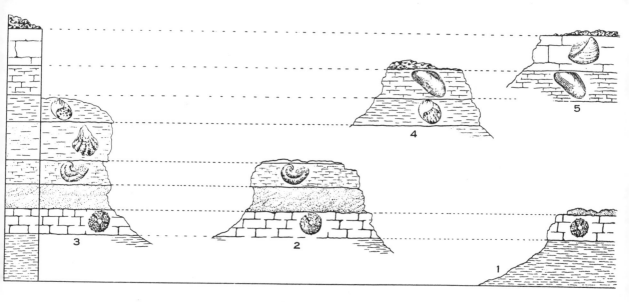

How index fossils are used to match, or correlate, beds of similar ages. The complete section of these varied strata (1–5) is shown at the left

into a greater one that shows formations and events in western North America during 35 million years of Late Cretaceous time.

Index Fossils. Still, we cannot always trace one deposit to the next or find thick series that overlap like shingles on a roof. When this happens, reliance must be placed upon index fossils.

An index fossil is found in rocks that formed in one limited part of earth history. A certain species of *Inoceramus,* for example, is common in Late Cretaceous shales that extend from Minnesota to Alberta, and formations containing shells of this species settled at about the same time. The snail called *Maclurites* is equally characteristic of certain much older (Ordovician) formations throughout eastern North America. The presence of an attractive coral known as *Pachyphyllum* means that rocks were deposited late in Devonian times, whether they occur in Iowa, Nevada, Arizona, or northern Canada.

A really good index fossil has three outstanding characteristics. First, it is easily recognized, which means that it cannot be confused with fossils that lived at other times. A good index fossil when alive also spread rapidly and widely, becoming common during one small division of time, or epoch, after which it became extinct. Finally, it was easily preserved, leaving a large number of fossils. Rare species may have index value when we find them, but they are much less useful than others that are plentiful.

Correlation. To make sure how index fossils are used, let us picture three isolated hills and two quarries. All contain strata in orderly sequence, but no two sequences match. Does this mean that different sediments settled in different places, as they did in Montana, Alberta, and South Dakota? Or do these beds form one continuous series, with the oldest at the bottom and the youngest at the top?

These questions cannot be answered by following strata, for they are hidden or missing in the stretches between our quarries and cliffs. Instead, we collect fossils from each place and then correlate, or match, them. At the top of Hill 1 we find some sea urchins identical with others collected at the bottom of Hill 2. High up in that hill is an oysterlike shell called *Gryphaea,* which also appears in Quarry 3. A plump snail links Quarry 3 with Hill 4, and a mussel shows that a bed near the crest of the hill is found at the bottom of Quarry 5. By matching strata that contain these index fossils, we arrange our exposures in one continuous series, or section.

Problems in correlation (facies problems) can be caused if certain fossils are found only in one kind of rock. In other words, when alive, these organisms lived in restricted kinds of environments or were preserved only under special circumstances. For example, graptolites are often restricted to black shales, whereas brachiopods are normally preserved in limestones and sandstones. So, when we try to correlate between shales and limestones that may have been deposited at the same time but in different places, we need to find some fossil that occurs in both. Pollen is often such a fossil; it settles from the air into many kinds of environments and thus forms a "time thread" connecting them all.

DIVIDING EARTH'S HISTORY

This method of correlating rocks by their fossils was first used during the 1790s by an English engineer, William Smith, and two French paleontologists, Georges Cuvier and Alexandre Brongniart. They also used differences between fossils to divide thick series of strata into related groups, formations, and beds. Both approaches appealed to geologists who were trying to escape from an outworn dogma which held that all fossil-bearing rocks had formed during one brief epoch that came soon after creation. Within forty years after Smith announced his ideas, his followers produced a classification of formations and larger units extending from the earliest Cambrian through the "Newer Pliocene." Though terms were defined in a number of ways and many details were lacking, this sequence included deposits from the last three eras of earth history—the only ones in which fossils other than stromatolites and a few single-celled fossils are common and well defined.

As a result of Smith's organization of rocks, the geological time scale was built up. It was not, however, constructed in an orderly fashion. Some units were originally defined by the physical character of the rocks and others by the fossils within them. The Jurassic was first defined by the rocks that occurred in the Jura Mountains, of eastern France and western Switzerland.

The geologic time scale showing major geologic and biologic events. Snowflake symbols indicate times of major glaciation. FA, first appearance; LA, last appearance. This chart demonstrates the immensity of Precambrian time relative to the short Phanerozoic, the time when fossils were most often preserved. (Modified after Harland and others, 1982)

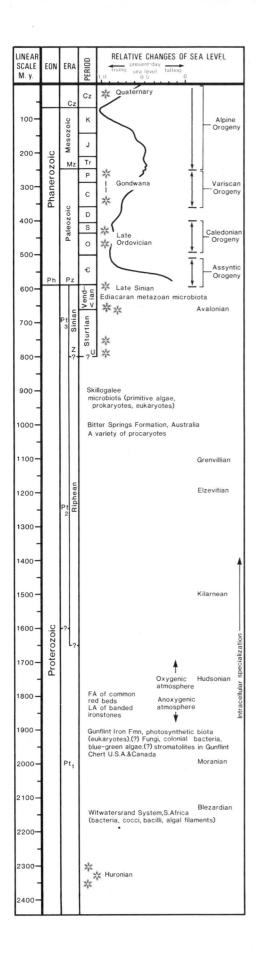

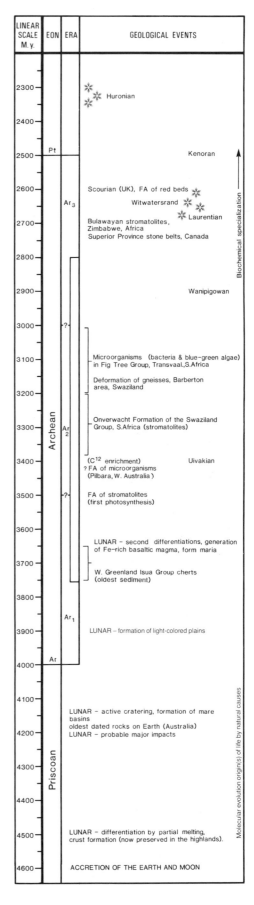

The geologic time scale emphasizing the Phanerozoic, the last 590 million years of time, showing major biologic events, sea level, magnetic polarity, and times of

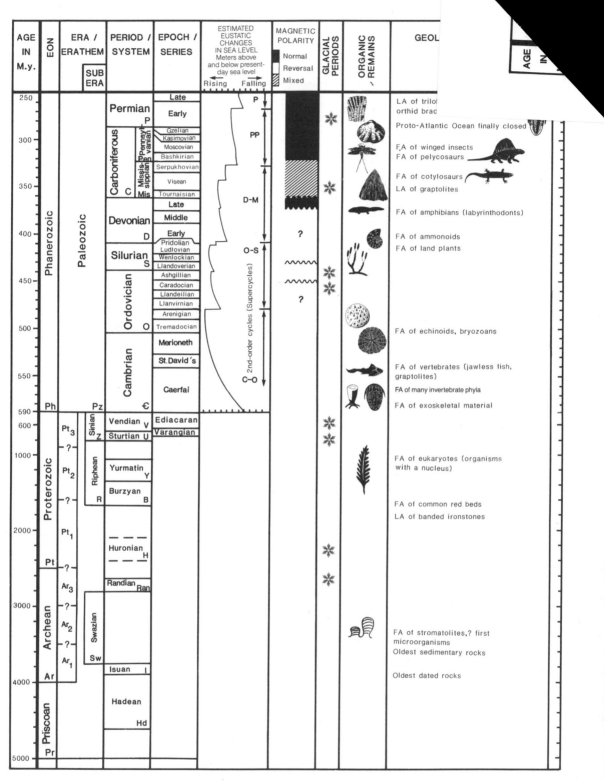

major glaciations (indicated by snowflakes). FA, first appearance; LA, last appearance. (Modified after Harland and others, 1982)

M.y.	EON	ERA / ERATHEM	SUB ERA	PERIOD / SYSTEM	EPOCH / SERIES	EUROPEAN STANDARD DIVISIONS	NORTH AMERICAN AGE / STAGE	AUSTRALIAN DIVISIONS AGE / STAGE	NEW ZEALAND DIVISIONS EPOCH/SERIES	NEW ZEALAND AGE / STAGE
				Pleistogene Ptg – Q	Pleistocene Ple	Several	Hallian / Wheelerian	Werrikooian	Hawera	Castlecliffian / Nukumarian
5				QUAT	Pliocene E / Pli	Villafranchian / Ruscinian / Messinian	Venturian / Repettian / Delmontian	Yatalan / Kalimnan / Cheltenhamian	Wanganui	Mangapanian / Waipipian / Opotian
10					L	Tortonian (Helvetian)	Mohnian	Mitchellian	Taranaki	Kapitean / Tongaporutuan
15				Neogene	M / Miocene	Langian (Vindobonian)	Luisian / Relisian	Barnsdalian / Balcombian	Southland	Waiauan / Lillburnian / Clifdinian
20		Cenozoic	Tertiary		E	Burdigalian / Aquitanian	Saucesian	Batesfordian / Longfordian	Pareora	Altonian / Otaian
25				Ng	Mio					Waitakian
30					L / Oligo- cene	Chattian	Zemorrian	Janjunkian	Landon	Duntroonian / Whaingaroan
35					E / Oli	Rupelian (Stampian)				
40					L	Bartonian	Refugian	Aldingian	Arnold	Runangan / Kaiatan
45				Paleogene	M / Eocene	Lutetian	Narizian			Bortonian
50					E / Eoc	Ypresian	Ulatisian	Johannian		Porangian / Heretaungan / Mangaorapan / Waipawan
55	Phanerozoic				L / Paleo- cene	Thanetian	Bulitian	Wangerripian	Dannevirke	Teurian
60					E / Pal	Montian	Ynezian			
65		Cz	TT	Pg		Danian				
70					Late / Senonian	Maastrichtian	Gulfian			Haumurian / Piripuan
						Campanian			Raukumara	Teratan / Mangaotanian / Arowhanian
				Cretaceous		Santonian / Coniacian / Turonian				
100						Cenomanian			Clarence	Ngaterian / Motuan / Urutawan
					Early	Albian	Comanchean		Taitai	Korangan
						Aptian / Barremian				
				K	Neocomian	Hauterivian / Valanginian / Berriasian				?
150		Mesozoic			Late / Malm	Tithonian / Kimmeridgian / Oxfordian			Oteke	Puaroan / Ohauan / Heterian ?
									Kawhia	
				Jurassic	Middle / Dogger	Callovian / Bathonian / Bajocian				Temaikan
						Aalenian				
200					Early / Lias	Toarcian / Pliensbachian / Sinemurian			Herangi	Ururoan
				J		Hettangian				Aratauran
					Late	Rhaetian / Norian / Carnian			Balfour	Otapirian / Warepan / Otamitan
				Triassic	Middle	Landian / Anisian	Spathian / Smithian / Dienerian		Gore	Oretian / Kaihikuan / Etalian
248	Ph	Mz		Tr		Scythian	Griesbachian			Malakovian

AGE IN M.y.	EON	ERA / ERATHEM	SUB ERA	PERIOD / SYSTEM	EPOCH / SERIES	MARINE			NEW ZEALAND DIVISIONS EPOCH / SERIES AGE / STAGE	
						EUROPEAN STANDARD DIVISIONS	NORTH AMERICAN AGE / STAGE	AUSTRALIAN DIVISIONS AGE / STAGE		
250	Phanerozoic	Paleozoic		Permian	Late	Tartarian / Kazanian / Ufimian	Ochoan / Guadalupian		D'Urville	Malakovian / Makarewan / Waiitian / Puruhauan
				P	Early	Kungurian / Artinskian / Sakmarian	Leonardian / Wolfcampian		Aparima	Braxtonian
300				Carboniferous	Pennsylvanian / Pen	Gzelian / Kasimovian / Moscovian / Bashkirian	14 named ages	Atokan / Virgilian / Missourian / Desmoinesian / Morrowan		Mangapirian / Telfordian
350				C	Mississippian / Mis	Serpukhovian / Visean / Tournaisian	11 named ages	Springerian / Chesterian / Meramacian / Osagean / Kinderhookian		
400				Devonian	Late	Famennian / Frasnian	Chautauquan / Senecan / Erian			
					Middle	Givetian / Eifelian				
				D	Early	Emsian / Siegenian / Gedinnian	Ulsterian			
					Pridolian					
				Silurian	Ludlovian / Wenlockian / Llandoverian	9 named ages	Cayugan / Niagran	Melbournian / Eildonian / Keilorian		
450				S						
				Ordovician	Ashgillian / Caradocian / Llandeilian / Llanvirnian / Arenigian / Tremadocian	16 named ages	Medinan / Cincinnatian / Champlainian / Canadian	Bolindian / Eastonian / Gisbornian / Darriwilian / Yapeenian / Castlemanian / Chewtonian / Bendigonian / Lancefieldian		
500				O						
550				Cambrian	Merioneth	Dolgellian / Maentwrogian / Menevian / Solvan / Lenian	Croixian / Albertan	Idamean / Templetonian / Ordian		
					St. Davids					
590	Ph	Pz		Є	Caerfai	Atdabanian / — ? — / Tommotian	Waucoban			

Major divisions of the geologic time scale during the Phanerozoic showing how different names are used on different continents, and in both marine and terrestrial sequences. The subdivisions are defined by the fossils in rock sequences. Boundaries between divisions are drawn using biologic events such as appearance and disappearance of various organisms. Tying together such subdivisions on different continents is not easy but is done by using both fossils and radiometric dating. (Modified after Harland and others, 1982) (Illustrations pages 36-38)

TERRESTRIAL LAND MAMMAL AGES				AGE IN M y.
EUROPEAN	NORTH AMERICAN	SOUTH AMERICAN	AFRICAN	
Oldenburgian Biharian	Rancholabrean Irvingtonian	Lujanian Ensenadan/Uquian		
Villafranchian	Blancan	Chapadmalalan Montehermosan	Rodolfian	
Ruscian			Lothagamian	5
Turolian	Hemphillian	Huayquerian	Ngororan	
Vallesian	Clarendonian	Chasicoan		10
Astaracian	Barstovian	Friasian	Tarnanian	15
Orleanian	Hemingfordian	Santacrucian	Rusingan	20
Agenian		Monte Leon		
	Arikarean	Colhuehuapian		
Arvernian	Whitneyan			25
	Orellan		Fayumian	30
Suevian	Chadronian	Deseadan		35
Headonian	Duchesnean			40
	Uintan	Divisaderan		45
	Bridgerian	Musterian		
	Wasatchian			50
	Clarkforkian	Casamayoran		55
	Tiffanian	Riochican		
	Torrejonian			60
	Puercan	Salamancan (marine)		65
	Lancian			70
				100
				150
				200
				248

The Eocene, on the other hand, was set up as those rocks in the Paris Basin, of France, that contained a suite of marine molluscs of which 3.5 percent were living species. New definitions were added, and over the next century and a half the geological time scale was standardized and expanded to include many units not in the original.

AN EARLY DIVISION OF THE TERTIARY PERIOD BY SIR CHARLES LYELL		
Formation and Epoch	*Meaning of Name*	*Percentage of Species Still Living*
Newer Pliocene	Newer More Recent	90–95
Older Pliocene	More Recent	35–50
Miocene	Less Recent	17
Eocene	Dawn of the Recent	3.5

Today our geological time scale is made up of three kinds of geological units: rock, time-rock, and time units. Rock units are ones that describe the physical (lithologic) characteristics of the rocks themselves; for example, the red beds, the Judith River Formation, or the Strezlecki Group. Time units refer only to the passage of time, and thus the Cenozoic Era is all of the time between 65 million years ago and today. The Cretaceous Period is the time between 130 and 65 million years ago. Time-rock units involve both time and rocks; that is, fossil sequences in rocks. And these time-rock units are what geologists often use when they organize the sedimentary rocks of the world in an orderly succession. The Cenozoic Erathem, then, is the rocks that were deposited during the Cenozoic Era, and it is the fossils that define the boundaries.

Time Units	Time-Rock Units
Era	Erathem
Period	System
Epoch	Series
Age	Stage
Phase	Zone

As you can imagine, time-rock sequences are not always complete in one area. So the Cenozoic Era means all the 65 million years from its beginning to its end; the Cenozoic Erathem, on the other hand, is not so continuous a unit. It is all the rocks and fossils deposited during the last 65 million years, and there may be breaks in this record caused by erosion, nondeposition, or nonrecognition because characteristic fossils are lacking. We must be careful, when thinking and talking about these three units, not to confuse them: time, rocks, and rocks deposited during a specific time as defined by fossils, are all different concepts.

From Fossils to Changes in the Earth.   Lyell's divisions did well enough so long as geologists knew more about fossils than they knew about rocks and the earth. In time, however, they discovered that this method of dividing earth history put effects in place of causes. The Cretaceous Period did not begin because certain molluscs and reptiles came into existence, nor did it end because they died out. It was a time when lands were low and seas spread widely, though there were progressive upheavals in the western United States. Similarly, the Pennsylvanian was more than a time of fernlike plants and primitive trees; it was one in which seas often spread and withdrew, turning their basins into swamps where the raw material of coal could settle. The Pleistocene, or Ice Age, on the other hand, was distinguished by high lands, changing climates, and glaciers that repeatedly spread in the Northern Hemisphere. These events are merely reflected by fossils, which adjusted themselves to the world in which they lived.

The number of time divisions has grown as knowledge of earth's history has increased. When Charles Lyell published his *Elements of Geology,* in 1838, he described sixteen epochs and formations distributed among three larger units, the Primary (or Transition), Secondary, and Tertiary. Today we recognize at least nine eras, as many as twenty periods, and a still larger number of epochs. These are listed in the accompanying table of earth history, in which names, events, and dates are correlated with outstanding developments in life.

As the number of periods and epochs increased, groups and formations grew smaller and smaller. Lyell's Cretaceous "group" is now a system; his Lias "formation" has become a series. Modern formations generally are limited to strata that settled during one compact portion of earth history, under essentially uniform conditions, and in one limited region. Many formations, therefore, contain one dominant kind of rock and take names from localities in which they are well developed. Others comprise rocks of two or more kinds, so intimately linked that they plainly belong together. These differences are reflected in names such as Brunswick Shale, Selma Chalk, St. Peter Sandstone, and Green River Formation. The last is a complex sequence of shales, sandstones, limestones, and marls deposited in two large, shallow lakes. Strata as varied as those along the Two Medicine River may be either a formation or a group.

AGES OF FOSSILS AND ROCKS

So far, we have seen how fossils can be used to set up a relative sequence of rocks. Dinosaurs, we know, occurred after trilobites became extinct and before woolly mammoths and humans arrived on the scene. But fossils themselves cannot give an age in years. It was this relative time scale that formed the basis of the geologic time scale we know today, based on the order of appearance and disappearance of various fossils in rock sequences. By the end of the 1800s, this relative time scale was well refined.

The question of how old in years the fossils were, however, remained unanswered. Soon after the discovery of radioactivity, in 1896, by Henri Becquerel, some geologists realized that it could provide a basis for determining the age of a rock in years. The reason for this was that radioactive processes were found to proceed at a constant rate under the range of temperature, pressure, and chemical conditions on the surface of the earth. A wide variety of dating techniques based on radioactive decay have been developed in this century. Each technique has its particular strength, which makes it possible to date certain types of samples that could otherwise not be dated. The well-known carbon-14 technique is commonly used to date samples of charcoal and plant material found in Late Quaternary sites no older than about forty thousand years. The potassium-argon technique is useful for dating samples no younger than about 1 million years and was used widely to date moon rocks on the order of 4,000 million years old.

Though the range of ages dated by the two techniques are so different, both are based on the same fundamental principle: after a known period of time called the *half-life,* the amount of the original radioactive material remaining in a rock sample is reduced by half because of radioactive decay. If a second period of equal duration passes, half of the remaining half, or one fourth, of the original radioactive material will remain. Thus, by measuring the amount of the radioactive material remaining and determining how much was originally present, it is possible to decide how much has decayed and thus how long it has been since the decay process started in the rock sample.

An analogous situation would be to determine how long it had been since a leaking bucket was filled. If the bucket leaks at a constant, known rate and you find it half full, you can determine how long ago the bucket was filled.

The time when a fast-leaking bucket was last filled can be determined within relatively narrow limits, because a large quantity of water is lost in a short time, making measurement easy. On the other hand, a fast-leaking bucket soon runs dry, and thus it is possible to determine the time of filling only if it is in the relatively recent past. A slow-leaking bucket can date the time of filling further into the past, but the limits of error of the age determination are much greater, because a small change in volume represents a long period of time.

In the same way, carbon 14, with a half-life of only 5,730 years, can give a date with an error of only a few years. But a mass of carbon 14 equal to that of the earth would not have a single original atom of cabon 14 remaining after one million years. In that period, the sample would have decreased, by half, 174.52 times. Or, in other words, there would only be one part in 3,434 followed by forty-nine zeros of the sample left. As such a qauntity of carbon 14 would "only" be about 25 followed by forty-nine zeros atoms, the chance that even a single one would have survived that long is slightly less than one in one hundred. It is for this reason that carbon 14 is useful only for dating events during the past forty thousand years. In geologic terms, that is the very recent past. But, even after that relatively short period, there is only about 1 part in 125 of the original carbon 14 remaining in the sample.

On the other hand, the oldest rocks on the earth and the moon, which have been dated by the potassium-argon method at about 4,000 million years, have about one-eighth the original potassium 40 that was in the sample to begin with, as the half-life of that isotope is 1,400 million years.

The "14" of carbon 14 refers to the total number of particles that form the nucleus of the carbon atom. Carbon 14 is a particular isotope of carbon that happens to be radioactive. Carbon 12, which is another carbon isotope, has twelve particles in the nucleus and is not radioactive. Almost 99 percent of the carbon on earth is carbon 12 and most of the rest is another stable isotope, carbon 13.

Carbon 14 is produced when cosmic rays from outer space bombard nitrogen 14 high up in the atmosphere. Approximately 70 tons of carbon 14 are produced in the earth's atmosphere this way each year. The carbon 14 so prduced is absorbed by plants (and sometimes in turn by animals that eat them). When the animals (or uneaten plants) die and are thus no longer incorporating any more carbon into their systems, half the carbon 14 is lost every 5,730 years. Dates can be determined by analyzing the relative amounts of the two isotopes carbon 12 and carbon 14. The ratio changes, as the carbon 14 decays and the carbon 12 does not.

The annual production of 70 tons of carbon 14 in the earth's atmosphere is an average that is known to have fluctuated over the past few thousand years. It is only one of the factors that leads to an error of measurement in a radioactive-decay age calculation. Therefore, such an age will be expressed with a $\pm$ error factor, for example as one date on South American sloth dung of 10,832 $\pm$400 years. In other words, the sloth may have lived as little as 10,432 years ago or as much as 11,232 years ago. Spruce trees in Manitowoc County, Wisconsin, were pushed over by ice of the last great glacier that reached the Mississippi Valley. They died at least 10,668 years ago or as much as 13,668 years ago.

Many other radioactive dating schemes exist and differ from the carbon 14 and potassium-argon techniques primarily in the ways the abundances of the isotopes involved are measured. Among the others is the first one developed, the well-known uranium–thorium–lead series. The basic underlying principle of all these techniques, however, is the same: the constancy of the rate of the decay process.

Some chemical processes proceed at uniform rates under special conditions. Amino acids are the building blocks out of which proteins are constructed and are present in all living cells. In a living organism, the structure of all the amino acids is referred to as left-handed. However, once an organism dies, the amino acids begin to convert to their right-handed, or mirror-image, structure, at a rate dependent on the temperature. Eventually, a 50–50 mixture of left- and right-handed amino acids is reached, and then the ratio remains constant. In situations in which the temperature in the past can be reasonably assumed to have been constant, such as the bottom of the deep sea or inside a cave, it is possible to date samples as old as one million years by this method.

Methods that depend on radioactive bombardment of samples have been developed as well. One of these is thermoluminescence. Trace amounts of radioactive isotopes present in all substances release particles as these isotopes decay. These emissions (alpha, beta, and gamma rays) disrupt the crystalline structure of the surrounding material. If the material is heated, at a certain temperature the flaws in the crystal start to disappear. As this happens, light is released. The more flaws, the more light is released. The amount of light released is therefore a measurement of how much radioactive bombardment the sample has undergone. By also measuring the trace amount of radioactive isotopes in the sample, the time since the crystals were formed can be determined. For a basalt flow, this would be the time the lava cooled. This method is useful for dating samples as old as one million years or as young as a dozen years.

Tree rings provide a method of accurately dating the past few thousand years. A major problem with tree rings is that "annual" rings may not occur each year. Drought, for example, can stop the formation of a distinct pair of rings for a given year. The relative widths of rings reflect the climatic conditions, and the sequence of widths of rings makes it possible to relate the cross sections of various tree. For example, a sequence of five wide bands followed by fourteen narrow ones followed by seven wide ones might occur only once in all of geologic time. If that sequence were found at the outer part of one tree and the inner part of a second, it would be possible to establish that the first was a mature tree when the second was young. By carrying the sequence from the second to the first, the overall sequence of tree-ring relative widths could be extended backward in time. Such tree-ring sequences must obviously be established for restricted areas, as the entire earth does not have the same climatic fluctuations. The best-established tree-ring sequence, or "dendrochronology," is for the bristlecone pine of the Sierra Nevada in California, which goes back about nine thousand years.

An analogous dating process that is worldwide in its scope is "paleomagnetic dating." On a time scale of hundreds of thousands to millions of years, the magnetic field of the earth reverses polarity. That is, after a reversal, the end of a compass needle that now points north would point south. As sediments accumulate, particles rich in nickel and iron become aligned with respect to the magnetic field of the earth. As the sediments harden into rock, the orientation of these particles is 'frozen' so that it is possible to determine the position of the magnetic poles when the hardening occurred, as more fully explained in Chapter III. Similarly, such particles in a lava preserve the orientation of the earth's magnetic field at the time of cooling and solidification, when movement was no longer possible.

Where long vertical unbroken sections of rock are preserved, it is sometimes possible to determine the relative thickness of the magnetically reversed and normal periods. These can be compared with the known sequence of reversed and normal periods that have been dated by such means as the potassium-argon method, mentioned above. Dating of the section in question can then be carried out if a plausible match of the sequences can be made or, as the process is aptly termed, the magnetic "signature" can be recognized.

Still another method of determing age relies upon dark and light layers of clay and silt that settled in lakes of glaciated regions and in some others besides. Each pair of layers, or varve, represents a year; to learn how much time one deposit represents, we count layers and divide by two. Longer series are secured by matching overlapping sections and estimating gaps where they do not overlap. By this method, one authority found that 13,500 years have passed since ice melted from the southern tip of Sweden. Another worker counted 6.5 million varves in deposits of the great Green River lakes of ancient Colorado and Wyoming. Those lakes, therefore, lasted 6.5 million years, an amazingly long time for inland waters whose basins were not very deep.

CHAPTER III

Continents Have Moved and Climates Have Changed

 Today if you stood on the tip of Sandy Hook, in New Jersey, and looked out to the east, you would see nothing but open ocean for as far as the eye could reach. Similarly, you would see only blue-gray water if you were to peer out to the south of the Great Australian Bight. This has not always been so. Were you to step back in time several millions of years, Africa could have been seen from New Jersey, and the great southern continent of Antarctica would have been clearly visible from southern Australia.

WEGENER'S CONTINENTAL DRIFT

The idea that continents have moved is not new. It was originally offered to explain the amazing parallelism of coasts on opposite sides of the Atlantic Ocean. Geologists were aware of such an idea by the beginning of the twentieth century. But not many took the idea seriously until Alfred Wegener published a book entitled *The Origin of Continents and Oceans,* first in 1912, with an expanded version in 1915. As support for this idea, Wegener and others, especially the South African geologist Alexander Du Toit, put together a long list of evidence. This list included data from paleontology (in particular, paleobiogeography—the study of the distribution of plants and animals in the past), paleoclimatology (the study of the distribution of ancient climates), the geometrical fit of continents on opposite sides of ocean basins, and structural and general geological studies that investigated sequences of rocks on opposite sides of ocean basins that seemed similar.

Although the evidence given by Du Toit and Wegener was suggestive, neither man could offer a convincing explanation of how the continents themselves could have moved. What was the force that drove continents through the oceans? Geophysicists argued that from what they knew about the physical properties of earth materials, continental drift was not possible.

But the geological and paleontological evidence hinting at continental drift was still there. How was the problem to be resolved? Geologists from many disciplines debated, argued, discussed, and continued to do so for several decades before any convincing solutions to this puzzle were reached.

After a stalemate of nearly thirty years, the debate about continental drift heated up again in the 1950s. This was not because of additional evidence of the kind that Wegener and Du Toit had compiled, but because of data from two other areas of geology: the magnetic properties of rocks and the nature of the ocean floor.

A GEOLOGICAL ARGUMENT

Many rocks contain particles of iron and nickel. Before the rocks harden, these particles tend to align themselves parallel to the prevailing magnetic field. Therefore, as the rock cools and hardens, a point (the Curie point) is reached, where the particles are no longer able to change orientation as the magnetic field shifts. By determining the "frozen" orientation of these particles, the direction of the magnetic field at the time the rock hardened can be measured. And in this way the former position of the magnetic north and south poles relative to the site where the rock sample was collected can be determined. Such a pole position is called a "paleomagnetic pole."

When a series of paleomagnetic poles of differing ages have been determined for a single landmass, it is possible to draw a "polar wandering curve" through these poles. Such a curve links the paleomagnetic poles in order by age and records the shifting position of the magnetic pole as seen from a single landmass. If the magnetic poles had wandered and there had been no continental drift, the polar wandering curves of all the continents would be the same shape. However, this is not the case, and the different shapes of these polar wandering curves imply that the various continents have moved with respect to one another.

Another kind of evidence bearing on the continental drift controversy was data being gathered on the topography of the ocean floor. Maurice Ewing and Bruce Heezen, working at the Lamont-Doherty Geological laboratories, in Palisades, New York, had plotted information being gathered by ships equipped with sonar devices. This allowed the mapping of the ocean bottom by bouncing sound waves off the seafloor. They discovered enormous mountain chains beneath the oceans, and these seemed to be connected all around the globe. This super chain was more than thirty-five thousand miles in length and, on the average, six hundred miles wide. Ewing and Heezen noted that the ridge in the Atlantic Ocean nicely split the ocean in half, with Europe and Africa on one side and the Americas on the other. They also noted that in the middle of the mountain chain and running the length of it was a central valley, like a rift valley (such as that in East Africa today), which might imply that this area was in a state of tension. This might be interpreted as an area of opening, the original split between the Americas and the Old World of Europe and Africa.

More evidence came to light. There was a high heat flow over the mid-ocean ridges: the ocean bottom was warmer in these areas than on either side of them. There were also frequent earthquakes in these areas. Another, seemingly unrelated, fact was that the ocean basins seemed to have relatively young features. With all the deep-sea drilling up until the early 1960s, the oldest rocks known in the ocean basins were of earliest Cretaceous or very latest Jurassic age. Therefore, the ocean basins that we know today had been in existence for only some 140 million years.

With all this in mind, some geologists suggested that the central mountain ranges, or ridges, in the ocean basins could be looked upon as areas where there was some sort of upwelling of hot material from within the earth. This rising material could explain the high heat flow, the rugged elevated topography of the ridges, and the tensional situation in the rift valley. To explain this, a convection-cell model was proposed. This is best likened to what happens when you boil a thick soup in a saucepan. Heat is applied from the bottom just as it would be if the heat came from deep in the earth. This warms the bottom layers of soup, causing expansion. The bottom layer of soup becomes lighter than the upper layers, moves to the top, and is then forced to move sideways as more hot liquid wells up from below. The path that an individual pea in a thick pea soup would take defines a convection cell. The cell is completed when the soup on top is cooled, contracts, and sinks to the bottom to begin the journey all over again. So geologists explained what might be happening in the earth's crust underneath the mid-ocean ridges and thus offered a general solution to the puzzle that had bedeviled Wegener and Du Toit as they tried to explain how the continents could have been "powered" on their drifting journey across the ocean basins.

In 1962, H. H. Hess, of Princeton University, drew all of the known information together about the ocean basins and convection cells. His paper, which he called "geopoetry," because it was a little short on data, was titled the "History of Ocean Basins." It became known to the everyday geologist as the theory of seafloor spreading. Basically, Hess said that the oceanic mountain ranges were the places where the convection cells of the deeper parts of the earth rose to the surface. Where the convection cell rose, it caused partial melting of solid-rock material, producing lava, which rose, resulting in volcanic eruptions, such as those in Iceland, as well as those that were purely submarine. As the lava solidified, it formed new ocean floor, which was in turn pushed sideways by more upwelling lava—thus the ocean basins grew. As an ocean basin grew, the continents were pushed along as passengers because of what was going on in the ocean basins. The continents did *not* plow through the ocean basins, as Wegener had supposed.

Hess also suggested that in areas where the convection cells went down, the ocean floor descended to depths to become part of the earth's interior once again. Oceanic trenches were the places where this happened. Thus he could explain why none of the present ocean basins were older than Jurassic in age; ocean-basin floors older than Mesozoic had simply been recycled!

A GEOLOGICAL REVOLUTION

Hess's proposal put geology on the brink of a real scientific revolution—a period when the basic assumptions or working rules are in a state of change. Shortly after Hess's "geopoetry" appeared, a young graduate student, Fred Vine, and a colleague, D. H. Matthews, made another intriguing discovery. They noticed a number of strange patterns (anomalies) in the earth's magnetic field over the Atlantic Ocean basin. They had plotted out a series of magnetized strips on the ocean floor, which they called "zebra stripes." They thought these could be explained by Hess's seafloor spreading theory. They knew that the polarity of the earth's magnetic field had periodically changed in the past—that is, for some reason not fully understood, the north pole became the south pole and the south pole became the north pole. This had happened many times in the past few hundred million years. They suggested that the magnetic patterns, the "zebra stripes," were formed by different parts of the newly generated seafloor being magnetized according to the prevailing magnetic field as the new lava was added along the mid-ocean ridges. When the magnetic field "flip-flopped," as the north and south poles traded places, the next lava produced at the mid-ocean ridge would be magnetized in the opposite direction to the solidified lava slightly farther away from the ridge. Only in the newly formed lava, still above the critical temperature, the Curie point, could the magnetic minerals orient according to a "new" prevailing magnetic field.

Vine and Matthews' brainstorm was the beginning of the most recent scientific revolution in the geological sciences. One of the most important results of this revolution was not that it gave strong support to continental movement, but that it united in one general theory many aspects of geology that had never been related before. Mid-ocean ridges, earthquake activity, heat flow, and location of volcanoes could be explained by a single, comprehensive theory. So, too, could such features as "zebra stripes" detected on horizontal traverses above the ocean floor be related to the pattern of alternating magnetic polarity observed in vertical sequences of rock found in both cores recovered from the ocean floor and in lava flows on land. The outcome was the theory of plate tectonics, which married the theories of continental drift with seafloor spreading, giving us the basic set of rules geologists play by today—until someone comes up with something better!

What is the theory of plate tectonics? The theory, stated simply, suggests

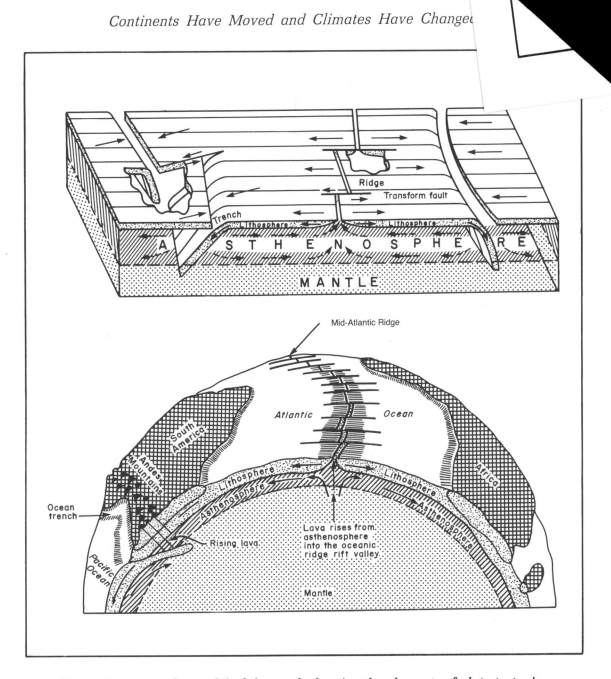

A block diagram and a model of the earth showing the elements of plate-tectonic theory. Ridges are where lava rises from the deeper layers of the earth to the surface and, once added to the surface, causes expansion of that surface; for example, the Mid-Atlantic Ridge. Trenches are areas where one lithospheric plate dives under another; for example, the trench along the western coast of South America that causes the devastating earthquakes of Chile. Transform faults are areas where crustal plates slide past one another laterally, such as those offsetting the Mid-Atlantic Ridge. It is the relative movement of these crustal (or lithospheric) plates that bring about the drift of continents. (With the permission of P. Wyllie and L. Sykes; drawings modified from their originals)

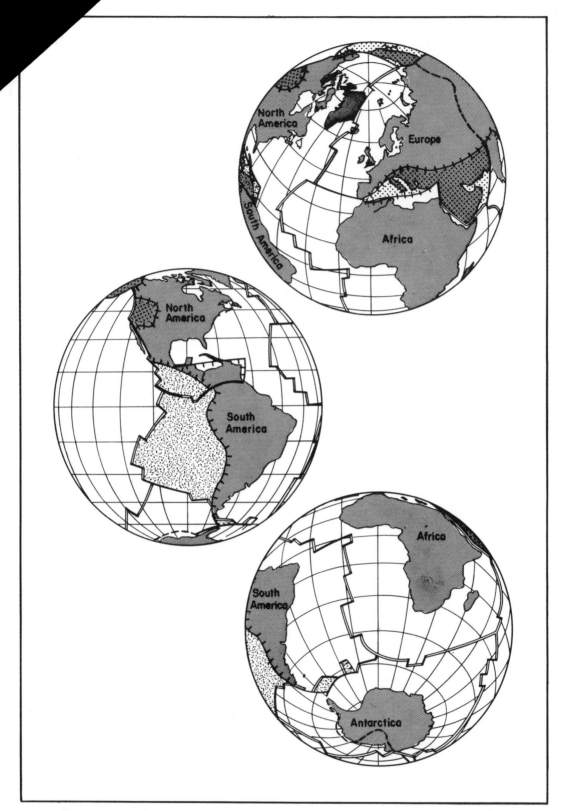

Three views of the earth showing the several crustal (or lithospheric) plates that exist today. Ridges are indicated by double lines, trenches by hatched lines, and transform faults by solid black lines. All these plates are in constant motion relative to one another. Continents are indicated by gray shading, and other textures are used to outline some of the individual plates. (Modified from F. A. Middlemiss and others, 1971)

that the upper few miles (up to sixty miles in continental areas) of the earth is divided into a series of thin, rigid plates. This part of the earth's crust is called the lithosphere. These plates meet one another along one of three kinds of boundaries: ridges, trenches, and transform faults. The plates themselves are relatively stable, and earthquake and volcanic activity is mainly confined to their edges. The *ridge,* such as the Mid-Atlantic Ridge, mentioned before, is a place where new material is being added from below, and an area of expansion. Such a boundary is characterized by high heat flow, volcanic activity, shallow to medium-depth earthquakes, and tensional faulting. A *trench,* such as the Marianas Trench, in the southwestern Pacific Ocean, is a boundary along which one crustal plate is moving below another such plate and material is being pushed or pulled into the deeper layers of the earth. Trenches typically have very low heat flow, earthquakes from shallow to deep (which take place all along the descending lithospheric slab as it sinks back into the deeper layers of the earth), and volcanoes above the deeper part of the descending slab. The third kind of boundary, the *transform fault,* is a most unusual kind of fault. It is an area where two plates move past one another laterally and is characterized by shallow earthquakes. It is unusual in that its observed movement is just the opposite of what it appears to be. All of this can be explained by using Hess's seafloor spreading idea—and a Canadian geologist, J. Tuzo Wilson, made a brilliant explanation of this kind of fault in the mid-1960s. Transform faults clearly show up on maps of the ocean basin floor as tremendous offsets of the mid-ocean ridges. They probably resulted in part from tension produced in these massive plates because spreading rates differed along the mid-ocean ridges.

Most geologists today use such a theory as a working model, but not all accept it or totally agree with it. As with science in general, it will stand as a useful idea until something more workable is put forward. Questioning the correctness of it is a necessity of good science and should always be heartily encouraged.

PAST PATTERNS OF CONTINENTS AND OCEANS

Geophysicists, using the information they have collected over the past twenty years on the location of fossil paleomagneticpoles, have constructed a number of paleogeographic maps for various times in the past. These maps show where the continents we know today have been in times past—relative to one another and relative to latitude and longitude. It is important for us to be aware of such maps as we look at the history of plants and animals, at least during the past 600 million years, when the record of life is good. Then we can see if the distribution of plants and animals supports the reconstructions based on geophysical data or not. If the biological data support the geophysical data, then the reconstructions are probably reasonably good. If, however, there are major contradictions based on different lines of evidence, then it is time to go back to the drawing board, so to speak, and find out whose data are incorrectly interpreted. This check-and-balance system in science leads to a continual reevaluation of observations and allows scientists to continually try to increase understanding of our earth and its inhabitants.

Let's look at some of the past continental distributions based on geophysical information and keep them in mind throughout the rest of the book as various animal and plant groups are explored. This should give a good overall view of what the world was like from both a physical and a biological point of view.

At the beginning of the Paleozoic, in the Cambrian Period, the world was very different from what it is today. As the map for this period illustrates, there was one, very large continent, Gondwana—formed by what are today Africa, South America, Australia, and Antarctica—which was surrounded by a number of smaller islands made up of bits of Asia and Europe. One other, smaller continent consisted of parts of Europe and North America. And then there was an even smaller continent, a fragment of eastern Asia.

As the Cambrian map shows, the continents were constructed of different jigsaw pieces from what they are today. They were also often situated in very different places. Antarctica, for instance, was not over the South Pole. It was instead near the equator, along with North America and Australia. In fact, most of the continental masses in the Cambrian were strung like beads on a string around the equator, and no landmass lay over either the north pole or the south pole. This kind of continental arrangement surely had an effect on the circulation patterns in the oceans and in the atmosphere as well, and thus had an effect on climate.

Because of lithospheric plate movements, by Silurian times, some 420 million years ago, many of the continental fragments had shifted positions. Gondwana had moved into a position over the south pole, bringing such continents as Antarctica, South America, and Africa far south. Australia, North America, parts of China, and Europe, however, were still strung around the equator. Gondwana remained the single large continent, and the few other landmasses were much smaller, all quite isolated from one another. In the Devonian Period, some 390 million years ago, there were essentially two large landmasses, Gondwana still the largest by far, but several parts of North America, Europe, and Asia had merged to form a second continent of significant size, Laurasia.

By the end of the Paleozoic Era, in the Permian Period, some 240 million years ago, all of the major landmasses had merged into one large unit, which Wegener named Pangaea. This, of course, meant that terrestrial animals and plants had the possibility of moving across a single large expanse, if they could tolerate local climatic conditions and cross barriers of inhospitable country. Antarctica was situated at the south pole at this time, and some of

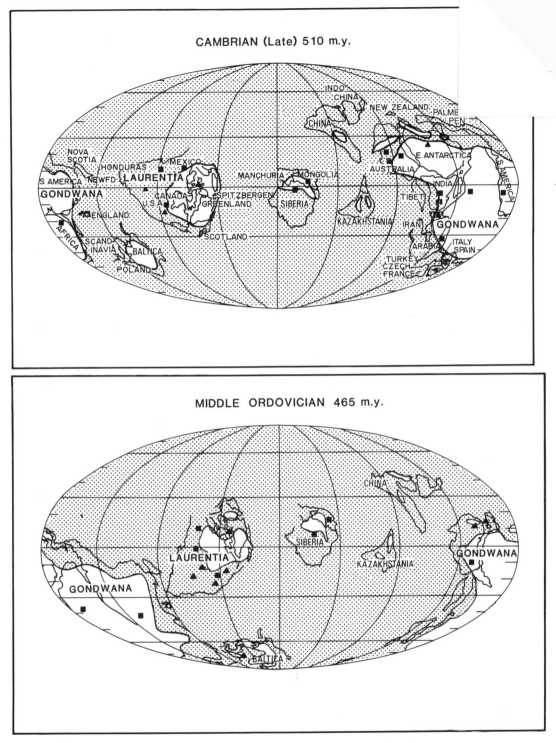

CAMBRIAN (Late) 510 m.y.

MIDDLE ORDOVICIAN 465 m.y.

Paleogeographic maps for the Phanerozoic (Cambrian into the future-page 53 to 58) of the world showing the location of each of the continents. The symbols on each of the maps show the information used to determine past climates: black squares are evaporites, thick sequences of salts that formed in relatively arid areas; black triangles are reefs, which today are restricted generally to within 30 degrees either side of the equator; black circles are coals that form under humid conditions, generally in temperate or cool–temperate areas. Stippled areas are oceans, white areas are continents, dark hatched areas are ice sheets. Arrows indicate the direction in which certain crustal plates are moving. (The last map in this sequence was modified after a map in Scientific American, *1970, Vol. 233, no. 4, p. 39)*

The Fossil Book

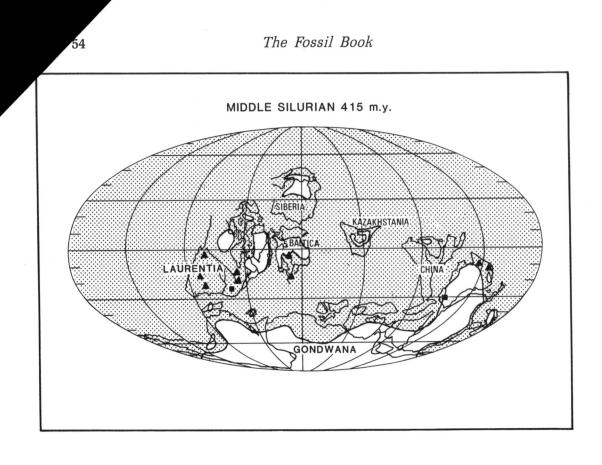

MIDDLE SILURIAN 415 m.y.

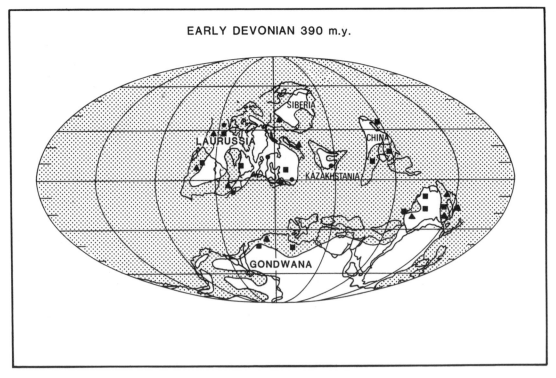

EARLY DEVONIAN 390 m.y.

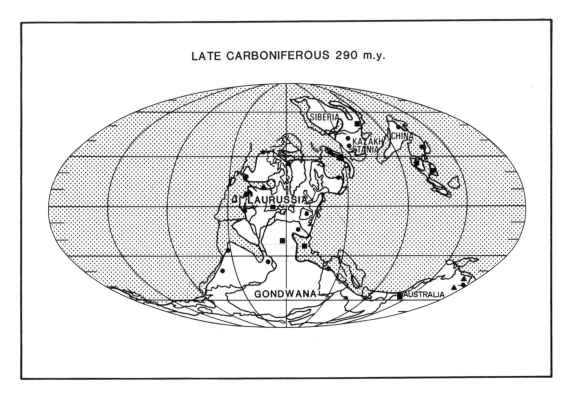

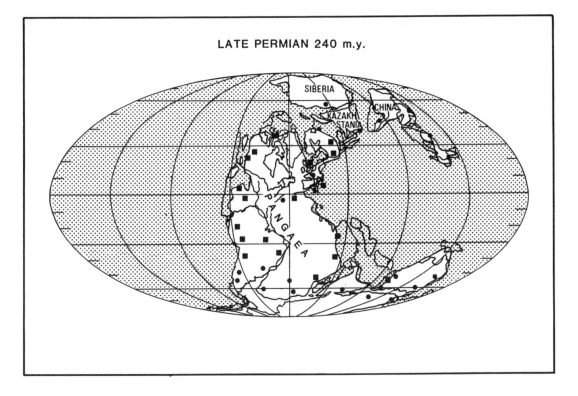

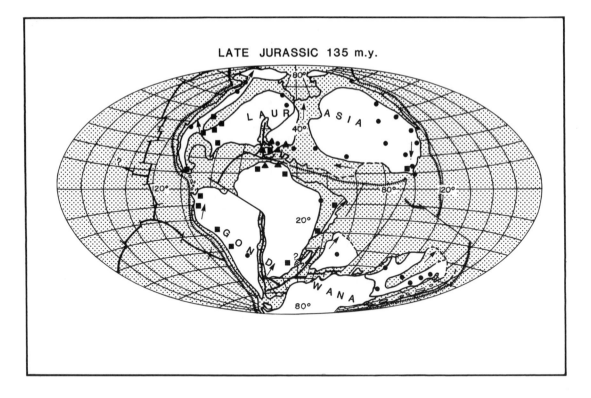

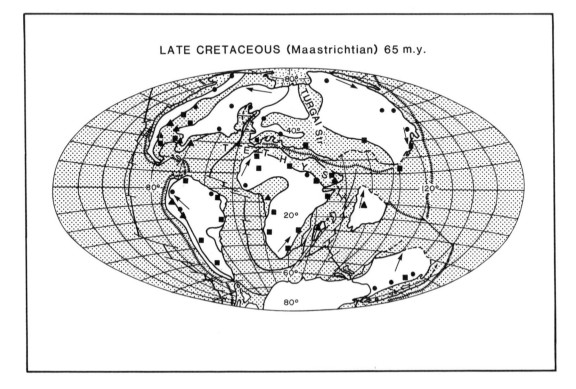

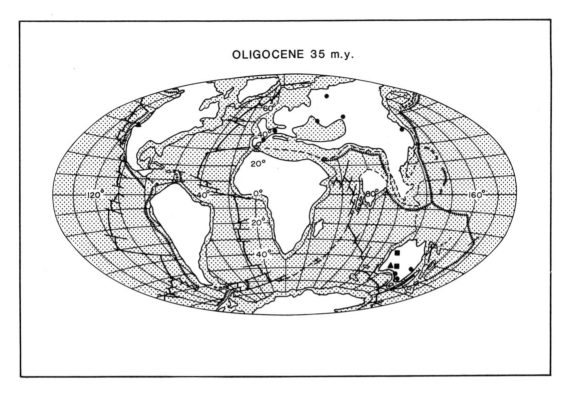

OLIGOCENE 35 m.y.

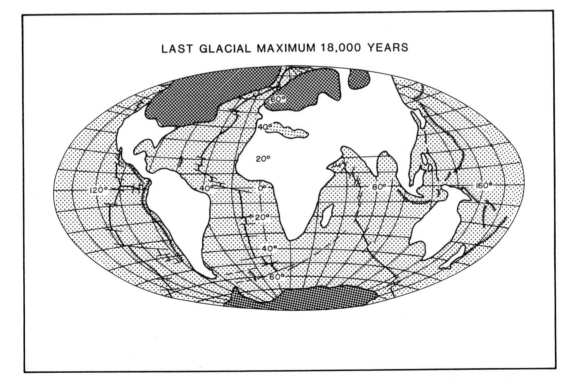

LAST GLACIAL MAXIMUM 18,000 YEARS

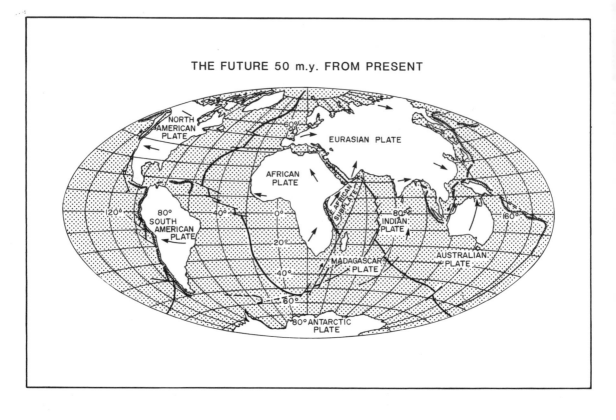

THE FUTURE 50 m.y. FROM PRESENT

what are now northern Europe and Asia were far north of the equator. Other parts of North America and Europe, including Russia, were closer to the equator than they are today. By contrast, South America and Africa were farther south of the equator than today. Australia and New Zealand, still attached to Antarctica, were far south indeed.

During Mesozoic times, the supercontinent, Pangaea, began to break apart. At first, the northern continents of North America and Eurasia broke away from Gondwana. Then Gondwana itself began to splinter, first Africa from Antarctica and South America, and then India broke away. Finally, New Zealand and then Australia began their northerly drift from Antarctica.

By the middle of the Cenozoic Era, the shapes of the modern-day continents were recognizable and in much the same positions they are in today, even though, of course, they were and are still moving. Earthquakes remind us of this movement. Africa and South America are still moving apart; so, too, are North America and Europe. Australia is moving northward, away from Antarctica, and, at the rate of a few centimeters per year, it should collide with Southeast Asia in about 50 million years. East Africa, at the same time, is on its journey away from Africa toward Iran and Asia Minor.

When you look at the paleogeographic maps, then, it is clear that the continents of today are rather ephemeral features. They do not remain constant through time. India and Asia are together today, but 150 million years ago, India neighbored Antarctica and Africa. It has made an incredible journey north across many degrees of latitude to join Asia, and during its collision with that continent threw up the mighty Himalaya Mountains. Australia, once connected directly with the great southern continent of Antarctica, is now on its voyage north to Asia. In the past few million years, as the collision between the crustal plates that bear these continents began, New Guinea has been thrown from the depths of the sea to the clouds forming the towering, snow-covered heights in the midst of the tropics. Continents that we know as solid blocks today have also had a checkered history. Asia today is actually formed of many blocks that in past times had varied associations with many other continents. So one must say that our continents of today are certainly not good reflections of the past. The magnetic properties of minerals in lavas and the past distributions of animals and plants are the clues that can help the geologist put the jigsaw pieces in the right places at the right time.

CLIMATES OF THE PAST

Besides the actual physical arrangement of continental masses and ocean basins, there are a number of other things that can affect the distribution of animals or plants. One of these factors, of course, is climate. It can serve as a barrier that can hinder or stop movement across an area even if the way is open on other counts.

Climate today, as in the past, is controlled to a great extent by latitude, as well as local topographic relief. Because there is more energy arriving on the earth's surface from the sun at the equator than near the poles, a series of climatic bands exist. The tropical band surrounds the equator, the polar bands straddle the poles, and the temperate band lies somewhere in between. The bands shift positions depending on the time of the year, as the tilt of the earth relative to the sun changes. The positions of these bands and their widths have also changed through geologic time. Their changing positions can now be explained mainly by the moving of the continents. The changing of the widths of the climatic bands, however, has a different explanation.

Several clues are used by paleoclimatologists to estimate what climates were. Tillites, chaotic sediments left behind by melting glaciers, are clues to cold climates. The salt deposits, left behind as evaporites, and reef accumulations hint at the location of the tropical belts. The location of coal deposits hints at moist temperate conditions. The measurement of the ratio of two isotopes of oxygen to one another (oxygen 18 / oxygen 16), as preserved in fossilized organisms, gives some estimate of the actual temperatures of the past. Armed with these tools, despite the problems of an incomplete record, reasonable attempts to sketch the past climate have been made.

Not much is known about climates before 2,500 million years ago, even though sedimentary rocks older than 3,800 million years are present in Greenland and Australia, indicative of the presence then of liquid water. Between 2,500 and 2,300 million years ago, the earth's first known glaciation occurred. We know this because there are large areas covered with tillites and other glacial debris of this age in Canada (the Huronian rocks), South Africa, and perhaps in Western Australia. This ice age was followed by warm and equable (even) climates until another glaciation began about 1,000 million years ago that lasted for 400 million years, ending about 600 million years ago. Many of the tillites left by the glaciers of this ice age are known to occur in very low latitudes; that is, near the equator. (They also occurred near the poles.) All continents except Antarctica have these late Precambrian tillites, and indications are that this was the coldest period that has ever occurred on the surface of the earth.

At the beginning of the Paleozoic, climates were warming, and the glaciers had all disappeared. Even continental fragments that lay at 55 degrees latitude seemed to enjoy warm climates. By the Ordovician Period, however, climates had begun to oscillate rather dramatically, and by the end of the period another glaciation was affecting parts of the world: Africa and, more marginally, North America and Europe. The evolutionary patterns of certain animal groups were markedly affected by this glaciation, as we will see later —both by the temperature drop itself and by the lowering of sea level, and the resulting loss of near-shore marine living space on the continental shelves, as the growing glaciers tied up more and more seawater.

The cold period ended in the Silurian, and warming continued into the Devonian Period. Temperatures were high throughout the Devonian, even though there may have been small glaciers in polar areas of South America. Some evaporites (salt deposits left behind by high evaporation rates in high-temperature conditions) extend to about 40 degrees of paleolatitude, at least 5 degrees farther than they do today. Such arid conditions changed to much more humid ones in the Carboniferous, as is suggested by the massive coal deposits of this age in North America, Europe, and Asia. Such high humidity may have triggered glaciation at the end of the Paleozoic, which had widespread effects. By the end of the Carboniferous and during the first part of the Permian, glaciers affected much of Gondwana, leaving behind their tillites, striated rock pavements grooved by the passage of the mighty glaciers, and oxygen isotope ratios suggestive of low temperatures. By the end of the Paleozoic, however, for some unknown reason, glaciation stopped, and warming began once again. Life, especially near-shore marine organisms, however, had been severely affected by the drastically lowered sea levels, many of them never to recover.

The warmest climates the world has ever experienced were characteristic of parts of the Mesozoic. Between the Middle Triassic and the Late Cretaceous, the thermal maximum of all earth history since life began was reached. It was only during the latest Cretaceous that the long, somewhat intermittant cooling began that eventually climaxed in our present glacial/ interglacial setting. Large-scale temperature drops occurred in the Late Eocene and the Middle Miocene. It was during the last major drop that the bulk of Antarctic ice built up. Ice advances and retreats have characterized the past 2 million years with a cyclicity of about a hundred thousand years. The last major ice advance ended about eighteen thousand years ago, but just what the future holds is not clear. There are a number of yet controversial theories. Man's addition of massive amounts of carbon dioxide to the atmosphere in the past century as a result of industrial activity will most certainly play a role in determining what comes next in the way of climates—but just what role and how quickly the changes will occur is still the big question.

What is clear from such an overview is that today's climate, and arrangement of continents, are not typical of the past. In fact, the glacial climate in which we do live is rather atypical for most of geologic time. More often, temperatures have been higher and climatic belts not so clearly defined on a north-south traverse as today. This is why it is sometimes rather difficult for us, looking back in time, to get an accurate feeling for what the world might have been like for a trilobite, or a dinosaur. Still, in the next few hundred pages we will try to do just that!

CHAPTER IV

Groups, Names, and Relationships

 Fossils once were alive, and most textbooks divide living things among two kingdoms, plant and animal. The former contains organisms that generally are green, do not move about, and make food from two lifeless materials, carbon dioxide and water. Typical animals, on the other hand, are not green beneath their skins, commonly move freely, and feed upon other animals or plants.

This division is respectably old, for it goes back some twenty-five hundred years. During most of them, however, it has required alterations and repairs. As early as 345 B.C. the Greek philosopher Aristotle added mushrooms and red seaweeds to plants, but transferred the sessile corals and sponges to the animal kingdom. Since Aristotle's time the plant kingdom has grown into a bewildering array of organisms that range from tiny and simple to large and complex; that may be green, purple, or other colors; that grow in one spot or move about; that make their own food or devour living and dead organisms. Animals have become equally varied. And many forms are assigned to both kingdoms. Others shift from plants to animals and back again as their activities change.

FROM TWO KINGDOMS TO FIVE
(OR MAYBE MORE)

These difficulties have convinced a growing number of biologists that the two traditional kingdoms are relics far removed from reality. To keep them is to squeeze here and stretch there; to put unlike things together while separating others that are related. The result is worse than confusing, for it gives an unnatural structure to the world of life.

Still, it has been easier to pronounce old kingdoms obsolete than to describe new ones. Everyone is accustomed to plants and animals, and all except a few puzzling groups have received places among them. But when other kingdoms are set up, the old rules must go, and experts do not agree on the new ones to be followed. Some authorities are content to add one new kingdom for the bacteria and their kin; others would do so for free-swimming "plants"; a few would make still a third new kingdom for fungi and their relatives. One expert divided the so-called algae into six groups, each of which he regarded as a kingdom. Then, "as a matter of convenience," he left all six, plus a few others, in the domain of plants. Others have suggested that within the nucleus-bearing organisms alone there are at least eighteen kingdoms. Obviously an abundant diversity of ideas exist!

We shall not do as these experts, and we need not make such sweeping changes as those they thought desirable. Many organisms that seem to form separate kingdoms did not become fossils. We know them only as very distinctive living forms. The others apparently can be accommodated in five kingdoms: monerans, protists, fungi, plants, and animals. The fourth and fifth of these are the "standard" kingdoms, redefined and restricted. The first and second were named by a German biologist, Ernst Haeckel, in 1866. Though Haeckel made monerans part of his kingdom Protista, later authors have separated them and have clarified both groups. The definitions accepted here were published by R. H. Whittaker in 1969. Whittaker's kingdoms are, for the most part, not derived from a single common ancestor, except for possibly the monerans. Because of this his groups are *polyphyletic,* or derived from several ancestors, not *monophyletic.* So his kingdoms are *grades* of structural organization, not *clades* of organisms drawn from a common "parent." The grades of structural organization of the three most complex groups are tied to the modes of feeding: plants, for example, produce their own food through photosynthesis, discussed below, and are producers; fungi feed by absorption and are reducers (or decomposers); animals are consumers.

Monerans, the Simplest Kingdom. Though some of Haeckel's monerans were results of faulty observation, this kingdom is now made to include two groups of very simple creatures, the blue-green algae (or cyanophytes) and bacteria. They agree in being very small and in consisting of a single cell each. Although some monerans are specialized in habits, shapes, and structures such as lashes for swimming, the basic plan of their cells remains simple. They are not divided, like cells of animals or plants, into one part of relatively minor importance and another (called the nucleus), which is essential for reproduction. Because they lack a distinct, organized nucleus, they are called *procaryotes.* The nuclear structures of monerans apparently are scattered through the cell, which seems merely to pinch in two when the time for reproduction arrives. This type of division is reflected in the term schizophytes ("fission plants"), which is used in many books that retain the two traditional kingdoms and put monerans among the plants.

Blue-green algae, as their name implies, include both blue and green material, the latter being chlorophyll. No one knows what the blue material does, but chlorophyll makes sweetish food by combining water with carbon dioxide, a gas now plentiful in the air and dissolved in seas, lakes, and streams.

Relationships of Major Kingdoms of Life

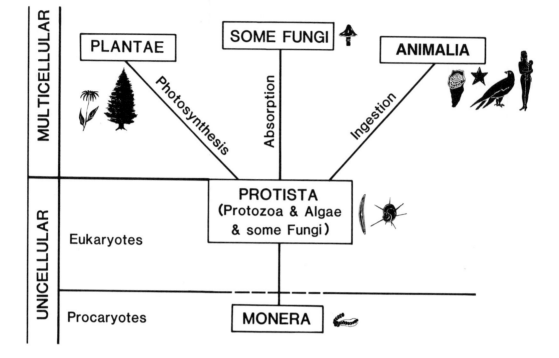

The five main kingdoms of life. (Modified after M. R. House. **The Origin of Major Invertebrate Groups.** *Academic Press, New York, 1979)*

The process (photosynthesis) uses energy from sunshine, and part of that energy is stored in the end product, which is a simple form of sugar.

Most living things now depend upon food made by chlorophyll, though it may be secured in roundabout ways. This fact, plus the simple structure of blue-green algae, was once supposed to mean that they were the earth's first organisms, making food that was eaten later by "degenerate" bacteria. We now reverse this theoretical order, for it seems that bacteria came first and fed on almost-living material that accumulated before they evolved. In time, some of the original grayish or whitish bacteria produced dull purple descendants whose color came from a mixture of red and green substances that made food much as chlorophyll does. Cyanophytes were born when this coloring matter became chlorophyll and the puzzling blue stuff was added. The swimming lash disappeared too, for blue-greens get along without that structure.

This sequence is inferred from things living today, not primarily from the fossils. If it is correct, blue-greens followed bacteria, yet the former are very old. Cyanophytes almost certainly helped build stromatolites, for their cells have been identified in Precambrian stromatolites. Both blue-greens and

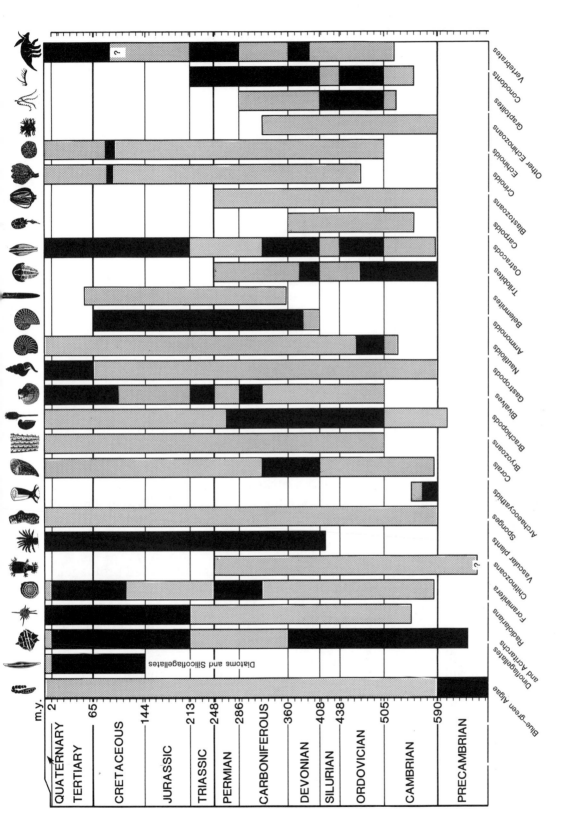

Geologic time span of organisms often found as fossils. Black
shading indicates times when a group is most useful in dating
rocks (Modified from M. S. Petersen and J. K. Rigby. Historical Geology
Laboratory Manual, W. C. Brown Co., Dubuque, Iowa, 1969)

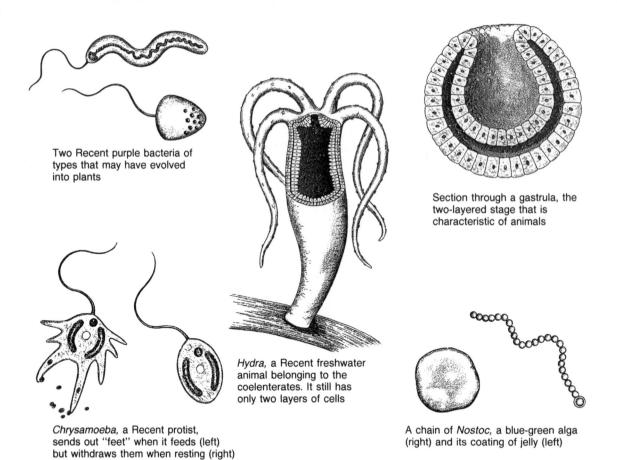

Two Recent purple bacteria of types that may have evolved into plants

Section through a gastrula, the two-layered stage that is characteristic of animals

Hydra, a Recent freshwater animal belonging to the coelenterates. It still has only two layers of cells

Chrysamoeba, a Recent protist, sends out "feet" when it feeds (left) but withdraws them when resting (right)

A chain of *Nostoc,* a blue-green alga (right) and its coating of jelly (left)

Bacteria and blue-green algae are monerans.* Chrysamoeba *is a protist, and the hydra is a simple animal

bacteria have been found in Huronian rocks of northern Michigan, the identifications having been made by experienced biologists. Bacteria apparently are common in coal and petrified plants of Devonian and later ages and have been found in coprolites. The commonest types are spheres and rods that may be joined end to end in short chains.

Protists Are Abundant Fossils. Protists are commonly called protozoans ("first animals") and are sometimes placed in the animal kingdom, though a few also are classed as green algae. This confusion comes from the fact that some protists contain chlorophyll. One, *Chrysamoeba,* even alternates between the traditional kingdoms. Part of the time it is egg-shaped, swims with a lash, and makes its own food, like a plant. At other times it loses its lash, sends out armlike "false feet," or pseudopods, and eats in the manner of animals.

The kingdom of protists is hard to define, for its members belong to various groups that differ enormously. All are one-celled, all have nuclei, and many build shells or other hard parts that readily become fossils. They are part of a group called *eucaryotes,* which have a distinct and organized nucleus. In fact, remains of certain protists make up beds of limestone, while others are equally plentiful in chert or are common in quartzite and diatomaceous earth. Paleontologists generally are content to determine the lesser groups to which these fossils belong and let biologists find the characters that bring them together in a single kingdom.

Plants and Fungi—Other Complex Kingdoms. Plants are better defined by what they have been than by what they are. They may have begun as one-celled descendants of green protists that swam with two lashes, not one. They combined carbon dioxide and water into a sugary food, using some of it to cover their cells with the woody stuff called cellulose. That characteristic persisted as plants evolved into a variety of one-celled groups as well as multicellular forms ranging from pond scums to trees. Cellulose even survived the loss of chlorophyll, which happened several times in the complex array of fungi (mushrooms, molds, rusts, and so on). Many modern fungi are parasites or live on dead plants; both habits are very ancient. Tubes and spores have been found in plants more than 300 million years old, as well as in less ancient trees. Ball fungi appear on Carboniferous leaves, and other parasitc types have been found in later formations. Some resemble modern rusts, which do great damage to grain and fruit.

Land plants arose during Middle Silurian times and became common near the end of the Devonian. Except for stony algae, most fossil plants come from Devonian and younger formations.

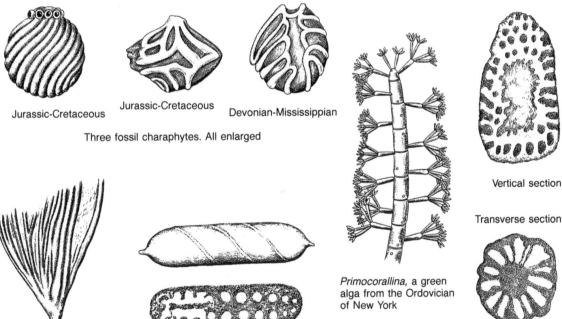

Jurassic-Cretaceous

Jurassic-Cretaceous

Devonian-Mississippian

Three fossil charaphytes. All enlarged

Vertical section

Transverse section

Primocorallina, a green alga from the Ordovician of New York

Macroporella, a green alga of Permian age

Oldhamia, perhaps the imprint of a red alga. Cambrian, New York

Surface and section of *Cylindroporella*, a green alga. Cretaceous

Fossil algae and charaphytes. All enlarged

The chlorophytes, or grass-green algae, are sometimes placed among the plants, but most paleobotanists now refer them to the protists. The group contains three families that are important as fossils. One of these families contains stony algae made up of small tubes that branch repeatedly. The dasyclads consist of short stems with tufts of leaflike structures; the fossils are short tubes or bulbs that are important in reef limestones. Charas are bushy plants as much as 2 feet (61 cm.) high that now grow in fresh waters and cover themselves with crusts of lime. Fossils include twisted stems and rootlike structures, as well as bulblike organs that once contained spores. Because they are very small, these fossils must be examined by means of a microscope. Many fossil charas are marine.

Animals, the Simple Kingdom. The bodies of animals become vastly more complex than those of plants, yet the kingdom they form is more closely knit. The first animals also were offspring of lash-bearing protists, but their ancestors had lost their chlorophyll and had grown into hollow, many-celled (multicellular) balls that formed coordinated colonies. In animals those balls collapsed and lengthened, so that each colony became one organism made up of two layers of cells. All animals still go through this stage unless they simplify the process of reproduction by starting from swellings or buds in the bodies of their parents. Most animals, however, add many cells to the two original layers and develop a third that is still more complex. The results may be traced in shells and bones produced by these layers, as well as in carbonized, dried, or frozen remains of actual ancient flesh. This versatile layer is the mesoderm, or "middle skin."

Sponges—Animals or Protists? Our statement that the animal kingdom is unified takes no account of sponges. They are usually called animals, yet their early development seems quite unlike that of other members of this kingdom, and they seem to represent an evolutionary dead end that gave rise to no offspring. Moreover, cells that line the digestive cavity of sponges seem to be inherited from protists with collarlike structures around their lashes. Multicellularity, in this case, seems to have come about by many protists joining together to form a colony. Some cells specialize for digestion, others for locomotion. Eventually the colony became a coordinated unit. At best, sponges are a loose federation of single protist cells.

WHYS AND HOWS OF CLASSIFICATION

We have been engaged in classification, which separates unlike organisms, and groups like ones together. This practice is far from novel, for it was used by the first human being who recognized his kinship with other men or gave different deer one general name because they all had branching antlers. Ever since that time, people have tried to distinguish different living things and put them together in larger and larger groups. In doing so, men were able to talk with one another about plants and animals. At the same time, they organized their knowledge of the animate world.

The Linnaean System. There have been many systems of classification, both rule-of-thumb and scientific. The one now used took form during the 1700s in the books of a Swedish explorer-doctor-professor named Carl von Linné (Carolus Linnaeus). He based classification upon the kind, or species, which for him was a unit that could be clearly defined. Species that resembled each other in structure or appearance were grouped together in genera, each group being a genus. Similar genera formed families, families formed orders, and orders made up classes. Linnaeus recognized six classes of animals and several more of plants.

Linnaeus assumed that species were divinely created and described them without pausing to explain how or why they had come into existence. Later naturalists and theologians abandoned his example, especially when skeptics began to suggest that species might vary, or that they might produce other species, and so on through genera, families, orders, and classes. To combat these heresies, clerics built up a dogma of divinely established classification, while natural philosophers explained that it revealed the "power, wisdom, and goodness of God as manifested in His creatures." Others invented a long series of catastrophes to get rid of fossil plants and animals, following each disaster by a new creation in which divine wisdom progressed enough to permit the creation of more and more advanced organisms. The culmination of this process supposedly took place in early November of 4004 B.C., when man was created as an improvement of a plan already tried, with limited success, in the anthropoid apes.

This sort of thinking prevailed until 1859, when Charles Darwin and Alfred Russel Wallace declared that species could and did produce other species by processes that also accounted for larger taxonomic groups and the general sequence of life that was revealed by fossils. Darwin's theory aroused bitter opposition but reoriented paleontology and gave new meaning to classification. Scientists began to study fossils in order to learn how they had varied and how they had changed, or evolved, as age succeeded age. Classification, besides distinguishing and naming the species and lesser groups produced

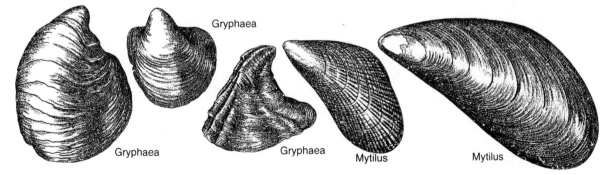

Examples of related but distinct species of **Gryphaea** *and* **Mytilus**

by evolution, began to show how these groups were related in genera, families, orders, and so on. Revising their sequence, to go from great to small, we may illustrate the system thus developed with the common Atlantic-coast oyster as an example:

KINGDOM: Animalia (all animals, either as they are restricted in this book or including the so-called protozoans)
  PHYLUM: Mollusca (the molluscs, most of which have limy shells)
    CLASS: Pelecypoda, or Bivalvia (the bivalves—clams, oysters, mussels, etc., whose shells contain two parts, or valves)
      SUBCLASS: Pteriomorpha
        ORDER: Dysodonta (jingle shells, scallops, oysters, marine mussels, etc.)
          FAMILY: Ostreidae (oysters and their close relatives)
            GENUS: *Ostrea* (true oysters)
              SPECIES: *virginica* (the common eastern or American oyster, a fossil as well as a living species)

These are the basic groups (kingdom, phylum, etc.) used for all organisms. Modern scientists have added such divisions as subphyla, subclasses, and superorders, as well as subgenera, subspecies, races, varieties, and others. Since these are recognized in some groups but not in others, we need not give examples of them.

Names and What They Tell. Every group of organisms needs a name, which is chosen according to methods established by Linnaeus and elaborated by later workers. With a few exceptions, Linnaeus gave one-word names to groups larger than species—*Ostrea* for all oysters, *Aves* for the whole class of birds, and so on. But a species requires two words, the first to place it in its genus and the second to distinguish it from related species. Thus, the dark blue edible mussel was called *Mytilus edulis,* while those tinted with buff and brown became another species. The name of genus always comes first, just as John Smith becomes Smith, John in an index or directory. To avoid tiresome repetition, however, the generic name may be indicated by its initial after it has been give once in full.

Two types of additions have been made to the names employed by Linnaeus. The first type recognizes divisions and includes them. If a genus is divided, the appropriate subgeneric name is inserted in parentheses, *Ostrea (Ostrea) lutraria* being a convenient example. When a species is divided, the varietal or subspecific name is added, as in *Homo sapiens sapiens.* Paleontologists tend to avoid triple names, or trinomials, by raising subspecies to the rank of species. This shortens labels and saves breath in discussion, but it obscures close relationships and so limits the value of classification. Then, too, the small differences that distinguish subspecies in the modern world are simply not detectable in many fossils.

The second type of addition comes from the fact that different people sometimes name the same genus or species, or give the same name to different groups. To show who named what, the author's name is added—*Mytilus* Linnaeus, for instance, or *Strophomena neglecta* James. If a species first named in one genus is moved to another, the author's name goes into parentheses. Thus, *Atrypa reticularis* (Linnaeus) was first called *Anomia* but later was transferred to *Atrypa*. Paleobotanists go still further, putting the original author's name in parentheses and adding that of the authority who gave the species its present generic assignment. Thus *Metasequoia occidentalis* (Newberry) Chaney 1951 was described as *Taxodium occidentale* by Newberry but was transferred to *Metasequoia* by Chaney in 1951.

Names in "Dead" Languages. Linnaeus wrote his books in Latin and chose names from that language or from Latinized Greek. Other scientists followed his example, Latinizing words from modern tongues when the classics became inadequate, and combining words of varied origins when that suited the author's purpose. The results have often been useful, even helpful, but they also included such bizarre or puzzling names as *Agassizocrinus, Chicagocrinus* (should it be pronounced Chi ca" go cri' nus?), and *Hesperopithecus haroldcooki.* Moreover, the whole practice of using "dead" languages has brought endless complaints from people who want things to bear familiar names. Why use polysyllables borrowed from or turned into ancient languages?

The best reason for doing so is the fact that familiar names do not exist. Most species, genera, and other groups were unrecognized, unknown, or unnamed until scientists described them: English, for instance, has no original, everyday names for fossils of such great groups as mammals, amphibians, vertebrates, or molluscs, or for the horde of families, genera, and species that are recognized today. Names, therefore, had to be invented, and the simplest way to do that was to take them from Latin and Greek. Just how would one make a familiar and truly English name for reptiles, protists, or *Astylospongia praemorsa?* And why are these names more "outlandish" than telephone, torque converter, or high-fidelity phonograph?

Another good reason for Latinized names is the fact that they can be used throughout the world, in accordance with recognized rules. But "familiar" names are parts of everyday language, which varies from place to place. Thus the creatures we call sea urchins are *poundstones* in one part of England, *oursins* to the French, *Seeigeln* in German, and *erizos de mar* in Spanish-speaking countries. Even if these terms could be turned into names for genera and species, they would differ in every language and mean nothing to all who did not speak it. And if only one of the terms were used, it would be "outlandish" in all other tongues. Just suppose an English-speaking collector had to use the Japanese sounds and symbol in place of echinoid!

No, the demand for "familiar" names is futile; most of them do not exist or would not work if we tried to use them. The most we can do is employ the few that are available and make a limited number of new ones by translating some technical names and by giving others familiar forms. The first method turns *Hyalospongea,* for instance, into "glass sponges"; the second writes *Reptilia* as "reptiles" and transforms *Mollusca* into "molluscs." It also takes the capitals from a few generic names, producing new English words such as eohippus and hydra. Little would be gained by translating the former into "dawn horse." Not only is the term unfamiliar; the creature itself fell so far short of being or even resembling a horse that such a name would be deceptive to all who do not understand its evolutionary significance.

When you are faced, however, with a scientific name, it is often helpful to be able to work out what the Latin and Greek parts of the word mean. One good book, besides various dictionaries, is R. W. Brown's *Composition of Scientific Words.* This can sometimes make a seemingly incomprehensible name make quite good sense.

Why Names Change.   The Linnaean method allows names to be used around the world, but it cannot keep them from changing.

Many names change because new discoveries show that old groups were so loosely defined that they included various unrelated things. In 1758, for example, Linnaeus named the fossil shell now called *Atrypa reticularis.* He did not illustrate his species, however, nor did he describe it in detail. During the next 160 years, therefore, paleontologists applied *A. recticularis* to a great variety of shells from Silurian and Devonian formations in many parts of the world. Other names were ignored or neglected, and the "species" became a catchall, a wastebasket, for shells of one general type that lived during periods that amounted to 90 million years.

This went on until the 1920s, when paleontologists began to reexamine this supposedly long-lived species. Looking closely and following modern

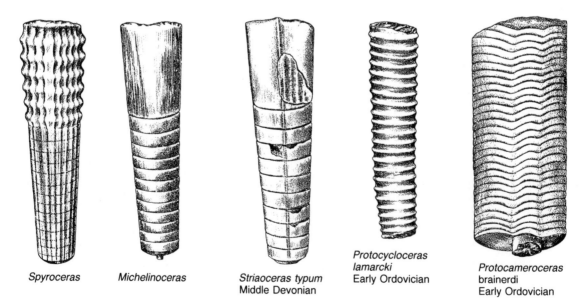

Spyroceras   Michelinoceras   Striaoceras typum   Protocycloceras   Protocameroceras
                                            Middle Devonian   lamarcki   brainerdi
                                                                       Early Ordovician   Early Ordovician

How names change. All these fossils were once called Orthoceras

standards of classification, they recognized forgotten species and described several new ones. Thus, fossils once called *A. reticularis* have been given names such as *A. nuntia, A. devoniana,* and *A. nevada.* Similar refinement has turned *Platystrophia lynx* Eichwald into *P. ponderosa, P. moritura, P. biforata,* and other species or subspecies.

Genera also are subject to refinement and renaming, a good example being *Spirifer.* It became a catchall that ranged from Silurian to Pennsylvanian, with a vast variety of species. Then it was divided into subgenera and genera—*Delthyris, Eospirifer, Syringothyris,* and so on. More than twenty of these groups are so common that some of their species are recognized as index fossils. The genus *Orthis,* named in 1828, has been divided even more thoroughly.

Other names change because of a rule that says the first name given a genus or species must hold, even though a later one may be more appropriate or better known. In 1839, for example, bones and teeth of a fossil whale were called *Zeuglodon* ("yoke tooth"). This name was used for many years, until an expert on whales found that identical bones had been named *Basilosaurus* in 1835. Though *Basilosaurus* means "king of reptiles," it now is the technical name of these whales, leaving zeuglodon—without a capital Z—only in popular usage.

Orthoceras illustrates another rule (the Rule of Priority), which says that when the same name is given to more than one genus or species the first usage shall be kept. For more than a century, *Orthoceras* was applied to straight-shelled cephalopods (Chapter XVII) found in Ordovician to Triassic formations. Then, in 1936, two authorities showed that this name had been given to clams and several other creatures before it was used for cephalopods. A clam, therefore, has become *Orthoceras,* and many American fossils once given that name are now called *Michelinoceras.*

Large groups, from orders to kingdoms, are practically exempt from rules; their names vary with the habits and opinions of authors. Thus, the kingdom Protista of this book appears (with a few omissions) as the phylum Protozoa in most older volumes. Corals are Anthozoa or Actinozoa, and the technical name of graptolites (Chapter XXI) may be Graptolithina, Graptolitoidea, or Graptozoa. Even duplication can occur if in widely differing groups, for both lampreys and a class of bryozoans are called Cyclostomata.

FAMILY TREES OF PHYLA AND CLASSES

In the old, simple days of special creation, biologists often arranged organisms in what was called an "ascending order." This meant that the simplest group was put at the bottom of a series. The one that seemed to rank next in complexity went above it, and so on through the living world. Everyone agreed that plants such as algae (bacteria were virtually unknown) belonged at or near the bottom of this sequence, and animals with backbones at the top. Between these extremes there was some variation, depending on how experts understood complexity.

Then came Darwin and the effort to make classification reflect relationships. But chapters in books follow in order, and so do printed lines on a page. To overcome this disadvantage, biologists began to draw "family trees" for the major groups of organisms. Such trees indicated descent and kinship among these organic groups, just as similar trees had traced kinships in human families.

If this book sought to describe phyla and classes in the order of their relationships, it would begin with monerans, progress with protists, and continue through plants, fungi, and animals with never a backward glance to tell what members of one great group lived with or upon those of another. Such a plan would serve very well in a textbook, but it would obscure important factors in life's progress, such as the dependence of land-dwelling vertebrates upon complex terrestrial plants. Even then, the order of chapters alone would not give relationships clearly unless the text itself went far afield into subjects such as biochemistry or embryology, which are seldom recorded by fossils.

We have chosen to avoid such digressions and to arrange chapters in an order that tells significant stories. Since the relationships of kingdoms have been discussed, we make no further effort to trace them. We also do not try to show connections within the kingdom of protists, which may contain several phyla commonly referred to as plants. This leaves relationships within the three kingdoms—plants, fungi, and animals—to be represented by so-called family trees.

The plant kingdom begins with green algae, whose ancestors apparently were green, lash-bearing protists. Some living green algae have only one cell; others, such as sea lettuce, are multicellular. Some of the most remarkable green algae cover themselves with plates or continuous deposits of lime, which make the plants resemble corals. In fact, "coralline" algae have often outranked corals as builders of limestone reefs.

Plants more complex than algae belong to eight or nine principal groups, which various authors divide among four to nine phyla. Simplest of these, and presumably oldest, are the mosses and liverworts. The latter are sheet-like affairs that grow on damp soil or rocks. Some authorities think they covered moist lowlands of very ancient times, while lichens (which are compounds of fungi and blue-green algae) grew upon dry rocks, as they do today.

"Higher" plants have roots, stems, leaves, and tubes that carry sap from one part of the organism to another. These tubes first appeared among aquatic or swamp-dwelling plants that presumably evolved from green algae. These higher plants probably lived near the mouths of rivers; some became large and abundant during the Late Carboniferous Coal Age, more than 280 million years ago.

Seed ferns also reached their zenith in Pennsylvanian times, and they seem to have formed an ancestral stock of all subsequent plant phyla. These include the cycads, conifers and their allies, and flowering plants (angiosperms), all of which developed during the past 200 million years.

Compared with plants, the family tree of animals seems to have suffered from lack of pruning. It begins with an inferred ancestor whose body probably was cup-shaped and contained two layers. This creature produced two types of offspring: the sea nuts, or comb jellies, and coelenterates. The latter diverged into several classes—but before going too far, it also produced two types of offspring. In one of these a third body layer (the mesoderm) developed from within the rim of the cup, expanding into muscles and other organs and enclosing a body cavity. In the second type, the third body layer came from the inner part of the cup, which was the digestive tract. Pouches that formed there became the mesodermal organs and contained the body cavity, whose technical name is coelom.

Now we see how little such terms as "higher" mean when they are applied to classification. Old systems would make this second body plan the "higher," since it is found in backboned animals and their relatives. Yet this "enterocoel" plan is limited to just a few phyla—including starfish, sea urchins, the acorn worms, and vertebrates. The "lower" (schizocoel) plan, on the other hand, is found in a much larger series of phyla. Though none of these phyla equals some chordates in size, intelligence, or complexity of structure, they vastly exceed the enterocoel groups in variety and abundance. Indeed, one schizocoel class (the insects) contains more individuals and species than do all other animal groups combined. So, who is to determine the "success" of these groups? Success is certainly a relative judgment.

FAMILY TREES AND CLASSIFICATION

One of the aims of studying animals and plants is to understand their relationships to one another. Once some understanding is gained, then a classification can be set up. As we have seen in this chapter, however, these classifications change as time passes. More information is gained on a certain animal or plant that increases our understanding and that may rate a shift in its position in the classification.

Another reason that positions within a classification can change can also be that the rules used by the paleontologist or biologist studying the group may be different. Certainly within the last few years there has been much discussion concerning just how to go about family-tree analysis and classification. At least three schools of thought exist. First there are the pheneticists, those who count up all the characters that an animal or plant group share. Those groups that share the greatest number are thought to be the closest relatives. Family trees are drawn up using the degrees of similar-

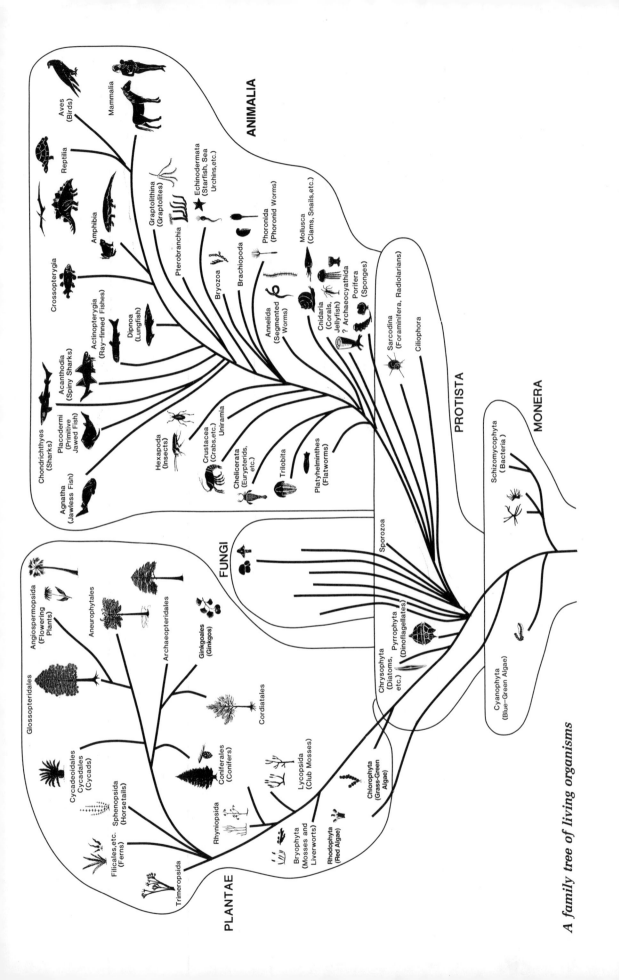

A family tree of living organisms

ity, using computers that consider often hundreds of characters at a time, to sort out the branching patterns.

Another group of scientists are interested in using only those characteristics that are specialized features, to tie organisms together. The more complex such features are, such as feathers for birds, the greater the chance that they represent a structure developed only once. Thus, the group will be monophyletic, that is from one ancestral stock. Sometimes, confusion is caused by unrelated animals and plants developing similar structures because they have a similar diet or a similar way of walking or running. This is called convergent evolution and can produce similar-looking forms that are not related at all. Thus, elephants have trunks and so do tapirs (though theirs are short). But these two groups are not all that closely related. Likewise, flightless birds, such as the dodo and the emu, reduced their wings to almost nothing, but this is not because they are related, but is simply a reflection of their lifestyle.

Among those scientists using specialized features to study animals, there are at least two major subdivisions, each of which uses slightly different rules. There are the cladists, who suggest that once an animal or plant develops a certain special feature, it must be classified with all those others that also possess that special feature. If you have a classification produced by a cladist, you can easily reconstruct the family tree (or phylogeny) from that classification. Another group would recognize the same family tree but would set up their classification in a somewhat different way: They would recognize the specializations but would also take into account the overall similarity of the animals and plants to one another when setting up their classification. Thus, organisms that had just branched off from an ancestral group but had the special feature of a new group might be classified with the ancestral group because it shared a large number of similarities with that ancestral group. It is not so simple a matter to reconstruct the family tree from a classification like this.

So, there is often not just one answer to the question of where an animal or plant should be placed in a classification or family tree. You as a reader of any papers or books on the subjects of taxonomy (the study of classification) or phylogeny (the study of family trees) must beware—and be aware of the philosophy, the set of rules, that each writer uses. Then you will better understand why classifications and family trees can be rather different, even though they begin with the same animals.

CHAPTER V

Earth's Oldest Remains

Many modern theories explain how the earth was formed, and the majority differ only in small details. Many of them postulate that our solar system started as a concentration of interstellar dust. Formation probably took place within a nebular cloud where interstellar dust and gas had already collected at more than ten thousand times the density of the rest (the nonnebular part) of space. The sun formed as this nebula fragmented and began to heat up to as much as 30,000 degrees Fahrenheit at the sun's center and to as little as 2,000 degrees Fahrenheit near Jupiter's present orbit. Through time, this entire nebular collection contracted, owing to the effect of gravity.

The earth and other planets then began to form, about 4,600 million years ago from the outer edges of the disk of gases and dust. They were divided into two groups: the inner, or terrestrial, planets, extending from Mercury to the asteroid belt, and the outer, or Jovian, planets, which included Jupiter and those beyond. The composition of the outer planets and their atmospheres more closely approximated the composition of the rest of the universe than did the denser, inner planets, of which our Earth is a prime example. As the inner planets were smaller and had weaker gravitational fields, as well as being closer to the sun, and thus warmer, the lighter, more volatile elements were able to escape into space.

After the initial high temperatures, the earth began to cool. Its core, mantle, and crust began to form about 4,200 million years ago, and a great deal of volcanic activity characterized the surface of this consolidating ball of celestial dust. Along with the moon, great craters formed on the surface of the earth as it was pummeled by large meteorites until about 3,300 million years ago.

The earth's earliest atmosphere probably formed in one of two ways. Either it was simply the gases of the nebula as a whole, less those light molecules such as hydrogen which evaporated into space. Or it was generated by volcanic activity bringing gases to the surface ("outgassing"). Besides water vapor, the principal components of the primeval atmosphere would have been either hydrogen, ammonia, and methane; or nitrogen, carbon dioxide, and carbon monoxide. Whichever group of three compounds plus water was dominant, the others, plus possibly hydrogen sulfide and hydrochloric acid, would have been present as minor constituents. No matter which compounds were dominant, it is clear that no free oxygen was present. Temperatures at this time were approaching what they are today, about 75–77 degrees Fahrenheit on the average.

The water that was ejected from the volcanoes as vapor, condensed as enormous and nearly continuous rainstorms. From these, pools, lakes, and the beginnings of the oceans formed. The rains also began to clear some of the volcanic dust particles from the air that must have given the sky a lingering red haze. The thunderstorms that yielded the rain also produced large-scale electrical discharges, lightning. Together with the heat from erupting volcanoes, a great deal of energy was injected into the environments on the earth's surface.

Whatever the original composition of the atmosphere, by 4,000 million years ago the one that lay above the ever-growing sea was made up largely of nitrogen. Only small traces of other gases were present, such as carbon dioxide. Most of the carbon dioxide was dissolved in the seas. To us this atmosphere would have been highly poisonous. There was no appreciable amount of oxygen to breathe. We could only have survived if we had a space suit or a diving outfit that would have provided air to breathe and a protection from the massive amounts of incoming ultraviolet radiation from the sun. At this time there was no ozone layer in the upper atmosphere, such as we have today, to act as a shield from this harmful radiation.

Prior to 2,000 million years ago, widespread deposits of banded iron cherts, and chemically unoxidized minerals such as detrital pyrite and uranite occurred. If even 0.1 percent of the atmosphere had been composed of oxygen, these deposits could not have formed.

The atmosphere remained much the same until about 1,500 to 2,000 million years ago. At this critical time, levels of oxygen that seem to have resulted from the biologic activity of plants had built up significantly in the atmosphere and in the oceans. For the first time, extensive red beds show up in the rock record, indicating that enough oxygen was around to oxidize the iron ions in the sediments. After this time there was no widespread deposition of unoxidized sediments. Such high levels of oxygen also provided for the development of a much more varied array of forms of life, which had already begun some 1,500 million years before, perhaps first recorded in the Warrawoona Group rocks of Western Australia nearly 3,500 million years ago.

THE BEGINNINGS OF LIFE

In order to try to understand how life began, scientists have used primarily two approaches, one of which involves carefully examining the fossil record for clues of what actually went on in Precambrian time. Another approach has been made by organic chemists, who have tried in the laboratory experimentally to produce the basic building blocks of life from simple compounds that were probably a part of the primitive atmosphere more than 3,500 million years ago. One famous experiment was carried out by a young graduate student, Stanley L. Miller, at the University of Chicago in 1953. He set up an apparatus through which he circulated a mixture of steam, ammonia, methane, and hydrogen. Through this mixture he passed a high-energy electrical spark, representing the lightning that might have existed in the early Precambrian world. He then condensed the steam before starting the process all over again. At the end of a full week, the water had turned a deep red and was cloudy. He analyzed the mixture and found it to contain a number of amino acids, the basic building blocks of proteins. He had gone from simple compounds to complex molecules that are directly associated with living systems. Over the years since Miller's work, other experiments using a variety of "atmospheric" compositions, and strong solar radiation, thunderlike sound waves, drying, and/or freezing have yielded a variety of complex molecules, including, most important, nucleotides, the structural units that form DNA, the basic building block of living systems. So far, no laboratory experiment has produced a DNA molecule capable of reproducing itself. But the experimental work is yet in its infancy, and it is very suggestive that eventually such a complex molecule will be constructed. We still have a long way to go, however, before there is an understanding of how complex molecules became organized into cells. We do know that, under certain special circumstances, such molecules, when suspended in water, will aggregate into small spheres separated from the water by a membrane. Why this happens, however, is not understood. But it is exciting experimental work that will undoubtedly continue to increase our understanding of life's beginnings.

THE "DAWN ANIMAL OF CANADA"

Where there once was life there may now be fossils; the problem has been to find them. Once found, they must be interpreted. What are they and how did they live? What do they tell about life's progress during very ancient times?

The first serious effort to answer these questions began in 1859. In that year, Sir William Logan, director of the Geological Survey of Canada, exhibited specimens "of probably organic character" from rocks supposed to be little younger than the so-called primeval crust. Logan submitted the fossils to his friend J. William Dawson, an outstanding paleontologist. He called them colonial foraminifers, one-celled creatures described in Chapter VI, which covered themselves with limy incrustations. Dawson named one species *Eozoon canadense,* the "dawn animal of Canada."

Filled worm burrows
from the Precambrian of Glacier
National Park, Montana

Eozoon canadense, from
the Grenville marble
of Quebec

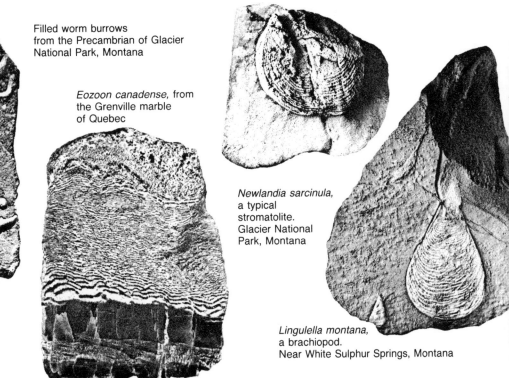

Newlandia sarcinula,
a typical
stromatolite.
Glacier National
Park, Montana

Lingulella montana,
a brachiopod.
Near White Sulphur Springs, Montana

Typical fossils of Late Precambrian (Proterozoic) or earliest Cambrian age

This he did in 1864, with the approval of an outstanding authority on modern "forams." Some scientists were enthusiastic, others were more reserved, and several became hostile. In 1866 two Irish mineralogists dismissed the "dawn animal" as a mere mixture of minerals developed as steam and heat from the earth's core changed beds of impure limestone to marble. Another critic compared the supposed fossils with blocks of limestone thrown out of Monte Somma, the ancient volcano on which Mount Vesuvius now stands.

Thus began an argument. On one side were Dawson and his supporters, who tried to prove that *Eozoon* was a fossil and described similar things from other very old formations. The opposition included geologists and mineralogists who maintained that all these supposed fossils were inorganic. Most of these critics based their opinions on thin sections, ignoring Dawson's insistence that *Eozoon* should also be seen in its native rock. One German, however, crossed the Atlantic to examine the dawn animal in ledges and quarries on the Quebec side of the Ottawa River. His verdict agreed with that of his fellows: *Eozoon* showed structures produced by both heat and pressure and therefore was not a fossil.

THE PUZZLING STROMATOLITES

This might have settled the problem had not Dawson found fossils resembling *Eozoon* in rocks of Hastings County, Ontario. Not only were these eozoons virtually unmodified by heat, steam, or compression; they were undeniably related to structures that have come to be known as stromatolites, a term that means "layer stones."

This relationship, however, did not immediately establish the Ontario eozoons as fossils. Stromatolites had been known for many years, and some of them had been described as calcareous protozoans. That theory, however, had lost standing; when interest in the fossils revived, they were transferred to the plant kingdom as algae. But several geologists promptly called them inorganic concretions, while an eminent paleobotanist declared that only fossils preserving cells could be referred to as algae. Other critics, less specific, were content to dismiss all concern with stromatolites as "unfortunate."

Unfortunate or not, the concern persisted. Today stromatolites are widely, if not generally, accepted as fossils produced by algae, though some are formed by bacteria, foraminifera, or even inorganic processes in caves such as slump structures. Indeed, stromatolites mainly constructed of calcium and magnesium carbonates are being formed today by algae inhabiting hot springs, lakes, and seas.

Here again we digress to clarify our words. The term *algae* is a general one; we apply it to plants or plantlike organisms that range from single cells in water or jelly to seaweeds with stalks and leaflike blades, or to jointed growths that resemble corals. Based on the studies carried out by Dr. Brian Logan in Shark Bay, south of Carnarvon, in Western Australia, stromatolites are the work of very simple blue-green "algae," or cyanophytes, and green algae (chlorophytes) which live in chains or mats and cover themselves with jelly. They also take carbon dioxide from water in order to make food, and in doing so compel limy material to settle in layers upon the jelly. Thus, the organisms build stony supports for their colonies, but not their cells, while they are still alive, by trapping sediments and shells of microorganisms in the algal mat. These structures, the stromatolites, are moundlike or headlike masses of laminated sediment that stand a few centimeters to many meters above the surface of deposition, in most instances.

Living stromatolites occur from shallow subtidal depths of about 15 feet to supratidal areas up to 6 feet above the low-water mark, and are also formed in mineral springs. Their shapes and growth forms can tell something of the environment in which they lived. Those that inhabited areas of breaking waves, for instance, tend to form circular heads, while those on the tidal flats form sheetlike structures. Stromatolite colonies today also align them-

Hadrophycus immanis *is one of the oldest and largest algal stromatolites, some masses being more than 16 feet in diameter. Found in Precambrian rocks of the Medicine Bow Mountains, Wyoming*

Modern stromatolites growing in Shark Bay, south of Carnarvon, Western Australia

Living algal mat that precipitates the stromatolite structure, Shark Bay

selves according to the prevailing currents, often into linear structures parallel to the current direction. Internal structure of the stromatolites will also vary, depending on the water depth, amount of wetting, drying, relief of the surface on which they grow, and the amount and rate of erosion, as well as on the actual species that are forming the mats. Attached to these living fortresses are any number of small encrusting foraminifers, minute molluscs, and serpulid worms that become incorporated into the heads as they grow, ultimately to be preserved as fossils too.

The living forms, however, may not represent the full range of possibilities for stromatolite-forming algae. In Devonian sediments of the Canning Basin, of Australia, gigantic stromatolite reefs nearly a mile wide have been found. These apparently were formed in water depths of 75 to 300 feet. So the tolerances of today's stromatolite-building organisms may be considerably narrower than they have been in the past.

With this knowledge of modern algal stromatolites, we come back to *Eozoon* and other very ancient fossils. *Eozoon* itself is found in limestone and marbles termed the Grenville Series, which may be more than 800 million years old. The fossils are convex or vase-shaped and consist of crumpled or gently convex layers whose structure suggests matted tubes and rods.

Hadrophycus ("mighty sea plant") includes stromatolites that form beds in the Medicine Bow Mountains of Wyoming. Colonies range from irregular sheets to flattened biscuits, swollen heads, and broad-based domes, and

Growth form of stromatolites subjected to prevailing currents that run parallel to the algal ridges. Knowledge of this modern effect on growth form permits prediction of current directions in ancient stromatolite concentrations

Growth form of stromatolites in water, with no prevailing current direction, in unprotected areas such as open headlands

structure varies with preservation. Fossils in which dolomite alternates with grainy chert show only crenulate layers. Others, made up of fine-grained chert, contain both layers and thick, irregular pillars. They show most plainly in broken, weathered domes and in those that were scraped smooth by glaciers of the last ice age.

Stromatolites have been found in other very old deposits of New Brunswick, the Northwest Territories of Canada, and the Macdonnell Ranges of central Australia. The most beautiful are those in the dark red iron ore known as jaspilite. Blocks make fine polished slabs, and selected blood-red pieces may be cut for gems.

Stromatolites have been used to subdivide rocks of the Late Precambrian in Russia, North America, Africa, India, and Australia, based primarily on their microstructure. This seems mainly controlled by the particular species of algae that are depositing the stromatolite layers. Stromatolites are particularly abundant and varied at that time, more so than at any other, probably because of the abundance of near-shore shelf seas (largely lacking in the Archaean), and the lack of grazers and burrowers, major destroyers in the Phanerozoic. Perhaps, too, the massive development of shelly organisms in the Cambrian meant less carbonate was available for deposition by algae, as so much was already tied up in shells.

Algae of Glacier National Park.   We now skip long ages and many miles to reach a happy hunting ground for algae in the northern Rockies. There a huge block of Precambrian rock has been broken and thrust upward and eastward over much younger formations for a distance of thirty-five miles. In the end it formed the spectacular mountains of Glacier National Park, Montana, and Waterton Lakes National Park, in adjacent Alberta.

Though shattered along the break, or thrust fault, rocks in the mountains have suffered little change. All show the layers in which their sediment settled, often rapidly but sometimes so slowly that the deposits of two centuries are only one inch thick. Ridges piled up by rippling waves are common, as are cracks that opened when the water retreated, leaving broad mud flats to dry in the sun. Other beds consist of fragments stirred up by floods or violent storms.

Amid these records of a shallow, shifting sea are vast numbers of stromatolites. Some form massive beds near the thrust fault; others are scattered through a thick formation of buff-weathering dolomite. Compact biscuits are found in the lowermost beds; flat-topped colonies appear higher in the series, beside trails and along a paved highway that crosses Glacier National Park. This road also cuts ledges made up of conical masses, and reefs as fine as those built by corals during later times. Those reefs grew while the muddy sea bottom was soft, for their weight squeezed the sediment below them and pushed it up at their sides.

Most surprising of all are algal biscuits found in red and green strata along the Continental Divide. These stromatolites almost always grew upon mud flats that had dried and cracked and then were covered by shallow water. Sudden storms often rolled the biscuits over; others were caught in floods of lava that issued from cracks. These lavas tore up mud and rolled it into twisted masses and turned stromatolites into lumps of iron-stained chert. So persistent were the algae, however, that they reappeared as soon as the lava hardened and was covered by a thin coat of mud.

Most of these fossils have been called *Collenia,* a name applied to stromatolites made up of convex layers that are flattened near the center. They form biscuit-shaped or columnar colonies, and many columns may unite in one larger colony. Stromatolites that grew on cracked mud or hardened lava are now placed in *Cryptozoon.* Unfortunately, stromatolites varied with the conditions under which they developed, and these variations do not fit under any name.

Again, careful studies of the living stromatolites in Australia and the Persian Gulf have shown that because of these environmental controls, the generic and specific names previously applied to these organisms were not realistic. It seems best to "classify" algal stromatolites according to structural types that always appear to be associated with a certain kind of environment. Thus, LLH-types (laterally linked hemispheroids) are formed as continuous mats with algal-bound sediments in marine intertidal mudflat

Collenia frequens *(left) and* **Collenia versiformis** *(right). Two types of algal stromatolites from late Precambrian (Belt) deposits of Glacier National Park, Montana*

environments, primarily in protected areas such as behind barrier islands. In addition to these structural names, generic and specific names can be given to the occasional remains of actual algae found preserved with these inorganic deposits.

STONY ALGAE OF LATER AGES

Stromatolites were not limited to the earliest eras but grew abundantly in seas of Cambrian and later times. Some may be called *Collenia,* but others must be placed in different genera.

Cryptozoon ("hidden or obscure animal") was named in the days when *Eozoon* was regarded as a foraminifer. It generally grew in crumpled layers that formed biscuits, or domes, whose upper surface resembled cauliflower, though at least one species spread out in undulating layers. The most spectacular form, *Cryptozoon proliferum,* was crowded into great barrier reefs around an island which now forms the Adirondack Mountains, in New York. Part of one reef, scraped smooth by glaciers, is to be seen in the "Petrified Sea Gardens," near Saratoga Springs. Good collecting grounds may be found near State College, Pennsylvania. A very different species occurs at Fountain, Minnesota, and in a bank beside U.S. Highway 52, 6.8 miles (11.3 km.) north of that town.

Solenopora is known to be a red alga, for its biscuits and heads are made up of tiny calcareous tubes that formed around algal filaments. *Girvanella* also is made up of tubes, but its small colonies are spheroidal or egg-shaped. *Ottonosia* looks like a little, crumpled *Cryptozoon* that developed around a shell, pebble, or some other solid body.

Algae of Freshwater Lakes.   Some 50 million years ago, a lake environment described in Chapter XXII covered parts of what now are Wyoming, Colorado, and Utah. Near the shores were rich growths of what seems to be a blue-green alga known as *Chlorellopsis.* Its cells were covered by small limy shells; the shells accumulated in layers, and the layers built biscuit-shaped masses resembling *Cryptozoon. Chlorellopsis* also grew around logs or upright stumps which finally were replaced by chalcedony. Some of these have been mistaken for geyser tubes or cones.

OTHER PRECAMBRIAN FOSSILS; TRACES OF EARLY LIFE

Two sorts of evidence of early life exist in Precambrian rocks. Of one sort are the actual remains of organisms, while the second consists of physical or chemical traces (chemical fossils) of their activities. Stromatolites are examples of the physical traces of organic activity and can sometimes incorporate in their structure remains of once living algae.

A reef of algal stromatolites called Collenia (above) in Belt strata, Going-to-the-Sun Highway in Glacier National Park, Montana. (Below) a bed of Cryptozoon proliferum, Late Cambrian of the "Petrified Sea Gardens," near Saratoga Springs, New York

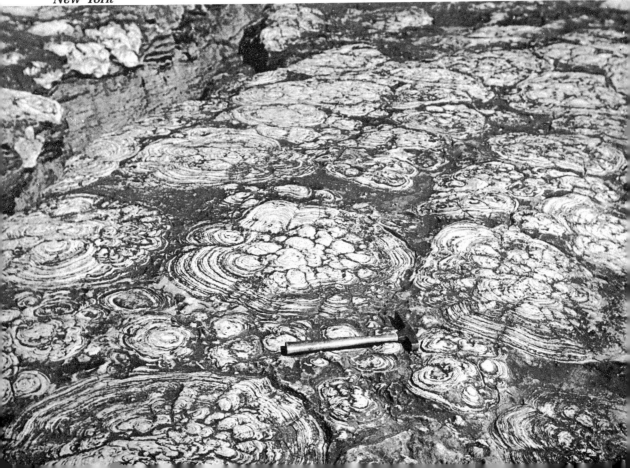

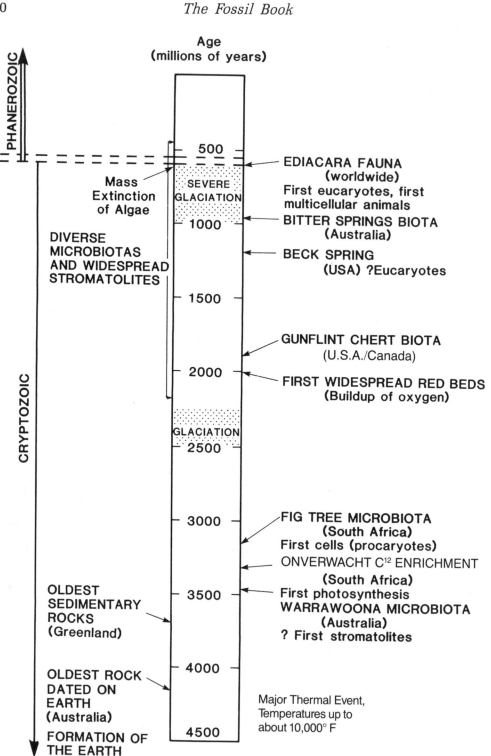

An outline of the significant events in the origin and early evolution of life (Courtesy of J. W. Warren)

The oldest evidence of life may be stromatolites dated at about 3,800 million years, though the identification of these laminated structures from Western Australia have not been fully accepted as organic.

Another indication that living things existed comes from complex carbon compounds found in rocks of about 3,350 million years in the upper part of the Onverwacht Group, in South Africa. Dr. D. Z. Oehler analyzed the carbon content of these rocks from bottom to top. She found that in the lower and middle parts of the Onverwacht there was a disproportionately high amount of C^{13} relative to C^{12}, whereas in the uppermost part there was a marked reduction of C^{13}. C^{13} and C^{12} are both naturally occurring isotopes of carbon and differ in that C^{13} has one more neutron in its nucleus. A certain ratio of C^{13} to C^{12} exists in the atmosphere, but when green plants remove CO^2 (carbon dioxide) from the air, they selectively concentrate the lighter C^{12} in the carbohydrates that they produce through photosynthesis. These carbohydrates are eaten by organisms and become cycled through other living systems. As a result, carbon compounds that are processed by living things have the C^{12} enrichment. So, Dr. Oehler's observations of the Onverwacht rocks suggest that photosynthesis had begun by the time the upper part was being deposited, and that this process left behind the chemical fossils as its "signature."

Remains of early cells. There are several places in the world where single-celled organisms are found in Precambrian rocks. The oldest of these to be accepted without doubt as organic come from a series of cherts, shales, and sandstones exposed in the Transvaal of South Africa. These rocks have been dated at about 3,200 million years. In the Fig Tree Group, the minute fossils are preserved in chert and are best studied by slicing the rock extremely thin and then examining it under a high-powered optical or an electron microscope. If the chert is dissolved with hydrofluoric acid, the residue left behind is the fossils, often highly deformed. At least two kinds of fossils are present: tiny rod-shaped forms that resemble living bacteria in cell-wall structure, size, and shape; and spherical structures resembling blue-green algae. Most of these are no larger than 20 microns (1/1,000 in.)! All of these "cells" seem to be procaryotes (have no distinct nucleus).

The Gunflint Chert, in northern Minnesota and neighboring Ontario, dated at about 1,900 million years, and the Bitter Springs Formation, in central Australia, with a 900-million-year age, contain a much greater variety of procaryotes. In the Gunflint sediments, which also includes stromatolites, three main categories of organisms exist: thin threads with wall-like partitions closely resembling today's filamentous bacteria and blue-green algae, a variety of spherical star-shaped, and umbrella-shaped bodies of unknown relationships. The younger Bitter Springs rocks contain an even greater diversity, especially of forms that appear to be related to blue-green algae. Some scientists have suggested that the diversity may be too great, for some of the different "species" may have been produced by the different ways

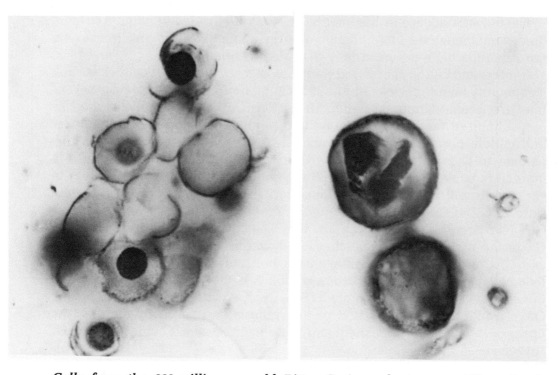

Cells from the 900-million-year-old Bitter Springs cherts, near Ellery Creek, Macdonnell Ranges, Northern Territory, Australia. These single-celled organisms were probably all procaryotes; that is, they lacked nuclei. The circular cells were about 10 microns (a micron is equal to 1/1000 of a millimeter) in diameter. The nucleuslike structures in these cells are pyrite crystals or other inclusions thought not to be nuclei. (Courtesy of J. W. Warren and I. Stewart, Monash University)

individual cells have dried after death. Further studies of both living forms and the fossils will help resolve such a perplexing problem.

Whether any of these fossils were actually eucaryotes (forms containing a nucleus where the genetic material controlling inheritance is concentrated) is not clear. Some cells look as if they have a nucleus, but on close inspection it is not at all evident whether this might not be merely an inorganic fleck or a drying flaw. The first undisputed occurrence of eucaryotes, however, was about 700 million years ago, when multicellular organisms first made their appearance.

The Multicellular Organisms: How complex organisms with many cells arose from single-celled forms is still not understood. One theory suggests that the cell walls of a single-celled organism infolded to produce such structures as the nucleus, mitochondria, and chloroplasts. The last two are involved in energy transfer and food oxidation. In procaryotes all of these functions are, in fact, carried out by the cell walls. Another theory suggests that certain procaryotes invaded others and then began to function as single units.

Regardless of just how this happened, by about 700 million years ago the first multicellular forms had appeared and diversified into a number of types. These forms were scattered at low paleolatitudes on just about every continent in the Late Precambrian, but probably are best preserved in the Flinders Ranges, of South Australia, where they were discovered as late as 1947. The fossils from this area gave their name to the time period that just precedes the Cambrian, the Ediacaran, from 670 to 550 million years ago. During this period, following the marked glaciation at the end of the Proterozoic, and the early part of the Cambrian, nearly all major phyla and most classes of invertebrates appeared.

Forms that may represent soft corals *(Charniodiscus)*, jellyfishlike animals *(Ediacara)*, worms *(Dickinsonia)*, arthropods *(Praecambridium)*, and many unknown groups *(Tribrachidium)* are represented abundantly in the Flinders Range rocks. All the animals were soft-bodied, they had no mineralized hard parts, and thus they have left behind only their impressions. They were certainly highly advanced over their single-celled predecessors, though they were relatively simpler than many of those multcellular animals that succeeded them in the Cambrian. Some, for instance, of the wormlike forms, were evidently extremely thin. This had been interpreted by certain paleon-

Reconstruction of the Ediacara fauna by Robert Allen and Mary Wade. (Courtesy of Alan Bartholomai, Queensland Museum)

Reconstruction of the Ediacara fauna by Frank Knight. Wormlike and jellyfishlike animals dominated. 1. Tribrachidium *and* 2. Parvancornia, *both of unknown relationships;* 3. *a sponge;* 4. Dickinsonia *and* 5. Tomopteris, *both worm-like animals;* 6. Pennatula, *a sea-pen-like animal;* 7. *a worm-like form in a sand burrow; and* 8. Ediacara, *a jellyfishlike animal*

Mawsonites spriggi,
a jellyfishlike animal

Several animals from the Ediacara fauna, late Precambrian, Flinders Range, South Australia. These are the oldest known multicellular animals and the first with organized nuclei in their cells. (Photographs by N. S. Pledge, reproduced by the courtesy of the South Australian Museum)

Charniodiscus longus, a sea-pen-like
animal; width about 5 centimeters (2 in.)

Spriggina floundersi, a segmented wormlike
animal; length about 4 centimeters (1.6 in.)

Dickinsonia costata, a segmented-worm-like
animal; length about 6.5 centimeters (2.5 in.)

Parvancornia minchami, an animal of
unknown relationships; about 2 centimeters
(slightly less than 1 in.) in length

Tribrachidium heraldicum, an animal of
unknown relationships; about 2.5 centimeters
(about 1 in.) in diameter

tologists to suggest that the circulatory systems of these animals were not highly developed and that they depended on oxygen intake through the skin. Thus, they could not become too thick, for oxygen could not be transported very far from the skin surface.

The Ediacaran animals most probably reproduced sexually. This advance over asexual reproduction vastly increased the variety of organisms. This gave decidedly more grist for the mill upon which natural selection could work to produce the vast array of life-forms which characterized the remaining Phanerozoic, the next 550 million years.

For some time, the interpretation of the Ediacaran animals has been that they are related to living groups, such as segmented worms and jellyfish. Another possibility is that they may have belonged to groups that have no modern descendants. Instead, however, they may represent a level of organization, an experiment in the basic way things are built, that failed and became extinct. The animals we see later in the Cambrian, according to this theory, would be the successful experiments, some of which ultimately gave rise to the groups we know today, including ourselves.

CHAPTER VI

A Variety of Protists

The theory holds that protists (Chapter IV) began when two or more single-celled organisms that lacked a distinct nucleus (procaryotes) came together to form a symbiotic relationship (mutually useful coexistence)—all inside one cell wall. This could have happened either by a "phagotroph" engulfing one or more cells, or alternatively a cell or cells penetrating the wall of a second organism. Each of the procaryotes that came together possibly provided the building blocks that led to a more complex, eucaryotic cell, which contained a distinct nucleus bound by its own membrane, cell organelles responsible for energy production and maintenance of the cell, and even in some cases the little whiplike flagella used for locomotion. The living amoeba *Pelomyxa* may resemble one of these early eucaryotes, for it lacks many of the specialized structures found in most of today's nucleus-bearing cells.

Such is only a theory, and there are others explaining developmental patterns in these early organisms. Decidedly more information is needed before we can thoroughly understand what really happened. For instance, did organisms capable of producing their own food (autotrophs, such as photosynthetic plants) develop after those requiring food from their environment (heterotrophs)? Many theories favor this idea, but more fossil material, as well as more understanding of living species of these types, are needed. At least the fossil record has strongly suggested, however, that the first organisms could not function in an environment with oxygen (they were thus anaerobic). Only about 2 billion years ago did forms develop the ability to survive under oxygen-rich conditions (aerobic), which is the case with the majority of living things today.

THE PROTISTS

Even deciding who belongs within the kingdom Protista is not entirely without problems. We will assume in this book that protists are the simplest of the eucaryotes, being more complicated than those cells without a distinct

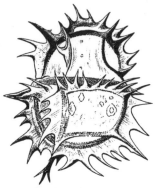

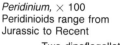

Ctenidodinium, × 700

Peridinium, × 100
Peridinioids range from
Jurassic to Recent

Cannopilus, × 450
A silicoflagellate. Cannopilids range
from Oligocene to Recent.

Two dinoflagellates common in the Mesozoic

Coccolithus, × 3,000,
a coccolithophore.
Cenozoic

Thoracosphaera.
Mesozoic–Cenozoic.
Greatly enlarged. A part
of the calcareous
nannoplankton whose
relationships are not certain

Actinoptychus, × 180.
Miocene–Recent

Melosira, × 250

Two diatoms of Cenozoic age

Two typical coccoliths

Though they have been divided often among plants and animals, these fossils find less confusing places among the protists

nucleus and less complex than land plants and multicellular animals. With this in mind, the protists comprise the protozoans, the algae, and some kinds of fungi. This includes "plant-like" organisms that generate their own food as well as "animal-like" ones that actively collect food particles. We should keep in mind that further work might well show that the protists are a rather unnatural group of organisms, which may include members more closely related to forms in other kingdoms. But, for now, the category Protista is a working model we will use until something better comes along.

Many protists are very common as microfossils in the rock record. They are often of great economic importance, because their small size means that thousands, even millions, of their skeletons can be preserved in very small rock samples. So, when wells are drilled into rock sections, the skeletons of these minute fossils can be used to precisely date the rocks in which they occur. This is particularly true in marine sequences, in which protist skeletons have supplied much of the "sediment rain" to the deep ocean floor, forming oozes. And, from collections of those tiny skeletons recovered from drill cores, the environmental and temporal history of the rocks can be reconstructed.

WHIP-BEARING CELLS

Dinoflagellates are named because of the two lashlike structures that propel them. Their name means "terrible whips." They range in size from 5 microns to 2 millimeters (0.0002–0.1 in.), and they include both "plant" and "animal" forms. Modern dinoflagellates include forms that cause "red rain" and "red snow" on the land as well as the "red tides" in the oceans. Still other types produce much of the eerie green phosphorescence that occasionally makes the seawater glow at night. They generally are free-floating marine dwellers, but some live in fresh water, some in sand, and yet others are even parasites.

Dinoflagellates have two phases in their life cycle: a mobile stage, in which they travel freely about by use of their flagellae, and a bottom-dwelling, sedentary, cyst stage. It is the skeletons deposited during the cyst stage that are most important in the fossil record. The cyst is composed of a resistant organic material very like the sporopollenin that makes up the outer walls of spores and pollen in terrestrial plants. Each cyst has a small "escape hole" in it.

Fossil dinoflagellates are frequent in Permian to Recent marine rocks, though the oldest record is in the Silurian. They come in a variety of shapes, sizes, and ornamentation types, ranging from frills and knobs to short, branched spines.

Acritarchs, another group of microscopic fossil cysts, resemble dinoflagellates. They are composed of sporopollenin. Their exact relationships, however, are not clear. They range from 20 to 150 microns (0.001–0.006 in.) in size and from Precambrian to modern times. The acritarchs were, however, most important as marine plankton in the Paleozoic. Their shell is normally made up of a spherical, ovoid, or triangular central body from which spines, processes, or linear ridges arise.

Coccoliths are single-celled planktonic flagellates with three whiplike or-

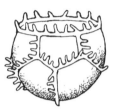

Cymatiogalea, *an acritarch, 0.02 millimeter (0.0008 in.) across. Middle Cambrian to Early Silurian. (Drawing by Frank Knight, modified from Brasier, 1981)*

Cyclococcolithina, *a living coccolithophore. Width is 0.017 millimeter (0.0007 in.). (Drawing by Frank Knight, modified from Brasier, 1981)*

gans. Their soft parts are protected by an armor of very small (3–5 microns, or 0.0001–0.0002 in.) calcium-carbonate scales. These fall apart when the organism dies and contribute to the deep-sea oozes and chalks present in both modern-day oceans and the fossil record. They are known in rocks of Jurassic age or younger.

MORE ORGANIC-WALLED PROTISTS

Tasmantids are yet another entirely marine microfossil group that may be related to the dinoflagellates. They have a sporopollenin wall, but the wall is very thick. Generally the tasmantids are spherical and range from 100 to 600 microns (0.004–0.024 in.) in diameter. They have many small canals that pass partially or completely through the thick walls. The first occurrence of this group is in the Cambrian, but they became extinct in the Miocene, depriving us of understanding much of their life history, unless the living *Pachysphaera* is really a member of this group.

No one quite knows where yet another organic-walled, minute, shelled group belongs, the Chitinozoa. Some paleontologists suggest that they were protozoans, while others have proposed that they have affinities with the graptolites. Chitinozoans are hollow and radially symmetric about a central long axis, and their shell is closed at only one end. Their size range is much the same as the dinoflagellates, 50 microns to 2 millimeters (0.002–0.079 in.). And they form a part of the marine plankton during the Ordovician, Silurian, and Devonian.

Many of these organisms—dinoflagellates, acritarchs, tasmantids, among others—have in the past been called hystrichospheres. Now this group has been found to be a "scrap basket" collection of forms that may or may not be related and so has been separated into several distinct categories.

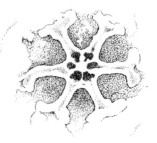

Discoaster, *0.01 millimeter (0.0004 in.) in diameter. A discoasterid. Tertiary marine sediment (Drawing by Frank Knight)*

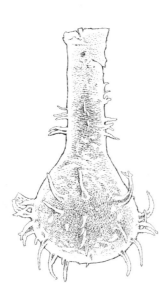

Gotlandochitina villosa, *a chitinozoan, 0.15 millimeter (0.006 in.) long. Silurian (Drawing by Frank Knight)*

STONY FLAGELLATES

Ebridians are flagellated forms that may be related to either dinoflagellates or silicoflagellates. They, too, are part of the marine microplankton, but they possess an internal skeleton made of silica, resembling in some ways the spicules of sponges or even simple radiolarian skeletons. Ebridians first occured in the Paleocene and continued to become more diverse until sometime in the Pliocene. After that they sharply declined in numbers.

Siliocoflagellates, as their name implies, use silica as the basis for their skeletons, just as do the ebridians. They possess the whiplike flagellae and are able to produce their own food by photosynthesis. So whether they are "plant" or "animal" is a debatable point. They have been a minor part of marine plankton since Early Cretaceous times and are especially important where calcium-carbonate fossils are scarce or lacking, such as in polar latitudes or in deep waters where carbonates are dissolved in the seawater. Silica, on the contrary, is not dissolved, and so the silica-based skeletons remain.

The silicoflagellate skeleton is made up of opaline silica, and it is built around a basal ring. Usually, more complex structures are built up along one side, so making most species asymmetrical.

Even though they have a long geologic history relative to other groups, silicoflagellates changed very slowly; thus, fine time divisions of rock columns will probably never be possible as a rule of practice with this group.

CILIATED PROTISTS

Some protists have not just two or three whiplike propulsive organs, but many; these are called cilia. Only a few of these types of protists are important as fossils, the main ones being tintinnids and calpionellids.

Tintinnids are known from the Ordovician to the present, but their record is very patchy. Their shells are cylindrical, conical, or even bell-shaped, with one end drawn out into a stalk. Calpionellids are calcareous forms in this group that are of use in zoning Mesozoic rocks; they are best studied in thin sections of the limestone rocks in which they occur.

DIATOMS

Modern diatoms are enormously abundant in cool seas as well as in streams and lakes or even soil or the sides of trees. All require some light, and in marine waters this means they live in waters less than 600 feet

(183 m.) deep. They are solitary or colonial creatures, lacking flagellae, that build ornate shells, or frustules, of silica. Each frustule contains two parts, one of which partly covers the other, as a lid fits over a box. Shapes vary endlessly, as does ornamentation, but marine species tend to be round (centric), while freshwater types are often elongated (pennate). The oldest marine diatoms are found in Late Cretaceous strata; freshwater species appear in lake beds of Tertiary age.

Modern diatoms form a large part of the sediment that settles on ocean bottoms, especially in Arctic and Antarctic regions. During the Tertiary period, diatoms were even more important in seas that encroached upon California, where the Monterey Shale, of Miocene age, exceeds 200 feet (61 m.) in thickness. It seems likely that many pre-Tertiary cherts also were first formed by these protists, whose boxlike shells disappeared leaving only their silica in the layers of compact rock.

ROOT FEET AND GLASSY SHELLS

A large number of fossil protozoans belong to the rhizopods, or Sarcodina. The former name means "root feet" and aptly describes the pseudopods, or "false feet," which these creatures put out as they feed, crawl, swim, or drift about in fresh and marine waters. Though some are bare, soft, and shapeless, others build up shells that are beautiful as well as complex, and are therefore frequently fossilized. Some rocks, in fact, are composed exclusively of these skeletons.

Radiolarians. If beauty were our criterion, radiolarians would rank as the most important rhizopods. The typical radiolarian consists of a spherical or compressed body supported by a shell of glassy silica that may contain several netlike layers and is commonly studded with spines. Another porous capsule lies in the jellylike flesh, or protoplasm, and divides it into two regions. The outer one sends out raylike pseudopods and digests food; the inner contains one or more nuclei and carries on reproduction. When necessary, the protist can use food produced by tiny algae that live in its protoplasm. The algae, in turn, utilize carbon dioxide and nitrogen-bearing wastes that are given off by the protists.

This is the typical plan, one that has many variations. Some radiolarians have a capsule but no shell, or exoskeleton. Others have no spines, are shaped like small pine cones, or are divided into radiating lobes. One group has shells made of strontium sulfate instead of silica.

Radiolarians were once thought to be rare and unimportant marine fossils. They are now known to be common in Paleozoic to Recent rocks. Especially rich deposits are found in Late Cretaceous and Tertiary rocks of California. They show drastic reductions in the Permian, when glaciation dramatically lowered global sea levels, as well as temperatures, and tectonic closure of

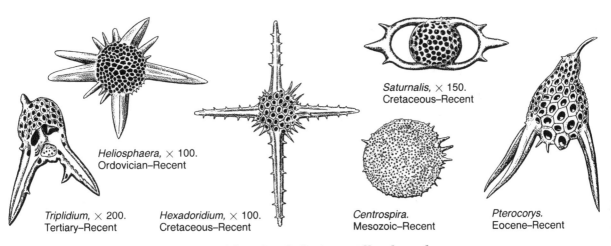

Heliosphaera, × 100.
Ordovician–Recent

Saturnalis, × 150.
Cretaceous–Recent

Triplidium, × 200.
Tertiary–Recent

Hexadoridium, × 100.
Cretaceous–Recent

Centrospira.
Mesozoic–Recent

Pterocorys.
Eocene–Recent

Recent and fossil radiolarians. All enlarged

some ocean basins occurred. Conversely, the opening of new ocean basins in the Jurassic and Cretaceous may account for radiolarians' broad expansion then.

THE VARIED AND USEFUL "FORAMS"

Many a paleontologist has lived a long and useful life without seeing fossil flagellates, ciliates, or even radiolarians. But no one who deals with so-called invertebrates can afford to overlook the Foraminifera, whose name is commonly shortened to "forams." Not only are they the most abundant and best-preserved fossil protists; they also are the most useful of index fossils. No one knows how many oil wells they have helped to locate or how many formations they have helped to identify and date.

The word *foraminifer* means "bearer of openings"—openings in a capsule or shell which is termed a *test.* Though some foraminifers have only a tough surface layer, the majority build tests provided with one or many openings. The jellylike flesh, or protoplasm, may be confined inside the test and send out pseudopods through one large foramen. More commonly, protoplasm both fills the test and covers it, flows freely through many foramina, and sends forth pseudopods from many parts of the surface. These "false feet" are slender and commonly branch, but they also run together and fuse. This happens when food is captured, forming islands of living material in which it is digested outside the central body and test.

Cells and Life Cycles. Long before anyone knew that "forams" were useful, students of fossils discovered that many species came in two forms. One, called megalospheric, began with a relatively large part called the proloculus ("first little chamber") but developed a small test. The other form, termed microspheric, began with a small proloculus but produced a test which was much larger than that of the microspheric form.

The reason for this contrast became clear when biologists got around to study reproduction in modern foraminifers. Microspheres are sexless crea-

103

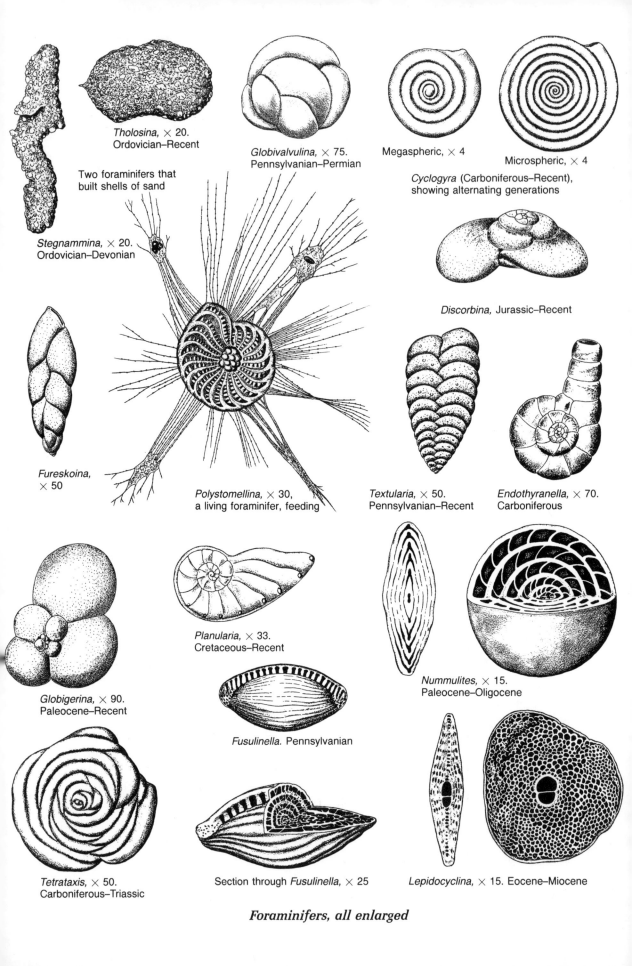

Tholosina, × 20.
Ordovician–Recent

Globivalvulina, × 75.
Pennsylvanian–Permian

Megaspheric, × 4

Microspheric, × 4

Cyclogyra (Carboniferous–Recent),
showing alternating generations

Two foraminifers that
built shells of sand

Stegnammina, × 20.
Ordovician–Devonian

Discorbina, Jurassic–Recent

Fureskoina,
× 50

Polystomellina, × 30,
a living foraminifer, feeding

Textularia, × 50.
Pennsylvanian–Recent

Endothyranella, × 70.
Carboniferous

Globigerina, × 90.
Paleocene–Recent

Planularia, × 33.
Cretaceous–Recent

Fusulinella. Pennsylvanian

Nummulites, × 15.
Paleocene–Oligocene

Tetrataxis, × 50.
Carboniferous–Triassic

Section through *Fusulinella,* × 25

Lepidocyclina, × 15. Eocene–Miocene

Foraminifers, all enlarged

tures whose nuclei divide until many are scattered through each cell. When the latter reaches maturity, its protoplasm flows from the test and divides into balls, one for each nucleus. These balls, which are young forams, construct large proloculi and go on to build megalospheres.

Though produced by asexual reproduction, the megalospheric form itself reproduces sexually. At maturity its nucleus divides into many tiny parts, each of which becomes the core of a lash-bearing swarm cell that resembles a small, gray *Chrysamoeba*. Many of these swarm cells die, but a few come together in pairs, unite, and build new microspheres. They, of course, later reproduce asexually and thereby continue the cycle of alternating generations.

This is the "typical" cycle—but, like many other things, it is subject to variation. This is true when megalospheres produce still more megalospheres for two, three, or even more generations before going back to microspheres. Since the proloculi of these generations can also differ in size, they seem to give such species more than their normal two forms.

Tests of Several Kinds. The tests of some foraminiferans are as small as 0.1 millimeter in diameter, or one two-hundred-fiftieth of an inch, and yet the largest have diameters ranging up to 7.6 inches (19.3 cm.). The commonest diameter, however, is roughly one fiftieth of an inch (0.05 cm.), or one-third that of a small pinhead.

Chitinous, or organic-walled, tests are the simplest and may be the most primitive. They are round, oval, or flask-shaped and consist of material that looks rather like clear plastic or the crisp layer that covers insects. This so-called tectin also survives in the early stages of very different tests; it is composed of proteins and polysaccharides. Allogromiine forams possess this kind of test.

Agglutinated tests are just what their name suggests. They consist of mud, sand, or other material glued together by cement that may be chitinous, limy, siliceous, or an iron compound. Some foraminifers use anything they can get; others use only one substance, such as sand, tiny flakes of mica, or tiny particles of shell. A few, such as Textularia, employ quartz sand where they inhabit cold water but select limy particles where the water is warm.

Calcareous, by far the most common, tests also are limy, but they are not agglutinated. They consist of calcite secreted by the living protists, just as snail shells are made of calcite secreted by living snails. The calcite may be either grainy or crystalline, and the shells may be either impunctate (that is, lacking holes) or full of foramina. Forams in the groups Miliolina, Fusulinina, and Rotaliina have this test composition.

Hyaline, or glassy, tests are common; many Rotaliina have this type of shell.

Varied Forms and Structures. Agglutinated forams are geologically oldest, occurring first in the Cambrian. Microgranular test walls developed during the Paleozoic and serve as a link between agglutinated foraminiferans and those with precipitated tests. Microgranular tests are made up of small calcite particles stuck together with a calcite cement, giving the shell a sugary texture.

Foraminiferans come in many shapes and sizes. They can consist of a single or many chambers. Generally the initial chamber is spherical or ovoid, but later chambers can be ovoid, spherical, or tubular. Chambers are added in a variety of ways, called chamber arrangements—and in what manner this is done is helpful in identifying forams. Uniserial forams have the chambers arranged in a single row, while biserial forms have two rows, and so on. If the rows are straight, they are called rectilinear, while if they are curved they are arcuate. If the chambers are coiled, the coiling can be in one plane (planispiral) or more than one plane (trochospiral). The shapes and ornamentation of apertures and openings, the presence or absence of pores, and the presence or absence of ornamentation of the entire test can all be of use in identification and definition of species.

Classification of Foraminifera. The Foraminifera are divided into a number of major groups, called suborders. The Allogromiina are probably the most primitive group and have a test made up entirely of organic material forming only a single chamber. Rarely found as fossils, they first appeared in marine rocks of Late Cambrian age and survive today.

The Textulariina have nonlaminated tests that are agglutinated and composed of organic or mineral material or other odds and ends glued together by calcareous, organic, or even iron-oxide cement. They, too, range from Cambrian to Recent times.

Forams in the Fusulinina had nonlaminated, calcareous, microgranular walls. These were mainly restricted to the Paleozoic, but some survived into the Triassic. Fusulinines probably gave rise to the living Rotaliina. As their name implies, they were fusiform, looking like rice grains, and were restricted to tropical waters.

The Miliolina have solid, imperforate, calcareous tests with porcelain-like surface texture. They first appeared in the Carboniferous, expanded in the Mesozoic, and survive today.

The rotaliine foraminifera possess a hyaline, calcareous test that is perforated and is made up of several distinct layers. The group is first known in the early Mesozoic and greatly diversified in the Cretaceous, prospering in the shallow continental chalk seas as well as in the opening Atlantic.

Telling Time with Forams. Foraminiferans for some time have been used to finely divide rock sequences and to tie one rock column with another that may be separated by a great geographic distance. The practice of using fossils for this purpose is called biostratigraphy. Forams appear to be most useful for this purpose in the late Paleozoic, the Late Cretaceous, and the Tertiary, even though they are useful throughout their entire occurrence.

In the late Paleozoic the fusulinid foraminiferans are most important. By examining the internal structure of their test walls in thin section, fine time divisions have been made in many parts of the world, especially in the ancestral Mediterranean Sea, called the Tethys, which stretched across Europe, North Africa, and central Asia. Fusulinids were tied to the tropical waters, however, and are unknown on continents that lay in the cooler climates, such as Australia and Antarctica, both of which were deeply affected by continental glaciation in the Late Paleozoic. Fusulinids were large forams, mostly with a wheat-grain-like shape and very complex internal wall structure.

In the late Mesozoic, the truly planktonic, or free-floating, forams developed. With this, forams once again became good biostratigraphic tools. They had broad geographic ranges over the oceans at any one time, and the "life span" of any single species was relatively short, say a few million years to even less than 1 million years.

By far the finest time divisions are based on Tertiary planktonic forms such as the globe-shaped Globigerinidae and the flattened spiral-like Globorotalidae, both rotaliines. Intervals as short as two hundred thousand years can be recognized using the appearance and disappearance of these protists. These planktonic forms have expanded (especially in the warmer Eocene and Miocene) and contracted throughout the Cenozoic, giving rise to a finely divided zonation of the marine rocks of the world.

Another historically famous Tertiary foram group, also rotaliines, were the nummulites *(Nummulites)*. They were large, discoidal forms that appeared in the Paleocene of the Old World but ranged through the Cenozoic; their descendents still survive in the Indopacific region. They were especially abundant in the Tethys Sea Basin. Limestone made largely from nummulite tests was used to build the pyramids of Egypt. Their shells were regarded as petrified lentils by the Greek historian Herodotus, who thought them to be remains of food the Egyptians provided for their slaves!

The orbitoids were also large, disklike rotaliine forams; they ranged from the Late Cretaceous to the Miocene. One well-known form is *Lepidocyclina,* which lived only in tropical waters from Eocene to Middle Miocene times.

Ways and Environments. Though most modern foraminifers are marine, some inhabit brackish water. A few have also been found in Hungarian lakes and in desert wells of Asia and North Africa. The vast majority of Paleozoic and early Mesozoic species lay or crawled on the bottoms of shallow seas, a way of life that was shared by nummulites and orbitoids. All were most abundant near shores, a condition that prevails among bottom dwellers today.

During the latter half of the Mesozoic Era, a variety of small foraminifers took up life in the open sea. There they drifted near the surface, where currents carried them far and wide. Some also evolved rapidly, developing new types at a rate rivaling that of the bottom-dwelling fusulinids. Since most of these new forms were short-lived, their remains were preserved in one or a few related formations.

Foraminifers also are limited by temperature and by conditions of the sea bottom. Off the modern Atlantic coast of North America, for example, four different groups of these protists are found in four zones that differ in temperature as well as in depth. A Lower Cretaceous formation in northern Texas contains one lot of bottom-dwelling species in dark, thin-bedded shale, another in brown to gray shales and marls, and a third in places where the rocks are yellow marls and limestones. Comparable differences are found in several other formations.

Tales Told by Forams.   These facts show that fossils can be used to trace conditions in long-vanished seas. An abundance of bottom-dwelling species means shallow water; if they grow more plentiful as we travel in a given direction, we are nearing the ancient shore.

One technique used to determine what kind of bottom conditions prevailed at the time the fossil-foram assemblage lived involves plotting the percentage of species in the whole collection in each of three categories: Miliolina, Rotaliina, and Textulariina. These percentages are recorded on a triangular graph. By knowing where assemblages of modern forams live today and plotting those on a similar triangular graph, we can then infer what the fossil environment was: open marine, brackish lagoon, and so on.

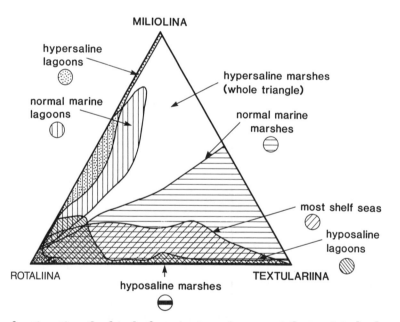

A method of estimating the kind of ancient environment that existed when fossil foraminifera lived. Percentages of species in each of the major groups of forams are plotted. When this is compared to modern distributions, shown on this diagram, a paleontologist can estimate if his or her foram assemblage lived in open-marine, marsh, or lagoonal environments. (Modified from Murray by D. Gelt)

Different types of bottom dwellers imply different bottoms, but varied drifting forms apparently record variations in temperature. If the fossils are closely related to modern species, we can tell which assemblages indicate warm water and which show that it was cool or cold.

Still of great practical importance is, however, the fact that many planktonic, or drifting, species are excellent index fossils whose value is increased by the fact that most of them are small enough to be found in the cores removed from test borings and oil wells. This means that they can be used to identify formations that lie deep down in the ground as well as those at the surface. Thus, one formation in an oil-bearing series has been traced from Nebraska to New Mexico by its fusulinids. An agglutinated species, *Vulvulina advena,* marks Late Cretaceous aged formations from Cuba to Alabama and eastern Mexico. So important are these index species that oil companies maintain staffs of experts to identify them and so guide geologists and drillers.

The same species of planktonic formanifera are often spread throughout the world's oceans. Their skeletons can be used to provide worldwide age correlations of great precision. Because of their sensitivity to temperature, however, separate zonation schemes are required for tropical, temperate, and high-latitude areas.

CHAPTER VII

Sponges, True and Problematical

Placing sponges among animals, we accept them as a phylum called the Porifera, or pore bearers. Those we see every day are soft-bodied creatures that have little chance of becoming fossils. Other sponges, however, build skeletons of silica or calcite, which are readily preserved. As a result, fossil sponges are found in Cambrian and many later formations. Some Precambrian sponges have been reported but are doubtful poriferans.

Though sponges are multicellular animals, with a higher level of organization than protistans, they are not regarded as metazoans. The reason for this is that their cells are not organized into tissues.

Throughout most of their history, sponges have lived in shallow seas, though a few have retreated into deep water, and one family of fifty-odd species now inhabits lakes, ponds, and streams. Young sponges may drift in the water, but adults are attached to muddy or sandy bottoms, to rocks, or to other organisms. The creatures range from a few simple branches to complex masses whose members interfinger and unite. Some sponges are smaller than a pinhead, but others reach 3 to 4 feet (1–1.2 m.) in diameter and height.

Though some sponges become complex, the basic plan of many sponges is simple. It consists of a cup-shaped or vase-like body that is attached at the bottom, open at the top, and pierced by many small tubes or canals. Half of these canals start at the surface through pores called ostia (the singular is ostium) and extend inward; the rest begin in the body wall and open into a central cavity commonly called the spongocoel. Water enters the outer canals, goes through the inner ones to the spongocoel, and then out the opening at its top, termed the osculum. During this journey, the sponge removes oxygen and bits of food but gives off wastes of various sorts and reproductive cells.

The cells in this simple body belong to three general types and are found in three layers. First among these is the ectopinacoderm ("board skin"), which covers the outside of the body. Most cells of the ectopinacoderm are thin and flat, but others overlap to form funnels that lead to the inner canals.

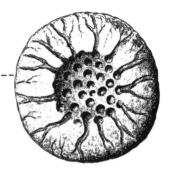

Astylospongia praemorsa, × 1.
Ordovician to Middle Silurian,
Tennessee and Mississippi Valley

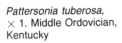

Pattersonia tuberosa,
× 1. Middle Ordovician,
Kentucky

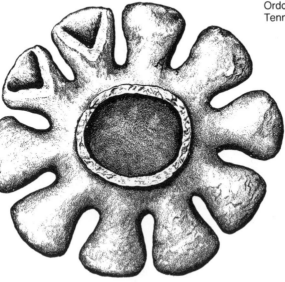

Spicules of Brachiospongia,
× 8

Brachiospongia digitata, × 0.5.
Ordovician, Kentucky

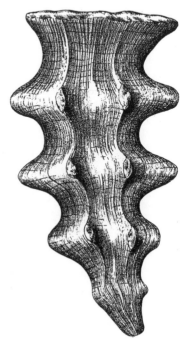

Titusvillia drakei, × 1.
Carboniferous,
western Pennsylvania

Prismodictya cercidea,
× 1. Late Devonian,
New York

Botryodictya ramosa, × 1.
Late Devonian,
western Pennsylvania

Hydnoceras bathense, × 0.5.
Late Devonian to Carboniferous,
western New York

Some typical Paleozoic sponges

These funnels can be closed, stopping the flow of water when that becomes necessary.

The endopinacoderm lines both the spongocoel and the incurrent and excurrent canals, through which water passes in and out. Cells in the cavity are thin, but those that line the choanocyte chambers, opening off the canals, are thick and have lashes surrounded by cuplike collars. As the lashes beat to and fro, they produce the currents that bring water into the sponge and send it out again. Food particles can be captured by the collar cells and carried into them for digestion.

The sponge's third layer lies between the inner and outer layers of pinacoderm. It consists of jelly in which lie irregular cells that send out pseudopods ("false feet"); it is quite different from the mesoderm ("middle

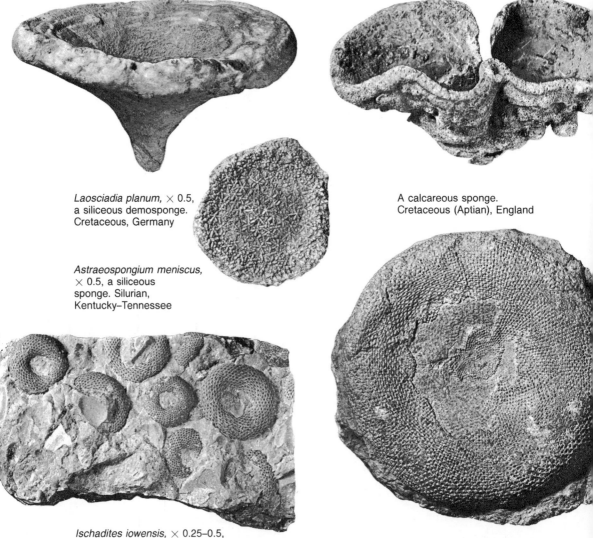

Laosciadia planum, × 0.5, a siliceous demosponge. Cretaceous, Germany

Astraeospongium meniscus, × 0.5, a siliceous sponge. Silurian, Kentucky–Tennessee

A calcareous sponge. Cretaceous (Aptian), England

Ischadites iowensis, × 0.25–0.5, Ordovician (Trenton), central North America

Receptaculites oweni, × 0.5 Middle to Late Ordovician, central United States and Wyoming

Sponges and two receptaculitids

skin") of other three-layered animals. Some of the cells (amoebocytes) wander about, digesting food or distributing it and collecting waste materials. Others build up fibers of tough spongin or make sharp-pointed spicules of calcite or silica. These fibers or spicules form the internal skeleton of the sponge.

A SURVEY OF FOSSIL SPONGES

Like most creatures that have lived through the ages, sponges have divided into several very different groups whose histories overlap. All three, indeed, seem to be so ancient that no one can tell which came first or how they developed.

Calcareous Sponges (Calcarea or Calcispongea). This group includes the simplest sponges, and on that ground it might be ranked as the most primitive. But these simple forms are known only from modern seas, which suggests that their simplicity may have come about through degeneration instead of being the product of survival from very ancient times.

The calcareous, or limy, sponges have skeletons made of calcite or the related mineral called aragonite. Though some spicules are needle-shaped, others are tuning-fork-shaped or have three or four branches. They also may be separate or fastened together in firm but porous masses.

Modern members of this group live near the shores of shallow seas, and fossils seem to have had similar habitats. They appear in the Cambrian and achieve some diversity in the Jurassic and Cretaceous. Modern forms are mostly tiny, whereas they have been relatively conspicuous in the past.

Astraeospongia is another calcareous sponge. It is a bowl-shaped organism that seemingly lay on the bottom without attachment. Its spicules, which are very coarse, have six rays arranged like those of a star and two more in the form of buttonlike bumps at right angles to the others. A single species, *A. meniscus,* is common in Middle Silurian rocks of Kentucky and Tennessee. Since it generally is silicified, it weathers out cleanly as beds of limestone are destroyed by solution.

Glass Sponges (Hexactinellida or Hyalospongea). These sponges have siliceous spicules with six rays, one of which may be so much longer than the others that it looks like a wisp of spun glass. Spicules often occur in two sizes, large (megasclere) and small (microsclere), as is the case in most sponges. Members of this group seem to occur mainly in deeper waters; their descendants are mostly found today at depths of 300 to 17,000 feet (90–5,200 m.).

Glass sponges were present in Early Cambrian seas and achieved great variety by Middle Cambrian times. The best specimens, with impressions of spicules and carbonized films representing the vase-shaped bodies, are found at the famous locality west of Burgess Pass, near Field, British Columbia, described in Chapter XI.

Glass sponges are rare in the Ordovician and Silurian but are preserved in enormous numbers in Late Devonian formations of western New York. The fossils lie in dark, fine-grained sandstone and are hardened fillings, or internal molds, which show the shapes of the fossils as well as impressions of their long, fibrous spicules. Anyone who wants to know what the skeletons looked like may compare them with the modern Venus's-flower-basket *(Euplectella)*, which lives in the Pacific Ocean near the Philippines and Japan. In this form the spicules have united to produce a single, rigid skeleton. Fossils range in length from a few inches to as much as 10 feet (about 3 m.).

Though glass sponges declined after Devonian times, they continued to live and evolve. One of the most interesting of later types is *Titusvillia,* from Early Mississippian (Early Carboniferous) deposits of northwestern Pennsylvania. It consists of branching colonies made up of cuplike individuals whose cavities are continuous. They open in a single osculum at the end of each branch.

Brachiospongia is an Ordovician form that may or may not be an aberrant glass sponge. It looks like a broad, ornate pot with its lower part squeezed out into a series of hollow fingerlike pouches. The most familiar species is found in Middle Ordovician deposits of Kentucky and Tennessee, but others occur in Late Ordovician rocks.

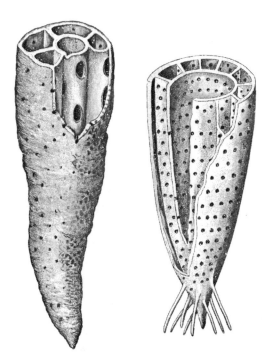

Diagram of an archaeocyathid or pleosponge (right), showing walls, pores, and props. (Left) Ajacicyathus nevadensis, *an Early Cambrian pleosponge from Nevada. Enlarged 8 times*

Vauxia dignata, *a colonial glass sponge of Middle Cambrian age. Burgess Pass, near Field, British Columbia. Enlarged about 4 times*

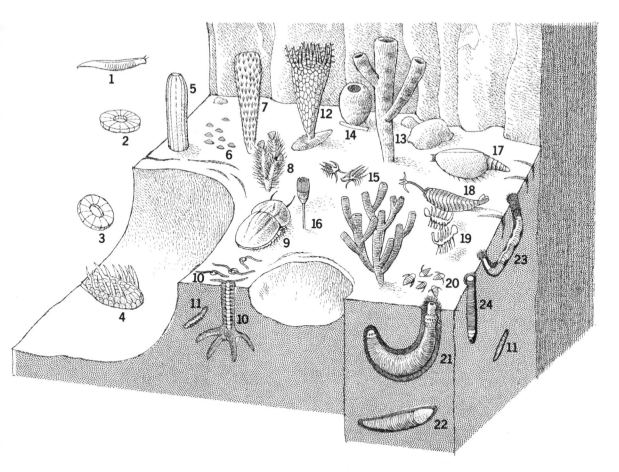

Underwater Restoration of the Middle Cambrian, Burgess Shale Community: (1)
Pikaia, *the only chordate animal in the fauna; chordates eventually gave rise to
the vertebrates;* (2–3) Pevtoia, *a free-swimming coelenterate;* (4) Wiwaxia, *a
scaled and spined, bottom-dwelling mollusc that fed on detritus;* (5) Mackenzia, *a
sessile coelenterate:* (6) Scenella, *a bottom-dwelling mollusc;* (7) Chancelloria, *a
sponge;* (8) Pirania, *a sponge;* (9) Naraoia, *a strange trilobite that retained some
larval characteristics in the adult;* (10) Burgessochaeta, *a polychaete worm that
used its tentacles to capture food:* (11) Peronochaeta, *a polychaete worm that
extracted its food from the silt it lived in;* (12) Echmatocrinus, *a primitive crinoid,
attached to an abandoned worm tube;* (13) Vauxia, *a sponge;* (14) Eiffelia, *a
sponge;* (15) Marrella, *an arthropod that may have swum above the
seafloor;* (16) Dinomischus, *belonging to a new invertebrate phylum;* (17)
Canadaspis, *an early crustacean;* (18) Opabinia, *of a new invertebrate phylum,
seen attacking a worm;* (19) Hallucigenia, *of another new phylum;* (20) Hyolithes,
a mollusc; (21) Ottoia, *a priapulid worm preparing to eat* Hyolithes; (22) An-
calagon, (23) Louisella, *and* (24) Selkirkia, *all three priapulid worms. (Based on
an illustration in Morris and Whittington, 1979; drawn by Frank Knight)*

Siliceous and Horny Sponges (Demospongea).   This is the largest and most complex group of sponges, with the longest history. It includes forms with needle-shaped or four-branched siliceous spicules, which may or may not be supported by spongin. It also includes many of our familiar "modern" sponges, from which spicules have disappeared, leaving spongin to form the skeleton of both single sponges and colonies.

Some of the first fossils that show entire bodies appear in the Middle Cambrian Burgess Shale of British Columbia, in Canada. After them come a long and varied array of spheroidal, vase-like, and irregular forms, some of which might be mistaken for corals. Rocks containing silicified specimens may be cut and polished to show their structure, which is made up of spicules cemented together into a firm network.

The best and most varied fossil demosponges are found in Jurassic and Cretaceous rocks of France and Germany. Shapes range from stemmed goblets to flattened mushrooms, cones, and crumpled cups.

Some modern demosponges grow upon rocks and shells and even into them, dissolving pits or tubes in them and then spreading over their surfaces. Similar cavities have been found in fossil shells of Devonian and later ages.

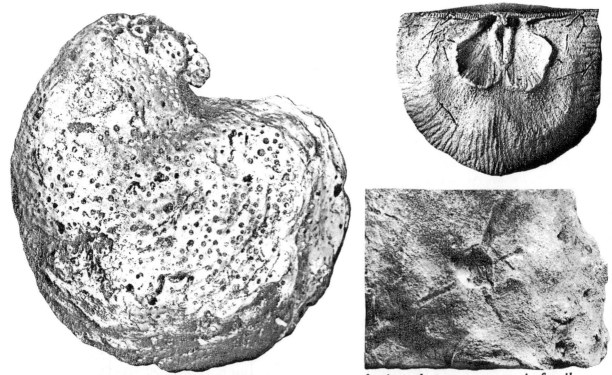

(Left) Cliona cretacica, *Late Cretaceous sponge borings that are common in fossil shells of the Atlantic and Gulf coastal plains. (Upper right)* Clionolithes hackberry-ensis; *burrows in Late Devonian shells of Iowa. (Lower right)* Topsentopsis devonica, *a supposed boring sponge found in Devonian formations from Iowa to New York,* × *1*

Some are assigned to the modern genus *Cliona,* but others have been given names such as *Clionolithes* and *Clionoides.*

Sponges have never been particularly important geologically. They have been minor elements of reefs, such as the Permian reef complex in West Texas. Likewise, in the Mesozoic of Europe, some reefs are primarily built of sponges. But after the Jurassic this seems not to occur.

ARCHAEOCYATHIDS (PLEOSPONGES) AND OTHER "PROBLEMATICA"

Pleo means "full" or "true," and some paleontologists think that pleosponges deserve their name. Others think they are only relatives of sponges, while a few paleontologists think they are aberrant descendants of very primitive corals. Still others believe that they form a separate phylum with a level of organization similar to sponges. It has even been suggested quite recently that pleosponges and some receptaculitids are related and belong in a separate kingdom. One novel proposal is that receptaculitids are a kind of green algae! An alternate name for the group, archaeocyathids ("ancient cups") implies relationship to horn corals.

These conflicting opinions add up to this: pleosponges may be related to sponges but possibly could be an independent group that developed a lifestyle like that of sponges. In shape they range from saucers to vases and cylinders; conical species generally are pointed at the bottom but have plate-like or root-shaped expansions that anchored them to or propped them up on the seafloor. The simplest species have only a thin, outer wall of calcite, but others possess an inner wall as well. The space between the walls is divided by vertical partitions perpendicular to the inner and outer walls, which, like the walls themselves, are pierced by many small holes, or pores. Crossbars, platforms, and curved plates that form blister-like structures appear between the partitions. Archaeocyathids ranged in size from 0.5 to 7 inches (1–15 cm.) in diameter and lived in shallow waters. Often they formed substantial reefs—some of the first in the world—together with algal stromatolites.

Pleosponges appear only in Early and Middle Cambrian formations. They ranged around the world except for the British Isles and northern Europe. Because they are so geographically widespread, and individual species have such a short "life span," they have been effectively used as index fossils to determine the age of rock sequences. The Russians especially have set up a highly detailed biostratigraphic scheme based on this quite biologically puzzling group.

Receptaculitids. These creatures are commonly called "sunflower corals." Their fossils generally are shaped like saucers or bowls, but these contain only the lower segments of creatures that actually resembled beets or broad turnips upside down. Most fossils also are hardened fillings or external molds and so are solid where the living creatures were soft, and have pits in place of the original skeleton, which consisted of thick calcareous pillars whose ends spread out into flat plates. Both plates and pillars were arranged in spiral rows. The pillars don't really resemble spicules, and no pores or osculum really existed. The shape of receptaculids is their main sponge-like character. So they are usually classed in a unique group of their own.

Receptaculites itself contains twenty or more species, one of which *(R. oweni)* reached diameters of 12 to 24 inches (30–60 cm.). During the Middle and Late Ordovician, *Receptaculites* ranged from Nevada to Wyoming, and

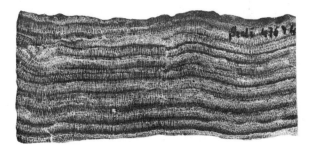

Section of *Actinostroma,* a stromatoporoid, × 3.
Late Devonian, Iowa

Three stromatoporoid colonies of Late Devonian age from
northern Iowa. Those at the left and right lay on the bottom;
the middle colony stood erect. The dark pits were made by the
supposed boring sponge *Topsentopsis devonica,* about one-third natural size

Stromatoporoids

from Missouri and Maryland to the Artic, but was most plentiful in the region that is now the upper Mississippi Valley. Several species also are found in Silurian formations, as well as in Devonian and Mississippian deposits of North America, Europe, and Australia.

STROMATOPOROIDS

Masses of layered and structured calcareous masses that vaguely resemble tabulate corals (discussed in Chapter VIII) have been called stromatoporoids. Their name, in fact, means "layered pores," rather appropriately. Their upper surface may be smooth or have small swellings, called mamelons, distributed at intervals, as well as star-shaped grooves called astrorhizae ("root stars"), which consist of central cavities and radial canals or tubes. Very often the structure of these fossils is studied in cross section.

Stromatoporoids have been found in lime-rich sediments from Cambrian to Cretaceous age and are particularly varied in Ordovician and Devonian sequences, where they form reefs.

The relationship of stromatoporoids has been unclear until recently. Different experts have considered them hydrozoans, encrusting foraminiferans, bryozoans, algae, sponges, or even members of some extinct phylum.

The discovery in 1970 of a group of unique encrusting sponges living in both the Pacific and the Atlantic oceans has led to the setting up of a new group of sponges called the Sclerospongia, to which the stromatoporoids seem to be related. The living sclerosponges have an aragonitic, layered skeleton with embedded spicules made of silica. The outer surface of living tissue is incised by incurrent and excurrent openings, which join to a stellate (star-shaped) canal system that remarkably resembles astrorhizae. The similarity between the skeletons of sclerosponges and some stromatoporoids is so close that they are now often put in the same group. *Chaetetes,* previously regarded as a tabulate coral, may also belong here. The stromatoporoids lack only one element that poriferans have, however, and that is spicules, so their placement with the sponges is still not an absolute certainty, but the best guess at present.

CHAPTER VIII

Simple Coelenterates: the Cnidarians

Along the Lackawanna railway near East Bethany, New York, lie gentle slopes of gray Devonian shale that is famous for its well-preserved fossils. Lampshells, or brachiopods, are abundant, snails of several kinds are common, and molds of clams are not rare. Most abundant, however, are massive, horn-shaped fossils whose structure shows that they belong to two of the four orders of corals.

Corals, in turn, introduce us to the coelenterates, which—with the possible exception of sponges—are the simplest metazoans with their cells organized into true tissues. Corals, however, do not rank as the simplest coelenterates. That honor, if it is one, belongs to the modern hydra, which inhabits quiet streams and freshwater pools and is illustrated in Chapter IV.

Though named for a mythical water serpent with many heads, the real hydra is a small creature whose body is a slender tube containing two layers of cells separated by a sheet of tough jelly. The base of this tube is loosely attached to a stick or a pebble; the upper end contains a mouth. Hollow tentacles stretch out to capture food, which is digested in a central cavity that takes the place of stomach, intestine, and several other organs. Cells in the two body layers feel, taste, sting prey and twine around it, contract as if they were muscles, and send messages through a network of nerves. Some cells also have pseudopods or lashes, but the latter are not surrounded by collars. This is one good reason for saying that *Hydra* is not closely related to sponges.

The body plan of *Hydra* is simple, but it has three great advantages. The first of these is efficiency, which has enabled the animal to live and prosper for untold ages. Second, the plan can be changed in many ways, producing creatures that range from delicate colonial organisms to massive polyps and free-swimming jellyfish. Third, early relatives of *Hydra* were able to produce a third layer of cells, thereby giving rise to all animals more complex than the phylum of coelenterates.

Both hydras and corals are cnidarians, a group characterized by having stinging capsules (nematocysts), asexual budding that yields polyps, sexual reproduction yielding medusoid forms, and often a skeleton (either internal or external) that is either aragonitic or chitinophosphatic in composition.

COLONIAL HYDROZOANS

Hydroids. Our first major group, the hydrozoans, disappoints collectors who want records of innovations made while they still were new. Hydrozoans such as the hydra itself presumably evolved in Precambrian times, since a diversity of specialized descendants appeared before the Paleozoic Era began. But simple hydrozoans are and presumably have always been too soft to be easily fossilized, and their nearest relatives first achieved that state during the Cambrian Period. Their chitinous skeletons have been found in Middle Cambrian and younger formations of Australia, Asia, Africa, Europe, and North America. North American occurrences range from Texas to Virginia and New York.

Many paleontologists would argue that the hydrozoans were the first cnidarians. But this theory, together with that suggesting whence the cnidarians are derived, is not at all generally agreed upon.

Millepores and Stylasterines. Millepores and stylasterines are colonial hydrozoans that build up limy hard parts and have tended to be reef formers. Each colony contains two basic types of animals or zooids. One type (the gastrozooids) captures food and swallows it; the second type is mouthless and therefore gets nourishment secondhand from the gastrozooids. The noneaters are further divided into relatively long, branched creatures (dactylozooids), whose tentacles help to capture the food they cannot devour, and short, reproductive zooids (ampullae), whose task is to produce young in the form of tiny jellyfish. These, in turn, develop cells that give rise to new colonies. The whole colony is joined by a fleshy sheet that covers the stony base and by tubes that run through it.

Fossil millepores appear in Tertiary rocks and continue into Recent deposits. Some are flattened mats, but many more branch; their surfaces show large pores that once housed gastrozooids and smaller pores that contained dactylozooids. Clusters of still smaller pores contained the reproductive polyps.

Spongiomorphida. These colonial forms make up massive colonies known from Triassic and Jurassic rocks. In these colonies, radial pillars are fused to form horizontal bars that vaguely resemble the astrorhizae of stromatoporoids.

ANCIENT JELLYFISH

Living jellyfish belong to two groups, the Hydrozoa and the Scyphozoa. The oldest supposed medusoid (jellyfish) was reported from rocks in the

Peytoia narthorsti, × 1, a jellyfish from the Burgess Shale. Middle Cambrian, British Columbia

Paropsonema, × 0.5, a hydrozoan jellyfish of Late Silurian to Devonian age, New York. Upper surface about 6 inches (15.2 cm.) wide

Paropsonema × 0.5. Late Devonian, Canandaigua Lake, New York

Fossil jellyfish

Transvaal, of South Africa, that were more than 1,200 million years old. It has a diameter of 48 millimeters (about 2 in.). This fossil, together with a large number of other Precambrian forms such as *Brooksella canyonensis,* from the Nankoweap Group in the Grand Canyon of Arizona, are very doubtfully organic. Some may be raindrop impressions, others gas blisters in sediments.

The earliest convincing jellyfish-like forms come from the Pound Quartzite in the Flinders Range of South Australia. Some of these have been assigned to either Hydrozoa or Scyphozoa, while others remain unassigned to any group: *Cyclomedusa plana, Ediacaria flindersi, Lorenzinites rarus, Mawsonites spriggi,* named after the geologist Sprigg, who made the fabulous discovery of the Ediacaran fossils in 1947. Some of these, or even most, may represent early experiments in multicellular animal evolution that led to no later forms.

From rocks of similar age, late Precambrian, in other parts of the world, medusoid forms have also been recovered. *Cyclomedusa,* for example, is relatively widespread in Russia. Throughout the succeeding Phanerozoic, jellyfish-like forms continue to be preserved sporadically. *Peytoia* is one example known from the Middle Cambrian Burgess Shale of British Columbia. Though it was thought to be a rhizostomatid schyphomedusan, it has now been removed from that group and recognized only as a medusoid form with unknown affinities.

Several groups of scyphozoans are known that have fossil records. The coronatids were thought for a long time to have first occurred in the Early Cambrian. *Camptostoma,* from the Early Cambrian of eastern Pennsylvania, once thought to be a member of this group, has been reassigned to the echinoderms. Now the coronatids appear to range from Jurassic to today. They have a discoidal bell, which has a circular groove separating the crown and the marginal areas, lappets, and tentacles that arise from grooves between the lappets. This group, Carybdeida, includes tropical forms with cubical bells that lack any lappets, have four tentacles, and live mainly on fish; they have extremely effective stinging cells. The Carybdeida range from the Late Jurassic to the present day. Another discoidal form, which has a low, saucer-shaped bell with scalloped edges, comprises the semontaeostomids, ranging from the Late Jurassic Solenhofen limestones of southern Germany to Recent. Today they are the only jellyfish commonly encountered in the temperate zones. The rhizostomids closely resemble this group but lack tentacles. Today the rhizostomids are generally confined to the tropics; they, too, extend back to the Late Jurassic.

Yet one more group, Lithorhizostomatida, is characterized by a dome-shaped bell and lappets with eight clusters of short tentacles. They are known only from the exquisite Jurassic-aged lithographic limestones of Solenhofen, where so many other medusan types are preserved. It seems ironic that such soft-bodied creatures preserve as well as they do in the fossil record, but when they lie on the beaches and dry out in the sun, they become tough, and thus better ready for preservation.

Conularians.   This group of invertebrates appears among worms or molluscs in some books and among jellyfish in others. It is typified by *Conularia,* a Cambrian to Permian genus, that has a pyramidal, chitinophosphatic horny shell with four sides, each with a lengthwise groove and many fine cross ridges. At first the shells may have been attached to the sea bottom or to other shells; later, many species broke loose near their tips and the animals drifted or swam. Some reconstructions show tentacles extending from the edge of the body, reaching upward while the creature was attached but hanging downward when it became a drifter. *Conchopeltis* departed from the norm by building a shell that was low and broad, with the four lobes one expects to find in a jellyfish. The tentacles, which were many, also were very short. Some paleontologists place this form in a group very distinct from the remaining conularids.

Fossils that resemble *Conularia* have been found in late Precambrian

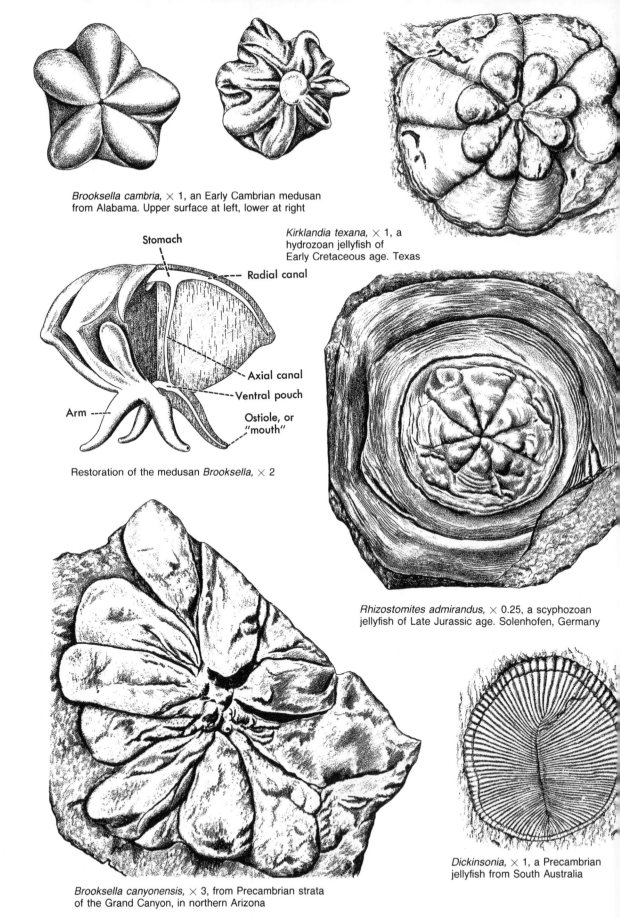

Brooksella cambria, × 1, an Early Cambrian medusan from Alabama. Upper surface at left, lower at right

Kirklandia texana, × 1, a hydrozoan jellyfish of Early Cretaceous age. Texas

Stomach

Radial canal

Axial canal

Ventral pouch

Arm

Ostiole, or "mouth"

Restoration of the medusan *Brooksella,* × 2

Rhizostomites admirandus, × 0.25, a scyphozoan jellyfish of Late Jurassic age. Solenhofen, Germany

Dickinsonia, × 1, a Precambrian jellyfish from South Australia

Brooksella canyonensis, × 3, from Precambrian strata of the Grand Canyon, in northern Arizona

Jellyfish, or medusae

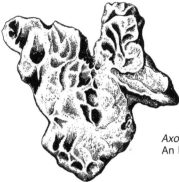

Axopora solanderi, × 1, surface × 20.
An Eocene millepore from France

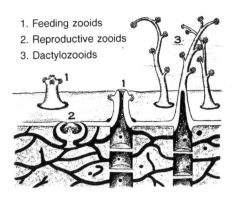

1. Feeding zooids
2. Reproductive zooids
3. Dactylozooids

Diagram of a millepore showing canals
(black) and the three types of zooids

Congregopora nasiformis,
× 1, a Late Cretaceous
hydrozoan from Denmark

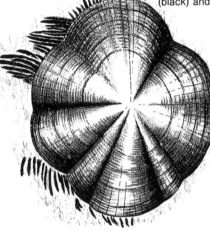

Conchopeltis alternata, × 1, a broad
and low conularian. Middle Ordovician
of New York

Congregopora, enlarged
to show pits of the
reproductive zooids (2)

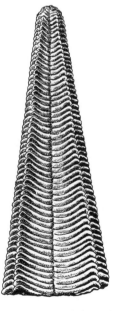

Paraconularia, × 1.
Mississippian

Conularia undulata, × 1.
Middle Devonian

Exoconularia (× 0.5)
in the free-swimming
state. Ordovician

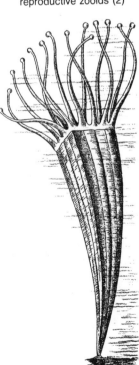

Archaeoconularia, × 1,
attached. Ordovician
and Silurian

Hydrozoans and conularians

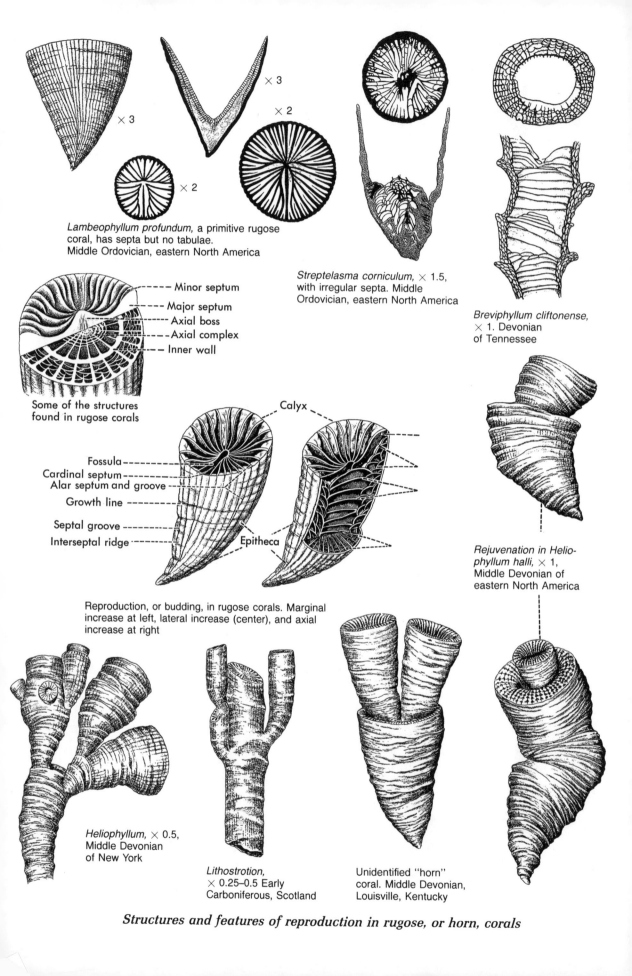

Lambeophyllum profundum, a primitive rugose coral, has septa but no tabulae. Middle Ordovician, eastern North America

Streptelasma corniculum, × 1.5, with irregular septa. Middle Ordovician, eastern North America

Breviphyllum cliftonense, × 1. Devonian of Tennessee

Some of the structures found in rugose corals

Minor septum
Major septum
Axial boss
Axial complex
Inner wall

Calyx

Fossula
Cardinal septum
Alar septum and groove
Growth line
Septal groove
Interseptal ridge
Epitheca

Reproduction, or budding, in rugose corals. Marginal increase at left, lateral increase (center), and axial increase at right

Rejuvenation in Helio-phyllum halli, × 1, Middle Devonian of eastern North America

Heliophyllum, × 0.5, Middle Devonian of New York

Lithostrotion, × 0.25–0.5 Early Carboniferous, Scotland

Unidentified "horn" coral. Middle Devonian, Louisville, Kentucky

Structures and features of reproduction in rugose, or horn, corals

rocks of Australia, among other places. Other conularians range through the Paleozoic and into Jurassic formations of Europe. The most familiar North American species come from Ordovician, Silurian, and Devonian rocks.

All conularids are quite small macrofossils, ranging from 0.1 to 6 inches (0.3–15 cm.) in length. They are often found in black shales and may well have been mainly planktonic animals.

Hydrozoans. Hydrozoan jellyfish range from Precambrian to Recent but are unusual fossils. Some Recent forms produce eggs that develop into new jellyfish, but the offspring of others settle down and become bottom-dwelling hydrozoans such as millepores. These jellyfish have a central mouth on the underside of the body, which is not divided into lobes. Tentacles hang down from the edge of the body, which may be either shallow and saucerlike, or bell-shaped.

Kirklandia is a hydrozoan jellyfish, of Early Cretaceous age, from Texas. *Crucimedusina,* from the Pennsylvanian of North America, had a quadrangular body that was bluntly pyramidal.

Siphonophores are colonial hydrozoans that include individuals of various specialized types. All bud from one original stem, which may be long and slender or may spread out in a disk that is attached to a float. Some fossils are related to the living *Velella,* which has a crest or sail; others lack that structure. All are rare, though specimens have been found in Ordovician and younger rocks.

Trachylina and Chondrophora are yet other hydrozoan groups in which only medusae occur; they are known in rocks of Jurassic to Recent, and Precambrian to Recent, respectively.

HYDROCONOZOA

From the Early Cambrian of Canada and Asiatic Russia, the hydroconozoans have been described as an independent major group of cnidarians. In the upper part of the skeleton, which reaches less than an inch (1.5 cm.) in height, is a depression that may have housed the soft parts. The skeleton often contains radiating plates, perhaps septa as well as tabula-like structures, and can be either laminar or entirely structureless. Hydroconozoans show a mixture of rugose-coral and scyphozoan features, but they seem to form an independent, distinct group.

CORALS AND THEIR KIN; THE ANTHOZOANS

Corals were once regarded as plants or plant animals (zoophytes). Actually they belong to the Anthozoa, a subclass made up of coelenterates that never go through the jellyfish stage and have a tubelike gullet, or stomo-

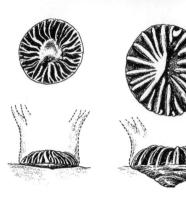

Microcyclus, × 1   *Hadrophyllum* × 2

These corals lay on the sea bottom during the Devonian

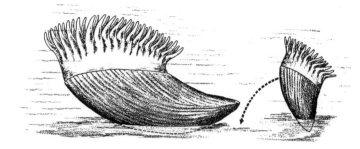

Aulacophyllum (× 0.5) stood upright while young. Later it sank on its convex side and lay upon the muddy bottom

Omphyma (× 1) kept itself upright by means of rootlike props

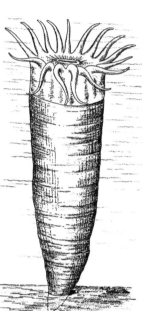

Streptelasma (× 2) remained upright by sinking into the mud. Ordovician–Silurian

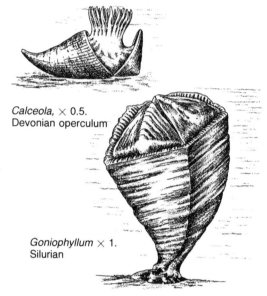

Calceola, × 0.5. Devonian operculum

Goniophyllum × 1. Silurian

Calceola and *Goniophyllum* covered their soft bodies with stony lids, or opercula. *Goniophyllum* is European; *Calceola* occurs in Europe, Asia, Australia, and North America

Caninia torquia (× 0.5), of the Carboniferous to Permian, fell over but turned its growth upward. *Cystiphylloides americanus,* × 0.5, of the Devonian, built buttresses, or talons

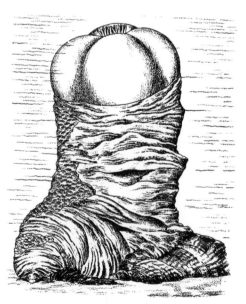

Life habits of some rugose corals

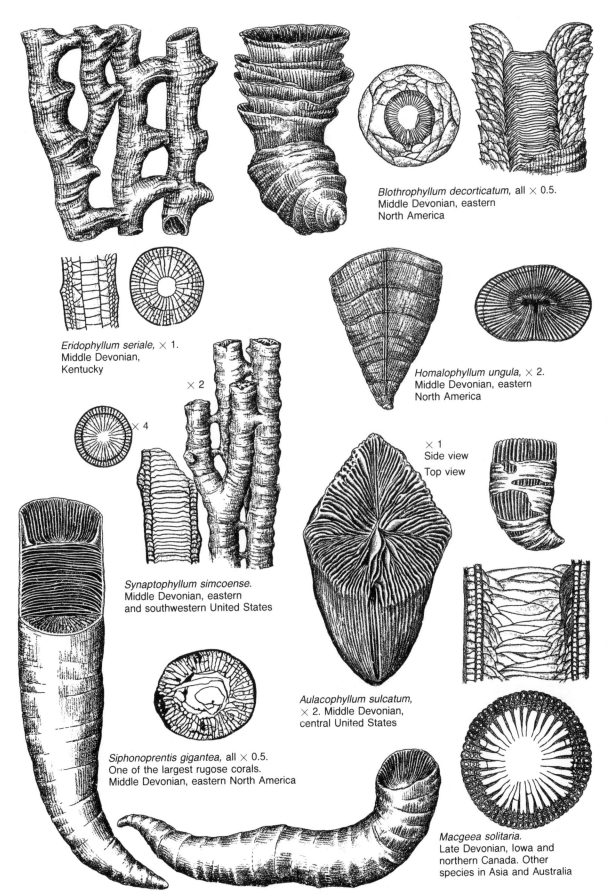

Blothrophyllum decorticatum, all × 0.5.
Middle Devonian, eastern
North America

Eridophyllum seriale, × 1.
Middle Devonian,
Kentucky

Homalophyllum ungula, × 2.
Middle Devonian, eastern
North America

× 2

× 4

Synaptophyllum simcoense.
Middle Devonian, eastern
and southwestern United States

× 1
Side view

Top view

Aulacophyllum sulcatum,
× 2. Middle Devonian,
central United States

Siphonoprentis gigantea, all × 0.5.
One of the largest rugose corals.
Middle Devonian, eastern North America

Macgeea solitaria.
Late Devonian, Iowa and
northern Canada. Other
species in Asia and Australia

Some typical rugose corals

daeum, that leads from the mouth to a large central cavity which does the work of a stomach. The tentacles are hollow, like those of hydra. One group, the sea anemones, has no hard parts; others build horny or stony structures that serve as external skeletons.

It is not hard to imagine how creatures with the body plan of hydra evolved into primitive corals. The first step, apparently, was to thicken the original body layers until each contained several sublayers and variously specialized cells. The mouth also became elongate, and upright radial folds of endoderm, called mesenteries, partly divided the body. The bottom of the tube began to secrete a limy base, or exoskeleton, whose function was to keep the soft body from toppling over into the mud, which would have smothered it. At first the base was a tiny disk, but since it increased in size with the growth of the coral, it took on the shape of a cup or a curved horn.

The oldest record of animals thought to be corals is in the Early Cambrian rocks of the White Mountains of Inyo County, California. There fossils of the Paiutiida, small (1–5 mm. in length), phosphatic, tube-like structures with a bilateral septal arrangement, occur. They lack mural pores, an axial structure, and dissepiments, but have a basic coral architecture. A definite assignment to the Anthozoa is still not a certainty, however.

Another old record of corals comes from the Middle Cambrian of Australia, the genus *Cothonion,* which has been assigned tentatively to the Rugosa. *Cothonion* has a conical skeleton with septa as well as an operculum.

The Structure of Rugose Corals.   Horn corals belong to the group Rugosa, so called because their surface is commonly marked by wrinkles. Rugose corals are common in Paleozoic rocks all over the world; they became extinct in the early part of the Triassic.

To find a primitive type we select *Lambeophyllum,* which appears in the Middle Ordovician of eastern North America. The name *Lambeophyllum* honors a Canadian paleontologist, L. M. Lambe, and is a cumbersome term for the exoskeleton of one small coral, also termed a corallite. This much-named structure actually is only a slightly curved cone of calcite (of which all Rugosa are composed) containing a cup, or calyx, in which the body rested. The cone is covered by an outer layer, or epitheca, marked by growth lines and lengthwise grooves that correspond to internal partitions called septa. Half of these septa are short and half are so long that they reach the center of the calyx.

Many books call *Lambeophyllum* a tetracoral, a term that explains itself when we find that two septa arise near the base (not at it) and are called cardinal and counter septa. They are followed by two alar septa, which divide the cone into unequal sections. Other septa, both long and short, are added in these basic quadrants as the coral increases in size. This arrangement, not surface wrinkles, is the feature that really distinguishes rugose corals from other anthozoans.

Such is one early tetracoral; since it starts out with nothing more than a cone, it seems to be close to the structural arrangement of the primordial form. But its simple plan, like that of *Hydra*, was one that could be elaborated—and this process began early. *Streptelasma*, which also appeared in Middle Ordovician seas, added curved plates (tabulae) under the calyx. Extensions from the septa also reached the central part of the corallite and seemed to twist at the bottom of the calyx.

Corals such as *Breviphyllum*, of Silurian age, added a zone of blister-like plates around the tabulae. Other forms developed gaps (fossulae) as one or more of the original septa ceased to develop fully. These and further elaborations appear in our diagram of tetracoralline structure.

Reproduction and Colonial Growth. Modern corals reproduce both sexually and asexually. The former method depends upon eggs and sperms produced by glands on the fleshy mesenteries, which grow between the septa. The sex cells pass out of the mouth and into the sea, where some sperms fertilize eggs, which then develop into simple larvae. These drift about for a while before they settle down to complete their development. Drifting, of course, gives them a chance to be widely distributed.

We must infer that ancient corals also used this method, since their soft parts have not been preserved. Asexual reproduction, however, is clearly shown by countless fossils. In some, new corallites developed by a process called peripheral increase or marginal budding. In it the outer portion of the old corallite divided into sections, or buds, which proceeded to grow upward and outward. The parent animal sometimes ceased to exist; at other times it became smaller but continued to live amid its offspring. In axial increase the parent polyps divided into two or more buds, which developed in the calyx of the parent and replaced it. Lateral increase took place when new corallites grew from the walls of old ones, building up branching colonies or adding to the size of those that were massive.

Rejuvenescence was almost as common as asexual reproduction. All rugose corals grew faster at some times than others, producing thickenings and wrinkles on the surface of horn-shaped species. Many corallites also suddenly became much smaller, lost some of their septa, and then began to grow larger again. This sometimes happened only once, but in many species it took place again and again during the life of every corallite, and it may well reflect "feast and famine" relative to food supply.

Both marginal budding and axial increase sometimes did no more than produce new corals that were independent even though they were attached to the skeleton of their parent. Commonly, however, asexual reproduction gave rise to colonies in which dozens, hundreds, or even thousands of individual polyps formed compact, branched, or netlike masses. Though some modern colonies are very large, few of those formed by tetracorals were more than 6 inches (15 cm.) thick or 8 to 12 inches (20–30 cm.) in width. In most of them the individual bases, or corallites, have characteristic shapes as well as the same internal structures found in their solitary relatives.

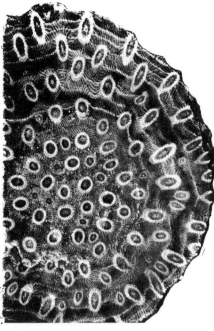

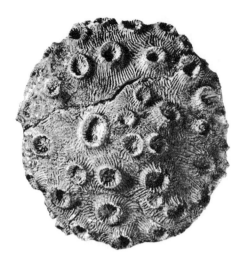

Pachyphyllum woodmani, × 1.
Late Devonian, Iowa. Related
species in northwestern Canada
and the West of the U.S.A.

Polished section × 0.5

Heliophyllum halli, × 1.
Top and lateral views.
Middle Devonian,
eastern North America

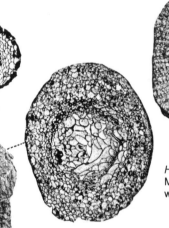

Heliophyllum obconicum, × 2.
Middle Devonian; Top view,
western New York

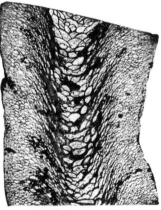

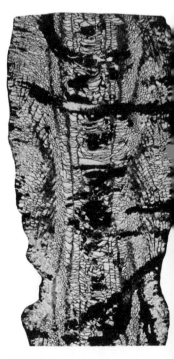

Cystiphylloides americanus. Two corallites;
two transverse, × 1 and × 2; and a longitudinal
section, × 5. Early to Middle Devonián,
eastern North America

Heliophyllum obconicum teres,
longitudinal, section, × 5.
Middle Devonian, New York

Rugose corals of Devonian age

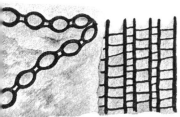

Sections of *Halysites amplitubatus,* × 2. Silurian, Anticosti Island, Quebec, Canada

Catenipora microporus, × 2. Ordovician–Silurian, North America

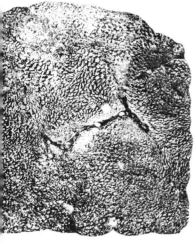

Alveolites goldfussi, × 1. Middle Devonian, eastern North America

Entelophyllum rugosum, × 0.25. Silurian, eastern North America

Aulopora michiganensis, × 1. Middle Devonian, Michigan

Hexagonaria percarinata, × 0.5. Often called "Petoskey stone." Middle Devonian, Michigan

Lithostrotionella, × 0.5. Carboniferous, North America; Early Permian, China

Tabulate and rugose corals

Devices for Support and Protection.   *Lambeophyllum* and *Streptelasma* must have kept themselves upright by letting their pointed tips sink into the mud, which also piled up around the corals and kept them from toppling over. But as tetracorals increased in size and built colonies, they outgrew this simple sort of support.

Some, it is true, evaded the problem by remaining small or by ceasing to build their corallites upward. Several genera of Silurian, Devonian, and later corals are smaller than *Streptelasma* and must have stood upon the mud just as easily. Others, forming the family of paleocyclids, built their corallites upward very slowly but grew outward into buttonlike affairs that could lie flat on the mud with small danger of being overturned.

Still other horn corals tipped slowly as they grew, but turned enough to keep their bodies erect. Those which turned in one direction became smoothly curved, but others, which rolled from side to side, assumed irregular shapes. One of the most amazing, *Siphonophrentis,* reached lengths of 7 to 24 inches (18–61 cm.). In closely packed banks it curved gently or remained almost straight, but in open places it fell over, rolled this way and that, and grew in directions changed by each new position.

A still better means of achieving support was to grow upon shells, stromatoporoids, or other corals. Some of these formed firm foundations throughout life; others tipped when the corals became top-heavy. Colonial species often spread out over the bottom, and some solitary species imitated sponges by sending out buttresses (talons) or rootlike projections that kept the creatures upright.

Modern coral polyps protect themselves with stinging cells on their tentacles and by contracting into tight balls when they are disturbed. Some small Silurian forms developed one or four lid-like opercula, which were hinged to the sides of the calyx. When such corals contracted, they pulled the opercula down, thus covering their bodies.

Sections.   Rugose corals, or tetracorals, once were identified like shells, by examining their external characters, especially those appearing in the calyx. Today most species and genera are based on internal structures, which are found by cutting thin sections lengthwise and crosswise through colonies or single corallites. Such sections show much that cannot be seen at the surface, and can be used even though calyxes have been destroyed or are filled with rock.

Most of the trends in rugose-coral evolution seen from studying such cross sections are clearly related to building a strong and firm skeleton. The development of dissepiments and the complication of other structures all reflect increase in stability and strength.

SIX ORIGINAL SEPTA; SCLERACTINIANS

Scleractinians are also called hexacorals. As the name implies, the septa and mesenteries are arranged on a basic plan of 6, with successive multiples

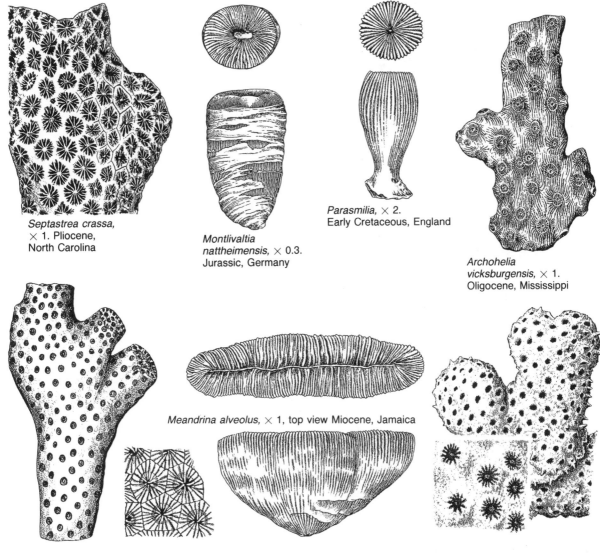

Septastrea crassa,
× 1. Pliocene,
North Carolina

Montlivaltia
nattheimensis, × 0.3.
Jurassic, Germany

Parasmilia, × 2.
Early Cretaceous, England

Archohelia
vicksburgensis, × 1.
Oligocene, Mississippi

Meandrina alveolus, × 1, top view Miocene, Jamaica

Haimeastrea conferta, × 1,
section × 5. Early Eocene, Alabama

Meandrina barreti, × 1.
Side view Miocene, Jamaica

Stylocoeniella armata, × 5 and × 1.
Recent, Bikini. Other species of
Tertiary age in North America

Some typical scleractinian corals

of 6: 12, 24, and so on. The shapes of these septa are also important in classification within the hexacorals. There is equally great variation in the manner of growth and the nature of the base, or exoskeleton. Some hexacorals are solitary and some colonial; though the former may be as much flattened as the paleocyclids, none has the height and hornlike shape of *Cystiphylloides* or *Siphonophrentis*. The individual corallites in colonies may be uniformly round or hexagonal, but they also may vary in shape and size or even run together, as they do in the modern brain coral. Fossulae are not developed, and the primary septa can be recognized only because they begin at the base instead of higher up in the growing corallite.

Scleractinians first left remains in Middle Triassic deposits, and, in fact, they are the only post-Early-Triassic corals. Before that period closed, they

135

were building reefs in southern Europe, southeastern Asia, California, and Alaska. Other reef-building epochs occurred in Middle and Late Jurassic, Early and Late Cretaceous, Tertiary, and later times. Most of the large coral reefs found in southern seas today have survived from the Pleistocene Epoch, and some may be even older.

Corals are not common in most Mesozoic deposits of North America, in spite of the fact that reefs were built in California, Alaska, and elsewhere. Collecting is much better in Europe, where Late Triassic, Jurassic, and Cretaceous rocks contain large numbers of well-preserved corals that once lived on great reefs formed in the old Tethys seaway. Solitary species are now common in the Gulf of Mexico, and colonial forms ("reef builders") were widespread in Miocene and later deposits. Some of the most attractive come from the Miocene "Silex" beds, near Tampa Bay, Florida. On the surface, they show cups and septa thinly coated with white limestone, but when broken or sawed they prove to be geodes lined with chalcedony.

Scleractinians may have been derived from a group of soft-bodied anemones or from the Cyathaxoniicae, a small, solitary, rugose coral group of very simple organization and known from the Ordovician to Early Triassic. Some paleontologists, such as Oliver, do not favor a rugose origin for the hexacorals, because the pattern of the septae is different and because rugose corals have calcitic skeletons and hexacorals have aragonitic skeletons.

The earliest hexacorals were shallow-water reef formers and probably contained the symbiotic algal zooxanthellae or dinoflagellates that restricted them to well-lighted waters (so the photosynthesizing algae could survive). These hermatypic (reef-building) corals were followed in the Early Jurassic by ahermatypic forms that no longer had the algal symbionts, and these, often solitary, forms invaded deep marine waters.

THE ABUNDANT TABULATES

A great array of Paleozoic corals makes up the subclass termed Tabulata —in English, the tabulates. They are confined to the Paleozoic and appear before the rugose corals in the Ordovician. All the members are colonial, consisting of small corallites that may spread out in chains or nets but generally are so closely crowded that they become prisms with four, five, or six sides. There are no dissepiments; tabulae are well developed and usually extend from wall to wall. Septa may be absent too; if not, they are few and may be reduced to mere ridges or rows of spines. The walls of the coral skeleton are riddled with holes called mural pores that connect the corallites (the cup in which the coral animal rests). Shapes range from creeping chains or nets to crusts, balls, curved cones, and branched colonies.

The Schizocorals. Schizo- means "split"; schizocorals reproduced by splitting, or fission, the pieces then growing upward into two or more new corallites. One of the best-known types, *Tetradium,* built massive sheaflike

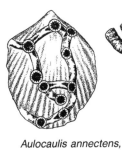

Aulocaulis annectens,
× 0.5. Late Devonian,
New York

× 1

× 2.5

Aulocystis jacksoni. Middle
Devonian, eastern North America

Heliolites interstinctus, × 5.
Middle Silurian, eastern
North America

Cladochonus beecheri, × 2 and × 5.
Mississippian, Mississippi Valley

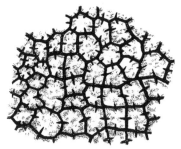

Tetradium fibratum, × 6. Middle and Late
Ordovician of eastern North America

Top view

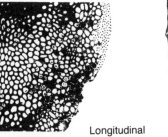

Longitudinal
section

Lichenaria typa, × 1, sections × 4.
Middle Ordovician, Mississippi Valley

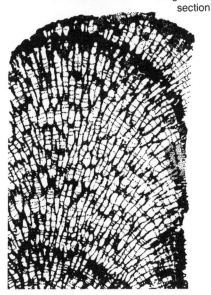

Chaetetes septosus, × 1 and × 4. Late
Mississippian (Viséan), France. First thought
to be a tabulate, it now appears to be a sponge

Syringopora retiformis, × 1, sections × 3. Middle Silurian,
Mississippi Valley and eastern North America

Tabulate corals

or branched colonies composed of tiny, prismatic corallites with four principal septa and few to many tabulae. After fission, the septa came together at the center, forming the outer walls of four new corallites.

Schizocorals may be as old as the tetracorals, for a supposed Middle Cambrian bryozoan seems to belong to this group. *Lichenaria* appears in Early Ordovician strata. *Chaetetes,* once thought to be a tabulate, and which ranges from the Paleozoic into the Mesozoic, now appears to be a sponge.

Tubes, Chains, and Honeycombs. Chain corals range from Late Ordovician to Early Devonian but are especially characteristic of Silurian deposits. The genus *Catenipora* consists of small oval tubes that grew side by side in rows called ranks, which resemble chains in cross section. Each tube contains twelve ridgelike septa whose edges are set with spines, but tabulae may not appear. The ranks are covered with wrinkled epitheca. *Halysites* resembles *Catenipora* in general appearance but has small angular corallites between those that are oval in section. Tabulae are well developed, but septa are absent.

Favosites, the honeycomb coral, is aptly described by its popular name. Colonies consist of closely packed corallites, most of which are prismatic and have thin walls that remain distinct, allowing large masses to split easily. Small pores extend through the walls, showing that the flesh of adjacent polyps was continuous; tabulae are well developed and extend from wall to wall. In some species, old corallites were covered by limy layers after the polyps died.

There are many species of *Favosites,* ranging from small sheets to massive domes and from compact cones to branched colonies. Some bear small corallites of uniform size, but others, such as *F. argus,* have large corallites scattered among what seem to be small ones, as autopores are scattered among siphonopores in *Heliopora.*

Several other genera are commonly grouped in one family with *Favosites.* Some differ in details; *Emmonsia,* for example, has incomplete tabulae that look like spines when we see them in section. Others possess such thick walls that they resemble branched hexacorals. Still others have large corallites with many coarse septal ridges and tabulae that form blisterlike structures. The collector who likes to cut, polish, and make sections can distinguish varied genera and species on a basis much firmer than the one used to classify them in most books.

Aulopora consists of small tubes with thick, wrinkled walls, faint septal ridges, and few or no tabulae. The polyps reproduced by budding, forming chains, networks, or even crusts, which spread out over firm through muddy bottoms or were attached to shells, stromatoporoids, and other corals. Related genera had tubes of differing shapes, grew upward into short columns, or formed bushy colonies.

Tabulates generally are not very important stratigraphic tools, other than on a gross scale. For example, we know that favositine and heliolitine corals

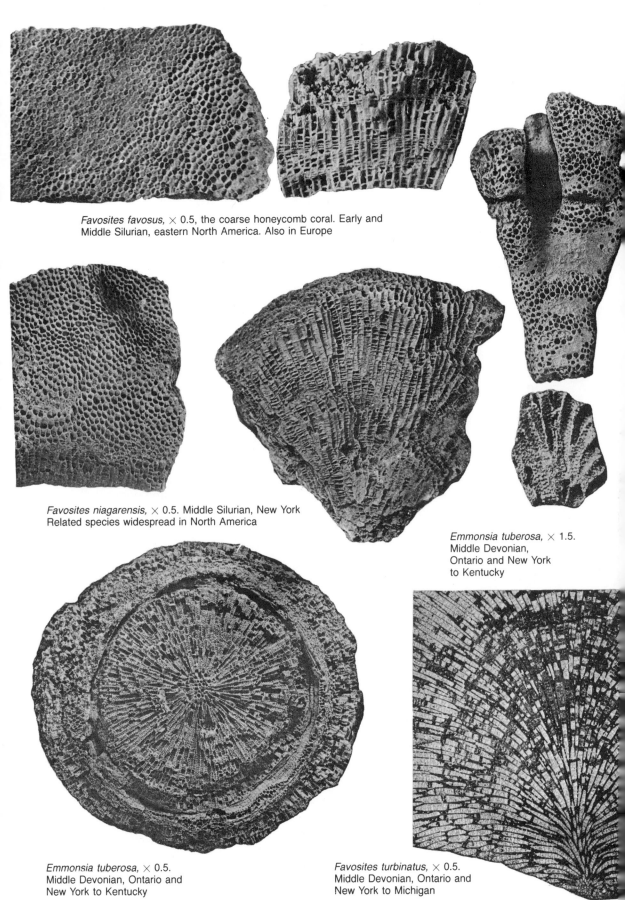

Favosites favosus, × 0.5, the coarse honeycomb coral. Early and Middle Silurian, eastern North America. Also in Europe

Favosites niagarensis, × 0.5. Middle Silurian, New York Related species widespread in North America

Emmonsia tuberosa, × 1.5. Middle Devonian, Ontario and New York to Kentucky

Emmonsia tuberosa, × 0.5. Middle Devonian, Ontario and New York to Kentucky

Favosites turbinatus, × 0.5. Middle Devonian, Ontario and New York to Michigan

Tabulate corals

dominated Silurian and Devonian tabulates, whereas forms related to *Syringopora* and *Aulopora* become dominant in the Carboniferous and Permian. Sometime during the Permian, the group became extinct, after a long survival: spanning more than 400 million years.

A STORY OF REEFS AND THEIR ARCHITECTS

Today, corals immediately come to mind when people think of reefs. They certainly are a major, though not exclusive, builder of tropical reefs, such as the Great Barrier Reef, in Australia. In the past, corals have sometimes not been as important as they are today, and during certain periods of the past were not even a part of the great reef complexes of the times.

The first reef structures are known from the Precambrian, more than 2,000 million years ago. These were constructed mainly of algal stromatolites, built up by filamentous blue-green algae. As far as we can determine, only plants, and no animals, built these massive limestone fortresses.

Cambrian organic mounds, or bioherms, show little change from their Precambrian counterparts. Stromatolites still dominated in most cases, but they were joined by archaeocyathids. Before the end of the Cambrian, however, the archaeocyathids had disappeared, and stromatolites alone were left on the reefs.

In the middle of the Ordovician (Chazyan) an invertebrate-algae complex developed in North America, moving into the ecological space occupied previously by archaeocyathids. These reefs were made up of red algae, bryozoans, stromatoporoids, and both rugose and tabulate corals, the oldest known "coral reef" community. Near the end of the Devonian, between the Frasnian and Famennian, this community was wiped out, after having survived for some 130 million years.

After the catastrophic crisis of the Middle Paleozoic, other reef complexes developed from associations of stromatolites, brachiopods, bryozoans, and calcareous sponges. This community diversified immensely, with thousands of reef-associated species developing.

Then, during the Permian, came another crisis, for as global temperatures cooled and large quantities of water were tied up in expanding polar ice caps, sea levels dropped, exposing large parts of the continental shelves. Since reefs are normally situated on continental shelves, as this environment was greatly restricted, widespread extinctions occurred.

During the Mesozoic, reefs came to include a large number of hexacorals, which first appeared in the Triassic. They lived alongside algae, as usual; stromatoporoids; and, in the Cretaceous, a strange group of coral-shaped molluscs, the rudists. The rudists, however, became extinct along with the dinosaurs by the end of the Cretaceous.

At the end of the Cretaceous came a worldwide collapse of many communities. It took more than 10 million years for the reef community to recover from this episode. In fact, coral reefs are almost unknown in Paleocene rocks in most parts of the world. The exact cause of this crisis is not generally agreed upon: perhaps it was related to the onset of seasonal oscillations in temperature and rainfall, or the disappearance of the shallow continental seaways, or even an asteroid or comet colliding with the earth.

Throughout the Cenozoic, coral-reef abundance and composition fluctuated with climatic factors and continental positions. For example, as Australia moved north from Antarctica, entering into tropical latitudes during the Miocene, reef corals colonized its then continental shelf. Certainly the makeup of the Eocene and younger reefs is strikingly modern, with many Eocene genera surviving to the present day.

So, reefs have been around for more than a billion years as topographic features of the marine environment. At times they have flourished, while at other times they have declined. What is clear, however, is that the communities of animals and plants that built these reefs have constantly changed through time.

CHAPTER IX

"Moss Animals," or Bryozoans

Shale banks near Cincinnati, Ohio, abound in fossils that suggest stony hydroids or corals dotted with minute openings. Some form biscuit-shaped or irregular lumps; others suggest twigs and crumpled leaves or are crusts that adhere to shells. A few are tapering blades marked by pits in neatly alternating rows.

These fossils actually are not corals, hydroids, or even coelenterates. Instead they belong to a phylum that contains branched, creeping, or encrusting creatures that now live in many streams and ponds but are much more plentiful in the sea. Their usual name, bryozoans, means "moss animals" and refers to the plantlike appearance of many species. The British, however, call them polyzoans ("many-animals") in recognition of the fact that they are colonial.

Unlikely as it may seem, these diminutive animals are related to brachiopods, for both have a structure called a lophophore, which they use in feeding. A third group, which has both a lophophore and a coelom (a body cavity), is the Phoronida, the tubicolous worms. This group may, in fact, be very similar to the ancestors of both the brachiopods and the bryozoans.

THE BRYOZOAN AND ITS WALL

Though tiny, the living bryozoan animal, or zooid, is much more highly organized than any coelenterate. Its sac-like body contains three layers: the same three found in flatworms and all other many-celled creatures more complex than coelenterates and sponges. The hinder end of the skeletal chamber is closed; the other (which is not a head) bears a ring or loop of tentacles (the lophophore) around the mouth. Cilia on these tentacles beat, producing currents that help transport food to the mouth. Digestion takes place in a U-shaped or V-shaped tube that terminates in an anus lying outside the tentacles and a little below the mouth. Supposed bryozoans whose anus lies inside the tentacles—the Entoprocta—apparently form a separate phylum.

Though the bryozoan has no head or brain, it does possess a nerve ganglion lying between mouth and anus. Muscles run through the fluid-filled zooid, causing it to retract when the creature is alarmed. Other organs extend the body when the zooid is ready to feed.

Each bryozoan can produce eggs and male sperm cells, though it may not do both at one time. After eggs are fertilized, they develop into larvae that swim feebly but are often carried far by currents. Most of these larvae are eaten by other invertebrates; the survivors attach themselves to seaweeds, shells, or other objects and establish new colonies. Thereafter they reproduce by budding and cover themselves with jelly, tough membranes, or walls that form open boxes, sacs, or tubes. These walls may be either chitinous—often called "horny"—or limy, composed of calcium carbonate. Bryozoans with limy walls are abundant as fossils, their colonies ranging from slender, branched structures to masses more than 24 inches (61 cm.) in diameter. The latter are exceptions, of course, for a bryozoan colony more than 4 inches (10 cm.) across is unusually large.

We say that the walls form boxes, sacs, or tubes, for these words describe their shapes. Technically, however, the wall around one bryozoan animal is a zooecium, the structure formed by many such walls being a zoarium. The living creature itself is a zooid or polypide. In colonies whose zooids belong to more than one type, zooecia of the largest zooids are called autopores. Smaller zooecia are mesopores. Still smaller, spine-like projections are termed acanthopores.

Interestingly enough, in almost all Paleozoic species of bryozoans the "shelly" framework of the colony was covered with soft tissue so that, unlike in brachiopods, the hard parts were not exposed directly to the water.

How to Tell Bryozoans from Corals. Many limy, or calcareous, bryozoans closely resemble corals. *Stomatopora*, for example, looks like a small

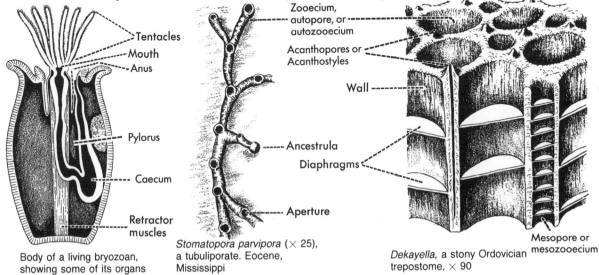

Body of a living bryozoan, showing some of its organs

Stomatopora parvipora (× 25), a tubuliporate. Eocene, Mississippi

Dekayella, a stony Ordovician trepostome, × 90

Structures of some modern and fossil bryozoans

Eliasopora siluriensis,
a ctenostome, × 10.
Silurian, New York

Vinella repens, a ctenostome, × 1,
attached to a brachiopod shell.
Ordovician–Cretaceous, Minnesota

Ropalonaria venosa,
a ctenostome, × 25.
Late Ordovician

Corynotrypa delicatula,
a tubuliporate, × 25.
Ordovician–Cretaceous,
Ohio Valley

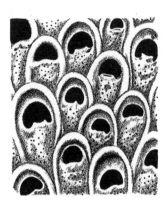

Floridinella vicksburgica,
a cheilostome, × 20.
Cretaceous–Recent, Alabama

Steginoporella magnilabris,
a cheilostome, × 25. Recent,
Gulf of Mexico

Flabellotrypa rugulosa,
a tubuliporate, × 15.
Devonian, Tennessee

Some typical bryozoans

Aulopora; Cyclotrypa resembles *Favosites; Polypora* reminds us of the modern sea fan, *Gorgonia*. Differences generally can be recognized in the small size of bryozoan zooecia and in details of structure. The best evidence, however, is provided by the earliest stages of colonies. The coral larva develops directly into an ordinary polyp as soon as it becomes attached, and that polyp produces others like itself. A larval bryozoan, however, becomes a round ancestrula, from which a tube-like zooid buds. This zooid buds again, thus starting the development of a colony. The ancestrula is most easily seen in attached, tubular forms such as *Stomatopora,* but careful search will show it in "coralline" types as well. Indeed, the round original zooid is the thing that finally convinced skeptics that these fossils were not corals.

Another distinctive feature of many, though not all, bryozoans is the ovicell, or chamber in which fertilized eggs lie while they develop into larvae. It may be a special, enlarged zooecium, or it may be a hollow swelling in an otherwise normal zooecial wall.

HOW "MOSS ANIMALS" ARE CLASSIFIED

Though bryozoans are abundant fossils, few come from rocks older than Middle Ordovician. The group is often neglected by collectors, who overlook small species or take specimens from clay or weathered shale but reject those in hard limestone, since these fossils cannot be separated from the rock.

The opinion that bryozoans do not reward careful study was once shared by many professional paleontologists. A glance through old books reveals that small species were neglected, while large ones appear under "omnibus" names such as *Stenopora fibrosa,* with descriptions based on such characters as shape and surface structure. Later, especially during the 1880s, came the discovery that fossils with few surface peculiarities may show quite different structure in sections cut lengthwise with and across the tubes. Such longitudinal and transverse sections, moreover, tell as much about specimens embedded in limestone as about those weathered from soft clay or shale. By this means, and by careful study under low-power microscopes, paleontologists have distinguished some four thousand living species and more than fifteen thousand fossil species.

Class Phylactolaemata.   The named species of bryozoans belong to three classes. One, the Phylactolaemata, contains several dozen species that now all inhabit shallow fresh waters and a few deep lakes; they are known from Mesozoic to Recent times. They differ from other bryozoans in that all but one genus have a horseshoe- or U-shaped lophophore, and tentacles that surround both the mouth and the anus. They also have a small liplike lobe of tissue overhanging the mouth. Some zoaria form chains or mats of leathery tubes; others are wormlike gelatinous masses that reach lengths of 8 to 10 inches (20–25 cm.).

Class Stenolaemata.   These bryozoans are calcified marine forms that have a rich fossil record from Ordovician to Recent times. The lophophores are extended by muscles, which deform the soft inner body wall and compress body fluids toward the front part of the zooid, thus forcing the lophophore to extend. They have complete interior vertical walls.

Class Gymnolaemata.   This group contains 650 genera. Living members of the class are distinguished by a complete ring of tentacles. Their lophophores are extended by muscles deforming a part of the outer body wall. Though some species live in brackish or fresh water, the vast majority are marine. Most gymnolaematous bryozoans also build calcareous walls, a fact that explains why fossils belonging to this class are known in Ordovician to recent rocks.

Hallopora ramosa, a trepostome, × 0.5. Ordovician, Ohio

Constellaria, × 1. Ordovician, Ohio

Upper surface of a dome-shaped zoarium of *Amplexopora,* a trepostome. Ordovician, Ohio Valley

Archimedes wortheni, a cryptostome, × 0.5. Axis and drawing showing the spiral fronds. Mississippian, Illinois

Lyropora subquadrans, a cryptostomate, × 1. Mississippian–Permian, Mississippi Valley

Broad frond of a fenestellid, crushed. Devonian, eastern Iowa

Batostoma implicatum, a trepostomate, × about 0.5 Ordovician, Ohio

Some typical bryozoans

MAIN GROUPS OF FOSSIL BRYOZOANS

The record of bryozoans begins with small fossils from the Early Ordovician rocks of Russia *(Profistulipora)* and eastern North America. The Russian forms appear to be cystopores, whereas the North American bryozoans may be trepostomes from the Black Rock Limestone in Arkansas and Missouri. Diverse bryozoan faunas are known from the Middle Ordovician Chazyan Series of Vermont and New York. By the Middle Ordovician, all of the stenolaemate orders as well as the gymnolaemate ctenostomes were established.

Bryozoans arose and expanded at a time when many other suspension feeding organisms also became abundant. Some paleobiologists, such as J. W. Valentine and E. M. Moores, believe this is because of availabilty of widespread suitable environments, which allowed efficient suspension feeding. Their ideas are based on the land-sea arrangements suggested by plate-tectonic paleogeographic reconstructions (see Chapter III). Yet other paleontologists, such as J. D. Farmer, think that even climates on a global scale meant greater stability of planktonic food items, which favored suspension feeding as an additional style to deposit feeding.

The fossil record of the phylactolaemates is negligible, because they lack limy skeletons.

The story is different, however, for the stenolaemates and the gymnolaemates. So we will briefly look at several subgroups within these two subdivisions. The stenolaemates were probably derived from the gymnolaemates early in the Paleozoic. When the stenolaemates first appear, in the Ordovician, they are already quite varied, and divided into at least four orders: Dyclostomata (also called Tubuliporata), Cystoporata, Trepostomata, and Cryptostomata. Some paleontologists recognize a fifth order, the Fenestrata, but this is not yet generally accepted. The gymnolaemates are represented by one order in Palaeozic faunas (Ctenostomata) and by yet another, which is first known in the Mesozoic, the Cheilostomata.

Cyclostomata, the "circle-mouths." Bryozoans belonging to this order are relatively large, varied, and complex members of the class Stenolaemata. Typically, however, the zooecia are simply limy tubes with round or polygonal apertures that have neither comb nor other means of closing. Walls are simple and thin, and contain many fine pores. Cyclostomes have large ovicells, specialized female zooids in which embryonic bryozoans are brooded.

Cyclostomes appeared in Ordovician seas and persisted throughout the Paleozoic with only moderate success. They were, however, the only group of calcareous bryozoans to survive the crisis at the end of the Paleozoic. In Jurassic times they began to prosper, reached their zenith in Cretaceous seas, where they were the dominant bryozoans, and continued in reduced numbers into modern times. They have varied greatly in size and general form, from simple chains of tubes or pear-shaped zooecia to sheets, disks, crumpled fans, and massive or many-branched colonies that stood erect upon expanded and attached bases. The simplest types, such as *Stomatopora* and *Corynotrypa,* consist of prostrate tubes cemented to shells, corals, or even other bryozoans. No diaphragms divide the tubes, which branch variously but do not form crusts or grow over each other.

Fistulipora is considered a cyclostome by some paleontologists, and it had massive, irregular zoaria; it was quite large, since it reached a diameter of 15 inches (about 40 cm.). The upper surface bore shallow pits and rounded elevations; the undersurface was covered by a wrinkled layer that resembles the epitheca of corals and sometimes is given that name. Large, tube-shaped zooecia (autopores) were separated by much smaller tubes with closely spaced transverse, curved partitions (cystiphragms). The rear wall of each autopore was thickened and abruptly curved, forming a lunarium that may appear as a hood over part of the aperture. Edges of the lunarium also may curve so abruptly that they project as pseudosepta that show plainly in transverse sections.

Some bryozoan specialists, however, would separate *Fistulipora* and some other forms into a separate order, Cystoporata ("sac-like passages"), a group distinctive in possessing cystiphragms and lunaria.

Trepostomata, the "changed-mouths." This order is mostly Paleozoic, since it appeared in Early Ordovician seas and died out in the Triassic. All trepostomes were stony, and many were large. Because of this, they outnumbered other Paleozoic bryozoans in specimens, though not in species.

Trepostome zooecia consist of long rounded or prismatic tubes. The inner (endozone) portion of each tube has thin walls and widely spaced diaphragms that suggest rapid and continuous growth. The outer (exozone) region, however, has thick walls and crowded diaphragms that are evidence of slower growth and many "resting" periods. The change from one region to the other explains the order's name.

The characteristics of trepostomes are well shown by *Dekayella,* a moderately thick-branched genus of Middle to Late Ordovician age. Longitudinal sections show that the immature region contains only large tubes, or autopores, with the usual thin walls and widely spaced diaphragms. With maturity the autopores thickened and turned obliquely outward. Small tubes called mesopores also appeared; their diaphragms were still more closely spaced. Transverse sections show even smaller tubes (acanthopores or acanthostyles), whose relatively thick walls commonly project as short spines. Acanthopores probably supported soft tissues, while mesopores were probably space fillers.

Mesopores were missing from some species of *Monticulipora,* and acanthopores commonly were few. Acanthopores were rare in *Prasopora,* a

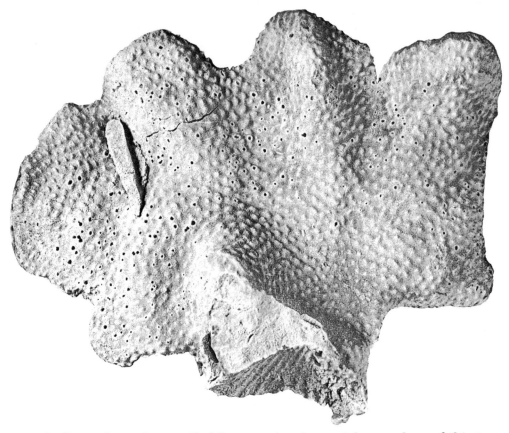

Monticulipora *(sometimes called* Ceriocava) molesta. *A large colony of this trepo-stome bryozoan, about natural size; it grew on a clamshell. Ordovician, Cincin-nati, Ohio*

buttonlike to subconical genus, one of whose species is sometimes called the gumdrop bryozoan. Its autopores contained steeply curved plates (cys-tiphragms), which lay outside or surrounded the diaphragms, very much as dissepiments surround tabulae in horn corals.

Some trepostomes have incomplete or perforated diaphragms; others, such as *Hallopora,* lack them. In several genera, clusters of mesopores are on a plane with the general surface or form shallow pits and therefore are called maculae, or spots. The attractive *Constellaria* had depressed maculae be-tween which autopores form starlike elevations. These stars resemble little flowers.

Virtually all the many species of trepostomes have been determined by structures shown in thin sections. Now that this basic work has been done, many of the fossils can be recognized by external characters, such as the stars of *Constellaria.* Internal characters may also be revealed by grinding transverse and longitudinal surfaces flat and etching them lightly with dilute

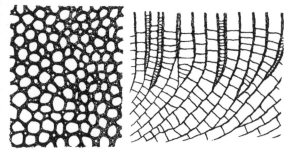
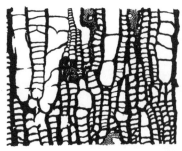
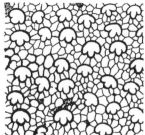

Transverse and vertical sections through *Dekayella,* a trepostome, × 10. This specimen is from the Middle Ordovician, Minnesota

Fistulipora, a stony cystopore, × 10. Carboniferous, North America

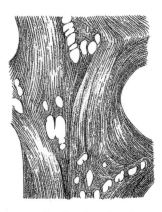

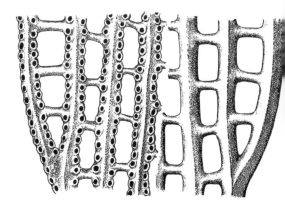

Section through axis, or "screw," of *Archimedes,* a cryptostome, × 20, showing layers, or lamellae

Structure of *Rhombopora,* a cryptostome, × 8. Ridges consist of acanthopores

A fenestellid cryptostome, × 15. Both sides of a frond. Middle Silurian, Ontario and New York

Some typical bryozoans

acid. This brings out acanthopores, mesopores, walls, and even tabulae, though a low-powered binocular microscope is needed to see them well.

The trepostomes diversified greatly in the Ordovician and Silurian but declined afterward, becoming extinct in the Triassic.

Cryptostomata, the "hidden-mouths." Many rocks of Ordovician to Permian age contain fossils that look like lacy nets or minute versions of the modern sea fan, the coral *Gorgonia.* Actually they are so-called Cryptostomata-bryozoans, with short autozooecia, whose apertures seem to lie at the bottoms of thick-walled vestibules, yet another group belonging to the class Stenolaemata. Many authorities, however, have decided that the supposed vestibules are merely the mature regions of zooecia, lying above projections known as hemisepta, which divide the zooecia. These mature regions contain no diaphragms. Some genera, such as *Rhombopora,* possess rows of large acanthopores; in others, the space between autopores or autozooecia is filled with vesicles. Lunaria are absent.

The group appears in Early Ordovician rocks, but reached its acme later in the Paleozoic. Members occurred as branched or blade-shaped colonies, most of which require thin sections for reliable identification. In the Ordovician, Silurian, and Devonian, the lacy genera, such as *Fenestella,* appeared. They grew in fanlike or conical colonies attached to shells and other supports by means of expanded bases or structures resembling roots. Their zooecia contain straight or flexuous branches joined by crossbars; apertures appear only on one surface.

Still more remarkable was *Archimedes,* in which a part of the lacy net had become a spiral extending from a central column in the form of a wide-flanged screw. The whole colony stood erect upon an expanded base but toppled over after death. Such a structure may have been an efficient feeding arrangement, as the combined effort of the lophophores would have set up a current moving down the screw from above, thus providing food for individuals in the colony. Fossils consist of screws with fragments of the lacy spiral or fragments of the latter separated from their central support. *Archimedes* is abundant in some Early and Late Mississippian deposits, is found in several Pennsylvanian formations in the western United States, and makes its final appearance in the Permian together with many other bryozoan groups that had been most successful during the Paleozoic.

Ctenostomata, or "comb-mouths." The ctenostomes belong to a simple but still living order whose zooecia bud from central stems, or stolons, and form clusters, chains, networks, or sheets, and which first appear in the Ordovician. The zooecia are gelatinous or horny, but the stolons may be calcified. Many of these bryozoans sink both stolons and tubes into shells or coral, so that fossils are mere depressions or holes. The order's name comes from a comblike structure that covers each zooecium after the tentacles are drawn in.

Vinella, whose stolons resemble tubular threads, is a ctenostome that appeared in Middle Ordovician seas and lived on to the Middle Silurian. *Ropalonaria* (Ordovician to Permian) is a network of stolons that swell into vesicles with porous walls that have an uncertain function. *Ascodictyon* (Silurian to Permian) had ovate or pear-shaped vesicles that formed clusters or were scattered along threadlike stolons.

Cheilostomata, the "lipped- or rimmed-mouths." Mesozoic to Recent rocks abound in Bryozoa whose zooecia are short, boxlike chambers of limy or horny material, or of both combined, which have a distal aperture. In life these chambers bear hinged, chitinous lids (opercula), which fit against narrowed lips, closing apertures when the body is contracted and the tentacles are withdrawn. The delicate colonies include mats, disks, and bushlike affairs with flat or chainlike branches. Small ovicells are present. The living animals possess stalked structures (avicularia) that snap like the beaks of birds in a constant motion that discourages predators and settling larvae. The vibracula bear lashes that whip to and fro, and when many in a single colony work together, they can, again, discourage predators or larvae or push away sediment. In certain kinds of bryozoans, the vibracula can be modified to leglike structures underneath the colony, making it possible for it to move.

Cheilostomes first appeared in Middle Jurassic seas; during the Cretaceous, they became the most abundant and varied of bryozoans. The order continued to prosper during the Tertiary Period, and today its species far outnumber those of all other groups. It is probably the most successful of all bryozoan groups. The expansion of these bryozoans seems to coincide with the decline of the cyclostomes. Today cheilostomes are the bryozoans most often washed ashore by storms, either loose, attached to shells and pebbles, or cemented to blades of seaweed.

THE USE OF BRYOZOANS IN TELLING TIME

Paleozoic bryozoan genera and species tend to survive for long periods of time and were restricted to certain kinds of environments, thus being found only in certain kinds of rocks such as calcareous shales or shaly limestones. Thus, they are called facies-controlled fossils. So, for determining the ages of rocks over large geographic areas by using fossils, when several kinds of rocks are involved, bryozoans are not generally very good as index fossils. Exceptions occur, however, if the paleontologist can examine species assemblages within one rock type (facies), especially in widespread carbonate sequences. The Soviets, for example, have made significant use of bryozoans in setting up biostratigraphic subdivisions. Perhaps the lack of use of this group in other parts of the world in part reflects the lack of effort made to establish such schemes. Some Cretaceous and Tertiary bryozoans do have limited time ranges that can be useful in determining the ages of rocks despite the overall trends in this group.

Undoubtedly, more work on this group in the future will increase its value as a "timepiece," but bryozoans will probably never have the biostratigraphic worth of the cosmopolitan and sometimes planktonic groups such as the foraminiferans and the graptolites.

CHAPTER X

The Sturdy Brachiopods

Among Late Precambrian fossils are a few brachiopods. Some authorities question their nature, however, and others agree that they tell little about this segment of the animal kingdom. For brachiopods, like other invertebrates, did not become important fossils until the Paleozoic Era. Then, after a laggard start, they filled the role now held by pelecypods among denizens of shallow sea waters. For more than 300 million years they prospered greatly and then declined before the Mesozoic Era dawned. Only slightly more than two hundred species inhabit modern seas.

Even as late as 1913, a standard textbook of paleontology grouped brachiopods with bryozoans in a phylum called Molluscoidea. Since that time the two groups have been separated, even though they appear in the same general part of the animals' family tree. Brachiopods are much more restricted in where they live than molluscs, both past and present, however. They have apparently always required nonstagnant water that is generally clear of much sediment, for otherwise their tentacle-like feeding organ, the lophophore, could not function properly.

The phylum Brachiopoda may have several ancestors, not just one, and so paleontologists would call it a polyphyletic, not monophyletic, group. The most likely relatives are the filter-feeding, tentacle-bearing worms, such as the Phoronida, which burrow into the sediments, extending only their tentacles to feed from the water. Brachiopods probably were able to move away from this infaunal existence by having protective shells that directed the feeding currents as well as having a supportive stalk that provided attachment to an unstable bottom environment.

WHAT ARE BRACHIOPODS?

Brachiopods are exclusively marine animals that cover their soft bodies with shells made up of two parts, or valves. In this, brachiopods resemble mussels, yet the two are not difficult to distinguish. The typical mussel has valves that are similar but mirror images; the shells can be divided into equal halves just by separating them. Brachiopods, however, have valves that are both unlike and unequal; to divide such shells into matching halves we should have to cut across both valves, not just pull them apart.

The Brachiopod Body.   Shells are essentially lifeless structures that organisms build as combined skeleton and armor and then leave to fate. The real brachiopod is a living body whose four main parts are mantle, brachia, internal organs, and stalk (or pedicle). The mantle is a sheet whose two halves are folded over the rest of the body and secrete the shell. Edges of the mantle bear fringes of hairlike setae, which are long and stiff in such genera as *Lingula* but short and soft in others. The mantle also encloses the body cavity and internal organs, which lie mainly in the hind part of the shell. Channels in the mantle provide for the flow of watery blood, their course being marked by depressions on the inside of the shell.

The brachia lie outside the body cavity but inside the mantle. Collectively termed the lophophore, they consist of two loops or spirals of flesh whose edges are set with tentacles. They bear cilia that beat to and fro, driving currents of food-bearing water over sticky mucus. When this mucus has trapped small creatures, it is swallowed by the mouth, which opens between the brachia. The lophophore once was thought to carry on respiration, but that seems to be done instead by the mantle.

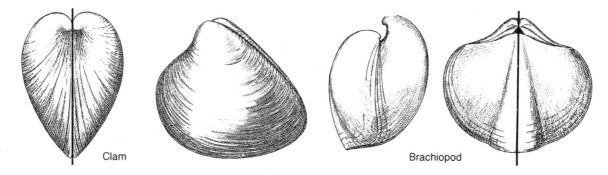

Clam   Brachiopod

A line drawn between the valves divides this clam into equal parts. In a brachiopod, the line must be drawn across the valves

Internal organs include muscles, a digestive tract, nerves, and glands of several kinds; there may or may not be a heart. The nervous system branches, but is very simple, with no distinct sense organs. In the digestive tract, the round mouth leads to an esophagus and sac-like stomach; then comes an intestine that is either short or long and V-shaped and is closed at its end. This, of course, means that waste matter passes out of the mouth when mucus is not being swallowed.

Muscles run through the body cavity; the hard parts to which they are fastened permit them to open and close the shell. The opening never is very wide, for even when a brachiopod feeds, its valves are separated by little more than a slit.

The pedicle is a fleshy or leathery stalk that projects between the valves or through an opening in one of them. In primitive brachiopods, this stalk is long and flexible and contains muscles that contract to cause shortening or even coiling. To lengthen the pedicle, muscles relax and fluid is pumped into the stalk from the body cavity. Many pedicles, however, are so short and stiff that they move little or not at all. They attach their owners to solid objects, and so do flexible pedicles that are not very long. Elongate—even wormlike—organs burrow into sand or soft mud.

The name *brachiopod* ("arm foot") was devised many years ago, when the brachia were regarded as molluscan feet that had somehow evolved into arms. Since that is not true, the name no longer has any real meaning, but the English lamp shell is not much better. It fits one valve of such genera as *Laqueus* and *Cranaena,* which do suggest an ancient bronze lamp with a spout to hold the wick. But the term does not describe the opposite valve and is even less appropriate for shells that are wedge-shaped, gently convex,

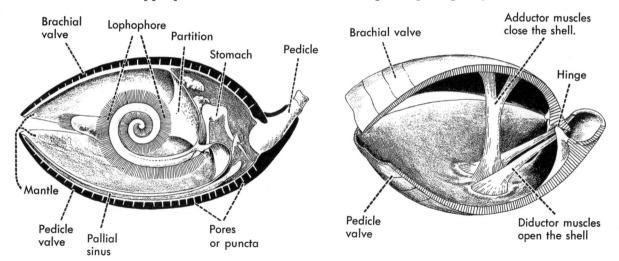

Section through the body of a modern brachiopod, and a diagram of muscles that open and close the shell

flattened, deeply and variously ribbed, or cuplike and covered with spines. Our best course in this case is to ignore translations and retain brachiopod, which at least enjoys the advantage of established scientific use.

Classes Based upon Shells. Brachiopods may be classified according to the way in which valves and pedicles develop, the microscopic structure of their shells, or the devices that hold the valves together. The first probably would distribute the creatures among two groups that closely but falsely resemble one another. Microstructure of shells would preserve one group but

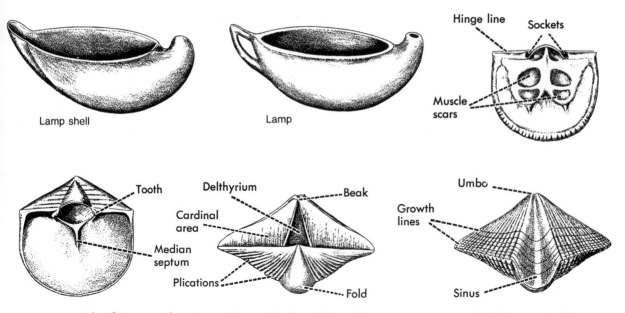

Labels in figure:
Lamp shell
Lamp
Hinge line — Sockets
Muscle scars
Tooth — Delthyrium — Beak
Cardinal area
Median septum
Plications
Fold
Umbo
Growth lines
Sinus

The first two drawings show why brachiopods are sometimes called lamp shells. The other drawings illustrate some terms used to describe brachiopods

divide it into one subgroup whose shells are pierced by tiny holes and another whose shells are solid. The third system of classification makes a much more obvious division based on the presence or absence of structures forming a hinge between the two valves. This again results in two groups, the Inarticulata and the Articulata. Though they may mean less than either of the other groupings, they are generally used by American paleontologists and are adopted here.

Inarticulate brachiopods are hingeless. They also occur early in the fossil record, even though they still survive in *Lingula* and *Glottidia.* Most inarticulates have thin—even flexible—shells whose valves are held together without ligaments or hinges like those to be seen in clams or oysters. The short valve may be moved from side to side, and the two often separate after death. Both valves may be so thin that fossils are almost flat.

Articulate brachiopods have valves that are hinged along a line that is either straight or curved and may extend beyond the rest of the shell. The hinge is strengthened by *teeth* that fit into pits or sockets, keeping the valves in line. In both classes the valves develop a variety of internal and external structures, as well as elevations, depressions, and so on. Since these are important in identification, they are illustrated and briefly defined.

Shell Materials and Structure. Most inarticulates, but by no means all, have chitinophosphatic shells. This means that the shells consist of calcium phosphate combined with chitinous material and minor substances. Such shells are always thin and commonly glossy, the latter being a character that survives in fossils, many of which are black. The two principal materials may be mixed or may combine in alternating layers, like sheets of varicolored paper piled up.

Almost all articulates and a few inarticulate brachiopods have shells composed chiefly of calcium carbonate in the form of the mineral calcite. Such shells have an outer, thinly laminate layer and a much thicker inner one made up of oblique fibers or rods. In impunctate shells, both layers are solid; punctate shells contain pores (puncta) left by threadlike projections from the mantle that extend into the laminar layer but stop just below the surface. Pseudopunctate shells contain rods of calcite in the fibrous layer. They formed pustules on the inner surface and look deceptively like true puncta in transverse sections of shells.

Naming the Valves.   For many years, scientists assumed that one valve of the brachiopod shell was upper, or dorsal, while the other was lower, or ventral. These two terms appear in many old articles and books.

The weakness of this assumption should have been shown by *Lingula* and other inarticulates that were known to burrow in muddy sand, thus keeping their shells upright. But *Lingula* received little attention before the early 1900s, and many more years went by before much was learned about ways of life among the articulates. Then it was found that species with short pedicles live in almost any position, though the "ventral" valve is often upward. Attached forms with long pedicles vary greatly, for the shells hang downward, slant obliquely upward, or have either valve in the dorsal position. Other types, especially fossils, started out with that valve obliquely

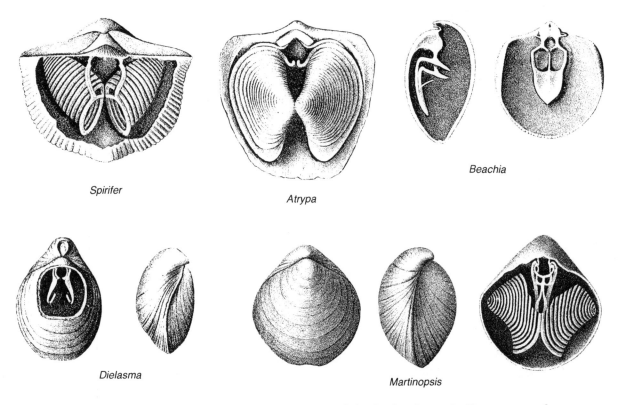

Spirifer

Atrypa

Beachia

Dielasma

Martinopsis

The hard structures, or brachidia, that supported the lophophores in five genera of brachiopods. Though Dielasma **resembles** Martinopsis, **the brachidia show that they are not related**

upward; but, as proportions changed, the animals turned till the pedicle valve became the lower. This also was true of most brachiopods that lost their pedicles and lay upon the bottom, though such genera as *Strophonella* and *Strophomena* apparently lay on the brachial valve.

Such facts made the terms *dorsal* and *ventral* almost useless and focused attention on other essential features. Since the pedicle of many brachiopods is attached to one half of the shell, it became known as the pedicle valve. The other valve, to which the brachia are fastened, was called the brachial. These terms are applied to primitive inarticulates as well as to specialized articulate genera.

THE ORDERS OF BRACHIOPODS

We already have divided brachiopods into two classes, the Inarticulata (hingeless) and the Articulata (hinged). The former contains at least four orders, but the latter includes eight.

Class Inarticulata

The inarticulates include four, or possibly more, orders, of which two are diverse and long-lived: the Lingulida and the Acrotretida. Both are represented by living forms. The remaining orders are restricted to the early Paleozoic, and their relationships to other brachiopods are uncertain. Some may not even be brachiopods!

Lingulida. The modern *Lingula* typifies this order, which includes some of the oldest brachiopods. Lingulids have an ill-defined pedicle opening formed by shallow notches in both valves, allowing the stalk to emerge between them, or it can be absent entirely. A common shape is that of *Lingulella*, which has an elongate, pointed pedicle valve and a shorter, blunter brachial, both with gently curved margins. Other genera became almost round, while yet others became elongate, with slender beaks or subangular margins. Plates on the brachial valve of some genera tended to force the pedicle to emerge from the opposite valve.

Forms like *Lingula,* the commonest living member of this order, ranged from the Early Cambrian to Recent, establishing a record for sturdy durability among animals. As things now stand, they have prospered for almost 600 million years. Studies have also shown that the preferences of *Lingula* have changed through time. It seems that, in the Paleozoic, this genus occurred over a much broader geographic area, living in both tropical and temperate areas (whereas today it is restricted to the tropics). It also lived in a much wider variety of environments, not restricted to fine sand substrates as it is today.

Acrotretida. Members of this Early Cambrian to Recent order have ei-

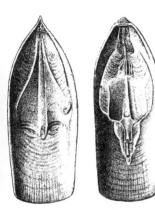

Lingula anatina, × 1. Interior of both valves, showing muscle scars. Recent, Philippines

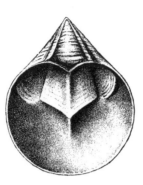

Dinobolus conradi, a lingulid, × 1. Pedicle valve. Middle Silurian, central United States and Europe

Lingula elderi, × 2. Internal molds, showing scars. Middle Ordovician, Minnesota, central United States

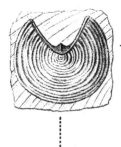

× 2

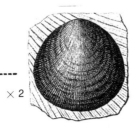

× 2

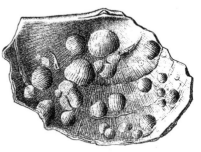

Petrocrania scabiosa, a craniid, × 1. Late Ordovician, Ohio Valley and Wisconsin

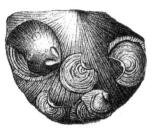

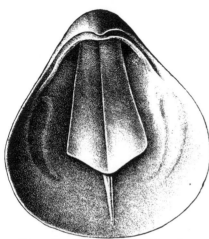

Schizocrania filosa. Cluster of shells on a strophomenid. Late Ordovician, Ohio Valley

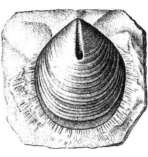

Schizambon canadensis, × 2. Pedicle valve. Late Ordovician, Ontario and New York

Trematis ottawaensis, × 1. Pedicle valve. Middle Ordovician, eastern North America

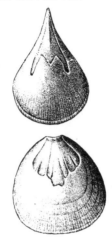

Trimerella ohioensis, a lingulid, × 1. Brachial valve. Middle Silurian, eastern North America

Lingulepis pinnaformis, × 2. Internal molds of both valves. Late Cambrian, North America

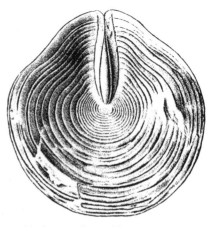

Lindstroemella aspidium, × 1. Pedicle valve. Middle Devonian, North America

Inarticulate brachiopods. (After Hall and Clarke)

ther a phosphatic or a calcareous shell. Most acrotretids are circular or subcircular in outline, with varying degrees of convexity. The pedicle is both present, as in *Acrotreta,* and exits through the pedicle valve only, or is completely absent, as in *Crania,* a limpetlike form. *Crania* cements the pedicle valve to the substrate. Craniids are most unusual in having a combination of both articulate and inarticulate characteristics as well as some unique ones of their own, such as the coalescing puncta of the shells and the types of shell proteins they possess. Perhaps, like the kutorginids, discussed later, they are not even brachiopods.

   Obolellida, Paterinida, and Kutorginida.   All three of these inarticulate groups appear at the base of the Cambrian and are extinct by the late part of this period. The obolellids had limy, biconvex shells that were subcircular or ovoid in outline. A "pseudointerarea" was present, which formed a curved surface between the beak and the posterior margin of the pedicle valve—where the pedicle itself occupied a variety of positions. The paterinids had phosphatic round or oval shells with "pseudointerareas" on both shells as well as a delthyrium, a notch beneath the beak of the pedicle valve, which housed the pedicle. A notothyrium was also present, essentially a notch in the brachial valve that also served as the exit of the pedicle.

   The kutorginids were the most enigmatic of the brachiopods, and because of this, paleontologists are not quite sure where to classify them, even whether to call them articulate or inarticulate. They had limy shells, the first for any of the brachiopods, as well as a hinge line, but no tooth and sockets along that hinge line. They had both a delthyrium and a notothyrium and in many respects looked like the articulates, but for now they are not easily placed in either of the two known brachiopod classes. Some paleontologists have suggested that they are not brachiopods at all, but one of the early tentacle-feeding groups that independently developed a skeleton—unique among invertebrates.

Class Articulata

   Unlike the inarticulates, the valves of articulate brachiopods are hinged together by teeth on one shell fitting into sockets on the other. Articulates appear in the fossil record at the same time as do the inarticulates, but they don't diversify very much until the Early Ordovician, well after several of the inarticulate orders have become extinct (in the Middle Cambrian). By the Ordovician, most of the articulate orders had appeared—only the terebratulids arose after that, in the Late Silurian. The time-range chart of the major brachiopod groups gives some idea of the waxing and waning of each of these groups as well as showing how severely the Permian glaciations affected almost all articulate groups. It also demonstrates how brachiopods were an extremely diversified group during the Paleozoic but are a mere shadow of their former selves today, with only three of the eight articulate

Rustella edsoni, × 2.5. Early Cambrian, Vermont

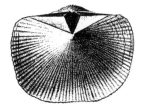

Kutorgina cingulata, × 3. Early Cambrian, Vermont

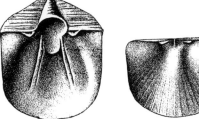
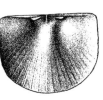

Billingsella pepina, both valves, × 3.
Late Cambrian, upper Mississippi Valley

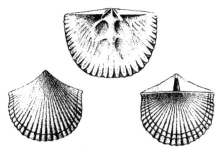

Retrorsirostra carleyi, × 1.
Late Ordovician, Ohio Valley

Hesperorthis tricenaria, × 1.
Middle Ordovician, eastern North America

Plaesiomys subquadrata, × 1.
Late Ordovician, Manitoba to Ohio,
Texas and New Mexico

Dinorthis pectinella, × 1.
Middle Ordovician, eastern North America

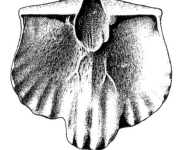

Platystrophia ponderosa, × 1.
Interiors. Late Ordovician, Ohio

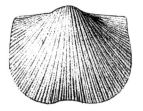

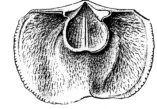
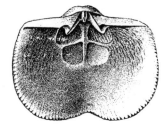

Hebertella sinuata, × 1. Late Ordovician, Ohio

Orthid brachiopods. (After Hall and Clarke)

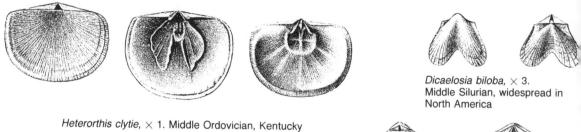

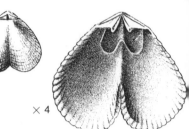

Dicaelosia biloba, × 3.
Middle Silurian, widespread in
North America

Heterorthis clytie, × 1. Middle Ordovician, Kentucky

× 2

× 4

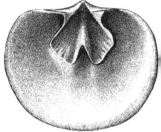

Dicaelosia varica. Early Devonian,
New York to Oklahoma

Rhipidomella hybrida, × 1.
Middle Silurian, eastern United States

Enteletes hemiplicatus, × 1.
Pennsylvanian, Nebraska to Texas

Levenea subcarinata, × 1.
Early Devonian, Oklahoma to New York

Schizophoria swallowi, × 1.
Mississippian, Mississippi Valley

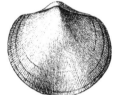

Schizophoria tulliensis, × 1.
Middle Devonian, New York

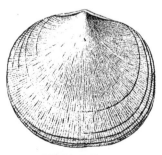

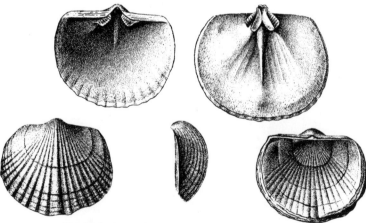

Rhipidomella penelope, × 1.
Middle Devonian, Ontario,
New York, Pennsylvania

Tropidoleptus carinatus, × 1. Middle to Late Devonian,
eastern United States and New Mexico

Orthid brachiopods (After Hall and Clarke)

orders and two of the inarticulate orders surviving, most in greatly reduced numbers.

Six and possibly eight orders of articulates are currently listed in most classifications of these marine animals; we will look briefly at what makes each of these groups distinct.

Orthida. Ranging from the Early Cambrian to the Late Permian, this is quite a varied order. Orthids are characterized by broad and generally unequally biconvex shells with radial costae, well-developed teeth, simple or divided cardinal processes, and a lack of brachidia. The delthyrium and notothyrium are usually open, but rarely can be closed by specialized structures. Beginning with small subquadrate forms of Early and Middle Cambrian, orthids achieved considerable variety and widths of 1 to 2 inches (3–5 cm.) before that period closed. Late Cambrian and earliest Ordovician genera included shells with rounded to high, pointed pedicle valves, sharp to obtuse extremities, and fine to coarse ridges called costae.

These brachiopods generally had impunctate shells, though a few have punctate ones. As far as shell shapes go, there are a number of genera that resemble those in other orders. One Ordovician orthid, for example, looked like a strophomenid, and another developed both shape and ornamentation that were paralleled in later times by the spiny productids. *Platystrophia* anticipated the spirifers in both shape and habit and even went through similar changes in the evolution of its species.

The earliest articulates were orthids, and from this group may have come several others, such as the pentamerids, the strophemenids, and the spiriferids. The orthids diversified swiftly in the Ordovician, only to become more and more restricted during the rest of the Paleozoic.

Dictyonellidina. Brachiopods assigned to this suborder are of uncertain affinities within the articulates. They first appear in the Middle Ordovician and persist until the Permian. *Eichwaldia* is typical of the group in having a globose shape and a peculiar triangular plate on the umbo of the pedicle valve.

Strophomenidina. These are the brachiopods most often referred to as "petrified butterflies," because of both their shape and their often flattened appearance. The strophomenid shell seems to be punctate but is not, so it is called pseudopunctate. What this means is that there were calcite rods, rather than hollow tubes, in the shell below the outermost layer. They give a false impression of open tubes in the fossil. The shell had a wide hinge line, a fine costate surface, and one concave valve (which was either brachial or pedicle). The pedicle foramen was very small or even lacking, and so these brachiopods often lacked the attachment stalk and were free-living. Most also did not have a brachial skeleton. Appearing in the Early Ordovician, strophomenids soon became both varied and abundant, reaching their acme in the Late Paleozoic. After a rapid expansion in the Early Permian, the group nearly became extinct during the Late Permian marine crisis, and only a few species survived into the Early Jurassic.

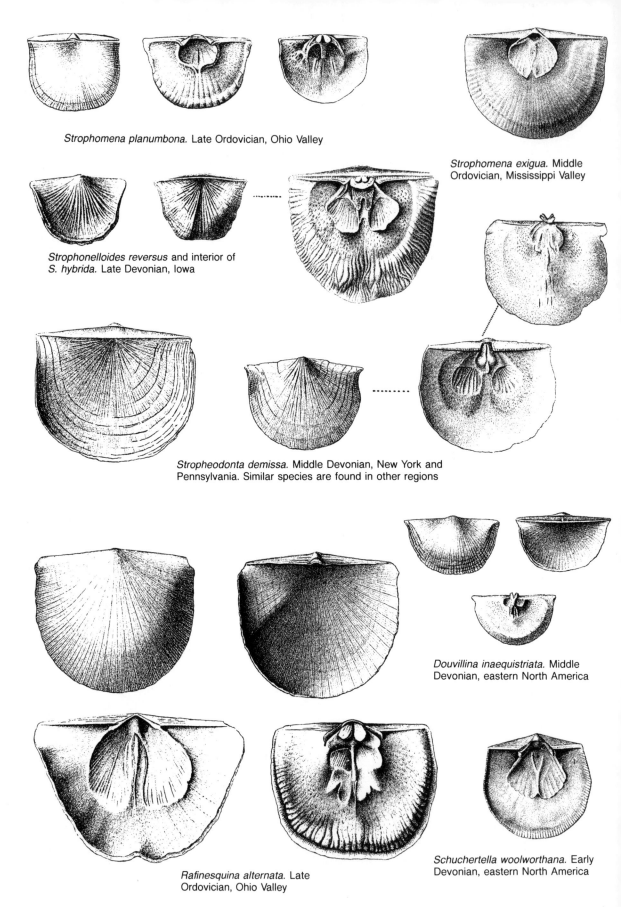

Strophomena planumbona. Late Ordovician, Ohio Valley

Strophomena exigua. Middle Ordovician, Mississippi Valley

Strophonelloides reversus and interior of *S. hybrida.* Late Devonian, Iowa

Stropheodonta demissa. Middle Devonian, New York and Pennsylvania. Similar species are found in other regions

Douvillina inaequistriata. Middle Devonian, eastern North America

Rafinesquina alternata. Late Ordovician, Ohio Valley

Schuchertella woolworthana. Early Devonian, eastern North America

Strophomenid brachiopods, all × 1. (After Hall and Clarke)

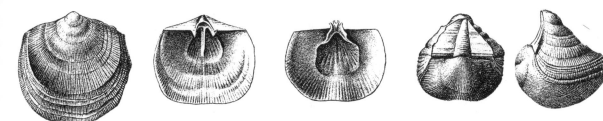

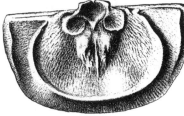

Derbyia crassa, × 1. Pennsylvanian, central United States

Derbyia bennetti, × 1.
Late Pennsylvanian, Missouri
and Nebraska to Texas

Leptaena rhomboidalis, × 1. A name used for wrinkled
leptaenas, which doubtless belong to several species.
Silurian and Devonian, North America

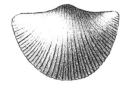

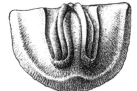

Plectodonta transversalis, × 2. Middle Silurian,
New York to Indiana, and Alabama

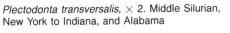

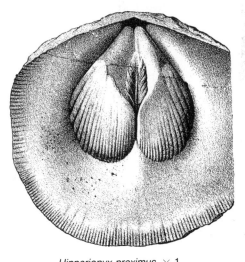

Fardenia subplana, × 1.
Middle Silurian, widespread
in the United States

Meekella striatocostata, × 1.
Pennsylvanian and Permian,
North America

Hipparionyx proximus, × 1.
Internal molds. Early
Devonian, Quebec to Oklahoma

Strophomenid brachiopods. (After Hall and Clarke)

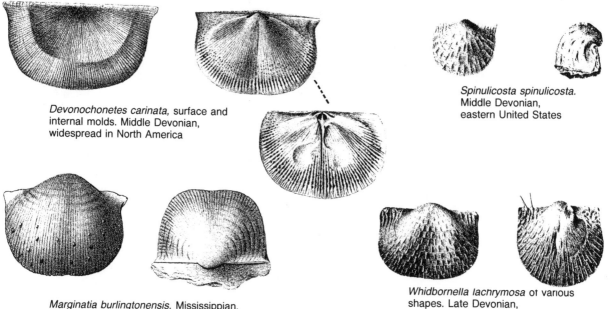

Devonochonetes carinata, surface and internal molds. Middle Devonian, widespread in North America

Spinulicosta spinulicosta. Middle Devonian, eastern United States

Marginatia burlingtonensis. Mississippian, Appalachians and Mississippi Valley

Whidbornella lachrymosa ot various shapes. Late Devonian, New York and Appalachians

Strophomenids, including the spiny productids. All × 1. (After Hall and Clarke)

Though the strophomenid body was very thin, it generally built a thick shell with prominent muscle scars. Such shells are abundant Paleozoic fossils, and well-cleaned pedicle valves are exceedingly attractive. Many species are marked by growth lines that show how shapes changed with increasing size.

One of the several suborders within the Strophomenida are the productids, a Devonian to Late Permian group. Some paleontologists, in fact, give the productids the status of their own order. The brachial valve is often flat, while the pedicle valve is deeply convex. Thus, the shell is called planoconvex in shape. Productids usually were very deep-bodied, and the pedicle valves tended to develop long "trails," or extensions. The delthyrium and notothyrium were often closed, and so these forms lacked the attaching pedicle. And quite frequently these forms had a series of spines, such as those on *Productella* and *Dictyoclostus.* The productids were very successful, because they took up a lifestyle that no other brachiopods had, that of living nearly buried in sediment, a part of the "infauna." This lifestyle gave them protection from predators as well as other environmental factors. The spines were evidently important in anchoring them within the sediments. The largest of all brachiopods, *Gigantoproductus,* which measured about 21 cm. (about 8 inches) wide, belonged to this unusual group. Productidines had a burst of diversification in the later part of the Paleozoic, after many groups of brachiopods had either become extinct or were severely restricted.

Pentamerida. These biconvex, impunctate brachiopods appeared in Middle Cambrian seas, became common in the Ordovician, and lived on to the end of Devonian times. They have short hinge lines, open notches for the

166

Anastrophia verneuili, × 1. Early Devonian,
Greenland and New York to Oklahoma

Gypidula romingeri, × 1.
Middle Devonian, Michigan

Conchidium nysius, × 1. Middle Silurian, Kentucky

Pentamerella arata.
Middle Devonian, Ontario
to New York and Indiana

Gypidula comis,
× 1. Devonian,
Iowa

Camerella volborthi, × 2.
Middle Ordovician,
Ontario and Quebec

Stricklandia castellana, × 1. Middle Silurian, Iowa

Virgiana decussata, × 1.
Middle Silurian, North America

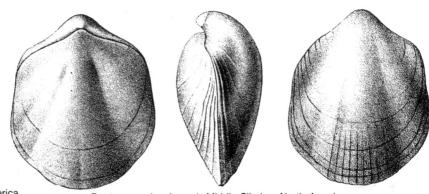

Pentamerus laevis, × 1. Middle Silurian, North America

Pentamerid brachiopods (After Hall and Clarke)

pedicle, and—with one exception—well-developed spondylia, which were essentially muscle-attachment areas on the pedicle valve. Directly opposite on the brachial valve often lay a structure of similar purpose, the cruralium. Some pentamerids had prominent folds and sulci. The Silurian *Pentamerus laevis* (often called *P. oblongus*) lived in closely packed colonies with pedicles sunk into the mud and elongate shells directed upward. Such colonies are often found on the underside of beds of fine sandstone. When cleaned and exhibited in museums, they appear upside down.

Rhynchonellida. These wedge-shaped, generally small brachiopods range from Middle Ordovician to Recent, being especially common in some Devonian rocks. They have short hinge lines, prominent beaks, and plications, which generally are coarse. Often they have a zigzag commissure (a line along which the opening margin of the shell meets), a fold and a sulcus, and always a pedicle. Some species are excellent index fossils; others belong to superficially similar genera that can be distinguished only by internal characters and whether the shells are punctate or impunctate.

Spiriferida. Derived from the rhynchonellids, these generally biconvex brachiopods, which range from Middle Ordovician to Jurassic, are united by spiral structures (brachidia), for which they are named. These supported the lophophore. Aside from this, the group varies greatly. Its oldest suborder, the Atrypidina, contained shells with short hinge lines, inconspicuous beaks, and spirals that were dorsally or laterally directed. Shells may have fine costae or coarse plications; some possess wide "wings," or alate lamellae, which are commonly missing from fossils. In other species, the lamellae fold

C. hamiltonensis   C. curvilineatea   C. alpenensis

Three species of *Cyrtina* of Devonian age from
New York, Iowa, and northern Michigan

Homoeospira evax. Middle
Silurian, New York,
Indiana, and Tennessee

Trematospira multistriata. Early
Devonian, New York to Oklahoma

Reticulariina spinosa.
Mississippian, Mississippi
Valley and Alabama

Spiriferid brachiopods with punctate shells. All resemble genera whose shells are not punctate. (After Hall and Clarke) (All × 1)

Rhynchotreta capax. Late Ordovician,
Ohio Valley; close relatives in many other regions

Rhynchotreta americana. Middle
Silurian, Ontario and New York
to Tennessee and Wisconsin

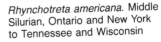

Camarotoechia congregata. Middle Devonian,
New York to Indiana

Orthorhynchula linneyi. Late Ordovician,
Tennessee and Ohio Valley

Hypothyridina venustula, with internal mold of pedicle valve.
Middle Devonian, Pennsylvania and New York

Pugnoides calvini. Late Devonian, Iowa.
Also internal molds of a related
species from the Chemung, of New York

Eatonia medialis.
Early Devonian,
Quebec to New York

Triplesia ortoni. Early Silurian, Ohio
to Tennessee and Oklahoma

Plethorhyncha speciosa. Early Devonian, Quebec to Tennessee
and Oklahoma

Rhynchonellid and triplesiid brachiopods, all × 1. (After Hall and Clarke)

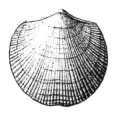 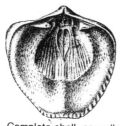 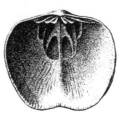 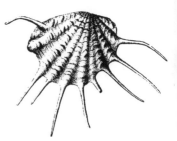

Atrypa sp., × 1. Complete shell, as well as interiors of both valves. Middle Devonian, Ontario and New York

Spinatrypa hystrix, × 1. Late Devonian, New York and Pennsylvania

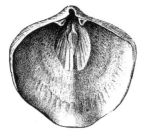   

Zygospira modesta, × 3. Late Ordovician, Quebec to Ohio Valley and Tennessee

Atrypa occidentalis, × 1. Middle Devonian, Iowa and Illinois

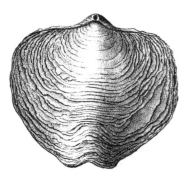  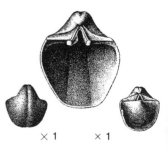

× 1   × 1

Athyris spiriferoides, × 1. Middle Devonian, Appalachians and New York

Torynifera setigera, × 1. Mississippian, Alabama and Kentucky to Arkansas

Ambocoelia umbonata, interior of pedicle enlarged. Middle Devonian, Ontario to Ohio and Kentucky

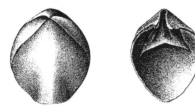  

Merista typa, × 1. Late Silurian, Pennsylvania and Maryland

 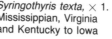 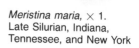

Syringothyris texta, × 1. Mississippian, Virginia and Kentucky to Iowa

Elita fimbriata, × 1. Middle Devonian, Ontario to Tennessee and Illinois

Meristina maria, × 1. Late Silurian, Indiana, Tennessee, and New York

Spiriferid brachiopods. (After Hall and Clarke)

Eospirifer radiatus.
Middle Silurian, eastern
North America

Cyrtia exporrecta. Niagaran of
Quebec, Indiana, and Kentucky

Mucrospirifer mucronatus.
Middle Devonian, New York
and Pennsylvania to Virginia

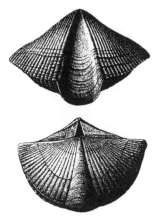

Costispirifer arenosus.
Early Devonian, eastern North
America and The Great Basin

Cyrtospirifer disjunctus. Late
Devonian, New York, Appalachians,
and Utah

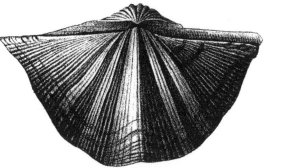

A spiriferid.
Mississippian,
Appalachians to Iowa

Mediospirifer audaculus.
Middle Devonian, eastern
North America

Neospirifer cameratus. Early
Pennsylvanian, Pennsylvania to Texas

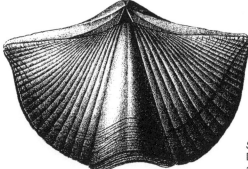

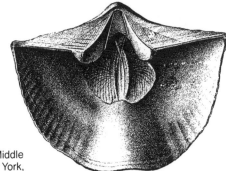

Spinocyrtia granulosa. Middle
Devonian, Ontario, New York,
and Pennsylvania

Spiriferid brachiopods, all × 1. (After Hall and Clarke)

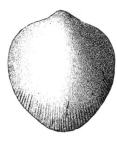 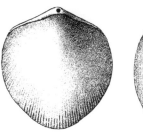   

Beachia suessana, × 1.
Early Devonian, Missouri to Quebec

Cranaena iowensis, × 1.
Middle Devonian, Missouri and Iowa

Cryptonella planirostra, × 1, with internal
mold of brachial valve. Middle Devonian,
New York and Virginia

Dielasma bovidens, × 1. Pennsylvanian
and Early Permian, Missouri to Texas

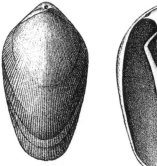  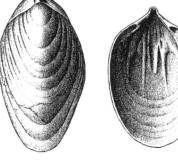

Rensselaeria johanni, × 1. Middle Devonian,
Iowa and Missouri

Rensselaeria marylandica, × 1.
Early Devonian, Maryland

Amphigenia elongata, × 1. Middle
Devonian, New York to Kentucky

Rensselaeria ovoides,
× 1. Early Devonian,
New York

Terebratulid brachiopods (After Hall and Clarke)

into spines, which also are easily broken. The delthyrium was open in some and closed in others, so some lived as animals moored to the sea bottom, while others were free-living.

This suborder contains *Atrypa reticularis,* which once was said to range through both Silurian and Devonian deposits. Actually *A. reticularis* is a complex lot of varieties and species, none of which lived through a whole period and many of which are so restricted in range that they serve well as index fossils.

Shells of the suborder Spiriferacea have, in the main, a characteristic "spirifer" shape, with a wide or extended hinge line, prominent beak, and well-developed sulcus and fold. The spiral brachidia extend outward toward the extremities, rather than into the brachial valve. The surface is either plicate or costate and may bear much finer markings.

Some spiriferids outwardly resembled rhynchonellids such as the Retziacea, which occur in Late Silurian to Permian rocks. Others came in a great variety of shapes including those with short hinge lines (Atrypidina), while others had very smooth shells (Athyrididina). In many cases, only the internal structure of these fossils can give an accurate guide to their relationships. Some paleontologists, in fact, think these groups are so different from the other spiriferids that they put them in separate orders. And there will continue to be different opinions on classification.

Spiriferids were most diverse in the Devonian and remained quite varied until the Late Triassic. After that, they quickly dwindled to extinction in the Jurassic.

Terebratulida. These punctuate shelled brachiopods apparently evolved in Late Silurian times and are characterized by short hinge lines and calcareous loops supporting the lophophores. Genera ranged from almost circular to elongate-oval in shape, with smooth or finely costate shells. During the Cretaceous and Tertiary periods, many shells became coarsely plicate. The pedicle is present but exits from the shell through a hole in the umbo, for the delthyrium is usually closed. Terebratulids are important today, especially in the Pacific. Some species inhabit rocky shores, though others are found in waters that are deep, quiet, and cold. Certainly in modern seas the species of terebratulids far outnumber those of all other brachiopods.

Thecideidina. This group of small, yet thick-shelled, articulates has been at times in the past assigned to the strophomenids, spiriferids, and terebratulids. They were usually cemented to something and lacked a pedicle, and, unlike most brachiopods, were evidently able to open their shells very wide when feeding. The brachidium had two horns that were bent back and ran parallel toward the mouth. Each of these had many lobes and is called a ptycholophe.

After first appearing in the Middle Triassic, the group become somewhat more varied in the Late Cretaceous, only to be restricted at the end of that period. It survives as a minor part of the brachiopod fauna until the present.

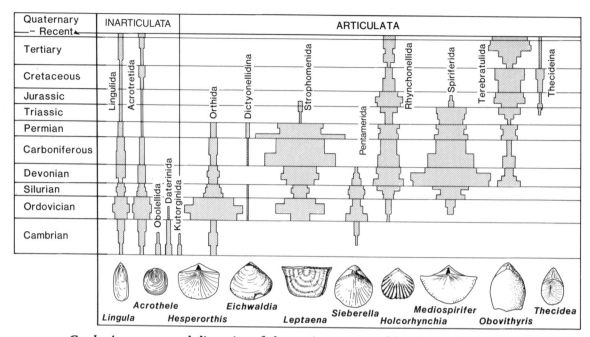

Geologic ranges and diversity of the major groups of brachiopods for the Phanerozoic. (Modified after Clarkson, 1979, by D. Gelt)

NATURAL HISTORY

As with other groups of animals and plants, we learn the natural history of brachiopods by comparing ancient with modern species, by examining strata in which the former are found, and by carefully studying the fossils themselves.

Depths and Habitats. Many brachiopods inhabit bottoms 150 to 1,500 feet (45–450 m.) deep, and others thrive at depths of 2,500 to more than 18,000 feet (760–5,500 m.). The majority, however, lived and still live in shallow water or even in the intertidal zone. Thus *Terebratalia* of the northern Pacific coast of North America often grows on rocks exposed by low tides, while *Lingula* and *Glottidia* burrow in sandy shoals where storms tear them up and sometimes wash them ashore in heaps that extend for miles and contain millions of animals. Though many shoals are brackish and hostile to most shelled invertebrates, modern linguloids apparently find them desirable habitats; they can tolerate large fluctuations in salinity. Today they prefer a fine sandy substrate and often are found in organically rich estuarine environments. Fossils in sandstone bearing rill marks and wave marks indicate similar habits as far back as the Cambrian. Prior to the Triassic, however, it appears that lingulids had even wider environmental tolerances. They were able to live in much colder water, for example in the Sydney

Resserella meeki *from the Late Ordovician of the Ohio Valley. These brachiopods lived near the place where their shells were buried, for most of them are not broken or worn. One shows a hole bored by a carnivorous snail*

A specimen of Atrypa *petrified where it lived on a colonial coral,* Hexagonaria, *from the Devonian of Iowa. The coral grew around the brachiopod but not against it, so the shell could be opened for feeding*

Basin of Australia, not far from active continental glaciers. Today, in contrast, they are restricted to the tropics.

Landlocked shallow epicontinental seas of the Paleozoic provided vast areas in which the water was rarely much more than 600 feet (180 m.) deep and commonly less than 150 (45 m.). There brachiopods and other invertebrates found sunlit, placid water and almost incredible supplies of microscopic food. Thus favored, brachiopods became both varied and abundant. The former is shown by the number of genera, species, and subspecies or varieties that are found; the latter, by the large number of specimens and by "banks" in which they are crowded as closely as blue mussels on modern shores. *Pentamerus laevis* colonies of this type are a good example.

There is no doubt that many ancient linguloids lived on sandy bottoms, as their descendants do today. There is a strong suggestion that some thin-shelled strophomenids also did so, and they may have been joined by wide-hinged spiriferids, whose sharp extremities acted as anchors. If so, these shells were buried where they lived and died. Many of the brachiopods found in limestone and shale also were buried where they had lived, since they preserve delicate frills, spines, and surface markings that would have been destroyed had they been washed into other regions. But some strata contain only worn shells or crowded fragments, which show that waves broke dead brachiopods to bits and mixed them with mud or swept them together in beds that resemble the coquina formed by Recent clamshells

Hesperorthis had a thick pedicle that could have been attached to a shell or might have dug into the bottom

Two specimens of *Terebratalia* (Recent). Both are attached by short, stiff pedicles that permit very little movement and cause distortion of the beaks

Barroisella, which looked and presumably lived like the modern *Lingula,* with its pedicle in the sea bottom

Compisita was attached by a strong pedicle, probably in varying positions, like *Terebratalia*

Composita was attached by a strong pedicle, probably in varying positions, like *Terebratalia*

Brachyspirifer had a thick pedicle that probably was attached to large shells, corals, etc., throughout the animal's life

Tritoechia. Its pedicle came from an opening near the beak and probably was attached to a shell

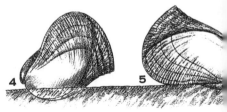

Stages in growth and orientation of a large *Atrypa*. A few old shells lay in position 4, but most came to rest in position 5

Schizophoria used its pedicle throughout life, though the pedicle valve sometimes rested on the bottom

Paraspirifer was attached when young, but its pedicle disappeared in maturity and the shell lay in the mud

Platystrophia also lost its pedicle and lay in the mud as it grew old

Orientation and attachment of typical brachiopods

along the coast of Florida. In other places, currents sorted broad valves, depositing brachials in one set of channels and pedicles in another. Death assemblages (thanatocoenoses) of brachiopods are thus quite varied.

Movement and Attachment. Larval brachiopods both drift and swim, but their travels are so limited that they generally settle down in clusters near their parents and relatives. Having done so, they cease to move about, spending the rest of their lives in one spot. Lingulids have one of the longest larval stages of any brachiopod group. They live up to two weeks as a free-moving form before settling, and so can be carried quite far by ocean currents.

Various groups have differing means of attaching themselves to the bottom. The primitive linguloids have a very long, tough pedicle that bores into sand or mud and covers its tip with a tough mucus to which sand grains are attached. By alternately contracting and relaxing its pedicle, the animal moves its shell up and down until it excavates a small burrow. When the creature is feeding, its shell extends about halfway out of the burrow. Any disturbance makes the pedicle contract, pulling the body into its hole.

We have found that storms often tear up banks of sand in which linguloids burrow. Those that are washed ashore perish, but the rest must burrow again. This they normally do with the pedicle, but injured animals may use their setae. Others travel short distances by pushing the setae into the sand and forcing themselves along on one side. In this way a creature that comes to rest in a crowd can pull itself away to a spot where it has room to burrow. Ancient linguloids doubtless shared these habits.

Many brachiopods kept their pedicles, though some were exceedingly small such as in the living *Curtia,* in which the pedicle serves only a tethering function, not support. Many others lost them, however, and were free-living. Others were cemented to corals or other shells, such as the thecideidines.

Pedicles appear to have been or are present in most terebratulids, rhynchonellids, orthids, and spiriferids, some pentamerids, and a few strophomenids.

In those that retain their pedicles, these organs differ greatly in flexibility and length. The short, stiff pedicle of *Terebratalia* holds both valves directly against the rocks or shells to which they are attached; such pedicles may be traced among fossils by thick shells that are worn or distorted by pressure. Thin-shelled genera such as *Laqueus* have longer, slender, more flexible pedicles that allow the shells to move freely. Some modern species attach themselves to seaweeds. Several ancient genera, such as *Oleneothyris, Rensselaeria,* and *Beachia* may have done the same. Both shapes and thin shells are consistent with this type of life.

Many Paleozoic brachiopods have openings that accommodate very large pedicles. Such shells also show little distortion or wear of the sort that might have come from attachment. We conclude that these brachiopods had long

Middle Devonian brachiopods of western New York and Ontario, shown in the positions they occupied during life; about half natural size. **1.** Spinocyrtia granulosa. **2.** Mucrospirifer mucronatus. **3.** Meristella barrisi. **4.** Athyris spiriferoides. **5.** Tropidoleptus carinatus. **6.** Pustulina pustulosa. **7.** Productella truncata. **8.** Atrypa reticularis. **9.** Camarotoechia sappho. **10.** Rhipidomella penelope. **11.** Str/Strophodonta demissa. *All these species are found in the famous exposures along Eighteen Mile Creek, Erie County, New York*

pedicles that either became stiff or remained so strong that the shells were held well above mud and solid objects to which the pedicles were attached. Indeed, it would not be hard to picture spirifers with deep valves and wide pedicle openings as creatures that reverted to habits much like those of *Lingula,* with stout pedicles that pierced the mud but held the shells above it.

Many brachiopods apparently were attached when young but lost their pedicles during maturity. This allowed the shells to lie upon the bottom or sink partway into it. *Rafinesquina, Strophomena,* and other concavo-convex genera apparently did this, resting upon their convex valves. *Hypothyridina* probably came to rest on its moderately curved pedicle valve, as did other genera of similar shape.

A variety of spines and wide projections kept aging specimens of *Atrypa* in position, though some probably rolled over onto their deepening brachial valves. *Paraspirifer* and *Platystrophia* apparently rested upon their deep pedicle valves, which sank more and more deeply into the mud. Some of these shells show growths of bryozoans, corals, and other encrusting organisms upon valves that must have been exposed.

Advanced as well as primitive brachiopods cemented themselves to solid supports. Many did so by means of spines, or by spines and part of one valve. In *Richthofenia,* of Permian age, the cemented valve comes to a point and is thickened so much that it looks like a horn coral. The uncemented valve is flattened and is little more than a lid.

The most amazing modification of the pedicle, however, occurs in the living *Magadina,* which is found along the southern coast of Australia. It inhabits areas where sediments are being rapidly deposited and may often threaten to cover the living brachiopods. *Magadina* avoids this by using its pedicle as a pogo stick to quickly and effectively move out of an inhospitable area.

LIFE HISTORIES AND ACCIDENTS

During the 1880s, two paleontologists washed and sieved a huge collection of Silurian fossils from Waldron, Indiana. They secured a large number of brachiopods, from very small shells to large ones whose size and irregular growth indicate that they were old. Four species were illustrated in *Memoir I* of the New York State Museum, published in 1889.

Methods of washing and sieving for fossils have been greatly improved, yet few "life histories" like those from Waldron have been collected and described. They are not always needed, however, for growth lines trace changes in shape and size from early stages to old age. Some genera also have minute surface markings that go through an equally precise sequence. Though they can be seen only through a good lens or a low-powered binocular microscope, they are well worth examination.

Ancient Injuries. Many modern brachiopods are sturdy creatures—linguloids live in wave-swept shallows, surviving storms that fill the water with sand or reduce salinity; *Terebratalia* endures beating surf and exposure at low tide. It also inhabits shallow, sunlit pools filled only by spray during storms, with long periods when the water bubbles with gas from decaying seaweeds. At least one terebratalian grew to good size inside the shell of a snail whose mantle had been torn.

Ancient brachiopods probably were as hardy as their modern relatives. Fossils show that they survived injuries that caused distortion and twisting of the valves or even sharply broken shells. A specially good example is seen in a shell whose valves grew around a bryozoan that had been forced against them. Though distorted and kept from opening normally, the brachiopod survived and almost regained its normal shape. Such specimens, like others that show attachment or change in orientation, are helpful clues to the natural history of ancient brachiopods.

CHAPTER XI

Worms, Burrows, Trails, and Other Problematica

The railroad town of Field, British Columbia, Canada, lies between precipitous mountains made up of Cambrian rocks. Northward from Field a trail climbs steeply until it crosses Burgess Pass. Beyond the pass another trail leads to the right, climbing above firs and spruces to beds of blackish Middle Cambrian shale exposed on a barren ridge. The shale was discovered in 1909, after Charles D. Walcott paused to push a stone from the trail. When Dr. Walcott last crossed the pass, many years later, he had collected forty thousand fossils from that one small exposure of Burgess Shale. Unknown numbers remain in ledges and frost-broken slabs.

These fossils are impressions and films of carbon that show both outer shapes and internal structures in amazing detail. To collect them is to carry our minds back to an age when the ridge was a quiet, muddy corner of a Middle Cambrian sea that extended southward from the Arctic Ocean and reached the Pacific near what now is Lower California. Algae were plentiful: green or blue-green species like tufts of silken threads, gracefully branched red seaweeds, and brown ones whose leaflike blades were pierced by many small holes. Little brachiopods were common too, and so were vaselike glass sponges described in Chapter VII. Jellyfish swam to and fro, sea cucumbers lay on the mud, and worms crawled across it. Some of those worms were small and plain, but others were showy, with brilliant scales and bristles that shimmered as their owners moved about.

The Burgess Shale fossils reflect how varied wormlike invertebrates were in the Early Paleozoic, and how diversified in the Late Precambrian.

WORMS OF VARIOUS PHYLA

The differing forms of these Middle Cambrian crawlers show that the word *worm* has only general significance. In everyday language it means almost any wriggling or crawling creature with an elongate body, from a caterpillar to a leech or intestinal parasite, from "blind worms" (legless lizards) to the hemichordates. Many old books about fossils, on the other hand, apply the term to only one or two classes in the phylum that includes earthworms and the most brilliant creatures that lived in the Burgess "pool."

The first of these interpretations is sometimes preferable to the second. It is true that caterpillars are young, or larval, insects and should be given their correct name. But even without them, "worm" remains a useful general term that fits a vast number of invertebrate animals that differ in shape, structure, and relationships and are now distributed among ten or more phyla. Four of these are known from petrified fossils or carbonized films, and at least three more can be traced in solidified burrows and tubes. Worms in these groups can range from the microscopic (0.1 mm. or 0.004 in.) to true giants, such as the living Australian earthworm *(Megascolecides),* up to 3 meters (10 ft.), or the ribbon worms, up to 24 meters (79 ft.). But of all the vermiform (worm-like) animals, the annelids are the most important as fossils.

Flatworms (Platyhelminthes).   Flatworms are the simplest of worms, as well as the simplest animals that have three distinct layers in their bodies instead of the two we have examined in coelenterates. This third layer forms organs such a muscles, as well as others that are lined with sheets of endoderm. Though this three-layered body is simple in flatworms, we have found that it becomes complex and precisely organized in many other phyla. Flatworms lack an anus and a coelom, so they probably branched off the "family tree" before these structures developed.

Since flatworms have no hard parts, they are poorly suited to fossilization. None are found in the Burgess Shale; in fact, no free-living flatworms are known as fossils, though a few parasites have been discovered in carbonized insects of Pennsylvanian and Tertiary ages. They show that some flatworms gave up independent life at least 250 million years ago and began to exist as flukes and tapeworms do today.

Roundworms (Nemathelminthes, or Nematoda).   Vast numbers of modern roundworms are parasites in plants as well as animals; some, such as trichina and the hookworm, are exceedingly dangerous. Others live in fresh water, soil, sand, and the sea; they are the most abundant of living animals and may outnumber all others combined. Parasitic species have been found in fossil insects and Quaternary mammals, including humans. One free-living form of the Burgess Shale is tentatively assigned to this phylum, which ranges from Cambrian to Recent.

Proboscis, or Priapulid, Worms (Nemertea).   This is a small group of mostly marine worms that are characterized by a wrinkled body, a straight digestive system, and a proboscis that is covered with spines. They range from the Jurassic to the present day.

Horsehair Worms (Nematomorpha).   A number of hair-shaped, unsegmented worms have been found in marine and freshwater sediments from Eocene to Recent times. They are not very important as fossils, however.

Arrowworms (Chaetognatha).   These forms are bullet-shaped, free-

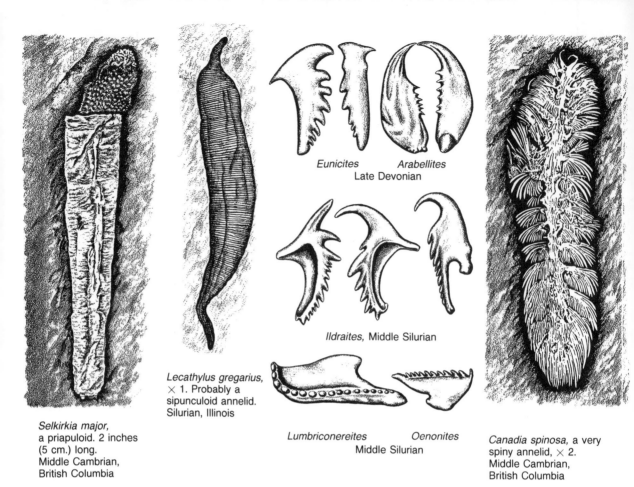

Eunicites   Arabellites
Late Devonian

Ildraites, Middle Silurian

Lecathylus gregarius,
× 1. Probably a
sipunculoid annelid.
Silurian, Illinois

Selkirkia major,
a priapuloid. 2 inches
(5 cm.) long.
Middle Cambrian,
British Columbia

Lumbriconereites   Oenonites
Middle Silurian

Canadia spinosa, a very
spiny annelid, × 2.
Middle Cambrian,
British Columbia

Priapuloid and annelid worms, and some typical scolecodonts (worm jaws, which are several times natural size)

swimming marine worms that are not segmented but, unlike the vermiform animals mentioned above, have a coelom. They have a distinct head, trunk, and tail. The head has a pair of eyes, and jaws constructed of chitin. They also possess both side fins and a caudal, or tail, fin, but apparently lack a circulatory or an excretory system. Arrowwormlike creatures are known from the Cambrian and survive today.

Peanut Worms (Siphunculoida). These worms, too, have coeloms, but are at best only weakly segmented. The body is tubular, and the front end may have several chitinous hooks. They range from Cambrian to Recent.

SEGMENTED WORMS (ANNELIDA)

These are the "Vermes" of many old books; they also are often called Annulata. As that name and Annelida imply, these are worms whose bodies are covered with rings, which correspond to internal sections in which some parts are repeated over and over again. This characteristic is shown plainly by the common earthworm. Annelids have a muscular body wall as well as reasonably developed nervous, excretory, and reproductive systems. They have a long geologic range, from Precambrian to Recent.

Though annelids are much less abundant than nematodes, most fossil worms belong to this phylum. One reason for this is the fact that annelids are covered with a tough layer, or cuticle, which resists destruction. Many annelids also possess hard, durable jaws or cover themselves with tubes or shells. The former are made of cemented grains or are provided with tough linings, while the latter are quite as sturdy as calcareous shells.

Ancient Marine "Earthworms."   The earthworm belongs to a group (the oligochaetes, meaning "few bristles," in reference to the chitinous bristles on each segment) most of whose members now live on land. A few, however, are marine, as were the only known fossils. The most familiar of these, *Protoscolex,* was a soft-bodied creature, with distinct rings, that was blunt at the forward end (there was no head) and tapered to the rear. Some specimens seem to possess a clitellum, the bandlike structure that forms a cocoon containing the eggs of a modern oligochaete. The oldest terrestrial earthworms occur in the Carboniferous.

Hunters and Jaws (Scolecodonts).   Earthworms and their kin are headless, have bristles instead of legs, and eat small organisms or dead, decaying food. Polychaetes ("many bristles") have heads and legs, and many of them (classed as Errantida, the "errant polychaetes") are active hunters whose mouths are equipped with two or three types of sharp, horny jaws.

Some carbonized worms of this type have been found, but most of them are known from their jaws, which are termed scolecodonts, or "worm teeth." The teeth contain large amounts of calcium, copper, silica, and magnesium. Their mineral composition is fluorapatite. They range from the Ordovician to the Recent, and from simple blades or prongs to complex structures with many points. Since scolecodonts are very small, they can be found complete in drill cores, and many are useful index fossils. Others give us a good idea of the abundance and variety of active annelids in seas in which more complete fossils are unknown. In certain parts of the world during certain periods of time, scolecodonts have been used as good rock subdividers: as biostratigraphic tools. Examples include Ordovician rocks of Poland and the Permian rocks of the central United States, for which a reference by Tasch and Stude (1966) is given in the Bibliography for this chapter.

Shell-building Worms.   Scolecodonts belonged to active worms that crawled, swam, or burrowed in search of prey, as does the modern clam worm *Nereis.* But annelids that build shells stay in one place, cover themselves with armor of calcite or cemented sand grains, and rely upon small food that can be captured by currents of water or by gills that are covered with sticky mucus.

Fossil shell builders are easily overlooked, for many of them are small. The commonest probably is *Spirorbis,* which looks like a tiny snail attached

Lumbricaria, about × 1, a trace fossil. Jurassic, Solenhofen, Germany

Serpula and Hamulus, about × 2, both annelids. Cretaceous to Recent

Arthrophycus allegheniensis, × 0.3 (annelid burrows often called A. harlani). Early Silurian, eastern North America

Tentaculites, about × 1. A fossil of uncertain affinities. Ordovician (?), Silurian–Devonian, nearly worldwide

Cornulites proprius, about × 5. A fossil of uncertain affinities. Silurian, eastern North America

Ottoia prolifica, × 1. A Middle Cambrian annelid

Trail fillings in shale. Though often called worms, such traces were commonly made by other animals

Two species, much enlarged, of Spirorbis, a polychaete annelid. Ordovician to Recent

Burrows resembling Diplocraterion, a Cambrian genus. Cretaceous, South Dakota

Annelids, trace fossils, and problematica

to other fossils and ranges from the Late Ordovician to the Recent, being very common on the brown seaweeds that often are washed ashore. *Serpula* is either coiled or irregularly twisted; some early species were not attached.

OTHER PROBLEMATICA SOMETIMES CALLED WORMS

A number of small, conical shells have been, and still are, a paleontologist's nightmare—when trying to understand relationships of these forms. They include *Hyolithes* and its relatives, tentaculitids *(Tentaculites)*, the cornulitids *(Cornulites)*, and others. Many of these have been shifted from one phylum to the next repeatedly, from snails to worms, for instance. We still don't have a clear idea what they are related to.

The major group of criconarids includes the tentaculitids, the styliolinids, and other fossils. They are all small (1–80 mm. in length: up to 3 in.), quite narrow and straight cones that have transverse rings, or striae, about them. They are restricted to marine rocks of the Paleozoic, the oldest known being *Tentaculites lowdoni,* from the Early Ordovician of Virgina. They reached their peak of diversity in the Middle Devonian but became extinct in the Late Devonian (Famennian). The last surviving criconarid was *Styliolina,* known from northeastern North America.

Hyolithids are bilaterally symmetric, conical fossils made up of calcium carbonate that taper to a closed point or a rounded end. They range from 1 to 150 millimeters (up to about 6 in.). Their walls are laminated, and they possessed an operculum, which presumably allowed closure of their shell to the outside world. They appear first in the Early Cambrian and survived until the Middle Permian. Because there were so many kinds of hyolithids in the Early Cambrian faunas, the group probably has a much longer record, extending back into the Precambrian. But, in the Precambrian, most organisms had no hard parts, and so the fossil record is lacking.

Hyolithids occur only in marine rocks and are usually found together with "shelly fossils" such as brachiopods and trilobites, only very rarely with reef-associated species such as corals. Paleontologists have suggested several lifestyles for hyolithids, ranging from sedentary forms that were basically filter feeders, to bottom feeders, to actively swimming (nektonic) forms, and even planktonic species. In the few well-preserved specimens, lateral finlike structures have been found: these may have acted as "wings," allowing the animal to move along the bottom like a modern ray, in search of a meal.

FOSSIL BURROWS AND CASTINGS

Fossil burrows and tubes were once called "fucoids" on the assumption that they were casts of brown algae. This was followed by an equally uncritical effort to assign them to the worms or to dismiss them as problematic affairs of little significance.

The error of this last assumption is shown by *Urechis,* a soft-bodied echiurid, or sausage worm, that lives in elongate U-shaped burrows on the California coast. Fossil sausage worms were unknown until G. E. MacGinitie, who had studied *Urechis* in its present-day home, dug the hardened filling of a typical burrow from the Pliocene Monterey Shale. Besides having the characteristic shape, the burrow filling contained a petrified crab, which is a commensal tenant in modern *Urechis* borrows only a few miles from the place where the fossil was found.

Nemerteans, or ribbon worms, have no hard parts that can be readily preserved and do not appear in lists of fossils. Modern species burrow almost constantly, however, searching for annelids and probably other food. First the worm extends its head forward like a pointed probe; then the head swells and retracts, pulling the body forward. The method is slow and laborious but well fitted to produce the alternately thickened and contracted burrows called *Arthrophycus,* of Silurian age. *Arthrophycus,* however, is generally regarded as the work of annelids that burrowed in this manner.

Many fossil burrows are smooth instead of annulate, and branch less commonly than *Arthrophycus.* Such burrows could have been made by either sipunculids or annelids that swallow sediment, extract food from it, and either cast it into the burrows behind them or discharge it at the surface. The common lugworm, *Arenicola,* does this; since food and sediment are collected on a sticky proboscis, grains that pass through the animal's intestine are smaller than those in the muddy sand around it.

Arenicola discharges its castings at the surface and sometimes lies in U-shaped burrows much smaller than those of *Urechis.* Similar burrows, called *Arenicolites,* often show that the worms looped their way upward or downward, making a series of U-shaped marks that extend through beds of sandstone. They are quite different from *Caulerpites,* which may have a similar form but lie on the surface of strata.

Some ancient castings resemble those of *Arenicola,* but others are much larger and longer. This may mean that they were made by bigger worms, but those called *Lumbricaria* closely resemble the castings made by modern burrowing sea cucumbers, which belong to the echinoderms.

Skolithos is a common fossil in rocks that range from Cambrian to Late Devonian age. It consists of filled tubes in beds of sandstone, tubes that are surprisingly straight and seldom form tangles or intertwine. They have been compared to modern "sand corals," which consist of tubes built by an annelid, *Sabellaria,* that is related to worms with shells. Actually *Skolithos* more closely resembles the tubes of phoronids, which are worms related to brachiopods. *Tigillites,* which as a funnel around the mouth of its tube, may also be the work of phoronids.

Burrowers Other than Worms. Though many burrows were made by worms, some were produced by other animals. Some sponges, for example,

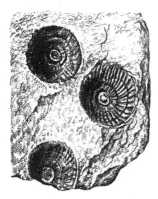

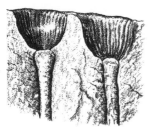

Diplocraterion, about natural size, a fossil annelid burrow. Early Cambrian, Europe, North America

Tigillites. Cambrian–Jurassic, Europe, North America, Arabia

Diplocraterion parallelum, × 1. Early Cambrian, Sweden

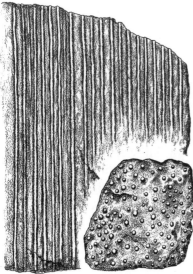

A living *Spirorbis* with its tentacles extended, about × 15

Rauffella, possibly a complex burrow. Ordovician, North America

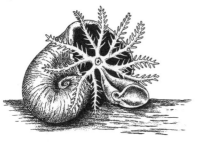

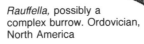

Skolithos is found in Cambrian to Ordovician sandstones of Europe, North America, Greenland, and Australia

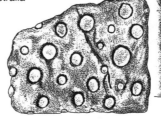

Skolithos linearis, burrows made by annelids or phoronids. Slender type, × 0.5

Skolithos linearis. Thick type, × 0.5

Tubes, burrows, and a modern shell-building annelid

have rootlike growths that extend downward into mud and serve as hold-fasts. Several sea anemones dig cup-shaped holes, but others make vertical tubes or even push their way through mud as they search for food. Some sea cucumbers are accomplished burrowers; that is how they get the mud for castings resembling *Lumbricaria.* Others lie in a U-shaped position, with both mouth and anus at the surface. Some crustaceans dig permanent holes, while others burrow through sand or mud and sift it to secure food. Some clams make holes 12 to as much as 30 inches (30–75 cm.) deep and either travel up and down their burrows or lie at the bottom and send their siphons to the surface. Snails such as *Olivella* crawl just beneath the surface, with the siphon projecting. The result is trails, or collapsed burrows, which can easily be recognized when they appear as fossils.

TRAILS—FEW MADE BY WORMS

Many formations, from Early Cambrian to Pleistocene, contain fossil trails and other marks or impressions, which at one time or another have been credited to worms.

Some supposed trails prove to be burrows: compressed mud or sand that filled burrows that were made just below the surface or along bedding planes between layers of sediment, where food probably was more plentiful than it was above or below. Other "trails" are marks made by shells that were dragged over the bottom by currents or by waves that reached to the floors of shallow seas. Many are preserved as hardened fillings that appear on the surface of beds that covered the marked layers. To see the original pits and scratches, one must make impressions in plaster of paris or plasticine.

Even when these pseudo trails are removed, we still have a large and interesting array of actual fossil trails. Some may have been made by large, heavy annelids that crept on soft bottoms and left marks made by their "legs," or parapods. But few annelids leave such marks today, and few fossil trails seem to have had this origin. Most of them, instead, belong to six types that may be credited to several groups other than worms:

1. Flat-bottomed furrows with ridges at each side, as well as cross ridges or wrinkles. They commonly end in pits or flattened impressions and were made by crawling snails that plowed into the soft bottom. Some ancient snails even left streaks of slime when they crawled, as slugs do today.

2. Marks that wind to and fro in closely spaced loops. They were made by snails that crawled about, eating films of plants that grew on mud.

3. Deep furrows that end in pits or short burrows. Some of the latter contain fossil clams; these and similar marks made by modern bivalves show that such trails were made by clams that lived in ancient seas.

4. Trails that show marks of two series of jointed legs, one at each side of

an apparently elongate body. There may also be marks made by dragging spines, and the trails may end in irregular burrows. Most of these fossils were made by trilobites (Chapter XII), though some probably are the work of eurypterids (Chapter XIV).

5. Somewhat less regular trails; the impressions of legs are sharper and less uniform. Some of these trails were made by ancient horseshoe crabs (Chapter XIV) and others by eurypterids.

6. Tracks that resemble the preceding but lack traces of dragging spines. Found in Pennsylvanian and later rocks, most of them seem to have been made by crabs and other modernized crustaceans.

This list is not complete, and it raises as many problems as it solves. Still, it is enough to indicate that fossil trails are much more than mere curios or hypothetical worms. They deserve careful collection and study, which will include experiments with modern bottom dwellers whose trails in soft mud and sand can be preserved by casting them in plaster. An example of such work is K. E. Caster's study of *Kouphichnium* (= *Paramphibius*), reported in the *Journal of Paleontology,* Vol. 12, pages 3–60, for 1938. Besides explaining some very interesting trails, Professor Caster proved that a supposed amphibian really was a fossil king crab.

TRACE FOSSILS

What we have been talking about are special cases of a much larger group of fossils called "trace fossils," those left behind as traces of an animal's (or plant's) existence and activities—not the actual remains of the organisms. Trace fossils, sometimes called ichnofossils ("track" fossils), include not only tracks and burrows, but also trails, borings, resting traces, escape tunnels, and many others. Though most trace fossils have very long time ranges, they are quite often characteristic of certain kinds of environments and so have become very important in paleoecological studies. Sometimes they are also the only fossils preserved in a rock sequence, and for the geologist who knows how to interpret them, they hold a wealth of information.

In order to try understanding trace fossils, scientists studying them have over the past few years developed several schemes of classification. One system organizes the traces according to the activity or behavior indicated by the fossil. Cubichnia are resting traces, usually shallow depressions, caused by the pausing of an animal in some spot. Sometimes the impression of the underside of the animal is preserved. Repichnia are crawling traces, tracks, or trails of the animal as it moves along, as we have seen earlier in this chapter. Pascichnia are grazing traces, much like those left behind in tide pools by snails removing plant material from the rocks. Fodinichnia are feeding traces of animals moving through the sediment, not just over it. Domichnia are dwelling structures, burrows in which marine worms or even denning coyotes spent some time. Generally these are rather permanent structures, often circular in cross section, and often with some compaction or cementation of the walls. Finally, Fugichnia are escape structures, traces made by rapid movement, either up or down, of an animal to compensate for rapid change in sedimentation, such as slumping or landslides on the one hand, and erosion on the other.

Another classification is based on the kind of environment that existed when the animals were alive—such as whether it was turbulent or quiet water, whether it had a high or a low rate of sedimentation. Several zones have been set up. The *Skolithos* and *Glossifungites* facies represent trace fossils formed in shallow, intertidal conditions. Suspension feeders live in this area today and depend on the waves and current to keep their food available. They must, however, be able to cope with storms, low tide, and sudden changes in temperature and salinity; so they often are capable of withdrawing far into burrows in the buffering sediments. Trace fossils are unbranched, deep, vertical burrows, often very concentrated, and there are generally only a few kinds of animals that make these traces. The next zone offshore is the *Cruziana* Facies. Waters there are much less turbulent, and the animals are most often deposit feeders. The trace fossils are more horizontally oriented burrows that are often branched, with back-filling structures such as lobes. Many kinds of animals inhabit this facies, and so the variety of trace fossils is much higher than in the *Skolithos* Facies.

The facies that generally lies on the continental slope is the zone of churners *(Zoophycos* Facies). This area is not affected at all by waves or massive downslope submarine landslides (turbidity currents). Sedimenta-

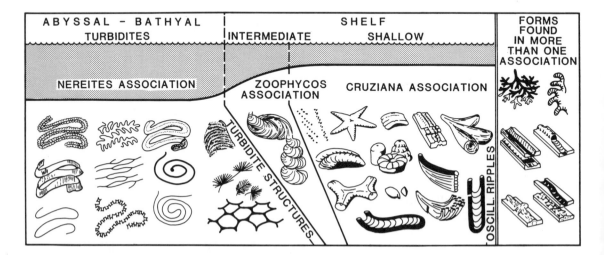

Frequent trace fossil associations and their environmental significance (Modified from A. Seilacher. Trace Fossil Concepts *by P. B. Basan et al., Soc. Econ. Paleo. and Mineral Short Course 5, S.E.P.M., 1978)*

tion is generally slow, continuous, and predictable, and there is a good supply of food but an ever decreasing supply of oxygen. Animals here intensively churn through the sediments, turning them over (bioturbate) again and again, and thus destroy any bedding that may have existed. Bioturbation is the main trace fossil.

The last facies is the *Nereites* Facies, also called the zone of systematic grazers and farmers. This facies today occurs in ocean depths that are affected by turbidity currents and are generally far away from the areas where abundant food is being produced. Waters are calm and environmental conditions generally rather constant. Trace fossils are complex, shallow burrows with densely meandering patterns, and these often have multiple exits.

By understanding where the many kinds of trace fossils are produced today, paleontologists have been able to make rather detailed reconstructions of past environments, using the present as a key to unlocking the past, our old principle of uniformitarianism. These reconstructions are important not only to the theoretical paleontologist, but to the company geologist as well, who is looking for the kind of paleoenvironmental conditions that could have led to oil accumulations. These rather nondescript fossils at first glance, can be of great help from Precambrian times to the present.

CHAPTER XII

Animals in Three Parts:
the Trilobites

No one can tell a simple, continuous story of fossils. For the world of invertebrates the story is not simple, and many of its phyla appeared abruptly at the beginning of the Phanerozoic, when hard parts were first acquired. Thus, origins of many are still not clearly understood. We can deal with them only group by group and, having told the story of one, must go back to remote antiquity to begin the record of another. In complex phyla, whose classes differ widely, we are forced to do this several times.

JOINTS AND "SKIN CRUSTS": THE ARTHROPODS

This is especially true of Arthropoda, a phylum so old and so varied that it is divided into seven major groups called by some "subphyla" and by others "superclasses," and an ever increasing number of classes. Several of these apparently were established in the Cambrian Period or even before, and only three have records limited to post-Silurian times. Many paleontologists have suggested that the phylum Arthropoda is really a group of unrelated animals, more a level of organization. Perhaps the crabs, the insects, the trilobites, and many other arthropods actually came from various ancestors and should each be made separate, distinct phyla.

The name Arthropoda means "jointed feet," but this is an understatement. From head to whatever serves as tail, the typical arthropod is a series of segments, or somites, connected by movable joints. More may be traced in grooves and constrictions where segments once movable have been fused into shields or plates. The legs or other appendages are similarly jointed.

The Useful Exoskeleton. Joints show plainly, because they bend, being soft parts of an exoskeleton that often becomes hard enough to be called a shell. It really is a crust secreted by the skin—a laminated crust that in most living arthropods is made up of three layers. At the surface is a waxy sheet

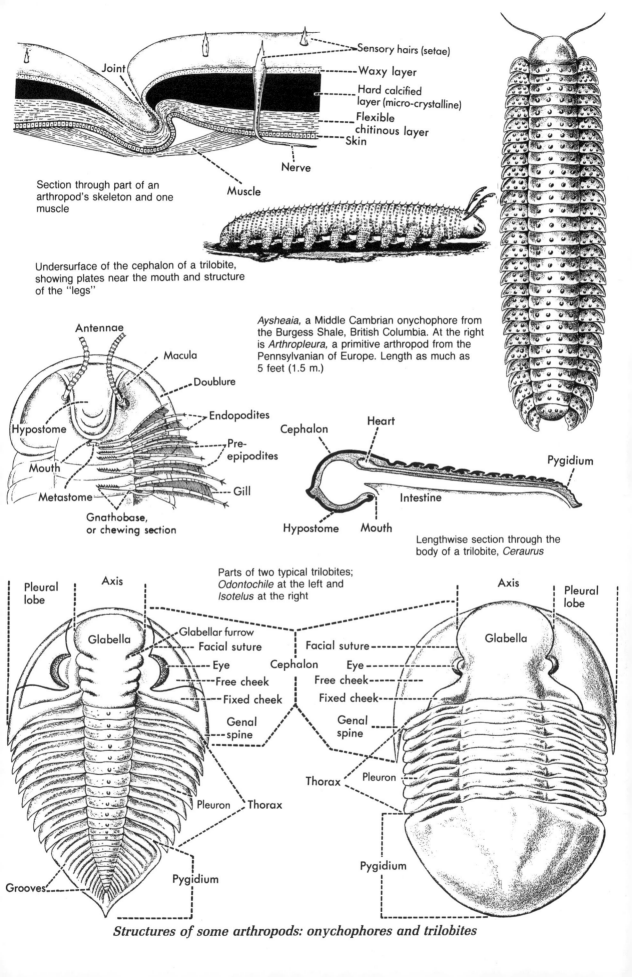

Sensory hairs (setae)

Waxy layer

Hard calcified
layer (micro-crystalline)

Flexible
chitinous layer

Skin

Joint

Nerve

Muscle

Section through part of an
arthropod's skeleton and one
muscle

Undersurface of the cephalon of a trilobite,
showing plates near the mouth and structure
of the "legs"

Aysheaia, a Middle Cambrian onychophore from
the Burgess Shale, British Columbia. At the right
is *Arthropleura,* a primitive arthropod from the
Pennsylvanian of Europe. Length as much as
5 feet (1.5 m.)

Antennae

Macula

Doublure

Endopodites

Hypostome

Pre-
epipodites

Mouth

Gill

Metastome

Gnathobase,
or chewing section

Cephalon

Heart

Pygidium

Hypostome

Mouth

Intestine

Lengthwise section through the
body of a trilobite, *Ceraurus*

Parts of two typical trilobites;
Odontochile at the left and
Isotelus at the right

Pleural
lobe

Axis

Axis

Pleural
lobe

Glabella

Glabellar furrow

Facial suture

Eye

Free cheek

Fixed cheek

Genal
spine

Cephalon

Facial suture

Eye

Free cheek

Fixed cheek

Genal
spine

Glabella

Pleuron

Thorax

Thorax

Pleuron

Pleuron

Pygidium

Grooves

Pygidium

Pygidium

Structures of some arthropods: onychophores and trilobites that seems to serve as waterproofing. Below this is a layer that gives stiffness and strength and therefore is fully developed only between the flexible joints. It may be chitinous, but in crabs and their relatives it contains secondary deposits of calcite. Last of all, in direct contact with the skin, is a tough but flexible layer of chitin. It forms most of the crust in soft-bodied insects and on newly molted, or "soft-shell," crabs.

Exoskeletons, as we know, support the soft structures inside them and generally serve as armor. The arthropod crust follows this rule—but, thanks to its joints, it also carries out some of the functions performed by bones in the vertebrate skeleton. Many vertebrate muscles run from bone to bone and, by contracting, produce movement in arms, legs, jaws, and so on. Arthropod muscles are fastened to skin, which generally is firmly attached to the crustlike exoskeleton. When muscles running from segment to segment contract, they can produce movements as rapid and precise as those of most vertebrates.

Molting and the Fossil Record.   In two respects, however, a crust is inferior to bones or even to ordinary shells. It is much less versatile than the former; no combination of arthropod organs can produce the variety of movements achieved by the vertebrate arm and hand. Once formed and hardened, the crust also is fixed; it cannot increase in size day by day as its owner grows. The developing arthropod must crowd more and more body into its casing until skin finally separates from crust, the latter splits, and its maker struggles out in a thin, soft covering. Then the body swells, the exoskeleton thickens, and the animal is again in an unyielding crust.

This process of shedding the crust, called molting, or ecdysis, takes place four to ten times in many arthropods and as many as thirty times in long-lived, ever-growing types such as lobsters. During early growth, molting also may be accompanied by radical changes in appearance and structure. Young crabs, for example, begin life as tiny, spiny drifters and go through shrimplike stages before reaching their final form. After that, molting results in little change in appearance except increase in size. Insects, on the other hand, stop growing when they achieve their adult form.

Ancient arthropods also molted and changed, or metamorphosed. This vastly increased the number of fossils, for castoff crusts were just as durable as dead bodies. Thus, one animal could leave several potential fossils, ranging from fragments to perfect exoskeletons. When castoff crusts show progressive changes in shape and structure, they reveal the development of individuals within a species.

LINKS BETWEEN ARTHROPODS AND WORMS

The record of arthropods may begin in Precambrian rocks of South Australia, whence came the very imperfect fossils mentioned in Chapter V. *Xenu-*

Aysheaia pedunculata, × 1.4.
A wormlike onychophore.
Middle Cambrian, British Columbia

Opabina regalis, × 0.9,
a "trilobitoid." Middle
Cambrian, British Columbia

Ceraurus pleurexanthemus, × 1,
a phacopid. Ordovician, eastern
North America

Phacops iowensis, a phacopid. Note
eye facets. Middle Devonian, Iowa

Dipleura dekayi, × 1, a phacopid, enrolled
(coiled). Middle Devonian, eastern United States

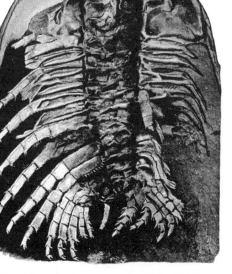

Olenoides serratus, a corynexochid, natural
size. Retouched to show the legs with their
chewing bases and gills. Middle Cambrian
(Burgess Shale), British Columbia. (After Walcott)

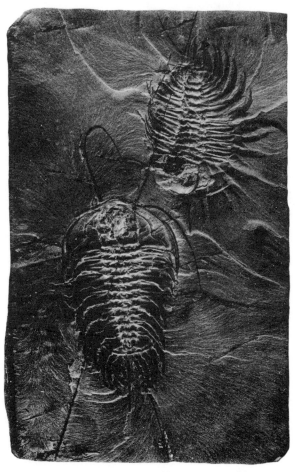

Olenoides serratus, × 0.5, with antennae and legs.
Middle Cambrian, British Columbia

An onychophore, some trilobites, and a "trilobitoid"

sion, from a glacial boulder found in Sweden, is probably also Precambrian. It is generally placed in the Onychophora, a subphylum or superclass of wormlike creatures that combine annelid-worm and arthropod characteristics (Chapter XIV).

Modern onychophores creep in damp tropical or subtropical forests, but *Xenusion* was marine. So was *Aysheaia,* of the Burgess Shale, a wormlike creature with twenty wrinkled legs that ended in claws, and with rings of bristles around its body. The head had one pair of branched antennae and two other projections that probably secreted ill-tasting slime when the creature was attacked. All in all, *Aysheaia* was so close to modern onychophores that the latter appear as "living fossils" which apparently have found refuge in surroundings very different from those in which they evolved.

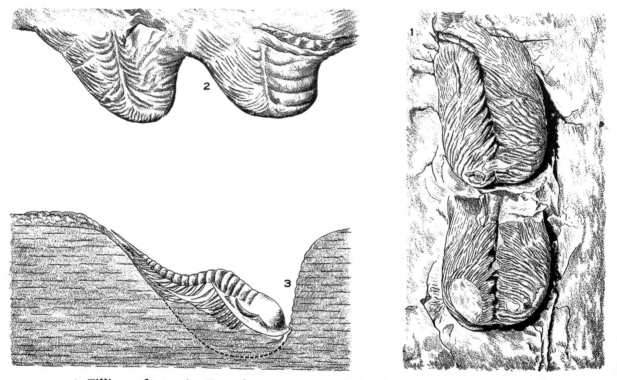

1. *Fillings of two pits* (Rusophycus) *apparently dug by an Early Cambrian species of* Olenellus. 2. *Side view of the fillings.* 3. *Restoration of the trilobite digging. The pits seem to have been resting-places.*

THREE-LOBED BODIES: THE TRILOBITES

Though onychophores and other arthropods took to land, they did not become diverse or abundant. Another group remained in the sea and there produced a bewildering array of families, genera (more than 1,500), and spe-

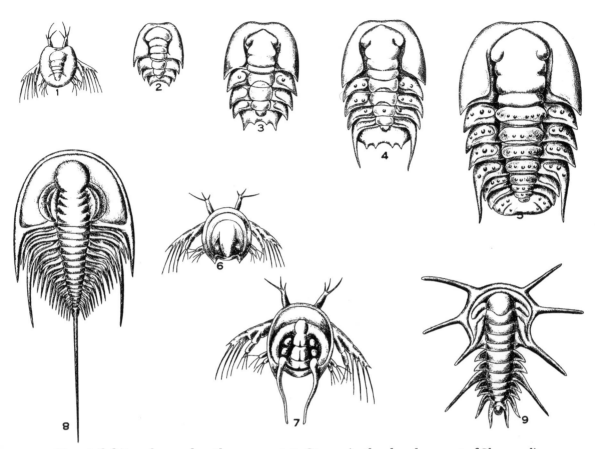

How trilobites changed as they grew. **1–5.** *Stages in the development of* Shumardia pusilla, *enlarged 40 times. The appendages have been restored in Stage 1. Though the last stage is only half the adult size, it has most of the adult characters.* **6–7.** *Two early stages of* Paedeumias transitans, *enlarged 20 times, with appendages restored.* **8.** *An adult of this species, natural size.* **9.** *An immature stage of* Olenelloides armatus, *showing spines on the cephalon. Enlarged about 7 times*

cies. For more than 300 million years, its members were the most plentiful and successful of arthropods. Trilobites are of special value in Cambrian and Ordovician rocks for determining their age. Besides this, they are fascinatingly complex and beautiful animals.

We call these creatures the Trilobita, or trilobites, a name that means "three-lobed ones." It might be interpreted in terms of a three-part plan that seems to consist of head, body, and tail. But, in fact, the name actually refers to parts that run lengthwise and are separated by furrows, not joints. These grooves divide every trilobite into an axial lobe in the middle and two pleurae—one at each side of the body.

Current theories suggest that trilobites descended from annelid worms in which the head increased in size by absorbing segments behind it, while the body spread broadly by developing pleurae on both sides of the original segments. Possibly a form like the Ediacara genus *Spriggina,* with its large, platelike head, may resemble a trilobite ancestor. Perhaps, too, all of the Ediacara forms failed to give rise to any later groups. On this basis, the most primitive group of trilobites now known are the olenellines, including *Olenellus,* which first occurs in the Early Cambrian of the eastern United States but ranges westward to Nevada and British Columbia. A primitive species is *O. vermontanus,* a flattened creature with a broad head and spiny segments that are narrowest and most like those of annelids at the hinder part of the body. A spine on the axial lobe of the fifteenth segment extends back to the tiny, buttonlike "tail." The group has been called micropygous, because the pygidium is minute when compared to the cephalon.

Throughout their history, trilobites developed an enormous diversity of forms while retaining the same overall body structure. We will now review this general structure and describe some of the more significant modifications it underwent.

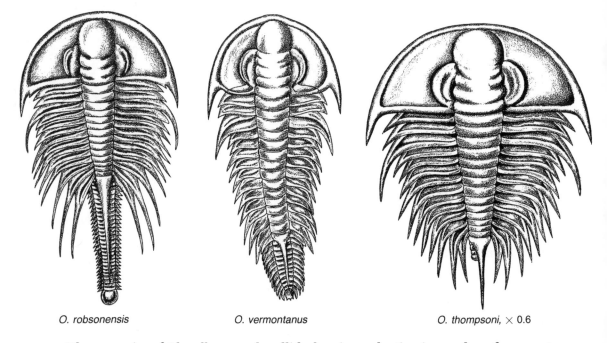

O. robsonensis   O. vermontanus   O. thompsoni, × 0.6

Three species of Olenellus, *an olenellid, showing reduction in number of segments*

Cephalon.   This structure, which is much more than a head, contains several segments that are fused into a single, continuous shield. In *Olenellus* it looks like a half moon, with curved margins that extend toward the rear in two genal spines. In other genera, it varies so greatly that even pictures can indicate only a few of its shapes. A most bizarre cephalon is that of the spiny *Terataspis,* though the rounded *Bumastus* also shows an extreme specialization.

Like the rest of the trilobite body, the typical cephalon shows three longitudinal lobes: the glabella and the lateral cheeks. Lines on the cheeks separating the fixed cheeks from the free ones are called the facial sutures. They mark the course of cracks in the exoskeleton along which the cheeks separated during molting to enable the old exoskeleton to be shed easily.

The glabella of *Olenellus* is a raised area that ends in a swollen bulb. Paired grooves at each side are all that remain of joints between segments in the cephalon. The grooves deepened in some later genera but became shallow or even disappeared from others. The glabella itself also changed shape, becoming narrow in some trilobites, but very broad and high in others.

The underside of the cephalon seldom shows plainly in fossils. When it does, it reveals a mouth, three pairs of legs, and bases of two jointed antennae. The mouth leads to a stomach that is largest under the glabella and tapers into an intestine running back to the pygidium. Since the stomach lay under and affected the shape of the glabella, this structure can give a clue to the kind of diet a trilobite had. Exceptionally well-preserved specimens show a simple heart above and behind the stomach. It apparently pumped blood into a segmented vessel running through the axial lobe. A "lip" plate (hypostome), lying in front of the mouth, is sometimes found separated from the remainder of the trilobite.

Eyes. The trilobite eye is the most ancient visual system. The lenses are composed of calcite. Most trilobite eyes are made up of many adjoining lenses that lie in cups, all covered with a single, clear visual area, or corneal membrane. At first the number of lenses was not large, but in some genera it increased to twelve thousand or even fifteen thousand. Others reversed this trend, reducing the number of facets to six hundred, two hundred, or as few as fourteen. In these eyes, called holochroal eyes, the lenses were all in contact with others. These kinds of eyes appeared in the Cambrian and lasted until the last trilobites became extinct. Another, more advanced type of eye, schizochroal, was confined to the Phacopina (Ordovician to Deveonian); for example, *Phacops.* These eyes were characterized by large lenses separated by thick portions of cuticle called sclera. Each lens had its own separate corneal membrane. Perhaps these eyes allowed 3-D vision or were used by nocturnal animals working under very dim conditions. One thing is for sure: schizochroal eyes were unusual.

Still more extreme was the complete loss of compound eyes, or their reduction to two or more new simple lenses on the free cheeks. This trend is seen in *Paraharpes* and some other members of the order to which it belongs.

Eyes differ almost as much in shape as they do in structure. Simple eyes are mere dots or granules. Compound eyes form crescents, lenticular elevations, knobs, or hemispheres at the ends of immovable stalks. A few small genera have relatively huge, convex eyes that were able to look downward and to the rear as well as forward, upward, and sidewise.

Thorax. The primitive trilobite thorax contained more than forty segments, fourteen or fifteen of which bore broad and well-defined pleural lobes

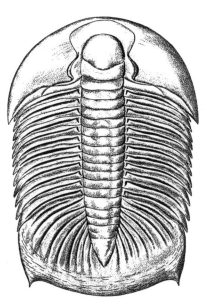

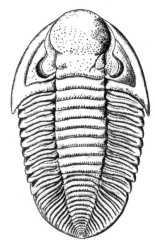

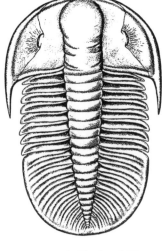

Dikelocephalus oweni, natural size, a dikelocephalid. Late Cambrian, Wisconsin

Griffithides, about × 2, a phillipsiid. Early Carboniferous, Europe and North America

Ogygopsis klotzi, × 0.75, an ogygopsid. Middle Cambrian, British Columbia

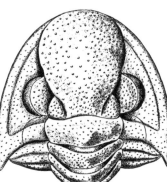

Phillipsia, × 3, a phillipsiid cephalon. Early Carboniferous, North America and Europe

Kaskia chesterensis, × 4, a phillipsiid. Mississippian, central to eastern United States

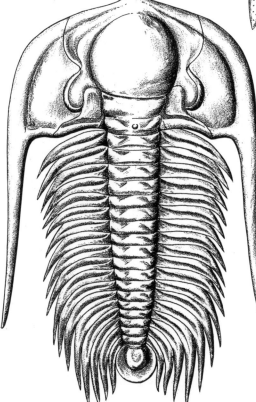

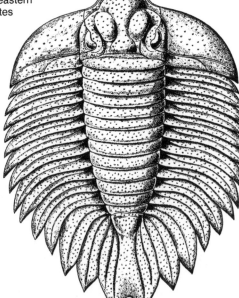

Paradoxides, natural size, a paradoxidid. This form is from the Middle Cambrian, Massachusetts

Arctinurus boltoni, a lichid, 5 to 6 inches (13–15 cm.) long. Middle Silurian, New York

Some typical trilobites

that ended in backwardly directed spines. The number of thoracic segments was often reduced; even some species of *Olenellus* got along with only eighteen to twenty. The ultimate in reduction was reached by agnostids, whose thoracic segments were very small and numbered only two.

Thoracic segments were reduced both by loss and by fusion into the pygidium. The latter is shown by such genera as *Ogygopsis* and *Trimerus,* whose pygidia contain many segments fused to form a single plate. In *Arctinurus* these segments still keep the spiny tips of their lateral lobes.

Several other trilobites kept eight to thirteen segments but lost all except the faintest traces of division into lobes. *Trimerus* and *Bumastus* are good examples of this trend.

Antennae and Legs.   Most fossil trilobites have lost their appendages, for these structures do not preserve well. A few specimens, however, retain them. Appendages have been described for *Olenoides,* from the Middle

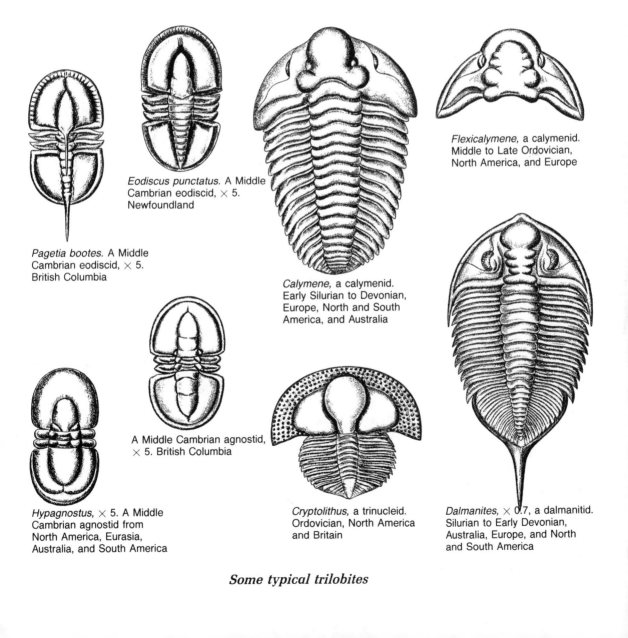

Pagetia bootes. A Middle Cambrian eodiscid, × 5. British Columbia

Eodiscus punctatus. A Middle Cambrian eodiscid, × 5. Newfoundland

Calymene, a calymenid. Early Silurian to Devonian, Europe, North and South America, and Australia

Flexicalymene, a calymenid. Middle to Late Ordovician, North America, and Europe

A Middle Cambrian agnostid, × 5. British Columbia

Hypagnostus, × 5. A Middle Cambrian agnostid from North America, Eurasia, Australia, and South America

Cryptolithus, a trinucleid. Ordovician, North America and Britain

Dalmanites, × 0.7, a dalmanitid. Silurian to Early Devonian, Australia, Europe, and North and South America

Some typical trilobites

Cambrian Burgess Shale, and for *Cryptolithus,* from the Ordovician. They begin with two many-jointed antennae that were attached to the lower surface of the cephalon beneath the sides of the hypostome and are single, not split. During life, the antennae probably carried small sensory organs perhaps of taste and smell, as do the antennae of modern lobsters.

The jointed legs (coxae) were borne in pairs on each segment on the underside of the cephalon, thorax, and pygidium, if the last contained several segments. Each leg is divided into a lower branch (endopodite), which was used in walking, and an upper branch (exopodite), with feathery gills, which both breathed oxygen and, in some, may have served as oars for swimming. Even though the exact function of the exopodite, or gill branch of the trilobite leg, is not fully understood, that of the walking leg is. Many tracks and trails of trilobites have been recognized, in the Paleozoic fossil record, as trace fossils (see Chapter XI).

The most common of these trilobite trackways are called *Cruziana,* ribbonlike tracks with paired chevron or herringbone patterns. We know these were made by trilobites because a few specimens, such as *Calymene,* have been found in resting excavations *(Rusophycus)* at the end of a *Cruziana* trail. *Cruziana* trails have also been found most abundantly in rocks of Cambrian and Ordovician age, less so in Silurian and Devonian rocks, and they are totally lacking in post-Permian rocks. This diversity, presence, and absence closely follows the appearance, diversity, and extinction of the trilobites. The tracks were, too, quite clearly made by legs of a similar and unspecialized type, such as those of trilobites. So, all the evidence seems to point to a trilobite origin for these trace fossils.

Trilobite trails indicate that these animals moved in a number of ways, sideways and forward, and they burrowed as well.

Pygidium. This structure is made up of one or more fused segments at the back of the trilobite and in its axis houses part of the intestinal canal and the anus. The pygidium is very small (micropygous) in primitive genera, such as *Olenellus,* but in other Early Cambrian forms it has grown by incorporating three or more thoracic segments. These forms are heteropygous—the pygidium is still smaller than the cephalon. This process continued during Middle Cambrian and later epochs, until some pygidia became as large as the cephalon (isopygous) and contained eighteen or more segments. Rarely the pygidium was larger than the cephalon, a condition called macropygous. The undersurface of such pygidia bore some of the legs of the segments that had been absorbed.

Many pygidia, as we have just seen, bore grooves marking the segments they have absorbed, as well as other grooves that once ran across the pleurae. In some genera these grooves remained deep and distinct; in others they became indistinct and finally disappeared. In still other genera some grooves were lost and others were kept, and those on pleural lobes of the pygidium do not match grooves of its axial lobe.

Color Patterns.   Though not much is known about the carapace coloring in trilobites, a few forms show stripes and spot patterns. *Isotelus maximus,* from the Late Ordovician of North America, preserves stripes along the axial furrows.

From Egg to Adult.   Trilobites must have laid eggs, as most arthropods do today. The female probably left the eggs in some sheltered spot and then went away, leaving the "nest" to be filled by drifting sand. If that is true, the male probably followed the female and waited beside her, ready to fertilize the ova as soon as they were laid. Sand washed into the "nests" was loose enough to let water reach the eggs and provide them with oxygen, and to let newly hatched young escape. At the same time, sand hid the eggs from scavengers and predators, including other trilobites.

Silicified fossils dissolved from limestone trace the development of many species of trilobites. During the first stage, the protaspid stage, the cephalon and the protopygidium (the latter composed of segments that were eventually incorporated into the anterior part of the thorax) are fused into a single shield. There is no way of telling exactly how many segments are fused into this shield, but the cephalon of some protaspids includes more than five segments, and the pygidium possibly includes another five. The onset of the meraspid, or second stage, is marked by the development of an articulation between the cephalon and the protopygidium. Throughout the meraspid stage, segments are progressively released into the thorax from the front of the protopygidium (during molting) until the full complement of throacic segments is acquired, at which time the holaspid, or adult, stage is reached. Changes during the holaspid stage are mainly confined to increase in size and changes in proportion.

Comparison with modern arthropods leaves no doubt that larval trilobites had branched, spiny legs that were used in swimming. These organs have been added to most of our illustrations of trilobite larvae.

Such development of the individual (ontogeny) from conception to death can sometimes be very useful in working out evolutionary relationships of trilobites. Though adults may be very different, similarities of the larvae can sometimes give hints about closer relationships.

SUTURES, MOLTING, AND CLASSIFICATION

Among most trilobites, the facial sutures were vitally important in molting, since they formed lines of weakness along which the exoskeleton could break. There must have been a great deal of wriggling, twisting, and squeezing before such animals as *Arctinurus* pulled themselves out of their armor. The process probably was carried on amid corals or under sheltering seaweeds, where the "soft-shelled" trilobite could hide while building its new skin crust.

At the left, Arctinurus *(× 0.3) walks on a muddy sea bottom. At the right, a second* Arctinurus *is molting and is partly out of its "shell."* Arctinurus *is a lichid*

We say that facial sutures were important to *most* trilobites, because one order lacks them. There also are genera, such as *Acidaspis,* in which the sutures are too faint to be seen. They could hardly have had much value when the molting season arrived.

Facial Sutures. Facial sutures were used in the past to distinguish the orders of trilobites. These sutures come in three main varieties: proparian, opisthoparian, and marginal (or hypoparian).

Proparian sutures are those in which the posterior branch passes in front of the genal spine. Opisthoparian sutures meet the margin of the cephalon between the genal angle and the occipital ring. Marginal, or hypoparian, sutures run around the edge of the cephalon and cannot be seen on the top surface. Yet another kind of facial suture is gonatoparian, in which the suture runs directly through the genal spine.

Even though these suture types were long used as a main feature for classification, they were finally discarded. Based on a variety of characters such as the nature of the cephalon and axial region, it became clear that a single kind of suture type had been developed more than once. So groups based on only the suture types contained a mixture of related and unrelated forms. Today the type of suture is only one of many features used to help determine the relationships of trilobites.

Classification. The classification used for trilobites today is based on several characters all considered together, not single features such as facial

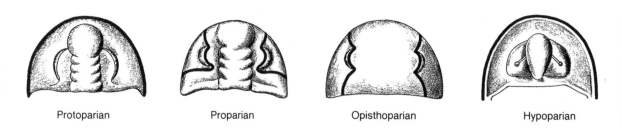

| Protoparian | Proparian | Opisthoparian | Hypoparian |

Types of facial sutures in trilobites. Sutures are marked by heavy lines

sutures. The class Trilobita is generally divided into eight orders, all of which will be briefly discussed.

Agnostida.   These minute creatures lived during Early Cambrian to Late Ordovician time. Most of them lacked eyes, had marginal sutures, and had two *(Agnostus)* or three *(Eodiscus)* thoracic segments. The cephalon and pygidium were of equal size—thus isopygous.

Redlichiida.   Members of this order are restricted to the Early to Middle Cambrian. The cephalon was a large half circle, usually with elongate genal spines. The pygidium was tiny (micropygous), and the thoracic segments were often spiny. Unlike the "blind" agnostids, the redlichiids had large eyes. *Olenellus* and *Paradoxides* are well-known members of this group. Facial sutures in this group were either fused or opisthoparian.

Corynexochida.   This group is restricted to the Cambrian. The glabella usually expanded toward the front or was parallel-sided, and the pygidium was often larger than the cephalon (macropygous). The thorax commonly had seven to eight segments, and the facial sutures were opisthoparian. *Olenoides* is a member of this group.

A group of Isotelus gigas *(a ptychopariid) in limestone. Ordovician, Trenton Falls, New York. The fossils are about 3 in. (8 cm.) long*

Ptychopariida. Occurring from the Early Cambrian to the Late Devonian, the ptychopariids included a diverse array of forms. All had more than three thoracic segments, and most had opisthoparian facial sutures, while a few had marginal or proparian sutures. The glabella usually tapered forward, but there was some variation in this pattern. Early forms had a large thorax and a small pygidium, but later ones had reduced the number of thoracic segments and enlarged the pygidium (for example, *Asaphus).* *Olenus, Elrathia, Cryptolithus,* and *Illaenus* are typical genera in this group.

Many early Ptychopariida were quite similar to Redlichiida, from which they probably arose. And, in turn, the Ptychopariida probably gave rise to most of the post-Cambrian trilobites, except the surviving agnostids.

Proetida. The Proetida was a long-ranging group, first appearing in the Ordovician and finally becoming extinct in the Permian. Like the agnostids, members of the Proetida were isopygous (with cephalon and pygidium of equal size), but the thorax had eight to ten segments. The glabella was large and bulbous, indicating an enlarged, complex stomach. The genal spines were present, the facial sutures opisthoparian, and the eyes large, with all the lenses touching one another (holochroal). *Proetus* and *Bathyurus* are in this group.

Phacopida. Though not as large an order as the Ptychopariida, this group was quite diverse. Phacopida were mainly proparian, while a few were gonatoparian (where the facial suture passed through the genal angle), and some were even opisthoparian. The glabella took on many forms. The thorax had eight to nineteen segments. The pygidium was often medium to large, but was small in some early representatives. *Calymene* belonged to one group of Phacopida that had gonatoparian sutures and a forward-tapering glabella with four or five pairs of lateral lobes and small, holochroal eyes. *Phacops* and *Dalmanites* belonged to yet another group of Phacopida which had a glabella that expanded forward, schizochroal eyes, and proparian facial sutures.

Lichida. Ranging from the Early Ordovician to the Late Devonian, the Lichida were medium to large-sized. The pygidium was often larger than the cephalon and had three blade-shaped pleurae, or side segments. The glabella was broad, and the sutures were opisthoparian. Often, too, the carapace was distinctive in having numerous bumps (tubercles) all over it; *Terataspis,* with its spiny and tuberculate appearance, is a good example.

Odontopleurida. These very spiny, rather small trilobites are known from Upper Cambrian or Lower Ordovician to Upper Devonian rocks. The pygidium was short and very spiny. The thorax, likewise, had spiny segments, eight to ten in number. The glabella had two or three pairs of lobes, and the facial sutures were opisthoparian. *Radiaspis* and *Leonaspis* are excellent examples of these bizarre trilobites.

When all of these trilobite groups are examined, several trends can be seen. Holochroal eyes gave rise to schizochroal eyes. Pygidia became larger,

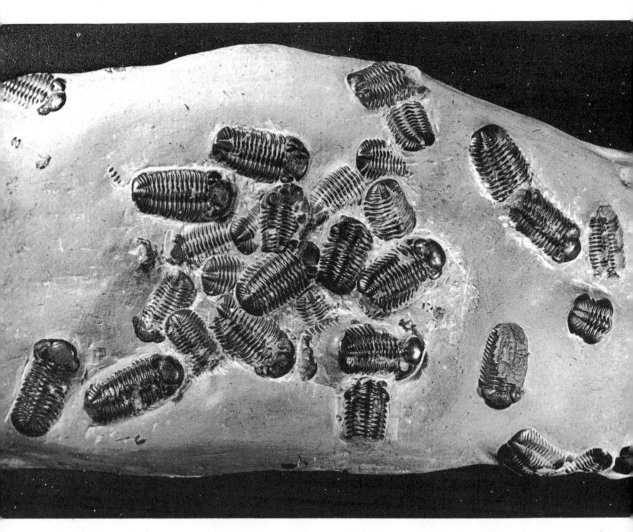

A cluster of Phacops rana *(a phacopid) on a limestone nodule found in shale. Middle Devonian, New York. The trilobites are about 1.25 inches (about 3 cm.) long*

changing from micropygous to isopygous or even macropygous types. Relatively simple, unornamented trilobites gave rise to highly spinose and tuberculate forms. Still, despite all these changes, trilobites didn't stray far from the original body design in all of their millions of years of history.

Some olenelline Redlichiida are among the oldest trilobites yet known in the fossil record. They were later joined by the Agnostida, Corynexochida, and Ptychopariida before the end of the Cambrian. At the end of the Cambrian a major crisis occurred. Only a few trilobite stocks continued into the Ordovician, with a great variety of forms developing in the early part of this period. Ordovician trilobites moved into many new environments they had not occurred in during the Cambrian; for instance, reefs. Another crisis occurred at the end of the Ordovician, as was the case with the graptolites. Silurian and Devonian trilobites belonged to similar stocks and were less diverse than they had been in the Early Paleozoic. After the Devonian, the only trilobites still in existence were some members of the Proetida. Then, possibly as a result of a lowering of sea level at the end of the Permian, trilobites, along with many other animals, became extinct.

HABITS AND ADAPTATIONS

All trilobites were marine; so far as we know, they did not even venture into brackish estuaries. But, within the oceans, they swam at the surface or below it, crawled or skimmed over the bottom, lay upon it, and plowed through sand or mud. Many small species burrowed into sediment, which also provided them with food. They varied from detritus eaters to filter feeders to predators.

The Ways of Olenellus.   Since elongate species of *Olenellus,* a member of the Redlichiida, are primitive, they provide the basic point of departure for other trilobite habits and adaptations. The newly hatched *Olenellus* was a tiny, rounded creature that may have drifted in the ocean waters. It continued to do so during the meraspid stage, but, with holaspid life, it settled down to bottom-dwelling existence under shallow water and often near the shores of seas.

Though *Olenellus* ranged across North America, Greenland, and Scotland, there is no better place to study its habits than the valley containing Lake Louise, in western Alberta. There, at the foot of ice-hung cliffs, talus slopes include slopes of Lower Cambrian quartzite and dark, micaceous shale. The latter contains crusts and impressions of trilobites, while the former is rich in traces of their activities.

Olenellus was able to swim using its gills or crawl with its endopodites. When swimming, it left no trail, but in crawling, the jointed endopodites dug into the sand, while spines on the cephalon and thoracic segments occasionally cut sharp furrows. Some of the trails so made became fossils, and so did pits bearing marks of endopodites and spines. Some of those pits were shallow and irregular; they may have been dug for food (possibly small, soft-bodied burrowing worms) or may have been resting burrows.

A Variety of Crawlers, Plowers, and Burrowers.   Crawling remained the dominant mode of trilobite travel, yet the shapes and sizes of crawlers changed greatly. *Olenellus vermontanus* was long and narrow, but the width of *O. thompsoni* almost equaled its length. Middle Cambrian and later times saw the development of many broad, flattened crawlers. Some, such as *Paradoxides,* had small pygidia and many thoracic segments; in others (*Dikelocephalus* and *Eobronteus* are examples), the thorax was reduced and the pygidium large. *Arctinurus,* of the Silurian, combined a very short, broad cephalon that ended in a snout with an exceedingly wide thorax.

Isotelus and its kin may have crawled, but their broad pygidia could dig into the mud, providing leverage for plowing. The long-snouted *Ectenaspis*

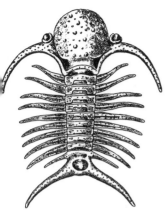

Deiphon forbesi, × 1.3, a cheirurid. Supposedly a drifter. Silurian, Bohemia

Cyclopyge, × 5, a cyclopygid. A big-eyed swimmer. Ordovician, Europe and eastern North America

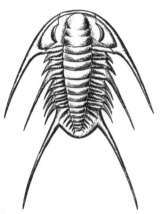

Albertella helena, × 0.6, a zacanthoidid. Middle Cambrian, northern Rockies

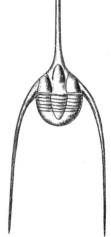

Ampyx, about 6 inches (15 cm.) long, a raphiophorid. Habits unknown. Ordovician, Sweden

Terataspis grandis, about 18 inches (46 cm.) long, a lichid. Apparently a crawler. Middle Devonian, New York

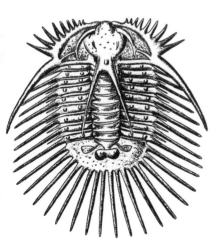

Radiaspis radiata, 1 inch (2.5 cm.) long, an odontopleurid. Devonian, Germany

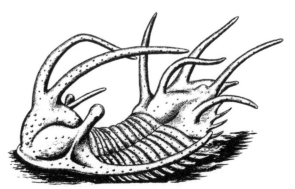

Ceratarges armatus, 1.5 inches (3.8 cm.) long, a lichid. Probably a well-armored crawler. Middle Devonian, Germany

Six spiny trilobites and a smooth swimmer

went much further, for the position of well-preserved fossils shows that it dug tail first into soft bottoms and lay with only its head at the surface. There it was ready to capture tiny crawlers or dead bodies as they drifted by.

Spiny and Fringed Trilobites as Bottom Dwellers.   Many theories have been proposed to explain the function of spines on trilobites. In the past, they have been said to indicate a planktonic mode of life, because they increased the surface area and so prevented sinking. But, more recently, spines have been interpreted to explain other lifestyles. Most spiny trilobites were too large for the spines to have given much extra capacity for floating. Spines were certainly at times protection against predators. But elongate side spines and ventral spines may have been very useful in spreading out the weight of the trilobite when it was resting on a soft sea bottom. Ventral spines also may have served to prop the trilobite slightly above the bottom. In the case of the odontopleurid *Acidaspis,* spines evidently supported the cephalon in a particular attitude that was efficient for grazing off the sea floor. Spines also may have aided in burrowing.

Some trilobites, such as members of the suborder Harpina (for example, *Harpes)* have a wide brim on the cephalon that is flat and extended backward into a pair of elongate horns. Such a broad surface area, just as with elongate spines, may have spread the weight of this sedentary trilobite over a wide surface, much like a ski or a snowshoe, and thus kept it from sinking. Another explanation for the harpid fringe is that it may have been a respiratory structure.

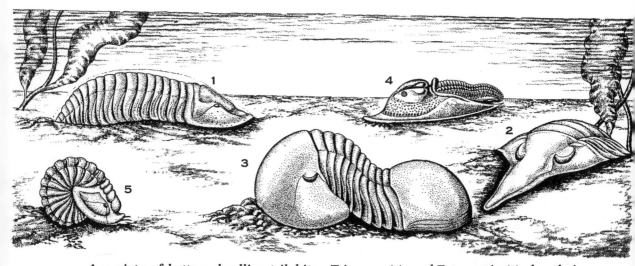

A variety of bottom-dwelling trilobites. **Trimerus (1)** *and* **Ectenaspis (2)** *dug their pygidia into the mud and lay in wait for dead food.* **Bumastus (3)** *plowed through the mud, and* **Paraharpes (4)** *crept upon it.* **Flexicalymene (5)** *could crawl or swim but rolled up when danger threatened*

Swimmers and Drifters. Free-swimming trilobites are typified by *Cyclopyge,* the genus with enormous eyes that could see in all directions. The term "enormous" is relative, however; though the eyes are huge in proportion to the body, a full-grown *Cyclopyge* was less than a half inch long (about 1 cm.). Some authorities believe that this creature hid during the day and came out at night, making its own light with round organs on its upper surface.

The tiny, blind agnostids may themselves have been part of the early Paleozoic plankton.

Besides swimming freely, a number of trilobites were probably floaters, or planktonic forms. Small size, such as in the agnostids, might also favor a planktonic existence. Such planktonic or nektonic forms had enlarged eyes, while others, such as *Agnostus,* were blind. Large eyes can be useful for more purposes than one: for good night vision, for wide vision, for stereoscopic vision. Blindness can occur in animals with widely varying lifestyles, such as those living in areas that are murky, where vision is impossible, or in areas lacking light. Burrowing forms are often blind, as can be planktonic forms. So you must be careful in using such information to reconstruct the life habits of a fossil. The total anatomy of the animal needs to be considered when carrying out such "rebuilding" of a fossil's day-to-day living.

Trilobite Giants. *Agnostus* is only one fourth of an inch (0.6 cm.) long, and the majority of trilobites are three fourths of an inch to 3 inches (1.8–8 cm.) in length. Some forms, however, became larger, and a few outstripped their relatives so much that we may call them giants.

The first giant was *Paradoxides harlani,* found in Early Cambrian strata of Massachusetts; it reached a length of 19 inches (48 cm.), and its cephalon was almost 12 inches (30 cm.) wide. The next giant was *Isotelus,* which reached lengths of 27 to 30 inches (69–76 cm.). More spectacular, however, were *Uralichas* and *Terataspis,* both of which had ornate crusts. The latter, which reached lengths of 19 to perhaps 27 inches (48–69 cm.), also was the spiniest of all large trilobites.

PROBLEMATIC CAMBRIAN ARTHROPODS
THE "TRILOBITOIDEA"

Cambrian rocks of Europe, North America, China, and Australia contain a variety of arthropods once called crustaceans. A few may actually belong in that group, but the rest seem to be different creatures, whose closest relationships are not understood clearly. They may have arisen during a major time of experimentation that gave rise to the arthropod groups that survived to later times. Conservative classifications have allied the "trilobitoids" close to the trilobites. More research and fieldwork are needed before we will have a reasonable understanding of these unusual and ancient "jointed

animals." A large number of specimens and species are found in the Burgess
Shale, though the group survived into the Devonian.

Marrella, often called the lace crab, has a very narrow thorax, four very
large spines, and many gill-bearing legs. It has been regarded as a newly
molted trilobite, but this interpretation seems to be ruled out by two pairs of
feathery antennae. Despite its delicate, lacy appearance, *Marrella* also is
common in the Burgess Shale.

Sidneyia is about 5 inches (about 13 cm.) wide, with a very broad cephalothorax and body, stalked eyes, and a finlike telson.

These and other problematic Cambrian arthropods included not only
swimming predators but bottom dwellers as well—a variety of early trials
that apparently ended mainly in extinction.

CHAPTER XIII

Crustaceans

Trilobites remind us of crayfish, lobsters, and even crabs, for all three have jointed exoskeletons and legs that mark them as arthropods. Yet they belong to different branches of that phylum, for crayfish, lobsters, and crabs are crustaceans—a group that also includes shrimps, barnacles, and several less familiar creatures, some microscopic. Though most of them live in salt or fresh water, a few make their homes on land, and some have become parasites.

The name Crustacea refers to the hard shell that characterizes this group —which is not always appropriate, as the shell is poorly developed or even absent in some crustaceans.

VARIED CRUSTACEANS

Some authorities call the crustaceans a class; others make them a subphylum or a superclass. The animals, however, do not change; all are distinguished from trilobites by having two pairs of antennae—not one—and by three pairs of legs that have become specialized into organs that chew food and push it into the mouth. Though these structures seldom appear in fossils, the latter generally show that the body consists of head, thorax, and abdomen, though the first two commonly are united in the cephalothorax.

Branchiopoda (Phyllopoda). Within the crustaceans are a number of groups, but only the Branchiopoda, Ostracoda, Cirripedia (the barnacles), and Malacostraca left fossil records of any note. So we will concentrate on these groups in this chapter. These tiny creatures (2–100 mm., 0.1–4 in.), whose name means "gill feet," are rather primitive crustaceans ranging from Devonian to Recent times. Like primitive trilobites, they have a large number of body segments; the jointed legs, which also are numerous, carry gills and are used for both breathing and swimming. In this group are the fairy shrimps and brine shrimps, small creatures with distinct head, stalked compound eyes, and segmented thorax that is not covered with armor. Modern members of this group rarely live in normal seas, but more often in briny lagoons or salt lakes, and in freshwater pools fed by rain or melting snow. One Oligocene genus, which lived in lakes, is almost identical with the fairy shrimps (Anostraca) of modern freshwater pools. Fairy shrimps also were abundant in the lake inhabited by Miocene arthropods of the Mojave Desert.

Many branchiopods had (or have) either a chitinous dorsal shield or a shell separated into two distinct parts. Some, however, have no carapace at all. Those with two shells differ from ostracods in having no interlocking structures for hingement.

Notostracans are more progressive, for they cover the head and thorax with a carapace. The best-known genus, *Triops*, includes Cenozoic, Mesozoic, and even Permian species. A few specimens preserve traces of a gland that secreted the carapace.

Conchostracans are the most frequently fossilized branchiopods. They cover their bodies with bivalved shells and so look like small clams unless their gill-bearing legs and antennae can be seen. Some fossil members of this order were marine, but others are found in freshwater deposits. *Daphnia* is a familiar freshwater form, often available in pet shops for sale as aquarium food. Several species of *Cyzicus* and related genera, all formerly called *Estheria,* occur in Devonian and later formations and are plentiful in modern ponds. Vast numbers of *Cyzicus* shells were found in freshwater shales of Triassic age at Princeton, New Jersey. These shale beds also contained many skeletons of the small bony fish *Diplurus,* which is described in Chapter XXII.

Fossil conchostracans can be very useful as index fossils in nonmarine sequences such as the Devonian of the Northern Hemisphere, the Permo-Carboniferous of the world, and the Asian Mesozoic. It is often difficult to find useful index fossils in these times and places, and so the tiny conchostracans take on added importance.

Ostracods. These crustaceans also have bivalve shells, but their bodies are shorter than those of branchiopods and they have one to three pairs of legs. The four pairs of appendages on the head are used for crawling, swimming, and digging; males also employ the first pair to clasp females during mating. Most species have only one eye, though some have two compound eyes, and a few are blind. The valves are hinged in all but the most primitive forms. Most species are 0.2 to 2 millimeters (0.01–0.1 in.) long, though one modern form reaches a length of 25 millimeters (1 in.), and some fossils exceeded 80 millimeters (3 in.).

Modern ostracods live in seas, brackish bays, and fresh water, where they swim, crawl, cling to plants, or burrow in mud. Though they probably originated in marine environments, they had invaded fresh waters by the Carboniferous and diversified there. Some even invaded forest soils. Their food consists of algae and diatoms as well as living and dead animals, gained from both filter and deposit feeding. One fossil sea scorpion (Chapter XIV) contains hundreds of shells of ostracods that apparently were trapped and covered with mud while they were feeding inside its shell. The sea scorpion had not dined on ostracods, for shells of the latter are not broken. They also are found in legs as well as in parts of the scorpion's body that once contained the digestive system.

Ostracods molt, like all other arthropods; some species did so many times before reaching their final shape and size. Most fossils consist only of valves whose proper position is determined by muscle scars. In general, the thin end is forward and the thick is to the rear, toward which spines and other elevations are directed.

Ostracods appeared in Early Cambrian seas and have been plentiful ever since. Some had smooth shells, but others were marked by ridges, knobs, pits, and furrows, all of which are used in identification. Since many species spread widely but did not live very long, they make excellent index fossils.

In fact, of all the Crustacea, the ostracods are by far the most useful fossils, being one of the better-documented groups of invertebrates. Surprisingly, it is the marine benthonic forms that are most important. The planktonic species have such weakly calcified shells that they are rare in fossil collections. Because of this, and because they don't produce planktonic (drifting) larvae, they are of use in intrabasinal, *not* intercontinental, correlation. Beyond this, they are very often used in paleoecological studies, as many crustaceans have rather specific environmental requirements.

Ostracods are generally divided into five orders (Archeocopida, Leperditicopida, Myodocopida, Beyrichicopida, and Podocopida) based the the construction and ornamentation of their shell (carapace), the nature of the hinge between the two valves (if present), the degree of calcification or phosphatization of the shell, and the arrangement of the scars on the valves left by the muscles that control opening and closing.

Barnacles, or Cirripedes. Until 1829, barnacles were regarded as molluscs, since most of them have thick, calcareous shells. Then they were found to be crustaceans that swim or drift about while they are young. After molting one to three times, they develop shells much like those of ostracods; then they settle down on their heads, usually lose their bivalved shells, and secrete others made up of plates that overlap or are held together by tough skin. Food is brought to the mouth by branched, fringed legs that resemble curved feathers, explaining the group's technical name of Cirripedia, or "fringe feet." The legs sweep to and fro with rhythmic movements, catching food which then is raked off by comblike organs near the mouth. The statement that the legs produce currents that take food into the mouth has been proved to be an error. A few barnacles have become parasitic, and they feed with piercing mouthparts or by direct absorption through their carapace or other parts.

The oldest known cirripede is *Cyprilepas,* found attached to the limbs of Late Silurian eurypterids. *Cyprilepas* belongs in the order Thoracica, the only cirripede group with much of a fossil record. This early form had a stalk like the modern goose barnacles. Goose barnacles are so called because they once were supposed to produce young wild geese. Modern species are attached by long stalks that are either scaly or naked, but some fossil genera have short stalks that are completely covered by plates. Plates on the body are separate and movable, being held together by leathery skin. Because of this, fossils generally consist of separate plates. They are limited to Mesozoic and Cenozoic formations. Acorn barnacles got their name from their shape, which is rounded or conical unless they are closely crowded. They have no stalk, and the plates that cover their bodies are firmly cemented, though those that close the shell are freely movable. Excellent specimens are found in some Mesozoic and Cenozoic deposits.

Though present in the Paleozoic, barnacles didn't really begin to diversify until the Mesozoic; they reached their peak in the Cenozoic. Some paleontologists have brought attention to this by calling the present day the "Age of Barnacles." This may be more a reflection of the poverty of the fossil record, however, than of *real* variety, for many of the living parasitic cirripedes lack hard parts and have very little chance of being preserved as fossils.

Barnacles probably developed from a group of arthropods called the Maxillopoda, which had five head segments, six thoracic segments, and five abdominal segments. Out of this group came a number of other arthropods, including the minute aquatic copepods, the ostracods, as well as the barnacles. Though a great deal of work on both living and fossil barnacles has been done since, it is interesting to be aware that Charles Darwin, famous for his theory of evolution through natural selection, wrote a massive monograph on fossil and living barnacles. His work was so thorough and careful that it still stands as a standard reference work on this group.

HARD "SOFT SHELLS," OR MALACOSTRACA

Ostracods may be the most abundant fossil crustaceans and barnacles the most highly specialized, but malacostracans are probably the ones we think of first when crustaceans are mentioned. They are the crabs and shrimps, the lobsters, the pill bugs (or slaters), and a whole variety of other forms we may never encounter, including the phyllocarids.

Malacostraca ("soft shells") is a poor name for these animals, since it fits them only during short periods that immediately follow molting. At other times, most malacostracans are well armored in shells that consist of tough chitin or of chitin hardened and thickened with limy material. The carapace, or shell, comes in a variety of shapes, varying from a nearly complete cover of the head and body to almost nothing. Generally, malacostracans have two compound eyes on stalks and five pairs of appendages behind the eyes that are modified into biramous (forked) antennae and mouthparts. The body is divided into two main sections, thorax and abdomen, each further divided into seven or eight, and six, segments respectively. Most segments bear a pair of limbs. Many have a tail fan. The group first appears in the Early Cambrian and continues to the present day.

Phyllocarids. These are an important group of malacostracans. They have a bivalved shell that covers only the front part of the body, unlike in the ostracods, in which the body is entirely encased by the shell. Phyllocarids ("leaf shrimp") are also macroscopic fossils (ranging from 8 mm. to 4 cm., 0.3–1.6 in.), not microscopic, and thus decidedly larger than the ostracods and branchiopods.

Phyllocarids are probably the most primitive of malacostracans, and forms like them undoubtedly gave rise to more advanced groups within this class. Phyllocarids first occur in Early Cambrian rocks and are alive today. Two genera of the many beautifully preserved fossils from the Middle Cambrian Burgess Shale are assigned to the phyllocarids: *Perspicaris* and *Canadaspis.* It is interesting that *Canadaspis* is the oldest known crustacean as well as one of the most primitive.

Decapoda. Unquestioned malacostracans include creatures that resemble *Triops,* as well as wood borers with fourteen legs and strange parasites that live on whales. But most fossil malacostracans are decapods—crustaceans with ten ordinary legs on the thorax, including six that are specialized as food handlers, or maxillae. The thorax contains six segments that are joined with the head in an armored cephalothorax, and the eyes are on movable stalks. The abdomen generally contains six clearly marked segments and ends in a tailpiece, or telson.

Shrimps and prawns are less specialized decapods, since they lack pincers and their crusts are not calcified. Decapods first appear in the Permian. They are rare in Triassic rocks, but many kinds have been found in the Jurassic lithographic limestones of southern Germany. Fossils preserve exoskeleton, antennae, legs, and abdominal appendages used in swimming, along with the fanlike tail.

Ghost shrimps are not true shrimps but are related to hermit crabs. The former are thinly armored burrowers; the latter have abdomens, which they hide in shells. Pincers of both are found in the Cretaceous and Tertiary. One ghost shrimp, *Callianassa mortoni,* is an index fossil in Late Cretaceous formations from New Jersey to Texas.

Spiny lobsters are sometimes called crayfish; modern species have prickly shells and massive antennae, and all ten legs are used for walking. Some fossils, however, have long, slim pincers; in others, the forelegs are very long and the last segment is covered with hairs that seem to have been used as feelers. Most fossil spiny lobsters are found in Mesozoic rocks of Europe, choice specimens coming from the Jurassic lithographic limestones. These also contain early true lobsters *(Eryma),* less than 2 inches (5 cm.) long, with pincers shaped like long-nosed pliers'. *Astacus,* the freshwater crayfish, has been found in Miocene and perhaps in Pliocene rocks of Idaho and eastern Oregon.

Crabs are the most modern crustaceans and are least like ancestral types.

Bradoria robusta, × 8.
An ostracod

Archaeoniscus brodei, × 3.
A sow bug, or isopod.
Late Jurassic, England and
Germany

Caryocaris curvilata, × 4. An early
phyllocarid malacostracan. Ordovician
(graptolite shales), widespread
in North America

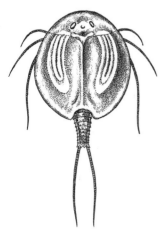

Triops, × 2. A notostracan
branchiopod, restored.
Permian, Oklahoma

Echinocaris punctata.
A phyllocarid malacostracan,
× 1. Middle to Late Devonian,
eastern United States

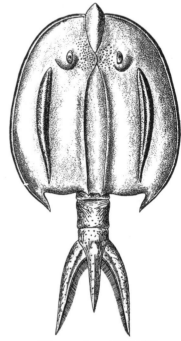

Dithyrocaris oceani, × 0.5.
A phyllocarid malacostracan.
Late Devonian, New York

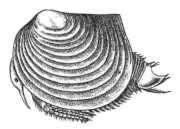

Cyzicus, × 10. A conchostracan
branchiopod, restored. Late Pennsylvanian,
Ohio. The genus occurs worldwide and
ranges from Devonian to Recent

Callianassa, × 1.4. Pincer of a ghost
shrimp, a decapod malacostracan.
Oligocene (?), Washington
and Oregon. The genus is cosmopolitan,
Cretaceous–Recent

Palaeopalaemon newberryi, × 2. A crayfish-
like malacostracan. Late Devonian of Ohio;
Early Mississippian of Iowa

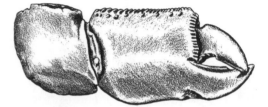

Callianassa, × 0.75. Pincer of a ghost
shrimp. Late Cretaceous, coastal
plain from New Jersey to Texas

Varied crustaceans

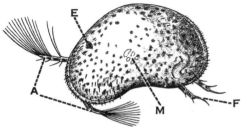

Cypris, modern podocopid ostracod, enlarged. E, eye; A, antennae; M, muscle scars; F, foot

Loxoconcha, × 15, a podocopid. Exterior and interior. Cretaceous–Recent, worldwide

A leperditiid, × 2, a leperditicopid. The family ranged from Ordovician to Devonian, worldwide

Cytheretta, × 25, a podocopid. Eocene–Recent, Europe and North America

Ranapeltis, × 30, a podocopid. Devonian, North America

Kirkbyella, × 16, a beyrichicopid. Silurian–Carboniferous, North America

Glyptopleura, × 30, a podocopid. Carboniferous, Europe and North America

Hollinella, × 20, a beyrichicopid. Devonian–Permian, North America and Europe

Paraechmina spinosa, × 20, a podocopid. Middle Silurian, Ontario to Maryland

Kloedenia, × 20, a beyrichicopid. Ordovician to Devonian, Europe and North America

Cytherura cretacea, × 120, a podocopid. Cretaceous–Recent, worldwide

Cytheropteron, × 35, a podocopid. Jurassic to Recent, worldwide

Drepanella crassinoda, × 15, a beyrichicopid. Ordovician, Virginia to Indiana

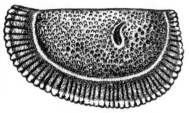

Eurychilina reticulata, × 20, a beyrichicopid. Middle Ordovician, eastern U.S.A.

Aparchites, × 30, a beyrichicopid. Ordovician to Devonian, Eurasia, North America, and Australia

Buntonia, × 80, a podocopid. Cretaceous–Recent, Africa, Europe, and North America

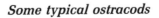

Some typical ostracods

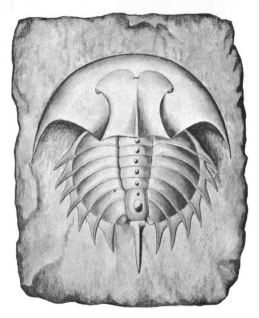

Euproops (Prestwichianella) danae, about × 1, a freshwater xiphosuran. Pennsylvanian, Illinois

Protobalanus, × 10, once thought to be a primitive barnacle, its relationships are uncertain. Middle Devonian, New York

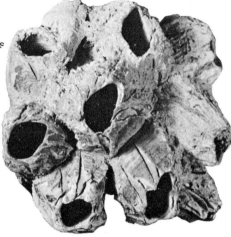

Balanus, acorn barnacles on a snail. This specimen from Miocene, of North America. The genus ranges from Eocene to Recent, all seas

Loriculina, a short-stalked barnacle. The genus occurred in the Cretaceous of Europe, the Middle East, and North America

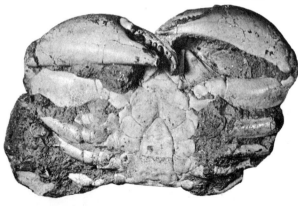

Balanus, acorn barnacles. These specimens from the Pliocene of California

Lower and upper surfaces of a swimming crab. A relative of the modern Pacific edible crab, *Cancer magister.* Tertiary, Panama

A shrimp, × 0.5. Early Jurassic, Solenhofen, Germany

Crustaceans and a xiphosuran, **Euproops (Prestwichianella)**

We see this in the broad, heavy carapace, the short abdomen that is bent under the thorax, the abbreviated antennae, and the lack of a tail fan. They appear in Middle Jurassic strata of Europe, in genera allied to modern forms that still bear traces of relationship to crustaceans with tails. Many bizarre crabs lived in seas that covered southern Europe and northern Africa during the Eocene Epoch; some (like a few modern crabs) seem to have looked like stony algae. Several genera and species of crabs are index fossils in Tertiary formations of North America, though they are much less common than molluscs. The eastern edible, or blue, crab *(Callinectes sapidus)* is found in Pleistocene deposits of Massachusetts and New Jersey. A relative of western edible crabs, *Cancer fissus,* is a Pliocene fossil of California.

All the major groups of decapods had appeared by Jurassic times. All of these continue to the present day, and many have broadly diversified during the latter part of the Cenozoic.

A Few Other Crustaceans. Among today's living invertebrates there are several more crustacean groups. But only a few of these, other than the groups already discussed in this chapter, have left a fossil record. These include the Triassic euthycarcinoids, the copepods, and the isopods (a kind of malacostracan).

The euthycarcinoides are known only from the Early Triassic of Europe and the Middle Triassic of Australia. They have a slender, elongate body divisible into three distinct parts and are small (0.5–6.5 cm., 0.2–2.5 in. in length). The head is solid, not divided into sections. The body ends in a solid, elongate tail called a telson. The five thoracic segments all bear a pair of appendages. Euthycarcinoids probably burrowed in the soft sediments in freshwater ponds and swamps, though they were capable of swimming. They probably were detrital feeders. They seem to combine some characteristics of merostomes and some of myriapods (see Chapter XIV). Despite the fact that euthycarcinoids are a small group with a limited geologic span, because they demonstrate links between two major groups they emphasize the importance of fossils in reconstructing family trees.

Copepods have only a Miocene to Recent record, and of these only the free-living, not the parasitic, forms have been found.

Isopods, such as the Jurassic *Archaeoniscus,* are a varied group that are known from Triassic to Recent. Their eyes are not on stalks, and much fusion of segments has taken place. Familiar isopods are the sow bugs, or slaters, often found near wet or rotting wood, which they eat. The isopods, however, have an amazing variety of feeding styles and are among the few successful land crustaceans.

CHAPTER XIV

Arthropods from Shoals to Air

Though many arthropods now live on land, earliest members of the phylum were aquatic. The first major radiation of arthropods, which occurred in Precambrian times, was played out in the shallow, epicontinental seas of the time, with many wormlike groups giving rise to various kinds. Arthropods apparently remained aquatic until true land plants—not lichens—covered the continents with vegetation, which provided shelter, moisture, and a variety of foods that opened a rich new environment to creatures that could solve the problems of living in air.

The solution of these problems was a gradual and slow process. Before the Cambrian period ended, a few trilobites had moved into estuaries. During the Ordovician, relatives of these animals invaded streams and evolved into chelicerates, or joint-legged animals whose antennae had vanished and whose second pair of appendages had become pincerlike jaws. At the moment, we are not certain of the ancestry of these animals, but it is quite likely that they were derived independently of the trilobites.

Land plants apparently appeared in Middle Silurian times, which we may roughly date at 420 million B.P. Before the period closed—that is, within some 15 million years—land-dwelling chelicerates were becoming fossils in Sweden, Scotland, Wales, and New York. Others, not yet terrestrial, were developing features that allowed them to live in shallow, brackish water or on intertidal flats. One of their descendant species can still live out of water for days, taking trips that range from a few feet to more than a half mile.

Chelicerates form a large group of arthropods and occur in rocks as old as Cambrian. They are still quite abundant. The body of all chelicerates divides into two parts: the prosoma, a fusion of the head and the thorax; and the opisthosoma, the abdomen. The name of the group, however, comes from the chelicerae (pinchers) that lie in front of the mouth, a characteristic of these animals. Spiders (Arachnida) are chelicerates, but so are two other groups, the xiphosurans (or horseshoe crabs) and the eurypterids (or water scorpions).

THE PERSISTENT XIPHOSURANS

This modern wanderer, the horseshoe crab, is famous as a so-called living fossil. Variously called *Limulus* and *Xiphosura,* it has survived with only minor changes since Early Permian times. For some 280 million years, therefore, the horseshoe crab has had a wide cephalothorax (also called the prosoma) that suggests a horse's hoof in outline and ends in genal spines. Like the cephalon of trilobites, the cephalothorax contains both head and visceral organs such as liver, stomach, and intestine. These continue into the spine-bordered buckler (also called the abdomen), which is followed by the telson.

There are two compound and two simple eyes; the mouth is centrally located under the cephalothorax; there are six pairs of legs but no antennae. The first two legs are chelicerae; the next eight are used for walking and are tipped with pincers; their spiny bases cut food to pieces before it enters the mouth. A sixth pair of legs is specialized pushers whose principal function is to force the creature forward through mud or sand. The undersurface of the buckler bears broad appendages that are flipped to and fro when the animal swims. These appendages also are used in respiration, for they bear "gill books," made up of 150 to 200 very thin leaves through which oxygen from water passes into the blood.

The best-known horseshoe crab, *Limulus polyphemus,* lives along the Atlantic coast from Nova Scotia southward and on the Gulf coast of Florida. *Limulus* plows and digs for worms and other small creatures, often covering itself with sand. In the spring it comes to very shallow bays, where it mates and deposits its eggs. Trails are easily seen between tides, some made by single animals and some made by pairs of animals—pairs in which the smallish male clings to the telson of his larger mate. These trails may be either shallow or deep; they often wind to and fro for long distances before ending in irregular pits in which the eggs are laid.

Ancient Relatives of Horseshoe Crabs. As the young limulus develops, it molts, grows, and changes shape at a rapid rate. It also resembles some of the stages through which the order passed during the Paleozoic. The first stage is reminiscent of *Aglaspis,* a Late Cambrian animal with a relatively short cephalon, eleven body segments, and sixteen pairs of legs besides the chelicerae. It belongs in its own order, which is restricted to the Cambrian. Then come stages resembling later forms with fewer and fewer segments. The Silurian *Bunodes,* for example, had nine; *Belinurus* (Devonian to Pennsylvanian) possessed eight, and *Euproops* (Pennsylvanian) had seven. *Palaeolimulus,* from Permian rocks of Kansas, had only the buckler, though grooves on its medial lobe are remains of six segments. From the oldest xiphosuran *(Palaeomerus,* of Early Cambrian age) to the living *Limulus,* the main changes have been to shorten the abdomen and to increase size.

Most ancient xiphosurans were marine, but *Belinurus* and *Euproops* in-

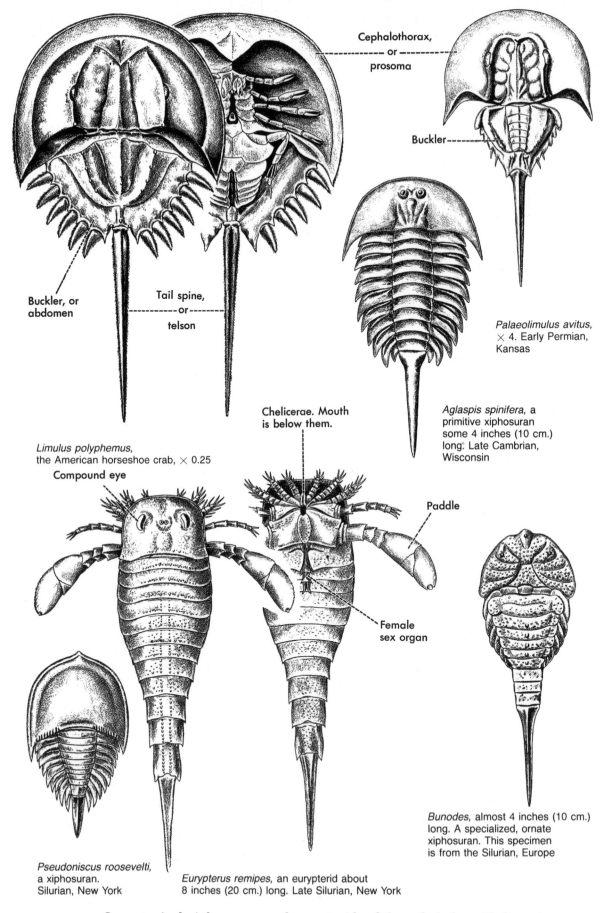

Cephalothorax, or prosoma

Buckler

Buckler, or abdomen

Tail spine, or telson

Palaeolimulus avitus, × 4. Early Permian, Kansas

Chelicerae. Mouth is below them.

Aglaspis spinifera, a primitive xiphosuran some 4 inches (10 cm.) long. Late Cambrian, Wisconsin

Limulus polyphemus, the American horseshoe crab, × 0.25

Compound eye

Paddle

Female sex organ

Bunodes, almost 4 inches (10 cm.) long. A specialized, ornate xiphosuran. This specimen is from the Silurian, Europe

Pseudoniscus rooseveltii, a xiphosuran. Silurian, New York

Eurypterus remipes, an eurypterid about 8 inches (20 cm.) long. Late Silurian, New York

Some typical xiphosurans and eurypterids of the subphylum Chelicerata

vaded brackish lagoons and even made their way into swamps. *Euproops,* especially, is a rare but characteristic fossil in the Coal Age concretions of Mazon Creek, Illinois, which also contain land plants and freshwater fish and molluscs.

As has been said, *Limulus* today crawls over sandy shores during the mating season. Ancient trails made by xiphosurans have been found in formations ranging from Ordovician to Cretaceous in age. Some of those from the Devonian of Pennsylvania were once regarded as amphibian footprints; others, from the Triassic of New Jersey, were ascribed to tiny reptiles. Most dramatic are Jurassic trails from Germany, which generally end in remains of the creatures that made them: *Mesolimulus.* Instead of coming ashore to mate and lay eggs, the German xiphosurans were frantically trying to get back to salt water but were failing in the attempt.

EURYPTERIDS, THE SEA SCORPIONS

Another fossil group belonging within the merostome chelicerates is Eurypterida, the water scorpions.

Varied species of eurypterids range from Ordovician to Permian of both North America and Europe, found in both brackish and freshwater sediments. Some forms known from the Late Silurian of Western Australia actually left trackways on dry land, the first evidence of life walking in a terrestrial environment. In general eurypterids remind us of slender aglaspids with blunt, narrow heads; tapering abdomens without pleural spines; and exoskeletons ornamented by knobs, scales, and ridges. Typical American species range from 5 to 17 inches (13–43 cm.) in length, and some were nearly 7 feet (2 m.) long.

Eurypterus had five pairs of legs: four short, spiny pairs that were used for walking, and one that had spread out into paddles. The chelicerae had become so small that the walking legs must have been used to hold food, but the bases of the paddles bore teeth used for chewing. Males had clasping organs on the underside; the female genital organs fitted over these claspers. Four pairs of stout walking legs followed. The last pair (the sixth) of prosomal appendages were the largest and had the terminal parts flattened— probably used in swimming. Two large compound eyes and two simple ones, all on the dorsal side of the prosoma, suggest that *Eurypterus* generally traveled with its "back," or dorsal surface, upward.

Eurypterus shows the basic plan of eurypterids. As ages passed, these creatures specialized in varied and often surprising ways. Some developed almost triangular prosomas, while the first six segments of the abdomen became very wide. Others had squarish prosomas, and the first four legs became long, with many slender spines, that look as if they were nets for trapping food. An Ordovician genus misnamed *Megalograptus* became spiny and developed pincers instead of a spinelike telson.

Stylonurus combined a long telson and tapering abdomen with a rather small and very rough prosoma on which the compound eyes moved closer and closer to the center. The first two walking legs were short and spiny, the second and third pairs were long, with comblike rows of spines, and the last two pairs were still longer and bore lengthwise ridges. They also looked alike, for the legs that were paddles in other eurypterids had evolved into slender organs tipped by sharp, curved claws.

Stylonurus apparently walked on its eight long legs and may have used the spiny ones to hold food, since its chelicerae were short. Silurian species were barely 5 inches (13 cm.) long, but one from the Middle Devonian of New York grew to 4 feet 6 inches (137 cm.). Even this did not equal *Pterygotus,* which reached lengths of 6 to 7 feet (1.8–2.1 m.). Its compound eyes were very large, its telson had become a wide plate, and its chelicerae were

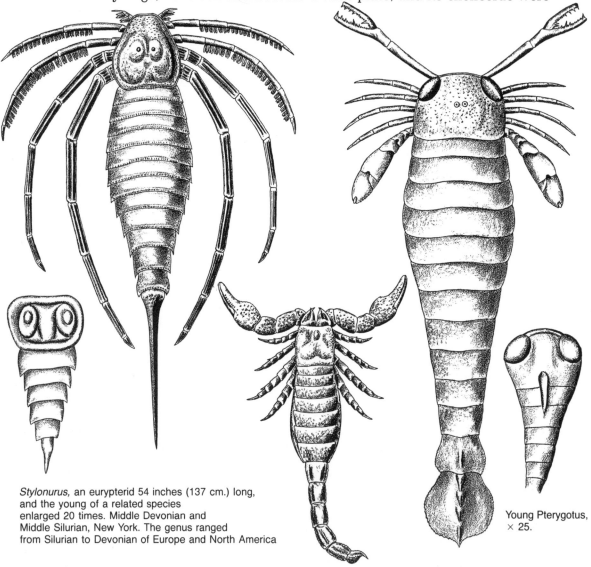

Stylonurus, an eurypterid 54 inches (137 cm.) long, and the young of a related species enlarged 20 times. Middle Devonian and Middle Silurian, New York. The genus ranged from Silurian to Devonian of Europe and North America

Young Pterygotus, × 25.

Palaeophonus nuncius, a true land-dwelling scorpion with stinging "tail." Late Silurian, Sweden

Pterygotus buffaloensis, 6 to 7 feet (1.8–2.1 m.) long. Late Silurian, New York

Three typical sea scorpions, or eurypterids, and a true scorpion

long, toothed pincers so jointed that they could reach the mouth. It could swim as well as crawl and was an active hunter and the most dangerous arthropod of Late Silurian and Early Devonian times.

Growth Stages and Habits. Cast-off crusts show that eurypterids went through extensive metamorphoses. The very young *Stylonurus myops,* for example, was short and broad, with eyes on raised oval areas and only five segments between carapace and telson. In succeeding stages, segments were added, their extremities became spinose, and the telson grew long and slender.

Early eurypterids were marine, but in Silurain times they took up life in wide lagoons or bays in which the water varied from exceedingly salty to brackish. Large numbers of young eurypterids in shaly layers at Otisville, New York, suggest that the area was a sheltered breeding place comparable to the shallow, protected bays in which *Limulus polyphemus* now deposits its eggs.

As time passed, more and more eurypterids moved into brackish bays, and from them into rivers and even swamps. Dead animals were buried in shales and limstones interbedded with coal, in regions as far apart as Germany, Nova Scotia, and central Illinois. *Lepidoderma,* from Pennsylvanian strata of Pennsylvania and Illinois, is a scaly form with spiny segments that is only 8 to 9 inches (20–23 cm.) long. It is found among plants of the swampy coal forests, in beds of shale that also contain freshwater mussels and snails. The last eurypterids, of Permian Europe, are also associated with fossil vines and trees of swampy woodlands.

SCORPIONS AND OTHER ARACHNIDS

Yet another major group of chelicerates is the Arachnida, which includes scorpions, spiders, and harvestmen.

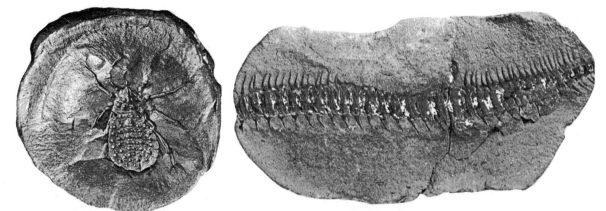

Eophrynus prestvici, a Pennsylvanian spider, from England. At the right is Euphoberia armigera, a millipede about 3.5 inches (about 9 cm.) long. Pennsylvanian, Grundy County, Illinois

Scorpions at one time were thought to have evolved from eurypterids such as *Pterygotus* whose chelicerae had become long, powerful pincers. Actually, the scorpion's chelicerae are short and inconspicious, its pincers being the first pair of walking legs, enlarged and modified. The fifth pair of legs never forms paddles, as it does in most eurypterids. The scorpion telson also has become a sort of hypodermic needle that can inject poison produced in a large gland at its base. The respiratory organs are book lungs, which take oxygen from air, not water.

These features suggest that scorpions are evolutionary nieces and nephews of eurypterids, not direct descendants. They also are respectably ancient, for fully developed specimens are found in Late Silurian rocks of New York and Sweden. Especially beautiful specimens come from Pennsylvanian deposits of Mazon Creek, in Grundy County, Illinois.

Spiders and Daddy Longlegs.   Spiders, like scorpions, are air breathers, though most of them use tubes that branch and run through the body. A few aquatic species are known to inhabit both marine and fresh waters. Spiders also lack pincers, and their bodies are short, without telsons. In spite of these differences, both spiders and scorpions belong to one group, the Arachnida, which also includes the spiderlike harvestmen, or daddy longlegs, and several other groups. Except in ticks and mites, the body is divided into a plated cephalothorax and a jointed abdomen. The former bears six pairs of appendages, four pairs of which are walking legs. There are no antennae.

Spiders are first found in Pennsylvanian rocks *(Palaeophorius,* for example), though their fully developed form and variety indicate that they evolved long before that time.

Spiders have much greater variety in the fossil record than they do today: only about half of the sixteen or so orders recognized are still alive, with major extinctions having occurred in the late Paleozoic. One truly gigantic spider, *Megarachne servinei,* from the Late Carboniferous of Argentina, had a leg span of more than 50 centimeters (about 20 in.).

Scorpions, too, show much variety in the past. During the Silurian to Carboniferous, the greatest number of types developed. After that, one group gave rise to all of the modern scorpions.

Another distinct group of arachnids, the Pycnogonida, or sea spiders, were once thought to be unique. Now it seems they were derived from an early group of marine arachnids. The pycnogonids have small abdomens with four pairs of walking legs that come in a variety of shapes. The third pair is modified in the males to carry eggs when they are being incubated. Pycnogonids range from a few millimeters (not much more than a tenth of an inch) up to 40 centimeters (16 in.) and are generally benthonic predators. The group is first known from the Early Devonian of Germany *(Palaeoisopus* and *Palaeopantopus)* and today is especially common in Antarctic waters, where more than one hundred species are known.

The oldest terrestrial arachnid is a spider, *Alkenia,* from the Early Devo-

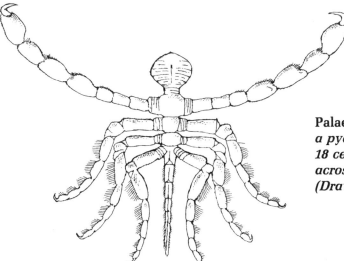

Palaeoisopus problematicus,
a pycnogonid,
18 centimeters (about 7 in.)
across. Early Devonian, Germany.
(Drawing by Frank Knight)

nian, decidedly older than the first land-dwelling scorpion. Throughout their history, both spiders and scorpions have tended to fuse and lose segments, making them more compact animals through time.

Some of the finest fossil arachnids come from Miocene nodules in California, the Oligocene Florissant insect beds of western North America, and from Tertiary amber deposits in the Baltic region of Europe. The amber, which is fossil tree resin, reveals even minute hairs on the bodies of these arachnids.

Another major division, sometimes called a phylum, of joint-legged animals includes the familiar millipedes and centipedes, insects, and the not so well known onychophorans. These belong in the Uniramia, all of which have limbs with a single central part (uniramous) that are not branched on the end like the biramous legs of trilobites. They also have jaws that bite with the tip of the whole limb.

Uniramians first appeared in the Cambrian and are still alive. *Aysheaia,* from the Middle Cambrian Burgess Shale, which reminds us in limb and cuticle structure of the onychophorans, is a uniramian. Often preserved alongside *Aysheaia* are sponge fragments, which may have been the food of this arthropod.

As the Burgess Shale fauna clearly reflects, the Cambrian (and probably the Precambrian) was a time of experimentation in many arthropod groups. Some groups struck on a successful body plan, but many others became extinct because of increasing competition with other invertebrates, including more advanced arthropods, by the mid-Paleozoic. The winners of the competition were heir to the future and gave rise to the living uniramians, crustaceans, and chelicerates.

ONYCHOPHORANS

Onychophorans are small, wormlike invertebrates that live in damp terrestrial environments, usually in logs or under stones—mainly in the Southern Hemisphere. So they are not the most familiar of the arthropods. None-theless, they are an intriguing group, because they are a mixture of wormlike and arthropodlike characteristics. Because of their mosaic nature, they have been placed in many groups, most recently among the uniramians. They have a simple head made up of three segments, and a wormlike segmented trunk that is not divided into major sections. The limbs are all single-branched. Much of the internal anatomy is arthropodan, and the embryonic stages of the onychophoran is very myriapod-like.

The onychophorans are first known in the Cambrian and survive until today, being one of the animal groups distributed mainly on the Gondwana continents.

THOUSAND-LEGS AND CENTIPEDES

Millipedes and centipedes are elongate, wormlike crawlers that form the class or subphylum of myriapods. Modern millipedes hide in the ground or under dead sticks and leaves, where they feed on decaying material or roots. They have hard, shiny exoskeletons, one pair of antennae, and two pairs of short legs on each of their many body segments. Their oldest know fossils come from Middle Paleozoic rocks. *Euphoberia,* from Mazon Creek, is a spiny form with relatively long legs and segments that seem to divide on the underside of the body. Another form from Mazon Creek reached a length of 8 inches (20 cm.) and ranks as the world's largest millipede.

Centipedes have only one pair of legs per segment, and those just behind the head have become poison fangs. Unlike the millipedes, they are fast-moving predators. There are undoubted centipedes in the Baltic amber, and fossils found at Mazon Creek may belong to this group.

Myriapods are all terrestrial, air-breathing arthropods with many seg-ments. Like the onychophorans, they have a distinct head, as well as a trunk that is simply segmented, not divided into a thorax and an abdomen. They have mandibles that are jointed for biting in a transverse plane, unlike many of the other arthropods. The most spectacular forms in this group are the gigantic arthropleurids, which reached up to 6 feet (nearly 2 m.) in length. These Carboniferous coal-swamp dwellers may have been herbivores, as lycopod fragments have been found within their fossils. They seem to have been closely tied to the coal-swamp environments, and they became extinct with the disappearance of the swampland floras after the Pennsylvanian.

THE AMAZINGLY SUCCESSFUL INSECTS: THE HEXAPODS

Insects are the largest and most successful class of arthropods; in fact, they are the most successful group in the entire animal kingdom. Not only do they live in a great variety of habitats—their million or more species form more than 67 percent of all living animal species. Many also exist in vast and everincreasing abundance, which seems not to be curbed by poisons and other devices employed against them by man. Yet, in many other cases, destruction of habitat by man's activities has caused species to become extinct, and many others are threatened with extinction.

The name *insect* comes from a Latin word meaning "cut into"; it refers to the fact that the insect body is sharply divided into head, thorax, and abdomen. The head is made up of six segments, the thorax of three, and the abdomen contains as few as six or as many as eleven or twelve. Antennae number a single pair, six legs are attached to the thorax, and the abdomen

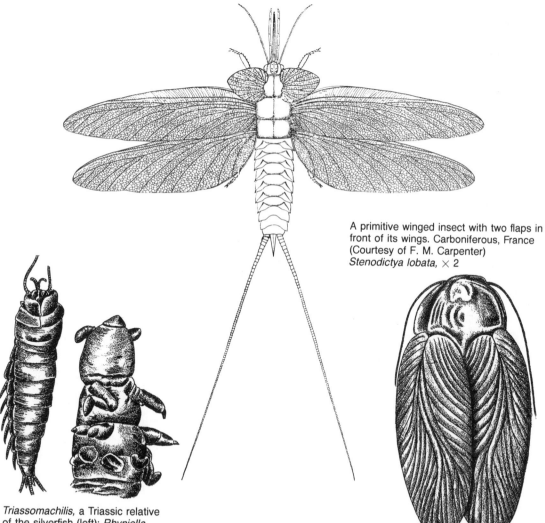

A primitive winged insect with two flaps in front of its wings. Carboniferous, France (Courtesy of F. M. Carpenter) *Stenodictya lobata,* × 2

Triassomachilis, a Triassic relative of the silverfish (left); *Rhyniella* (right), once thought to be a Devonian fossil, has now been recognized as a modern insect inadvertently "trapped" in a crevice in Devonian rocks

Adeloblatta columbiana, a cockroach 1 inch (2.5 cm.) long. Pennsylvanian, Illinois

Three primitive insects of Paleozoic age

bears none. Three pairs of mouthparts are used for chewing. The legs have eight or nine joints and generally bear claws. Young, or larvae, may be aquatic and breathe with gills, but adults take air into tubes vastly more complex than those possessed by spiders. Most adult insects also have hard, chitinous exoskeletons.

Primitive Wingless Insects (Apterygota).   We often picture insects as agile creatures, with two or four wings, that spend much of their time in flight, though they may rest or hunt food on the ground. Actually, great numbers of insects are terrestrial and almost flightless, and the class began as wingless creatures. Primitive types still survive in springtails (Collembola) as well as bristletails and silverfish (Thysanura). The first of these are very small, with short antennae and simple eyes; they run on short legs or jump with forked "tails" attached to the underside of the body.

Bristletails, which seem to be slightly more advanced than springtails, have been discovered in rocks of Carboniferous age. Silverfish go back to the Triassic. Not only are these creatures ancient; they are outstanding examples of insects' pliancy and success. At a time when silverfish should be living fossils threatened with extinction, they are pushing their range over most of the world in man's well-heated buildings. There, removed from their natural foods, silverfish thrive on starched clothing, books, and slick-paper magazines, and crumbs that collect in kitchens.

Early "Ancient-wings" (Paleoptera).   Many animal organs are made-overs; legs have turned into pincers, other legs serve as jaws, and so on. Wings, on the other hand, are new, for they developed from four out of six flaps that appeared on the first three thoracic segments. This is shown by fossils such as *Stenodictya,* from Pennsylvanian deposits of France. *Stenodictya* has two flaps on the first thoracic segment but true wings on the second and third. Flaps and wings are essentially alike, for both are thin, both have supporting veins, and both possess tiny hairs scattered over the upper surface.

Flaps must have evolved into wings during Mississippian times, since insects fully equipped for flight have been found in the Lower Carboniferous. We call these early winged forms paleopterans, because their vein patterns are archaic though complex and because the wings themselves could not be folded back when their owners were at rest. They were hinged and had an assortment of muscles that could move them in many directions. Modern mayflies (Ephemeroptera) are very like these first fliers, though the first fossils of this group are not known until the Late Carboniferous.

Most paleopterans had wingspreads of 1 to 4 inches (2.5–10 cm.), but many were a great deal larger. Some species of Protodonata, often called ancestral dragonflies, had wingspreads of 28 to 30 inches (70–76 cm.) and bodies 12 to 15 inches (30–38 cm.) in length. Like true dragonflies, they were swift-flying predators with spiny legs used in capturing prey. The Protodonata range from Carboniferous to Permian and from Europe to Australia; exceptionally

Wing of Typus gracilis, *an ancestral dragonfly from the Permian of Oklahoma; length 14.5 centimeters (about 6 in.). Below is a remarkably perfect fly from Baltic amber. (Photographs by F. M. Carpenter)*

Two termites in amber. Both insects are in the winged stage, showing that they were trapped in resin during the spring mating season. (Photograph by P. S. Tice, from Buchsbaum's Animals Without Backbones)

fine specimens have been found in thin layers of Permian limestone at Elmo, near Abilene, Kansas. True dragonflies (Odonata) evolved in Early Permian times and continue to Recent.

There were several orders of Paleoptera living in the late Paleozoic, but only two orders, Ephemeroptera and Odonata, survive today. These are overshadowed by more advanced forms, such as the cockroaches, grasshoppers, and related forms.

Neopterans with Folding Wings. Wings were life-saving acquisitions; they enabled their owners to escape from spiders, scorpions, and small vertebrates that hunted on the ground. Yet the primitive wing was also a nuisance, since, by spreading sideways, it kept paleopterans from hiding under branches and leaves. New rewards could be won by wings that would fold, permitting ready concealment as well as escape by flight.

Several insect groups evolved wings that would fold, some in an order whose other features are those of paleopterans. Long before the Pennsylvanian period came to an end, there was a considerable array of neopterous ("new-winged") insects, whose wings folded backward, one pair over another. Among these newly evolved groups were cockroaches (Blattodea), whose fossils may be recognized by their large forewings with characteristic venation, as well as by the broad thorax, which in many species almost hides the head. Some Pennsylvanian roaches reached lengths of 3 to 4 inches (7.6–10 cm.), but later species were not so large. Since early cockroaches lived on damp ground under swampy forests, their remains were readily buried in mud and, therefore, are disproportionately common among Paleozoic insects.

Complete and Incomplete (Simple) Metamorphosis. Early neopterans such as cockroaches went through an incomplete metamorphosis. This means that their eggs hatched into tiny nymphs that looked and lived very much like their full-grown parents. A cockroach nymph, for example, sheds its skin-crust several times, but it does little more than grow, become mature, and add two pairs of wings that are lacking when it hatches. As countless people know, the nymph runs about like its parents, eats as they do, and lives amid the same surroundings.

There is nothing wrong with this: witness the fact that cockroaches remain prosperous and abundant after more than 280 million years. Still, many insects have found improved chances for life when the young live in one environment and the adults in another. This can be done with incomplete metamorphosis; young dragonflies, for instance, creep at the bottom of pools, but adults take to dry land and hunt or escape enemies in the air. But the range of environments is still greater when young have one form, adults have another, and an intermediate stage, or pupa, makes provision for extensive change. We see this in the butterfly, whose young is a wormlike larva that crawls upon plants and devours their leaves. This larva becomes a chrysalis —legless, mouthless, and encased in armor that gives protection while the body is reorganized. The adult then emerges with four broad wings, legs adapted to clinging, and mouth parts that suck juices such as the nectar of flowers. No butterfly can crowd out its own young ones or take food from them, nor does it need to spend its life in one habitat. This is complete metamorphosis.

From the early cockroach-like ancestors came three major groups or superorders of insects. One is the orthopteroids: Blattodea, cockroaches (Late Carboniferous to Recent); Orthoptera, the grasshoppers and crickets (Late Carboniferous to Recent); Dermaptera, the earwigs (Jurassic to Recent); Isoptera, the termites (early Tertiary to Recent); Plecoptera, the stone flies (Permian to Recent) and Ambloptera or Embioptera, the web spinners (early Tertiary to Recent), all of which have a simple metamorphosis and a large lobe on the hind wing, among other characteristics. Another group includes the hemipteroid orders: Mallophaga, the bird lice (Recent only); Anoplura, the sucking lice (Pleistocene to Recent); Thysanoptera, the thrips (Jurassic to Recent); and Hemiptera, the bugs (Early Permian to Recent). These also undergo a simple metamorphosis and lack the large lobe on the hind wing; also, the fine venation in the wings is reduced. The third group, the neuropteroids, is characterized by a complete metamorphosis, with larvae and pupae that don't resemble the adult. Included in this category are Hymenoptera, the bees, wasps, and ants (Triassic to Recent); Coleoptera, the beetles (Late Permian to Recent); Neuroptera, the ant lions (Early Permian to Recent); Mecoptera, the scorpion flies (Early Permian to Recent); Siphonaptera, the fleas (a questionable Cretaceous record in Australia; Early Tertiary to Recent); Diptera, the flies and mosquitoes (Triassic to Recent); Trichoptera, the caddis flies (Permian to Recent); and Lepidoptera, the butterflies and moths (Cretaceous to Recent).

These advantages were apparently won at least by Permian times, since some of the Early Permian insects belonged to two groups (orders) that now go through larval, pupal, and adult stages. They accounted for only 5 percent of the known species then living, but the proportion increased during subsequent ages. Today more than 80 percent of the world's insects go through a complete metamorphosis.

Modern Insect Faunas. Though insects we meet with today are a mixture of ancient (cockroaches and dragonflies) and more recent stock, those in the neuropteroid and orthopteroid orders predominate.

Protolindenia wittei, *a true dragonfly with a wingspread of more than 4 inches (about 10 cm.). Jurassic, Solenhofen, Germany. (Photograph by F. M. Carpenter)*

Clatrotitan andersoni. A relative of crickets, with a very large chirping organ. Length 5.4 inches (13.8 cm.). Triassic, New South Wales

Raphidia mortua, a snake fly 0.7 inch (1.7 cm.) long. Oligocene, Florissant, Colorado

Dunbaria fasciipennis showing color pattern on wings. Width 1.5 inches (3.7 cm.). Early Permian, Elmo, Kansas

Lithosmylus columbianus, related to dobson-flies. Oligocene, Florissant, Colorado. Length about 1 inch (3.0 cm.)

A robber fly (family Asilidae) about 1 inch (2.5 cm.) long. Note hairs on the legs. Oligocene, Florissant, Colorado

Prodryas persephone, a butterfly showing color pattern. Width about 2 inches (5.3 cm.). Oligocene, Florissant, Colorado

Permian, Triassic, and Oligocene insects. (Photographs by F. M. Carpenter)

Corcorania trispinosa,
*about 3.5 centimeters
(1.4 in.) in length, from
the Early Ordovician
(Lancefieldian) of
southeastern Australia.
In its own family, its
relationship to other
arthropods is unknown.
(Photograph by F. Coffa
with permission of P.
Jell and The Museum of
Victoria)*

Beetles appeared in Late Permian times and were abundant by the beginning of the Mesozoic Era. About two thousand Tertiary species have been described, and their hard, shelly forewings are abundant in the Pleistocene tar deposits of California, and elsewhere in the world in rocks of this age.

Modern flies have lost one pair of wings, indicated by their group name of Diptera, or "two-wings." Primitive moths (Lepidoptera) appeared first in the Early Cretaceous. Those found along with a great variety of plants and other invertebrates in the Oligocene lake beds of Florissant and elsewhere in Colorado (Chapter XXXII) preserve color markings as well as antennae and the hairlike scales that covered both abdomen and thorax. Primitive species related to ants and bees (Hymenoptera) occur as far back as the Triassic, but more specialized types, such as those with social behavior, are not known until the Cretaceous.

In general, fossil insects are significant without being plentiful. They tell a great deal about the evolution of their class, but they are found in only a few regions and formations, and even in those they may be overshadowed by fossil plants. Sometimes, however, the two combine, as they do in carbonized galls or Florissant leaves that were trimmed or perforated by leaf-cutting bees.

CHAPTER XV

Snails and their Kin

Snails belong to the molluscs—phylum Mollusca—whose name comes from a Latin word for "soft." The molluscs form the second-largest group of invertebrates, with more than a hundred thousand living species. In everyday language, molluscs are "shells," edible types often being called "shellfish." Actually, many animals that have shells are not molluscs, and some molluscs have either lost their shells or have tucked them away where they cannot be seen. To learn what the phylum really is, we must emphasize bodies and give secondary attention to shells.

The molluscan body is soft; its lower part has become a muscular structure that is generally used for locomotion and therefore is called a foot. The upper part of the body is spread out into a mantle that folds downward over the rest of the creature. Since the mantle builds the shell, if there is one, the latter does not completely cover the body, as does the shell of a crab or a lobster. The molluscan shell is limy. Limy shells are largely calcite, but they may contain layers of a related mineral called aragonite, which dissolves readily. Such shells are likely to form casts or molds, not petrified fossils.

The mollusc body plan is certainly different from that of the brachiopod. Molluscs are mobile animals and thus not anchored in one spot. They have both a mouth and an anus, not a "blind gut," so that waste is not passed out through the mouth, as it is in brachiopods. All of these "advances" have produced an animal capable of invading a great many different feeding niches and seemingly more versatile than the brachiopods, whose dominance they displaced.

Molluscs are probably descendants of free-living flatworms. The dorso-ventral muscles of worms formed the ancestral molluscan foot.

MONOPLACOPHORANS

The monoplacophorans are a group of limpet-shaped marine molluscs that have not undergone tortion and seem to be quite primitive. They have pseudo-segmented muscles, gills, and internal organs. The foot is circular

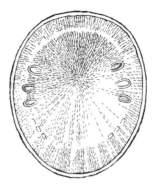

Neopilina galathae, *a living monoplacophoran from the west coast of Central America. Top (dorsal) view of shell, about 1 centimeter (less than 0.5 in.) long. (Modified after Tasch, 1973, by Frank Knight)*

Scenella, *a monoplacophoran from the Middle Cambrian of Canada. Underside (ventral) view showing U-shaped, segmented muscle scars; about 1.2 centimeters (0.5 in.) long. (Modified after Tasch, 1973, by Frank Knight)*

and surrounded by the mantle cavity. Because they are the only molluscs with segmentation, they hint at an ancestry for this phylum within the segmented worms or the arthropods. They occur first in rocks of Cambrian age, as well as in today's seas, for example *Neopilina.* The group was first known from fossil remains, and so when *Neopilina* was found alive, in 1957, it was looked upon as a "living fossil."

CHITONS AND TUSK SHELLS

The earliest, simplest molluscs are virtually unknown, for they were part of the horde of soft-bodied creatures that evolved, died out, and disappeared during Precambrian times. But we can get a fair picture of those pioneers by looking at the simplest of living molluscs, the chitons.

Chitons, or Amphineura. The technical name of chitons, Amphineura, refers to their nervous system, which forms a double series around the mouth, in the head, and through the body. A living chiton is an oval creature with an indistinct head and a foot that is merely the flattened underside of the body. They range from 0.25 inch (0.6 cm.) long to the giant *Cryptochiton* of the West Coast of North America, which is 14 inches (36 cm.) in length. The mouth contains a rough tongue supported by a radula in the form of a ribbon-like structure with rows of sharp, horny teeth and lies at the front of the animal. Muscles thrust the radula forward and pull it back and forth over a base, thus scraping algae from rocks over which the animal crawls. The digestive system is simple, and the shell (which some species have lost) consists of seven or eight separate plates, one behind another on the back. Gills are generally well developed.

Though chitons are very primitive molluscs, their fossils may occur in

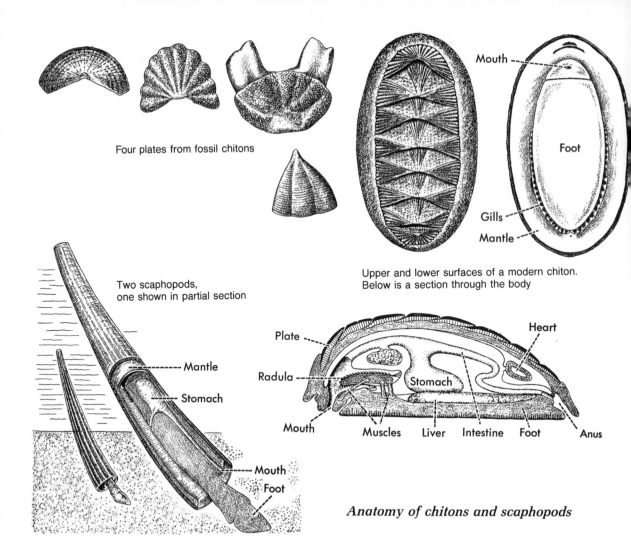

Four plates from fossil chitons

Mouth

Foot

Gills

Mantle

Upper and lower surfaces of a modern chiton.
Below is a section through the body

Two scaphopods,
one shown in partial section

Mantle

Stomach

Mouth

Foot

Plate

Radula

Mouth

Muscles

Liver

Stomach

Intestine

Foot

Heart

Anus

Anatomy of chitons and scaphopods

rocks of Late Cambrian age; e.g., *Matthevia,* from North America. Paleozoic species can be recognized by the fact that their plates fitted end to end; those of Mesozoic and later types overlapped like movable shingles, just as they do in modern species.

Scaphopods, or Tusk Shells. Modern members of this group were often used as beads by American Indians. They are strangely specialized molluscs whose shells are slender, curved cones that are open at both ends; most species are less than 3 inches (7.5 cm.) long, but one from the Pennsylvanian of Texas reached the amazing length of 2 feet (about 60 cm.). Living scaphopods burrow in the sea bottom at depths ranging from the level of low tide to at least 15,000 feet (4,500 m.) The shell is carried obliquely and extends into the water, the foot is used for creeping and digging, and short tentacles around the mouth capture food in the form of small animals. The mouth is permanently embedded in the sediment. The gut exit, or anus, lies at the upper end of the shell, and the gills are quite reduced. Fossils range from the Ordovician onward but are most common in Cenozoic strata, for instance the genus *Dentalium.*

SNAILS AND THEIR ALLIES: THE GASTROPODS

The word gastropod means "stomach foot," but a stomach that lies in the foot is a character these molluscs share with the chiton. Gastropods are better characterized as snails and their kin, whose shells (unless they have been lost) consist of a single structure.

The Gastropod Body. Most fossil gastropods are shells, but to understand them we must picture the creatures to which they belonged. A typical gastropod has a foot that can be spread out very broadly or pulled back into the shell. The body is either tumid or coiled and is covered by the sheetlike mantle. The head, a structure present only in snails and cephalopods among the molluscs, has two tentacles, each with an eye on its outer surface about midway between the base and the tip. The mantle is thickened at the edge and at one place forms a pocketlike cavity between itself and the body. In most aquatic species this cavity contains one or two gills, to which water may come through a tube-shaped fold, the siphon. After the gills have taken oxygen from it, this water passes out through the slit that separates body and mantle. All gastropods have undergone torsion, or twisting the top part of the body around so that it sits back to front on the bottom (or ventral) half.

Gastropod Shells. Gastropod shells vary greatly, but all are secreted by the mantle. At the surface is a thin coat, the periostracum, which consists of horny material (a dark-colored protein) that protects the shell from wear. It is seldom, if ever, preserved in fossils and is not developed by gastropods whose shells are covered by broad folds of the mantle.

Most of the shell is made up of aragonite deposited in a series of layers, or prisms. The innermost layers commonly are of very thin aragonite whose structure lies parallel with the inner shell surface; it is smoothly "polished," or pearly. Because shells contain much aragonite, they often dissolve before they can be preserved. Others, formed of coarse fibers and prisms, crumble when their fossils are weathered out of limestone, marl, or shale.

Most snail shells are coiled, but a few are not; these characteristics alone tell nothing about relationships. Snails seem to have been derived from an uncoiled ancestor sometime in the Cambrian or before. A few primitive ones, the bellerophontids, are symmetrically coiled, but most are asymmetric about an axis. Perhaps the symmetric forms don't even belong with the snails; some paleontologists have suggested they are instead monoplacophorans.

The Operculum. The gastropod shell forms a sturdy and ever ready coat of armor into which the builder can tuck its soft and compressible body. In some groups, no further protection is needed; cowries and cone shells, for example, have such narrow apertures that almost nothing can reach into

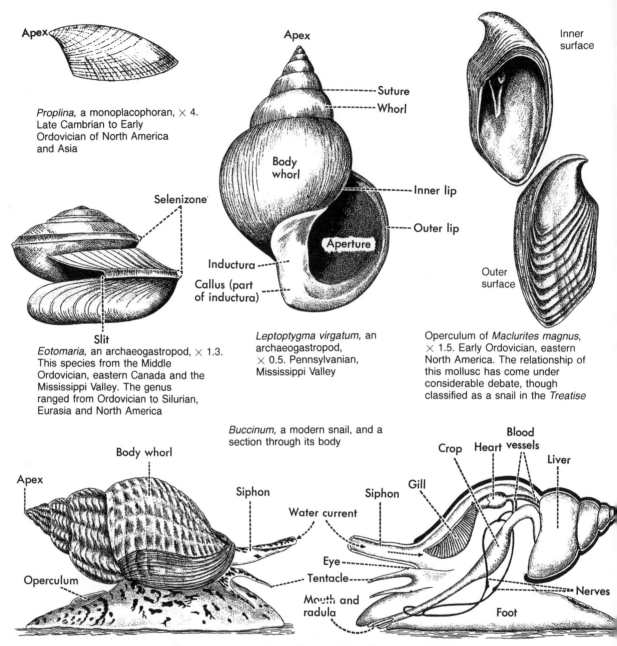

Apex

Proplina, a monoplacophoran, × 4. Late Cambrian to Early Ordovician of North America and Asia

Apex

Suture

Whorl

Body whorl

Inner lip

Outer lip

Aperture

Inductura

Callus (part of inductura)

Inner surface

Outer surface

Selenizone

Slit

Eotomaria, an archaeogastropod, × 1.3. This species from the Middle Ordovician, eastern Canada and the Mississippi Valley. The genus ranged from Ordovician to Silurian, Eurasia and North America

Leptoptygma virgatum, an archaeogastropod, × 0.5. Pennsylvanian, Mississippi Valley

Operculum of *Maclurites magnus,* × 1.5. Early Ordovician, eastern North America. The relationship of this mollusc has come under considerable debate, though classified as a snail in the *Treatise*

Buccinum, a modern snail, and a section through its body

Crop   Heart   Blood vessels

Liver

Gill

Body whorl

Apex

Siphon

Water current

Siphon

Operculum

Eye

Tentacle

Mouth and radula

Nerves

Foot

Terms used to describe snail bodies and shells

them. But limpets, abalones, and other conical or slightly coiled snails have apertures as large as their shells. To secure protection, these molluscs cling tightly to rocks and other objects with their broad, muscular feet. The rough area in an abalone shell shows the size and suggests the strength of the muscle that contracts, turning the animal's flat foot into a vacuum cup.

Most gastropods have apertures that are wider than those of cowries but lack the abalone's powerful foot. Such snails protect themselves by means of an operculum, which is a horny or calcareous plate secreted by glands above the hind part of the foot. Though this plate looks absurdly small on an expanded snail, it fits tightly against the shell when the animal draws far back into the body whorl.

Horny opercula are seldom, if ever, preserved as fossils, but those that are strengthened by calcite may be thicker and sturdier than the shells into which they fit. Some of the thickest and commonest fossil opercula belonged to snails called *Maclurites,* of Middle to Late Ordovician age.

The Radula. The main feeding structure in gastropods is the radula, a strip of horny teeth that lies in the mouth. This has allowed snails to take on a variety of feeding styles: herbivorous, carnivorous, as well as scavenging. The radula can rasp, tear, bite, grasp, pierce, bore, or even stab snake-fashion. Radulae are found in the fossil record and are useful in classifying many groups of snails.

Growth and Length of Life. Many snails grow to large size; one modern species becomes 2 feet (60 cm.) long. Many others, both fossil and modern, are covered with growth lines, or wrinkles, which make them look very old. The fact is that snails grow rapidly and have rather short lives. Tube snails reach lengths of 4 to 5 inches (10–13 cm.) in only two or three years; a thick-shelled *Murex* added a frill one fourth to one half inch (0.5–1 cm.) wide in only three days. Though some snails are known to live twenty years, one to five years is the rule.

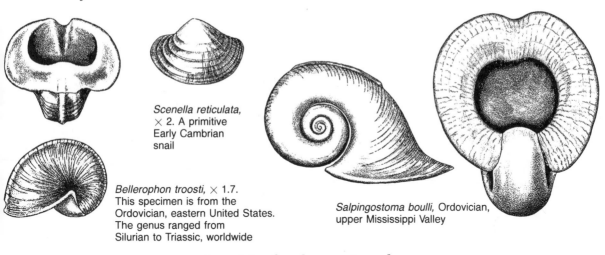

Scenella reticulata, × 2. A primitive Early Cambrian snail

Bellerophon troosti, × 1.7. This specimen is from the Ordovician, eastern United States. The genus ranged from Silurian to Triassic, worldwide

Salpingostoma boulli, Ordovician, upper Mississippi Valley

A variety of archaeogastropods

ARCHAEOGASTROPODS

Snails doubtless evolved during Precambrian times, but their oldest known shells are found in Early Cambrian rocks. *Aldanella,* from the Early Cambrian (Tommotian) of Siberia, is considered by some paleontologists to be the oldest known gastropod. *Pelagiella,* an enigmatic Cambrian fossil, seems to be somewhat intermediate in shape between *Aldanella* and monoplacophorans, giving us a hint at the ancestry of snails and their kin. *Aldanella* may belong to the archaeogastropods, a primitive class containing some forms that coil in one plane but are not "twisted," or spiraled. Marks, or scars, on places where muscles were attached, show that the body filled the forward part of the shell, while two leaf-shaped gills lay to the rear, in a pocket covered by the mantle. The gills have filaments that were lined up in a double comb and were free at one end. Occasionally only one gill was present. The tip, or apex, of the shell, therefore, pointed forward, and growth was toward the rear. Archaeogastropods apparently crawled on muddy sea bottoms, "inching" along from side to side and feeding upon small algae.

In Greek mythology, Bellerophon was a hero who rode to battle on Pegasus, the winged horse. Among fossils, *Bellerophon* is a snail whose shell coils symmetrically in one plane. The outer lip flares at both sides and has a central notch or slit that becomes a ridge when it is closed. Several related genera are not closely coiled, have still more widely flaring lips, and show other peculiarities.

There is still some doubt as to where bellerophontids belong in molluscan classification. Some paleontologists consider them archaeogastropods, directing their coils forward and their apertures toward the rear. Other authorities think bellerophontids were more closely related to the monoplacophorans. It is quite clear that much more work is needed before the relationships of many Cambrian mollusc-like forms, including these, will be understood.

The bellerophontids had a great variety of shapes, and ranged from Cambrian to Triassic times. They were most successful, however, during the Ordovician, Silurian, and Devonian.

THE PROSPEROUS PROSOBRANCHS

The archaeogastropods were members of one of the three major groups of gastropods, the Prosobranchiata, which ranges from the Early Cambrian to the present. The prosobranchs are the vast majority of Paleozoic gastropods, as well as a significant part of post-Paleozoic faunas. Their gills and mantle cavity lie near the head, the aperture is directed forward, and the shell's apex points toward the rear. The digestive tract also had become so abruptly and deeply curved that the anus opens above the head.

Undoubted prosobranchs appeared in Cambrian seas and are abundant today. Even though muscle scars may not be visible in some forms, most members of this class can be recognized as marine snails that coil spirally. They range from *Euomphalus,* whose shell goes into a reversed spiral that is flat on one side and sunken on the other, to tall, slender spires such as *Ectomaria* and *Turritella.* Some are as smooth as well-glazed china; others

Platyceras, an archaeo-
gastropod. This specimen is
from the Silurian, central
United States. This varied
genus ranged worldwide
from Silurian to Permian

A gastropod from the Late
Cretaceous, New Jersey to
Texas and Utah

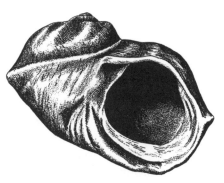

Turbonopsis shumardi, an
archaeogastropod, × 1.
Middle Devonian,
Mississippi Valley

Vermicularia, a
mesogastropod.
Miocene to Recent,
eastern North and
South America

Helminthozyga vermicula,
a mesogastropod, × 25.
Pennsylvanian, North America

Holopea symmetrica, an
archaeogastropod, × 3.
Middle Ordovician, eastern
North America

Murex mississippiensis,
a neogastropod, × 1.5.
Oligocene, Mississippi

Straparolus, an
archaeogastropod.
Worldwide from the
Silurian to the Permian

Turritella, a mesogastropod.
Internal mold. Cretaceous, New Jersey

Turritella, a mesogastropod. This species is from the Paleocene and
Eocene, Maryland to Texas. The genus ranged from Oligocene to
Recent in Eurasia, North Africa, and tropical to subtropical America

Hormotoma whiteavesi,
an archaeogastropod,
× 0.9. Middle Silurian, New York

A variety of fossil snails

are wrinkled, ridged, elaborately spiny, or sculptured with dead odds and ends cemented into the shell. Colors of living species range from white or gray to red, green, and purple, all hues of the rainbow.

Habits of Some Prosobranchs.   Habits vary as greatly as shapes, ornamentation, and colors. Modern periwinkles *(Littorina)* and dog whelks *(Thais)* dwell on rocks that lie bare and dry at every low tide and are pounded by waves during storms. Olive shells crawl beneath the surface of loose sand, producing marking almost identical with some that are found in Pennsylvanian strata. Many other snails crawl on sandy or muddy bottoms, cling to submerged rocks, or creep over coral reefs. Creeping generally is done with the sole of the foot, which may also be covered with fine channels that serve as suckers with which the snail holds fast to shells or rocks. But *Strombus* and a few other prosobranchs have clawlike opercula that are thrust forward and hooked into sand or mud. Foot muscles then contract, pulling the animals forward.

Most prosobranchs now feed on algae, which they scrape from rocks or the sea bottom with their radulae. Moon snails and oyster drills, however, bore into other molluscs, whose flesh is then devoured. This, too, is a long-established habit, for bored molluscs are found in many Tertiary and Mesozoic formations, while bored brachiopods go back to the Late Ordovician. They suggest that Paleozoic carnivores preferred lamp shells to clams, but we cannot be sure, because our samples are quite uneven, or biased. Most early pelecypods are too poorly preserved to show borings even if the latter once were common.

Several carnivorous gastropods pry into pelecypods or barnacles by means of a tooth or spine on the outer tip of the shell. *Strombus* and others are scavengers that feed on dead fish and invertebrates.

Many limpets, which are prosobranchs whose shells no longer coil, spend most of their lives in particular resting-places, creeping forth at night to feed upon algae but returning before morning. After settling down, the gastropods cling so tightly that their shells grow to fit the spots in which they rest.

Fossil limpets may or may not have had this habit, but there is no doubt that some other prosobranchs had definite resting-places. Several species of *Platyceras* and *Cyclonema,* for example, clung to the sides or tops of crinoids so tightly that the gastropods fitted the contours of their hosts and even left marks upon them. Since these snails could not push through the barrier formed by the crinoids' arms and creep about eating algae, we conclude that the molluscs probably fed upon waste material discharged by their hosts.

An even more unusual prosobranch is *Vermicularia.* When it is young, its shell is a slender spire resembling that of *Turritella.* Then the mollusc ceases to coil and builds an irregular, twisted tube that is often mistaken for that of an annelid. *Vermicularia* tubes may be free or attached to other shells or rocks, and they often form tangled masses. *Helminthozyga* is a Pennsylvanian fossil that also became very loosely coiled.

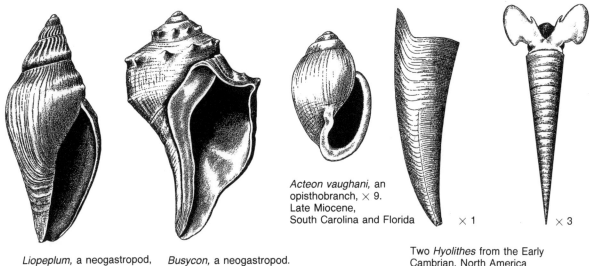

Liopeplum, a neogastropod,
× 1.6. This species is from
the Late Cretaceous,
Maryland to Texas

Busycon, a neogastropod.
This species is from the
Late Cretaceous, Tennessee

Acteon vaughani, an
opisthobranch, × 9.
Late Miocene,
South Carolina and Florida

Two Hyolithes from the Early
Cambrian, North America

Three snails and two Paleozoic fossils once thought to be pteropods (on right)

Mesogastropods and Neogastropods. Two other groups of the prosobranchs are recognized in addition to the archaeogastropods. One, the mesogastropods, first appeared in the Ordovician and are still extant. Again, they are recognized as a distinct group mainly on the basis of their soft parts. They have a single row of gills and a single auricle in the heart. Various groups within the mesogastropods are determined by the form of their radula. The shapes of the shells are quite variable, though many tend to be high-spired with many whorls. Mesogastropods are not very diverse during the Paleozoic when compared to the Mesozoic, particularly in the Cretaceous, and have continued to expand in the Cenozoic.

The neogastropods first appeared in the Cretaceous and have gills very much like those in the mesogastropods. They, like several mesogastropod families, have a tube called a siphon, which takes water into the mantle cavity, and usually a groove in the shell that houses this tube. In these two groups are many of the familiar marine gastropods of today, such as the high-spired *Turritella,* the delicate, spiny *Murex tribulus* (a prize of modern shell collectors), as well as other species of *Murex,* and the highly poisonous *Conus!*

Gastropods became diverse in the Early Ordovician and continued to flourish until the end of the Devonian. These early Paleozoic faunas were replaced by other groups that persisted until the end of the Triassic, affected somewhat by mass extinctions at the end of the Permian. By Cretaceous times the modern suite of forms gradually evolved, with increasing numbers of neogastropods and a lesser number of mesogastropods appearing. Most of these were not affected by the extinction events at the end of the Cretaceous. The dominance of these forms has continued into the Cenozoic and up to the present day.

247

OPISTHOBRANCHS: PROGRESS BY DEGENERATION

Acteon is an egg-shaped or slender gastropod whose varied species range from the Pierre and Bearpaw formations (Chapter II) to modern temperate seas. They also typify the opisthobranchs, a class that has progressed largely by degeneration. Some, such as *Acteon,* retain a well-developed shell, a mantle, and one gill, though it has twisted around to the rear; in other words, undergone detorsion and straightened itself out. In sea hares, the shell has become very small, and that of nudibranchs has vanished except from the embryo. Nudibranchs are unknown as fossils, but the group to which *Acteon* belongs appears in the Mississippian and continues to the present. Several species are useful index fossils in Late Cretaceous and Tertiary deposits, and it is in the Mesozoic and Cenozoic that this group is most varied. Shell shapes vary considerably, and though most have thin, delicate shells, a few have thickened ones suited for preservation in the fossil record. All are marine.

The Free-swimming Pteropods. The majority of pteropods are as bare and soft as nudibranchs, but others have thin, coiled, or conical shells. The head has become indistinct, but the foot is spread out in a pair of winglike fins *(pteropod* means "wing foot"), with which the animals swim. They are generally quite small, less than 0.5 inch (1 cm.) in length. Fossil pteropods are thin-shelled and slender; some have opercula to close their apertures.

The oldest pteropods are of Eocene age, and like their living relatives, they were part of the marine plankton of the time. Because of this, they had and have a wide geographic distribution.

Hyolithes, a Cambrian form, was once thought to be a pteropod. Today, however, we are uncertain of just where it belongs in a classification of the invertebrates. It may be somehow related to the molluscs but in a separate phylum.

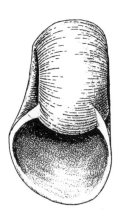

Helisoma, *a pulmonate, twice natural size. This freshwater snail now ranges from the Atlantic Coast to the Pacific and northward to Alaska. Helisoma also is a Pleistocene and Pliocene fossil*

PULMONATES: AIR-BREATHING MOLLUSCS

Anyone who has collected in a damp woodland knows that some snails and slugs live on land and breathe air. Freshwater snails share the latter habit, securing bubbles of air at the surface and using them when they submerge. In both groups, the gills have been lost and breathing is done with a lunglike organ developed from the mantle cavity. These gastropods are really the only molluscs that have made a success of living on land.

Freshwater pulmonates have shells, though they vary greatly in shape. There also are four tentacles on the head, with simple eyes at the base of the back pair. These snails may have evolved during the Paleozoic, but their known record begins in the Mesozoic. Several pulmonates are index fossils of Late Cretaceous rocks, and one characterizes the Morrison Formation, in which a great variety of North America's largest dinosaurs and early mammals have been found.

Many land snails retain their shells, which may be high-spired or low, thick or thin and brittle. A few slugs, such as *Helisoma,* however, have lost their shells completely, and in others they are reduced to thin plates that are hidden by the mantle.

Though pulmonates form only a minor part of the fossil record of snails and their kin, they have their own story to tell. Stephen Jay Gould, as a part of his work as a graduate student at Columbia University, in New York City, studied a large collection of fossil pulmonates that had lived over the past three hundred thousand years on the island of Bermuda. He was able to detect a number of small changes that occurred throughout this time in various populations of these small snails as they were repeatedly isolated on small islands around Bermuda when the sea level rose and fell during Pleistocene interglacials (warm periods) and glaciations. He was able to show that evolutionary changes occurred rapidly, not gradually, in his snails, which led to a new outlook on how evolution takes place. And so, in this case, the fossil record of a rather insignificant group led to the proposal of an important and exciting scientific idea.

CHAPTER XVI

Bivalves: Clams, Mussels, and Oysters

 Snails are the most widely distributed class among molluscs and the only ones that live upon land. Bivalves, or pelecypods, are more familiar, however, for they include such edible "shellfish" as oysters, scallops, and clams.

Here again, names become troublesome, for the molluscs called pelecypods in Canada and the United States are lamellibranchs in Europe and many other parts of the world. The former name means "hatchet foot" and refers to the characteristic shape of that organ. Lamellibranch, or "plate gill," aptly describes the structures with which many of these molluscs breathe.

Bivalves, named because two valves are present, first appear in the fossil record in the Early Cambrian. They are limited in diversity in the Paleozoic but expand in the Mesozoic. Today they are the dominant hard-shelled invertebrates in shallow marine environments.

WHAT IS A BIVALVE?

Bivalves are built on a plan that is both simpler and more complex than that of a primitive snail or chiton. Simplicity appears in the body, which has no head with its tentacles, eyes, and rasping radula. Complexity appears in the shell, which consists of two parts, or valves, that may resemble one another or may differ in function and shape.

The body has two sides, right and left, and is neither coiled like a typical snail nor spread out like a limpet. The foot still is the underpart of the body, but in all except some highly specialized forms, it has become narrow and hatchet-shaped or wedgelike, rather than broad and flat. The gills lie below the body proper, not above it, and range from leaf-shaped organs to folded sheets or even flattened rods. They are covered by two broad flaps of the mantle, which is pierced by holes for the muscles that are attached to the shell.

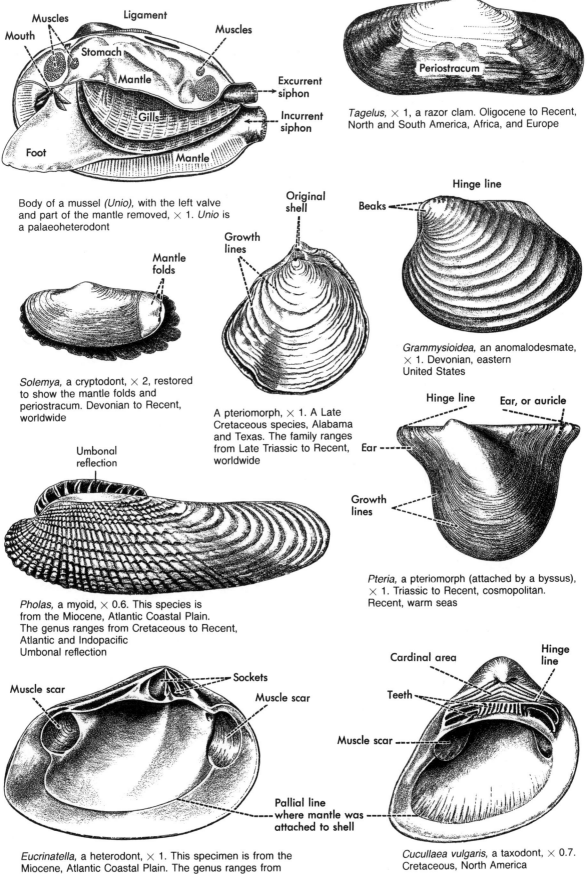

Muscles
Ligament
Mouth
Muscles
Stomach
Mantle
Gills
Excurrent siphon
Incurrent siphon
Foot
Mantle

Body of a mussel *(Unio)*, with the left valve and part of the mantle removed, × 1. *Unio* is a palaeoheterodont

Periostracum

Tagelus, × 1, a razor clam. Oligocene to Recent, North and South America, Africa, and Europe

Mantle folds

Solemya, a cryptodont, × 2, restored to show the mantle folds and periostracum. Devonian to Recent, worldwide

Original shell

Growth lines

A pteriomorph, × 1. A Late Cretaceous species, Alabama and Texas. The family ranges from Late Triassic to Recent, worldwide

Hinge line
Beaks

Grammysioidea, an anomalodesmate, × 1. Devonian, eastern United States

Umbonal reflection

Pholas, a myoid, × 0.6. This species is from the Miocene, Atlantic Coastal Plain. The genus ranges from Cretaceous to Recent, Atlantic and Indopacific Umbonal reflection

Hinge line
Ear, or auricle
Ear
Growth lines

Pteria, a pteriomorph (attached by a byssus), × 1. Triassic to Recent, cosmopolitan. Recent, warm seas

Muscle scar
Sockets
Muscle scar

Pallial line where mantle was attached to shell

Eucrinatella, a heterodont, × 1. This specimen is from the Miocene, Atlantic Coastal Plain. The genus ranges from Cretaceous to Miocene, Europe and North America

Cardinal area
Hinge line
Teeth
Muscle scar

Cucullaea vulgaris, a taxodont, × 0.7. Cretaceous, North America

Structures of bivalves

Varied Methods of Feeding. Since bivalves cannot devour large creatures, they dine on microscopic organisms in the water from which their gills
take oxygen. This means that each animal must bring water into the cavity
covered by its mantle, must remove food and reject or excrete sand or mud,
and must take the food to its mouth while it gets rid of rubbish, waste, and
water from which oxygen has been removed. These tasks are performed by
organs that vary with the habits of various bivalves.

We see these organs at their simplest in *Solemya* and its primitive relatives, of Devonian to Recent age. The mantle is folded into two indistinct
channels inside the hinder part of the shell. Beating cilia produce a current
that brings water into the lower, or incurrent, channel and takes it over the
gills. There the blood absorbs oxygen and gives up waste, both of which
pass easily through the thin gill membranes. At the same time, food is caught
on sticky mucus that covers the gills and is carried to the mouth. Another
current takes sand, mud, waste, and "used" water into the upper (excurrent)
channel and so back to the sea.

In more advanced pelecypods, and especially in those that burrow, the
channels become tubes called siphons, which may be separate or covered by
a tough sheath of skin. Lengthwise muscles shorten the siphons or pull them
into the shell when danger threatens; other muscles can close the tubes and
so keep mud or sand out of the mantle cavity. Further protection is given by
the mantle itself, whose muscular edges may close its two lobes much as
muscles close our lips. The edges may also fuse, forming an envelope whose
only openings are the siphons and a slit through which the foot can project.

The giant clam *(Tridacna)* lives on coral reefs where low tides expose
most of its shell though high tides cover it. As water returns, the valves open
and the mantle spreads out in thick, beautifully multicolored folds containing algae that grow in the flesh and use energy from sunlight and carbon
dioxide to make food. The clam and the algae have a symbiotic relationship,
for each benefits the other.

Tridacna is found in Tertiary rocks; the fossil molluscs may or may not
have grown algae in their mantles. But there is no doubt about the feeding
habits of some ancient clams that bored in wood, like modern "shipworms."
As they burrowed, they scraped the wood into powder, which would have
filled their holes had it not been devoured. We may safely assume that the
fossils digested cellulose, just as their relatives do today.

THE BIVALVE SHELL

Most fossil bivalves are shells, though casts and internal or external
molds are common, some even preserved in opaline silica. Modern shells,
like those of gastropods, generally contain three layers. The horny periostracum ranges from thin to thick; it covers a limy layer that generally con-

Ostrea, a pteriomorph, × 1.
Cretaceous to Recent, worldwide
in nonpolar seas

?Pterotrigonia, a schizodont,
× 1. Late Cretaceous, Oregon

Unio, a palaeoheterodont, × 1.
This species is from the Late
Cretaceous, Montana. The genus
ranges from Triassic to Recent,
Eurasia and Africa

Lopha, a pteriomorph. Triassic
to Recent, generally restricted
to the tropics or subtropics.
Small to medium size, up to about
4 inches (11 cm.) long

Venus, a heterodont, interior of
left valve, × 1. The genus ranges
from Oligocene to Recent,
Eurasia, North America

Venus, × 1. This specimen is
from the Miocene,
Atlantic Coastal Plain

Ostrea, a pteriomorph.
Length of this species is
to 50 inches (1.3 m.).
Miocene, California

Chlamys (Lyropecten), a pteriomorph, × 0.5.
This species is from the Miocene, Virginia
to Florida and California. The genus
ranged from Miocene to Pliocene, eastern
Pacific and West Atlantic

Some freshwater (Unio) *and saltwater bivalves*

Types of burrowing bivalves. All are fossils, restored to correspond to related living species. 1. Crassatella; 2. Tellina; 3. Macoma; 4. Mactra; 5. Ensis; 6. Martesia; 7. Pholas. *Incurrent and excurrent siphons are marked by arrows showing directions in which currents flow*

sists of needles and angular prisms of calcite, which may look like coarse fibers in weathered fossils such as the thick-shelled *Inoceramus*. The inner layer contains thin sheets of calcite or aragonite, which may alternate with material that resembles the periostracum. If the limy sheets are thick and smooth they resemble china; if they are thin and crumpled they appear lustrous and are known as mother-of-pearl. Though pearly luster is sometimes found in fossils, neither it nor the china-like appearance usually survives petrifaction. Besides these three typical layers, at least three more are known in bivalves. The combination of these layers and number present are useful in figuring out the relationships of these animals.

Shell Changes and Structures. The bivalve shell begins as a convex plate that divides into two smooth and almost circular valves. If growth were uniform, this shape would persist, but growth takes place at various rates and in different directions. Because of this, the valves generally become convex, forming umbos that stand out prominently when curvature is reduced and the shell begins to spread. Each umbo terminates in a beak whose tip would be the original shell were the latter not worn away.

The beak may come close to the hinge line, along which the two valves are joined. On the other hand, each valve may have an intervening cardinal area that is either flat or convex. The general surface may be smooth except for growth lines, which mark "resting periods" determined by low temperature, lack of food, or reproductive activity. Generally, however, growth lines are combined with radial ridges or wrinkles, concentric ridges, frills, or spines. The hinge line may also be prolonged by ears, or auricles, which are specially well developed in the shells of scallops *(Pecten).*

254

Shells vary greatly in size; some are no larger than a pinhead, but others are very large. The most massive is *Tridacna,* which reaches a width of 54 inches (1.3 m.) and a weight of 500 pounds (about 225 kg.) *Haploscapha,* from the Late Cretaceous of Kansas, is not so heavy but is as much as 3.3 feet (1 m.) wide and 5 feet (1.5 m.) long. The life span of these giants is unknown, but many modern clams of moderate size live eight to eighteen years.

Internal Structures. The bivalve shell, like that of any other shell-bearing mollusc, is built up by the mantle. This is firmly attached to the inner surface of both valves, but its edges are always free. Attachment ends at the pallial line, which shows plainly in most modern and fossil species but can be indistinct in some. If there are siphons, the pallial line curves round them, and the depth of the curve (called the pallial sinus) shows whether the siphons are small or large. Since long siphons go with burrowing life, the sinus gives a clue to the habits of many fossils. This clue, however, should be supported by shape of shell, relationships, and other evidence.

Most bivalve shells also show one or two rough scars that serve as attachment for muscles that close the shell. Since they do this by pulling the valves together, the muscles are called adductors. The scallops we eat are adductor muscles of pelecypods belonging to the genus *Pecten,* which has already been mentioned because of its auricles.

Hinges, Teeth, and Opening Devices. A shell with loosely joined valves can be useful; we have found shells of just that sort in *Lingula* and other

Some free-moving and attached bivalves, restored. 1. Lima *swimming (L. reticulata, Miocene, Maryland)* 2. Cardium *thrusting out its foot to pull itself forward* (C. coosense, *Miocene to Recent, Pacific coast)* 3. Cornellites *lying on the bottom* (C. flabella, *Devonian, eastern U.S.A.)* 4. Anomia *cemented to a shell* (A. micronema, *Late Cretaceous, western North America)* 5. Mytilus *attached by a cluster of threads, or byssus* (M. conradinus, *Miocene, New Jersey to Texas)* 6. Byssonychia *attached by byssus* (B. radiata, *Late Ordovician, eastern U.S.A.)* 7–8. *Two twisted forms cemented to dead shells* 7. Toucasia patagiata, *Early Cretaceous, Texas and Mexico;* 8. Monopleura texana, *Early Cretaceous, Texas and Mexico*

× 3

Martesia, a pholadacean. Shell and shell in tube. Jurassic to Recent, worldwide, nonpolar seas

Exogyra, a pteriomorph, × 1. Early to Late Cretaceous, nearly worldwide except South America and Australia

× 1.5

Gryphaea, a pteriomorph, up to 7 inches (about 16 cm.) long. This species is from the Early Jurassic, Europe

Exogyra, a pteriomorph, × 0.5. This species is Late Cretaceous, New Jersey to Mexico

Venericardia planicosta, a heterodont, × 0.5. Eocene, Europe

Myalina, a pteriomorph, × 0.5. Pennsylvanian, southwestern U.S.A. The genus ranged from Carboniferous to Permian, worldwide

Some free-living, attached, and tube-building bivalves

primitive brachiopods. But bivalve valves are all hinged, and in most genera the hinge is strengthened by projecting teeth and sockets into which they fit, thus locking the valves together when the adductors contract. Both teeth and sockets are arranged in patterns that differ in the major groups.

Though bivalve shells must be closed by muscles, most of them are automatically opened by structures called the ligament and the resilium. The former is a tough and sometimes very thick band that runs from valve to valve above the hinge, but the resilium is a spongy pad between two limy plates inside the shell. When the latter is closed, the pad is compressed; when the muscles relax, the pad expands, forcing the valves to open.

A strange specialization is found in *Pholas* and its kin (piddocks and angel wings), whose fossils date back to the early Tertiary. *Pholas* has lost its ligament, and one adductor muscle has moved outside the shell. There it is attached to plates whose curvature is opposite to that of the valves. When this muscle contracts, it opens the shell instead of closing it.

Classification of the Bivalves. Paleontologists have always found bivalves somewhat difficult to classify and to relate to one another, but not as difficult as the snails. The main reason for this is that bivalve shells have

256

on them a limited number of clues to relationships, a recurring problem with fossils. At the higher levels of classification, such as the subclass, the soft parts, such as the gill structure, are more useful for determining relationships. But, of course, in fossils, these parts are not usually preserved. Often, too, shells can be recrystallized during petrification, so that it is sometimes hard to decide whether the shell was originally made of calcite or of aragonite. Fortunately, at the family-genus-species level, classification is not such a problem, and shell shape can often provide enough information.

One classification that is used widely today takes several characters into account: the microstructure of the shell, the nature of the hinge area of the shell, as well as the nature of soft parts such as the gills and the stomach. Six subclasses are recognized in this scheme. The paleotoxodonts are small forms with leaflike (protobranch) gills, a hinge line with numerous teeth that lie parallel to one another (taxodont dentition), and an aragonitic shell. They are "infauna," living and feeding within the sediments. *Nucula* is a typical genus in this group, which ranges from Ordovician to Recent and is thought to be relatively primitive within the bivalve group.

Cryptodonts have also lived from the Ordovician to the present day. They generally lack teeth, or have only very simple teeth near the edge of the articular part of the shell (dysodont). They also have aragonitic shells and live in the sediments. Today only *Solemya* represents the group, which reached its peak in the Paleozoic.

The pteriomorphs first appeared in the Ordovician and still live in today's oceans. They are quite a variable group that commonly developed byssal threads (the byssus) as organs of attachment in the adult. They have both calcitic and aragonitic shells, and include such familiar genera as *Mytilus* (the mussels), *Pecten, Inoceramus, Ostrea* (oysters), and *Exogyra.*

Another Ordovician-to-Recent group is Palaeoheterodonta. Bivalves in this group have either heterodont or schizodont teeth in the hinge area. Heterodonts generally have two or three large (cardinal) teeth just below the umbo, and long lateral teeth both in front of and behind the cardinal teeth. Schizodont teeth occur only in one group, which includes *Neotrigonia,* a living fossil found off the Australian coast. Close relatives of it were long known in North American and European Mesozoic rocks before early French explorers dredged it still alive off Australia's southeast coast in the early-nineteenth century. Also in this subclass are the unionids, heterodont nonmarine clams.

Heterodonts first appeared in the Ordovician and are the most abundant of modern shallow- and deepwater bivalves. The hinges are either heterodont or desmodont, the latter where the teeth are very small or missing. Ridges that run parallel to the hinge margin can take the place of the teeth. Heterodonts nearly all have aragonitic shells and have become especially varied as infaunal forms that feed through an elongate tube, the siphon, which extends above the sediment to collect food by filter feeding, leaving the clam protected in the sediment. *Mya, Pholas,* and *Venus* are examples.

Another group of burrowing clams and boring forms is Anomalodesmata. The first of these turn up in Triassic rocks and have continued to today, including, for example, *Pholadomya.* They have desmodont dentition and aragonitic shells.

Fossil History. Though *Fordilla* (known from North America and Eurasia) is the first known bivalve and occurs in the Early Cambrian, it wasn't until the Early Ordovician that bivalves began to diversify. As is true for the whole phylum Mollusca, bivalves were of low diversity and of small size until the end of the Cambrian—then a second, major radiation of forms took place. The first bivalves lived in the sediments, but by the Ordovician there were both infaunal and epifaunal types that had moved into several kinds of feeding styles. One lifestyle that gave the bivalves a great advantage over articulate brachiopods was burrowing very efficiently with the foot. Some burrowers also developed elongate siphons at the end of the Paleozoic that made it possible for them to bury themselves quite deep and still feed from the water above. With such structural changes, they successfully invaded the intertidal environment that was often churned by waves or left open to the air at low tide. Deep or rapid burrowing made them ideal pioneers in this hostile land, and very successful pioneers they were, as told by their great expansion during the past 200 million years.

Despite their success, bivalve genera and species are often very long-ranging and so not always useful to the paleontologist wishing to date rocks. They are generally used only on a broad scale. But there are exceptions, such as the nonmarine-bivalve zones of the Carboniferous, the *Buchia* zonation of the mid-Jurassic and Early Cretaceous, and the inoceramid divisions of the Cretaceous. Certainly their greatest use lies in paleoecology, for their shell form, as we have seen earlier, can give a very good clue to their lifestyle and the environmental conditions around them when they lived.

Rostroconchs. Rostroconchs were a small Paleozoic (Early Cambrian to Permian) group of molluscs that were quite tiny. They ranged from a few millimeters to a few centimeters and superficially resembled bivalves. They probably were similar to bivalves internally as well and apparently had a functioning foot. They differed, however, in that they lacked a proper hinge on the shell. Though they had two valves, or shells, the shell layers continued right across the hinge area. In some advanced forms, such as *Conocardium,* however, the outer shell layer did not cross the hinge. Because of this, some paleontologists, especially J. Pojeta and B. Runnegar, have suggested that this might be a step in the direction toward bivalves and have set up the class Rostroconchia to emphasize the distinctiveness of this group. Some scientists even make a further suggestion: that rostroconchs may have had ancestors among the monoplacophorans. Perhaps, then, the rostroconchs gave rise to the bivalves and possibly the scaphopods. More work will need to be done before we really understand the varied array of molluscan animals that lived in the Cambrian and probably before. Localities with beautifully preserved silica replicas, such as Mootwingee, in the Middle Cambrian Coonigan Formation, of western New South Wales, will continue to shed light on this very interesting phase of rapid change within the Mollusca, and offer a satisfying explanation of rostroconch relationship.

Though bivalves lived during Cambrian times, they did not become common until the Middle Ordovician. The most primitive group, called palaeotaxodonts, is characterized by thin, elongate valves and hinges in which the teeth are poorly developed or lacking. Modern representatives have small, leaflike gills much like those of gastropods and chitons.

Shells and Feet for Creeping. Palaeotaxodonts established a basic pattern from which their successors could and often did diverge. The changes that were most easily made added strength to the shell, improved it as armor, or reduced the labor of crawling. During the Ordovician Period, several bivalves shortened and thickened their shells and added teeth to their hinges. Others, of Ordovician to Devonian age, became elongate and wedgelike, with narrow lower margins. Such shells were able to slip through mud with a minimum of friction.

We often think of creeping in terms of pushing, but bivalves are built to pull. The foot is thrust forward and gets a hold in soft mud or sand; strong muscles then are contracted, pulling the shell forward. The result generally is a slow, halting form of progress, but some creepers can contract their muscles so quickly that they actually jump forward. *Cardium* is able to do this, and so do some burrowers when they are at the surface. Razor clams *(Solen* and *Tagelus)* sometimes leap 10 to 12 inches (25–30 cm.)

Nestling and Burrowing. Burrowing is a way of life that has developed several times in various groups of bivalves. We see one early stage in *Encrintella (Crassatellites),* which nestles in a pit that is dug by shifting the shell from one side to the other. The quahogs *(Venus)* go a little further: they dig down until most of the shell is covered, though the hind part and short siphons are exposed. *Mya,* the soft-shelled, or sand, clam, is completely buried and its siphons are a good deal longer than the shell. As *Mya* burrows, its shell moves from side to side, cutting its way through the sand.

Macoma also burrows in muddy sand. One species, *M. nasuta,* lies on its left side and sends up a long incurrent siphon that moves about over the sand, sucking up slimy food. When no more can be found, the siphon is pulled back and thrust up through the sand to a new feeding ground. The excurrent siphon, which is short, discharges its wastes below the surface.

Many bivalves are able to dig very rapidly. Some of these have thick shells and live in sand; *Venus* is a good example. Razor clams *(Solen, Ensis, Tagelus,* and *Siliqua)* dig almost vertically in sand and have siphons of various lengths. One species of *Siliqua* burrows in sandy beaches along the Pacific coast. When the water is quiet it stays near the surface, but as storm waves crash or ground swells roll in, *Siliqua* pulls itself down below the danger zone.

Boring Clams and "Shipworms." No clam ever bothered its missing head with the difference between burrowing and boring. We take the former to mean digging, chiefly with the foot, in sediment that has not become compact. Borers, however, wear their way through firmly packed clay, shells, wood, concrete, and granite.

Piddocks and angel wings belong to a family that bores into firm sand or clay and rocks that range from crumbly sandstone to granite. An early stage is seen in *Pholadidea,* which fastens its suckerlike foot to some firm surface and then moves the shell up and down. Its forward portion is covered with ridges that scrape away the surrounding clay or stone. Some members of the family keep on boring and growing throughout their lives. Others reach their full size, cover the sucker foot with shell, and spend the rest of their lives feeding and reproducing.

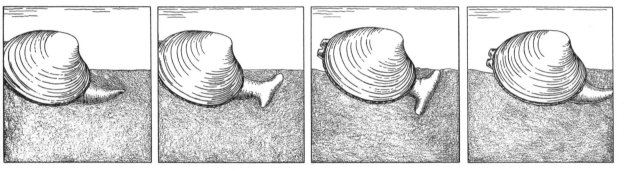

| A creeping clam pushes its foot through mud or sand | Then the tip of the foot begins to swell into an anchor | Muscles in the foot contract, pulling the body forward | Soon the foot is pushed out and the process begins again |

Lithophaga, the date clam, attaches itself with a cluster of threads and secretes a calcium complexing compound that dissolves the rock and living corals into which this creature bores. The periostracum is very thick, protecting the shell's layers.

"Shipworms" are not worms at all; they are clams whose valves are often quite small and have become small rasping organs and two little plates that seem to protect the siphons. The young shipworm hatches in the spring, swims for a week or two, and then settles down on a sunken log or some other form of wood. Into this the clam bores, making a tube which it lines with a thin calcareous layer. When shipworms are common, they fill large timbers with their borings, making the wood so weak that it crumbles under the impact of waves.

Martesia includes bivalves related to *Pholas,* though they do not resemble it. They have well-developed shells, which are used for boring while the clams are young. Later the valves are cemented together and to a calcareous tube that is built around the siphons. *Martesia* shells and tubes are found as fossils in brackish-water deposits along the Two Medicine River, of Montana (Chapter II), as well as in other formations.

Anthraconaia ("Anthracomya")
elongata, a pteriomorph, × 4.
Pennsylvanian, Europe.
The genus is restricted to
the Carboniferous of Eurasia

Naiadites carbonarius, a pteriomorph,
with byssus restored, × 1.5. Late
Carboniferous of Scotland

Archanodon catskillensis,
a palaeoheterodont,
× 0.5. Middle and Late Devonian,
Pennsylvania and New York

Three freshwater mussels of Late Paleozoic age

Scallops and Swimming Clams. Pteropods swim by flapping their feet, and some other gastropods swim or use their expanded feet as rafts. Some bivalves are swimmers too, but they propel themselves by opening and closing their shells.

A number of groups invented this process. The family of pectens began with forms which had a straight hinge line, pointed auricles, and a right valve that generally was deeper than the left. Species with equal valves may have crawled, but others lay on the sea bottom. In time, some of their descendants began to fasten themselves to seaweeds or shells with threads—the byssus—which emerged from a notch under one auricle. Others took to opening their shells and snapping them shut, thus forcing water out quickly. The result was a jerky type of swimming in which the creatures moved with

Plagioptychus partschi, *a rudistid heterodont "clam" that grew upright with one valve as a lidlike structure covering the body,* **× 0.5.** *Cretaceous of Austria. This group superficially looked like corals, a case of convergent evolution toward a similar lifestyle*

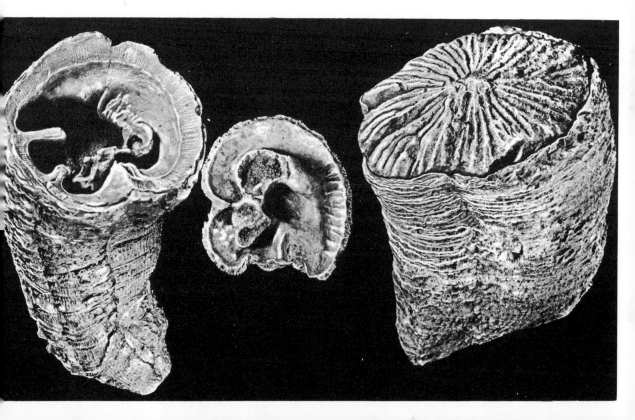

the hinge line forward, but only as an escape strategy, not a way of life. Shell shape indicates that late Paleozoic species of *Aviculopecten* swam in this way, as do *Pecten* and its relatives in Recent seas. Their mantles are fringed with tentacles and bear eyespots that seem to give warning of approaching danger.

Lima, the other swimmer, is known as a fossil and still lives in both the Atlantic and the Pacific oceans. Is tentacles are many and long, though the shell seldom reaches 2 inches (5 cm.) in length. When some spieces are not swimming, they settle down in cavities and secrete tough threads which are tangled into nests open at both ends. A food-bearing current enters one end and waste goes out at the other.

Attachment by Threads and Cement.   Pectens were not the first molluscs to develop a byssus; this structure appeared in the Ordovician *Byssonychia,* whose anterior margin bears a wide notch through which the threads emerged. A byssus also is found in *Mytilus* and other sea mussels, in jingles *(Anomia),* in the young of *Tridacna,* and in several other groups. One of these, the Pteriidae, ranges from the Devonian to Recent and includes modern pearl oysters as well as ancient shells that superficially resemble *Aviculopecten.* The Pernidae, also byssus bearers, include such important Mesozoic genera as *Gervilliopsis* and *Inoceramus.* Juvenile bivalves of many types also secrete byssal threads for initial attachment.

Threads of the byssus are spun by a gland on the foot, which is slender and reaches out to fasten each thread into place. Some spinners, such as *Mytilus,* move about by placing one thread far ahead, dissolving the base of the other threads, and then pulling shell and body forward. In *Anomia,* however, the byssus becomes a horny plug or is calcified, and the right valve grows around it. Such shells are firmly attached for the rest of their lives.

Oysters typify the attached, or sessile, bivalves. After a brief clamlike existence, *Ostrea* attaches itself to a rock, a shell, or a sunken log, to which the left valve is cemented; it thereupon becomes longer, wider, and deeper than the right, which sometimes is not much more than a lid covering the cavity filled by the body. *Ostrea* appeared in Triassic seas, became plentiful during Cretaceous times, and is widespread today. Both eastern and Pacific North American species are found in Pleistocene deposits. The former, *Ostrea virginica,* grew as much as 15 inches (nearly 40 cm.) long in days before white men began to gather and sell it for food.

ABERRANT BOTTOM DWELLERS

Oysters are not "normal" bivalves, since they live on one side and have shells that are much higher than they are long. Other bivalves became still more abnormal, developing valves that coiled like snails or even assumed the shape of horn corals.

Exogyra costata *(left) and* Gryphaea mutabilis *(right), two Late Cretaceous mol-*
luscs related to oysters. They are shown as they lived on the sea bottom in what is
now McNairy County, Tennessee

Gryphaea and Exogyra. We first find coiling in *Gryphaea* and *Exogyra,*
two members of the oyster family that appeared in shallow Jurassic seas.
Like true oysters, they first developed smooth, symmetrical shells that
looked as if they were destined to creep or burrow just beneath the surface.
Soon, however, these "spats" settled down upon the left valve, which then
grew much more rapidly than the right. In early species of *Gryphaea,* the left
valve first assumed the form of a primitive snail shell, but with further
growth became massive and coiled. It also broke loose from its attachment
and sat on the mud, where weight and shape kept it in its original position.
The right valve became a flattened plate that could be raised or lowered to
open or close the shell.

During Late Cretaceous times, large species of *Gryphaea* lost most of their
tendency to coil and became cup- or bowl-shaped. Some individuals still
broke away from the shells to which they had been cemented, but others
remained attached throughout life. Shells of both types are plentiful in formations of the Atlantic and Gulf coastal plains of North America, the latter
extending as far northward as Tennessee.

Exogyra differs from *Gryphaea* in having an indistinct tooth on the hinge,
a very narrow pit for the ligament, and valves that are always spirally

coiled. The left valve generally is much larger and thicker than that of *Gryphaea.* In large species—some exceed 6 inches (15 cm.) in height—the shell is marked by costae and growth lines that extend into laminae.

The left valves of *Exogyra* range from short or loose spirals to massive structures that are closely coiled at the beak. Most shells seem to have outgrown the bases to which they were cemented, and some evidently broke loose in the manner of *Gryphaea.* Others became so large and so heavy that they sank into the mud, tipping enough to bring their flat right, or upper, valve into a horizontal position. Surprisingly few valves are distorted by contact with other shells. Though *Exogyra* was abundant in many places, it apparently did not grow in such closely packed colonies as those formed by modern oysters.

Double Spirals and Cones.   Though both valves of *Exogyra* are spirals, the right one is virtually flat. Other bivalves developed shells that were spirally coiled and almost equal, so that complete shells look rather like two snails clinging lip to lip. Having achieved this form, some genera went on to turn one valve—either left or right—into a massive spiral, horn-shaped, or conical structures that lay or stood upright on the sea bottom, while the other valve became little more than a plate covering the body. Several of these strange shells are important Cretaceous index fossils in Texas, New Mexico, and Mexico.

Most remarkable of all are the rudistids, which lost all trace of coiling. The lower valve became conical—a complex structure composed of plates and layers that looked like a rugose coral and sometimes reached 40 inches (102 cm.) in length. The upper valve was reduced to a mere lid whose under-surface bore very long teeth that projected into sockets in the lower valve. Rudistids are limited to the Late Jurassic and Cretaceous and are more plentiful in Europe than in North America, where they form sizable reefs.

FROM SALT TO FRESH WATER

Bivalves appeared in the sea, and throughout the ages most of them have lived in that environment. Some, however, moved into brackish bays and, during Devonian times, adapted themselves to life in fresh water. One well-known genus, *Archanodon,* contained slender thin-shelled clams about 3 inches (about 8 cm.) long. It lived in streams that crossed the great Catskill Delta, which spread across Pennsylvania and New York during the Middle and Late Devonian.

While *Archanodon* and its offspring crept in streams, related forms called *Naiadites* developed a byssus and fastened themselves to submerged logs. Their shells are found among the famous Pennsylvanian fern nodules of Mazon Creek, Illinois, as well as in Ohio and Nova Scotia. In the last region they are mingled with other genera, one of which *("Anthracomya")* resembles a tiny horse clam.

Most of our modern freshwater clams, or mussels, belong to the genera *Unio* and *Anodonta*. Fossils from Triassic formations of Massachusetts, Pennsylvania, and the Southwest once were referred to the former genus, but they now seem to belong to other types that survive only in South America. *Unio* apparently developed in Triassic Europe or Asia, reached North America in the Late Jurassic, and has thrived on this continent ever since. Fossils are found in beds containing bones of the great Jurassic dinosaurs, as well as in Cretaceous and later formations. Though some shells were preserved, most specimens are only internal molds. As a tool in prospecting, unionids are a good sign to those paleontologists searching for terrestrial vertebrates. They signal past environmental conditions that could have trapped and preserved these remains as fossils.

CHAPTER XVII

Feet Before Heads: the Nautiloids and Their Relatives

Fishermen in the southwestern Pacific often set woven bamboo traps to catch molluscs of the genus *Nautilus*. They have ivory-white and reddish-brown shells, eyes with pinholes that focus light, and about ninety soft arms that are used in crawling or are stretched out to capture food. Their flesh is boiled or made into soup, and their shells bring good prices from collectors.

Nautilus is the lone survivor of a much larger group that met with success by moving into a lifestyle utilized by few others at the time: that of an active hunter, particularly of prey in the open water. They were able to do this mainly because of the buoyancy of their shells and their specialized "jet propulsion" system discussed later in this chapter. They did this at a time when there was an explosion of organisms that made their living as suspension feeders, in the Early Ordovician—and which served as the nautiloids' prey. These times were certainly a change over the Cambrian, when deposit feeders were dominant and mostly tied to the sea bottom.

NAUTILUS, A SAMPLE CEPHALOPOD

Nautilus is more than an unusual and beautiful shell; it also is a sample of an entirely marine class of molluscs known as cephalopods. Their name, which means "head foot," makes sense when we realize that the arms actually are elongate sections of a highly specialized foot. It and the head have come together, so that the arms lie in front of the eyes and cluster around the mouth.

Other features distinguish this cephalopod from molluscs such as snails. Its mouth still contains a radula, but it also is equipped with horny, parrot-like jaws or beaks that are used for biting. The head region is well developed, with an impressive brain and sophisticated eyes. The mantle is wrapped around the body and encloses a cavity that contains the anus and four leaflike gills. The arms, or tentacles, are parts of the foot; they stretch out to seize food and pull it to the mouth and are used in crawling or anchoring. But when *Nautilus* needs to move swiftly, it fills the mantle cavity with water and squirts it out through a tube, or funnel, below the body and arms. This funnel also is part of the foot and consists of two fleshy flaps that fold together, forming a tapering tube. Jets of water driven from it enable *Nautilus* to swim quickly, but jerkily. If the funnel (also called a hyponome) points forward, its owner swims backward, but when the tube is turned to the rear, the creature darts ahead. This is generally done to capture unwary fish or other food.

The Many-chambered Shell.   The shell of *Nautilus* suggests a large, narrow snail coiled in one plane, but that resemblance is superficial. Its outer part (the wall) has a surface layer that resembles china, a middle layer that is pearly, or nacreous, and an inner one that is clear. The first and second of these layers are formed by the mantle, but the third is secreted by a continu-

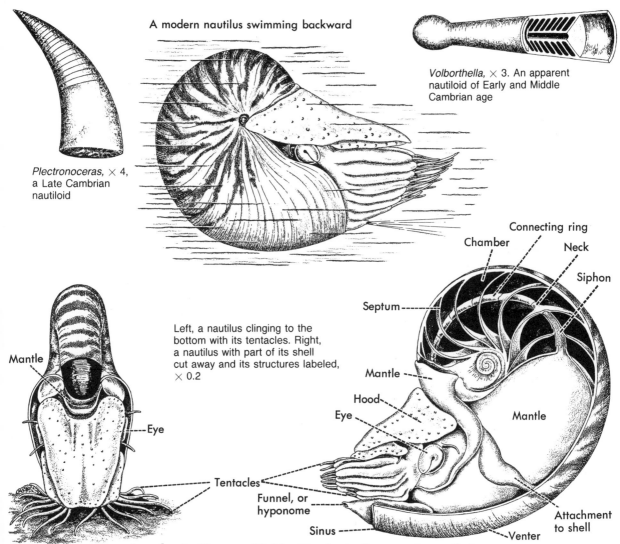

A modern nautilus swimming backward

Volborthella, × 3. An apparent nautiloid of Early and Middle Cambrian age

Plectronoceras, × 4, a Late Cambrian nautiloid

Left, a nautilus clinging to the bottom with its tentacles. Right, a nautilus with part of its shell cut away and its structures labeled, × 0.2

Connecting ring
Chamber
Neck
Siphon
Septum
Mantle
Hood
Eye
Mantle
Mantle
Tentacles
Funnel, or hyponome
Sinus
Venter
Attachment to shell
Eye

Recent and primitive nautiloids. The tentacles are also called arms

ous ring of muscles that fasten body to shell. All three, however, consist of aragonite.

Still greater differences appear in the way the shell is built. A snail's shell is undivided; if we could unroll it, it would form one irregular, but continuous, cone. The shell of *Nautilus,* however, is generally divided into thirty or more chambers (or camerae) that are separated by pearly partitions called septa. Each septum is secreted by the mantle at the back of the body, cutting off the abandoned part of the shell from the living chamber. As *Nautilus* grows, the mantle builds the living chamber forward while the hind part of the body becomes more and more cramped. At last muscles establish a new line of attachment, the old one is released, and the animal slips forward. This leaves an empty space at the rear, but it is soon closed off by another septum.

Siphon and Siphuncle.   We have said that the shell is empty behind the living chamber, but that is not quite true. As the body moves forward, a fleshy stalk, or siphon, remains and the septum is built around it in a backwardly directed neck. This is not very long, but a connecting ring secreted by the siphon continues to the septum behind. Necks and rings together form a tube, the siphuncle, that runs back through chamber after chamber to the very beginning of the shell. So does the siphon, which is well supplied with blood vessels and seems to carry gas into the chambers. Liquid, called cameral fluid, can also be added or removed from the chambers in much the same way—thus making the shell heavier or lighter.

The connecting rings of *Nautilus* are thin and disappear when the animal dies. In many fossils, however, they were thickened by deposits of aragonite. The result was siphuncles that often outlasted walls and septa, with shapes that can be used to distinguish genera and species.

FROM SIMPLE SNAIL TO CEPHALOPOD

Doctors often disagree, and those who classify cephalopods are not exceptions to that rule. Yet many in the past seem to be unanimous in saying that the ancestor of these creatures differed in no essential respect from a primitive cap-shaped snail. It was supposed to have had a flat creeping foot, a mouth at the front, and gills and anus at the rear. It was thought to creep over firm but muddy bottoms, instead of living on rocks in the manner of modern limpets.

As ages passed, the descendants of this pioneer developed deeper and deeper bodies. This meant that the foot shortened and the digestive tract curved sharply, while the shell became conical or slightly horn-shaped to fit the ever deepening body. Still later, the foot began to curve upward, the mantel secreted a few septa, and part of the body extended through them, forming a primitive siphon. In the final stage of our hypothetical sequence, the digestive tract bent into a V, and the siphon and shell became elongate. The foot continued to grow around the head, dividing into arms and two flaps that curved toward each other. When they met, they formed the funnel, with which the newly evolved cephalopod swam when crawling became too slow. So went the story until an American paleontologist, E. L. Yochelson, and his colleagues came upon a very interesting little fossil. The fossil was *Knightoconus antarcticus,* from the Late Cambrian of a most unlikely place today, West Antarctica. It was a monoplacophoran with a high, slightly curved conical shell, and was distinct in having a few septa near the apex. All that was needed to make this into a nautiloid was the development of the siphuncle, so characteristic of cephalopods. So it seems that cephalopods, including nautiloids, as well as snails (see Chapter XV), were all drawn from the ancient monoplacophorans.

THE VARIED AND LONG-LIVED NAUTILOIDS

Nautilus is both a typical cephalopod and the only surviving member of the subclass Nautiloidea. Though its members differ enormously, nautiloids are all similar in having relatively simple septa, which generally resemble watch glasses with the concave side forward or are relatively shallow cones. Each septum arches backward below the funnel, forming a hyponomic sinus. Each septum produces a line, or suture, where it joins the wall. The suture may be straight except for an indentation at the sinus, or it may be variously curved. Some forms, such as the early Tertiary *Aturia,* had septa as complex as some Paleozoic goniatitic ammonites.

At one time, the oldest known nautiloid was thought to be *Volborthella,* from Early Cambrian rocks of northern Europe and Canada. *Volborthella* had a straight calcareous shell a few millimeters long. It lacked septa and had radial, not bilateral, symmetry. The shell was made of laminar structures that were formed of fragments and detrital grains. Yochelson was able to describe this fine internal structure because of new, well-preserved fossils found in Norway. A specialist on early molluscs, Yochelson further suggested that both the Volborthellidae and another group, the Salterellidae, should be put in a separate, new phylum, which he called the Agmata, distinct from the molluscs.

Some paleontologists accept *Plectronoceras,* of the Late Cambrian, as the oldest and simplest nautiloid. *Plectronoceras* is curved instead of straight, with a deep living chamber and closely spaced septa that are curved like tiny watch glasses. The siphuncle is near the lower side, not at the center of the shell.

The soft parts of these and other early cephalopods are unknown, for none has been found among carbonized films. But we may safely assume that the animals looked much like *Nautilus,* with eyes that had narrow slits ending in

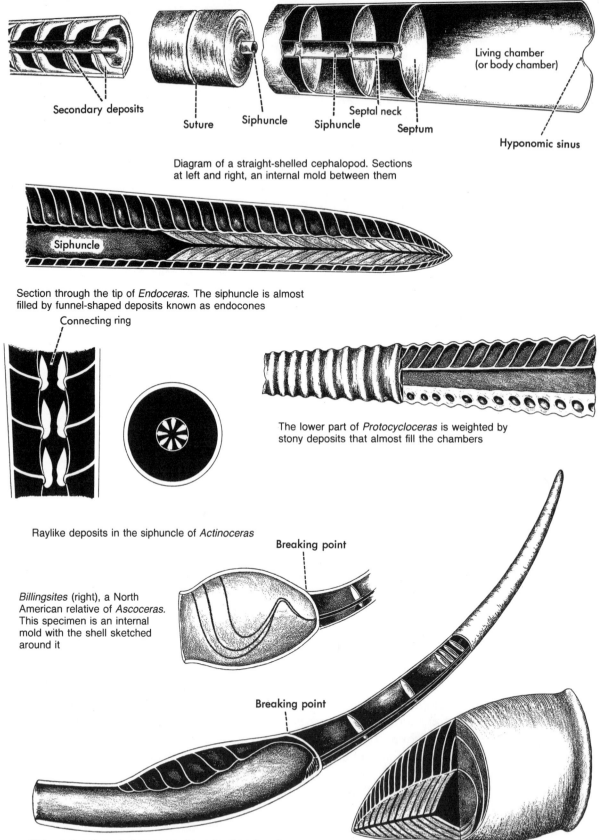

Secondary deposits

Suture

Siphuncle

Siphuncle

Septal neck

Septum

Living chamber
(or body chamber)

Hyponomic sinus

Diagram of a straight-shelled cephalopod. Sections
at left and right, an internal mold between them

Siphuncle

Section through the tip of *Endoceras.* The siphuncle is almost
filled by funnel-shaped deposits known as endocones

Connecting ring

The lower part of *Protocycloceras* is weighted by
stony deposits that almost fill the chambers

Raylike deposits in the siphuncle of *Actinoceras*

Breaking point

Billingsites (right), a North
American relative of *Ascoceras.*
This specimen is an internal
mold with the shell sketched
around it

Breaking point

This section through *Ascoceras* shows its changing shape,
its structure, and the place where the shell breaks off.
Silurian, Czechoslovakia

The siphuncle of *Cassinoceras* is large
and is almost filled by endocones

Structures of ancient nautiloids

pinholes and a tough hood that closed the shell when body, head, and arms were drawn into it. The arms almost certainly had no suckers, but they were longer and less numerous than those of *Nautilus.* Impressions suggest that in some species they numbered only ten.

Why Call Them "Horn Shells"?   The names of nautiloids deserve comment, since many of them end with *-ceras,* from the Greek word for "horn." Many fossils do resemble curved or coiled horns, and the first use of *-ceras* was based upon that resemblance. In time, it became a custom that was extended to other cephalopods with external shells. New genera became "Cassin horns," "Knot horns," "Moore's horns," and so on. Though there are a few exceptions, any fossil whose name ends in *-ceras* is almost sure to be a cephalopod.

HABITS AND CHANGING SHELLS

Primitive cephalopods may have been straight, like *Volborthella,* but they probably were slightly curved. Since their chambers contained only gas, the shells weighed less than water and much less than the body. Light weight must have made them tip upward, like the shell in the final stage of our supposed evolutionary change from snail to cephalopod.

This probably caused no trouble when shells were small as well as short and were more than counterbalanced by bodies. But as ages passed and shells became large, difficulties appeared. Large shells, much lighter than water, would tip upward and bob to and fro, at the mercy of every wave or current. This would have reduced speed, causing difficulty in steering. It may also have kept cephalopods that built such shells from staying right side up.

These things might have happened, but we cannot be sure that they *did.* Nautiloids that became unfit to live efficiently probably were weeded out by predators, accidents, or starvation before they departed far from the norm. Their places were taken by relatives that avoided the obstacles we have mentioned, yet increased in size.

Several theories attempt to explain why and how these new and better-adapted nautiloids developed, but some theories contradict others. Let us, therefore, ignore the hows and whys and concentrate upon actual changes in shells and their apparent relationships to orientation and habits.

Ballast and Bottom-dwellers.   The first cephalopods were creepers or crawlers, and some of their earliest changes maintained and even increased fitness for bottom-dwelling, or benthonic, life. They are conspicuous in the so-called orthoceracones, whose shells were straight and slender and sometimes very large. One Ordovician genus, *Endoceras,* reached lengths of 9 to 12 feet (2.7–3.6 m.).

Such shells, had they been empty, would have drifted with their tips upright and their builders hanging downward at the bottom. But rare speci-

Habits of some Paleozoic nautiloids. **1.** Gonioceras, *a flattened bottom-dweller.* **2.** Gigantoceras, *which both crawled and swam; this one is eating a trilobite.* **3.** Cyrtoceras, *which apparently crawled like a snail, using its tentacles.* **4.** Michelinoceras, *a crawler that could swim.* **5.** Mandaloceras, *a drifter with egg-shaped shell*

mens with stripes, blotches, and zigzag bands of color on the upper, or dorsal, half of the shell leave no doubt that orthoceracones lived in a horizontal position, with funnel below and head above. This was made possible by stony deposits on the walls and septa and in the siphuncle, which generally lay well below the center of the shell. Deposits on septa and walls also were thickest on the lower side, or venter.

Siphuncular ballast took three forms: some was deposited in rings, some in raylike plates, and some in conical layers called endocones, or "inner cones." The last of these sometimes formed in large siphuncles, which lay very near the venter or in direct contact with it.

Actinoceras is one of the commonest cephalopods that filled the siphuncle with raylike plates. *Endoceras* is a straight-shelled example of shells that possessed endocones, especially near the tips. *Cassinoceras,* on the other hand, was short and thick, with closely spaced chambers that curved partway around the siphuncle and its massive endocones. The aperture is tipped downward just a little, as if the heavily weighted cone raised it well above the mud on which the animal lived.

Strangest of all was the device developed by *Ascoceras* and its relatives, of Ordovician and Silurian age. These creatures began by building slender shells with gentle curvature and no ballast except a siphon that moved closer and closer to the venter. The living chamber also became longer, and during Late Ordovician times it began to swell, allowing septa to cut off gas-filled chambers that curved broadly over the dorsal region, thus allowing the body to become its own ballast. At last, as the body moved into the enlarged living chamber, it closed the siphuncle and allowed the rest of the shell to drop off. Thus a long, pointed shell became short and better suited to active life than it had been during its youth.

Gonioceras, a Groveler.   A very different adaptation to bottom life is seen in *Gonioceras* ("angle horn"), of the Ordovician. Its shell was very wide and low, with a moderately convex central portion and "wings" which thinned to sharp edges that explain the name. The undersurface was almost flat, and the siphuncle was not very heavy; during adult life the aperture narrowed until the lateral wings were closed. This has been interpreted as a device that kept the creature from pulling itself out of its shell as it crept among seaweeds and corals.

This idea is dubious for two reasons. First, the broad shell and rayed siphuncle gave much better attachment, in proportion to weight, than we find in the massive, straight cones whose apertures were not restricted. Second, *Gonioceras* probably did very little crawling. Its wide shell reminds us of flounders, which lie on the bottom waiting for food but swim from one place to another. *Gonioceras* probably did the same, reaching out for food with its arms and gliding backward through the water when it felt impelled to swim.

Conical and Horn-shaped Crawlers.   Both structure and coloration show that long, straight nautiloids crawled and swam in an essentially horizontal position. But some short, wide shells preserve bands of color that went all the way around. These bands, plus shapes and lack of ballast, leave little doubt that the shells were carried upright while their owners crawled.

The simplest of these crawlers are generally called *Rizoceras* and *Cyrtoceras*. One was conical and the other slightly curved, the outer side of the curve being the venter. At least one paleontologist believed that the builders of these shells crawled snailwise on a flat surface that was a remnant of the original gastropod foot. This would make the creatures seem to be primitive cephalopods, relics that managed to survive throughout most of the Paleozoic Era. It seems more likely that they were true nautiloids whose shells had shortened and whose bodies were specialized to provide whatever creeping surface was essential to locomotion.

Curved shells were not limited to *Cyrtoceras* and its kin; they appeared in several families and even in another order. They also followed two contrasting plans, one with the siphuncle and venter at the outer side of the curve (exogastric), the other with those parts inside (endogastric). The former offers no new problems, especially if the shells had siphuncles containing

deposits that served as ballast. But endogastric shells, with weights or without, are quite different. Did they contain bodies that were heavy enough so
the creatures could crawl with the tips of their shells directed downward?
Or, since the shells were lighter than water, did they tip upward until their
owners drifted with only their arms resting upon the bottom?

Bizarre Crawlers and Drifters.   These questions are answered by short,
curved   shells   of   Silurian   and   Devonian   age.   Some,   such   as
Protophragmoceras, had living chambers that were compressed but open;
their builders must have lived in the manner of *Cyrtoceras.*

Genera such as *Phragmoceras* are shorter, and the shell expands rapidly
to a large but greatly compressed living chamber. The aperture also is constricted—not merely made narrower, but pinched greatly here and not so
much there until it is roughly I-shaped or even more elaborate. Even when
the siphuncle is weighted, it is not very heavy. In *Phragmoceras* it must have
tipped the shell slightly to the rear but left the task of stabilization primarily
to the body. *Phragmoceras* apparently crawled most of the time, with its
eyes and arms projecting from the large part of its aperture and its funnel at
the rear. The empty chambers provided buoyancy, which was most useful
when the animal swam. This it did in a forward direction, not backward,
since its funnel was turned to the rear.

Forms such as *Hexameroceras* were not so narrow or so abruptly coiled.
They almost certainly drifted, and the shape of the living chamber suggests
that the place where eyes and arms emerged was lower than the funnel.

Another type of adaptation to drifting life is found in short-shelled nauti-

Eutrephoceras dekayi, × 1.4.
Late Cretaceous, widespread
in North America

Armenoceras, an actinoceratoid,
about × 0.75. Ordovician
to Silurian, Eurasia, Greenland,
Australia, and North America

Endoceras, an endoceratoid.
Middle and Late Ordovician,
North America and Eurasia

Straight-shelled and coiled nautiloids. Eutrephoceras *was related to* Nautilus

Lituites lituus, about × 0.5. A nautiloid that coiled and then grew straight like the ammonoid *Baculites.* Ordovician, northern Europe

Actinoceras, an actinoceratoid, 8 inches (20 cm.) long. This specimen shows an internal mold (left), a weathered section (center), and a section cut through the siphuncle (right). Middle Ordovician to Early Silurian, Eurasia, Greenland, and North America

Siphuncle only

Huronia bigsbyi, an actinoceratoid, 5 inches (13 cm.) long. Middle Silurian, northern Michigan

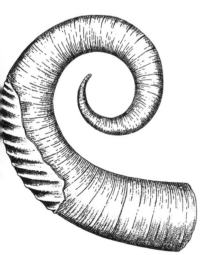

Bickmorites bickmoreanus, a nautiloid, about 9 inches (23 cm.) long. Middle Silurian, Indiana

Hexameroceras, a nautiloid, × 0.6. Middle to Late Silurian, Europe and North America

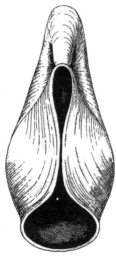

Rutocerus, a nautiloid, × 0.5. Devonian, Europe and North and perhaps South America

Phragmoceras, a nautiloid, × 0.5. A short, open coil with a narrow aperture. Middle Silurian, Europe and North America

Straight and coiled nautiloids

loids such as *Mandaloceras* and *Ovoceras,* of Ordovician to Devonian age. Their shells became both short and wide, with scarcely a trace of curvature and Y- or T-shaped apertures. Crossbars of the Y or T accommodated the eyes, and the rear (really the ventral) extension provided an opening for the funnel, with the arms emerging between. These animals apparently drifted head downward, sinking to the bottom at times but rising by forcing water through the funnel when it was directed downward. By slanting it to the rear, they were able to move obliquely forward.

Neither movement could have been very rapid, and the drifting position indicates that food was found on the bottom. The slitlike aperture led an Austrian paleontologist to conclude that these and other constricted cephalopods ate only very small food. He is opposed by those who argue that the beaks could project from even narrow slits, biting into any victim the arms were able to hold. Actual eating was done by the radula, which probably could extend farther and work more efficiently than that of *Nautilus.*

Coiled Crawlers and Swimmers.   One theory says that certain early cephalopods curved like *Cyrtoceras* but did not become short or constrict their apertures. Next they began to coil; first loosely, but then more and more tightly, until the last whorls overlapped and even hid their predecessors.

There is nothing wrong with this theory, but it has not yet been supported by an actual series of fossils. It is true that the Early Cambrian *Volborthella* is almost straight and that the Late Cambrian *Plectronoceras* is fairly long and moderately curved. But Early Cambrian seas also contained two groups of closely coiled shells, without intermediate stages. Three other groups or orders that appeared during Devonian and Mississippian times seem to have had ancestors that already were closely coiled. How they got that way remains a subject for speculation.

Coiled shells are given various names, depending upon the closeness of coiling. More important, so far as habits are concerned, are the size of the body and the width and general shape of the shell. Cephalopods such as *Titanoceras* and *Solenocheilus,* which had wide shells and relatively large, heavy bodies, must have spent most of their time crawling, swimming only short distances and then mostly when they were alarmed. Tight or open coiling of shell had little effect upon these habits.

Forms such as *Eurystomites* built discoidal shells that were light in weight and had long but not large living chambers which finally became almost straight. The body evidently was heavy enough to serve as ballast, but the shell must have been so buoyant that the aperture pointed obliquely downward. These animals half crawled and half drifted and could swim more easily than *Titanoceras.* Still, their high, empty shells must have been difficult to guide.

Nautilus typifies coiled cephalopods that developed stubby bodies and compact shells that still were not very narrow. A grown *Nautilus* is just a little heavier than water; so little that it can crawl without much effort and

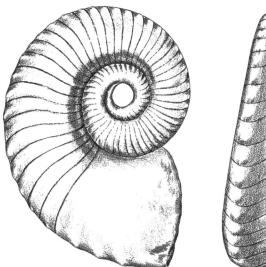

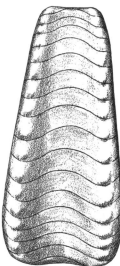

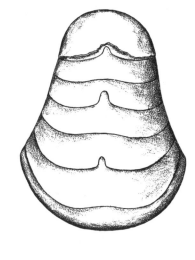

Solenochilus, about 2 inches (5 cm.) high. Carboniferous to Permian, worldwide

Titanoceras ponderosum, × 0.35. Late Pennsylvanian, Illinois to Nebraska

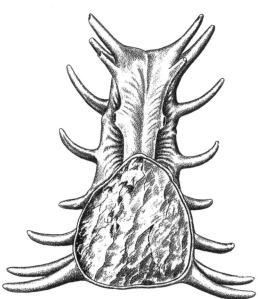

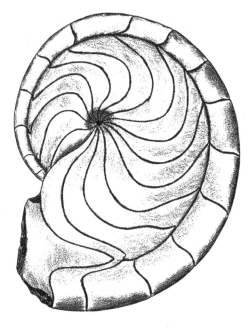

Cooperoceras texanum, × 0.6. Permian, Glass Mountains, Texas

Aturia, × 0.5. This specimen is from the Eocene, New Jersey. The genus ranged from Paleocene to Miocene, worldwide

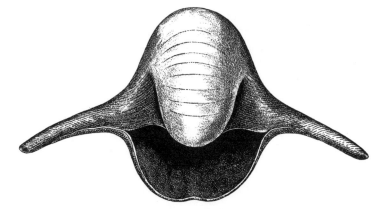

Endolobus, about × 1. Carboniferous–Permian, Europe and North America

Acanthonautilus, about × 0.5. This specimen is from Russia. The genus was restricted to the Early Carboniferous of Europe and North America

Coiled nautiloids, some with long spines

can drift or hover above the bottom with only the slightest use of its funnel. A strong current from that organ sends *Nautilus* swimming shell first. Modern species stay in deep water (as much as 1,785 ft., 550 m.) during the day but often swim toward the surface at night, and extinct animals represented by fossils may have shared this habit. Since water would crush the shell at a depth of 1,180 feet (350 m.), *Nautilus* apparently is able to force gas into its chambers, enabling them to withstand the pressures at greater depths. There is no evidence, however, that gas becomes dense enough to help the animals sink or is reduced so much as to make them rise.

Still better suited to swimming were coiled nautiloids with very narrow shells. Some of these appeared in Pennsylvanian seas, but others evolved during the Mesozoic and Cenozoic eras. Many of these creatures had smooth shells, and their septa were deeply curved or folded, prod cing more complex sutures.

Some Aberrant Nautiloids.   Most ancient nautiloids hau smooth shells bearing faint lines and wrinkles marking brief interruptions in growth. Others developed ridges or annular costae, and a few built grids of ridges. The Rotoceratida went still further, for their shells were ornamented by frills, nodes, spines, and grooves. Some of these must have made swimming almost impossible and apparently interfered with crawling. It is hard to believe that the spines of *Cooperoceras* did not become entangled in seaweeds, or that the frills of *Ryticeras* did not impede creeping and swimming. *Ryticeras* also had to stay away from massive corals, which would have caught and broken those graceful frills.

Several nautiloids whose ancestors had developed coiled shells gave up swimming for drifting or crawling. We see this in such genera as *Schroederoceras,* of Ordovician age. At first its shell was tightly coiled; then it became only slightly curved, suggesting that its builder compromised between drifting and crawling. The Silurian *Lituites* went much further, for most of its shell was straight and its aperture was constricted. Since neither siphuncle nor walls were weighted, *Lituites* must have drifted head downward like an elongate *Mandaloceras.*

Another Silurian genus, *Mitroceras,* typifies nautiloids that coiled spirally, as if they were snails, though some Devonian genera also uncoiled during maturity. These nautiloids must have crawled with the shell half floating above them, though nothing suggests that the body had any broad, flat structure analogous to the foot of a snail.

NAUTILOIDS AS FOSSILS

Since the nautiloid shell consists of aragonite, which dissolves readily, most fossils belonging to this group are internal molds. They show the shape of the shell and its varied chambers as well as its siphuncle. Septa appear as curved surfaces or lines across broken specimens or as other lines (the sutures) that show where septa joined the walls.

There are many exceptions, of course, to this rule that shells disappeared while fillings were preserved. The most important are silicified fossils, in which aragonite was replaced by silica colored by impurities such as iron oxide. These remains stand out prominently on weathered slabs of limestone and may be removed by dissolving the latter in commercial hydrochloric (muriatic) or acetic acid.

For full understanding of fossil nautiloids we need specimens showing how the shell developed from early stages to maturity. Yet much can be learned from incomplete specimens. Casts are enough to distinguish most genera and species, and others can be determined from bits of siphuncle. Weathered sections in rock are useful too, though they almost never reveal surface ornamentation.

Much more difficult than identifying species is the task of determining genera. Before 1925, many straight or curved nautiloids were placed in the genus *Orthoceras* ("straight horn"), whose siphuncle was near the center and whose shell was smooth except for growth wrinkles and lines. *Nautilus* included a great variety of coiled shells whose siphuncle started out near the center but moved toward the venter. *Gomphoceras* denoted short curved shells that were not much flattened, and so on.

Such genera were simple, but most of them were based on superficial resemblances and were really "form genera," scrap baskets of superficially similar forms. When *Orthoceras* was critically studied, only a few species were found to deserve that name, which is now spelled *Orthoceros*. Many species went into new genera, such as *Michelinoceras* and *Geisenocerina*. Other catchall groups suffered a similar fate, so that nautiloids are now divided into a bewildering number of genera distributed through many tens of families and eleven orders.

There is nothing wrong with this; classification must correspond to differences and relationships, even though they can be complex. But it does pose a problem for collectors, who can use up-to-date names only for nautiloids illustrated here, in available textbooks, and in the ever useful *Index Fossils of North America,* by Shimer and Shrock. Others must be identified as to species, using technical publications and the collections and paleontological experts found in museums, universities, and other institutions discussed in Chapter XXXVI.

The earliest nautiloids, such as *Plectronoceras,* were small (the oldest only about 10 mm., or 0.4 in. in length) with gently curving (cyrtocone) shells, typical of Cambrian forms. From these, in the Early Ordovician came a great variety of forms that were generally larger and came in a much greater number of shapes. Both cyrtocone and orthocone (straight) shells were dominant in the Paleozoic, however.

By Middle Ordovician times, nine major groups had appeared, many of which lasted most of the Paleozoic. The last of the nautiloid orders to appear, in the latest Silurian or earliest Devonian, was the one that has as one of its members the living *Nautilus.*

At the end of the Paleozoic, most nautiloid groups came to an end, with only the Nautilida lasting through the Mesozoic and then on to the present day. Perhaps the nautiloid extinctions were tied with the great expansion of the ammonites, which came to dominate Mesozoic seas.

CLASSIFICATION OF NAUTILOIDS

Nautiloids and their near relatives are arranged by some, but not all, paleontologists in a classification that is based on the location and shape of structures associated with the siphon. Three subclasses are recognized: Endoceratoidea, which is known only in Ordovician and Silurian rocks; Actinoceratoidea, know from the Ordovician to the Carboniferous; and Nautiloidea, from the Late Cambrian to the present.

Endoceratoids are either orthocone or cyrtocone. Their siphuncles are usually near the margin of the shell and are large. All actinoceratoids have orthocone shells. They have balloon-like septal necks that are short, and complicated sets of radial canals lie between them. The nautiloids have orthocone and cyrtocone shells as well as those that are completely coiled—the whole range of variety. Orthocone types survived into the Triassic, but after this the coiled forms took over. Siphuncles of this group are also highly varied. Early nautiloids had septal necks connected by rings, but these were lost in some post-Paleozoic forms.

CHAPTER XVIII

"Ammon's Stones" and Naked Cephalopods

The word *Ammonites* means "Ammon's stones"; it was given to fossil shells whose wrinkled whorls suggest rams' horns, which often appeared on the Egyptian god Ammon. Today we recognize ammonoids—*Ammonites* is a genus—as a subclass of cephalopods that developed increasingly complex septa. Shells ranged from thick to thin, from broad to narrow, and from smooth to incredibly ornate. Most were medium-sized animals, but some forms reached huge proportions, such as *Pachydiscus seppenradensis,* which was 1.7 meters (5.6 ft.) in diameter. Many members of the group, and perhaps all, could close the shell with a horny plate (anaptychus) or a double calcareous structure (aptychus) when the body was completely drawn into the living chamber. Body, eyes, and arms have usually been reconstructed like those of nautiloids, but, in fact, ammonoids may have more closely resembled the coeloids, including the squid and the octopus. Like the coeloids, ammonoids had a radula, for feeding, that had seven rows of teeth, jaws that looked very like the "parrot beak" nippers of the octopus, and an ink sac, Nautiloids have thirteen rows of teeth on their radulae and differ from both ammonoids and coeloids in lacking the ink sac; ammonoids further differed in normally having the siphuncle in a ventral, or bottom, position, and septa that were convex forward, not concave. So, in fact, perhaps the soft parts of ammonites should be reconstructed using the squid and its relatives as a model.

CRUMPLED SEPTA AND SUTURES

Ammonoids apparently were descended from straight-shelled Bactroidea, another subclass of cephalopods, but the new group did not become well established until Middle Devonian times. Called "goniatites" ("angle stones"), almost all of these Devonian forms had smooth shells that ranged from wide to narrow and were compactly coiled. Their name is explained by angular zigzags in their sutures.

How Septa Crumpled.   Primitive septa, as we know, were only a little
larger than the shell and produced straight or gently curved sutures. In ammonoids, as well as in such nautiloids as *Aturia,* the septa grew so large that
they were forced to become fluted or deeply lobed. The process is analogous
to that of forcing pieces of paper into a glass tumbler. A little bending will
make the paper fit if it is not much larger than the available space. But when
the paper is much too large, it crumples as it goes into the glass.

This is only an analogy, for it ignores two facts. First, septa were not
pushed into cephalopod shells; they were built there by the mantle and correspond to its surface. Second, crumpling is a hit-or-miss process; no two
papers pushed into a tumbler bend in identical ways. But folds and furrows
in cephalopod mantles were definite characters and follow definite patterns
that reveal themselves in the sutures. The latter are divided into saddles,
which extend forward, and lobes, which are directed backward. For study,
they generally are drawn flat on cards. If the sutures are long, as they are in
large fossils, only half is shown.

Three Types of Sutures.   Goniatites lived and prospered for 170 million
years, for they appeared in Middle Devonian times and lived through the
Triassic, with a major decrease in number at the end of the Permian. During
that time, members of the group changed greatly, some becoming so wide
that they were almost spheroidal. At least one aberrant type became roughly
triangular; another resembled a vastly overgrown foraminiferan. Goniatites
also increased the size of their septa, thereby adding to the saddles and
lobes in their sutures. Neither saddles nor lobes were divided, however, and
their simplicity distinguishes the type of suture called goniatite.

Ceratite sutures had subdivided lobes, though the saddles were undivided.
Sutures of this type appeared during the Mississippian and continued to the

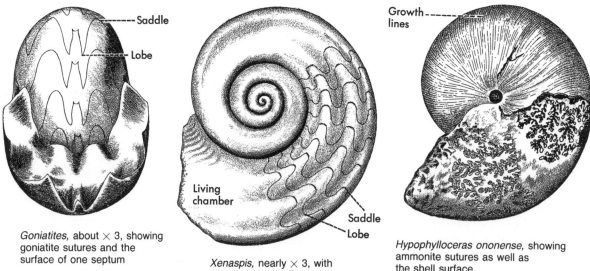

Goniatites, about × 3, showing
goniatite sutures and the
surface of one septum

Xenaspis, nearly × 3, with
ceratite sutures. Permian,
Texas and Mexico

Hypophylloceras ononense, showing
ammonite sutures as well as
the shell surface.
Early Cretaceous, California

Cephalopods with goniatitic, ceratitic, and ammonitic sutures

end of the Triassic. Cephalopods possessing them then died out, but ceratite sutures were developed anew by Late Cretaceous genera that simplified their septa. These were called pseudoceratites (false ceratites). Not all members of the order Ceratitida had ceratitic sutures, but most did. This group underwent an explosive diversification in the Triassic after the crash of the goniatites, only to become extinct themselves at the end of the Triassic.

Ammonitic sutures appeared early in the Triassic Period. In it both saddles and lobes were divided and subdivided, producing patterns that suggest the tracings of frost on windowpanes or the outlines of ferns with unbelievably delicate leaves. With these changes went others in shape and ornamentation, which led to shells more elaborate and often more grotesque than the strangest of nautiloids.

High specialized ammonoids of the Triassic died out as that period closed, leaving conservative types to carry on. Their descendants, however, soon evolved even more elaborate sutures. Later came secondary simplification, so that descendants of genera whose sutures had grown increasingly complex reverted to the ceratite type. Some, in fact, developed sutures that were almost as simple as those of early goniatites.

Why Did Sutures Become Ornate?   Many writers have tried to explain why ammonoid septa crumpled, making more and more ornate sutures. One theory calls this an orthogenetic trend, a tendency to one type of variation that became established and then continued even though its results ceased to have discernible value to the ammonite. Opposed to this is the theory of selection, which holds that cephalopods with elaborate septa enjoyed a selective advantage because crumpled septa increased the strength of shells. This idea finds support in the fact that many smooth, thin shells of ammonoids that live in relatively deep water show elaborately crumpled septa, while those of some thin shells in shallow-water deposits are much simpler. Many smooth shells also have more elaborate septa than ornate contemporaries that were strengthened by ribs and bosses. On the other hand, we know of no ammonoids with the smoothest of nautiloid septa that lived in water deep enough to crush shells. Moreover, some well-ribbed shells of the shallows have more elaborate sutures than do smooth deepwater genera.

Further difficulty comes from the fact that ammonoids did not change all their septa and sutures each time a new pattern developed. Instead, the new character appeared only after a series of stages that repeated the adult sutures of earlier, ancestral genera. If the final character was advantageous and had triumphed over its predecessors, how did the growing ammonoid manage to live through those preliminary stages? One answer might be that the young lived in different places from the adults, or that the smaller shells were stronger than the larger ones, in which septa might be farther apart to accommodate the larger living animal.

Regardless of exactly what were the advantages of complex or less complex septae, the mere fact that there are so many kinds, with quite limited

Lytoceras, about × 0.5.
Jurassic to Cretaceous, worldwide

Leioceras, filled with calcite crystals.
Lines on shell are ornament, not sutures.
Jurassic, Eurasia, North Africa

Scaphites. Cretaceous,
Australia, Northern
Hemisphere, and Madagascar

Baculites "ovatus," about × 2,
showing pearly layer.
Late Cretaceous,
North America

Baculites "ovatus," about × 1,
showing sutures. Late Cretaceous,
North America

Dipoloceras. The keel does not show
in this internal mold. Early
Cretaceous, Europe, Africa,
and North America

Aptychus from the aperture
of an ammonoid. Jurassic
limestone, Solenhofen, Germany

Nipponites mirabilis, about × 0.75.
Cretaceous, Hokkaido, Japan

Some typical ammonoids

time ranges, means that ammonites are terribly important as biostratigraphic tools. They are extremely useful for dating rocks, particularly those of the Mesozoic.

SHAPES, ORNAMENTS, AND HABITS

Early ammonoids were coiled, though some did not have the whorls in contact. Paleozoic and Mesozoic members of the group developed typical swimming and crawling forms. Many of the former looked and probably lived like *Nautilus;* others had streamlined shells so narrow that we wonder how they remained upright while at rest. Their arms must have spread out as props to keep the creatures from toppling over.

Crawlers appeared as broad, smooth goniatites in Mississippian seas. During the Pennsylvanian and Jurassic periods several genera developed wide shells with flattened sides, such as the sluggish pond snail *Helisoma,* once known as *Planorbis.* Several Permian crawlers were almost spheroidal, as were some of Late Triassic and Jurassic age. Other types that must have crawled were egg-shaped, triangular, or resembled enormously overgrown foraminiferans. The second and third of these appeared in Late Devonian seas.

Frills and Other Ornaments. We recall that some nautiloids covered their loosely coiled shells with frills built like mantles spread out. When each frill reached full size, the mantle contracted, built a short length of ordinary wall, and then flared outward again. Ammonoids such as *Lytoceras* duplicated this process, though fossils seldom show more than broken bases of frills.

An enormous number of ammonoids developed ridges and furrows that ran lengthwise or around the whorls, as well as knoblike bosses and even spines. Most of these structures strengthened the shell, just as corrugations make sheet steel rigid and repoussé decorations give strength to a silver coffeepot or bowl. Many genera so ornamented and strengthened resembled *Nautilus* in overall shape and apparently had similar habits. Other genera became streamlined, with keels, which show that they were relatively rapid swimmers. Many more, however, had features that go with a sluggish, crawling life. *Zemistephanus,* for example, looked like an abnormally broad, squat *Helisoma,* and *Arcestes* had an almost globose shell. Not merely did such shapes reduce speed; they seem to mean that the creatures almost always crawled.

Beaks, Ears, and Funnels. Again like nautiloids, many ammonoids narrowed their apertures during maturity. Others developed beaks (rostra) that grew forward from keels, or ears (auricles) that were added at each side of the aperture. One theory says that constricted apertures kept the body from being torn from its shell—an explanation that assumes that many young

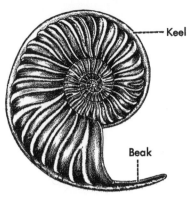

Schloenbachia, about
× 1, with keel
and beak. Cretaceous, Europe,
Greenland

Lytoceras, slightly less than × 1,
showing ornamentation.
Jurassic–Cretaceous, Europe

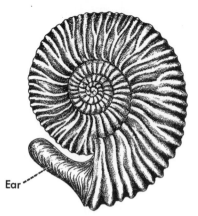

Normannites, showing the
prominent ear. Middle
Jurassic, Europe

Dufrenoyia, about × 1, a narrow
ammonoid with coarse ribs.
Early Cretaceous, Europe, North
and South America, Africa

Arcestes, about × 2,
a rounded crawler.
Shows ceratitic suture
pattern. Worldwide range
in the Middle to Late Triassic

Prodromites gorbyi, × 0.5.
Early Mississippian,
central United States

Zemistephanus, a crawler that
resembled some snails. Jurassic,
British Columbia

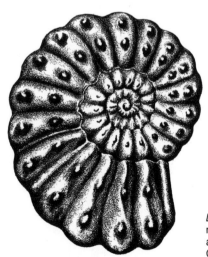

Mortoniceras, × 1.
Genus was restricted to
the Early Cretaceous of
Africa, Eurasia, and North
and South America

Diploceras, a
narrow ammonoid with
a keel, about × 1.
Cretaceous

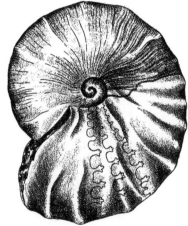

Engonoceras, about × 1. Cretaceous, Europe,
North Africa, and North and South America

Ammonoids of varied shapes

animals were pulled out through their wide apertures, or that mature animals became less and less firmly attached to the walls of their shells. Unfortunately there is no evidence in favor of either assumption and some evidence that all ammonoids, both old and young, had very sturdy attachments.

Beaks and ears have been said to mean that their owners seldom or never swam. This theory robs keels of their function as water cutters and stabilizers and gives beaks and ears a nuisance value they seemingly did not possess. If these structures were troublesome, they were so when their owners crawled forward, not when they swam backward with their arms trailing as rudders. Narrow, keeled ammonoids such as *Dipoloceras* "make sense" only as swimmers. Perhaps some of these structures were stabilizers.

Aptychi and Anaptychi. In Mesozoic rocks, often found together with ammonites, are paired calcite structures that look like bivalves. Rarely, these have been found inside body chambers of ammonites and apparently worked like old saloon swinging doors, swinging open in the middle. These are called aptychi and evidently could close the ammonite, protected, in its shell. Anaptychi are other structures found in ammonites, but are made up of chitin or some other organic material. They are a single plate often in the shape of a butterfly. In the rare specimens in which they are found, these plates are opposite one another; they may have been jaws.

Uncoiled Ammonoids. Two nonswimmer ammonoids, the triangular *Soliclymenia,* and *Parawocklumeria,* had shells no less grotesque than their names. Other genera gave up regular coiling and assumed a variety of shapes that we may summarize as follows:

High-spired types appeared in the Late Triassic and in Middle to Late Cretaceous times. They looked and probably crawled like snails, doing little if any swimming.

Open-coiled ammonoids are found in Early Jurassic deposits and throughout the Cretaceous. Some merely have whorls that do not touch; others are considerably shortened; a few form open curves. The first two groups could either crawl or swim, and so could some members of the third. Others may have drifted near the bottom, but that is only a guess.

Baculites, after coiling for a few whorls, built a straight, compressed shell that ended in an unusually wide beak. Some experts think it drifted head downward; others say it crawled. Fragments with pearly nacre or excellent sutures are common fossils in the Late Cretaceous Pierre Shale.

Hamulina and its kin, of Early Cretaceous age, grew straight forward for a while, made a sharp turn, and then grew straight to the rear. We can picture young and fully grown individuals as creepers and occasional swimmers; in maturity, the tip of the shell projected above and beyond the arms. But what did the animals do while they were making that hairpin turn?

Equally puzzling are *Hamites* and *Macroscaphites,* of Cretaceous age. All have been regarded as drifters, with form dictating their orientation in the water.

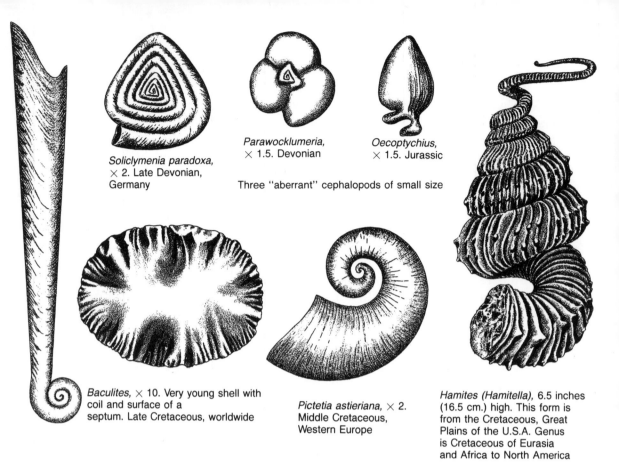

Soliclymenia paradoxa,
× 2. Late Devonian,
Germany

Parawocklumeria,
× 1.5. Devonian

Oecoptychius,
× 1.5. Jurassic

Three "aberrant" cephalopods of small size

Baculites, × 10. Very young shell with
coil and surface of a
septum. Late Cretaceous, worldwide

Pictetia astieriana, × 2.
Middle Cretaceous,
Western Europe

Hamites (Hamitella), 6.5 inches
(16.5 cm.) high. This form is
from the Cretaceous, Great
Plains of the U.S.A. Genus
is Cretaceous of Eurasia
and Africa to North America

Uncoiled and aberrantly coiled ammonoids of Devonian to Late Cretaceous age

Scaphites is little more than a very short *Macroscaphites,* with the same problems of habit and orientation. In youth it may have been a swimmer and crawler, but in maturity and old age it was poorly adapted to crawling and perhaps became a drifter. It prospered and became an abundant fossil in the Pierre Shale and other Late Cretaceous formations.

The ultimate in bizarre form is found in *Nipponites,* from the Cretaceous of Japan, and certain species of *Helicoceras.* The former became an irregular tangle, which could not swim but was probably a specialized bottom feeder. *Hamites* included both open loops and species that began by coiling, then built their shells into hairpin U's, coiled spirally for a few whorls, stopped coiling, and began to bend back toward the apices of their spirals.

HABITATS OF CRETACEOUS AMMONOIDS

Cretaceous rocks of Texas and northeastern Mexico range from soft sandstones to shales and limestones, and settled in situations ranging from deltas and tidal flats to reefs, extensive shoals, and waters more than 600 feet (about 180 m.) deep. These formations also contain enormous numbers of ammonoids, with shells so little broken and worn that they plainly were buried close to the places in which they had lived. With them are snails, clams, oysters, sea urchins, foraminiferans, and many other remains. Fossils and rocks give the following record of conditions under which ammonoids lived and creatures with which they associated:

1. Ammonoids did not inhabit the ponds, streams, and brackish bays of deltas. This is not surprising, since no cephalopod of any sort has been found in fresh water or in freshwater deposits.

2. Ammonoids seldom lived in shallow, near-shore waters where sand was deposited. Such waters probably were too shallow for these molluscs, became too nearly brackish after hard rains, and grew too warm during the summer. The eggs of many modern cephalopods die very quickly when the water around them becomes warm.

3. Ammonoids also avoided the extensive shallows in which large dinosaurs sometimes waded. There the water ranged from 8 or 10 to perhaps 20 feet (2.5–6 m.) in depth, and waves often reached the bottom, piling up small ripple marks. Sometimes, indeed, the seawater vanished, leaving mud flats to dry and crack under the blazing sun or to be pitted by drops of rain. Large snails and thick-shelled clams found this habitat inviting, as did sea urchins and uncountable billions of the "foram" *Orbitolina*. Ammonoids probably were kept out by the same factors that excluded them from sandy shoals.

4. Few ammonoids thrived where empty clamshells covered the bottom, forming beds of coquina. Still, the narrow but thick-ribbed *Dufrenoyia* is common in one coquina deposit.

5. Ammonoids also avoided reefs built by corals and rudistids, where the water was both shallow and rough. Banks of *Gryphaea* and *Exogyra* formed more favorable habitats; narrow ammonoids such as *Engonoceras* and *Diploceras* thrived there, though other types were rare.

6. These same narrow ammonoids reached enormous numbers in seas 30 or 40 to as much as 120 feet (9–37 m.) deep. There temperature and salinity did not change much, the muddy bottom was never exposed, and the largest waves produced only oscillations that piled oyster shells into giant ripples. Other molluscs and sea urchins also were plentiful.

7. Ammonoids reached their greatest abundance and variety in waters 120 to about 600 feet (37–180 m.) deep, but various kinds apparently needed different bottoms or the conditions that went with them. Sandy limestones and shales contain ornate shells of several types, as well as the narrow ones found in deposits of shallower water. Partly uncoiled forms, such as *Scaphites,* are rare.

Fine-grained shales and soft, marly limestones contain an enormous variety of ammonoids—smooth and rough, squat and narrow, closely coiled, spiral, and partly uncoiled. If there was an ideal habitat for Cretaceous ammonoids, it was a marly bottom under water more than 120 feet (37 m.) deep, with abundant algae that provided food for varied animals, including those eaten by ammonoids.

8. Seas more than 600 feet (180 m.) deep filled a trench that extended

Hamites, length 3 inches (7.6 cm.). Early Cretaceous, Africa, Eurasia, and North America

Macroscaphites yvani, 5 inches (13 cm.) long. Early Cretaceous (Neocomian), Europe

Spiroceras bifurcati, natural size. Middle Jurassic (Bajocian), Europe

Hamulina astieriana, 12 inches (30 cm.) long. Early Cretaceous, Europe

Four European ammonoids that uncoiled. All except Hamulina *were small*

westward from what now is the Gulf of Mexico. There water was too deep and too dark for seaweeds, and snails and clams were rare or absent. Near the edges of the trough, smooth-shelled ammonoids were surprisingly plentiful. At greater depths the water was cold and contained little oxygen, a factor unfavorable to normal animal life. Snails could not live in such depths, and pelecypods were rare, thin-shelled creatures very different from those of the shallows. Ammonoids were more successful; species with wide, smooth shells were almost the only animals whose remains became fossils. Most of them are preserved in pyrite, good specimens being very attractive. But perhaps their presence there means only that they lived in the waters above these trenches and *not* in the trenches themselves.

9. Ammonites themselves were preyed upon by a number of animals, both invertebrates and vertebrates, including large crabs and fish. Marine reptiles, mososaurs, are a classic example of ammonite predators. One ammonite specimen of *Placenticeras,* for example, from the Late Cretaceous of South Dakota, was severely bitten sixteen times by a mososaur as determined by the sets of tooth marks on the shell.

One more fact appears in this record: Ammonoids were gregarious and, except in hostile habitats, lived in large schools. They shared this habit with most other cephalopods, from *Volborthella* to the modern *Nautilus* and squids. Only the octopus and the cuttlefish are solitary. Both prowl for food alone, and both tuck their soft, unprotected bodies into crevices between

290

rocks. Some ammonites may also have fed on carrion and vegetable matter, and it seems the majority may have lived on or near the bottom. Diets for several ammonites are specifically known. Stomach contents show that *Arnioceras* preferred foraminiferans and ostracods. *Hildoceras* was a predator on other ammonites, while yet others ate sea lilies.

Jaws of many ammonites indicate that they were not primarily predators, for the jaws were not designed for cutting. The shovel-like lower jaws of many may have been used to stir up bottom sediments and benthonic organisms, which were then consumed. Also, some forms may have been planktonic and ingested microplankton.

DARTLIKE SWIMMERS—THE BELEMNOIDS

While ammonoids were developing more elaborate shells, some of the orthocone cephalopods reduced the shell until it was hidden under the mantle. Thus, they became belemnoids, the first rapid swimmers among cephalopods.

Belemnoids are a member of yet another subclass of cephalopods, the Coleoidea, which includes all forms having two gills in the mantle cavity (and called dibranchiates). This includes the octopus and squid as well. All other cephalopods (Endoceratoidea, Actinoceratoidea, Nautiloidea, Bactritoidea, and Ammonoidea) had or have four gills and are thus called tetrabranchiates.

Belemnoid Anatomy and Habits. A few fossils preserving impressions of flesh show that belemnoids looked and presumably acted like the modern squid. The body had become torpedo-shaped and was surrounded by a mantle that spread out into two lateral fins that kept it right side up and could be moved to guide the animal upward or downward. There was a constricted "neck" behind the head; the eyes were large, round, and dark and apparently focused light with lenses, rather than through pinholes. The ten arms

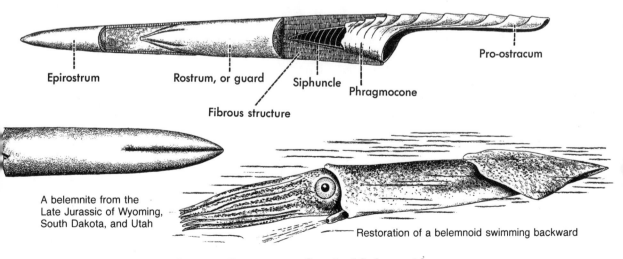

Epirostrum — Rostrum, or guard — Fibrous structure — Siphuncle — Phragmocone — Pro-ostracum

A belemnite from the Late Jurassic of Wyoming, South Dakota, and Utah

Restoration of a belemnoid swimming backward

Shape and structure of typical belemnoids

were not smooth, like those of *Nautilus,* but were set with hooks that increased their efficiency in catching and holding food. Fossils tell nothing about the diet, but resemblance to squids suggests that it included small fish plus tidbits such as crabs, prawns, and injured belemnoids.

Like most other cephalopods, belemnoids swam by taking water into the mantle cavity and forcing it out through the funnel. When the latter pointed forward, its owner swam backward; when the funnel was turned to the rear, the belemnoid darted ahead. Alarm caused the creature to release a thick dark liquid from an ink sac that opened into the cavity and through the funnel. The ink spead out in an opaque cloud which supposedly blinded any enemy while the belemnoid darted away. But the ink of modern squids paralyzes the organs of smell, with which predaceous fishes (the squids' chief enemies) do their hunting. Fishes blunder about aimlessly long after they have swum out of the blinding clouds. Belemnoid ink probably had the same effect.

Shells Inside Bodies. Belemnoids apparently evolved when some descendant of early nautiloids outgrew its living chamber and wrapped its mantle around the inadequate shell. That shell includes a guard plus the phragmocone. In the upper, or dorsal, region there was sometimes an elongate shield, the pro-ostracum, which supported and perhaps protected the forward portion of the body.

The long empty shells of early belemnoids enabled them to float their bodies with a minimum of effort. But phragmocones were delicate, and as the creatures gained speed there were many collisions. There also was need

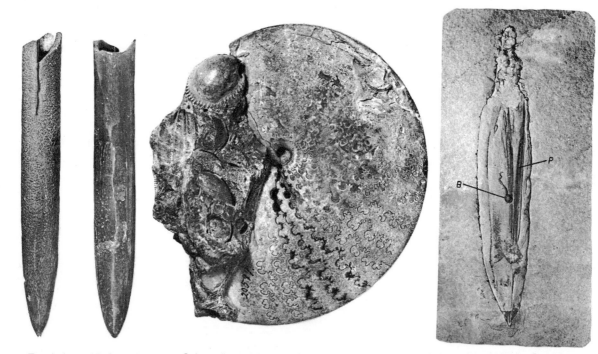

Two belemnoids from the
Late Cretaceous, New Jersey
to Texas

Sphenodiscus lobatus, × 0.3.
Late Cretaceous, Atlantic and Gulf coastal plains

A Jurassic squid from Germany.
B is the ink bag, **P** the pen

for some ballast at the tip of the body so it could cut the water without turning or wobbling.

Both requirements were met by the guard, or rostrum, a solid bullet-shaped structure built behind and partly around the shell. It consists of radial fibers arranged in alternating light and dark layers. The latter contain large amounts of organic material, but the former were pure calcite. Both show plainly in broken or polished sections, which also trace changes in shape as guards became larger and longer. Many also reveal fractures and dislocations—ample proof that belemnoids often bumped into other objects as they darted backward.

Some belemnoids added a fourth internal structure, attached to the guard much as the latter capped the tip of the phragmocone. This epirostrum (the pro-ostracum) contained no fibrous layers and was easily destroyed after death. It is known in only a few fossil genera.

Belemnoids appeared in Mississippian seas but did not become plentiful until the Late Triassic. Countless billions swam in schools during the Jurassic and the Cretaceous, but the creatures declined rapidly at the end of the latter period. Their last fossils—aberrant phragmocones and guards—are rare in Eocene rocks.

FROM CONES TO CUTTLEBONE

Belemnoids had hardly become abundant when some of them produced offspring that evolved into sepioids. As they did so, the phragmocone coiled or changed its structure, the guard became small or vanished, and sucking cups replaced hooks on the animals' arms.

These changes, which began in the Jurassic, followed two different paths. In one, the shield and guard vanished, the siphuncle became marginal, the shell coiled like a tiny *Gyroceras,* and both body and arms became short. The result was *Spirula,* a small creature (about 10 cm., or 4 in., long) that drifts and swims in modern oceans—the only shelled cephalopod known to be truly pelagic. Some of its predecessors stayed in shallow seas, for their shells and shortened guards have been found in Tertiary rocks of North America and Europe.

The second group of sepioids kept a little of the guard, added a new and very wide dorsal shield, and turned the phragmocone into a spongy mass of aragonite in which the septa and other plates are connected by small rods or pillars. Thus it became "cuttlebone," which is given to canaries and other caged birds as a source of calcium carbonate. Fossil cuttlebones and shields are found in Tertiary rocks of Europe, but the modern cuttlefish *(Sepia)* ranges around the world. It is a short, plump creature with two long arms and eight short ones. It can swim rapidly by means of its funnel and slowly by rippling the finfolds that run along both sides of its body.

SQUIDS AND OCTOPODS

When belemnoids died out, their place was taken by the teuthoids, or squids. These creatures lost the phragmocone and guard but kept a horny "pen" that often looks like a quill pen and may or may not be a remnant of the belemnoid dorsal shield. Squids also have always been very rapid swimmers, and their sucking cups are superior to hooks for capturing and holding food. Squids appeared in the Early Jurassic, made slow progress for millions of years, and then became the most abundant of cephalopods. Since they lived in the manner of belemnoids, it is probable that they crowded the latter out of the seas soon after the beginning of the Tertiary period. Squids could have done this both by eating food on which belemnoids depended and by actually devouring their less able and active relatives.

Octopods, as their name suggests, reduced the number of their arms from ten to eight, at the same time losing all trace of ancestral guard and shell. Because of this, they almost never formed fossils, but one genus with round body and lateral fins has been found in Late Cretaceous strata of Lebanon. Another group, the argonauts, developed a new and delicate "shell"—really a brood pouch that held developing eggs or even a captured and much smaller male—between two of the female's arms. A few of these pouches have been found in Tertiary rocks.

As the name suggests, modern paper nautiluses *(Argonauta)* are swimmers at the surface of warm seas around the world. Thus, their habits are very different from octopods', which live along rocky shores, and from giant squids', which inhabit dark, cold depths of the oceans. Among the latter is the great *Megateuthis,* which reaches overall lengths of 55 to 66 feet (17–20 m.) and weights of 1,000 to 4,000 pounds (450–1,800 kg.). This is one case in which living giants exceed anything of the past. Fossil squids are few in number but first occur in early Tertiary times.

It is interesting to note that most of the shelled cephalopods were extinct by the end of the Mesozoic. Certainly there was a crisis at the end of that era, but some paleontologists have suggested that the extinctions might have been building for some time, as shelled cephalopods came under increasing stress from competition with bony fish, which were moving into the upper marine waters. The unshelled cephalopods that were able to invade deeper waters without the risk of shell implosion perhaps survived because the competition was not quite so marked in those waters. At least it is an interesting suggestion worthy of further thought.

Despite their extinction at the end of the Mesozoic, however, we should remember that ammonites were some of the most varied marine animals during that time. Their shelly remains allow a very fine subdivision of the rock sequences and correlation of formations over a very broad geographic range.

CHAPTER XIX

Mostly Stemmed Echinoderms

A limestone quarry near Le Grand, Iowa, has long been famous for its fossils. Though some beds and layers are barren, others contain well-preserved remains, which quarrymen as well as collectors call sea lilies (crinoids). Both names (the Greek word *krinon* means lily) are justified by these fossils that look like flowers on jointed stalks.

Sea lilies introduce us to the phylum of echinoderms, or spiny-skinned animals. This entire group, like the brachiopods, is marine; of its numerous classes only six are still living, including such creatures as starfish, sand dollars, and sea cucumbers, as well as crinoids and their relatives. Some have stalks, but many lack them; some are hard, while others are soft-skinned; they include sessile stay-at-homes as well as drifters, burrowers, and crawlers. Colors of living animals range across the spectrum from the dingy gray-green of mud to blue, purple, and vermilion.

In spite of these differences, echinoderms have a few basic characters in common. Generally their skeletons are arranged in five starlike sections (they have fivefold symmetry). Some, however, such as the sea urchins, have a secondary bilateral symmetry. Still others, such as the homalozoans, lack any trace of radial symmetry. Most echinoderms also possess skeletal supports in the form of plates or spines of crystalline calcite, which looks porous or netlike under the microscope yet splits into flat-sided blocks. These supports are built from an embryonic tissue called mesoderm, which also gives rise to muscles. The plates may be joined together but generally are not fused, which means that they can increase in size as long as their owners live. Growth is often recorded in fine lines or wrinkles that show up on plates, though spines merely grow longer and thicker with age and increasing size.

Another characteristic of echinoderms is their water-vascular system. This is an interconnecting, internal plumbing of tubes and bladders filled with fluid. Extensions of this reach the outside as tube feet, which are used in feeding, breathing, and moving. Though probably present, this system has not been recognized in all fossil echinoderm groups.

Echinoderms appear at the beginning of the Paleozoic. They are so distinct from other invertebrate groups, however, that their ancestry is not clear. *Tribrachidium* (see Chapter V), from the Late Precambrian Ediacara fauna in South Australia, may be an echinoderm, but, also, it may belong to an extinct group that only superficially resembled the spiny-skinned animals. It is embryology that hints at relationships of the group. Hemichordates, including acorn worms and *Rhabdopleura* (see Chapter XXI), and the chordates share similar larvae and similar modes of formation of the coelom (or body cavity) among other developmental features of the embryo.

As with some other phyla, such as Arthropoda, there was a great diversification of echinoderm classes in the Cambrian and the Ordovician. These experiments worked for a time when there was no better design, and new environments were being invaded. Then they became extinct with increasing competition, and only a few gave rise to later, more efficient classes. Efficiency of respiration and filter feeding and better protection were critical to survival of several groups.

Diversity of echinoderms, measured by counting the number of genera per million years, rose from the Cambrian to the Carboniferous, fell to a low point in the Triassic, and climbed to a peak in the Tertiary.

Though the fossil record has little to say about the origin of echinoderms, it certainly tells much about the evolutionary patterns within this group over the past 590 million years. What it tells is that most of the basic echinoderm body designs had developed by the end of the Ordovician. After that, echinoderm history was one of minor design changes in a basic ground plan.

THE STEMMED ECHINODERMS: THE BLASTOZOANS

During much of the Paleozoic, a great variety of stemmed echinoderms dominated the world's marine environments. Their variety was far greater than today, and they predominated in the echinoderm faunas. Today most classes are extinct, and starfish and sea urchins are the most diverse echinoderms. This gives a false impression of what groups have dominated the phylum over the past 500 million years.

The stemmed echinoderms fall into two major groups: the blastozoans (blastoids) and the crinozoans (crinoids). We will look at both subphyla, the blastoids and their relatives first.

Eocrinoids. These small (6–7 cm., 2–3 in.) early echinoderms usually had an elongate, tapering stalk, though a few were stemless. Their vase-shaped theca was built of solid polygonal plates of crystalline calcite with thecal pores situated along suture lines between the plates. The theca had several simple brachioles (just as in cystoids and differing from the biserial, branching structures in crinoids), which generally lacked branches. During life, the brachioles probably carried cilia that took food to the mouth, which lay on top of the theca. Though eocrinoids never were very diverse, they did live for

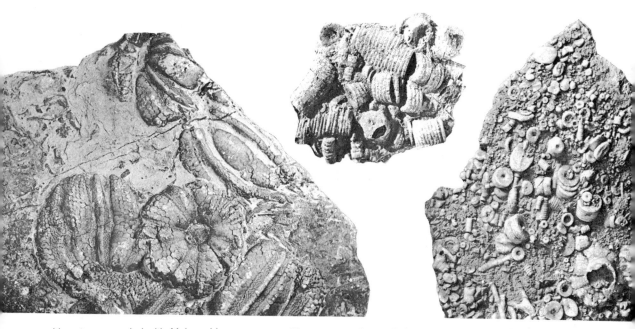

Limestone crowded with *Melonechinus multiporus,* about × 0.5. Early Carboniferous, Illinois and Missouri

Limestone made up of pieces of crinoid columns cemented together. Mississippian, × 1

Typical encrinal limestone, × 1

These specimens show that remains of echinoderms form a large part of some limestones. The sea urchins (Melonechinus) *are well preserved, but the crinoids have fallen apart. Many of those in the encrinal limestone have also been severely worn*

more than 200 million years, from the Early Cambrian to the Silurian. We certainly can't argue against their success.

Cystoids (Diploporita and Rhombifera). These creatures, whose class name means "bladderlike," had compressed egg-shaped or spherical bodies covered by a theca of plates that were perforated by pores used for respiration. Some genera were attached directly to other objects; some had short stalks (columns) made up of round flat sections (columnals), each with a central hole through which ran a stalk of soft tissue. The stemless state seems to be primitive, and so does one in which plates number more than two hundred and have no definite arrangement. A small number of plates, with distinct shapes and positions, is a specialized character.

The cystoid mouth lay on the upper surface, generally at the center of radiating grooves (ambulacra), which must have been lined with cilia that beat to and fro, carrying food to the mouth. These food grooves were covered by calcite plates. Some genera lacked appendages; others had armlike brachioles that rose in a cluster around the mouth or ran along both sides of food grooves that extended far down the sides of the theca. Food grooves branched and extended along brachioles, which may also have borne jointed branches called pinnules. The brachioles were always short and slender. The anus lay to one side of the mouth and was covered by plates.

Cystoids are divided into two groups (Rhombifera and Diploporita) by

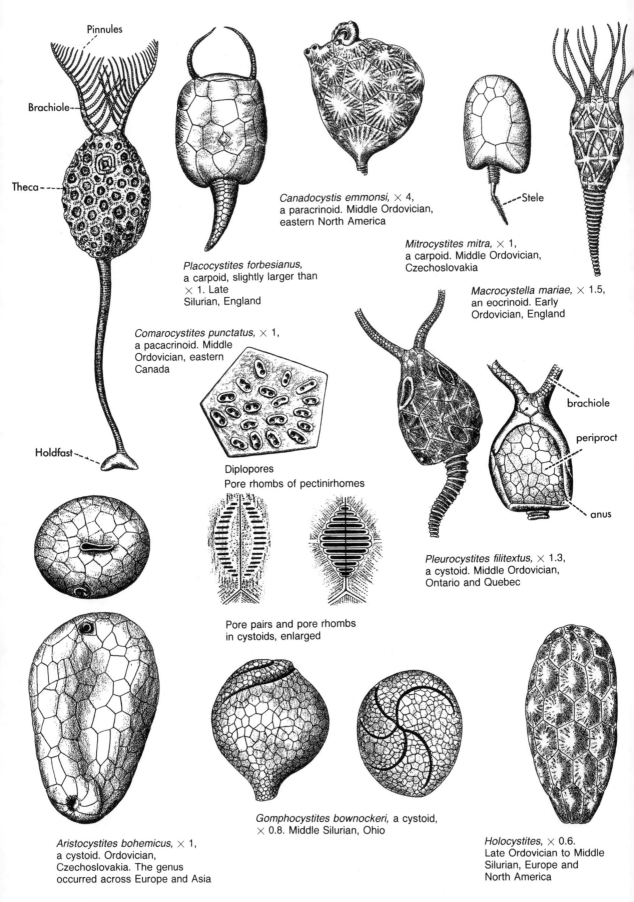

Pinnules

Brachiole

Theca

Holdfast

Canadocystis emmonsi, × 4, a paracrinoid. Middle Ordovician, eastern North America

Placocystites forbesianus, a carpoid, slightly larger than × 1. Late Silurian, England

Stele

Mitrocystites mitra, × 1, a carpoid. Middle Ordovician, Czechoslovakia

Macrocystella mariae, × 1.5, an eocrinoid. Early Ordovician, England

Comarocystites punctatus, × 1, a pacacrinoid. Middle Ordovician, eastern Canada

Diplopores
Pore rhombs of pectinirhomes

brachiole

periproct

anus

Pleurocystites filitextus, × 1.3, a cystoid. Middle Ordovician, Ontario and Quebec

Pore pairs and pore rhombs in cystoids, enlarged

Aristocystites bohemicus, × 1, a cystoid. Ordovician, Czechoslovakia. The genus occurred across Europe and Asia

Gomphocystites bownockeri, a cystoid, × 0.8. Middle Silurian, Ohio

Holocystites, × 0.6. Late Ordovician to Middle Silurian, Europe and North America

Carpoids, eocrinoids, paracrinoids, and cystoids

differences in the pores that took water through plates of the theca, apparently to secure oxygen. The groups together do not necessarily form a natural, monophyletic group. In one group the pores are arranged in parallel sets in rhomblike patterns and open either through slits or small holes shared by adjoining plates; in the second group the pores are arranged in pairs that are confined to one thecal plate. Most of the twenty-two families of cystoids lived from Cambrian to the end of Silurian times. Very few are known from Devonian strata.

Most cystoids were attached filter feeders. They used their brachioles to move organic particles toward their mouths and were probably not too bothered by some sediment being suspended in the shallow marine water, where they thrived.

Some forms, however, were rather highly modified. *Pleurocystites* may in fact have been a mobile form. It had a flexible stem and lacked a holdfast. This sort of stem could have propelled the cystoid through the water near the seabed by undulating to and fro.

Parablastoids. Though distinct from all echinoderm groups, the parablastoids superficially resembled blastoids. They were small, *Blastoidocrinus* being slightly less than 3 centimeters (slightly more than 1 in.) in diameter. The stem was made up of thin discoidal columnals, and the theca consisted of a large number of plates. In top, or dorsal, view, the theca had a five-pointed star shape with deeply indented areas, between the arms of the star, called interambulacral areas. The aboral (or dorsal) region was very distinct from the oral (or ventral) surface. The aboral surface had three or more circlets of plates and a series of tiny ambulacral plates along each of the five branches of the food-gathering grooves. Pores were present along plate margins. Only two genera, each with one species, are known from the Early Ordovician of Russia and the Middle Ordovician of eastern North America. Their relationships to other echinoderms are not well understood.

Blastoids. These fossils are often called "petrified nuts," though their technical name means "budlike." They were most often small, stemmed echinoderms with the diameter of the calyx being less than 2.5 centimeters (1 in.). Ranging from Silurian to latest Permian, they are most plentiful in the Early Carboniferous. Weathered rocks sometimes provide thousands of fine specimens.

The blastoid theca or calyx may be recognized by its shape, its five broad, cross-ribbed ambulacra, which are deeply grooved at the center, and the V-shaped plates that partly enclose them. Generally the theca was composed of eighteen to twenty-one main plates, plus a number of smaller ones, a markedly different arrangement from that of the crinoids, where there was a myriad of small plates. The mouth lay at the apex of the "bud"; around it were five holes (spiracles), one of which often served as an anus. During life the mouth was covered by small movable plates, and so were the ambulacra. These plates are generally missing from fossils, and so are the numerous jointed brachioles that once extended at both sides of the ambulacra and carried branches of the food grooves.

The respiratory apparatus of blastoids begans with rows of pores on both sides of the ambulacra. The pores led to thin-walled folded structures called hydrospires, one or more of which opened through each spiracle. These structures are distinctive of the blastoids. Water came in through the many pores, gave up oxygen to soft membranes lining the hydrospires, and passed out of the spiracles.

Most blastoids had stalks that were anchored to the sea bottom by means of rootlike extensions. A few became stemless, however, and lay on the mud or were partly embedded in it. Some of these stemless genera, such as *Timoroblastus,* developed winglike extensions or structures resembling the feet of old-fashioned jardinieres.

Blastoids, like many of the blastozoan groups, were never very abundant, except locally especially in cronoid bank deposits atop reefs. Silurian blastoids are only known from North America, but in the Devonian they are known all over the world.

Paracrinoids and Edrioblastoids. Paracrinoids appeared, diversified, and became extinct all in the Middle Ordovician. Because they are of local abundance only, however, it is quite possible that in the future they will be found in older and younger rocks. They were similar to many stemmed blastozoan groups. Their theca was like that of cystoids, their arms like those of

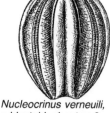

Tricoelocrinus woodmani, a blastoid, × 12. Mississippian, Indiana and Missouri

Stephanocrinus angulatus, a coronoid, about × 4. Silurian, New York and Indiana

Pentremites robustus, a blastoid, showing structure, enlarged

Orophocrinus stelliformis, a blastoid, × 1.5. Mississippian, Mississippi Valley

At left, *Pentremites godoni,* restored as in life, × 1

Timoroblastus coronatus, a stemless Permian blastoid, × 1.5. East Indies (Timor)

Nucleocrinus verneuili, a blastoid, about × 2. Devonian, Mississippi Valley

Blastozoans of various ages

crinoids, and their stems like those of blastoids. The irregularity of their plates and their pore system was different from that in blastoids. Their uniserial ambulacra and pinnules, or small branches on their arms, distinguished them from eocrinoids and cystoids. These pinnules must have provided an excellent strainer for gathering food.

The edrioblastoids were a primitive group of attached echinoderms that have been classified as blastoids, cystoids, or edrioasteroids (Chapter XX). They have been found only in the Middle Ordovician of Canada and Australia and are extremely rare even there. They were of small size, only about 2.0 centimeters (less than 1 in.) in diameter, and the theca was composed of only twenty major plates arranged in four circlets, every circlet made up of five each of basals, radials, deltoids, and orals—giving rise to a fivefold, or pentameral, symmetry. The theca was bulbous and blastoid-like. There were no

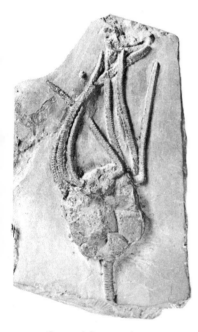

Caryocrinites ornatus, a cystoid, × 1. Middle Silurian, eastern North America

Three views of the blastoid *Pentremites* showing plates and apex; upper left × 1, others × 2

Troosticrinus reinwardti, a blastoid, × 1.5. Silurian, Tennessee

Pleurocystites filitextus, a cystoid, × 1.3. Ordovician, Ontario and Quebec

Blastoids and cystoids

brachioles and no pores in the thecal plates, thus distinguishing them from the cystoids. The irregularity of the smaller plates between the major plates made them different from blastoids. Only one species, *Astrocystites ottawaensis,* is known from this group, and its relationships to other echinoderms is not yet clear.

Coronoids. Several genera, including *Stephanocrinus,* once thought to be inadunate crinoids, among other things, have been placed in a blastozoan group of their own. They were restricted to the Ordovician and Silurian. They had coiled, biserial, and branching armlike appendages that were not connected to the body cavity, resembling the brachioles of blastozoans. The theca, fused into a solid structure, or corona, was pyramidal, with three circlets of plates. Five ambulacra were restricted to the top of the theca. Within processes or horns on this corona were U-shaped coelomic canals, unique among the blastozoans and probably used in breathing. Coronoids had a column of moderate length and were cemented by a holdfast that was disk-shaped. The closest relatives of the coronoids appear to be the blastoids.

THE VARIED AND SUCCESSFUL CRINOIDS

Crinoids, the so-called sea lilies, include the most complex and beautiful group of stalked echinoderms. During the Paleozoic Era, they also were the largest, the most successful, and the most abundant. Crinoids had appeared by the Early Ordovician. *Echmatocrinus,* known from the Middle Cambrian Burgess Shale, is thought by some paleontologists to be a crinoid; if so, it would push the origin of this class further back in time. Though many crinoids died out at the end of the Paleozoic, others lived on into modern times. Their range is as wide as the seas and oceans and extends from sunlit shoals and reefs to dark, frigid waters at depths of 13,000 feet (nearly 4,000 m.) or more. A few modern species are 50 to 60 feet (15–18 m.) long; a Cretaceous genus bore arms 4 feet (1.2 m.) in length. Vast colonies lived in shallow seas of the Devonian and Carboniferous, where their remains built up beds of limestone. One of these series in the Rocky Mountains near Banff, Alberta, reached a total of 200 feet (60 m.).

Most beds of crinoidal, or encrinal, limestone consist mainly of broken columns and separate colmnals, with only a few calyces. This may mean that mature crinoids broke loose from their stalks and drifted away, to be scattered widely when they died. It also may mean that the calyces disintegrated very soon after death, whereas the columns held together for a while.

The basic plan of crinoids resembles that of eocrinoids and cystoids; it also has been compared to a starfish resting bottom side up on a jointed column, with both mouth and anus directed upward. The arms always begin

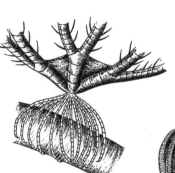

Crinoid columnals showing the axial canals. American Indians sometimes used columnals for beads. Somewhat enlarged

Base of *Antedon,* a comatulid, clinging by means of cirri, × 10. Recent

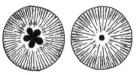

Cirrus —

Nodal - - -

Inter- <
nodals

Cirrus Nodal Internodals
Parts of a crinoid column

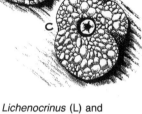

Lichenocrinus (L) and *Cystoidosaccus* (C), plate-covered crinoid holdfasts. (L) Ordovician–Silurian; (C) Ordovician. North America

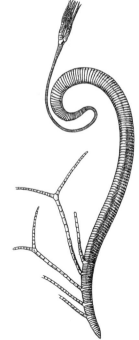

Myelodactylus, × 1.5, an inadunate whose cirri were specialized to conceal an elongate, slim crown. Middle Silurian to (?) Late Devonian, Europe and North America

Anchor-shaped base of *Ancyrocrinus,* an inadunate, × 0.8. Devonian, Europe and North America

Plate-covered, bulblike base of *Scyphocrinites,* a camerate, × 0.25. Silurian and Devonian, Eurasia and North America

Halysiocrinus, an inadunate, × 1, had a prostrate column, and its calyx rested on the bottom. Middle Devonian to Early Mississippian, North America

Eucalyptocrinites crassus, a camerate, restored, about × 0.5, showing the calyx, stalk, and divided roots. Silurian, central United States

Hemicrinus astierianus, an aberrant articulate crinoid with solidified column fused to the calyx and thick base, × 3. Late Cretaceous, Europe

Structures and habits of crinoids

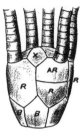

Plates in the calyx of three crinoids.
B, basals; IB, infrabasals; R, radials; X, anal;
AR, aniradial; RA, radianal

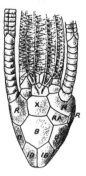

Carabocrinus, an inadunate
with very short arms.
Ordovician, Europe and
North America

Cornucrinus mirus,
an armless inadunate crinoid,
× 0.9.
Middle Ordovician, Europe

Arms of Petalocrinus,
an inadunate, × 1.6,
became broad plates radiating
from the calyx.
Middle Silurian, North America

Uperocrinus, a camerate, × 0.7,
had a long,
spiny anal tube.
Mississippian, Mississippi Valley

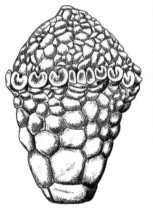

Cactocrinus, a camerate, × 1.4,
had smooth plates. Early
Mississippian, Iowa and
Missouri

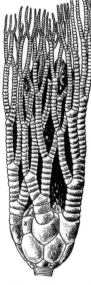

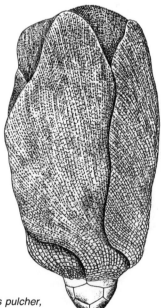

Arms of Cyathocrinites (about × 1)
divided several times; an inadunate.
Silurian to Mississippian (?) and Permian, worldwide

Scyphocrinites elegans,
a camerate, × 0.5, had great numbers
of plates in its calyx.
Late Silurian to Early Devonian,
Africa, Eurasia, and North America

Arms of Crotalocrinites pulcher,
an inadunate, × 0.8,
formed wide, fanlike structures.
Late Silurian, Gotland, Sweden

Structures of various crinoids

with only one series of brachial plates. Water enters the body through a perforated plate, as in edrioasteroids, passed through a ring and radial canals, and fills tube feet that extend through pores in the arms and are used for breathing. Cilia along grooves in the arms and their branches gather food and take it to the mouth.

This is the general plan; it allows for a great deal of variation and a corresponding abundance of terms. Most of these may be ignored, but we must note that the arms and calyx together are often called the crown, while the stalk, with its roots or base of attachment, becomes the pelma. The latter term appears in Pelmatozoa, a grouping sometimes used for all echinoderms that have or once had stalks, as well as the edrioasteroids.

Roots and Other Bases. Variations begin at the very bottom of the pelma. In many crinoids it consisted of rootlike structures that grew into mud as the roots of land plants grow into soil. The stalk also may have spread into a plate that was cemented to a shell, a coral, or some other hard object. This foundation was sometimes overturned by waves; a Late Ordovician formation in the Cincinnati, Ohio, region contains many flat, thin concretions that have had crinoid bases attached to both sides and even to their edges. Crinoid rootlets also have been found on petrified wood of Devonian age, suggesting that some of these echinoderms hung downward from floating logs.

Lichenocrinus and perhaps *Cystoidosaccus* are plate-covered bases of crinoids. Each base must have covered a pad of flesh. *Ancyrocrinus* is another base, which generally bore four prongs that enabled it to serve as an anchor. The roots of *Scyphocrinites* grew into a thick, plated bulb that was divided into sections and sometimes separately called *Lobolithus* or *Camarocrinas.* Once regarded as a float, which enabled the crinoid to drift with its body hanging downward, the bulb apparently provided fixation on rocky bottoms or on solid objects such as shells as well as stems of other crinoids.

The Stalk, or Column. Restorations sometimes show crinoids waving gracefully in the water or coiling and bending this way and that to reach levels where food might be plentiful or avoid disturbing currents. Such pictures somewhat ignore the nature of the stalk, which generally consists of flat columnals fastened face to face, with only a little freedom of movement allowed by the ligaments running between columnals. In some genera, however, the columnals are narrow with ridged or curved faces, which allowed them to tip from side to side. Columnals of platycrinitids also are twisted, so that perhaps the sum of their tiltings enabled the column to bend in several directions.

Columnals vary greatly in shape, from round to elliptical, quadrangular, star-shaped, or even crescentic. Their surfaces bear ridges and varied flutings whose principal function must have been to strengthen their linkage. In many crinoids the columnals changed shape during growth. One of the commonest changes led some to become larger than others, the two types being distinguished as nodals and internodals. Branchlets from stalks are called cirri, which appear only on nodals.

Since both stalks and bases grew throughout life, they had to be supplied with food and dissolved lime salts that could be turned into calcite. Most of this was done by a fleshy cord that ran through the axial canal seen in columnals or fragments of stalks. These canals range from large or small cylindrical tubes to others with five well-defined sections.

Most stalks served as means of support that were firmly anchored or cemented at the base. But *Myelodactylus* had no base, only a tip that could coil around corals, crinoids, or some other convenient object, and cling to them by means of cirri that were single-branched. The lower part of the stalk generally was thick, but more than halfway up to the calyx it contracted and commonly curved so abruptly that the column surrounded the crown. Except for a few species that were long enough to direct their bodies upward, *Myelodactylus* must have resembled a living question mark.

Still more extreme were changes in which the stalk was lost. That happened several times in various orders, producing such forms as the modern *Antedon* and *Uintacrinus,* of Late Cretaceous age and worldwide distribution. The former builds a stalk, breaks away from it, and clings to shells or other objects with a tuft of clawlike cirri, releasing its hold to swim or crawl slowly by using its arms. *Uintacrinus* did not even have cirri, but floated as plankton at the surface in hordes that sometimes drifted into shallows, where they were stranded and thus preserved by the hundreds.

The Calyx or Theca.　The crinoidal calyx consists of two parts: the cup, or dorsal cup, and the tegmen. The former is aptly described by its name, for it is a cuplike, bowl-shaped, or vase-shaped structure made up of plates that have definite forms and occupy definite positions in various genera. The tegmen ranges from a leathery covering over the cup to a roof of thick plates that may rise in a tall anal sac or tube or may form a solid roof over both the mouth and the food grooves.

The oldest and most primitive crinoids, inadunates, had small, rigid, elongate cups with two circlets of plates (monocyclic) called basals (B) and radials (R), the former being attached to the stalk, while the latter supported the arms. Some of these early inadunates were dicyclic, that is they had a third circlet of plates below the basals, called the infrabasals. Another plate, the anal (X), rested between two radials and above a plate called radianal in some genera and aniradial in others.

Other crinoids added infrabasals, inserted new plates near the anal, took arm plates into the cup while increasing their number, and developed new intrabrachial plates that were not connected with the anal. Because of these additions, even small crinoids such as *Uperocrinus* and others such as *Ichthyocrinus* and *Scyphocrinites* had large numbers of plates in their calyces, often numbering more than one hundred. Paleozoic genera then died out, and most of those that lived in the Mesozoic and Cenozoic eras reduced

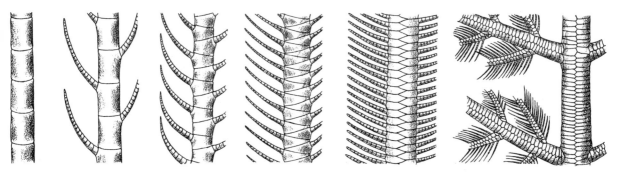

A variety of brachial structures found in crinoids. As brachials became shorter and shorter and formed two series, the number of pinnules on crinoid arms increased

both the size of the calyx and the number of its plates. *Uintacrinus,* however, retained a bulbous calyx that contained a large number of plates.

We have mentioned crinoids whose stalks were coiled so deeply that they surrounded the calyx. These aberrant types were erect, but *Halysiocrinus* lay on the bottom or arched down to it with the calyx bent sharply upward. One side also was flattened, as if to form a surface on which the calyx could lie.

Hemicrinus, of Cretaceous age, had a short stalk that was broadly attached at its base, the calyx turned sidewise at right angle, and its plates as well as its columnals were fused into one solid mass from which thick arms projected. This crinoid may have lived amid strong currents or in turbulent areas where waves reached the bottom.

Some peculiarities involved both calyx and tegmen. In *Eucalyptocrinites,* for example, the calyx has a deep concavity at its lower end, so that the stalk is attached in an inverted cup. The tegmen forms a tube and then spreads out; around it are ten partitions that form compartments, each of which holds two branched arms.

Arms, or Brachia. The arms of crinoids come in a variety of shapes too. The arms of crinoids differ from those of most other stalked echinoderms in that they are direct outgrowths of the central body mass and carry extensions of the food grooves and water-vascular system. At their base there is an opening into the body cavity within the theca. In relatively primitive types, the arms branch only once, the two branches are of equal size and are formed by single rows of jointed plates known as brachials. In *Carabocrinus,* these arms were short; in *Petalocrinus,* the arms developed into plates that grew so large that they resembled petals curved backward toward the base. Other changes may be summarized as follows:

Many crinoids kept a single row of brachials but may have added greatly to their length.

In other, uniserial arms the brachial plates became wedge-shaped. Further shortening and narrowing allowed them to lie side by side with only their edges alternating, leading to biserial arms, however, which retain a uniserial base.

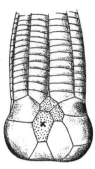

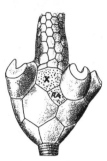

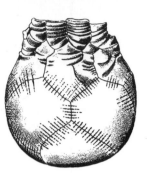

Phanocrinus, × 1.6. Carboniferous, Africa, Europe, and North America

Botryocrinus, × 1.5. Silurian to Devonian, Europe and North America

Marsupites, an articulate, × 0.8. Late Cretaceous, Africa, Australia, Eurasia, and North America

A fragment of *Pentacrinites,* an articulate, × 0.7. Jurassic, Europe and North America

Two inadunate crinoids. X, anal plate; RA, radianal

Rhizocrinus, an articulate, about × 10. Recent

Glyptocrinus decadactylus, a camerate, × 1. Middle Ordovician, North America

Eutrochocrinus christyi, a camerate. Mississippian, Mississippi Valley and New Mexico

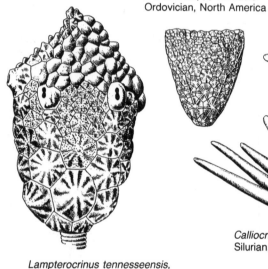

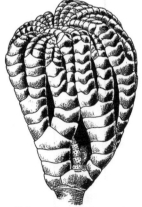

Calliocrinus, a camerate, about × 1. Silurian, Sweden

Lampterocrinus tennesseensis, a camerate, × 1.4. Middle Silurian, Tennessee

Eutaxocrinus fletcheri, a flexibilian, × 1.1. Mississippian, North America

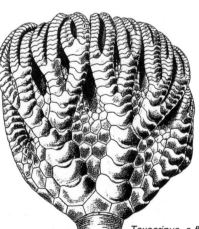

Eutaxocrinus whiteavesi, a flexibilian, × 1.5. Middle Devonian to Early Carboniferous, Europe and North America

Taxocrinus, a flexibilian, × 0.5. Devonian to Early Carboniferous, Europe and North America

Sagenocrinites clarki, × 1.1, interbrachials dotted; a flexibilian. Silurian, Tennessee

Inadunate, articulate, camerate, and flexible crinoids

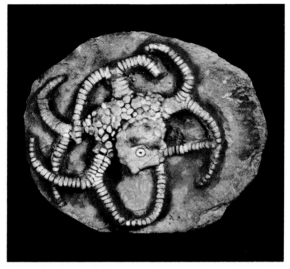

This wood has been replaced by silica, preserving cells, growth rings, wood rays, and distortion produced by disease. Colors are due to iron minerals and are not those of the original wood. (Courtesy of the United States National Museum of Natural History, Washington, D.C.)

This mineralized crinoid contains some of its original calcite. It also shows the shape and structure of plates in the calyx and arms. Mississippian, Burlington, Iowa. (Courtesy of the United States National Museum of Natural History)

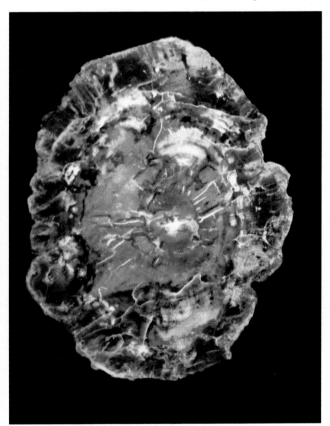

Wood replaced by silica, colored brightly by iron compounds. It preserves none of the original woody structure. Triassic, Petrified Forest, Arizona. (Courtesy of the United States National Museum of Natural History)

Impression of a leaf showing its shape and its veins; the color is due to mineral deposits. Oligocene, Republic, Washington. (Courtesy of the United States National Museum of Natural History)

FOSSILS PRESERVED IN VARIOUS WAYS

Internal mold of a gastropod, from Andamooka, South Australia, of Early Cretaceous age. The shell was filled with material that was later opalized. None of the original shell material remains. (With permission of Brian Shelton, from his collection)

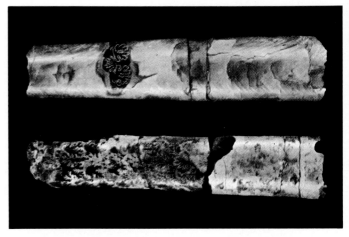

(Above) two species of *Baculites* from Pierre Shale of Pennington County, South Dakota. (Below) Bearpaw Shale, Valley County, Montana. Both specimens preserve the nacreous structure and show the sutures made by septa dividing the shell into chambers. (Courtesy of the United States National Museum of Natural History)

Pinus, a pinecone from Oligocene deposits of Florissant, Colorado. It shows both the shape of the cone and the scales that enclosed its seeds. (Courtesy of Princeton University)

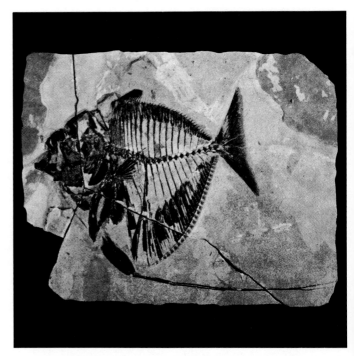

Mene rhombeus, a deep-bodied fish related to the modern pompano. Hundreds of petrified bones make up this fossil, which shows the shape and structure of the fish and its strange hind, or pelvic, fins. They have moved far forward and have degenerated into bony spines. (Courtesy of the United States National Museum of Natural History)

FOSSILS SHOWING BOTH FORM AND STRUCTURE

Silicified cones of an araucarian "pine," one cut to show its structure. Triassic of Argentina. (Courtesy of Princeton University)

A snail, *Euconospira*, that preserves its color pattern. Pennsylvanian, near Alamogordo, New Mexico. (Courtesy of the United States National Museum of Natural History)

Leaf of *Platanus*, a sycamore. This impression shows shape and venation; colors are due to minerals. Late Miocene, Faraday Dam, Washington. (Courtesy of the United States National Museum of Natural History)

Uintacyon, a small carnivore whose bones and teeth are petrified. Eocene (Bridger Formation) of central Wyoming. (Courtesy of the United States National Museum of Natural History)

An external mold showing one valve of *Derbyia*, a brachiopod. Mississippian, Galena, Kansas. (Courtesy of the United States National Museum of Natural History)

Coenites, a silicified tabulate coral that shows only the surface of the colony. Silurian, Louisville, Kentucky. (Courtesy of the United States National Museum of Natural History)

FOSSILS SHOWING SHAPES, COLORS, AND STRUCTURES

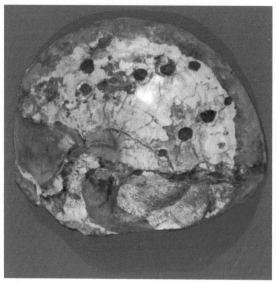

Placenticeras, a large ammonoid from the Cretaceous Pierre Shale, of South Dakota. Holes in this shell show that it was bitten by a hungry mosasaur, or marine lizard. (Courtesy of the University of Michigan)

FOSSIL CEPHALOPODS AND CORALS

Restoration of a spiny nautiloid, among corals, glass sponges, and other animals of a Permian sea bottom in the region that now is southwestern Texas. (Courtesy of the University of Michigan)

Emmonsia, Coenites (both tabulates), and other corals in a piece of weathered limestone stained by hematite. Middle Devonian near Louisville, Kentucky. (Courtesy of the United States National Museum of Natural History)

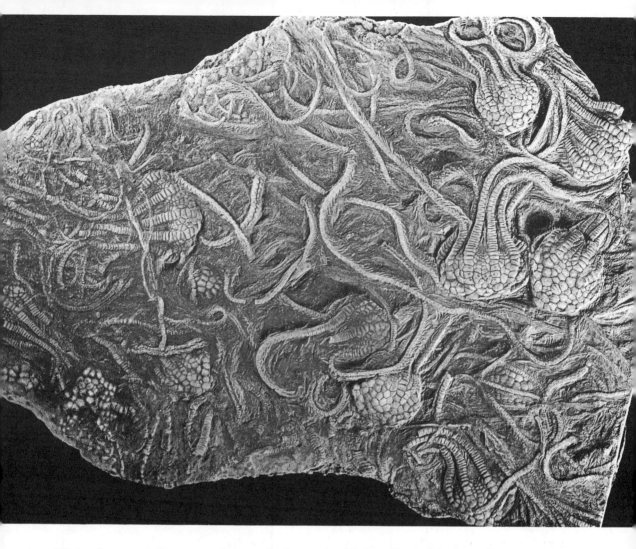

Uintacrinus socialis, *a stemless articulate crinoid that floated in Late Cretaceous seas of Europe and North America. This slab was found near Elkader, Iowa. About* × *0.4*

Both uniserial and biserial arms repeatedly developed side branches, or pinnules.

The arms of some crinoids ceased to branch, and developed long, slender plates, as in *Petalocrinus.*

Many crinoids developed arms that branched again and again, becoming both large and complex. Examples of this type include the many-branched pentacrinds of Mesozoic and modern seas. In *Crotalocrinites,* of Silurian age, the abundant branches are linked in flexible nets that either form broad, fanlike fronds or partially enfold each other. Still more extreme is *Barrandeocrinus,* from the Silurian of northern Europe. Its pinnules are free only at the tips; below this they consist of flattened plates that interlock, forming ten structures that curve downward and suggest the sections of an orange. The mouth was buried in a pit amid these overdeveloped arms.

Cornucrinus lost its free arms, retaining only ambulacra and food grooves that really were parts of the calyx.

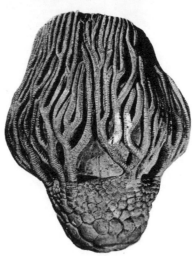

Cactocrinus, a camerate, × 0.3.
Mississippian, North America

Aesiocrinus magnificus,
an inadunate, × 0.6. Late
Pennsylvanian, Missouri

Megistocrinus evansi,
a camerate, × 0.4. Mississippian,
North America

Cusacrinus nodobrachiatus,
a camerate, × 0.5. Mississippian,
North America

Onychocrinus, a flexibilian, × 0.4.
Early Carboniferous, Europe
and North America

Megistocrinus nobilis, × 0.4. Mississippian,
North America. From Le Grand, Iowa

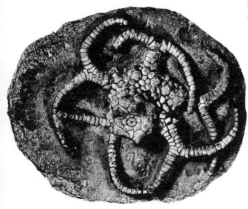

Gilbertsocrinus, a camerate, × 2.5.
Devonian to Early Carboniferous,
Europe and North America

Dorycrinus mississippiensis, a long-spined
camerate, × 0.5. Mississippian,
Mississippi Valley

Typical crinoids

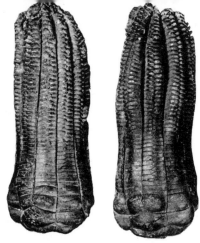

Cupressocrinites,
an inadunate, × 0.7.
Devonian, Europe

Encrinus liliiformis,
an inadunate, × 1. Triassic, Europe

Cyathocrinites, an inadunate, × 0.5.
Silurian to Early Carboniferous,
worldwide

Onychocrinus ulrichi,
a flexibilian, about × 0.4.
Mississippian, Indiana

Onychocrinus ramulosus, × 0.2.
Mississippian, Indiana

Ichthyocrinus laevis,
a flexibilian, × 1, Silurian,
North America

Crinoid bases on a
slab of shale.
Ordovician, Ohio

Eucladocrinus, a
camerate, × 1.
Mississippian,
North America

Inadunate, camerate, and flexible crinoids

Spines. Crinoids were the first echinoderms to deserve the name "spiny skins." Many genera had thick, rough plates in the cup; in others, the plates extended into spines that projected from cup, tegmen, arms, stalk, and even from long anal tubes. *Ancyrocrinus,* as we have seen, also developed basal spines that served as prongs of an anchor. Spines of *Arthroacantha,* from the Devonian of Europe and North America, were even attached, by joints, to small tubercles and were thus moveable.

MAIN GROUPS OF CRINOIDS

There are more than six thousand species of fossil crinoids. In modern seas there are some twenty-five stalked genera and ninety more that lack stalks. Living and fossil forms can be grouped into four well-marked categories, often called orders. Three of these orders are for the most part confined to the Paleozoic Era, when they often formed dense "crinoid gardens," some functioning like kites in the submarine currents. Only one of the four orders survives to the present day.

Inadunata. These are relatively simple crinoids which include the oldest known and most primitive members of the class and survived until the Early Triassic. There is a possibility, however, that the living *Hypocrinus* might be a "living fossil" survivor of this group. The plates of the calyx are rigidly fastened together, the tegmen covers the mouth, but the food grooves are above it. The arms are uniserial or biserial and nonpinnulate or pinnulate; in most genera they are free or loosely connected above the radial plates. Often, the fivefold (pentameral) symmetry of the calyx has an extra plate, the radianal, in the radial circle. The oldest inadunates had long, straight cups, but in younger, Paleozoic genera, the calyx was expanded sideways and flattened, and the crown took on a flowerlike appearance.

Flexibilia. Another Paleozoic group (Ordovician to Permian) were the flexible crinoids. Joints between plates of both cup and tegmen show that these structures were flexible during life, only loosely united. The lower brachials formed part of the cup, and interbrachials and interradials ranged from few to many. The upper surface of the tegmen bore both mouth and open food grooves; the arms were uniserial and had no pinnules and were generally much wider than they were high. As in the inadunates, there was a radianal plate and an anal plate. These crinoids developed similar specializations to those of the inadunates but were less diverse.

Camerata. The camerates were the most diverse of all Paleozoic crinoid groups. All plates of the calyx were rigidly united and commonly were thick. The tegmen covered both mouth and food grooves. The lower brachial plates formed part of the cup, and so—in most genera—did the interradials. The arms were uniserial or biserial and pinnulate. The radianal plate was absent. Camerates ranged from Ordovician to Late Permian and were especially abundant during the Mississippian. The earliest camerates shared many characteristics with the inadunates, from which they may have originated.

Articulata. In this extremely varied group of stalked and stalkless (the comatulids) crinoids, the cups commonly are small and contain few plates. The ability to move and not remain forever attached opened up a great many possibilities for the articulates—thus explaining their success. Plates of the cup are united by slightly flexible joints; their pinnulate arms are very flexible and always uniserial; the tegmen is a leathery affair that bears the mouth and open food grooves and may be studded with small plates. Nearly all of the Mesozoic and Cenozoic crinoids were/are articulates.

The articulates must have evolved during the Permian Period, though their oldest known members did not appear until other orders were completely or nearly extinct. There also are hints that they form two major groups, not one, some having come from inadunates while others are descendants of the Flexibilia. Be that as it may, the articulates achieved little variety during the Mesozoic and early Tertiary, though series such as *Uintacrinus socialis* existed in vast numbers. Expansion began during the Tertiary, and the articulates now number more than six hundred widely differing species. Ranging from shallows to abysses and from tropical to near-polar seas, they compare in importance with the camerates of Early Carboniferous times.

THE PUZZLING HOMALOZOANS: ANIMALS IN SEARCH OF A PHYLUM

Animals whose relationships are not obvious often stir the imaginations of paleontologists, and perhaps get more attention than they deserve. Conodonts and graptolites are certainly two such puzzling groups, but equally or more problematical are the homalozoans, some also known as the calcichordates, or carpoids. They have generally been classified with the echinoderms, but some workers, in using the name Calcichordata, have suggested that they have chordate, and thus verbetrate, similarities.

Unlike many echinoderms, the homalozoans had no radical symmetry. For that matter, many forms had no symmetry at all. Some carpoids, however, did have a nearly bilaterally symmetric skeleton, just as in many of the chordates.

Three basic kinds of carpoids have been recognized, the stylophorans, homosteleans, and the homoiosteleans.

Homosteleans were made up of a theca and a stele, which was a narrowed extension of the theca. The theca was flattened and had two very dissimilar sides: one flat and presumably the one on which the animal rested, and an opposite, concave side. The carapace was made of a middle section of many small plates (centralia) and a peripheral area with large

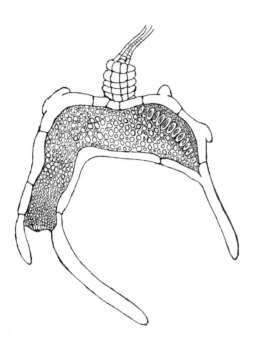

Cothurnocystis, *a stylophoran carpoid, about 5 centimeters (2 in.) wide. Ordovician, Europe. (Drawing by Frank Knight from Moore, 1967)*

marginal plates (marginalia). The stele, a narrow, taillike structure attached to the theca, had a double series of plates divided along the midline by smaller plates, and there was no arm attached to the theca. The homosteleans were restricted entirely to the Middle Cambrian. They may have had a sedentary life with their stele embedded in the sea bottom while they filtered food from the water. Or perhaps they were mobile bottom detrital feeders. At present we don't know which, if either, is the best model to explain their lifestyle.

Stylophora is another carpoid group. *Cothurnocystis* was a typical stylophore, which was laterally flattened. It was boot-shaped and had a stalk. The stylophores had large marginal plates and a mosaic of small median plates. Along the margin were several spines projecting away from the stalk. A series of slitlike pores lay near the toe of the "boot"; some paleontologists have thought these functioned like vertebrate gill slits. Not all paleontologists would agree with this interpretation, and so the controversy goes on. The group ranges from Middle Cambrian to Late Devonian.

A third group of carpoids is the homoiosteleans. They were very similar to the homosteleans but had a single arm and a stele that had only a double row of plates. The theca was made up entirely of a series of small plates. The group ranged from the Cambrian of Nevada to the Early Devonian of Victoria, in Australia.

On the basis of embryological studies, as well as developmental and biochemical work, echinoderms and chordates seem to be related. So it is quite possible that carpoids may well fall in the twilight zone between these two major phyla. Further studies on the internal anatomy, in rare specimens where it is preserved as well as the discovery of more fossils, will be needed before the controversy is convincingly resolved.

CHAPTER XX

Stars, Urchins, and Cucumbers of the Sea

 We have likened crinoids to starfish resting upon joined stalks with the mouth directed upward. We now come to the groups of echinoderms in which the mouth is on the underside or at one end of a sausage-shaped body.

SEA STARS AND THEIR ORIGIN

Books about living animals generally describe two great groups of starshaped echinoderms, one of which includes true starfish (asteroids), while the other is made up of brittle and serpent stars (ophiuroids). Paleontologists add a third group, the somasters, and place all three groups in a class termed the Stelleroidea, or "starlike ones." A useful English equivalent is "sea stars," leaving "starfish" for the animals technically called asteroids.

Somasters ranged from Early Ordovician to Late Devonian, especially in western Europe. They have short, thick arms and large openings, which once contained the mouth, surrounded by tough skin. Plates with large pores, which accommodated tube feet, appeared at the edge of this opening and ran in two adjacent series along the middle of each arm. Many rows of rodlike plates called virgalia branched off at each side, completing a structure that resembled the arms and pinnules of a crinoid. Exceptionally good specimens show that the upper surface was covered with tough skin studded with little spicules. Skin also covered the virgalia on the undersurface.

If these fossils mean what they seem to, sea stars are descendants of Cambrian crinoids that lost their stalks, lay mouth downward, and began to crawl with tube feet, which their ancestors had used only for respiration. The spicules of Ordovician somasters probably are specializations, since the oldest true starfish have plates resembling those of crinoids.

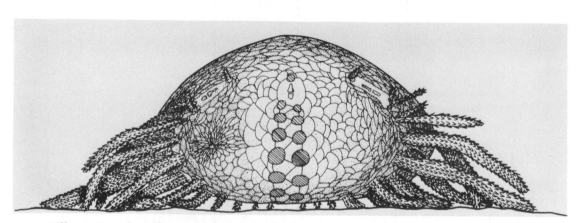

Gillocystis polypoda, an ophiocistioid, about 4 centimeters (1.6 in.) across. Early Devonian, Victoria, Australia. (Drawing by and courtesy of P. Jell)

STARFISH WAYS AND FOSSILS

This resemblance appears only in Paleozoic starfish; the plates of most later types interlock and generally are rough or spiny. Typical asteroids have thick arms that contain lobes of the stomach, digestive glands, and reproductive organs. Water can be absorbed and then forced out through the skin, but it also is taken into the body through a porous plate (madreporite) that lies on the upper surface, near the point where two arms join. Water goes from this plate to the tube feet through canals that suggest those of crinoids and edrioasteroids.

How Starfish Feed. A starfish feels for food or tastes it by means of specialized tube feet near the tips of its arms. Shorter feet, which line the well-developed ambulacra, are used mainly for clinging or for crawling at speeds that vary from an inch or two to almost a foot (2–30 cm.) per minute. Often, however, the animal lies in one place for hours, scarcely moving an arm.

Starfish use foods of several kinds and devour them in various ways. Some species eat organic debris that drifts across the sea bottom, catching it in sheets of slime which then are swallowed and digested. When such carrion becomes scarce, the secretion of slime is halted, and the stomach, which is a membranous sac, begins to flow out of the mouth. There it dissolves seaweeds, small algae that grow on rocks, or even astringent sponges. A similar method is used to devour sea urchins and chitons, though starfish that feed on snails usually swallow them whole by pushing them into the mouth with their tube feet. Mussels, clams, and oysters are pulled open by means of the tube feet, after which the stomach surrounds the victim and rapidly digests its flesh.

Fossil Starfish. Such are the ways of living starfish; fossils seem to have had similar habits. They begin with such creatures as *Hudsonaster,* of middle to Late Ordovician age. *Hudsonaster* is less than an inch wide and has stubby arms. Its upper surface is composed of smooth, thick plates that are arranged in regular order suggesting that of a crinoid cup. *Palaeaster* and

Devonaster have longer, more slender arms and small plates between rows of large ones. Though the latter still form definite patterns, the small plates between them do not.

Some basically primitive starfish developed unusual forms. *Stuertzaster,* for example, had broad, petal-shaped arms and a bulbous body that resembled the mushrooms called earth stars. *Cheiropteraster* was even more aberrant; it had a very large opening for the mouth but no arms, its ambulacra being directly attached to a baglike body without plates or spicules. *Loriolaster* had a small mouth and well-developed ambulacra that formed arms, though the rest of the body lacked ossicles. Like *Cheiropteraster* and several other unusual starfish, this genus is found in hard Devonian shales (often miscalled slates) of Bundenbach, Germany.

Starfish are rare in the Paleozoic and are even less plentiful in Mesozoic and Cenozoic formations. Most of the fossils belong to genera that developed large, thick plates that were either smooth or spiny; they include living genera as well as others that are extinct. *Metopaster,* for example, is a Cretaceous genus which, like its modern relatives, had massive plates and arms that were not much more than angles on the sides of the body. *Oreaster* is a modern genus that appeared in Jurassic seas. Most fossils have rather slender arms, but the most familiar living species has short arms and a thick, well-armored body whose color may be red, yellow, or blue.

BRITTLE STARS; THE OPHIUROIDS

The Ophiuroidea ("snakelike tails") are so called because most of them have thin, snaky arms; their popular name refers to the fact that those organs are easily broken. Types whose arms branch again and again are called basket stars.

Brittle stars are specialized descendants of somasters whose bodies became disk-shaped and whose arms grew slender. The stomach does not extend into the arms, and the mouth is star-shaped and narrow. Instead of being hollow, the arms contain plates that are articulated like vertebrae in a backbone. In living species these so-called vertebrae are embedded in tough tissue set with wide plates and spines, while epidermis covers the plates. The creatures crawl by pulling with some arms and pushing with others, in a complex of wriggling movements. The arms also are used to hold large pieces of food and pass them to the mouth. Small particles are passed along by the tube feet. *Onychaster,* of Mississippian age, clung to the arms or anal tubes of crinoids, apparently feeding on waste materials. These may have been gathered in slime like that secreted and then swallowed by some modern starfish.

Brittle stars first appear in Early Ordovician strata and are sparingly found in deposits of later ages and epochs. Though the best specimens come

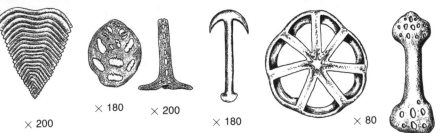

× 200   × 180   × 200   × 180   × 80

Spicules of varied holothurians, or sea cucumbers, from Europe and North America

× 130

Cheiropteraster giganteus, an ophiuroid, × 0.25. Devonian, Germany

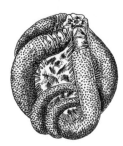

Onychaster flexilis, a brittle star, × 1. Mississippian, Indiana

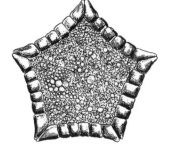

Metopaster, an asteroid. Cretaceous to Miocene, Europe, North America, and New Zealand

Madreporite

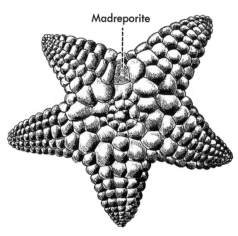

Villebrunaster thorali, a somaster. Ordovician, France

Hudsonaster incomptus, an asteroid, × 2. Late Ordovician, Ohio

Aganaster gregarius, an ophiuroid, or brittle star, × 1. Mississippian, Indiana

Madreporite

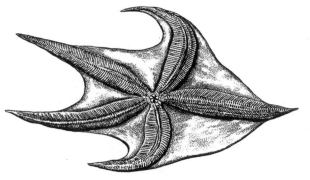

Loriolaster mirabilis, an ophiuroid. Early Devonian (Bundenbach "slate"), Germany

Devonaster eucharis, an asteroid, × 1. Middle Devonian, New York and Ontario

Sea stars and spicules of sea cucumbers

318

from Early Devonian black shales of Europe, good examples have been found in Middle Ordovician rocks of eastern North America.

ECHINOIDS, OR SEA URCHINS

The word *urchin* once meant "hedgehog" *(Erinaceus)*—plump, spiny mammals that range from Western Europe and North Africa to China, and which have been introduced to New Zealand. Sea urchins, or Echinoidea, are echinoderms that have neither stalks nor arms and commonly are much more spiny than the mammals for which they are named. They also have a great range, being found in seas around the world and in formations ranging from early Paleozoic to Recent.

Armor and Anatomy. This long geologic record reveals the development of armor that became increasingly sturdy and so was readily petrified. The most primitive echinoids had tests—they should not be called shells—made of smallish plates that overlapped, were movable, and often fell apart after death. In progressive types, the plates are firmly fastened and commonly are thick or are reinforced by secondary deposits that fill as much as half of the test. Several genera whose plates remain relatively thin possess clublike, massive spines. Though the internal structure of the plates is lacy or netlike, many of them are strong enough to survive burial and petrifaction.

The oldest and most primitive echinoids are spheroidal; later types may be flattened at top and bottom, subconical, discoidal, or so irregular that only pictures can adequately describe their shapes. The ventral surface commonly is flattened and has a central opening, the peristome ("around the mouth"), which in life is covered by tough skin studded with calcareous plates. The dorsal surface is moderately to steeply arched; in most regular echinoids (called Regularia in older classifications), its central section is occupied by two sets of plates termed the apical system. One set, the periproct, surrounds the anus; the other, the oculogenital ring, includes five plates at the tips of the ambulacra and five more containing large pores through which reproductive cells pass out of the body.

In most irregular echinoids (Irregularia, of older classifications), the apical system is divided. The oculogenital ring remains at or near the center of the upper surface, but the anus and periproct move to the rear. They may even lie on the ventral surface, a short distance back of the mouth.

The regular and the irregular echinoids are similar in having one genital plate that is a sievelike madreporite, through which water is taken into canals leading to the tube feet. They reach out from the ambulacra, as they do in crinoids, starfish, and other echinoderms. Each starfish foot, however, comes from one pore and is filled with liquid from one muscular, contractile sac. An urchin's foot starts out as two sacs which send tubes through a pair of pores. The tubes then join and form a single organ, which may be very long.

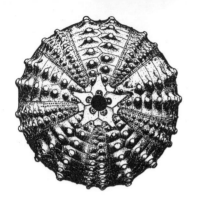

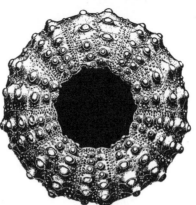

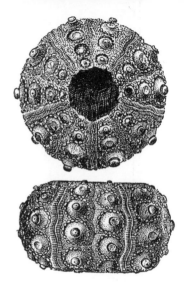

Goniopygus. Jurassic to Eocene, Eurasia, North Africa, and North and South America

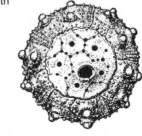

A cidaroid from the Paleocene, New Jersey

Salenia. Cretaceous to Recent. Fossils known from the Northern Hemisphere and Australia. Recent, worldwide

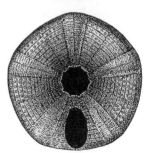

Holaster. Cretaceous to Eocene, worldwide

Holectypus. Jurassic to Cretaceous, Europe and North America

Diplopodia. Triassic to Cretaceous, Eurasia and North America

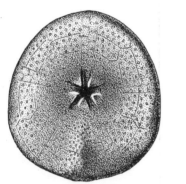

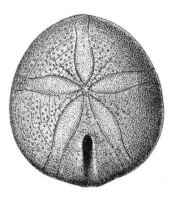

Hardouinja. Late Cretaceous, North America

Typical sea urchins, or echinoids, all euechinoids except one cideroid. (After Clark and Twitchell)

Ambulacra vary almost as much as the entire test. Some are narrow and almost straight; some are flexuous; others are petal-shaped. They may run from peristome to apical system or may be limited to part of the dorsal surface. In primitive genera they contain two rows of large plates, but some Paleozoic fossils have several rows of small ones. Mesozoic and Cenozoic sea urchins combined small plates and rearranged them until many formed single large compound plates.

All sea urchin tests bear tubercles, which may be large and conspicuous or may be too small to be seen without a magnifying glass. During life, the test is covered with skin, while the tubercles serve as attachments for spines that are held in place by ligaments and moved by cordlike muscles. In primitive genera, these spines are borne only on plates between the ambulacra, but they appear on the ambulacral plates of Mesozoic and Cenozoic urchins.

Echinoids eat with a complex device called the lantern, or Aristotle's lantern. It contains five pointed teeth and as many as thirty-five bonelike plates, all operated by some sixty muscles. The plates form five identical sets, which serve as sheaths and guides for the teeth as well as attachments for muscles. As teeth wear at one end, they grow at the other, and so are slowly pushed downward through notches in the lantern.

Two other groups of structures demand attention, since they are important in identifying the various kinds of echinoids not often found as fossils. First come the pedicellariae, tiny nipperlike or jawlike structures that move to and fro, capturing or removing things that settle upon the skin. The other structures are plates, rods, and hooks of calcite that are found in the intestine, reproductive glands, tube feet, and several other structures. Like pedicellariae, they are so small that they must be examined through a microscope.

We have already mentioned irregular and regular echinoids. Until the mid-1950s, urchins were divided between these two groups. Soon after this, it was found that "irregularity" had probably developed more than once, and so this character could not be used to group closely related animals. Instead, classifications, and thus relationships, had to be decided upon by looking at a larger number of anatomical details.

The new classification to emerge was based on the general makeup and strength or rigidity of the test or shell, the number of ambulacral and interambulacral columns, and the actual structure of the ambulacral plates, Aristotle's lantern, and perignathic girdle, flanges inside the test around the peristome that supported the chewing apparatus of the echinoid—the lantern. The detailed structure of the apical disk and regularity are factors used in ordinal and lower levels of classification.

Two major groups are recognized, the perischoechinoids, which range from Ordovician to Recent, and the euechinoids, which don't appear until the Late Triassic and survive to recent times. We will look at both of these groups in some detail.

Perischoechinoids. These are the primitive members of the Echinozoa, including all the extinct Paleozoic echinoids as well as the fossil and living cidaroids. The Paleozoic forms differ from younger echinoids in several ways. The test is usually globular and always regular; very few flattened forms are known. The periproct lies in the center of the apical disk. Many have flexible tests and are large. Because of the flexible tests, specimens are quite often found in a collapsed and flattened state. Ambulacral plates never have more than one pair of pores per column, even though there may be many columns.

The cidaroids were the only Paleozoic group to survive the Permo-Triassic crisis and live on until today. They probably gave rise to all Mesozoic and Cenozoic echinoid stocks. The cidaroids themselves have changed little since the Mesozoic, and like the lingulid brachiopods and the ginkgo tree, are looked upon as "living fossils."

Cidaroids have large interambulacral plates that each have a single, big tubercle in the center, onto which a spine attaches. They have narrow, snakelike ambulacra made up of small plates, each pierced by a single pair of pores. The Aristotle's lantern is very simple. They have a wide variety of spine types. Shallow-water forms have club-shaped or fusiform spines that probably acted as stabilizers in rough water. Deeper-water, mud-dwelling forms had elongate, slender spines. Cidaroids may extend back to the Silurian, but certainly are known in the Devonian.

Euechinoids. All post-Paleozoic echinoids except the cidaroids belong in this group, which first appears in the Late Triassic. Euechinoids all have five ambulacra and five interambulacra, which are composed of two columns each. Individual plates can have more than one pair of pores; these are called compound plates. Unlike the perischoechinoids, they can be either regular or irregular. Likewise, the Aristotle's lantern may be present, but it can be lost in irregular forms. The euechinoids were able to move into a great many more lifestyles than their predecessors had, even going so far as to become good burrowers.

Within the euechinoids there are four major groups, and among these are about eighteen orders. We will look briefly at the four major groups.

Diadematacea. These first appear in the Late Jurassic and survive today. They usually have simple plates, though a few have some compound ones. The Aristotle's lantern is simple, as in the primitive cidaroids, which probably gave rise to the euechinoids. Though there are many species that live at depths, those probably most memorable are reef species that have elongate, poisonous spines, such as *Diadema*.

Echinacea. The echinaceans range from Late Triassic to present-day and are all regular echinoids, with more complex structures than occur in the diadamataceans. They have a complex perignathic girdle, plates with more than a single pair of pores, gill slits, and a complex Aristotle's lantern.

Gnathostomata. The gnathostomes are irregular echinoids that first appeared in the Jurassic, one group of which is familiar to us today as sand dollars, which are clypeasteroids. All have ambulacral plates with only one pair of pores. The Aristotle's lantern has keeled teeth present, and the peristome and apical system are about opposite one another except in the clypeasteroids, in which they both are often on the oral surface. The clypeasteroids appeared rather late in echinoid history, in Paleocene rocks. In most respects they are highly specialized, since the oculogenital ring (plates surrounding the periproct and anus) is fused and the test assumes unusual shapes and is generally strengthened by internal ribs, plates, and pillars of calcite. The spines on these forms are small, generally of two types, and numerous. They have many minute accessory food-gathering tube feet outside the petals.

Early clypeasteroids were tiny and egg-shaped, with ambulacra that were not quite petals. Later genera, including *Clypeaster* itself, became larger and thicker, with well-developed petals and the mouth at the top of an inverted funnel. Most clypeasteroids, however, are sand dollars, depressed creatures with a flattened undersurface crossed by food-collecting grooves that commonly branch. Spines are so short and delicate that they can look like fur.

Since clypeasteroids have sturdy tests, they are abundant fossils. In some places they almost fill beds of soft limestone; in others, they litter the ground as rain wears away deposits of soft marl, shale, or sandstone.

Atelostomata. This last major group of euechinoids are all irregular forms that lack an Aristotle's lantern as well as a girdle in adults. The peristome and apical system are seldom opposite, and the ambulacra generally form a flowerlike pattern. Cassiduloids are in this group. They appeared first in the Jurassic and still exist; their petal-like ambulacra have lost the compound plates and are limited to the dorsal surface, forming blunt petals. A double ring of flowerlike plates, the floscelle, surrounds the mouth—a structure that exists in no other group of urchins.

The spatangoids and holasteroids, or heart urchins, are atelostomates as well. They are shaped like domes and biscuits or scones, as well as hearts, and range from the Early Jurassic to the Recent; the spatangoids appeared in the Early Cretaceous and continue to the present. Their ambulacra are petal-shaped and may number four instead of five. The mouth is forward from the center, and the periproct lies in an almost vertical area, which is really part of the dorsal surface. Spines are delicate and silky and are either short or very long. Several genera are marked by grooves (fascioles) in which the tubercles are microscopic and the spines are correspondingly small.

One of the best-known spatangoids is the genus *Micraster,* abundant in the Late Cretaceous chalk deposits of Western Europe. Detailed studies beginning in 1899 on large numbers of relatively complete specimens have led to an understanding of evolutionary patterns of *Micraster* species, which developed from nonburrowing types to shallow burrowers, such as *Micraster leskei,* to deeper burrowers, like *M. coranguinum.* These studies

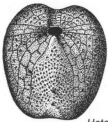

Heteraster. Cretaceous, Arabia, Mediterranean, and North and South America

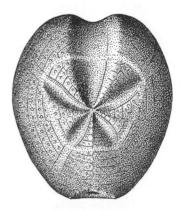

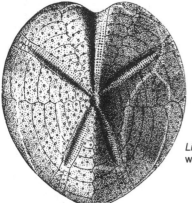

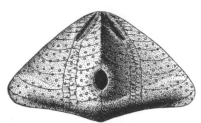

Linthia. Cretaceous to Pliocene, worldwide

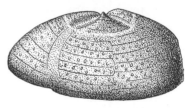

Hemiaster. Cretaceous to Recent, worldwide

A nucleolitid from the Late Cretaceous, Alabama and Mississippi

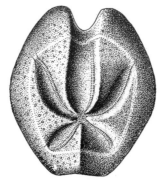

Hemiaster, a form from the Late Cretaceous, south-central Texas

Rhopostoma. Paleocene, North America

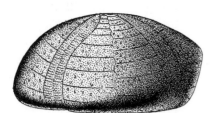

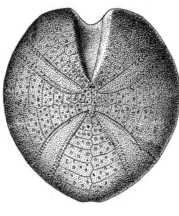

Holaster. Paleocene, nearly worldwide

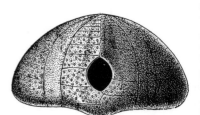

Late Cretaceous and Tertiary sea urchins, or echinoids. (After Clark and Twitchell)

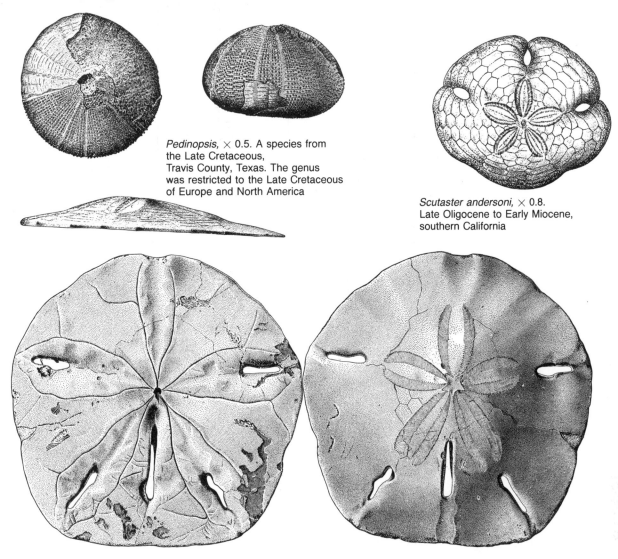

Pedinopsis, × 0.5. A species from
the Late Cretaceous,
Travis County, Texas. The genus
was restricted to the Late Cretaceous
of Europe and North America

Scutaster andersoni, × 0.8.
Late Oligocene to Early Miocene,
southern California

Mellita, a sand dollar, × 0.5. A specimen from the
Pleistocene ("Ice Age"), South Carolina and Georgia to Texas

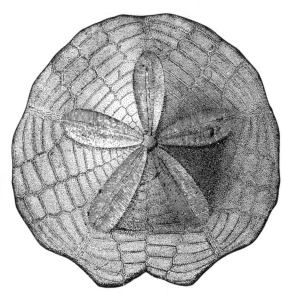

Abertella, a sand dollar, × 0.5.
Middle Miocene, Maryland

Clypeaster, × 0.6. Pliocene, southern California.
The genus ranges from Eocene to Recent, worldwide

Sea urchins and sand dollars, or echinoids, all euechinoids

have provided a better understanding of the function of the spatangoid test as well as a fine subdivision of the very monotonous shallow marine rocks that make up the chalk sequences in Europe and England.

HOMES AND HABITS OF URCHINS

Sea urchins have many habitats, from reefs and sandy shoals to deep water that is seldom disturbed by waves. Some even live in shallow bays and rocky shores that are exposed at low tide.

In such varied surroundings, echinoids live in a variety of ways. Almost all are gregarious, forming swarms of schools that number dozens, hundreds, or even thousands of individuals. Many regular species cling tightly to rocks or brace themselves in cracks and crevices by means of spines and tube feet that end in sucking disks. Others excavate burrows, not merely in limestone and shale, but in granite, basalt, and hard, gritty sandstone. Such rock is much more resistant than calcite, and no one knows just how urchins wear it away.

Other regular urchins lie on mud among rocks and corals or upon smooth, firm bottoms. There they crawl by means of their tube feet or by using their spines as stilts. Since the spines fit on ball-and-socket joints, they can be moved in almost any direction.

The foods of these regular urchins fit their habits and habitats. Some eat

Part of a slab of starfish, Crateraster, *in the University of Oklahoma Museum. From the Cretaceous Austin Chalk, near Austin, Texas. (Photograph by Hubert Gotthold)*

small algae that cover the surface of rocks, but others catch pieces of seaweed on their spines and pass them down to the mouth by means of tube feet. Rock-dwelling urchins devour sponges, hydroids, bryozoans, and tube worms when they can get them, but species that live in crevices or burrows are limited to foods that crawl or drift into their niches. Pedicellariae seize tiny creatures and pass them along to the mouth, and some bottom-dwelling urchins swallow mud and digest whatever food it contains.

Irregular echinoids inhabit muddy or sandy bottoms, where they crawl or burrow. Many heart urchins plow along slowly, scooping mud into their mouths and digesting its organic content. Others lie in burrows 4 to 6 inches deep, getting water for breathing through a chimney that extends to the surface. Long tube feet also reach up through this chimney, picking up food and pulling it down where it can be passed to the mouth.

Many sand dollars crawl under a very thin coating of sediment. But some species that live in estuaries rest on edge, partly in water and partly below it, wedged in the sand but always across the direction of tidal flow. When the tide recedes, they dig in, cover themselves with sand, and either rest quietly or creep to new feeding grounds. They also burrow at the approach of starfish that eat echinoids, but they are not disturbed by other species.

Feeding, for a sand dollar, is a complex process. Its spines, of course, are covered with skin; those on the upper surface also secrete mucus and carry cilia that beat to and fro. They produce currents that flow toward the lower surface, making eddies that wash tiny organisms against the mucus, in which they are trapped. The mucus, in turn, is driven to the undersurface, where it collects in grooves and is taken to the mouth. Not until the teeth grind it up does the sand dollar actually eat.

It seems clear that ancient sand dollars fed like their modern descendants, that most fossil heart urchins plowed through mud, and that reef dwellers devoured both plants and small animals. Beyond this, however, there is little to tell about the feeding habits of specific echinoids.

SEA CUCUMBERS, OR HOLOTHURIDEA

Sea cucumbers are soft-bodied creatures with leathery skin, whose appearance is well suggested by their names. The mouth lies at one end of the body and is surrounded by tentacles. The anus usually lies at the opposite end. Rows of tube feet run along the body in most species, and tiny porous plates (sclerites) of calcite or iron phosphate are scattered through the tissue. Many of the plates are anchor-shaped, while others are grate- or wheel-shaped. In the mouth region, there is a single continous ring of plates. Most sea cucumbers lie or crawl on sea bottoms, swallowing mud or trapping small animals with their tentacles. One group consists of burrowers. Members of one modern group (Elasipoda) swim by pulsating an umbrella-shaped

Edrioaster bigsbyi × 1.1.
Ordovician, North America

Foerstediscus splendens, × 1.
Ordovician, Minnesota

Two typical edrioasters

web of skin that is stretched between elongate tentacles, and feed on plankton.

The oldest sea-cucumber remains are possibly of Cambrian age. Spicules that undoubtedly belong to this group, however, are found in Devonian rocks. Some forms are almost completely plated, but most fossil and recent forms have greatly reduced the skeleton.

Today holothurians are at home in warm, shallow waters as well as the deep sea.

THE EXTINCT ECHINOZOANS: EDRIOASTEROIDS AND OTHERS

A number of other echinozoan groups are much rarer in the fossil record than the echinoids. All are now extinct and were restricted to the Paleozoic, generally the early Paleozoic, an experimental period in the history of the spiny-skinned animals.

Edrioasteroids. Edrioasteroids are a small worldwide group with five distinct, usually sinuous ambulacra and five corresponding interambulacral areas that are restricted to the upper surface of the animal. These converge on a central mouth. The interambulacral areas are covered with a series of flexible plates that are irregularly arranged. By flexing these plates, some may have been able to move, but others were sedentary or attached.

The ambulacral system is somewhat like that in the crinoids, but edrioasteroids lacked brachioles. They seem to be related to the echinoids and are considered by some as a possible ancestral group to them.

The oldest member of this group was *Stromatocystites,* from the Early to the Middle Cambrian, one of the earliest echinoderms. It was five-sided, with five narrow, straight ambulacra and a mosaic of tiny plates in the interambulacral area. It was a free-living form. Other, later edrioasteroids were free-living, but many were permanently fixed by the marginal ring to the seafloor or rocks or other invertebrates.

328

Helicoplacoids.   From high up in the White Mountains of eastern California in Early Cambrian shales that represent an ancient sea come numerous fossils of helicoplacoids, an early and unusual group of echinoderms. They are also found in rocks of similar age elsewhere in western North America. These were radially symmetric, generally lentil-shaped animals with spirally arranged columns of plates forming a flexible test. Apical and oral areas were at opposite ends. Much detail about the anatomy of the helicoplacoids is yet to be learned, for instance the precise structure of the peristome and the location of the anus.

Helicoplacoids may have been free-living, but at times perhaps stationary, with the apical pole buried in the soft sea bottom upon which they lived. They also might have lain on the sea bottom, crawling about like holothurians.

Together with helicoplacoids, other early echinoderm groups are known, such as the edrioasteroids, carpoids, and eocrinoids. The diversity of echinoderm types early in the Cambrian record suggests that differentiation within the Echinodermata must have begun before the Cambrian itself began. The Australian *Tribrachidium,* from the Ediacara fauna, has been suggested as a possible ancestor by some paleontologists. These early fossils also suggest that the ancestral echinoderm must have been free-living.

Besides helicoplacoids and edrioasteroids, a number of other little known but distinctive groups of Paleozoic echinozoans are known—such as the Ordovician to Devonian ophiocystioids and cyclocystoids. Each is discussed in some detail in the *Treatise on Invertebrate Paleontology,* edited by R. C. Moore, a reference that examines in depth invertebrate groups with fossil records, and one that any serious paleontologist, amateur or professional, will find a must. Very recently the classification of the echinoids has been slightly modified in an important book by Andrew Smith (1984). He also presents much new information on their anatomy, biology, and paleobiology.

CHAPTER XXI

Nets, Wrigglers, and "Teeth" Without Jaws

Many early Paleozoic formations contain small carbonized fossils that once were chitinous or horny. Since they resemble pen or pencil marks, they were named graptolites, or "written stones."

Though graptolites are plentiful, their nature has long been a puzzle. Linnaeus called them "false fossils"; others mistook them for plants, sponges, coelenterates, and bryozoans. In 1948 a Polish scientist linked them with *Rhabdopleura,* a wormlike modern animal whose fossils have been found in Ordovician to Tertiary strata.

This was the most surprising interpretation of all; though the tiny (less than 0.5 mm., 0.02 in.), rare, marine *Rhabdopleura* looks like a sedentary worm, it has a rodlike projection (the diverticulum) beyond the mouth. The creature, as with most pterobranchs, builds colonies by budding; a muscular stalk links each animal, or zooid, to a branched, flesh-filled tube (the stolon) that runs through the colony. When undisturbed, *Rhabdopleura* extends its body to feed by setting up currents with its cilia, but it can quickly pull itself back into shelter by contracting its stalk. Pterobranchs live inside chitinous tubes or cups called thecae, which consist of half rings that join in zigzag patterns. In four of the six graptolite orders, the similar thecae are also linked, by stolon tubes, to form a colony called a rhabdosome. And it is such striking similarities in the structure of the hard parts that led to these groups' being placed near one another.

Though pterobranchs and graptolites show similarities, it took a third species to establish how all these were related to other animals. That group was the acorn worms, or Enteropneusta, which commonly burrow in tidal flats. They have long, slender bodies that resemble worms, thus their names, but differ in having an acorn-shaped snout that extends beyond the mouth. This snout is a burrowing organ. Behind the snout, or proboscis, is a collar region, and there lies a dorsal hollow nerve cord. This type of nerve cord is characteristic of chordate animals, including the vertebrates. In this area, too, is a solid structure that has been interpreted by some zoologists to be the beginnings of a supporting rod, the notochord, also a feature of chordate anatomy. Not all zoologists would agree with this conclusion, however. But probably most important is the type of gill system that the acorn worms have. It is very similar to that seen in *Amphioxus,* a fishlike primitive chordate animal, one of the invertebrate experiments that eventually led to the vertebrate, or back-boned, animals.

Amphioxus, acorn worms, pterobranchs, and another group called the tunicates, or sea squirts, all are called invertebrate chordates and lie intermediate between typical invertebrates and vertebrates. Graptolites apparently belong in this twilight zone, too, the unlikely relatives of our ancestors.

TWO GROUPS OF GRAPTOLITES

Graptolites, as we have said, are divided among six orders. Four of these, however, are so uncommon that we may ignore them. They are bottom-dwelling or encrusting forms with very restricted distributions.

Dendroidea.   These are the most primitive graptolites and those most like *Rhabdopleura.* Thin thecae bud in groups of three and are joined by stolons. Characteristically, each colony begins with one tubelike theca (the sicula), from whose base a threadlike nema extends. A chitinous patch served as attachment to the sea bottom or some other object, such as a seaweed or a shell. Dendroids remind us of fine nets.

Dendroids have three kinds of thecae. The stolothecae, or "budding individuals," make a continuous closed tube, through which the colony is interconnected. The other thecae developed open ends, which means that their occupants ate, breathed, and reproduced sexually. Since one open theca is always large (autotheca) and the other is small (bitheca), we infer that the former may have contained a female zooid, while the latter enclosed a male.

Dendroids ranged from Late Cambrian to Carboniferous—a life of more than 250 million years. Some genera, such as *Inocaulis,* have sometimes been called seaweeds.

Graptoloidea.   The dendroids gave rise to a very successful group, the graptoloid graptolites. The anisograptids lie somewhat intermediate between these two major orders. This advanced order had lost the variety of budding zooids and retained only one type of open cup or tube. Any zooid, therefore, was able to bud and build up its colony, as well as to reproduce sexually. Stolons were present but were not enclosed in a skeletal sheath.

Graptoloids are the most abundant, most varied, and most specialized members of their class and are the ones most often found. In spite of this, they are limited to Ordovician and Devonian rocks. Though many of these forms were benthonic, some became planktonic, drifting widely in the oceans of the world. Because of this, they are good index fossils for much of the Paleozoic, especially the Ordovician.

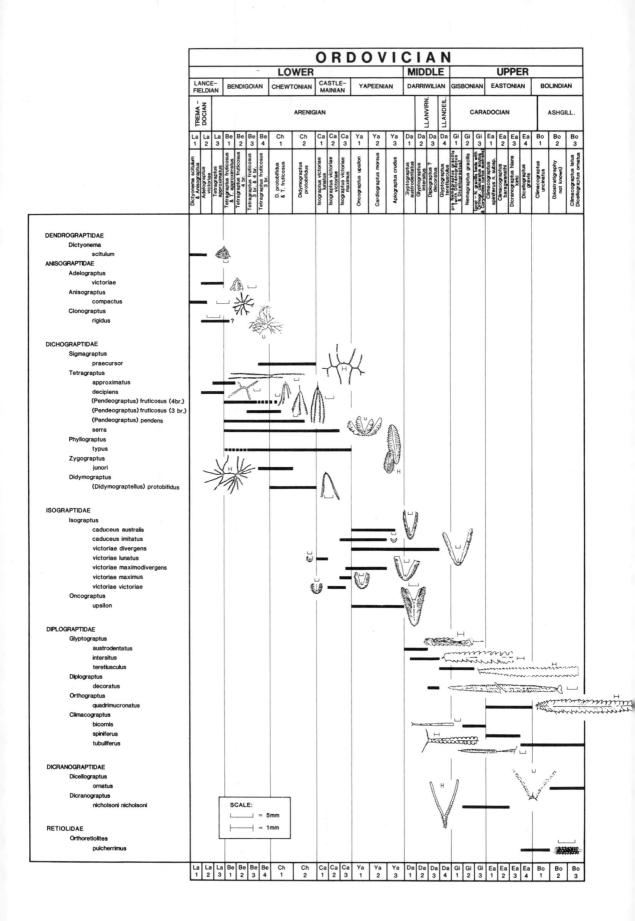

SHAPES, HABITS, AND HOMES

The earliest graptolites formed small colonies with slender branches that grew upward from a base attached to shells or firm mud. Before the Cambrian Period closed, however, colonies had assumed several forms. A great variety of forms developed during Ordovician times.

Dendrograptus typifies branched, or bushy, dendroids. In them the nema was a short stalk or had almost vanished; the colonies were attached to shells or to hardened mud. Such habits limited the spread of both adults and larvae, and few species of bushy dendroids are widely distributed. They can be useful, however, in paleoenvironmental studies.

Callograptus and *Dictyonema* show two types of colonies with very different habits. The former is fanlike and consists of branches that divide again and again and are connected by dissepiments, or crossbars. There is either a short stalk or none, with a base attached to the sea bottom. These graptolites lived much like the bushy dendroids, and their species did not spread widely.

The graptolites in the genus *Dictyonema* or closely related to this form are either benthic or planktonic (floating). *Dictyonema* itself was a fanlike colony that attached to the substrate either by a disk that encrusted hard objects or by penetration of soft bottoms with fibrous holdfasts. Other genera in this group, such as *Rhabdinopora* spent their lives floating in the open ocean.

Most fossils of *Diplograptus* and *Glossograptus* are fragments, but a few fine specimens contain clusters of rhabdosomes whose nemas are fastened to a central disk. This, in turn, was covered by an umbrella-shaped float surrounded by smaller floats of cylindrical shape. The whole structure formed a supercolony, or synrhabdosome, that drifted on Paleozoic seas as the Portuguese man-of-war jellyfish drifts upon waves and currents today. Zooids may even have been specialized for various functions, as are those in the Recent Portuguese man-of-war.

We do not know how many other graptolites built supercolonies, for most

(Opposite) Time ranges of several dendroid (Dendrograptidae, Anisograptidae) and graptoloid (Dichograptidae, Isograptidae, Diplograptidae, Dicranograptidae, and Retiolidae) graptolites found in Australian Ordovician rocks. The heavy black lines show the total time ranges of each of these graptolites. Based on the first appearance, last appearance, and simultaneous occurrence of these various graptolites, many zones have been set up in southeastern Australia, such as the Lancefieldian and Chewtonian. Sometimes it is possible to tie these sequences in with similar ones in Nevada, Idaho, England, and Scandinavia (Tremadocian, for example), by use of the graptolite fossils. These fossils have been very useful in dating highly folded and complex black shales, which often bear no other fossils but graptolites. (Chart prepared by Ian Stewart and Penny Morrison)

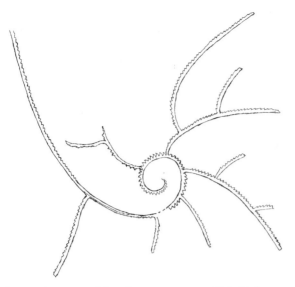

Cyrtograptus murchisoni, *a monograptid. Colony about 6 centimeters (2.4 in.) across. Middle Silurian, worldwide except for South America. (Drawing by F. Knight after Moore, 1970)*

Monograptus turriculatus, *a monograptid. Colony about 2 centimeters long (0.8 in.). Early Silurian, Europe. (Drawing by F. Knight after Moore, 1970)*

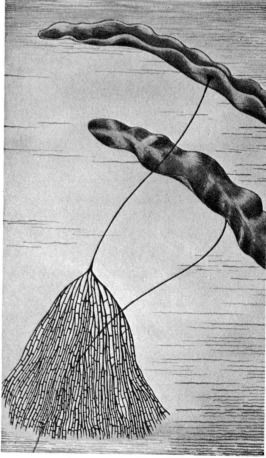

Rhabdinopora flabelliformis, *of Early Ordovician age, nearly worldwide. The drawing shows how this dendroid graptolite looked when it was alive,* × 1

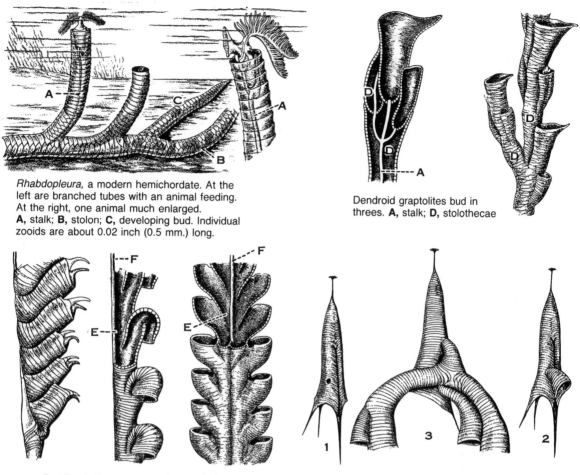

Rhabdopleura, a modern hemichordate. At the left are branched tubes with an animal feeding. At the right, one animal much enlarged. **A**, stalk; **B**, stolon; **C**, developing bud. Individual zooids are about 0.02 inch (0.5 mm.) long.

Dendroid graptolites bud in threes. **A**, stalk; **D**, stolothecae

Budding in three genera of graptoloids. **E**, central canal; **F**, the nema

Early stages of a graptoloid. **1**, shows only the sicula; **2**, the sicula and one bud; **3**, the beginning of branching

Graptolites and a modern hemichordate

fossils are scattered fragments whose arrangement cannot be determined. Several genera, however, formed branched or spiral colonies that hung from floating objects in the manner of *Rhabdinopora*.

Depending on how the budding occurred, whether forming one or many branches, various colonial forms developed. If two branches, called stipes, grew up from the first-formed theca, the sicula, the colony was called biserial. If only one branch formed, it was a uniserial rhabdosome. The direction in which the branches grew away from the sicula is important as well. If the stipes grew upward from the sicula, the colony is called scandent. Whereas if the branches drooped down, they were pendent. Paleontologists studying graptolites also use such characters as the shape of individual thecae and the shapes of their openings, or apertures, to determine different species.

By studying changes in graptolite assemblages in long sequences of rocks in places like southeastern Australia, western North America, Spitzbergen, and Britain, very fine subdivisions can be made. Graptolites are complex

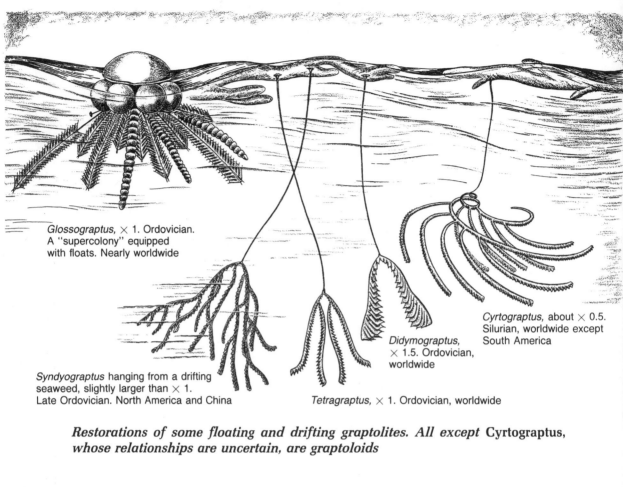

Glossograptus, × 1. Ordovician.
A "supercolony" equipped
with floats. Nearly worldwide

Cyrtograptus, about × 0.5.
Silurian, worldwide except
South America

Didymograptus,
× 1.5. Ordovician,
worldwide

Syndyograptus hanging from a drifting
seaweed, slightly larger than × 1.
Late Ordovician. North America and China

Tetragraptus, × 1. Ordovician, worldwide

Restorations of some floating and drifting graptolites. All except **Cyrtograptus,**
whose relationships are uncertain, are graptoloids

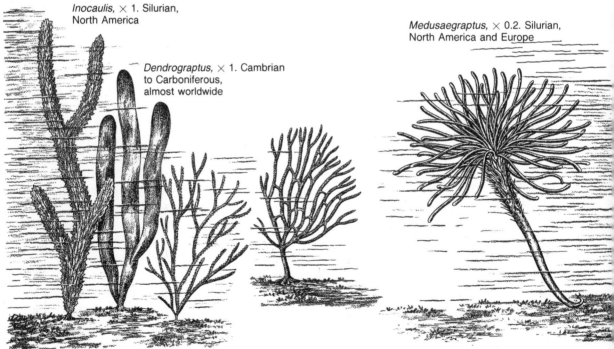

Inocaulis, × 1. Silurian,
North America

Medusaegraptus, × 0.2. Silurian,
North America and Europe

Dendrograptus, × 1. Cambrian
to Carboniferous,
almost worldwide

Restorations of some bottom-dwelling graptolites. All are dendroids, except
Medusaegraptus, *whose relatives are uncertain*

fossils that changed rapidly, and many spread widely, so it is sometimes even possible to use them to correlate between these areas. The major trends in graptolites we can see are mainly related to simplifying and making the colonies lighter in weight. There are losses of branches, going from many-stiped to single. The external skeleton becomes thinner. Floats are also developed to help keep the colonies in midwater, or perhaps near the surface. Related to the development of floats and a planktonic lifestyle, too, growth of the colonies changes from pendent to scandent.

During the Ordovician, graptolite variety reached a peak. As temperatures

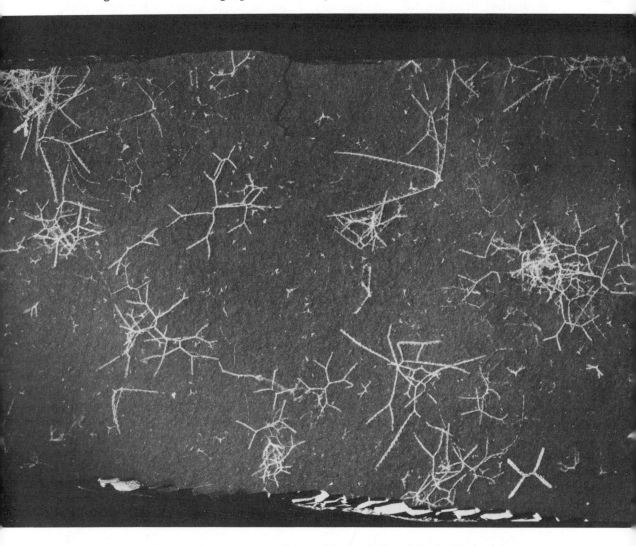

Several kinds of graptolites preserved in a black shale of Early Ordovician age, southeastern Australia. Four-branched form (upper left) is Tetragraptus decipiens; *large three-branched form (lower middle) is* Kiaerograptus antiquus *(single branch 2 centimeters [0.8 in.] long); many-branched form (right middle) is* Clonograptus; *small form (lower middle) is* Adelograptus victoriae. *All are Early Ordovician, worldwide. (Photograph by F. Coffa, courtesy of the Museum of Victoria, Melbourne)*

cooled throughout this period, worldwide provinces (temperate and tropical) developed, as climatic zones became more marked, much as they are today.

Toward the end of the Ordovician, a major glaciation lowered temperatures of the globe, including the seas. This rather drastically affected marine faunas, causing most groups of graptolites to become extinct. Only a few species survived this great biologic crisis, and these gave rise to the much less varied Silurian graptolite faunas, dominated by the monograptids, uniserial pendent forms.

Habitats and Preservation. Graptolites occur in chert, limestone, and shale. But they are most commonly found in black shale. There are many reasons why this is so. Their colonies were so delicate that sand would have soon ground them to bits, and so would trilobites and lesser scavengers that often swarmed where lime mud accumulated. But most black shale settled in stagnant regions where the water contained little oxygen and was poisoned by hydrogen sulfide from slowly decaying rubbish. Since few scavengers lived in such surroundings, dead graptolites lay undisturbed until they were preserved and pyritized or replaced by a silvery micaceous mineral. Often these were areas of quiet water, too, where there was little mechanical destruction. Furthermore, sedimentation rates were low and a great accumulation of organic matter resulted with little associated clay.

"TEETH" WITHOUT JAWS: THE CONODONTS

Another group of fossils that some paleontologists have thought related to the vertebrates are conodonts (from a Greek word meaning "cone tooth"). Conodonts are puzzling marine fossils. Other paleontologists suggest that conodonts may have been more closely related to animals with lophophores such as brachiopods, bryozoans, and phoronids. One of the Burgess Shale fossils, *Odontogriphus,* a worm-shaped animal about 6 centimeters (2.4 in.) long, from the Middle Cambrian of British Columbia (Chapter XI) contains conelike structures that resemble conodonts. These cones lay at the base of each of the twenty to twenty-five tentacles and evidently served as an internal support for these food-gathering "arms" (or lophophores). The body of *Odontogriphus* was soft, with regular constrictions and a distinct head. They are unusual in that they were constructed of calcium phosphate and first appear in the fossil record when phosphatic hard parts were more common in invertebrates than they are now. Conodonts definitely are found in Ordovician to Late Triassic rocks, but may range back into the Cambrian or even late Precambrian, and some may have survived until the Late Cretaceous.

Conodonts are microscopic (0.1–5 mm, 0.004–0.2 in.), toothlike or platelike structures whose function is not really understood. Sometimes conodont fossils look like tiny teeth, and often are found together in many sets of pairs, as are teeth of vertebrate animals. But the conodont "teeth," unlike vertebrate

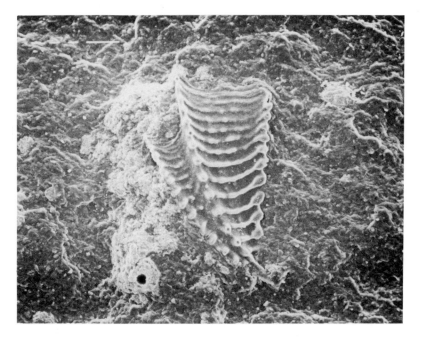

Scanning-electron-microscope picture of Pygodus anserinus, *a conodont element, 510 microns (0.51 mm., 0.02 in.) long. Late Ordovician, worldwide. (Courtesy of I. Stewart and J. Warren)*

Scanning-electron-microscope picture of Pygodus serra, *a conodont element, 370 microns (0.37 mm., 0.01 in.) across. Middle to Late Ordovician, worldwide. (Courtesy of I. Stewart and J. Warren)*

or worm teeth, have no wear facets on them, so probably were never used to chew food directly. More likely, conodonts were internal structures that supported a soft tissue, such as a gill or the walls of the pharynx, or "throat," region.

Four basic kinds of conodonts are known: simple cones, thin bars, blades, and platforms. On these structures are often one or more cusps, or conelike structures, similar to cusps on our own teeth. Both the outside ornamentation and the internal structure of the conodont are important in classifying conodonts and in working out their relationships to one another.

Classifying conodonts causes some problems, because there may be several kinds of conodonts in one animal, much as we have several kinds of teeth in our jaws. In the past, paleontologists gave each conodont element a name. But discovery of several different elements in clusters led to the recognition that the conodont "animal" must have contained a particular arrangement of elements. Now this arrangement, or conodont apparatus, is also given a separate name.

The conodont animal was probably a free-swimming or free-floating marine invertebrate. Many species occurred nearly worldwide, from North America and Europe to Australia. Because of this, as well as their small size and resistance to decay, they are excellent index fossils, especially when drill cores are being used. Thousands of these tiny fossils can be preserved in a tiny piece of a core recovered by a drilling rig. Techniques of how to prepare rock samples to recover these as well as other microfossils are described by M. D. Brasier in *Microfossils.*

Besides providing a good basis for determining the age of rocks, conodonts can be used to estimate the depth of water represented by certain rock sequences. Depending on their color, too, whether pale amber or black, they can give some idea of the influence of temperature, depth, and length of burial of rocks. This information is useful to oil geologists in evaluating the oil- and gas-bearing potential of certain areas. Despite our uncertainty of the relationships of the conodont animal and the function of the conodonts themselves, these fossils are extremely helpful in biostratigraphic and paleoecologic studies, especially in the Middle Ordovician and Late Devonian, when they reach their greatest diversities.

CHAPTER XXII

From Starfish to Fish, Lords of the Water

While graptolites died and sank to ocean bottoms that lacked much oxygen, something new appeared in the oceans. This new organism had an internal support in the form of a flexible rod, called a notochord, that ran the length of the body. This animal probably resembled the living lancelets, *Amphioxus*, small (4 in., or about 10 cm., in length), fishlike invertebrates that live today in near-shore seas partly buried in the sand. They have a series of segmented muscles along the body, a series of gill slits and gills supported by a cartilagelike internal "skeleton," and a tubular nerve cord that lies above the supporting notochord. A fossil form called *Pikaia,* from the Middle Cambrian of North America, resembles *Amphioxus* and thus demonstrates that such animals actually existed quite long ago.

THE INVERTEBRATE CHORDATES:
LINKS BETWEEN SPINY-SKINS AND BACKBONED ANIMALS

Amphioxus, a cephalochordate, is important in any understanding of where the backboned animals, the vertebrates, came from. *Amphioxus* and a menagerie of other odd-looking creatures form a link between the invertebrate world, especially the echinoderms, and the vetebrates. In this twilight zone between major animal groups are the acorn "worms" and pterobranchs, thought to be related to the graptolites and together known as hemichordates. Also included as invertebrate chordates are the sac-like sea squirts, or tunicates (urochordates), whose adult form bears no resemblance to fish. Its larval form superficially resembles a tadpole.

Chordates are animals that possess a notochord at some stage in their development. In *Amphioxus,* the notochord is an important adult structure, giving the body its main support. In fish and man it is greatly reduced and mainly an embryonic feature.

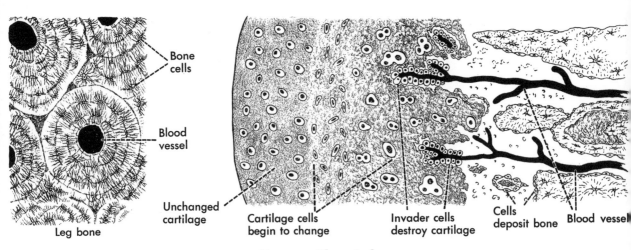

Bone cells

Blood vessel

Unchanged cartilage

Cartilage cells begin to change

Invader cells destroy cartilage

Cells deposit bone

Blood vessel

Leg bone

From cartilage to bone

The invertebrate chordates are of special interest because they demonstrate that echinoderms and vertebrates must have had a common ancestry. Echinoderms and chordates have a similar kind of mesoderm development. Mesoderm is the embryonic body layer that lies between the outer layer, or ectoderm (which develops into skin and the nervous system), and the inner layer, or endoderm, which develops into the gut and its appendages such as the appendix. The mesoderm in starfish, *Amphioxus,* and humans similarly forms as an outgrowth from the gut wall. A space is left inside this outgrowth and forms the body cavities in which such organs as the lungs and the liver are housed. In worms, molluscs, and arthropods, the mesoderm forms in an entirely different fashion and the body cavities develop initially as slits in a solid mass of tissue, not as an outpocket.

Echinoderms and some invertebrate chordates also have very similar larvae, which are quite distinct from those of other invertebrates. Similarly, proteins of the blood serum are alike, differing from those of other invertebrate groups. On the other hand, several invertebrate chordates share many unique characters with the vertebrates: gill slits, a notochord, a tubular dorsal nerve cord, and so on—either in juvenile or adult stages.

Even though starfish and sea urchins, with their radial symmetry, do not very much resemble primitive vertebrates, such as fish, there are "spiny-

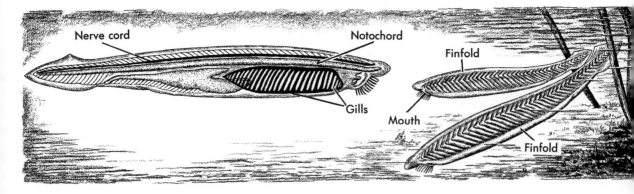

Nerve cord

Notochord

Finfold

Gills

Mouth

Finfold

Amphioxids are modern sea-dwelling chordates about 2 inches (5 cm.) long. The diagram shows the notochord below the nerve cord

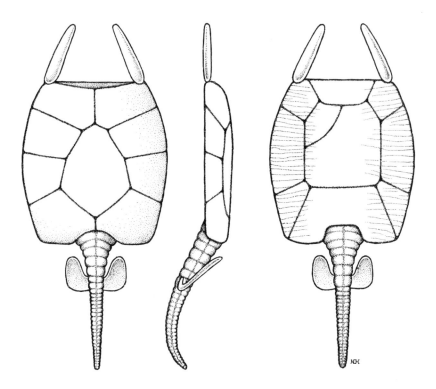

Reconstruction of Notocarpos garratti, *in three views: A, dorsal; B, ventral; and C, side. (Courtesy of G. M. Philip)*

skins" that form closer links. The carpoids, mentioned in Chapter XX, include species that were bilaterally symmetric or nearly so, just like vertebrates. Some, such as *Notocarpos,* even seem to have had distinct "head" and "tail" regions and were dorsoventrally flattened and mobile. Some paleontologists, such as R. P. S. Jefferies, have suggested that this group gave rise to the chordates and thus all vertebrate animals, but this has been disputed by G. M. Philip and others.

The First Vertebrate Chordates

Though *Amphioxus* is quite fishlike, it still lacks many features that true vertebrates possess. For a start, it lacks a backbone. It also lacks teeth and is obliged to filter-feed for a living. There is no enlargement in the nervous system that might serve as a brain, and there is no heart, even though the circulatory system is laid out on the vertebrate plan.

The first fossils thought to be remains of vertebrates occur in the Late Cambrian and Early Ordovician of North America, Greenland, and Spitsbergen, all in marine rocks of the Northern Hemisphere. Often called ostracoderms, or "shell skins," the remains of these early fish are phosphatic and fragmentary, mineralogically formed of apatite, just as is living bone, but with a microstructure different from that of the bone we know today. Many of these scale-like fossils have been assigned the name *Anatolepis,* but not all paleontologists would agree that they belonged to the vertebrates.

Middle Ordovician rocks in central Australia have produced some of the oldest known vertebrate remains of an entire jawless fish, *Arandaspis*. No bone is preserved, only impressions, but these show both the internal and the external structure. This early fish had a series of large dorsal and ventral plates and a single row of smaller plates over the gill openings. Small scales covered at least the front part of the body, if not its entirety. *Arandaspis* was 12 to 14 centimeters (about 5–5.6 in.) in total length, and its body was oval in cross section, not dorsoventrally compressed as were so many of the early armored fish. This early fish probably fed on organic debris and microorganisms and had an erratic, tadpole-like motion, for it lacked paired fins for more delicate swimming control. Other forms, such as *Porophoraspis*, are also known from Middle Ordovician rocks in Australia, but none are so complete as *Arandaspis*. Very recently, in 1987–1988, further complete remains have been recovered from both North and South America.

From slightly younger Ordovician marine rocks of the Rocky Mountains of North America come the first unquestionable bony remains, in the Harding Sandstone. The bone, called aspidin, consisted of four layers: a basal laminar layer, followed by a cancellous layer, followed by a dentine layer and then an enamel layer. Many of the fossils are fragmentary, but a nearly complete form, *Astraspis disiderata*, has been recovered. The armor was made up of a series of small polygonal plates. Another form, *Eriptychius*, possessed an internal skeleton composed of calcified cartilage. Both, like *Arandaspis*, were jawless filter feeders.

OTHER PTERASPIDOMORPHS, OR "WING SHIELD FORMS."

Besides the Ordovician ostracoderms, a number of other Silurian and Devonian jawless fish seem to be related. They all had a single opening for their gills (not several), paired nasal sacs, and a relatively solid head shield. Most did not possess paired fins. These jawless fish included the cyathaspids, the amphiaspids, the pteraspids, the psammosteids, and possibly the thelodonts.

Cyathaspids. This group of ostracoderms first appeared in the Middle Silurian and didn't become extinct until the early part of the Devonian. Though the earlier forms are primarily found in marine rocks, many had moved into brackish or fresh waters in the Devonian. The cyathaspids were quite similar to some of the Ordovician ostracoderms, with the head shield being made up of dorsal and ventral plates separated by long, relatively narrow brachial plates. Individual plates were ornamented by rounded dentine ridges that ran parallel to the plate margins. These fish, like their immediate ancestors and *Amphioxus*, are probably filter feeders.

The body of cyathaspids was slightly compressed dorsoventrally, and the eyes lay on the side, not top, of the head shield. The tail was nearly symmetrical. Most of the later ostracoderms, which became quite varied in the Devonian, were probably derived from this group.

Arandaspis prionotolepis, *an early jawless fish from the Stairway Sandstone, Early to Middle Ordovician, central Australia. (Reconstruction by Frank Knight, courtesy of the Museum of Victoria and Pioneer Design Studios)*

Amphiaspids.   Known only from the Early and Middle Devonian of Siberia, these very specialized ostracoderms had a nearly solid, fused carapace (head and thoracic shield). They also had nearly, if not completely, lost their eyes, which suggests that they lived in very sediment-laden water or were actually mud burrowers. Some had the mouth situated at the end of a long tube.

Pteraspids.   Like the amphiaspids, these ostracoderms probably arose from the cyathaspids. As in the amphiaspids, there was much plate fusion, but there were a few more individual plates. Pteraspids differed, too, in having bony structures protruding from the top and sides of their carapace that may have acted as stabilizers. The bottom, or ventral, lobe of the tail was markedly more elongate than the dorsal. Rather characteristic of this group was a forward-projecting rostral plate that extended far beyond the mouth, and some forms even developed elongate lateral "horns" on the head shield. They were most bizarre fish indeed!

Psammosteids.   Exhibiting a trend quite opposite to that seen in cyathaspids, these dorsoventrally flattened fish first occurred in riverine environments (in the Early Devonian), and then some moved into the oceans. They survived until the Late Devonian and were widely dispersed across the Northern Hemisphere.

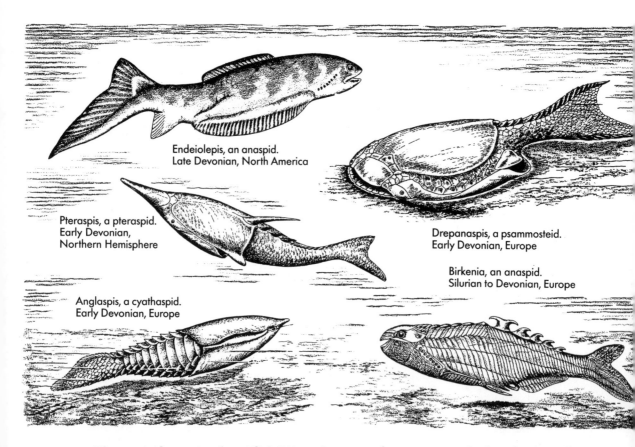

Endeiolepis, an anaspid.
Late Devonian, North America

Pteraspis, a pteraspid.
Early Devonian,
Northern Hemisphere

Drepanaspis, a psammosteid.
Early Devonian, Europe

Birkenia, an anaspid.
Silurian to Devonian, Europe

Anglaspis, a cyathaspid.
Early Devonian, Europe

Five agnaths, or jawless "fish." Lengths range from 2.5 to 12 inches (6–30 cm.)

Some psammosteids reached considerable size, up to two meters (6.5 ft.). Just how they fed is not quite clear; even though they were flattened, as many bottom-dwelling forms are, their mouths faced upward.

Thelodonts. The thelodonts, or coelolepids, are a group of extinct jawless fish that are very useful in dating rocks, but, as with conodonts, much is still unknown about their anatomy. Their bodies were covered with tiny, rhombus-shaped nonoverlapping scales. No fusion of these plates seems to have occurred, and, like most other early fishes, there was no ossification of the internal skeleton. It evidently consisted of cartilage only. It is the isolated scales that are used in dating rocks.

The body of thelodonts, usually preserved as a flattened impression, was evidently slightly compressed dorsoventrally, but still basically fusiform. The eyes lay on the side of the head, and the mouth was at the front of the body, neither on the ventral nor the dorsal surface. Separate gill openings were present along the side of the body, unlike the single branchial opening characterizing all the other pteraspidomorphs.

Thelodonts also seem to have possessed a variety of fins, including a pair of pectoral (or lateral) fins, a small dorsal fin, and an anal fin lying in front of the hypocercal tail fin, with its enlarged dorsal lobe.

Scales of thelodonts are known from rocks as old as the Late Ordovician, and the group survived into the Devonian. Their nearest relatives, however, remain elusive. On the one hand, they had lateral eyes and lacked a median nostril, such as in pteraspidomorphs (heterostracans). On the other hand, the presence of several separate gill slits and paired fins is more akin to the cephalaspidomorphs, to be discussed later. Before their true relationships are known, better-preserved specimens are needed, but this doesn't detract from their geologic usefulness.

The Cephalaspidomorphs

A second large group of jawless fish were the cephalaspidomorphs. They differed from all the heterostracans in several ways, one in having a nasal sac that had a single opening in the middle of the heavily ossified head shield. These have been studied extensively by the Swedish school of paleoichthyology, led by Erik Stensiö. Stensiö, over several decades, serial-sectioned many specimens of these ancient fishes and was able to reconstruct minute details of their brain cavities and cranial nerves, and their entire cranial anatomy.

There are three groups of cephalaspidomorphs: the anaspids, the osteostracans ("bony shells"), and the galeaspids. They differ quite radically in body form, which is basically related to their lifestyle.

Anaspids. These creatures were torpedo-shaped and covered with nar-

row, overlapping scales. Their eyes lay on the sides of the head. The notochord bent down into the bottom lobe of the tail fin, producing a reversed
heterocercal (or hypocercal) tail, which some researchers think tended to
push the fish upward as it swam. In any case, the fish probably spent time *in*
the water and not simply tied to the bottom. All were relatively small fish,
with mouth at the front of the skull. Their feeding styles could have varied
considerably. Several gill openings (6–15) ran diagonally down each side of
these fish, and behind those gills lay a spine. Attached to that spine on either
side was a scaled fin. Perhaps such fins were derived from ventrolateral
finfolds that occurred on the primitive chordates such as *Amphioxus.*

Anaspids first appeared in the Late Silurian, as shown by such well-armored forms as *Birkenia.* Later forms, for instance the Late Devonian *En-
deiolepsis,* were almost naked, with little or no ossification of scales.

Jamoytius belongs in this group, though it was once considered a
nonvertebrate chordate. It is also unusual in that it occurs in marine rocks,
whereas most anaspids come from freshwater deposits.

Osteostracans ("Bony Shells")

Probably the best known and the most complete of the Paleozoic jawless
fish were the osteostracans. Their bottom-dwelling lifestyle is clearly reflected in the construction of their dorsoventrally flattened head shield.

In a typical, rather specialized genus, *Cephalaspis,* the plates of the head
formed a shield that was rounded in front but projected backward in
"horns" resembling the spines of many trilobites. The two eyes lay close
together and faced upward; a single nostril opened in front of them, and
between the eyes lay the pineal opening—perhaps remnants of a second set
of eyes.

The underside of the head bore an oval mouth near the front of openings
for ten pairs of gills. From the brain, branching tubes ran toward three dorsal
areas covered with small plates. Once regarded as electrical organs, these
areas are now thought to have been sensory fields that detected pressure
differences and vibrations in the water, which were then transmitted to the
inner ear.

The body of *Cephalaspis* tapered to the tail, where the vertebral column
bent upward to support a plated fin that contained cartilaginous rays. This
type of tail, called heterocercal, is found in many agnaths and among primitive jawed fish and sharks. Narrow plates allowed the body to bend freely,
and a dorsal fin kept the fish from rolling too much from side to side. Two
pectoral flaps, one on either side of the body near the head, probably served
as balancing organs, but they were not true fins.

Cephalaspis seemingly could have swum fairly well, though its tail perhaps tended to force it downward instead of straight ahead. The creatures
probably spent most of their time in lakes, rivers, and estuaries, where they

Cephalaspis, *an ostracoderm of the Old Red Sandstone. About 7 inches (about 18 cm.) long. At the right is the head shield of* Sclerodus, *natural size, from the Early Devonian of Europe*

fed by sucking mud into the mouth vacuum-cleaner style and strained out bits of food as they passed over the gills. These habits were shared by other osteostracans.

Osteostracans first occur in Late Silurian rocks, but were quite diverse when they first appeared, suggesting a long previous history. They were the first group to develop what we consider true bone, which includes spaces, or lacunae, for bone cells. Their exoskeleton had a complex structure, resembling that of heterostracans. Each had a three-fold division: a laminar layer at the base, a layer with blood vessels passing through it in the middle, and a third, external layer made up of an underlying dentine-like zone and a hard enamel-like surface zone.

Though the group moved into many benthonic feeding niches in the Early Devonian, all osteostracans were extinct by the end of that period.

Galeaspids.   Early Devonian rocks of China have produced yet a third distinctive group of ostracoderms, which probably developed in isolation. Though the group shows a mixture of characters of both heterostracans and osteostracans, galeaspids appear to be more closely related to the latter.

Galeaspids looked more like osteostracans. They had a heavily ossified head shield with dorsal eyes, and two inner-ear (semicircular) canals, both oriented vertically. But they seem to have had two nasal sacs. The underside of the carapace was made up of a mosaic of small plates, and there was a series of gill openings on either side. The mouth lay on the ventral surface, suggesting that these fish were bottom-dwelling detritus feeders. Unlike the osteostracans, however, they had no dorsal sensory fields and had a hypocercal, rather than a heterocercal, tail.

Cyclostomes

Ostracoderms became common during Late Silurian times but dwindled in numbers and disappeared at the end of the Devonian Period. Some experts say they vanished without trace; others suspect that the anaspids left descendants in the form of lampreys and hagfishes, collectively termed cyclostomes ("round-mouths"). They are eel-shaped, limbless, and jawless creatures that are found in both fresh and salt water. Their skin is smooth, they have only one nostril, and some feed by attaching themselves to living fish. There they rasp through skin and flesh until they reach the body cavity, where they feed upon the viscera and body fluids of their still living victims.

Perhaps an anaspid such as *Jamoytius* gave rise to the living cyclostomes, for they have similarities in gill and mouth structures.

Definite cyclostome fossils are also known, one of the oldest from the Middle Pennsylvanian rocks of Mazon Creek, Illinois. *Mayomyzon,* from this locality, has a remarkably similar arrangement of cartilaginous supports for the mouth region to the living lamprey *Lampetra. Mayomyzon,* however, did not have the specialized, fused gill supports present in modern lampreys. *Hardistiella* is the oldest known cyclostome, known from the Early Carboniferous of Montana.

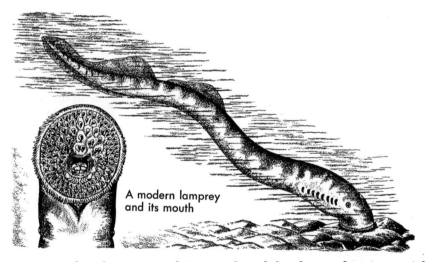

A modern lamprey
and its mouth

A modern lamprey and its mouth. Adult, about 2 feet (61 cm.) long

THE FIRST FISHES WITH JAWS: THE PLACODERMS

Several theories suggest how the first jaws formed in vertebrates, but transitional stages are not known. True jaws appear to be modified gill arches and were a major innovation allowing gnathostomes (jaw-bearing forms) to try out a vast array of feeding styles not possible for agnathans.

The first of these jaw-bearing forms appeared in the Late Silurian, in both fresh and marine waters. Even on their first appearance, they were quite varied, suggesting that they had a much longer history.

Four groups of jaw-bearing fishes are known in the Early Devonian: the armored placoderms, the Chondrichthyes, or cartilaginous fishes (sharks, skates, and rays), the Osteichthyes, or bony fish, and the acanthodians, or spiny sharks. These were all so different from one another that we are not even certain they came from a single ancestral group. Perhaps jaws, and the paired fins so important in increasing maneuverability, evolved more than once. The fossil record may yet provide some more definite answers.

Placoderms. Placoderms were among the first fish to possess both paired fins and jaws, though none of the gill arches were involved in jaw support. The veterbral column was quite primitive in this group, for the notochord persisted throughout life, and vertebrae were represented only by Y-shaped spines that developed above and below it.

Placoderms were quite varied in the earliest Devonian, probably because they were the first vertebrates with jaws that gave them a real advantage over other forms. Acanthodians are known as fossils before the placoderms, so may have been the first forms with jaws, but placoderms were the first to diversify widely.

Placoderms generally had a heavily ossified external skeleton. The bony covers of the skull and thorax were separate, not fused, and generally could move with respect to one another. Their bone was very similar to the three-layered, lacunae-bearing material already seen in osteostracans. Many groups of placoderms are known from Devonian rocks, and their fossils are of particular use in Devonian biostratigraphy. Though they started out as diminutive forms early in their history, placoderms reached large size. *Titanichthys,* a highly predaceous arthrodire found in the Late Devonian Cleveland Shale of Ohio, reached more than 6 meters (19.5 ft.).

A great variety of placoderms developed during the Devonian, and then the group became extinct, the only major fish group not to have a living representative. The greatest variety of placoderms by far belonged to the Arthrodira ("joint-necked").

Arthrodires. Some of the earliest arthrodires, such as *Sigaspis,* were completely covered with bony armor including the tail. The thoracic shield continued back that far, and the pelvic area was protected by large, imbricated scales. In this genus and other primitive arthrodires, the trunk and head shields actually met in a sliding articulation and not a ball-and-socket joint as in later forms.

The head and thoracic shield of arthrodires were composed of a series of large plates that remained distinct throughout the fish's life. Because it is difficult to decide how these bones tie in with those in the skulls of more advanced fish, like the trout and the goldfish, a series of distinctive names have been given to their skull and thoracic plates. For example, in the early arthrodires the thoracic shield consists of a large Median Dorsal Plate flanked on either side by anterior and posterior dorsolateral and lateral plates. Their names basically suggest their anatomical positions.

The bones of the head and thoracic shields were dermal bones, formed in the skin of these fish. The braincase, on the other hand, was heavily ossified but was made up of endochondral bone; that is, it first formed in cartilage, which later was replaced by bone when bone cells invaded the cartilage. One important form that provided a great deal of information on the brains of these fish was *Kujdanowiaspis,* from the Early Devonian.

The jaws of early arthrodires were made up of the upper palatoquadrate, another endochondral bone, like the braincase. Attached to this bone and the braincase were two pairs of dermal bones, the superognathals. These were lined with little denticles that must have served as teeth. The lower jaw was supported by another endochondral bone, the Meckelian bone; and just as in the upper jaw, there was a dermal bone attached that actually did the cutting up or grasping of the food: the infragnathal.

More is known of some of the specialized arthrodires, such as *Coccosteus,* than more primitive forms, but the main trends in the evolutionary history of arthrodires is to lighten and reduce the area covered by the head and thoracic shields and free the cheek unit from the skull roof. Much of the endochondral bone of the braincase and jaws reverted to cartilage. All this meant that less of the trunk of the fish was enclosed by armor and so al-

Some Middle and Late Devonian arthrodires. **Dunkleosteus** *(left) reached lengths of 30 feet (9 m.), but* **Coccosteus** *(right) was smaller, reaching up to 2 feet (60 cm.) in length. Both occur widely across the Northern Hemisphere continents and North Africa*

lowed more effective swimming, as did the general lightening of the whole skeleton. Spines were even reduced or lost as a lightening measure. Many of the advanced arthrodires became highly effective carnivores, such as the giant *Dunkleosteus* (= *Dinichthys* ["terrible fish"]).

Antiarchs.   Modified for a bottom-dwelling and a less active mode of life, are the antiarchs. They remained heavily armored fish for much of their history, superficially resembling the living armored catfish of South America today, though they are unrelated to these more advanced fish. The oldest antiarchs are the yunnanolepids from the Late Silurian and Early Devonian of China.

Most antiarchs were dorsoventrally flattened, and their eyes were facing upward, reflecting their bottom-dwelling existence, where they must have fed like vacuum cleaners. Most antiarchs had jointed pectoral fin spines that probably acted as props more than having anything to do with swimming.

One well-known antiarch is the "wing fish," *Pterichthys,* found in the Old Red Sandstone of Scotland. *Pterichthys* was so well armored that it was first mistaken for a crab. Bony plates completely enclosed its head and trunk, and thick overlapping scales continued to the tail. The resemblance of the paired pectoral spines to wings probably led to its name. *Pterichthys* was tied to the ponds in which it lived, for it was not capable of breathing air outside of water. Quite probably, many of the well-preserved specimens found in the Old Red Sandstone resulted from fish left stranded when temporary ponds dried up after seasonal floods.

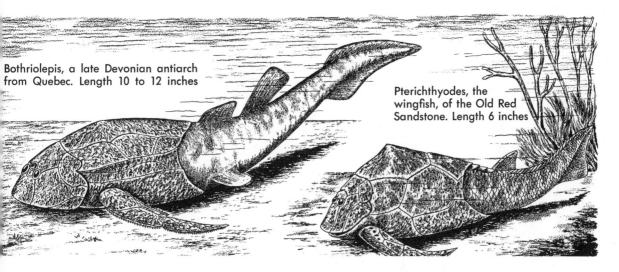

Bothriolepis, a late Devonian antiarch from Quebec. Length 10 to 12 inches

Pterichthyodes, the wingfish, of the Old Red Sandstone. Length 6 inches

Bothriolepis, a Late Devonian antiarch with nearly worldwide distribution. Length 10 to 12 inches (25.4–30.5 cm.)

Pterichthyes (or *Pterichthyodes*), the "wing fish," of the Old Red Sandstone. Middle Devonian; known from the Early Devonian of Australia. Length 6 inches (15 cm.)

Two armored antiarchs that resembled ostracoderms

Bothriolepis, meaning "pitted scale" in reference to the ornamentation of the armor, is yet another well-known antiarch. The oldest forms are known from the Middle Devonian of China and Australia, but by Late Devonian times this genus had a wide distribution across the globe. One famous locality producing *Bothriolepis* is on the Gaspé Peninsula, in Quebec. There, fishermen who catch modern herring also dig petrified antiarchs from beds of gray shale and soft sandstone exposed along the shore. A frequent find is *Bothriolepis,* about 10 inches (25 cm.) (though some reach 1 m. in length) long, a fish with a blunt head and a broad body encased in elaborately pitted plates. The tail and part of the trunk of this fish were naked, the armored and jointed pectoral fins relatively long and lined with rows of short spines along their edges.

There were many species of *Bothriolepis* around the world, and their armor reflected a variety of bottom-dwelling lifestyles. One Australian form, *B. gippslandiensis,* developed a bony crest on top of its short trunk armor that may have served as a stabilizer in the swift-flowing mountain streams where it lived. Another armored fish with a worldwide distribution, *Groenlandaspis,* also developed such a crest.

Phyllolepids.   Another placoderm group thought to be related to both antiarchs and arthrodires were the phyllolepids. *Phyllolepis* was a very dorsoventrally flattened bottom-dwelling fish with a distinctive pattern on the head and thoracic shields, a fingerprint pattern: ornament was a series of curved ridges. The median plates of the shields were very large, and the lateral ones much smaller.

Phyllolepids were restricted to fresh waters of the Late Devonian, and their anatomy and external armor are reasonably well known, particularly in Australian fossils.

A variety of other Placoderms: Several other groups of placoderms are known from Devonian rocks of the world. The petalichthyids were marine fishes that ranged from the Early to the Late Devonian. They, too, were benthonic, or bottom-dwelling, as is reflected in their dorsal eyes and flattened shields. Though they were similar in many respects to some of the more ancient arthrodires, they had very short thoracic shields. In the petalichthyids that developed a head-trunk articulation, it was oriented differently from that in the arthrodires.

The Acanthothoraci were Early Devonian marine placoderms that were similar in many ways to the arthrodires. They, however, like the antiarchs, had dorsally oriented noses.

Ptyctodonts had very limited armor, an elongate body, and a very elongate, slender tail. They occurred in mainly marine Middle and Late Devonian rocks and possessed a pair of unique upper and lower crushing teeth. In fact, they were quite distinct and bizarre among placoderms, really more resembling the ratfishes, or chimaeras, of today, even to the extent of having claspers associated with the pelvic fin in the males, used presumably for holding the female during mating. Only sharks and their close relations (including the ratfishes) have these. Without a doubt, the lifestyle of these placoderms, if in fact they belong in this group, is very different when compared to all others.

The rhenanids possessed a few large dermal plates that covered the head and trunk, but the rest of the body had a variety of small plates and scales. Jaws were rather sharklike and had individual, toothlike denticles. Many of these fish, for example *Gemuendina,* were relatively small, only 30 centimeters (12 in.) or so in length. They were mainly flattened, benthonic forms, resembling skates, known in the Early Devonian from marine rocks but generally quite rare.

The stensiöellids (named after the famous Swedish paleoichthyologist Erik Stensiö) and the pseudopetalichthyids are very poorly known fishes from the Early Devonian marine rocks of Germany. All were small and dorsoventrally flattened. They superficially resembled the rhenanids and had a similar jaw structure. But they are so poorly known that it will be some time before we fully understand their relationships.

The placoderms were an early series of evolutionary "experiments" in "jawed" and "finned" lifestyles that were successful for some time. It was only toward the end of the Devonian and afterward that they were displaced by the cartilaginous fishes (Chondrichthyes) and the bony fishes (Osteichthyes), which dominate the world today.

Acanthodians

The acanthodians, or "spiny sharks" as they have been called by many, first appeared in the Early Silurian and survived until the Permian. They are the oldest group of jaw-bearing vertebrates known. Their name comes from the fact that they had many paired as well as unpaired fins supported by spines. They possessed a variety of bony-fishlike and sharklike features, and have been at times even classified as placoderms. They resembled some of the early bony fish, except for their spines and heterocercal tail. They had a mosaic of small, nonoverlapping plates over the head and minute, regularly arranged scales over the body. As in many of the higher fish, a bone called the hyomandibular aided in the attachment between palatoquadrate, or upper jaw, and the braincase. Acanthodians differed from all higher fishes, however, in that those with teeth lacked enamel and had no regular tooth replacement.

Acanthodians were small fish, most no more than a few centimeters (or inches) in length, though one genus did reach more than 4–5 feet (about 1.5 m.). They had a heterocercal tail with the upper lobe more elongate than the lower. They also had enlarged scales covering the gill area.

Climatius is a typical advanced acanthodian. It was small, with adults averaging 3 to 5 inches (7.5–13 cm.) in length, with a blunt head, a sharklike

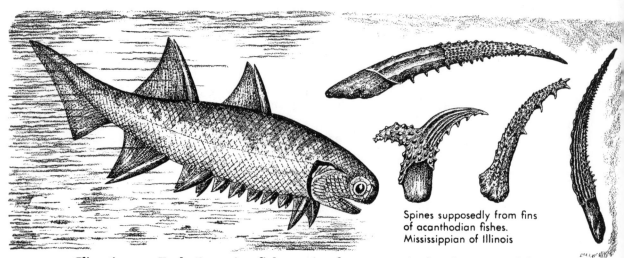

Spines supposedly from fins
of acanthodian fishes.
Mississippian of Illinois

Climatius, *an Early Devonian fish ranging from 3 to 5 inches (7.5–13 cm.) long. It
had jaws and several pairs of fins supported by spines*

tail, and hard, diamond-shaped scales that covered its entire body. The
paired fins were numerous, but most were little more than spines, and strong
spines supported the unpaired dorsal and ventral fins.

Climatius lived in fresh waters of possibly the Late Silurian and definitely
the Early Devonian, but many later forms increased in size and tended to
reduce the scale covering and the size and number of fins. *Acanthodes,* from
the Early Permian, was, in fact, an elongate form that was only partly scaled
and had no teeth, very different from its Early Devonian relatives.

SHARKS AND THEIR KIN: THE CHONDRICHTHYES

In the past, sharks were often regarded as rather primitive fish, because
their skulls and skeletons were made up of cartilage and not bone. In some
sharks, the cartilage became calcified, but they never developed true bone,
and all except the ratfishes have a series of separate gill slits that are not
covered.

Though paleontologists are still debating the details of relationships,
acanthodians, sharks, and bony fishes seem quite different from placoderms.
One difference is that, in the modern fishes, including the sharks, the jaw
musculature lies lateral to the palatoquadrate, whereas in most placoderms
it is internal. There are other differences, but it's likely to be a while before
the detailed family trees of all these groups and their relationships to one
another are understood.

The first cartilaginous fishes are represented in the Late Silurian by small
denticles, which are known to occur in the skin of living sharks. These fossils come from marine rocks, and these sharks (including skates and rays—
the Elasmobranchii) and their relatives the ratfishes (Holocephali) remained
in the sea, with only a few exceptions.

During the history of sharks, there have been two major times of diversification, one in the Devonian and a second in the Mesozoic, which gave rise to our modern fauna. During the entire history they have remained important predators in marine realms. But a few others have become plankton feeders and mollusc crushers as well. The teeth of sharks were derived from scales that concentrated along the jaw regions and have taken on a variety of cusp patterns depending on diet.

Six or seven major groups of sharks lived during the Paleozoic Era, and their relationships to one another are not at all clear. Again, the diversity signals experimentation for a successful body style, one of which gave rise to most, if not all, of the living forms. Paleozoic groups include the cladoselachids, the symmoriids, the xenacanthids, the eugenodontids, the squatinactids, the petalodontids, the orodontids, and the ctenacanthids. We will only look briefly at three of these.

Cladoselachids. *Cladoselache* is the best known of these primitive sharks. Remains of this form are well preserved in Late Devonian nodules from the Cleveland Shale in Ohio. This genus was made up of slender, torpedo-shaped fish, up to 4 feet (just over 1 m.) in length, with a broad heterocercal tail. Its pectoral fins had narrow bases, whereas many other primitive sharks' often had broad bases. All these features point to a fast, maneuverable fish.

The upper jaw was fused or tightly bound to the braincase, a jaw suspension called amphistylic.

Cladoselache had no anal fin, but two dorsal fins. It also had unique fin

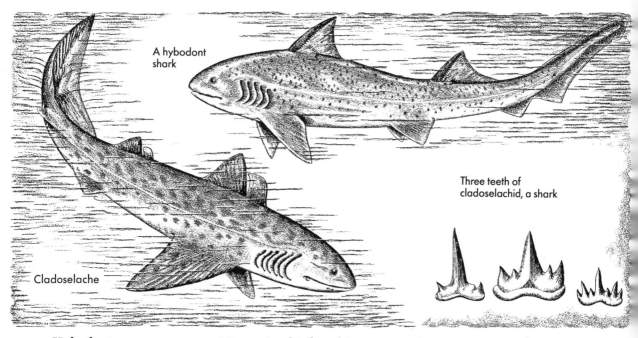

Hybodonts were common Mesozoic sharks, this one ranging up to 7 or 8 feet (2–2.4 m.) in length. **Cladoselache,** *which ranged up to 4 feet (1.2 m.) long, is best known from fossils in Late Devonian shales near Cleveland, Ohio*

spines that were built of dentine. The skin lacked scales except for the fin margins and around the eye.

Xenacanthids (Pleuracanths).   Very unusual among sharks, the xenacanths took up life in fresh water. Their teeth are always recognizable in that they had two lateral developed cusps, and a small one in between that met the next tooth. Based on isolated tooth remains in many cases, the range of the group is from Late Devonian to Late Triassic, with a wide geographic range on the globe from North America to Australia and Antarctica.

In some respects, the xenacanths resemble the cladoselachids and may have been derived from them, but in many other respects they are unique and bizarre. The dorsal fin was long, extending the full length of the body from just behind the head. A clasper was present on the pelvic fin. The pectoral fin had a long central axis with small supports radiating from it in a featherlike fashion, a fin called archipterygial. One large fin spine was often attached to the back of the braincase.

Ctenacanthids.   This group of Paleozoic sharks probably gave rise to all of our modern sharks. In general they didn't look too different from *Cladoselache*. They differed mainly in structure of the fins and fin spines. The spines had an extra layer of hard material called vitrodentine that apparently formed in the outer layer of the skin, not the deeper layers. Ctenacanths also

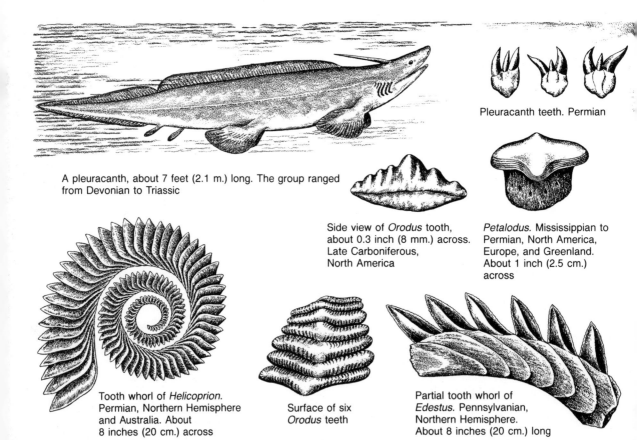

Pleuracanth teeth. Permian

A pleuracanth, about 7 feet (2.1 m.) long. The group ranged from Devonian to Triassic

Side view of *Orodus* tooth, about 0.3 inch (8 mm.) across. Late Carboniferous, North America

Petalodus. Mississippian to Permian, North America, Europe, and Greenland. About 1 inch (2.5 cm.) across

Tooth whorl of *Helicoprion*. Permian, Northern Hemisphere and Australia. About 8 inches (20 cm.) across

Surface of six *Orodus* teeth

Partial tooth whorl of *Edestus*. Pennsylvanian, Northern Hemisphere. About 8 inches (20 cm.) long

A pleuracanth "shark" and teeth of several primitive sharklike fish

had an anal fin and the beginning of the three-part basal support to the fin that all modern sharks possess.

Ctenacanths appeared in the Devonian and lived into the Triassic but were probably most successful in the Carboniferous. Hybodonts were one of the first groups to develop from the ctenacanthids in the Carboniferous in the direction of modern sharks. And within the hybodonts a variety of tooth types developed, demonstrating that these fishes were adapted to many feeding strategies. Many of these and other Paleozoic sharks probably occupied feeding niches that bony fish moved into during the Mesozoic.

Modern Sharks (Neoselachii). The modern sharks, skates, and rays became the dominant cartilaginous fish from the middle Mesozoic to the present. The first appeared in the Jurassic and rapidly spread around the world. Some fossils of these show traces of skin and flesh and general body outlines, but the majority are teeth that range from minute affairs with many cusps to broadly triangular blades. Each individual shark had dozens or

(Left) Two slender shark teeth from the Pliocene (Red Crag) of England. (Right) Tooth (about 8 in. or 20 cm., long) of a giant shark, Carcharodon. *Miocene deposits near Chesapeake Bay, eastern North America*

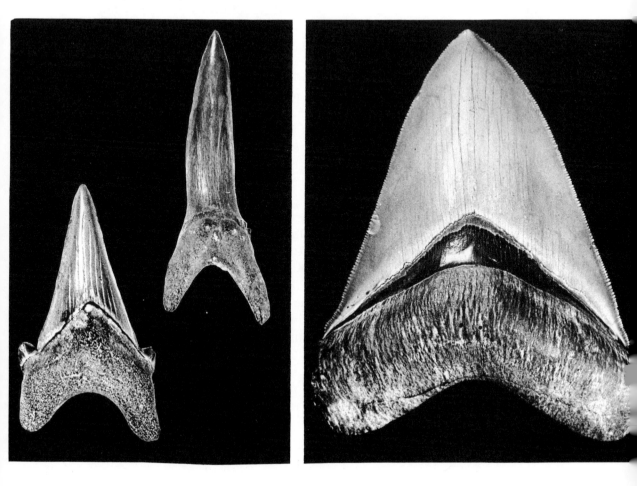

hundreds of teeth in its jaws at one time and new ones moved quickly to replace old ones broken or lost in feeding or battle.

The changes that took place between the primitive Paleozoic sharks and those of today are as follows: the vetebral centra calcified, the fins became more flexible, spines were reduced, and the upper jaw became movable relative to the braincase. All of these led to a more maneuverable fish with a greater versatility in what it could do with its jaws. For instance, the jaws of many modern sharks can be protruded relative to the braincase allowing small pieces of large prey, like plugs of flesh from whales, to be removed without taking the whole prey. Paleozoic sharks had mainly a scissorlike action to the jaws, not allowing such an activity.

Some sharks reached enormous sizes, such as *Carcharodon,* a genus that still survives in the white shark, sometimes called a man-eater. A large white shark can reach 30 to 40 feet (9–12 m.) and has teeth up to 3 inches (about 8 cm.) long. Several Tertiary species had teeth 6 to 8 inches (15–20 cm.) long, set in thick, gristly jaws that were 6 feet (1.8 m.) or more wide. These creatures were, thus, decidedly more massive than the white sharks and had larger heads, and must have reached lengths of up to 50 feet (15 m.), formidable predators even to the largest of marine creatures.

Skates and rays (also known as batoids) are sharks that became flattened bottom dwellers by greatly expanding the pectoral fins, with which they "fly" through the water. The eyes, as in most bottom-dwelling forms, moved into a dorsal position. Most other fins were reduced or absent, and the tail evolved into a whiplike structure.

The jaws in these forms became quite detached from the braincase. Skate and ray teeth are generally flattened, forming a crushing surface. They can thus feed on organisms, such as clams, that have hard shells.

The oldest batoid is *Squatina,* from the Late Jurassic, and, of course, the group survives today.

Holocephalans, or Ratfishes.　　The chimaeras, or ratfishes, are the final, and probably most memorable, of the cartilaginous fishes that we will look at.

The ratfishes are difficult to relate to any other shark group. They are unique among sharks in fusing the upper jaw with the braincase and in having the gills enclosed by a single cover, called an operculum, much as in the bony fishes. Teeth are two pairs of plates in the upper jaw and a single pair in the lower, perhaps functioning in the same fashion as in the batoids. The front vertebrae are fused into a solid structure called a synarcual, and onto this a dorsal spine articulates. The tail is but a narrow whip. Like the sharks, ratfishes have claspers, not only on the pelvic fins but also on the head.

Ratfishes may extend as far back as the Carboniferous if *Echinochimaera,* from the Late Mississippian, is indeed, as suspected, a member of this group. In addition to forms that clearly are related to living ratfish, a number of other odd Paleozoic forms, such as the iniopterygians, from the Pennsylvanian of North America, may belong in this assemblage. How these are all related, and indeed where the ratfishes came from, however, are still tantalizing questions.

OSTEICHTHYES, THE BONY FISH.

Near a crossroads called Fossil, not far from Kemmerer, Wyoming, rise cliffs of white marly limestone and pink shale. Their age is Eocene, and they settled in one of the many lakes that spread across southwestern Wyoming and nearby parts of Utah and Colorado. These rocks, which are part of the

Cliffs of the Eocene Green River Formation, west of Green River, Wyoming. The finely bedded shale settled in a lake, but sandstone at the top of the cliff was deposited by a river. The shale contains fossil fish

Green River Formation, are famous for their abundant and well-preserved fish.

Many placoderms and sharks, as we have seen, had bony plates in the skin, but their internal framework was cartilage. The group to which most of the Green River fish belong had the former structure but changed the latter. Their complex internal skeletons were of true bone, and more and more dermal bones were added to the skull, jaws, and shoulder girdle. Their caudal fins were modified until, in the most advanced forms, a bilaterally symmetrical, or homocercal, tail resulted.

Two major groups of bony fish are known: the "ray-finned," or actinopterygian, fishes, and the "Lobe-finned," or sarcopterygians. Both groups had appeared by the Early Devonian. Perhaps some isolated scales from the Late Silurian belong in this group as well.

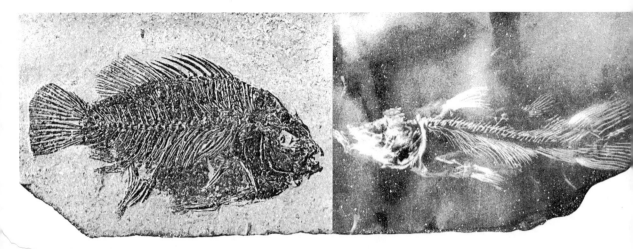

(Left) A bony fish, Priscacara, *from the Eocene Green River Formation of Uinta County, Wyoming. (Right) An X-ray photograph of a fossil fish in red Triassic shale from near Princeton, New Jersey*

Actinopterygians

The "ray-finned" fish are so named because they have paired and median fins stretched over delicate bony rays, which extend directly from the body and not as fringes on both sides of a bony or muscular lobe.

Actinopterygians, of all the bony fish, seem most similar to the acanthodians, but, of course, still differ in a number of ways, such as their regular tooth-replacement pattern.

Primitive "Ray Fins" (Chondrosteans). The chondrosteans had greatest success in the Paleozoic and early Mesozoic, but several species survive today. Chondrosteans may first have appeared in the Late Silurian. These, and in fact most of the Paleozoic forms, were palaeoniscids. Most were small, though such Late Devonian forms as *Cheirolepis* may have been as much as 2 feet (just over 0.5 m.) in length.

Cheirolepis was a slender, blunt-nosed fish with a V-shaped heterocercal tail fin that had an unrestricted notochord continuing right into the top lobe of that tail, single dorsal and anal fins, and paired lateral fins that all had broad bases. The skull was composed of a series of flexible bony plates, which were pierced by a pair of small eyes. More typical palaeoniscoids had large eyes.

The body of palaeonisciforms was covered by a series of small, rhombic scales that were quite thick. They were composed of three layers, including a thick outer one of ganoine, which is very enamel-like. Such scales could have been derived from acanthodian scales, which are similar in some ways.

The jaws of these fish were long, giving an elongate, scissorlike bite, and articulated behind the braincase. From such a beginning the early ray-finned fishes evolved in divergent ways. Some developed larger eyes and thicker bodies, and reduced the paired fins until they were nearly useless. Others became deeper-bodied and thinner than sunfish, which they resembled in size, a body form often associated with quiet water. Some reduced the bone of the skull and the vertebral column, as well as reducing the number of scales to a few rows of large, bony plates. One result of such a trend was the naked, nearly scaleless sturgeons *(Acipenser),* a group of bottom scavengers that live in bays, lakes, and large streams today. Paddlefish *(Polydon),* known first in the Cretaceous and also alive today in the Mississippi River, of North America, and several rivers in China, have lost even more. They have only a few small scales left at the base of the tail. Both retain relatively primitive fins and a heterocercal tail. A few, however, that have left living

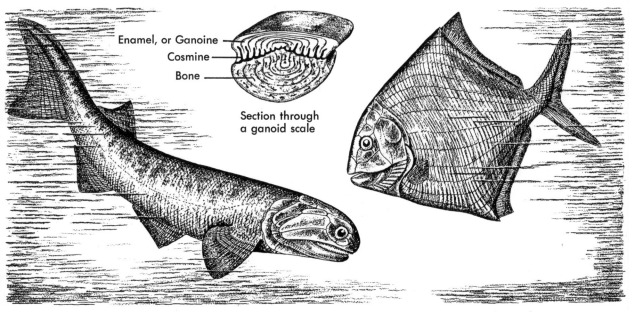

(Left) Cheirolepis, *a primitive Devonian "ray fin," may have reached 2 feet (about 0.5 m.) in length. (Right)* Amphicentrum, *a deep-bodied Carboniferous ray fin about 6 inches (15 cm.) long. It may have been a reef dweller, certainly living in some form of quiet water*

representatives, such as *Polypterus,* the African bichir, retained a thick armor coat of shiny scales. It has a peculiar set of sail-like dorsal fins and a diphycercal tail, and retains a pair of ventral lungs, which probably explains its survival in regions affected by seasonal drought.

This radiation of primitive ray fins occurred through much of the Devonian to Permian, with the development of a variety of fin and body forms.

Lepisosteus, the living gar pike, probably also belongs with these primitive ray fins, retaining its heavy scales and heterocercal tail. It occurs in Cretaceous rocks nearly worldwide, and its abundant scales, rhomboidal affairs with bright, shiny surfaces, have been called "fossil figs" by some collectors in the Hell Creek area of Montana. Their presence led to the discovery of one of the richest early-mammal microfossil sites in the world, the Bug Creek Anthills, near Fort Peck, Montana.

Neopterygians, the Modern Ray Fins.   Besides the chondrosteans, all ray-finned fishes are now considered to form one major group. The group first appeared in the late Paleozoic and came to dominate waters, both salt and fresh, in the Mesozoic and Cenozoic eras.

The main changes that occurred in the transition from ancient to modern ray fins was in the bones and musculature associated with feeding and locomotion. In modern ray fins, the maxilla bone separated from the rest of the cheek bones, new bones were added, and the muscles controlling jaw action expanded, no longer contained in a small area. These changes allowed a much larger gape and a stronger bite, and in many cases the front of the jaws could actually be pushed forward: the mouth protruded. In many forms, food can actually be sucked into the mouth.

Advanced ray-finned fishes also lost the heavy, multilayered scales. Though these had served as good protection, they were also very heavy. Their loss allowed more agile, rapid movements. The new, lightweight scales, generally circular, rather than diamond-shaped, are called cycloid. Along with these changes there was, likewise, a tendency toward cylindrical, spool-shaped centra to the vertebrae, so characteristic of the bony teleosts we eat today.

Fins became more mobile, and pelvic and pectoral fins often occurred in unusual positions, such as pectorals directly above pelvics, providing rather fine-tuned maneuverability. The caudal fin tended to become symmetrical, probably as a result of the lightening of the fish due to scale reduction and the effect of the swim bladder in providing buoyancy.

The most primitive of these modern ray fins have often been called "holosteans," but their interrelationships have not been clearly deciphered—so it seems best to recognize them only as primitive modern ray fins until more is known.

Semionotus was one such early modern ray fin, which lived during the Triassic. It was a fusiform fish looking somewhat troutlike in its body form. Other semionotids, however, such as *Dapedium,* were deep-bodied fish,

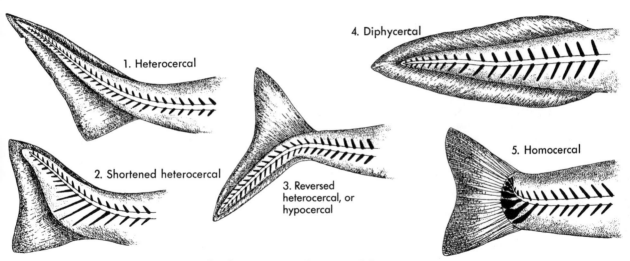

The five principal types of fish tails

1. Heterocercal
2. Shortened heterocercal
3. Reversed heterocercal, or hypocercal
4. Diphycertal
5. Homocercal

more resembling a modern angelfish. *Dapedium* had blunt, peg-shaped teeth with which it may have crushed molluscs and other invertebrates.

Bowfins *(Amia)* are other primitive modern ray fins. Close relatives of this form first appeared in fresh waters of the Jurassic. *Amia* first appeared in the Late Cretaceous. They were and still are powerful predators, reaching more than 30 inches (76 cm.) in length, with a long dorsal fin and a blunt tail, which has a few upturned vertebrae—not quite symmetrical. Bowfins feed largely on small fish but also consume a variety of invertebrates and other odds and ends. The males dig nests and guard the eggs, and both sexes are able to use the air bladder as a lung.

A variety of other fish, such as the deep-bodied, massive-toothed pycnodonts of the Triassic to Eocene and the Mesozoic macrosemiids,

(Right) Dapedium, *a deep-bodied Jurassic "holostean" 14 inches (36 cm.) long.* *(Left)* Semionotus, *a freshwater "holostean" of Triassic age. This species, 7 inches (18 cm.) long, inhabited Arizona. Both were primitive neopterygians*

among others, were fish transitional between chondrosteans and the most advanced actinopterygians, the teleosts.

Teleosts. The Most Modern of Ray Fins. The Late Triassic pholido-phorids are the oldest teleosts, the actinopterygian group that is most abundant and varied today and which has dominated the fish world since the Late Mesozoic. They range from goldfish to sea horses, from angelfish to trout.

We are tempted to define teleosts as the boniest of bony fishes and let it go at that. Unlike the chondrosteans and the lobe-fins, already discussed, they have fully ossified internal skeletons in which long-established structures are often supplemented by a variety of new spines and bones. The tail has become homocercal, which means that the backbone stops at the tail base, with the fin rays growing out from it to support the caudal fin. Scales have no trace of the ganoid, or enamel-like, layer, and they normally overlap like shingles. They also may be reduced in size or disappear.

The most primitive of all modern teleosts are probably the osteogloss-omorphs, freshwater fish with a mainly Southern Hemisphere distribution. Only a few are known from Southeast Asia and North America. They first appeared in the Jurassic of China.

Another major group of teleosts, the elopomorphs, also had appeared by the Late Jurassic. Tarpons and eels are members of this carnivorous, mainly marine group, which shares a peculiar, nearly transparent form called the leptocephalous larva.

The "bulldog tarpon," *Portheus,* known from Cretaceous rocks of both Europe and North America, belongs in this group. The American form had a blunt head and jaws set with a row of impressive teeth. *Portheus* reached a length of 12 feet (3.7 m.) and weighed 500–600 pounds (225–275 kg.). It fed upon smaller fish and young marine reptiles that plied the shallow epicon-tinental seas of Kansas and southern England. One huge *Portheus* even gulped down a 6-foot (1.8 m.) neighbor, but died before digesting it. This event is clearly recorded by the skeletal remains left behind in the fossil record.

Yet another teleost group includes the clupeomorphs, which appeared at least by the Early Cretaceous. The herring *(Clupea)* are typical of this group, as are sardines and anchovies.

All other teleosts belong in the euteleosts, which are first known in the Late Cretaceous. Most have a cellular bone and are characterized by specialization in the bones of the caudal fin. Generally the euteleosts are subdivided into the salmoniforms, including the salmon and the trout; the ostariophysi, including the carp *(Cyprinus),* catfish (siluriforms), and electric eels; and the neoteleosts, including most of the more highly modified teleosts such as the beautiful but bizarre angelfish as well as the cod, perches, flying fishes, and the like.

Though spines, and even whole skeletons, of many of these groups of teleosts are often preserved, the fossil record is enriched by preservation of "ear stones," or otoliths, of many forms. A cavity of the inner ear, the sacculus, is practically filled with crystalline calcite. As a result, the shape of the otolith reflects the sacculus shape and is very characteristic of each species. Many of otoliths can be recovered from a small drill core, and thus otoliths are becoming increasingly useful for determining the age of rocks in addition to identifying the fish that left them behind.

Another "hearing aid" occurs in the ostariophysians, the carps and catfishes. They have processes on the front vertebrae that develop as small, detached bones called Weberian ossicles. These articulate with one another and basically connect the air bladder with the ear region, acting very like the chain of ear bones in mammels to amplify and transmit the sound vibrations of the air bladder to the inner-ear liquids, which stimulate the nerve endings connected to the brain.

Certainly the bony fishes must be considered the most successful of all the vertebrates, if numbers and variety are any measure of success.

THE LOBE-FINS, MIRRORS OF CREATURES TO COME

In contrast to the actinopterygians, the sarcopterygians, or lobe-finned fishes, have left few living representatives. These consist of three living dipnoans, or lungfish, one each occurring in South America, Africa, and Australia, and the coelacanth *Latimeria.*

When the fossil record is consulted, three major groups of lobe-finned fish can be recognized. These include the lungfish, coelacanths *(Latimeria),* and rhipidistians confined to the Paleozoic. All these groups appeared first in the Devonian. The lungfish are placed in a group of their own, the Dipnoi,

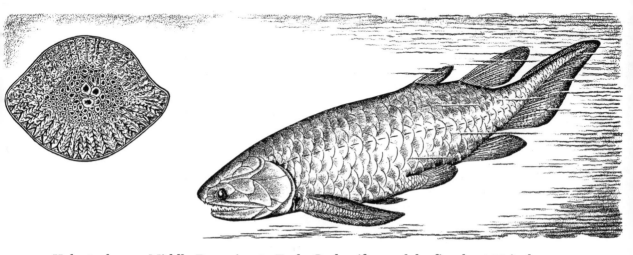

Holoptychus, *a Middle Devonian to Early Carboniferous lobe-fin about 30 inches (76 cm.) long. The cross section through one of this fish's teeth shows how the enamel is folded into a "labyrinthine" pattern.* Holoptychus *ranged widely around the world, including Antarctica*

whereas the remaining two groups are sometimes linked and called cross-opterygians.

Lobe-fins are characterized by fins with fleshy bases, or lobes, containing a jointed series of bones distinct from those in the fringe-like fin membranes. It is from fish in this assemblage that the first tetrapods, the amphibians, developed. So, even though they are not successful in numbers today, their "offspring" have succeeded in a variety of lifestyles as the tetrapods.

The Lungfish, Dipnoi. The Devonian genus *Dipterus* was typical of the lungfish, which are somewhat like other lobe-fins until they open their mouths. Then many reveal a specialized dentition, with broad, fanlike, ridged teeth that suggest their owners may have crushed hard objects such as shelled invertebrates. In modern lungfish, these teeth and the adductor musculature working the jaw produce a strong bite and allow them to feed effectively on a wide variety of foods, including hard objects. The skull was composed of a mosaic of small bones, whose arrangement shows little similarity to that in any other bony-fish group.

One significant feature of *Dipterus* is that the teeth and skull bones link it to the living lungfish. And we know a great deal about the lifestyles of the few living forms, so we can suggest what the fossil species were like as living fish. Though the living lungfish have gills, they can breathe air and get oxygen from it in sac-like lungs that were derived from the air bladder.

But how could a lung be of use to a fish? Today, lungs serve such fish well in times of drought, when ponds are stagnant or completely dry up. Lungfish can survive by breathing air. The African *(Protopterus)* and South American *(Lepidosiren)* lungfish actually dig burrows in which they estivate until the wet season returns. Members of the Permian *Gnathorhiza* must also have done this, for fossils have been found in burrows, still awaiting the next wet season!

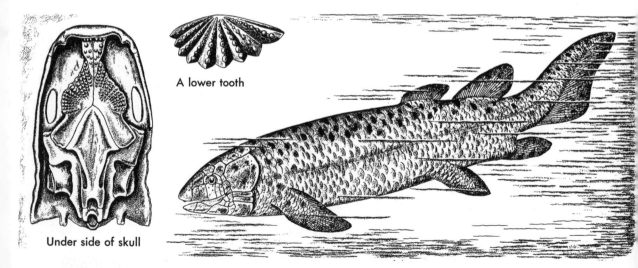

A lower tooth

Under side of skull

Dipterus, *a primitive lungfish of Devonian age with a wide distribution around the world*

Protopterus. Eocene to Recent, Africa

Tooth of Ceratodus

Scaumenacia. Late Devonian, North America and Europe

Ceratodus, Early Triassic, Early Tertiary, cosmopolitan. Up to 6 feet (1.8 m.) in length

Three specialized lungfish. Two of them are now extinct, though one similar to Ceratodus, Neoceratodus, *still lives in eastern Australia*

Though the earliest lungfish lacked the unique fan-shaped teeth and were highly ossified, by the Middle Devonian much of the skeleton had become cartilaginous, and the special dentition had developed. The scales were also much reduced. Throughout their history, lungfishes diversified several times, at first in marine and fresh water, but certainly during the later Paleozoic and Mesozoic mainly in fresh water. Today, however, their rare leftovers are restricted to the fresh waters of the southern continents, relicts of a previously much wider distribution.

Crossopterygians, the Tassel, or Fringe Fins. Rhipidistians are perhaps to us the most important of the fringe fins, for they gave rise to amphibians sometime in the Devonian, and therefore, somewhat later and indirectly, to us.

Eusthenopteron, *a Late Devonian rhipidistian fish that breathed air. Length 40–45 inches (1–1.2 m.)*

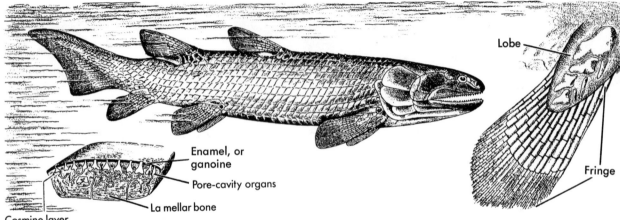

Osteolepis, *a rhipidistian lobe-finned fish from the Middle Devonian Old Red
Sandstone of Europe. It occurs in several other parts of the Middle to Late Devonian of the Old World and Antarctica. At the left is an enlarged section through a
lobe-fin cosmoid scale; at the right is a fin with skin and scales removed, showing
bones in the lobe.* Osteolepis *was about 9 inches (22.5 cm.) long*

Rhipidistians appeared at the base of the Devonian and continued to the
Early Permian. During that time, they were the major freshwater predators of
all the bony fish.

Many features of the early rhipidistians are similar to primitive actinopterygians. Besides that, the skulls of some rhipidistians, such as *Eusthenopteron,* were very like those of early amphibians. The teeth of rhipidistians are characterized by complexly folded dentine, which has given them
the name labyrinthodont. Many primitive tetrapods, including amphibians,
have this sort of tooth structure. So we have some idea of where this group
came from and what it led to!

Eusthenopteron and other osteolepiform rhipidistians also had a number
of other features that were good credentials for amphibian ancestors. These
include a lacrimal duct, perhaps related to the near-surface lifestyle where
eyes and nasal openings were out of the water for sufficient periods to require bathing of the eyes. They developed an internal nostril, which presumably give them the ability to sense smells within the mouth. Their braincase
was divided into two distinct segments, and the remnants of such a division
have been observed in the first amphibian skulls, those of *Ichthyostega,* from
Greenland. The vertebral centra of both *Eusthenopteron* and *Osteolepis* are
quite similar to those of primitive labyrinthodont amphibians, there being
two pairs of segments, a dorsal pleurocentrum and a ventral intercentrum. In
all three cases the centra are associated with a large notochord.

Like other parts of the anatomy, the limbs in rhipidistians are quite distinctive from other fish. It was such limbs that gave rise to the tetrapod limb
capable of supporting an animal's weight out of water. In the pectoral fin
there was a large proximal bone quite comparable to the humerus, and beyond that analogues of the radius and ulna. Beyond that were carpals, but

further distally were no major support elements, so metacarpals and bones of the digits must have been newly added in tetrapods. Much the same situation existed in the hind limb.

The Persistent Coelacanths. Rhipidistians gave rise not only to tetrapods but also to another group, the coelacanths, which have one living, though rare, form, *Latimeria.*

The first coelacanths are known from Middle Devonian rocks. The link with the rhipidistians is mainly based on the structure of the braincase, which was divided into two parts. Their bodies were short and they usually had deep, somewhat blunt heads. Lobes of the paired fins were relatively short, and the diphycercal tail has a three-part fin.

Diplurus, *a freshwater coelacanth of the Late Triassic of New Jersey, was 4 to 5 inches (10–13 cm.) long.* **Holophagus,** *from Late Triassic and Jurassic strata of Europe and other parts of the world, was marine and reached a length of 2 feet (0.6 m.)*

By the Late Devonian, both marine and freshwater forms existed, but most of the Mesozoic coelacanth record is marine, on a worldwide scale. Until 1938, the group was thought to have become extinct in the Late Mesozoic. But then a living coelacanth, named *Latimeria,* was dredged up from the depths of the Indian Ocean near the coast of South Africa. This specimen, plus several collected more recently near Madagascar have given us an excellent idea of what the soft-part anatomy was like of a group known only as fossils before the discovery of *Latimeria.* It truly was a "living fossil," just like the *Ginkgo* tree, first found alive in China.

CHAPTER XXIII

The Greening of the Land

 We have reviewed monerans, protists, animals, and lowly plants whose story runs through more than 3,000 million years. Most of these organisms were aquatic, and the vast majority were marine. Exceptions, such as freshwater snails and terrestrial insects, were latecomers. They appeared ages or even eras after their relatives had become plentiful in the sea.

This fact shows that we did not begin our survey with marine fossils just for convenience and are just getting around to the others. If that were true, we could now turn back to Precambrian deposits and begin a new series of chapters on inhabitants of the land. Lands existed in those ancient times, forming shores of the constantly shifting seas and providing most of the sediment that filled burrows, covered trails, and enclosed dead shells or corals. Yet, from those lands have come few fossils, none at all that antedate the Silurian period. Insects, which now outnumber all other terrestrial creatures, did not appear until Devonian times.

THE PROBLEMS OF BECOMING TERRESTRIAL

Plants existed billions of years in watery environments before they appeared on land. There are reasons for that. Many new problems faced plants and animals living in the harsh land environment: avoiding drying out, and getting nutrients, namely carbon for use in photosynthesis, and reproducing in a dry situation. Terrestrial plants have solved some of these problems by developing such materials as cutin, made up of a hydrocarbon that forms a waxy or fatty layer, preventing water loss. They also have developed specialized cells called stomata in the leaves that normally act as one-way valves: they let in carbon dioxide (CO_2), needed for the carbon used in photosynthesis, but don't allow the water out. A system of roots in terrestrial plants not only anchor them to the ground but also take up water and nutrients needed for growth and survival. Larger plants also developed a series of vessels to transport water and nutrients from the roots to stems and leaves.

They also developed special tissues that gave them support so that large size could be reached. And finally terrestrial plants developed reproductive structures, such as spores and seeds, that protected them from drying out.

THE ANCESTORS OF LAND PLANTS

Where did the land plants that are so dominant today come from? This question is one better answered by looking at living forms than by the fossils, because the record is rather sparse during the Late Cambrian and Early Silurian, when the terrestrial environment was invaded.

Much evidence points to the chlorophytes, the grass-green algae (such as pond scum), as the group that gave rise to terrestrial plants. Like the terrestrial tracheophytes, chlorophytes have both chlorophyll a and chlorophyll b, as well as true starch, and cellulose in their cell walls. This type of algae also has what is called "alternation of generations," which means it goes through phases of both sexual and asexual reproduction, in much the way a modern fern does. All of these characteristics together single out chlorophytes, of all the lower plants, as most similar to tracheophytes, with which they share a number of features.

THE EARLIEST LAND PLANTS

Thick-walled spores with shapes similar to those of some modern terrestrial plants have been found in Early Cambrian rocks of India and Russia.

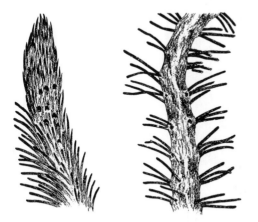

Baragwanathia longifolia, a lycopod. Late Silurian (once thought to be Early Devonian), Australia. About 4–11 inches (10–28 cm.) long

Yarravia. Late Silurian, Australia

Some very early land plants

Aldanophyton consists of a series of carbonized imprints from Siberia with shoots up to 5 inches (13 cm.) wide. It resembles a small lycopod (club moss) with spirally arranged leaves, each about 3 inches (8 mm.) wide. But whether, indeed, it was a vascular plant, and whether or not the fossil spores recovered from rocks of this same time period were contaminant, is not really known. So until more and better material from Cambrian and Ordovician rocks is found, paleobotanists will remain wary of accepting any of these early fossils as true land-plant material.

When land plants first appear in the fossil record, they are a mixture of simple and complex forms, hinting at a previous history we have not yet uncovered. Though there are nonvascular plants (in other words, plants lacking tubes that can carry nutrients and water) in Early Silurian deposits, no true vascular plants are known until the later part of this period.

Baragwanathia, from Australia, is one of these early "vesseled" plants in rocks of either Late Silurian or Early Devonian age. These were of reasonable size, with branches up to 10 to 11 inches (26–28 cm.) in length and 0.5 to 2.5 inches (1–6 cm.) in diameter. The stems were slender and bore a large number of tiny, pliable leaves. At places along the stem or leaves there were cases (sporangia) that contained spores, for *Baragwanathia* reproduced much as ferns do today. It is interesting that the overall structure, both

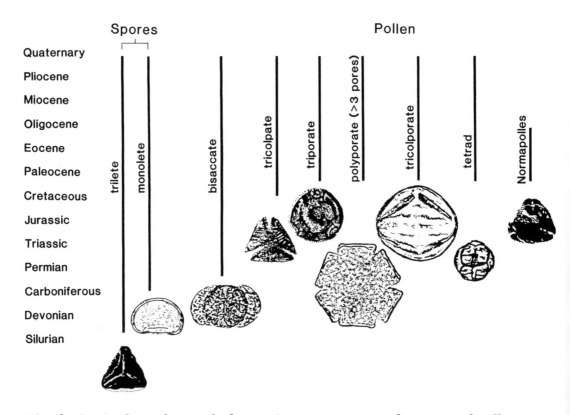

Distribution in the rock record of some important groups of spores and pollen. (Modified from Brasier, 1981; Microfossils, *by D. Gelt)*

internal and external, of *Baragwanathia* was like living lycopods, or club mosses, at this supposedly early stage of land-plant evolution.

In contrast to the complex *Baragwanathia, Cooksonia* was a very simply organized, small plant, only a few centimeters high. The stems were slender and naked, with no leaves, and sporangia occurred at the ends of branches. *Cooksonia* occurred in the Middle Silurian of Ireland but survived as late as the Early Devonian of Wales and Australia. In many ways it resembles what a number of paleobotanists think the most primitive vascular plants looked like, especially in lacking true leaves and roots.

DEVONIAN BOGS AND FORESTS

Tourists who use the Silver Gate entrance to Yellowstone National Park pass the site of another early land flora. To reach it they climb some thousands of feet by automobile and travel across an ancient and now uncovered seafloor dotted by glacial lakes. Beside one of these, rises Beartooth Butte, a cliff of marine strata, that range from Cambrian to Devonian in age. Near the top is an Early Devonian river channel, worn in older beds while northwestern Wyoming was a lowland crossed by meandering streams.

Photographers pause to "shoot" the lake, but fossil hunters park their cars and climb the southern face of the butte. Near its base they find green to brown shales and sandstones, some showing filled burrows of Middle Cambrian annelids. Then come dolomites and limestones containing stromatolites, followed by red, buff, and gray river deposits whose thickness reaches 150 feet (45 m.). Laid down near the mouth of a sluggish stream, these sediments contain eurypterids, ostracoderms, fish, and a variety of land plants. The most common of these is *Psilophyton,* a prickly leafless shrub.

Plants much like those of Beartooth Butte lived in eastern Canada during Early to Middle Devonian times; their remains, generally poorly preserved, may be found in the Gaspé sandstones, of southeastern Quebec. Our best record of Early Devonian vegetation comes from Western Europe. There, in what once were sheltered valleys between mountain ranges, grew fungi and a variety of more complex plants. The best-known types were found in a onetime peat bog near the village of Rhynie, in Aberdeenshire, Scotland. Fed by silica-bearing water from nearby hot springs, this bog produced fossils that preserve the delicate cell structure in thin sections cut from layers of chert. *Rhynia,* one of these plants, was simple. It possessed rootlike structures, but not true roots, and lacked leaves. Several species varied in size from very small plants to those reaching 20 inches (50 cm.) or so in height. *Horneophyton,* another Rhynie plant, is important because it forms an intermediate stage between the bryophytes (mosses and liverworts) and forms such as *Rhynia,* in which the sporophyte (spore-bearing) and gametophyte

Beartooth Butte, Wyoming. Fossil plants and vertebrates are found in dark-colored river deposits above the letter R

(male- and female-sex-cell-bearing) plants are completely independent of one another. In *Horneophyton*, sporophyte and gametophyte plants grew together, but the sporophyte was much larger when compared to the gametophyte.

Both *Rhynia* and *Horneophyton* are in the Rhyniopsida, a group restricted to the Siluro-Devonian. Perhaps they are related to the living, inconspicuous *Psilotum*, of the world's tropics. It, too, is a plant of few accessories; no roots or vesseled leaves are present, and spore cases are situated at the tips of short stems.

LATE DEVONIAN FORESTS

Returning to North America, we find that mountains thrown up as the Proto-Atlantic closed were probably islands, extending from Georgia to Newfoundland during Late Devonian times. Those mountains were moist,

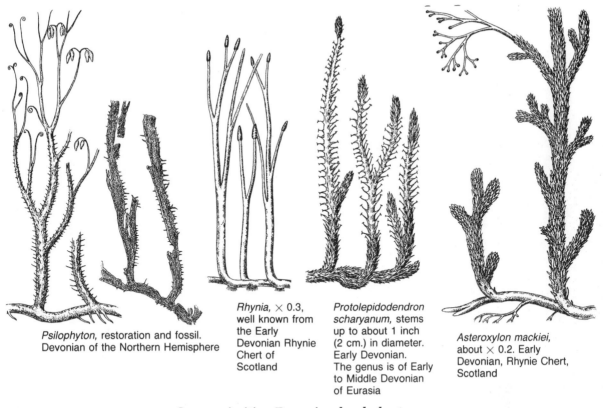

Psilophyton, restoration and fossil. Devonian of the Northern Hemisphere

Rhynia, × 0.3, well known from the Early Devonian Rhynie Chert of Scotland

Protolepidodendron scharyanum, stems up to about 1 inch (2 cm.) in diameter. Early Devonian. The genus is of Early to Middle Devonian of Eurasia

Asteroxylon mackiei, about × 0.2. Early Devonian, Rhynie Chert, Scotland

Some primitive Devonian land plants

with many streams that flowed toward the retreating sea. Where the streams reached salt water, they built up piles of sediment such as the Catskill Delta, in New York. These deltas spread until they formed an almost continuous lowland covered by some of the earth's first forests.

The existence of those forests had been suspected since 1869, when a freshet raged down Schoharie Creek, wrecking bridges, washing out culverts, and exposing a few fossil tree stumps near the village of Gilboa, New York. Additional fragments were found in 1897, and in 1920 collectors discovered a forest stratum higher than the one reached by the freshet. At last, in 1921, the city of New York opened two quarries to get stone for dams. The dams were built to hold back water, but the quarries completed the story of Gilboa's ancient forest.

"Eospermatopteris."   The most plentiful trees in the Gilboa forests had straight trunks 20 to 40 feet (up to 12 m.) high, with swollen, onion-shaped bases 3 to 4 feet (about 1 m.) in thickness. The roots were slender and straplike, running out in all directions, like the roots of present-day palms. The leaves were fernlike and 6 to 8 feet (up to 2.7 m.) long, and their tips bore pointed structures resembling seeds. Because of them the trees were assigned to a group called the seed ferns and were named *Eospermatopteris.*

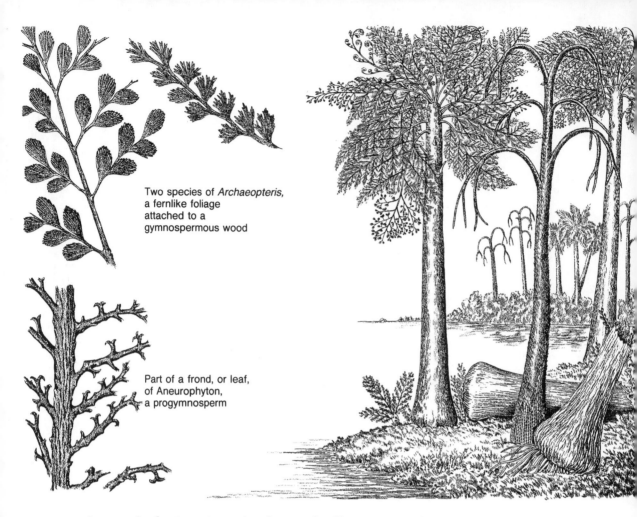

Two species of *Archaeopteris*, a fernlike foliage attached to a gymnospermous wood

Part of a frond, or leaf, of Aneurophyton, a progymnosperm

A scene in the Late Devonian forest of Gilboa, New York, and fossils of some late Devonian plants. The trees with fernlike leaves are Archaeosigillaria, a genus of lycopods known from the Early Devonian to the Late Carboniferous

Later studies have shown that some of the "seeds" still contain spores, while the trunks and leaves are identical with others long known as *Aneurophyton. Aneurophyton* and other plants such as *Callixylon* are often referred to as progymnosperms. They have a fernlike method of reproduction, but their woody structure is very coniferlike. They form an important structural link between two large groups of plants.

Callixylon. Occurring often with *Archaeopteris* is another plant, *Callixylon,* that seems somewhat intermediate between ferns and true gymnosperms (the plants with naked, but true, seeds). Permineralized specimens representing this form are abundant, including everything from tree trunks, with a diameter of up to 1.5 meters (5 ft.) and a height of more than 8 meters (about 26 ft.), to small twigs and branches. In cross section the wood has a structure typical of modern conifers. *Callixylon zalesskyi,* found in many rock sequences in the northeastern U.S.A., is of great importance, for it has the spore-bearing fronds of a fern attached to a stem with gymnospermous wood. In fact, the fernlike fronds attached to the *Callixylon* stem had been named *Archaeopteris macilenta* long before they were found associated. Since *Archaeopteris* was named first, in 1871, the whole plant, including both stem and fronds, had to take on this name, now that all the parts had been found attached to one another. And that name became *Archaeopteris macilenta.* Much of the Late Devonian fossil wood from the U.S. Northeast belongs in this group of plants, which formed a major part of the forests of the time.

Early Lycopods. Much less common in Gilboa's swampy woods were two species of lycopods, plants that still survive in the form of club mosses *(Selaginella)* and ground pines *(Lycopodium).* Those of Gilboa were slender trees with drooping branches. One species had narrow leaves about 12

Lepidodendron   Sigillaria   Cordaites   Calamites

Tree Fern

Plants of a swampy Pennsylvanian forest in many parts of the Northern Hemisphere. Lepidodendron *may have had a more drooping foliage, more like that of the living* Araucaria. Sigillaria *may also have had foliage restricted more to the top of the tree and the leaves decidedly more elongate and hanging, completely covering conelike structures concentrated around the trunk* inches long (about 30 cm.), but those of the other species were wider and shorter and overlapped like scales. They grew upon both trunk and branches and must have made the trees look as if they were covered with moss. Cones at the tips of some branches were filled with spores, not seeds.

This matter of spores versus seeds is important in plant classification. At its simplest, a spore is a single cell that can grow into a new plant. Such spores are found among molds, fungi, mosses, and ferns. In many other plants, however, two cells must interact and form a single new one before development can begin. These "marrying cells" may be identical, as they are in lycopods and some algae. They also may differ in size and shape, as they do in horsetails and pine trees, to choose only two examples. As with simple spores, the product is always a new plant that must make its way unassisted through the early stages of its life.

A seed, on the other hand, is a new plant enclosed in parental stores of food and in armor. The seed begins when two cells—always different—unite and grow into a partly developed plant known as an embryo. This embryo is supplied with food and covered with a husk or shell that furnishes protection. When this structure, the seed, is fully developed, the embryo in it may begin to grow. It also may lie for months or even years before it germinates, developing into a new plant that itself later reproduces sexually.

Lycopods or plants close to the ancestry of lycopods are first known in the Late Silurian or Early Devonian. A number of forms, such as *Zosterophyllum,* lie somewhat intermediate between psilopsids and lycopsids. Many of the Devonian lycopods are small herbaceous forms, not so different in overall shape and form from the small, inconspicuous living *Lycopodium.* Some forms, such as *Baragwanathia,* mentioned earlier in this chapter, did reach larger sizes. These lycopods were, and are, distinguished from other plants by having microphylls ("little leaves") and adaxial sporangia, which means the spore containers are borne on the top surface of the leaves. The lycopods and their immediate ancestors were the first plants with leaves, which probably developed as spine-like outgrowths of the stem.

COAL AGE AND COAL FORESTS

The Devonian Period came to an end as rocks crumpled into mountain ranges that stretched from Newfoundland to what is now North Carolina, as the Proto-Atlantic Ocean closed, causing orogenies in both North America and Europe. The debris of the North American Acadian Mountains created the Catskill Delta, in which the Gilboa forest had been buried. Then came the Early Carboniferous, or Mississippian in North America, a period or subperiod that lasted 40 million years. During most of those years, shallow seas spread widely across the interior of North America, but much of the eastern region was lowland. Fossils show that the bulbous-trunked

Aneurophyton had vanished, along with the drooping trees of Gilboa. In their stead grew other lycopods, as well as ferns, seed ferns, and trees related to living horsetail rushes. To get a really satisfying picture of Carboniferous plant life, we must go to the next subdivision of this period.

That subdivision bears various names: Pennsylvanian, Late Carboniferous, and Coal Age (which really applies to all of the Carboniferous). It was a time when seas repeatedly advanced, especially noticeable in the Northern Hemisphere, only to retreat as streams filled them with sediment. Other streams flowed to inland basins, which sank about as rapidly as they were filled by detritus. The result was a vast series of swamps whose waters sometimes were clear, sometimes were muddy, and sometimes were almost choked by deposits of mud, gravel, and sand.

Those swamps were a paradise for plant life, offering rich soil, an equable and humid climate, and a generous supply of moisture. As a result, vegetation grew in such abundance that its decaying remains built up beds of peat, which then hardened into coal as it was buried deeper and deeper. Late Carboniferous formations of western Pennsylvania, for example, contain thirteen important coal beds, one of which—the Pittsburgh "seam"—is 6 to 14 feet (about 2–4.3 m.) in thickness. The number of leaves, stems, and trunks in such deposits defies imagination. The almost predictable repetition of marine, swampy, coal-seam, and riverine deposits are called cyclothems. These banded rock successions can often be seen in interstate highway road cuts in the eastern U.S.A. and are a reminder of how different conditions were in the past. They are a record of fluctuating shorelines: marine transgressions and times when shorelines regressed (moved away from the land).

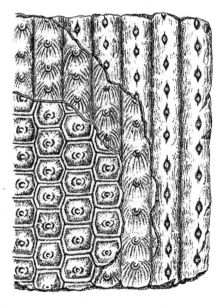

Sigillaria, showing three different layers of bark. The outermost is at the left

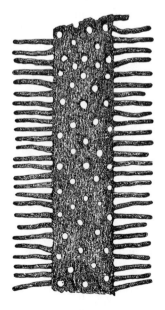

Stigmaria ficoides, the rootlike organ of a tree such as *Lepidodendron*

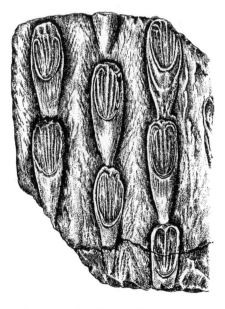

Psaronius, the stem of a late Paleozoic tree fern. The scars show where leaves were attached

Bark, roots, and a stem from typical Pennsylvanian (Late Carboniferous) plants

Besides forming beds of coal, land plants of Pennsylvanian times left an abundance of fossils. Some of them are films of carbon left in fine sand and mud as leaves, stems, and roots decayed. Others are mere impressions in sandstone, but many are perfect petrifications found in lumps of calcite, or "coal balls." Trees range from carbonized layers to casts made of sediment that filled holes left by trunks or stumps after their pulpy wood had decayed. In many places, these fossil stamps and trunks have been found standing erect in rock. Those at Joggins and Sydney, Nova Scotia, are among the finest and most famous in North America. In some of these trunks, which had rotted before being covered with sediment, are some of the finest early reptiles and amphibians, which will be mentioned later in this book.

Anyone who identifies Pennsylvanian plants soon finds that they are widely distributed. Many species that are plentiful in Nova Scotia, West Virginia, and Illinois or Kansas were discovered and named in Europe. These wide-ranging fossils are a great help in correlating formations. And since each species generally fits a definite set of surroundings, wide distribution also indicates uniformity of climate and other conditions in places thousands of miles apart. In the Southern Hemisphere, somewhat in contrast, major coal deposits were not all Carboniferous in age. In Australia, for instance, major coal deposition during the Paleozoic occurred in the Permian.

SOME TYPICAL PENNSYLVANIAN PLANTS

No one book, and assuredly no single chapter, can describe the vast array of Pennsylvanian plants. We can, however, mention the genera most likely to be found in the Northern Hemisphere fossil deposits, which also are the ones that establish the general character of the flora in Coal Age forests and swamps.

Lycopods. Modern lycopods, as we already know, include the club mosses and ground pines: small plants that creep on the ground, send up stalks and branches, and reproduce by means of spores borne in conelike organs. Most Pennsylvanian lycopods were, quite the contrary, trees, and *Lepidodendron* was one of the tallest. Some species reached heights of 100 to 125 feet (about 30–40 m.). The trunk was straight and simple at its base, but higher up it formed two branches that bifurcated again and again. Young parts of the tree were covered with dagger-shaped leaves that grew close to the thick bark. When leaves dropped from the trunk and older branches, they left scars that look like diamond-shaped scales and gave the plant its name, which means "scale tree." The spore-bearing cones were long and grew either at the tips of branches or along their sides. The species of *Lepidodendron*—they number more than a hundred—are distinguished largely by the shape and detailed structure of these scars.

The base of each *Lepidodendron* trunk divided into underground parts

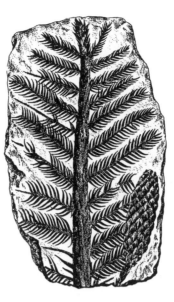

Annularia and *Asterophyllites*, × 1.
Both are branches and leaves
of scouring rushes, or sphenopsids

Lebachia (sometimes called
Walchia), × 1. An early conifer

Sphenophyllum, a small
creeping plant that ranged
from Devonian to Permian

Four typical Pennsylvanian plants

that formed a network of woody organs bearing the deceptive name of root-stocks. Each rootstock gave off what botanists often call "lateral absorptive appendages," since they may or may not have been true roots. They left small round scars on the rootstock—scars that are more widely spaced than those on the bark of branches and trees.

Stigmaria. Before the nature of the rootstocks was known, they were named *Stigmaria.* There is little doubt that most so-called stigmarians belong to *Lepidodendron,* though some may be the underground stems of other lycopods. The commonest type bears the specific name *ficoides* (figlike), because it slightly resembles the branchlets of fig trees. *Stigmaria ficoides* tapers gradually to a blunt tip about one inch (2.5 cm.) in diameter. The "rootlets" seldom measure more than a quarter inch (0.6 cm.) in width and look like narrow black ribbons on layers of gray shale that once was soil.

Another prominent tree in the Pennsylvanian forests was *Sigillaria.* It was sturdier than *Lepidodendron,* but not so tall; one species reached 6 feet (nearly 2 m.) in diameter at the base, tapered to 12 inches (30 cm.) at a height of 18 feet (5.5 m.) and measured less than 40 feet (12 m.) overall. The leaves were slender, pointed, and longer than those of *Lepidodendron,* some resembling very large blades of grass. When the leaves fell, they left scars that seldom were closely crowded. In some species, the bark between scars was smooth; in others, it bore ridges that ran up and down the trunk. Most species did not branch, or branched only once or twice. The cones, 4 to 8 inches (10–20 cm.) in length, hung from long stems on trunks or branches, just below the leaves.

"Pecopteris," a form genus of fernlike foliage borne by both ferns and seed plants

Lepidostrobus, cone of an arborescent lycopod, × 0.25

Calamites, × 0.5, internal mold of a calamite, or scouring rush, stem

Branches of *Lepidodendron,* a lycopod ("club moss")

Neuropteris, foliage of the seed fern *Medullosa*

Alethopteris, a seed-fern form genus found attached to *Medullosa,* × 0.4

Lepidodendron, × 1. Outer section of a trunk

Mariopteris, a fernlike gymnosperm

Fernlike leaves, lycopods, and a scouring rush, all Pennsylvanian

Horsetails and Their Kin. Modern horsetails, also called scouring rushes, live in both wet and very dry places. Their straight, slender stems are jointed and are made gritty by large amounts of silica. *Calamites,* the chief Pennsylvanian genus, grew 2 or 3 to as much as 40 feet (12 m.) high, with stems that were smooth or had lengthwise ridges. Specimens 3 inches (8 cm.) in diameter are common, and some plants must have been 10 to 12 inches (25–30 cm.) thick. The upright, woody stems grew from rootstocks and were supported by roots that came from the lowermost joints, like the prop roots of corn. Some species were unbranched, but others had branches that grew from the joints, or nodes. Clusters of slender leaves also grew from nodes, especially on young branches, though they often remained on good-sized stems.

Calamites formed extensive jungles beside rivers and lakes, as well as in shallow swamps. Petrified stems are found on some shales, and carbonized leaves are common. Still more familiar are sandstone casts replacing the pith which once filled upright stems. These casts generally show ridges as well as nodes and pits to which branches were attached, but the ridges do not correspond to those that once appeared on the surface.

Annularia and *Asterophyllites* are names applied to leaves of calamites. The leaves are needle-like or bladelike, with a single vein, and form clusters around branches or stems. Isolated fragments of calamite roots are often given another name, *Astromyelon.*

The horsetails, or Sphenopsida, have a long geologic range, from Devonian to Recent, but certainly reached their heyday in the late Paleozoic. Their origin lies somewhere within the ferns, as plants, such as *Hyenia,* intermediate between the two groups, demonstrate.

Much evolutionary experimentation was occurring during the Middle and Late Devonian within such groups as ferns and early gymnosperms. Because of this, there are several plant groups that are difficult to classify. *Sphenophyllum* is one of these "difficult" plants.

Sphenophyllum was a small herbaceous plant that had small leaves that were triangular or divided into lobes, and grew in whorls. Roots grew from joints on the slender stem. First known in the Late Devonian, it reached its greatest abundance in the Late Carboniferous and disappeared by the Late Permian. Sometimes thought to be related to the horsetails, this group shows similarity to the club mosses. Now it is recognized as a unique, extinct group, the Sphenophyllales.

True Ferns. Ferns first appear in the Middle Devonian at a time when there was much diversification occurring in tracheophytes. They probably developed from a group of plants not all too different from *Rhynia:* the trimerophytopsids. Ferns diversified greatly during the Carboniferous, only to undergo a great reduction in the Early Permian. Later, in the late Mesozoic, they again diversified, this time in concert with the flowering plants, and continue to be varied today.

Pennsylvanian ferns had a staggering variety of growth forms, ranging from plants resembling the living Royal Fern to some that formed trees. The impressive marattiaceous tree ferns, such as *Psaronius,* crowd the Late Carboniferous swamps of North America and Europe. *Psaronius* had a tall, tapering, slender trunk and a crown of leaves, much as some tree ferns do today. The fronds of *Psaronius,* when found isolated from the stem, have often been called *Pecopteris,* and reached up to 3 meters (nearly 10 ft.) in length. The roots were very like those of living ferns.

Cordaites and Conifers.   These fossil plants remind us that trees are not a natural group but merely are large, woody plants that may or may not be related. Most Coal Age trees were lycopods, but *Cordaites* was an early conifer and may have been related to *Callixylon,* of Devonian times. *Cordaites* itself was a tall, slender tree with a trunk that bore a crown of branches. The leaves were wider, strap-like, and less pointed than those of lycopods; as fossils they suggest broad, blunt cattail leaves 8 to 40 inches (20–100 cm.) long. Flattened, heart-shaped seeds were borne on stalks among the leaves.

The group Cordaitales is another example of plants whose separate parts were discovered and named before anyone suspected that they were related. As a result, the seed-bearing stalks became *Cordaianthus,* casts of pith in the trunks were named *Artisia,* and roots were called *Amyelon.* It will be some time yet, however, before all the various bits and pieces can be related to one plant.

Cordaitaceans became an important part of the forests in Pennsylvanian times and flourished on into the Permian. They were nearly worldwide in distribution, known on all continents except for Antarctica. Some grew nearly 100 feet (30 m.) high, but many others were 15 feet (4.5 m.) or less. Some had mangrove-like stilt-roots, obviously related to their life in swampy conditions, while others had shallow systems that extended far laterally, just as do the living *Eucalyptus,* or gum trees.

Lebachia (sometimes referred to as *Walchia)* was another early conifer present in Carboniferous forests. It belonged to the Voltziales, a group sometimes believed to be transitional between cordaitaceans and true conifers. Though the Voltziales are mosaics of these two groups, there are still many information gaps that need to be filled, especially with regard to pollen and cone structure, before the relationships of all these groups can be worked out.

Lebachia and related forms resembled the living Norfolk Island pine *(Araucaria excelsa),* with branches coming off in whorls along the main trunk. Both groups had needle-like leaves, very unlike the cordaitaceans.

The Beginnings of Seeds.   The origin of seeds, during the Middle Paleozoic, is certainly one of the most important developments for land plants—just as the amniote egg was to reptiles. Seeds freed plants from dependence on water or at least a moist environment for reproduction, and thus plants were able to colonize a much greater part of the terrestrial environment.

A number of plant groups that occur in forests of Carboniferous age either are seed bearers or are nearing this state. Some plants, the protogymnosperms, are a mixture of fern and gymnosperm features. The gymnosperms themselves show great variety in styles of reproduction and leaf and wood types. Such variety has often been confusing if an isolated part of any of these plants is found. It is often difficult to determine what major group such a fragment belongs to.

Within this variety of gymnosperms appear to be two genealogical lines, one to the cycads and another to the conifers. Whereas the cycads have large, frondlike leaves and stems with a broad area of pith, conifers generally have simple leaves and compact woody stems.

Cycadophytes come in three varieties: Cycadales, Cycadeoidales, and Pteridospermales (seed ferns).

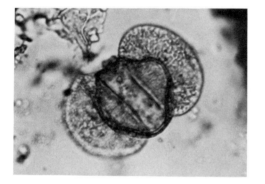

Podocarpidites ostentatus, *a gymnosperm pollen grain from the LaTrobe Valley, southeastern Victoria. Late Miocene. About 5.8 microns (0.0058 mm., 0.002 in.) wide. (Courtesy of J. McEwen Mason, Monash University)*

Seed ferns. Coal Age deposits (Carboniferous) in the Northern Hemisphere contain great numbers of fossil leaves that were once thought to be true ferns or plants that combined characteristics of ferns and cycads. In shape some resembled tree ferns, while others grew close to the ground or formed vines. Fronds were normally spirally arranged on the stem. Seeds or seedlike structures, and sporangia, were situated on the foliage and were not borne in cones, thus differing from the conifers.

Medullosa is one of the better-known medullosacean seed ferns, which range from the Early Carboniferous into the Permian. As with so many other plants discussed earlier, many parts of *Medullosa* were given other names until all were found attached in one specimen. Detached petioles were called *Myeloxylon*. Detached fronds were *Neuropteris* and *Alethopteris,* among other names. *Colpoxylon* referred to isolated stems. To the nonexpert, this becomes all very complex and confusing, but it does help point out how very important the rare complete or nearly complete plant fossil can be in deciphering relationships and making reconstructions of extinct species.

Cycads and Cycadeoids. Today cycads are a minor part of the world's vegetation, but in the late Paleozoic and Mesozoic they were a much more

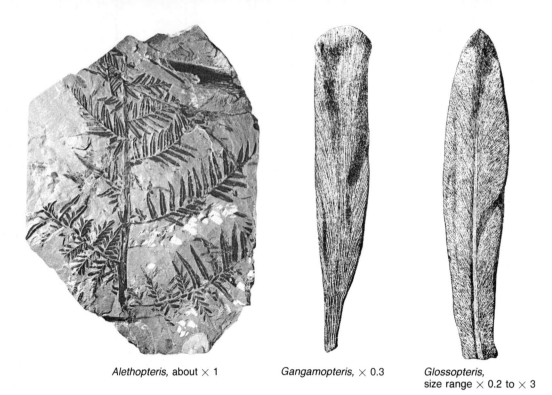

Alethopteris, about × 1   Gangamopteris, × 0.3   Glossopteris,
size range × 0.2 to × 3

Alethopteris *is a Pennsylvanian seed fern. The other genera belong to the Permian* **Glossopteris** *flora characteristic of Gondwana*

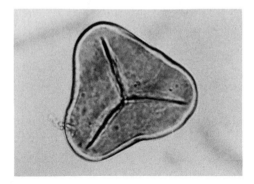

Cyathidites australis, *a fern spore from Early Cretaceous floodplain rocks at Kilcunda, Victoria. Highly magnified, 5.7 microns (0.0057 mm., 0.002 in.) in diameter. (Courtesy of B. Wagstaff, Monash University)*

important group, reaching their acme in the Mesozoic. Living cycads look like palms (which are actually flowering plants) with stout trunks. They are and have been both small plants and proper trees. Seeds and pollen-bearing organs are situated on conelike structures called strobili and on cones. Pollen is borne on one plant, while seed cones are borne on another. Pollen from cycads has a characteristic boat shape.

Several problematical plants from the Carboniferous, such as *Lasiostrobus,* and Permian, such as *Spermopteris,* may be early cycads. It is not until the Triassic, however, that plants such as *Lyssoxylon,* a beautifully preserved stem genus from the Chinle Formation, of Arizona, establishes without a doubt that cycads existed.

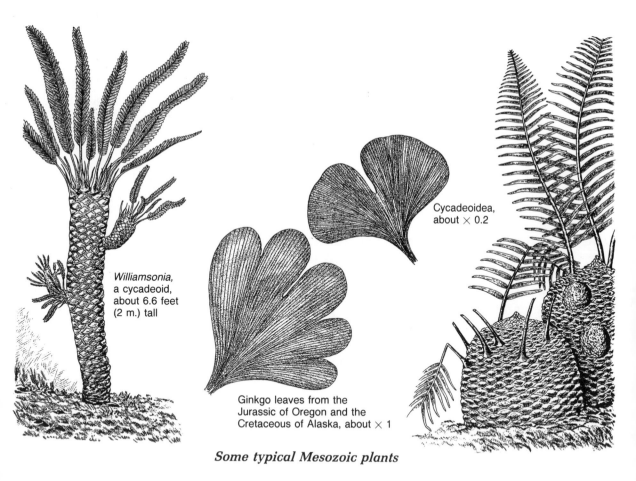

Williamsonia,
a cycadeoid,
about 6.6 feet
(2 m.) tall

Cycadeoidea,
about × 0.2

Ginkgo leaves from the
Jurassic of Oregon and the
Cretaceous of Alaska, about × 1

Some typical Mesozoic plants

Cycadeoids are another group of palmlike plants, related to cycads, that are prominent in Mesozoic floras. *Williamsonia* is probably one of the better known of these because of the beautiful reconstructions produced by the famous Indian paleobotanist Sahni. Reproductive structures of cycadeoids are very like flowers. Both groups were probably derived from the seed ferns sometime in the Late Carboniferous.

Ginkgophytes and Other Mesozoic Seed Bearers

During the Mesozoic, along with cycadophytes grew a number of seed-bearing plants, some of which have survived to the present. *Caytonia* and *Glossopteris* left no survivors, but the Ginkgoales did in the maidenhair tree, or *Ginkgo.* An abundance of the fan-shaped leaves of this genus are known from Mesozoic and Tertiary rocks, and one species, *G. biloba,* was discovered as a "living fossil" growing in the gardens of some temples in China. Since then it has been successfully introduced to various areas of the world, in many cases where the group it belongs to had lived successfully, and in greater variety, millions of years before. Probably derived from cordaites, ginkgos share a number of characteristics with cycads and other gymnosperms of this time period.

Additionally, in Mesozoic floras, conifers and related forms became more dominant, only to be superseded in the Late Cretaceous by the flowering plants, or angiosperms, which will be discussed in Chapter XXXII.

PARADISE PAST: THE PERMIAN FLORA

Coal Age swamps were a paradise for plant life, but a paradise that disappeared as conditions changed. This happened at the end of the Pennsylvanian Period and during the Permian, when glacial ice spread, causing sea levels to drop as more and more water was tied up in ice and as global temperatures dropped. Between glaciations came epochs of moisture and somewhat warmer conditions.

These changes affected the Southern Hemisphere more than the Northern, where broad and often swampy lowlands persisted for some millions of years. We find, therefore, that Early Permian plants of the Northern Hemisphere are much like their Pennsylvanian ancestors. In the Southern Hemisphere, however, where many continents were loaded with ice sheets, a very different sort of flora developed.

Glossopteris and Its Kin. This hardy flora contained a variety of plants: true ferns, conifers, small calamites, and so on. Its foremost member, however, was *Glossopteris,* a seed fern with thick bladelike leaves, which was abundant in both Permian and Triassic rocks of the Southern Hemisphere. Each leaf contained a network of veins and a sturdy midrib, but the latter was lacking from the leaves of another seed fern, *Gangamopteris.* A third genus, *Neuropteridium,* had a coarse central stalk with lobed leaflets that were broadly attached at the base.

Glossopteris was a tree of substantial size and had a trunk of *Araucarioxylon* gymnospermous wood reaching up to 40 centimeters (16 in.) in diameter.

The Hermit Flora. An array of Permian plants have been found along trails that descend into Arizona's Grand Canyon. The Hermit flora preserved in a deposit of shale built up as a delta that contains casts of salt crystals and is deeply marked by mud cracks. These sediments plainly formed in a region where torrential rains were followed by droughts, during which streams ran dry and ponds became sun-baked flats.

Swamp-dwelling plants could not have survived in such a habitat. Instead, the red rocks contain mats of algae that spread over muddy slime, and leathery seed ferns that grew beside both ponds and intermittent streams. There also are a thick-stemmed species of *Sphenophyllum,* a *Walchia* with little leaves, and several other conifers. It is interesting to note that the total number of species in this flora was low, suggesting harsher conditions than in many other North American areas producing Permian plants.

THE END OF AN ERA

The Permian was certainly a time of floral change as well as marked climatic fluctuation. Many of the groups dominant in the Paleozoic were drastically reduced even if they expanded again in the Mesozoic or Cenozoic. Groups such as cycads and their relatives, along with glossopteroids, expanded.

Though many fern groups became extinct in the early part of the Permian, one, the Osmundaceae, was expanding. What happened in the later parts of the Permian was certainly a herald of what was to come in the Mesozoic as far as floral makeup is concerned.

CHAPTER XXIV

Amphibians, Ancient and Modern

 The word "amphibian" means "living a double life" and refers to the fact that most members of this group spend part of their life in water and part on land. Frogs, for example, often lay their eggs in water. When the tadpoles hatch out, they breathe with gills and are totally aquatic. Later, they undergo metamorphosis, gain lungs and legs, and are able to live on land. Amphibians can be subdivided into three major groups: labyrinthodonts, lepospondyls, and lissamphibians. Exactly how these groups are related to one another, to the fish from which they were derived, and to the reptiles which arose from them is not clear. The Lissamphibia, in fact, may not be a natural group, and its members (frogs, salamanders, etc.) may be derived from different groups.

Labyrinthodonts, a most ancient group. The name of one of these groups, labyrinthodonts, means literally "maze teeth" and refers to the way the enamel of the teeth is intricately folded. When a thin slice of a tooth is cut, it appears to have a maze-like structure.

The most primitive labyrinthodonts are the ichthyostegalians, of which the Late Devonian *Ichthyostega,* from Greenland, is the best known. With four short and thick but well-developed legs, stubby toes, and strong limb girdles, the animal was able to get about on land, but probably in an awkward fashion when compared to most modern terrestrial animals. That they actually did so is supported by fossil footprints found in Australia. However, these early amphibians still retained several features of their fish ancestors, including a tail fin, a lateral line system on the side of the skull, and a remnant of the preopercular bone, which in fish connects the rest of the skull with the operculum, the covering for the gills. All the external surfaces of the skull and opercular apparatus were deeply sculptured with long ridges of bone typical of later labyrinthodonts. With its large teeth and powerful jaws, *Ichthyostega* must have been a ferocious predator.

In labyrinthodonts and *Ichthyostega,* there are two bones which form the centrum of the vertebra, the pleurocentrum and the intercentrum. In one of the labyrinthodont groups, the temnospondyls, the intercentrum came to dominate the centrum, and finally the pleurocentrum completely disap-

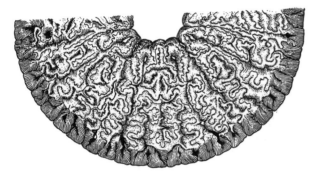

Section through half of a labyrinthodont tooth, showing the crumpled enamel

peared in some forms. In the other group, the anthracosaurs, it was the pleurocentrum which became dominant and the intercentrum which was reduced, and, in some instances, finally disappeared. To get ahead of the story somewhat, the reptiles and their descendants have vertebrae formed of the ancient amphibian pleurocentrum. Because of this, anthracosaurs are thought to be the most likely group to have given rise to reptiles.

Temnospondyls, a group of labyrinthodonts whose name means "divided spools," in reference to the division of their centra, are not particularly well named. Other labyrinthodonts also have centra composed of more than one bone. Be that as it may, these were the most successful amphibian group, having by far the greatest number of families.

During the Carboniferous and Early Permian, the temnospondyls radiated into a myriad of forms and became more and more terrestrial in their adaptations. Their skulls became deeper and their limbs better developed. Among these was the 8-centimeter (3-in.) -long *Amphibamus,* from the early Late Carboniferous of Europe and North America. Two slightly later forms from the Early Permian of Texas were *Eryops,* about 5 feet (1.5 m.) long, and *Cacops,* about 16 inches (40 cm.) long. Both of these animals were carnivores, as were all the labyrinthodonts and lepospondyls.

Eryops was a fully terrestrial, active predator feeding on the smaller amphibians as well as fish. *Cacops* was probably the most terrestrially adapted temnospondyl that ever lived, as is hinted at by its robust limbs and limb girdles. With its head forming one third its total body length, though small it must have been a rapacious and effective predator. Armor was frequently developed as a defense mechanism on these very terrestrial temnospondyls, and one of them, *Platyhystrix,* even had elongated spines on its back, a condition we shall see again and again among various reptilian groups but nowhere else among amphibians.

The temnospondyls during this phase are grouped together as the rhachitomes, the "cut spines," in reference to the fact that the centrum of the vertebrae had a major contribution from the pleurocentrum as well as the intercentrum.

From the Permian onward, the earlier trends toward a greater adaptation

Ichthyostega, *a Late Devonian amphibian from Greenland. It had four legs, but fins on its tail. Length slightly less than 1 meter (3 ft.)*

Late Devonian trackway of one of the oldest tetrapods. From the Genoa River Beds, Victoria, Australia. Length of trackway about 2 meters (6 feet, 7 inches). (Photo courtesy of J. Warren)

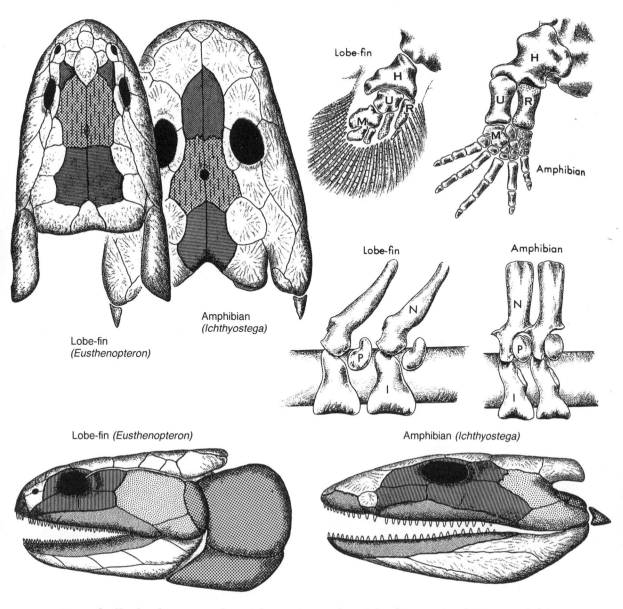

How skulls, leg bones, and vertebrae changed as lobe-fins evolved into amphibians. Identical bones in the skull are marked by similar shading. In the front fin, foreleg, and vertebrae, the identical bones are indicated by the same letter: H, humerus; I, intercentrum; M, metacarpals; N, neural arch; P, pleurocentrum; R, radius; and U, ulna

to a terrestrial existence were reversed by a second group, the stereospondyls, the "solid spools," in reference to the tendency for the centrum to be formed primarily by the intercentrum and the pleurocentrum, reduced or, in extreme cases, absent. The bodies, and particularly the heads, of these animals became flatter and flatter through time. In some groups, the metoposaurs, the eyes moved forward, toward the snout. Their limbs became reduced, and these animals became more and more fully aquatic. In appearance, they resembled crocodiles. *Metoposaurus,* from the Late Triassic of

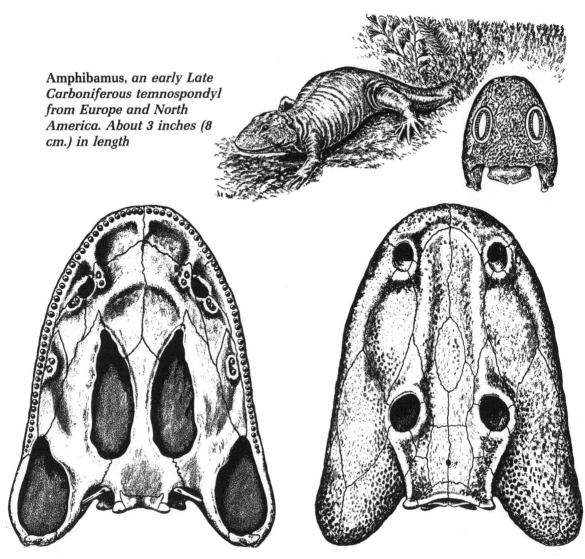

Amphibamus, *an early Late Carboniferous temnospondyl from Europe and North America. About 3 inches (8 cm.) in length*

Skull of Eryops, *from the Permian of Baylor County, Texas. Length about 18 inches (46 cm.)*

Eryops *was a big, powerful, and active amphibian of Early Permian times. Length 5 feet (1.5 m.)*

Cacops, *a labyrinthodont 16 inches (41 cm.) long, from the Permian red beds of* **Texas**

North America, Europe, and Asia, may have never left the water. Another member of this group was *Mastodontosaurus,* from the Triassic of Europe. This animal had a skull nearly a meter long and a body length of more than 4 meters (13 ft.).

One subdivision of this group was the brachyopoids, which means "short faces" in reference to their remarkably shortened skulls. One of the last surviving members of this group as well as the labyrinthodonts was *Siderops,* from the Early Jurassic of Queensland, Australia. Another Jurassic form is known from China, but the youngest labyrinthodont to date is an Early Cretaceous form from Australia. Brachyopoids probably spent most of their time on the bottom of freshwater ponds and lakes, gazing upward for prey, which they seized from below when it swam overhead.

The most completely aquatic of all of the temnospondyls were the plagiosaurs. One of these at least, *Gerrothorax,* retained gills throughout its life, not just during the juvenile stage. The retention of juvenile structures into adulthood is termed neoteny and is a common method of adapting to changing conditions. All that is required is for the developmental timing mechanism of the organism to be altered. This can be seen in the living axolotl, often available at pet stores, which retains gills throughout life, instead of resorbing them.

Elongated skulls and teeth, developed into long, needle-like structures, typify the trematosaurs, active fish catchers of the Early Triassic. Some may

Metoposaurus, *of Late Triassic age, had a broad, flattened body and head, and weak legs. This labyrinthodont may never have left the water. Length 8 feet (2.4 m.)*

Bones and six skulls of Metoposaurus *found in what once was a pool. Triassic near Santa Fe, New Mexico. (Photo from U.S. National Museum)*

Siderops, *from the Early Jurassic Evergreen Formation of Queensland, Australia. It is one of the youngest labyrinthodont amphibians. Evidently Australia served as a refuge for this as well as many other groups. Length of skull 49 cm. (20 in.). (Photo courtesy of A. Warren)*

Painting of Siderops *by Frank Knight. (Courtesy of the Museum of Victoria and Pioneer Design Studio)*

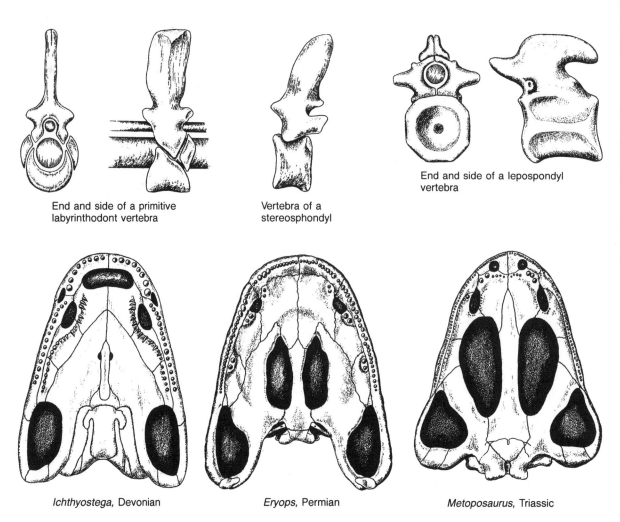

End and side of a primitive
labyrinthodont vertebra

Vertebra of a
stereosphondyl

End and side of a lepospondyl
vertebra

Ichthyostega, Devonian

Eryops, Permian

Metoposaurus, Triassic

How vertebrae and openings in the palate changed

have lived marginally in oceans around Greenland and Spitsbergen. If this is true, they were most unusual, for most (but not all) modern amphibians cannot tolerate salt water, and none of the other extinct amphibians appear to have been adapted to it. Perhaps, though, these unusual occurrences represent deltaic deposits where freshwater rivers emptied into oceans, mixing marine and freshwater organisms. However, the trematosaurs apparently followed their prey, the actinopterygian fishes, into the sea when these fishes diversified in the ocean during the Triassic.

This return to the water was probably related to the rise of the fully terrestrial reptilian carnivores in the Permian. Against this competition, one solution was to leave the land and become aquatic carnivores.

Yet another labyrinthodont group, the anthracosaurs, or "coal lizards," were so named because their remains are common in the Carboniferous coal deposits of Europe. They were not lizards at all, but the classical Greek word *sauros* is commonly used in the scientific names of both reptiles and amphibians, as there is no more appropriate word in either that language or

Latin. It is from these two languages that new scientific words are usually formed.

Never as numerous or 'diverse as the temnospondyls, anthracosaurs may have evolved from a common ancestor somewhat resembling *Ichthyostega* in the Late Devonian or Early Carboniferous. They became extinct at the end of the Permian.

Though the pleurocentrum was the dominant bone in an anthracosaur vertebral centrum, one group of them had an intercentrum that was nearly as large and also formed a complete ring around the notochord, the flexible support rod that was large in primitive vertebrates. These were the embolomeres, typical of which was the long-bodied, aquatic *Pteroplax,* an animal 5 meters (16 ft.) long from the early Late Carboniferous of Great Britain. As a typical embolomere, it had small limbs and even had redeveloped a dorsal fin. Though fully aquatic, it did not evolve into the flattened form that the later labyrinthodonts assumed. A smaller contemporary from Czechoslovakia, *Diplovertebron,* was about 15 centimeters (6 in.) long. Unusual for an embolomere, the body was not particularly elongated or the limbs reduced, and apparently it was not fully aquatic.

All other anthracosaurs had a large pleurocentrum with the intercentrum reduced to a small wedge of bone, if present at all. Of these, *Seymouria* for many years was considered to be the closest link between the amphibians

Pteroplax, *a Late Carboniferous anthracosaur about 15 feet (4.5 m.) long, from* **Great Britain**

Diplovertebron, *a Late Carboniferous labyrinthodont, had a slender body and rather weak legs. The head was not very large, nor was it much flattened. Length 6 inches (15 cm.)*

and the reptiles. It was named for the town of Seymour, Texas, near where the first specimen was found. In the structure of the skeleton other than the skull, it is quite reptile-like. However, it retains amphibian features such as a prominent notch for the ear at the rear of its skull, which is not present in any reptile. A close relative even retains gill arches in the larval stage. No reptile once hatched from an egg still has gill arches.

Another problem with *Seymouria* being a direct reptilian ancestor is that it occurred too late in time to be an actual ancestor; it lived during the Early Permian, while the oldest reptiles were early Late Carboniferous in age. But it may have been a form not all too different from the ancestors that gave rise to the reptiles.

Seymouria *(left), 20 inches (51 cm.) long, was similar to the link between amphibians and reptiles but lived too late.* Trimerorhachis *(right) was a specialized labyrinthodont. Both are from the Permian of Texas*

In recent years, another anthracosaur has been carefully described which appears to be closer to the ancestry of the reptiles. This is *Gephyrostegus,* from the early Late Carboniferous of Czechoslovakia. It lived at the same time as the earliest reptiles and thus was still not an actual ancestor to them. However, its skull, as well as the rest of the skeleton, is quite similar to those of primitive reptiles, differing principally in details of the structure of the vertebrae of the neck and the form of the palate (roof of the mouth) of the skull.

The Enigmatic Branchiosaurs. Many Late Carboniferous and Early Permian amphibians were small creatures, once called branchiosaurs. They had short skulls, long tails, and bones that were mostly cartilaginous. The fossils of some show external gills like those of modern mud puppies (or axolotls) and tadpoles. Critical study finally proved that these supposed adults actually were partly developed, or larval, stages of labyrinthodont amphibians. Thus, the branchiosaurs as a distinct group of amphibians never existed.

Larval "branchiosaur" from the Late Carboniferous and Early Permian of Europe. Length 1.6 to 6 inches (4 to 15 cm.)

The Aberrant Lepospondyls. Unlike the labyrinthodonts, the lepospondyls, or amphibians with "husk spools," are characterized by a single, hollow bone forming the centrum of the vertebra. Appearing in the Early Carboniferous and becoming extinct at the end of the Permian, the group was rather conservative in its evolution.

All lepospondyls tended to be small, the largest only about 1 meter (3 ft.) long, and most were only 30 cm. (12 in.) or less. Typically, they had elongated bodies with reduced limbs and limb girdles, if any at all. Some, such as *Ophiderpeton,* from the early Late Carboniferous of Europe and North America, might have easily been mistaken for a snake about 75 cm. (30 in.) long.

One of the most bizarre lepospondyls was *Diplocaulus,* from the Late Pennsylvanian and Early Permian of North America. The skull was flattened, and broad "horns" projected from the body. Though it still possessed

Diplocaulus, *a wide-skulled lepospondyl amphibian 2 to 3 feet (60–90 cm.) long*

legs, they were tiny and hung beside its long, but flattened, body. The head of *Diplocaulus* was a massive crescent or triangle of bone, which varied in shape from species to species, but invariably ended at the sides in a point. Eyes and nostrils were directed upward, but the small mouth lay underneath. *Diplocaulus* must have spent its whole life in the water, where it sometimes lay in one spot for hours or even days at a time. Waking, it probably ate such small fry as it could find on the bottom. It breathed with gills, probably internal, whose openings lay in folds of skin behind the massive head.

Frogs and Salamanders, the Lissamphibians.

All the amphibians living today are grouped together in the lissamphibians, the "smooth amphibians," in reference to their smooth, scaleless skin. These include the frogs and toads; the salamanders; and the caecilians, or apodans. These latter are tropical forms which are rarely seen. They look and behave something like a large earthworm, lacking both limbs and limb girdles and being nearly blind.

For many years it was thought that frogs were derived from the labyrinthodonts, and the salamanders and apodans from the lepospondyls. However, the gaps in the fossil record are so great that no one really knows if the lissamphibians are related to other amphibians or evolved from a separate fish ancestor. Some structures such as the unique zone of weakness at the base of the teeth, found nowhere else among vertebrates except for the temnospondyl *Doleserpeton,* support the idea that they branched off from other amphibians long before their earliest Middle Permian record.

Lissamphibians do not become common in the fossil record until the Late Jurassic, though there are a few vertebrae that have been assigned to frogs and salamanders as early as Middle Permian. The oldest undoubted record is *Triadobatrachus,* a frog known from an entire skeleton in the Early Triassic of Madagascar.

In becoming superbly adapted for hopping, modern frogs have skeletons that are among the most highly modified of any vertebrate. *Triadobatrachus,* though undoubtedly a frog, was primitive in several respects, as might be expected of the earliest representative of its group. In the arm there are both a radius and an ulna, rather than the single bone that characterizes later frogs. The same is true of the bones of the hind limb. The tail was formed of a series of separate vertebrae, the normal condition for a vertebrate. In other frogs it is a single, spike-like structure, the urostyle, formed by the fusion of about a dozen vertebrae.

When *Triadobatrachus* lived, the lepospondyls were extinct and the labyrinthodonts were to last only into the Early Cretaceous. Between the Late Triassic and the Late Jurassic, the amphibians nearly became extinct, for only a few species survived into the Cretaceous. This is only one of many instances of a group's declining in prominence only to flourish again at a later time.

Today frogs are found on all the continents except Antarctica and have

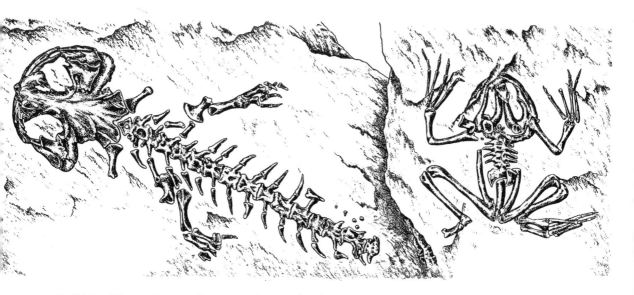

(Left) Andrias, *a Late Miocene salamander from Europe. Length 2 to 4 feet (60–120 cm.). (Right)* Palaeobatrachus, *a North American Miocene frog 3 inches (8 cm.) long*

reached many remote land areas such as New Zealand. Salamanders, on the other hand, failed to reach not only Antarctica, where they could hardly be expected to survive today in the harsh conditions, but also are unknown in Australia and New Zealand.

Even though most living salamanders are only a few centimeters (or inches) long, the largest today is *Andrias,* from China and Japan, which reaches a length of more than 1 meter (40 in.). A Miocene specimen of *Andrias* from Europe was first named *Homo diluvii testis* (the name means "man who witnessed the flood") in the seventeenth century, because it was then thought to be the remains of a poor sinner who had perished in the biblical Deluge.

It is singularly unfortunate that fossils of Early Carboniferous tetrapods are almost unknown anywhere in the world. This was the time not only when the labyrinthodonts and the lepospondyls diverged from one another, but also may have been when, within the labyrinthodonts, the temnospondyls split from the anthracosaurs, though this may have occurred ever earlier. It was also the time when the reptiles differentiated from the anthracosaurs. Clearly the Early Carboniferous was the most important period of amphibian history, when most groups, except possibly the lissamphibians, appeared.

Fortunately, the situation in the Late Devonian and Late Carboniferous is somewhat better, giving us at least glimpses before and after this major event. Terrestrial vertebrates are known from the Late Devonian of eastern Greenland, southeastern Australia, and possibly Canada and Russia, and from the Late Carboniferous of Europe and eastern North America. This short list of areas does emphasize, however, that even at these times the record of land vertebrates is extremely spotty.

CHAPTER XXV

A Myriad of Reptiles on Land

SKULL OPENINGS AND THE GROUPS OF REPTILES

 Hylonomus, the oldest vertebrate recognized as a reptile, comes from the Early Pennsylvanian of Joggins, Nova Scotia. Unlike most of the amphibians, these animals were generally not tied to water for reproduction, but laid eggs that were able to survive in a terrestrial environment. So they were able to move onto the land and exploit resources not generally used by vertebrates before.

Hylonomus had an unbroken expanse of bone behind each eye opening, or orbit. Other reptiles had one or more gaps, the temporal openings, occupying various positions and enclosed by various bones. Though these patterns vary in details, the gaps themselves—or lack of them—are the basis for splitting the reptiles into four major groups, or subclasses:

Anapsids. Most primitive of these groups are the anapsids, creatures such as *Hylonomus,* which had no temporal openings. Behind each eye, five bones fit tightly, as we see in cotylosaurs, turtles, and tortoises. The first of these died out as the Jurassic Period dawned, but turtles and tortoises still prosper.

Synapsids. This old group, extinct since the Early Jurassic, was not truly primitive. Its members had one temporal opening on each side of the skull, *below* two bones called the postorbital and the squamosal. Pelycosaurs and therapsids, the "mammal-like reptiles" (See Chapter XXXI) are placed in this group.

Euryapsids. Animals in this group had a single temporal opening on each side of the skull *above* the postorbital and squamosal bones. Euryapsids were all aquatic and include nothosaurs, plesiosaurs, placodonts, and ichthyosaurs.

Diapsids. As their name suggests, the skull of these reptiles contains two temporal openings on each side—one above and one below the squamosal and postorbital bones. Since their appearance, in the Late Carboniferous,

Meiolania, *a giant horned turtle from Quaternary sediments on Lord Howe Island, southwestern Pacific Ocean. (Reconstruction by Frank Knight, courtesy of the Museum of Victoria and Pioneer Design Studio)*

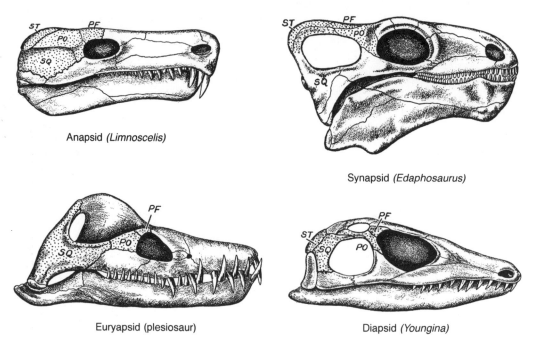

Anapsid *(Limnoscelis)*

Synapsid *(Edaphosaurus)*

Euryapsid (plesiosaur)

Diapsid *(Youngina)*

Skulls in the four main groups, or subclasses, of reptiles. The anapsids have no temporal opening; diapsids have two openings; euryapsids have an opening above, and synapsids have an opening below, the postorbital-squamosal bar

diapsids have evolved into two principal groups: "scaly reptiles" (lepidosaurs) and "ruling reptiles" (archosaurs). The former group includes lizards, snakes, and mosasaurs; the latter includes dinosaurs, crocodiles, flying reptiles, and their varied relatives. For more than 200 million years, they have outranked most other reptiles in abundance, variety, and size.

No neat formula will summarize the story of these four subclasses. Some reptiles have grown large, while others have become dwarfs; a few groups started out on one course and abruptly switched to another. In many families, the number of bones was reduced in both skull and skeleton. Others added many new ones, and some—notably the snakes—lost the bones of such organs as legs but multiplied their primitive allotment of vertebrae and ribs. Lizards and their kin have taken up life in swamps, deserts, seas, and even in trees; ichthyosaurs, among the euryapsids, became more fishlike in outline than several specialized fish. Although sphenodontids made no such changes and have lived for more than 150 million years without a major innovation in habits, structure, or shape, divergence is the one factor we can usually count on in the history of reptiles. Let us trace its principal patterns and examine the results.

Upright tree trunk in the Joggins Formation, Cumberland County, Nova Scotia, Canada. In many of the trunks that rotted out before burial, skeletons of amphibians and reptiles have been recovered that are Pennsylvanian in age. (Photo courtesy of R. M. Hunt and D. Baird)

COTYLOSAURS AND AN ANCIENT PITFALL TRAP

The Bay of Fundy, between New Brunswick and Nova Scotia, is widely noted for having the greatest rise and fall of the tide anywhere on earth. Less well known, but quite important as a key link in documenting the history of vertebrate evolution, is the fossil site at Joggins, Nova Scotia, on the shore of that bay.

Three hundred million years ago, in the Early Pennsylvanian, the area was a coal-forming swamp with extensive forests of lycopods (see Chapter XXIII) such as *Sigillaria*. These trees were 3 to 4 feet (0.9–1.2 m.) in diameter and up to 100 feet (30 m.) tall. Unlike modern trees, however, they had only a hard outer layer a few inches (about 10 cm.) thick. The inner part of the tree was either hollow or formed of material that decayed rapidly. From time to time, the bases of the trees were rapidly buried in sediment up to 10 feet (3 m.) deep. The trees died, the tops collapsed, and a hole developed on the surface into which unwary reptiles and amphibians fell.

All the bones in each skeleton separated from one another. This fact, together with the presence of numerous coprolites, indicates that the fall into these natural pit traps did not kill the animals. Rather, they lived long enough within these traps to feed on one another.

One of the two reptiles that occurs at Joggins is *Hylonomus,* whose length was about 8 inches (20 cm.). Structurally, it makes almost the perfect ances-

Skull of Elginia, *a Late Permian pareiasaur of Scotland, length 10 inches (25 cm.).* Bradysaurus *(right) measured about 8 feet (2.4 m.). This pareiasaur lived in South Africa during the Middle Permian*

tor for later reptiles as diverse as tuataras, lizards, snakes, crocodiles, and turtles, plus a variety of extinct Mesozoic groups. In general appearance, it looked quite similar to tuataras and primitive modern lizards and differed from them primarily in having the solid skull of an anapsid, rather than the two-holed, diapsid condition. The vertebrae, limbs, and girdles are essentially the same as those in modern tuataras and lizards.

Pareiasaurs. Most cotylosaurs were small animals not significantly different from, or larger than, *Hylonomus*. However, the Middle and Late Permian pareiasaurs were an exception.

By the Middle Permian, this group had evolved into bulky, grotesque creatures. Known from South African rocks of that age, the largest were 10 feet (3 m.) long, with thick legs, barrel-shaped bodies, and weights exceeding a ton (0.9 t.). The skull had become massive and knobby, the skin was studded with bony plates, and teeth on the jaws were serrated like a steak knife. Skeletons have been found in standing position, just as the animals sank into mud while they were feeding on swamp plants. In the Late Permian, when the last pareiasaurs lived, they were rare in Africa but better known in Scotland, China, and Russia.

SYNAPSIDS, ANCESTORS TO THE MAMMALS

A rarer fossil than *Hylonomus* from the tree trunks at Joggins is possibly the oldest known synapsid, *Protoclepsydrops*. It is known only from a humerus and a few vertebrae, so there is some doubt as to whether it was a synapsid at all. From another fossil tree trunk locality nearby, at Florence, Nova Scotia, came *Archaeothyris*. The rocks at Florence are slightly younger than those at Joggins: Late Pennsylvanian. Several other synapsids of this age are known, but none is as well preserved as *Archaeothyris*.

Late Pennsylvanian and Early Permian synapsids are all called pelycosaurs. Within pelycosaurs, there were two groups of meat eaters and two of plant eaters. All are well represented from the Early Permian deposits of north-central Texas.

Today that region is rolling plains dotted with cattle ranches and farms. Mesquite is the principal tree; rattlesnakes are the largest reptiles; and occasional torrential rains are the fossil hunter's best friend. Their waters, rushing through "breaks," or broad gullies, expose the multicolored clays, red shales, and sandstones of the red beds, in which vertebrate fossils are often found.

When those strata were accumulating, northern Texas was a series of deltas at the edge of a shifting ocean shoreline. Inland climates may have been arid, but the deltas themselves were well watered and supported lush vegetation, much like that of the earlier coal swamps. *Calamites,* an ancient scouring rush (See Chapter XXIII), grew as tall as small trees; conifers and lycopods formed forests; true ferns were plentiful. *Medullosa,* with its finely lined, fernlike leaves was prominent among the seed ferns.

The most fearsome of the meat-eating pelycosaurs that occurred in those swamps was the sphenacodont *Dimetrodon.* What made it look so fierce was not only the twinned, daggerlike teeth at the front of its mouth, but also the slicing ones behind. In addition to that, there was a prominent "sail" along its back formed by elongated spines from the vertebrae. Stretched between the spines was a membrane of skin that was well supplied with blood vessels. When the sail was perpendicular to the rays of the sun, it may have served as a way for *Dimetrodon* to rapidly warm its blood. Though all sphenacodonts were carnivorous, like *Dimetrodon,* not all had "sails" along their backs.

About the same size as *Dimetrodon, Ophiacodon* lacked a "sail." It was more at home in the water and preferred to eat fish, rather than other reptiles.

One of the reptiles that undoubtedly figured prominently in the diet of

Dimetrodon, *a fin-backed pelycosaur of Early to Middle Permian age from North America. Maximum length 10 to 11 feet (3–3.3 m.)*

Dimetrodon was the plant-eating pelycosaur *Edaphosaurus.* It, too, had a "sail" along its back, but there was an addition. Projecting outward from the vertical spines were short horizontal crossbars. There were no daggerlike teeth, and all the teeth were much alike.

Edaphosaurus was about the same size as the other two pelycosaurs discussed so far, 10 or 11 feet (up to 3.3 m.) in length. However, not all pelycosaurs were this big. *Varanosaurus* was a smaller ophiacodont carnivore, only 5 feet (1.5 m.) long, and even smaller was *Mycterosaurus,* a herbivore only 2 feet (0.6 m.) long.

The next phase of synapsid history was dominated by the origin and diversification of the therapsids. Most paleontologists think these reptiles evolved from sphenacodont pelycosaurs. The skull became more rigid as bracing was added, yet the temporal opening on the side of the skull in most cases became larger, allowing for expansion of the jaw muscles when they contracted. This produced a more powerful bite.

Another area in which the therapsids were advanced over the pelycosaurs

The fin-backed **Edaphosaurus** *and its skull. Length of entire animal about 11 feet (3.3 m.). At the lower right is* **Ophiacodon,** *fish eater. Both are from the Permian of Texas*

Some smaller animals from the Permian red beds of Texas: Varanosaurus, *an ophiacodont, length 5 feet (1.5 m.);* Labidosaurus, *a cotylosaur, length 2 feet (60 cm.).* Diadectes *was either an advanced amphibian or a primitive reptile, length 5 to 6 feet (1.5–1.8 m.)*

was in the structure of the hind legs. Instead of sprawling outward so that the femur, or upper hind limb bone, moved in the horizontal plane, the limb was brought under the body, so that it moved entirely in the vertical plane. This was a much more efficient arrangement for rapid movement. The front limbs continued to have a sprawling posture until the advent of some of the most advanced therapsids in the latest Permian.

The earliest therapsids are known in the Middle Permian, which is the top of the sequence of terrestrial Permian rocks in North America. Fortunately, it is also the base of a sequence of terrestrial Middle and Late Permian rocks in European Russia. There, the initial diversification of the therapsids can be followed. The Russian rock sequence overlaps with the bottom of an even longer section of rocks in South Africa, where the therapsid record extends into the Late Triassic. One therapsid survived into the Middle Jurassic in Europe. So, the evolutionary history of the synapsids is one of the best-documented by fossils of all vertebrate groups.

Most paleontologists think that all of the therapsids came from only one group of pelycosaurs, the carnivorous sphenacodonts. However, it has been suggested that some of the herbivorous therapsids may have evolved from caseid reptiles.

Among vertebrates, it has generally been true that it is from carnivores, not herbivores, that more advanced major groups have evolved. Most often, even the herbivores among the advanced groups are derived from the carnivores and not the herbivores of the more primitive ones. Exceptions are known to this generalization, however, so it would not be unique if caseids did give rise to some or all of the herbivorous therapsids.

Most numerous of the therapsids, both in individual specimens known and in numbers of genera, are the anomodonts. When this entirely herbivorous group first appeared, in the Middle Permian, all of its members were small, ranging from 25 to 50 centimeters (10 to 20 in.) in length. This may have been due to the presence then of large herbivorous dinocephalians, another therapsid group, and pareiasaurs, both of which were greater than 2 meters (nearly 7 ft.) long. Dinocephalians became extinct later in the Permian, and that was the time when the anomodonts increased in size.

Kannemeyeria, *an Early Triassic dicynodont from South Africa and possibly Russia and Australia. Length about 6 feet (1.8 m.). At right is the skull of* Dicynodon *itself, from the Late Permian of South Africa. Length 6 inches (15 cm.)*

All but a few of the earliest anomodonts were dicynodonts (therapsids that had lost all incisors and lower canines). In their place was a horny beak. An upper canine was present and generally developed as a large tusk. Cheek teeth were present behind the canine in some dicynodonts.

Three groups of dicynodonts evolved in the Late Permian, and all but one of them became extinct at the close of that period. In the Triassic, there was only one group of dicynodonts; it reached every land area on earth and persisted to the end of that period.

One of the more unusual and most widespread of the dicynodonts was *Lystrosaurus.* This animal had an extremely shortened, downturned face. Unlike most dicynodonts, its feet were formed mainly of cartilage. In addition, it had a rounded, barrellike body. Probably, *Lystrosaurus* lived much like a modern hippopotamus, spending much of its time in rivers and lakes but able to walk about on land. *Lystrosaurus* was one of the first fossil vertebrates discovered in Antarctica, showing that during the Early Triassic, reptiles and amphibians of that continent were quite similar to those of South Africa. *Lystrosaurus* itself, however, is known much more widely, having been found also in India, China, Asiatic Russia, and Indochina.

Another group of reptiles appeared at the beginning of the Triassic. Like the dicynodonts, forms in this group had reduced the teeth and developed prominent beaks for dealing with vegetation. These were the rhynchosaurs, one of the many diapsid groups. It may be that the dicynodonts never regained their dominant position after the major episode of extinction at the end of the Permian, because the rhynchosaurs arose in the Triassic and

A Triassic scene in Antarctica or South Africa. A Thrinaxodon, *a carnivorous mammal-like reptile, stands over a* Procolophon *that it has just killed. In the background a crocodile-like thecodont,* Chasmatosaurus, *lurks in the water, while two of the three herbivorous mammal-like reptiles* Lystrosaurus *look on (Reconstruction by Peter Trusler)*

Outcrops of the Triassic Fremouw Formation, of Antarctica, interbedded with the Jurassic Ferrar Dolerite, a diabase in the Transantarctic Mountains 350 miles (560 km.) from the South Pole. Many of the same fossil reptiles and amphibians found in the Early Triassic of other parts of Gondwana have been collected from the Fremouw Formation. South Africa and Tasmania also show another similarity to this region in that, in those areas as well, Jurassic diabases formed thick sills that intruded into continental Triassic sedimentary rocks

Collecting Middle Triassic therapsids in Argentina. (Photo courtesy of J. A. Jensen)

417

occupied herbivorous roles in the animal community that otherwise a dicyn-odont might have evolved to fill. Rhynchosaurs and dicynodonts both be-came extinct near the end of the Late Triassic.

A much more short-lived group of therapsids were the dinocephalians. They were confined to the Middle Permian and are known only from North America, Russia, and South Africa. Typically, they were large animals, about 2 meters (nearly 7 ft.) long with massive skulls. Thick layers of dense bone, particularly above the tiny brain, suggests that males may have com-peted for females by butting heads, much as modern mountain sheep do.

Dinocephalians were both herbivorous and carnivorous. Though some were meat eaters, it is difficult to conceive of a ponderous dinocephalian running down its prey. Perhaps they were scavengers or ambushed their victims.

The more lightly constructed and smaller gorgonopsians may have been active predators. Typical in size was *Lycaenops,* an animal about 60 cm. (2 ft.) long from the Late Permian of South Africa. A large canine in both the skull and jaw was common to all gorgonopsians, and most of these teeth were large enough to be called saberlike. The teeth behind the canines were typically quite small and, in some forms, nonexistent. Gorgonopsians simply cut off flesh from their prey and bolted it down without chewing it into smaller pieces.

It is rare for a carnivore to have horns, but the Russian Late Permian *Proburnetia* had a well-developed pair at the back of its skull, as well as bony protuberances above the eyes.

Gorgonopsians were the dominant carnivorous therapsids during the Mid-dle and Late Permian, but they became extinct abruptly at the end of that period, without any descendants.

A much smaller group of contemporary, primarily carnivorous therapsids were the therocephalians. Besides carnivores, some therocephalians were adapted for a number of other feeding habits. A few were herbivorous, a not uncommon therapsid mode of life. But three evolved structures that suggest rare or unique adaptations for these reptiles. Behind the canines of one form thought to be a scavenger were a series of horny tooth plates, rather than teeth. No other therapsids were as small as some therocephalians, which were probably insect eaters. Behind their canines were tiny, pointed teeth, well adapted for piercing the cuticle of beetles or cockroaches, both of which had appeared by the Permian (See Chapter XIV).

One therocephalian, *Euchambersia,* probably had a venomous bite. The bone surrounding the base of the upper canine is filled with small holes such as might be associated with a venom gland. On the outside of the canine or fang is a groove running downward along which venom could have flowed into a wound when *Euchambersia* snapped its jaws shut onto an animal it was trying to kill.

In the latest Permian, the therocephalians gave rise to the cynodonts ("dog teeth"). Ultimately, it was from the cynodonts that the mammals arose, in the Late Triassic.

Soon after the beginning of the Triassic, the cynodonts evolved into at least six families. As time went by, these became more mammal-like in their features, each in different ways.

In common with other advanced therapsids, the cynodonts had developed a new sheet of bone in the skull; the secondary palate. This served to separate the mouth from the nasal passage. In more primitive therapsids, it was not possible to breathe and eat at the same time. For animals such as lizards today, this does not matter, as their bodily processes operate at a slow enough rate that they can simply stop breathing while eating. But, for active animals such as ourselves, it is easier if not necessary to do both at once. Think of the last time you had a cold and could only breathe through your mouth. Eating can be a bit more difficult then! This is just one indication that cynodonts were quite active animals.

As far as it can be reconstructed, the pattern of blood vessels in the skull of cynodonts is more like that of mammals than reptiles. In addition, the relative sizes of the ribs suggest cynodonts had a diaphragm between the lungs and the lower body cavity. Finally, the bone around the margin of the skull is smooth and lacks fine grooves and small holes except near the snout, where deep pits are present. This is the condition seen in animals with well-developed, fleshy lips, and vibrissae, or sensory hairs.

The mammalian circulatory system, with its four-chambered heart and a diaphragm, are associated with the greater efficiency required for transporting blood and breathing in warm-blooded animals. The presence of lips enabled manipulation of the food so it could be chewed into small pieces before being swallowed. In living reptiles, food is swallowed in large chunks. As cynoconts became more mammal-like, they probably developed hair and suckled their young as well.

Cynognathus, *a mammal-like reptile from the Early Triassic of South Africa. Length about 5 feet (1.5 m.)*

Later, cynodonts were advanced in other respects. The forelimbs no longer sprawled but, rather, became like the hind limbs long before. They were drawn in under the body so that they moved in the vertical plane, instead of the humerus moving in the horizontal. Advanced cynodonts also lost the bony bar that separated the temporal opening from the orbit, where the eye was housed.

After the earliest Triassic, cynodonts radiated into a number of families. Most became extinct by the end of the Triassic. However, the Early Jurassic *Oligokyphus* did manage to last a bit longer. This small animal, only 18 inches (45 cm.) long, had a highly specialized dentition. The canines were absent. Where the canines might be expected, there was a large gap in the tooth row. In front were incisors, and behind the gap were elaborate cheek teeth, each with many cusps or bumps. The pattern of the tooth crowns is similar to that seen today in animals that eat seeds or nuts.

However, the teeth of *Oligokyphus* are rather unusual for a cynodont. Most cynodonts, such as *Cynognathus,* from the Early Triassic of South Africa, were well adapted as carnivores. Out of one of these cynodonts with a carnivorous dentition arose the first true mammals, in the Late Triassic, which led at the beginning of the Cenozoic to an explosion of life-forms—but not before a long quiescence while the "terrible lizards," the dinosaurs, reigned.

CHAPTER XXVI

Farewells to Land

Reptiles evolved when the changing earth gave four-footed verte-brates a chance to succeed on land. No sooner was this accom-plished, however, than some of the newly developed creatures took up aquatic life. Perhaps some never fully emerged from the water at all.

We already know *Ophiacodon,* a fish-eating Permian synapsid that must have been an active swimmer, though it could also walk on dry ground. More truly aquatic was *Mesosaurus,* a short-lived genus from the Early Per-mian of southern Africa and South America. A slender creature about 40 centimeters (16 in.) long, *Mesosaurus* had jaws full of needle-shaped teeth. It apparently used its forelegs as balancing organs as it drove its body through the water with its broad hind feet, swimming in pursuit of crustaceans. It had an interesting geographic distribution, occurring only in Brazil (eastern South America) and southern Africa. When *Mesosaurus* lived, these two Gondwana continents were still parts of a single landmass.

Mesosaurus, *an aquatic reptile of Early Permian age from southern Africa and South America, length 16 inches (40 cm.)*

THE STURDY AND NOT SO CONSERVATIVE TURTLES

When we speak of aquatic reptiles today, most of us think of turtles and tortoises, or Testudines, which appeared by Late Triassic times and have been common during all subsequent ages. They invaded swamps, lakes, rivers, and seas, and developed the finest armor to be found among four-footed vertebrates. Most of them clung to this early anatomical trait, which may explain why they have been successful for 200 million years. However, during that span of time, two separate groups of turtles independently modified the skull and neck in ways unique among vertebrates, so the group was far from evolutionarily static from the Triassic to the present day.

Turtles evolved from unknown Permian anapsids that settled down to life in quiet, and probably swampy, waters, where their bodies widened while their feet became paddles with webs between the toes. A shell, or carapace, appeared on the back and fused with the ribs and vertebrae; it consisted of bony plates that formed in the skin and were covered by scales that expanded into horny scutes. Scutes also covered the ventral armor, or plastron, which was joined to the carapace at both sides. Parts of the limb girdles were incorporated into the plastron. Teeth became small and finally vanished, while horny beaks grew on the jaws.

Groups of Turtles.   With this beginning, turtles evolved into three principal groups. One, the Proganochelydia, is typified by *Proganochelys* itself. Specimens of it have been found in the Triassic of Europe and Thailand. Its jaws were already toothless, but tiny teeth remained on the palate. Neither head nor tail could be tucked into the shell, but both were protected by spines. The legs, which also may have remained outside the shell, were protected by long, sharp-edged scutes.

The other two groups of turtles are more advanced than the Proganochelydia in a number of ways. Early in their histories, both developed solid skulls that no longer contained movable joints. At the same time, each group separately developed a pulley arrangement that changed the direction of action of the jaw muscles. Later, probably at the end of the Mesozoic, the necks of the two groups became modified in different ways so that the head could be pulled back into the protection of the shell.

Modern members of one group, the pleurodires ("side necks"), swing their long necks sidewise and so tuck their heads under shelter. Fossils, which date back to the Cretaceous, are surprisingly like forms that still live in the Southern Hemisphere. All surviving turtles of Australia belong to this group.

Cryptodires ("hidden necks") include all other turtles. All living cryptodires tuck both head and neck away by bending the latter into an *S* between the shoulder blades. However, not all Late Cenozoic cryptodires could do this. *Meiolania,* from eastern Australia, and *Niolamia,* from Argen-

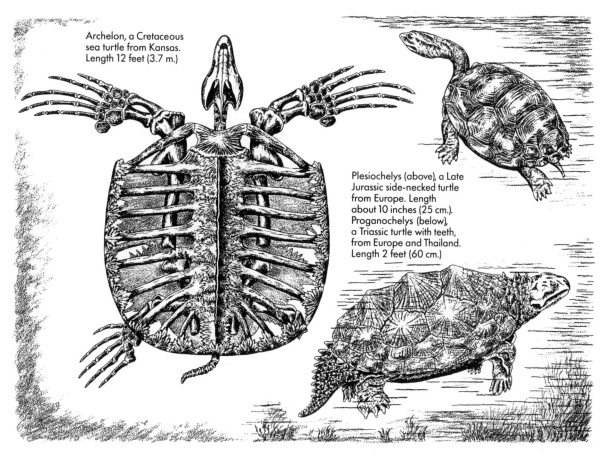

Archelon, a Cretaceous sea turtle from Kansas. Length 12 feet (3.7 m.)

Plesiochelys (above), a Late Jurassic side-necked turtle from Europe. Length about 10 inches (25 cm.). Proganochelys (below), a Triassic turtle with teeth, from Europe and Thailand. Length 2 feet (60 cm.)

Mesozoic Turtles

tina, undoubtedly would have been most uncomfortable had they done so, for these tortoises had well-developed horns!

Early cryptodires began as marsh dwellers that swam well, often sunned themselves on logs or sandbanks, and frequently walked on land. Some of their descendants became more completely aquatic but remained in rivers and swamps, though others took to the sea. Foremost among these was *Archelon,* a giant more than 12 feet (3.7 m.) long, with a narrow head, hooked beak, huge flippers, and a weight of about 6,000 pounds (2.7 t.). *Archelon* lived in Late Cretaceous seas of South Dakota, Kansas, and adjacent regions, which swarmed with large fish and savage reptiles closely related to lizards. The finest skeleton of *Archelon* has one hind paddle missing. It may have been bitten off by one of these predators.

At this point we encounter more of those contrasts and contradictions that mark the evolution of reptiles. Turtles began by developing shells and taking to water; some forms, such as the modern snapping turtle, almost never leave it. Others gave up armor or went back to the land, though none of them did both.

Archelon was one of the turtles that lost most of its armor, covering the

(Left) shell of Toxochelys, *a North American Cretaceous sea turtle that resembled the modern loggerhead. Length about 12 feet (3.7 m.). (Right)* Testudo ammon, *a land tortoise from the early Tertiary of Egypt. Shell 40 inches (1 m.) in length*

bones that remained with tough skin. Two other groups of marine turtles repeated the process, and so did the stream-dwelling soft-shells. Early Tertiary members of the last group had shells made up of thin, pitted plates; later types lost all their armor and appeared in leathery carapaces. Broken bones of Tertiary soft-shell turtles are so common on bare hills near the Continental Divide of North America, in south-central Wyoming, that they make up a large part of the pebbles. Apparently both shells and skeletons fell to pieces soon after death, for complete specimens are rare.

Pond turtles often venture upon land today and have done so for ages. Perhaps the best-known fossil pond turtle is *Stylemys,* which lived on the moist plains of South Dakota, Nebraska, and eastern Wyoming during the Oligocene but was less common in Miocene times. Typical specimens are 5 to 8 inches (13 to 20 cm.) long, but shells 20 to 36 inches (51 to 91 cm.) long have been reported.

Tortoises are terrestrial turtles with club-shaped feet that have lost the webs between their toes. Large shells called *Stylemys* may actually belong to *Testudo,* a fully terrestrial genus that includes the modern gopher and desert tortoises as well as the giant species of the Galápagos and the Aldabra islands. Appearing in the Eocene, tortoises had became quite varied by the Early Oligocene. Once named *Colossochelys,* the largest specimens of *Testudo* have been found on the flanks of The Himalayas in the Siwalik Hills, of India. These animals were of Pleistocene age, with shells reaching 2.2 meters (7 ft. 3 in.) long, 1.5 meters (4 ft. 11 in.) wide, and 88 centimeters (2 ft. 10 in.) high, and weighed in excess of 1 tonne (1.1 T.). This was no mean record for a terrestrial reptile whose undersized ancestors had abandoned the land!

ICHTHYOSAURS

Ichthyosaurs progressed a great deal during the 120 million years of their known history. Their most primitive members, which appeared in Middle Triassic seas of California, Spitsbergen, Europe, and Indonesia, were slender creatures whose tails were compressed but almost straight, with narrow finfolds above and below. In time, the backbone began to bend downward, while its upper lobe enlarged. At last the tail became a reversed heterocercal type, a swimming organ equal to that possessed by the swiftest shark. The slender jaws had many teeth; the front flippers were larger than the hind,

Cymbospondylus

Ophthalmosaurus

Tail of Mixosaurus, of Triassic age. Vertebrae were bent downward, and the upper lobe of the tail fin had begun to expand.

Cymbospondylus *was a primitive ichthyosaur found in the Middle Triassic of Nevada. Length 40 feet (12.2 m.). The backbone did not bend downward in the tail, and there may have been no fin on the back.* **Ophthalmosaurus,** *from the Jurassic of Wyoming and England, was highly specialized. Its tail was sharklike, and its teeth were very small. Length 10 feet (3 m.).* **Mixosaurus** *was known from Europe, North America, Spitsbergen, and Indonesia.*

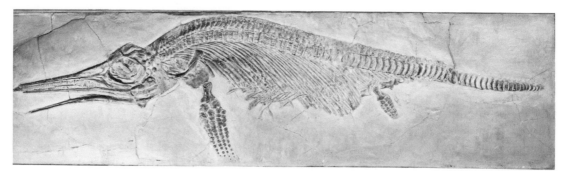

Stenopterygius, *from the Early Jurassic of Germany. Length 5 feet (1.6 m.). (Photo by Frank Coffa, courtesy of the Museum of Victoria, Melbourne)*

Front flipper of Stenopterygius *showing the addition of phalanges to the toes (hyperphalangy) but not the addition of further toes (hyperdactyly). Length of flipper 9.5 inches (24 cm.). (Photo by Frank Coffa, courtesy of the Museum of Victoria, Melbourne)*

426

though, in both, the leg bones were shortened while the toes were lengthened by the addition of phalanges, a condition called hyperphalangy. In many cases, more rows of bones were added alongside the original toes, making the flippers broader. Vertebrae also were short and numerous, and the enormous goggle eyes were strengthened by sclerotic rings of bone. Ichthyosaurs plainly hunted by sight, and their eyes were equipped to catch a maximum of light.

In reconstructing fossil vertebrates, we usually have to restore their soft parts from evidence supplied by their bones. Not so with ichthyosaurs. Dark-colored Jurassic rocks of Germany contain skeletons surrounded by carbonized films which show the streamlined body, the broad flippers, the tail, and the shark-type dorsal fin, which was boneless. These carbonized films also prove that the skin was smooth, with only a few small scales on the forward edge of the flippers. Tiny pigment grains show that "fish lizards" were dark above with whitish beneath, coloration which increased their resemblance to sharks and dolphins and helped conceal the reptiles from their prey, both above and below.

Though ichthyosaurs still breathed air, they led purely aquatic lives. They fed upon fish, squids, and belemnites, whose remains sometimes are preserved as fossils between their ribs. Ichthyosaurs probably never went ashore and, instead of laying their eggs, allowed them to hatch internally. Specimens show skeletons of very small ichthyosaurs inside large ones, with no hint that the former were eaten instead of belemnites or fish. On other slabs, young animals appear to be coming from the region in which eggs were kept. Either the mother ichthyosaur died during "childbirth" or the young ones emerged soon after her death. The latter sometimes happens in lizards and snakes whose eggs hatch inside the body, after which the young wriggle out.

FROM CRAWLERS TO PLESIOSAURS

In the Late Permian, the island of Madagascar moved away from the east coast of Africa. Living along the then newly formed coast on the west side of Madagascar was *Claudiosaurus,* a reptile about 70 centimeters (2 ft. 4 in.) long. It had a small head, moderately long neck, and hind limbs larger in size than the front ones. It alternated between basking seal-like on the warm rocks and hunting small crustaceans in the waters of the nearby ocean.

Claudiosaurus is the first glimpse we have of the great variety of nothosaurs and plesiosaurs that were to evolve later and become so successful in the Mesozoic. It arose from a Permian diapsid ancestor, and like the lizards, it lost the lower bar on the lower skull opening, thus gaining the euryapsid condition.

As the Triassic Period began, close relatives of *Claudiosaurus,* the

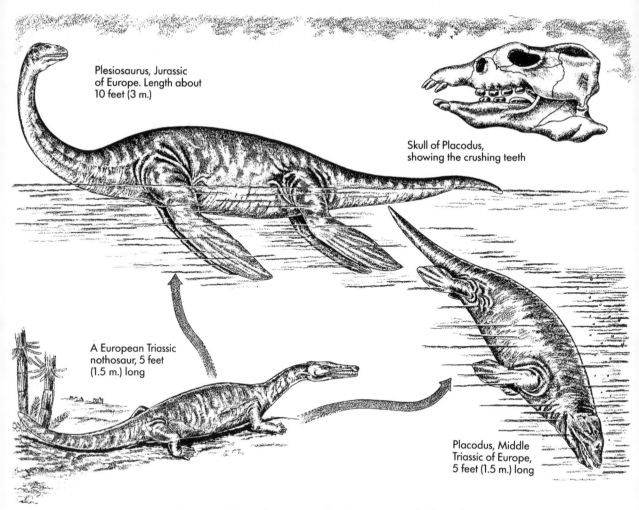

Plesiosaurus, Jurassic of Europe. Length about 10 feet (3 m.)

Skull of Placodus, showing the crushing teeth

A European Triassic nothosaur, 5 feet (1.5 m.) long

Placodus, Middle Triassic of Europe, 5 feet (1.5 m.) long

The aquatic nothosaurs, plesiosaurs, and placodonts

nothosaurs, became more fully aquatic, with increased specialization of the skeleton for life in the water. Like modern seagoing crocodiles, they probably went ashore whenever they wished to do so. Their bones have been found in marine deposits associated primarily with the Tethys Seaway, in southern Europe, Asia, and North Africa.

Plesiosaurs. The name of these descendants of nothosaurs means "like lizards" or "almost lizards," but few creatures were less lizardlike in appearance and habits. Plesiosaurs were marine reptiles adapted to life on the open sea, though they sometimes invaded swamps, estuaries, and rivers. One group of these reptiles had short, flattened heads, long necks, and plump oval bodies strengthened by mats of abdominal ribs. Their tails, though fairly long, were finless; they swam by means of legs and feet that had developed into oarlike paddles. Bones of the hips and shoulder were broad, providing attachment for the powerful muscles, which brought the paddles down and backward. The length ranged from 8 to 50 feet (2.4–15.2 m.), and the number of neck vertebrae generally varied from thirty to almost eighty.

428

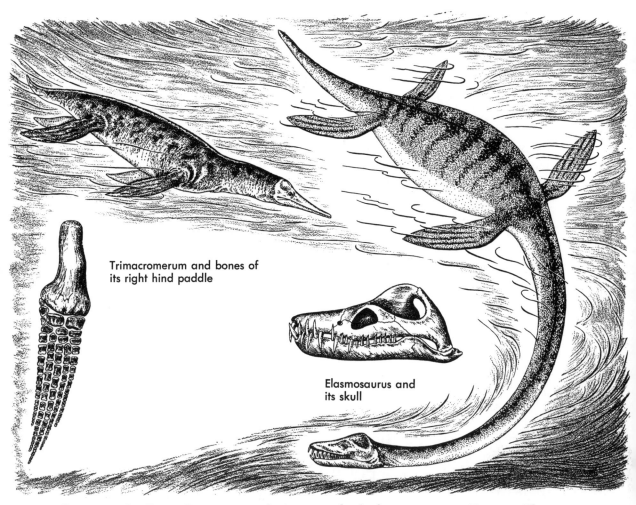

Contrasts in Late Cretaceous plesiosaurs, both from western Kansas. Elasmosaurus *was 40 to 50 feet (12.2–15.2 m.) in length, but the short-necked* Trinacromerum *was barely 10 feet (3 m.) long*

A second group of plesiosaurs were similar in paddles and tail, but their bodies were deeper and their skulls were extended by long, slender jaws. Their necks also were short, those of some species containing only thirteen vertebrae.

Both long- and short-necked plesiosaurs appeared in Early Jurassic seas of Europe; for millions of years they were plentiful there but scare or absent elsewhere. Then, during Cretaceous times, they both spread widely and became very large. *Kronosaurus,* of Australia, had a skull almost 9 feet (2.7 m.) long; elasmosaurs in seas of the Great Plains region of North America possessed slender tails and necks as much as 23 feet (7 m.) long. These elongated necks and tails explain why plesiosaurs are sometimes described as snakes threaded through the bodies of turtles. No known plesiosaur was armored, however, and though the neck was flexible, not even the longest species coiled and twisted the neck like a serpent. Plesiosaurs apparently swam at the surface or just below it, diving infrequently. When underwater, they "flew" with their paddles much as a penguin does. Prey consisted largely of fish, belemnites, and squids, seized with a forward rush or a quick thrust of the head. Victims too large to be swallowed whole were torn to pieces by jerks, a method now used by crocodiles and alligators.

Placodonts. Less certainly related to nothosaurs was another group of marine euryapsids, the placodonts. Like the nothosaurs, they have been found only in Triassic marine deposits of the Tethys regions: southern Europe, northern Africa, and southwestern Asia. Placodonts became streamlined creatures with blunt heads, plump bodies, and paddle-shaped legs. They resembled the modern manatee, or sea cow, and evidently paddled through shallow waters, eating molluscs and crushing their shells with broad, low teeth on the jaws and bony palate. In *Placodus* the ribs of the back were very thick, while a "basket" of abdominal ribs (gastralia) protected the underside. Both also acted as ballast to keep the animal floating upright on top of the water. *Placochelys,* of the Late Triassic, had its back covered with armor.

CHAMPSOSAURUS, AN ARCHAIC SURVIVOR

Many diapsids took to the water; all the remaining reptiles described in this chapter belong to that group. Most conservative of all these was *Champsosaurus,* which superficially looked like a gavial with its narrow snout. Like it, *Champsosaurus* was a highly efficient fish catcher. However, in the structure of its skull it is quite primitive and fits what might be expected of a Triassic reptile. However, it lived from the Late Cretaceous to the Eocene in North America and Europe and is also known from the Late Cretaceous of eastern Asia. It has the distinction of being the largest vertebrate to have survived the severe extinction episode that marked the end of the Cretaceous.

MOSASAURS, TRUE AQUATIC LIZARDS

Early accounts occasionally described plesiosaurs as "savage monsters of horrid mien." Actually, such lurid adjectives apply more aptly to the great aquatic true lizards known as mosasaurs.

Mosasaurs were bizarre reptiles, and their introduction to science was equally spectacular. In 1780, workmen discovered a petrified skull in a subterranean sandstone quarry under the Pietersberg (Peter's Mount), near the city of Maastricht, the Netherlands. The men sent for an army surgeon and naturalist who had collected fossils from the quarry. He directed work so skillfully that the entire skeleton was removed.

A Dr. Hofmann recognized the specimen's value, paid for removing it, and prepared it for exhibition. But land above the quarry was owned by one

Canon Goddin, who went to court, won his case, and seized the fossil. Then, in 1795, a French army besieged Maastricht, and so famous had the fossil become that the general in command told his gunners to spare the part of the city containing Canon Goddin's house. Suspecting the reason for this favor, Canon Goddin hid his specimen, trying to keep its loation secret after the city surrendered. The French thereupon offered a reward—said to have been six hundred bottles of wine—for the specimen, and a band of thirsty grenadiers soon found it. Taken to Paris, it was described as a "primordial whale" or a "breathing fish," and then as "the Great Lizard of the Meuse," the river that flows past the Pietersberg. A British author translated this long-winded description into the Latin *Mosasaurus*.

Mosasaurs ranged around the world during the Late Cretaceous, reaching their zenith in seas that spread inland from the Atlantic Ocean and the Gulf of Mexico. The finest specimens come from chalk deposits of western Kansas and reach a maximum length of 30 feet (9 m.). However, jaws and teeth

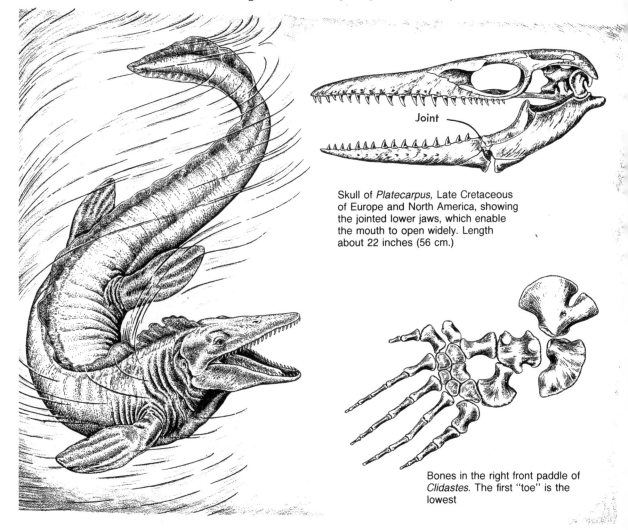

Joint

Skull of *Platecarpus*, Late Cretaceous of Europe and North America, showing the jointed lower jaws, which enable the mouth to open widely. Length about 22 inches (56 cm.)

Bones in the right front paddle of *Clidastes*. The first "toe" is the lowest

Mosasaurs, or marine lizards, of Late Cretaceous age. Tylosaurus, *from Kansas and New Zealand (left), was about 22 feet (6.7 m.) long*

found in greensand beds of New Jersey, U.S.A., suggest a giant mosasaur some 45 feet (14 m.) long. The strangest member of the group was *Globidens,* of the southern United States, South America, Africa, Europe, and Asia. It apparently fed upon the sea bottom, where it grubbed for clams, snails, and other sluggish molluscs whose shells it crushed between bulbous teeth that had all but lost their once-sharp points.

A more typical mosasaur, such as *Tylosaurus,* of Kansas and New Zealand, was an active swimmer with a long body, flattened tail, and feet that had become broad, webbed paddles with well-developed toes. Bony plates covered the top of the head; neck, body, and tail were covered by lizard-type scales still preserved in a few carbonized fossils. Sclerotic rings strengthened the eyes, and the eardrum consisted of thick cartilage. The lower jaws were each armed with sixteen to eighteen sharp teeth. At the back of each was a rod of bone, the quadrate. The quadrate had a hinge connection with the jaw at one end and a second such joint at the other uniting it with the skull. This and a ligament linking the two jaws together at the front meant that, like serpents, mosasaurs were able to drop their jaws and spread them widely in order to swallow oversized food.

Petrified stomach contents show that fish formed the chief food of mosasaurs. With lengths of 20 to 30 feet (6.1–9.1 m.), they were the only vertebrates that could capture such forms as the "bulldog tarpon" *(Portheus molossus),* which weighed 600 to 800 pounds (270–360 kg.) and was as dangerous as most marine reptiles. Another item in the mosasaur diet was ammonites. Ammonites have been found with puncture marks in their shells that match the teeth of mosasaurs. Because old, dull teeth dropped from the jaws and were replaced by new ones, mosasaurs never lacked weapons with which to attack rivals or prey.

THE WRONGLY NAMED PHYTOSAURS

When mosasaurs went into streams, they sometimes saw crocodiles as much as 50 feet (15.2 m.) in length. Yet they were much too late to encounter the creatures whose habits, form, and bony structure mark them as false crocodiles. Technically, we must call these creatures phytosaurs ("plant lizards"), not because the name fits them, but because an almost forgotten professor thought they were herbivores. Actually, phytosaurs were carnivorous reptiles that ranged from about 6 to 20 feet (1.8–6.1 m.) in length and were covered with bony armor overlain by horny scutes. The skull resembled that of the modern gavial, a crocodilian with bulging "forehead" and slender jaws. The gavial's nostrils, however, are on his snout; those of the phytosaurs lay close to the eyes, generally on mounds of bone rising above the rest of the skull.

The oldest known phytosaurs are found in the Middle Triassic of Europe. They spread around the world during the Late Triassic and persisted into the

Rutiodon, *a Late Triassic phytosaur from the Painted Desert, of northern Arizona; skull 42 inches (107 cm.) long. The plants include cycads, calamites, ferns, and araucarians. The tree at the extreme right is* Araucarioxylon; *to the left of it is* Woodworthia

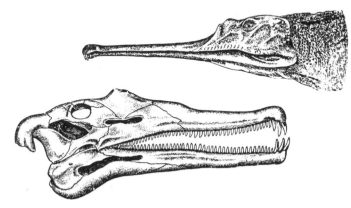

Mystriosuchus, Late Triassic of Europe, a long-snouted phytosaur. Skull length 33 inches (83 cm.).

Skull of Rutiodon, *Late Triassic of North America, 42 inches (107 cm.) long*

Early Jurassic. Their bones have been found in Europe and South America, across the Hudson River from New York City, in North Carolina, and at many places in the American Southwest. These reptiles lived in sluggish streams and in swamps, swam with their compressed tails, and often lay with only their nostrils above the water. Though they doubtless ate amphibians and other reptiles, their principal prey must have been fish.

CROCODILIANS

Crocodilians form a long-lived order that includes true crocodiles, gavials, alligators, caimans, and their fossil relatives. The first of these appeared in the Late Triassic of Europe, South America, and East Africa. The famous Petrified Forest, of northeastern Arizona, is one of the areas where fossils of the most primitive crocodilians are found. The bright-hued semideserts of today contrast quite markedly with the swamps that existed there when *Protosuchus* was alive. It was a reptile about 30 inches (76 cm.) long, with a relatively short head, large eyes, and a tail of moderate length. Its back, belly, and tail were encased in rectangular plates, which probably gave protection from the teeth of hungry phytosaurs. Limbs were typically crocodil-

Protosuchus, *an ancestral crocodile from the Early Jurassic of Arizona, about 30 inches (76 cm.) long*

Geosaurus, *a Late Jurassic marine mesosuchian crocodile (metriorhynchid) from Central Europe and Argentina with paddles and shark-like tail. Length 5 feet 8 inches (1.7 m.). At the right, skull of* Alligator thomsoni, *a freshwater reptile from the Late Miocene of western Nebraska. Length 14 inches (36 cm.)*

ian and could be used for either walking or swimming. The hind legs were longer than the forelegs, a condition that still prevails. It also is one of several features that crocodilians share with the majority of dinosaurs.

Mesosuchians. Crocodilians enjoyed two bursts of diversification. One came during the Jurassic Period, when a group called the mesosuchians ranged over both the New World and the Old. The smallest were less than 12 inches (30 cm.) long and had almost no armor; the largest were slender-snouted creatures that resembled modern gavials and reached lengths of 15 to 20 feet (4.6–6.1 m.). All had large upper temporal openings and vertebrae that were flattened or slightly concave at both ends. Those vertebrae and isolated teeth are the commonest mesosuchian fossils.

Most mesosuchians were active hunters that prowled along coasts and in swampy shallows, seeking fish or reptilian prey. The metriorhynchids were the most unusual of these crocodilians, because their bodies were extremely modified for life at sea, where they competed with icthyosaurs and mosasaurs. They were smooth-skinned, armorless reptiles with slender bodies, long snouts, and very long tails in which the backbone bent downward as in ichthyosaurs, indicating a terminal fin. Also like ichthyosaurs, the top lobe of the tail fin did not have any bones in it, but its presence is known from fossils preserved in fine black shale in which the outline of the body is preserved. Most of their swimming was done with the tail; the limbs, which had become flippers, served as balancing organs. Most metriorhynchids lived in Jurassic seas of Europe and South America, but other mesosuchians ranged the seas, rivers, and swamps of Europe, Africa, and the Americas, surviving through the Cretaceous and into the Eocene.

Modern Crocodilians. The next great wave of crocodilian progress began at the dawn of the Cretaceous, or Chalk Age. Within that long period, the three groups originated that still exist: snouted gavials, sharp-nosed crocodiles, and broad-nosed alligators. Except for a few alligators, all these modern crocodilians, or eusuchians, lack armor on their sides and bellies. Their temporal openings are small, and their vertebrae are concave in front but convex behind. They also had an improved solution to the problem presented by external nostrils on a long nose or snout. The phytosaurs did not have the problem, because their nostrils remained near the eyes. In mesosuchians, bones of the upper jaws and palate produced a tube that lay under the true roof of the mouth and took air to openings below and back of the eyes. In eusuchians, nostrils remained on the snout, while the air tube stretched to the hinder part of the skull near the opening of the windpipe. With this improvement, plus a membrane that closed the throat, these reptiles were able to breathe without getting water into their lungs, even when their mouths were open.

Deinosuchus, a crocodile found in Cretaceous rocks of Europe and North America, had a skull more than 6 feet (1.8 m.) long and reached lengths of 45 to 50 feet (13.7 to 15.2 m.). Vastly larger than living species—the modern

Indian gavial reaches 30 feet (9 m.) in length, while the saltwater crocodile, which ranges from India to the Solomon Islands and northern Australia, grows to lengths of over 33 feet (10 m.)—in both bulk and length *Deinosuchus* dwarfs the metriorhynchids, though it is not so highly specialized for aquatic life. Thus, its limbs still are legs and feet, and its tail, though a first-rate swimming organ, shows no trace of a fin.

Though most crocodilians are aquatic, two groups appear to have thrived as land predators during the Cenozoic. Both have flattened, daggerlike teeth reminiscent of the large carnivorous dinosaurs such as *Tyrannosaurus*. Such teeth are called ziphodont, which is Greek for "dagger tooth." One, the pristichampsines (or ziphodonts) were eusuchians, which were present in the Northern Hemisphere until the end of the Eocene. They may have survived into the Miocene in Africa, and the most recent were known from the Pleistocene of Australia. The second were the carnivorous Sebecidae, which thrived in South America until placental carnivores reached that continent,

Outcrops of marine Triassic rocks in central Arabia. From these deposits have come placodonts and nothosaurs such as are also found in northern Africa, southern Europe, and southwestern Asia, the site of the Tethys Seaway

(Left) snails, clams, and uncoiled ammonoids *(Baculites)* in a Cretaceous sea. *(Right) Placenticeras,* a coiled ammonoid. Above it swim two belemnoids, whose shells are covered by their fleshy mantles.

SOME MARINE FOSSILS AS THEY LOOKED DURING LIFE

(Dioramas from the Exhibit Museum of the University of Michigan)

(Below) part of a Devonian coral bank in New York or Ontario. It shows corals, brachiopods, trilobites, an ammonite, and a straight-shelled nautiloid.

(Left) Leptaena and other Late Ordovician brachiopods, Oxford, Ohio. *(Right)* arthropods, sponges, and jellyfish of the Middle Cambrian Burgess Shale. The large animal is *Sidneyia*. The small animals are *Marrella*.

BRACHIOPODS AND RESTORATIONS OF FOSSIL INVERTEBRATES

A Mississippian crinoid bank in what is now Indiana. One starfish lies on the bottom; another clings to the yellow crinoid at the right. (This and the Burgess diorama from the University of Michigan)

Mud that filled these footprints of an amphibian has hardened into red shale. Mississippian (Mauch Chunk Formation) near Pottsville, Pennsylvania. (Courtesy of the Museum of Comparative Zoology, Harvard University; photograph by Dr. Don Baird)

Two jawless vertebrates, or agnaths. *(Left)* armor from the back and head of *Cyrtaspis. (Right)* restoration of *Protaspis* as it looked when alive. Early Devonian riverbed, Beartooth Butte, Wyoming. (Courtesy of Princeton University)

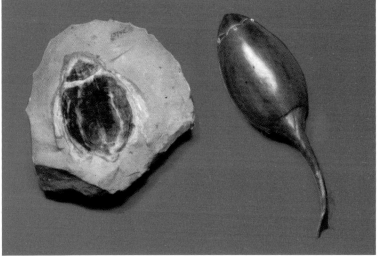

AMPHIBIANS AND TWO ARMORED AGNATHS

Impression of a frog's skeleton *(Palaeobatrachus)* in shale. Remains or impressions of frogs are very rare fossils, and this specimen from the Oligocene of Germany is unusually good. (Courtesy of the Museum of Comparative Zoology, Harvard University; photograph by Dr. Don Baird)

Skull of *Stegoceras,* a relatively primitive "boneheaded" dinosaur. Late Cretaceous, Alberta, Canada.

TWO REPTILES AND A PERMIAN AMPHIBIAN

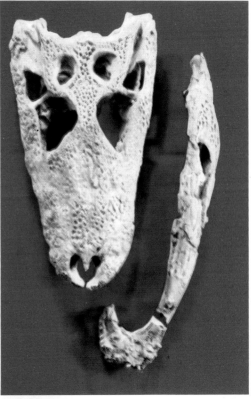

The skull and part of the lower jaw of *Alligator prenasalis* from the Oligocene of the White River Badlands near Scenic, South Dakota.

A skeleton of *Dissorophus,* a labyrinthodont amphibian of Early Permian age from Baylor County, Texas. The skull is thick, and bony armor plates cover the back. The scale is 20 centimeters, or almost 8 inches, long.

Specimens are in the Museum of Comparative Zoology, Harvard University. Photographs by Dr. Don Baird.

in the Late Tertiary, with the opening of the Panamanian land bridge. The sebecids either are regarded as peculiar mesosuchians or are put into their own group, the sebecosuchians.

Earlier, another group of less common crocodilians, the hsisosuchids, of the Jurassic of China and the Cretaceous of Austria, had also developed ziphodont teeth.

Two factors impress us most deeply as we trace crocodilian history. One is the apparent ease with which the reptiles evolved the body form of phytosaurs—not once but at least three times, the others being crocodilians and champsosaurs. The second fact is that unspecialized animals seem to have survived, while others became extinct. Living crocodilians are less specialized than ichthyosaurs, plesiosaurs, mosasaurs, and many extinct crocodilians. Yet these more specialized forms became extinct, while the generalized crocodiles persisted. Like the turtles, they still survive—not as relicts on the verge of extinction, but as a large and vigorous group. Unless humans willfully destroy them, they seem destined to live and prosper through millions of years to come.

CHAPTER XXVII

Scale Bearers and Lizard Hipped Dinosaurs

We have found, again and again, that important ancestral organisms seldom were imposing. Most of them were small, ordinary in appearance, and relatively unspecialized. Few of them became abundant; fewer still managed to live through more than one or two epochs. As one expert has said, organisms can seldom spend long ages as generalized ancestors. They either die out or produce descendants that, in habits as well as anatomy, become specialists at the job of living. As these specialists become established, they displace their primitive forebears, which often become extinct.

There are exceptions to this rule of simplicity and short life, and the ancestral diapsids were one of them. They first appeared in the Late Pennsylvanian of North America, persisted through the Permian, and were finally replaced by more progressive descendants as the Triassic dawned. One of the earliest and best-known types was *Petrolacosaurus,* an animal with a lizardlike build, long tail, slender legs, and a skull about 2.3 inches (5.9 cm.) long. The jaws were set with pointed teeth; other teeth, shorter and not so sharp, were scattered over the roof of the mouth. Both temporal openings were well developed, and the pineal "eye" was relatively large.

SCALES, SKULLS, AND SNAKES

From this beginning came a varied array of more progressive reptiles in the Triassic. One group, the lepidosaurians, developed scales and other modifications. Of these, some genera changed very little and clung to a crawling mode of life. These were the sphenodontids, which survive today as the tuatara, of New Zealand. More radical in the changes from the ancestral diapsids were the rhynchosaurs, which developed powerful jaws, blunt teeth, and parrot-type beaks, suggesting that they fed on tough plant material. This group flourished through the Triassic and then became extinct by the end of the period. The champsosaurs were a group of lepidosaurs that

438

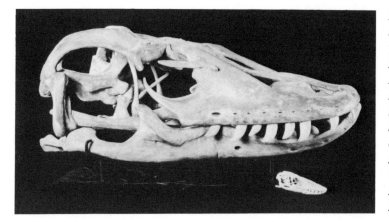

Reconstruction of the skull of **Megalania prisca**, *a giant varanid lizard from the Pleistocene of Australia. Length of skull 23 inches (74 cm.). Below it is the skull of a living species of* **Varanus**, *the closest relative. (Photo by Frank Coffa, courtesy of the Museum of Victoria, Melbourne)*

became secondarily aquatic and efficient fish eaters, having assumed a croc-odilian form. They persisted from the Triassic to the Eocene (see Chapter XXVI).

A more important group of lepidosaurs lost one cheekbone and reduced the size of two others, thereby becoming true lizards. Early types were re-lated to the iguanas and monitors that survive in our modern tropics. They were followed by chameleons and other specialized saurians.

Certain Early Cretaceous monitors produced descendants whose legs be-came shorter and shorter, while their backbones added vertebrae and their ribs increased in number. The first result of these changes was a group of long-bodied, short-legged lizards that crept by wriggling. These aberrant liz-ards then produced snakes: stocky serpents related to modern boas and pythons, which still keep traces of legs. Early snakes also lost the remaining arc of bone lying back of the eye, so that what once were two temporal openings became a single broad gap. As in the mosasaurs, the jaws also became loosely attached and double-jointed, able to spread so wide that their owners could swallow creatures thicker than themselves.

Most ancient snakes were nonpoisonous; though fossils that may repre-sent vipers have been found in Cretaceous and Paleocene formations, the first convincing specimens came from Miocene rocks. They include both cobras and true vipers. Pit vipers, which include rattlesnakes, appeared in the Pliocene. Venomous snakes also include the only true sea serpents, the hydrophids. Concentrated today mainly in the Australian region though ranging from Madagascar to Panama, some sea snakes never leave the wa-ter even to reproduce but, rather, bear their young alive at sea.

FROM THECODONTS TO DINOSAURS

Besides the lepidosaurs, the primitive diapsids gave rise to a second group of reptiles, the archosaurs, or "ruling reptiles." This group dominated the

Megalania *(length 18 feet, 5.5 m.), feasting on a carcass of* Diprotodon. *(Painting by Frank Knight, courtesy of the Museum of Victoria, Melbourne, and Pioneer Design Studio)*

land from the Middle Triassic to the Late Cretaceous. Most well known among its members were the dinosaurs, but Archosauria also included the primitive thecodonts, out of which the other archosaurs arose, the flying reptiles, or pterosaurs, and the only living survivor, the crocodiles.

We now return to the Triassic world. The evolving thecodonts developed new characters of the skull, jaw, and hip girdle, or pelvis, which were related to the success of the archosaurs. An opening appeared in the skull in front of each eye. Another characteristic opening was developed in the lower jaw. Modifications to the pelvis included broadening of the surfaces for the attachment of muscles, deepening of the socket for the head of the upper leg bone (the femur), and the attachment of more vertebrae to the pelvis so that the linkage to the backbone was strengthened. All these were essential to semierect, bipedal life and large size, which many thecodonts and their descendants assumed.

Among the bipedal thecodonts was *Euparkeria,* which ran about on long hind legs, balancing its half-erect body with a long, stiffly held tail. Length ranged from 3 to 4 feet (1–1.3 m.) and height from 10 to 15 inches (25–37 cm.).

Among the thecodonts that continued to walk on all fours were the aetosaurs. Occurring in the Triassic, they were among the first heavily armored terrestrial vertebrates. Another four-footed thecodont group was Phytosauria (see Chapter XXVI).

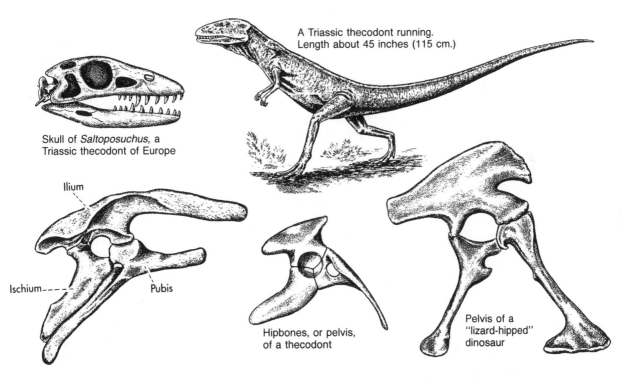

A Triassic thecodont running. Length about 45 inches (115 cm.)

Skull of *Saltoposuchus,* a Triassic thecodont of Europe

Ilium

Ischium

Pubis

Hipbones, or pelvis, of a thecodont

Pelvis of a "lizard-hipped" dinosaur

Thecodonts and contrasting pelvic bones of the two orders of dinosaurs

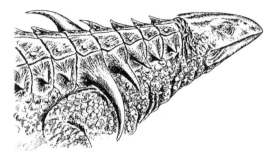

Typothorax, *a Late Triassic aetosaur from North America. Body length about 12 feet (3.7 m.)*

Two Dinosaurian Orders.— Out of the thecodonts in the Triassic came a most fantastic array of reptiles, the dinosaurs.

This term *dinosaur,* which means "terrible lizard," is both useful and deceptive. It is useful because it can be applied to a great variety of archosaurs that prospered during Mesozoic times and have no other everyday name. It is deceptive because it implies that all these reptiles were huge and ferocious carnivores that belonged to a single natural group. Actually, the so-called dinosaurs ranged from massive creatures weighing 40 or 50 tons down to delicately proportioned reptiles smaller than a barnyard rooster. Though many species were carnivores, they were outnumbered by contemporaries that ate only plants. Finally, these varied reptiles formed two distinct orders, even though both were descended from early thecodonts.

The chief difference between these orders appears in the hipbones, or pelvis. In the saurischians, or "lizard hips," this structure retains the three-pronged form developed by early thecodonts and found in the skeletons of crocodiles. Among ornithischians ("bird hips"), the pubic bone normally has two branches, one of which reaches forward while the other extends backward under the ischium. The teeth of saurischians also extend to the very front of the jaw, while those of most ornithischians stop short of it. In all ornithischians except a few genera, the jaws were covered by horny beaks. Both they and the character of the teeth show that all but one group of the ornithischians were herbivores, but the saruischians include about equal numbers of meat and plant eaters.

THE MOST ANCIENT DINOSAURS

The change from thecodont to saurischian dinosaur was not great and apparently took place before Middle Triassic times. During the latter half of that period, saurischians roamed across Europe, Asia, and the valleys of eastern North America. There they left a few skeletons and countless footprints in beds of dark red, muddy sand that hardened into stone. Now hard to find, these tracks were common in the days when Triassic "brownstone" was quarried to build churches, mansions, and even railroad culverts and jails.

Coelophysis, *a primitive dinosaur from the Late Triassic of northern Arizona and New Mexico. Length to tip of tail about 8 feet (2.4 m.)*

Triassic Dinosaurs.   Both bones and footprints show that many Late Triassic dinosaurs were carnivorous, with slender legs, long necks, small heads, and long tails. Many were 3 to 4 feet (90–120 cm.) long, those that measured 7 or 8 feet (2.1–2.4 m.) were large, and creatures 16 to 20 feet (4.9–6.1 m.) were giants. All walked on their hind feet, which had three—rarely four—long toes and one more so short that it seldom left an impression. For this reason their fossil footprints were first mistaken for those of birds.

A good picture of Late Triassic life is provided by the Chinle Formation, of northeastern Arizona and adjacent parts of Utah and New Mexico. It shows us uplands covered with forests of cone-bearing araucarian "pines," whose fallen trunks were washed downstream and deposited on mud banks to form the Petrified Forest, of Arizona, and other forests of less spectacular beauty. Large ferns grew under the trees, small cycads filled openings, and horsetails formed thickets along the streams (see Chapter XXIII). The climate was moderate, though clouds of ash from volcanic eruptions sometimes filled the air.

Streams, ponds, and shallow lakes were the home of mussels, lungfish, ganoids, and large amphibians. Armored thecodonts reached lengths of 12 to 15 feet (3.6–4.6 m.); preying upon them were saurischian dinosaurs, up to 20 feet (6 m.) long, which roamed about on two stout hind legs. Phytosaurs, up to 45 feet (14 m.) long, were common in swamps, and at least one dicynodont *(Placerias),* with tusks and beaked jaws, apparently lived in upland forests. There it encountered smaller saurischian dinosaurs that were slender bipeds about 8 feet (2.4 m.) long, with high, narrow skulls and hollow leg bones. Like their thecodont ancestors, they walked and ran on their hind legs, captured prey with forelimbs and jaws, and balanced their swaying bodies with stiffly extended tails. Their weight has been estimated at 40 to 50 pounds (18 to 23 kg.). Those of the Painted Desert and northwestern New Mexico belong to the genus *Coelophysis*.

THE REIGN OF GREAT SAUROPODS

As the Jurassic Period dawned in the western United States, swamps gave way to deserts that spread from New Mexico and Colorado to southern Nevada. Winds howled across this barren land, piling sand into dunes that today form cross-bedded sandstones 3,500 feet (1,100 m.) thick. Travelers see them in the Vermilion and Echo cliffs; in the red, buff, and white walls of Zion Canyon; and in the arches, towers, and spectacular chasms in the region of Moab, Utah.

Deserts made poor homes for dinosaurs, but some of their bones have been discovered in hardened Jurassic dunes. Other regions were more inviting, and lizard-hipped saurischians thrived in their warm and often swampy lowlands. The saurischians were subdivided into two groups, called theropods ("beast-footed") and sauropods ("lizard-footed"). Neither name is very appropriate, but the groups themselves are important. With a few exceptions, the theropods were bipeds that walked on three birdlike toes, had short forelegs, and were carnivorous. Sauropods, however, walked on four feet, developed massive legs both fore and aft, and had teeth that were suited only to a diet of soft, juicy plants.

Ancestors of Giants. This twofold division of the lizard-hipped dinosaurs had begun in Triassic times. Among the slender reptiles that ranged through eastern valleys was a heavier creature, with stocky hind legs, called *Anchisaurus.* It had a smallish head, blunt teeth, and five toes on each foot, four being usable; and it apparently could walk half erect or on all fours and ate plants as well as animals. While feeding, it may have waded into shallow swamps.

This creature was a prosauropod, or "first lizard-foot." Prosauropods were a very widespread group in the Late Triassic and Early Jurassic, with specimens known from all the continents except Antarctica. *Plateosaurus,* from Germany, France, and Argentina, was about 20 feet (6.1 m.) long and probably spent even more of its time on all four feet than did *Anchisaurus,* but it still was able to get about on its hind legs alone.

Unlike their descendants, the sauropods, not all prosauropods were strictly herbivorous. *Thecodontosaurus* may have preferred some of its thecodont cousins to plant food.

The largest prosauropod was *Euskelosaurus,* from the Late Triassic of South Africa. With a length of 40 feet (12.2 m.) and a weight of 2 tonnes (2.2 T.), this dinosaur was the largest of the prosauropods. It was unusual in

(Left) Plateosaurus, *a primitive sauropod of the European and Argentinian Triassic; 16 to 20 feet (4.9–6.1 m.) in length.* Anchisaurus *(right) of eastern United States, was about 8 feet long (2.4 m.)*

that it does not show signs of having descended from bipedal ancestors in the recent past. It is generally held that all later archosaurs were descended from bipedal thecodonts. However, the existence of *Euskelosaurus,* with a fully quadrupedal stance so early in the geologic record of archosaurs, suggests it is possible that the sauropods evolved directly from four-footed stock that never had bipedal ancestors.

The Triumph of Sauropods. Generally larger than prosauropods and never bipedal, sauropods can be quickly distinguished by the structure of the front feet. Sauropods have only one claw on the front foot, and it is on the thumb. By contrast, prosauropods have claws on at least the first three digits.

Sauropods appeared in the Early Jurassic, but their record is scanty until the Late Jurassic. Then they are well known, particularly from the Morrison Formation of North America, from Tendaguru, Tanzania, East Africa, and from Sichuan, China. By the Late Jurassic they had achieved abundance and variety as well as enormous size.

The Morrison Formation is made up of a complex series of clays, shales, and sandstones that settled in swamps, shallow lakes, and broad streams that wandered over low-lying plains. Cycads, ginkgos, and conifers formed forests, shading an undergrowth made up largely of ferns. Horsetails and succulent plants grew abundantly in swamps. All indications are that the climate was mild and equable, though it alternated between wet and dry seasons.

Brachiosaurus *(left) and* Apatosaurus, *the brontosaur (right), were two of the largest "lizard-hipped" dinosaurs. Both lived in Colorado and adjacent regions during Morrison times.* Brachiosaurus *also inhabited central Africa. Since this restoration was drawn, it has been learned that the skull of* Apatosaurus *was actually quite similar to that of* Diplodocus, *and not* Camarasaurus *as shown here*

One Morrison sauropod, *Camarasaurus,* was a relatively unspecialized creature 30 to 60 feet (9 to 18 m.) long when fully grown, with slender neck and tail and short forelegs—the last condition reminiscent of theropod ancestors. Both fore- and hind feet were stubby, and the former had only one complete toe.

Apatosaurus—better, though wrongly, known as *Brontosaurus,* the "thunder lizard"—was a huge and highly specialized sauropod. *Apatosaurus* was 65 to 77 feet (20 to 23 m.) long, with a deep, short body, a flexible neck, and a tail that was massive near the hip but ended in a whiplash tip. The legs formed thick columns ending in broad feet as much as 26 inches (66 cm.) wide, padded like those of an elephant. The fully developed toes bore claws

446

—one on each forefoot and three massive claws behind. The total weight of this reptile is estimated at 30 to 35 tons (27.2–31.8 t.).

Apatosaurus often encountered a relative known as *Diplodocus*. This creature reached lengths of 80 to 87 feet (24–27 m.) and was 13 feet (4 m.) tall at the curve of its back, forward from the hips. Almost one third of the length was neck, and more than half consisted of tail that ended in a slender lash. Even so, *Diplodocus* was a giant, weighing up to 20 tons (18.2 t.) or more, or about five times as much as a large elephant.

In front of this enormous bulk was a weak-looking head about two feet (60 cm.) long. The nostrils opened through a single hole between and above the eyes; the muzzle sloped down to the jaws; blunt teeth were tipped outward and must have been used to pull plants, not to nip them off.

The brain was a small, smooth organ weighing only a few ounces, about the size of that of a rabbit. Though small, the brains of sauropods such as *Diplodocus* were not so tiny that they could not function well. When the brain sizes of smaller reptiles are plotted against the weight of the animal and then extrapolated to the size of sauropods, the "expected" brain size for a reptile as large as *Diplodocus* is about five times the actual size measured in the fossils. So they probably were not among the more intelligent dinosaurs. However, sauropods did survive for more than 100 million years, during which time many other dinosaur groups came and went. So the brains must have been quite sufficient for life as a sauropod.

Diplodocus, then, must have been a sluggish creature that ate moderate amounts of food. The brain was able to sort out messages of sight, hearing,

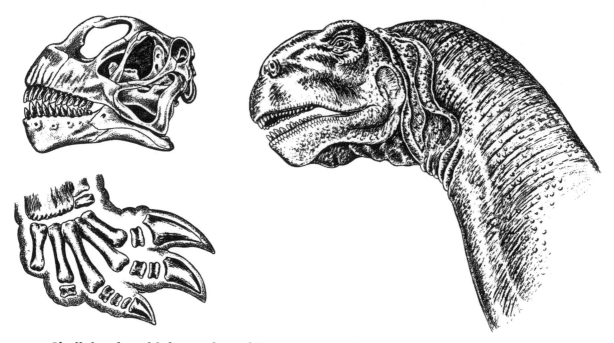

Skull, head, and left rear foot of **Camarasaurus,** *from the Late Jurassic Morrison Formation. The full-grown reptile was 30 to 40 feet (9.1–12.2 m.) long*

and smell and pass them to ganglia above the shoulder and hips. These nerve knots coordinated such jobs as walking and swinging the tail. These activities, plus reaching out for food, mating, and possibly roving in herds, filled the life of *Diplodocus* and other sauropods. Abstract thinking was a luxury in which they did not indulge.

Larger still was *Brachiosaurus,* whose remains have been found in western North America, Portugal, and North and East Africa. Unlike other sauropods, this giant had forelegs longer than the hind, so that the back of the massive body sloped tailward like that of a giraffe. The upper "arm" bone, or humerus, was 7 feet (2.1 m.) long; the height above the shoulder was 19 feet (5.8 m.), the neck was almost 28 feet (8.5 m.) long, and the head was carried more than 39 feet (11.9 m.) above the ground. Though the tail was much shorter than that of *Apatosaurus,* the total length was more than 74 feet (22.6 m.). A massive body—the ribs were 8 feet 7 inches (2.6 m.) long— brought the weight to at least 40 tons (36.3 t.). The brain, however, weighed only 7 ounces (200 gm.).

These are measurements made from one skeleton, that of a brachiosaur whose growth was not complete. Other bones are larger by as much as 13 percent. They indicate that full-grown animals were as much as 44 feet (13.4 m.) high and 84 feet (25.6 m.) long and weighed 45 to 50 tons (40.8–45.4 t.).

Two sauropods are known from the Morrison Formation that may be even larger. However, the remains are quite incomplete. The smaller and better known of the two was *Supersaurus,* which may have had a total body length between 80 and 100 feet (24.4–30.5 m.). *Ultrasaurus* may have been more than 100 feet (30.5 meters) long and weighed as much as 150 tons (136 t.). If so, it would have been as long as, but heavier than, the living blue whale, up to now the largest known animal that ever lived.

But even *Ultrasaurus* may have looked small when compared to *Breviparopus,* a sauropod from Morocco known only from its tracks and a newly discovered form from the American Southwest, nicknamed *Seismosauris* or "Earthshaker." The size of the tracks and the spacing between them suggested to the scientists who first described them that this animal was 157 feet (48 m.) long.

The Sauropod Skeleton.   Sauropods were not only the world's largest reptiles; they also were the largest of terrestrial animals. Size and environment together posed problems which were solved by a complex of bones, ligaments, muscles, habits, and reproductive organs.

The first and most obvious problem was that of providing a framework for the body. Part of that framework was ribs, but its critical portion was the backbone. Vertebrae had to be large and strong but not solid, for solid vertebrae would have added more weight than legs were able to support. As sauropods became giants, therefore, they developed "excavated" vertebrae, which seem to be made up largely of holes. Actually, evolutionary changes omitted bone where it did no good but added it in bars and ridges that met

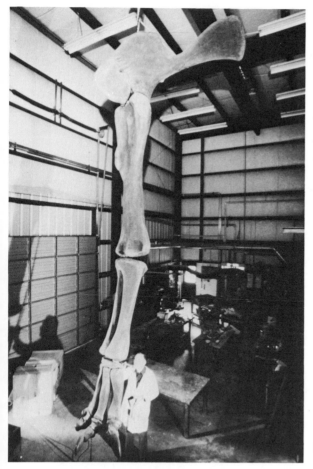

Front leg of a model of the gargantuan dinosaur Utrasaurus, *a sauropod from the Late Jurassic Morrison Formation, at Dry Mesa Quarry, Colorado. (Photo courtesy of J. A. Jensen)*

Scapula (shoulder blade) of Ultrasaurus *in the ground at Dry Mesa Quarry. (Photo courtesy of J. A. Jensen)*

every normal stress. The result was a structure much like that of a modern steel bridge, held together by ligaments and interlocking joints instead of by welds, rivets, or bolts.

Once framed, the body had to be supported and moved from place to place. For these tasks the sauropods used long, massive legs that stood upright. Their size is indicated by the humerus of *Brachiosaurus,* which was 7 feet (2.1 m.) long. The thighbone (femur) of *Apatosaurus* was more massive, with a length of 6 feet 6 inches (2 m.) and a girth, near the middle, of more than 3 feet (90 cm.).

Sauropod Ways. There is a long-standing argument as to whether even these massive legs could support the huge sauropod body. Those who say they did not, point to long bones, which were capped by cartilage that presumably would have been crushed by weights of 20 to 50 tons (18.2–45.4 t.),

Mamenchisaurus *had the longest neck of any sauropod. From the Middle or Late Jurassic of Sichuan, People's Republic of China (Courtesy of the Museum of Victoria, Melbourne)*

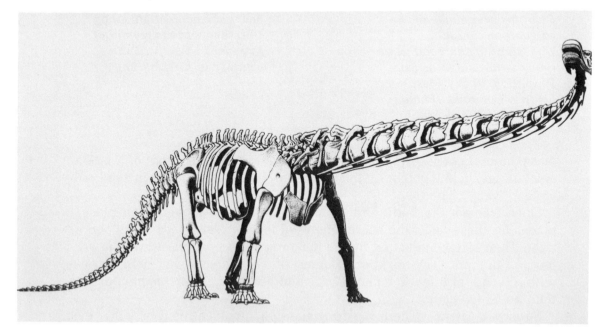

Mamenchisaurus. *(Drawing by Peter Trusler, courtesy of the Museum of Victoria, Melbourne)*

Outcrops of the Jurassic Shaximiao Formation, in Sichuan, People's Republic of China. Mamenchisaurus *is just one of the many different dinosaurs that have been found in these rocks. (Photo courtesy of Minchen Chow and the Institute of Vertebrate Paleontology and Paleoanthropology, Beijing)*

leaving the reptiles unable to move. This disaster would have been avoided, however, if the sauropods waded in water deep enough to partly float their bodies and ponderous tails.

All this is inference, but it seems to be supported by sauropod trails found in early Cretaceous rocks along the Paluxy River (or Creek) near Glen Rose, Texas. The trail makers probably were closely related to *Apatosaurus* and *Diplodocus,* though the hind feet bore four claws instead of three, and the forefeet had none. The creatures evidently waded in coastal marshes of a very early Cretaceous sea, leaving footprints in beds of limy sand that also contained oyster shells and other marine remains. Prints of the hind feet were as much as 38 inches (96 cm.) long and 26 inches (66 cm.) wide and were separated by 12-foot (3.7 m.) strides.

Most of the footprints were made by animals that walked on all fours, with their tails off the ground or bottom. One dinosaur, however, dragged its tail for some distance; another walked on its forefeet while its hindquarters floated. In order to turn, this reptile struck outward and upward with only one hind foot. Its claws dug deep gashes that remained when the sediment became stone.

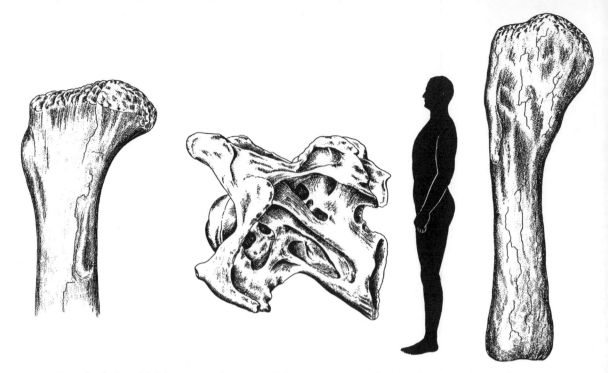

Head of the thighbone, or femur, of Camarasaurus *(left). The pits show that the end of this bone had not hardened but was covered with soft cartilage. A bone from the neck of* Apatosaurus *(center) shows the bars and plates that gave strength, while hollow spaces reduced the weight. A man 5 feet 8 inches (1.7 m.) tall (right) beside an upper "arm" bone, or humerus, of* Brachiosaurus. *The bone, found near Fruita, Colorado, is 7 feet (2.1 m.) in length*

Apatosaurus *wading with its forelegs but swimming with its hind legs. Below* Apatosaurus *is* Diplodocus *wading in shallow water; its tail is half afloat*

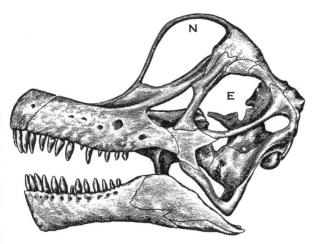

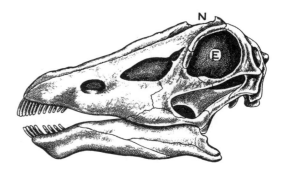

Skull of Brachiosaurus, *30 inches (76 cm.) long. The nostrils were at N, the eye at E*

Skull of Diplodocus, *about 2 feet (60 cm.) long. The orbit of the eye is marked E; the nares are shown by N*

Critics do not question these facts, but give them another interpretation. The leg bones, these critics say, prove only that sauropods grew throughout life. Cartilaginous ends, therefore, were not replaced by bone, but the cartilage might have been strong enough to bear the weight of the body. More important, the Glen Rose trails combine proof that big dinosaurs often waded, with strong hints that they did not always do so. Tracks of the former type are deep but indistinct, as if wet, soft sediment slumped into them as soon as the reptiles walked away. Other tracks are clear-cut but relatively shallow, as if the sediments were firm and drier. The usual absence of tail marks suggests that the sauropods kept their tails off the ground most of the time when on dry land.

Furthermore, though the skeletons of sauropods are massive, they are as light as possible. If sauropods were completely aquatic, like whales, there would be no need for lightening the skeleton. Sauropod feet are not large relative to the size of the animals, and because of this, they might easily have gotten bogged on a soft, muddy swamp bottom. They seem better adapted to movement over hard ground. The bodies of sauropods are deep and narrow, like the terrestrial elephant, not round, like the amphibious hippopotamus.

Thus stands the argument; a solution awaits the finding of sauropod tracks in sediments laid down on land or in shoals whose depth can be determined within a foot or two (about 0.5 m.). Meanwhile we can only say that sauropods, at least from time to time, did wade in water that buoyed up their bodies, and that they could swim.

One problem still remains to be solved: that of producing young. In southern France, fossil eggs 12 inches (30 cm.) in diameter are found in the same deposits as the sauropod dinosaur *Hypselosaurus.* In Argentina, an entire skeleton of a juvenile of the prosauropod *Mussaurus* only about 10 inches (24 cm.) long has been found close to a fossil egg about 1 inch (2.5 cm.) in diameter. These associations strongly suggest that sauropods probably laid eggs, rather than bore their young alive. Perhaps, like modern crocodiles, they protected their young after hatching.

How Long Did the Sauropods Last?   Sauropods reached their zenith in the Northern Hemisphere in the Late Jurassic and Early Cretaceous times. We once thought they then went into a rapid decline, with only a few stragglers of moderate size lingering into the Late Cretaceous. Recent discoveries, however, suggest that large sauropods persisted until the end of that period. A great variety of Late Cretaceous sauropods has now come to light in Argentina, the largest of these being *Chubutisaurus,* which was 75 feet (23 m.) long. Elsewhere in the world, the occurrence of large Late Cretaceous sauropods is not as frequent as in the Late Jurassic. However, the existence of *Alamosaurus,* from North America, which weighed 30 tons (27.2 t.) and was 69 feet (21 m.) long, shows they did exist then.

THE PREDATORY CARNOSAURS

The sauropods provided vast amounts of meat, weighing from a few hundred to 90,000 pounds (100 kg. to 41 t.). Thanks to these riches, carnivorous dinosaurs also were able to evolve into giants.

We have met early meat eaters among the little three-toed, bipedal theropods of the Middle Triassic. Before that period closed, some of their descendants became 8 to 12 feet (2.4–3.7 m.) long, weighed upward of 150 pounds (70 kg.), and were much stronger than most modern lizards. They doubtless preyed on such creatures as *Plateosaurus* while those awkward reptiles were turning into sauropods.

Perhaps meat eaters even got ahead of their prey. The oldest known sauropods are found in Early Jurassic rocks, but full-fledged carnosaurs may be represented in Late Triassic deposits of Europe and South Africa. The fossils in question are so fragmentary, however, that they could have belonged to large, carnivorous thecodonts instead of dinosaurs. In Early Jurassic times, one family, appropriately called the megalosaurs, or "large saurians," included members 12 to 30 feet (3.7–9 m.) long, with 12-inch (30-cm.) skulls and serrate teeth that became recurved when fully developed. The forelegs were shorter than those of *Plateosaurus,* the hind legs were long and powerful, and the feet bore long, curved claws. Megalosaurs probably lay in wait for their prey, rushed upon it, and killed it by biting through the backbone. The claws held food while it was being eaten, as vultures use their claws today.

Few Middle Jurassic carnosaurs are known, but the group became large and varied during the Late Jurassic. One of its best-known members is *Cer-*

atosaurus, found in steeply tilted rocks near Canyon City, Colorado. When walking, this reptile measured 17 feet 6 inches (5.3 m.) from nose to tail tip and was 7 feet (2.1 m.) high. The head was 20 inches (51 cm.) long and 13 inches (33 cm.) high, with saber-shaped teeth that extended 2 inches (5 cm.) beyond the jaws. The nose bore a blunt, narrow horn, and a bony knob rose in front of each eye. Like the megalosaurs, *Ceratosaurus* walked and ran on its hind legs, with its body balanced by its long tail.

Though a powerful and savage hunter, *Ceratosaurus* seems small when placed beside *Allosaurus.* This reptile was 42 feet (13 m.) long, stood more than 8 feet (2.4 m.) high as it stooped to eat, and when aroused could raise its head to 14 or 15 feet (4.3 or 4.6 m.). The head was 36 inches (91 cm.) in length, and the 6-inch (15-cm.) teeth had serrate edges. The lower jaw was hinged far back on the skull, giving a tremendous gape to the savage mouth. Thus, the creature could deliver powerful, slashing bites and could also gulp down food in massive, unchewed lumps.

We must guess what many ancient reptiles ate, but not so with *Allosaurus.* At Dinosaur National Monument, Utah, remains of *Allosaurus* have been

Allosaurus
34 feet long

Ceratosaurus
17.5 feet long

Ornitholestes
6 feet long

Three carnivorous dinosaurs of Late Jurassic age. They lived in what now is the Rocky Mountains region of the western United States. The largest, Allosaurus, *was 34 feet (10.4 m.) long;* Ceratosaurus *was 17.5 feet (5.3 m.) long; and the smallest,* Ornitholestes, *was 6 feet (1.8 m.) long*

(Right) Struthiomimus, *the "ostrich mimic," of Cretaceous Alberta, Canada. Height 8 to 9 feet (2.4–2.7 m.). (Left) an early species of* Gorgosaurus, *7 feet (2.1 m.) high at the hips. Cretaceous of Alberta*

found among those of *Diplodocus* and other sauropods. At the famous Bone Cabin dinosaur quarry, near Como Bluff, Wyoming, bones of *Apatosaurus* and other sauropods are scratched by the teeth of *Allosaurus,* which also lie among the remains. Evidently the huge carnivore bit so hard that it broke off some of its 6-inch (15-cm.) teeth and left them with the refuse of its meal.

Only one question remains. Did *Allosaurus* kill the great, defenseless sauropods, or was it a carrion eater? Some experts say one and some the other, and both may be correct. It seems probable that allosaurs captured young giants and forms such as *Camarasaurus*. Moreover, at least one carnosaur as large as *Allosaurus* stalked a sauropod in the coastal swamp whose deposits are found near Glen Rose, Texas. Not even plunging into deep water would necessarily have saved a sauropod in such circumstances, because theropods, too, were good swimmers.

Tyrannosaurids, the "Tyrant Lizards." During the first half of the Cretaceous Period some of the theropods evolved into the tyrannosaurids ("tyrant lizards"), probably the largest of all terrestrial carnivores.

Among the earlier tyrannosaurids was a relatively slender species of *Gorgosaurus* that ranged through moist, thickly forested lowlands in what is now the province of Alberta, Canada. Standing about 7 feet (2.1 m.) high at the hips, it had a low skull armed with surprisingly long teeth. There were two toes on each forefoot and four on the hind, with a remnant of a fifth. Ventral ribs protected the belly, a primitive character.

Tyrannosaurus, *a carnivorous dinosaur 47 feet (14.3 m.) long and 18 feet (5.5 m.) high, and its skull, about 50 inches (127 cm.) long. Cretaceous of Montana*

This, however, was only the beginning; a later species of *Gorgosaurus* reached a length of 29 feet (8.8 m.), stood 9 feet (2.7 m.) high at the hips, and had a low skull some 22 inches (56 cm.) long, armed with recurved teeth. Ventral ribs still were well developed, but the vestigial fifth hind toe had been lost. The reptile probably walked with a stoop, as did *Ceratosaurus* and *Allosaurus,* but could run swiftly for short distances. Its forelegs, however, were small and presumably useless. So were the diminutive forefeet, which had only two toes.

Last of all came *Albertosaurus* and its better-known cousin, *Tyrannosaurus.* Both were massive, erect dinosaurs with the largest heads known among saurischians. *Tyrannosaurus* was 47 feet (14.3 m.) long, 18 feet (5.5 m.) tall, and weighed 8 to 10 tons (7.3–9.1 t.). Its knee joint was 6 feet (1.8 m.) above the ground; the claws on its hind feet were 6 to 8 inches (15–20 cm.) long; its skull measured 51 inches (130 cm.) from front to back; its teeth were serrate blades 3 to 6 inches (8–15 cm.) long and an inch (2.5 cm.) in

Skull of **Tyrannosaurus,** *length about 50 inches (127 cm.). (Photo by Frank Coffa, courtesy of the Museum of Victoria, Melbourne*

width. The forefeet had only two toes and were too small to be of much use in handling food.

We are tempted to picture the food of *Tyrannosaurus* in massive proportions to match its size. Actually, the great carnivore lived during latest Cretaceous times, when *Diplodocus* and *Brachiosaurus* had been extinct for 50 million years and lesser sauropods were rare. The tyrant saurian's prey consisted of herbivorous reptiles 20 to 30 feet (6 to 9 m.) long that waded, swam, and walked on lowlands of western North America. What they lacked in bulk they made up in numbers. The tyrant seldom went hungry; he merely took more meals than his predecessor, *Allosaurus.*

Spiny Carnivores. Strangest of all theropods were the spinosaurids. They lived in Europe and northern Africa during the Late Cretaceous. Though the fossils are far from perfect, the North African *Spinosaurus* was a large creature whose back bore neural spines resembling those of *Dimetrodon* and were as much as 6 feet (1.8 m.) long. One wonders how such reptiles walked on two legs and killed active prey. Did they merely lie in wait for victims, or did they eat carrion?

The tetrapods with highly developed neural spines such as the Permian pelycosaurs *Dimetrodon; Edaphosaurus,* of Texas; the Triassic thecodont *Ctenosauriscus,* of Germany, and the North African Late Cretaceous dinosaurs *Ouranosaurus* and *Spinosaurus* all lived close to where the equator was at those times. This suggests that the "sails" on their backs may have been useful for getting rid of excess body heat. By sending blood into the sail when the animal was in the shade or even when the plane of the sail was parallel to the sun's rays, the temperature of the blood would be lowered. In the event the animal was cool, it could heat itself up more rapidly in the sun than those animals without a sail, by turning so the plane of the sail was perpendicular to the rays of the sun.

Another use for these "sails" may have been to make an animal appear larger to rival males during the breeding period or carnivores that might prey upon it.

The Long-armed Theropods. During the Late Cretaceous in Asia there were at least two theropods known only from their arms. But what arms they are! Each is about 8 feet (2.5 m.) long, and each terminated in three powerful claws. *Deinocheirus* had relatively slender arms, but those of *Therizinosaurus* were quite stocky. Because a whole skeleton of neither of these animals is known, we have no clear idea of what they looked like. The most reasonable guess is that they resembled a *Tyrannosaurus* with enlarged forelimbs.

Bird Catchers and Bird Mimics. While some theropods evolved into giants, others became slender and agile. Some even developed legs, bodies, and necks much like those of the modern ostrich.

This trend began with such Triassic forms as *Coelophysis* or with the slender, bipedal *Compsognathus,* which lived on forested seashores of Late Jurassic Germany. Because two thirds of its 30 inches (76 cm.) were neck and tail, this dinosaur probably weighed less than a good-sized rooster. The toes were long and bore claws, and the small jaws were set with sharp teeth. *Compsognathus* probably ranged through underbrush and preyed upon still smaller reptiles. In fact, the remains of such a meal still lie in the abdominal region of one specimen.

Ornitholestes, from the Late Jurassic Morrison Formation, of Wyoming,

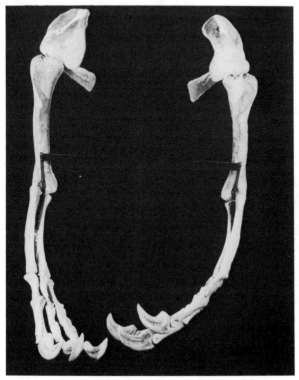

Forelimbs of **Deinocheirus,** *an otherwise virtually unknown theropod from the Late Cretaceous of the People's Republic of Mongolia. Each forelimb is 8 feet 6 inches (2.6 m.) long. (Photo by Frank Coffa, courtesy of Zofia Kielan-Jaworowska, Institute of Paleobiology (Warsaw) and the Museum of Victoria, Melbourne)*

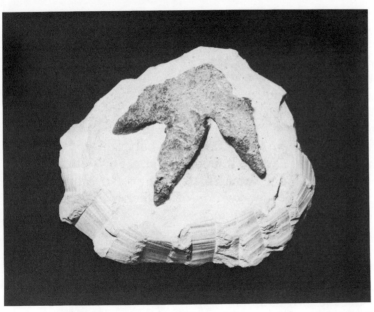

Footprint of a small dinosaur from the Early Cretaceous of Victoria, Australia. Length about 8 inches (20 cm.). (Photo by Frank Coffa, courtesy of the Museum of Victoria, Melbourne)

U.S.A., was 6 feet (1.8 m.) long, with a stout body and a rather long, inflexible tail. Forefeet had become three-toed grasping organs; hind legs and feet were long, slender, and well adapted to running. Often pictured in the act of catching a bird, *Ornitholestes* (the name means "bird robber") probably dined chiefly on small, agile reptiles such as the early lizards.

Deinonychus, from the Early Cretaceous of Montana, was 8 to 13 feet (2.4–4 m.) long and had a large head. It was an unusual dinosaur in a number of ways. First, the second digit on each hind foot bore an enlarged claw. Using it as a hook, *Deinonychus,* with a swift kick, was able to slash open the belly of its prey or competitor. Unlike most other dinosaurs, *Deinonychus* could see in three dimensions, because the field of vision of its two eyes overlapped. The eyes were also very large, suggesting that it could see in the dark as well as in the daylight. Perhaps it hunted at night. Compared to the size of the body, the brain of *Deinonychus* was much larger than in any other dinosaurs, about the same size as to be expected of an equally large modern bird such as an ostrich.

A Late Cretaceous Mongolian relative of *Deinonychus, Adasaurus,* had a pelvis more like that of a bird than a typical theropod. Instead of the pubis being directed downward and forward, it ran downward and backward, parallel to the ischium.

Another family of small theropods with this same peculiar arrangement of the pelvis were the Late Cretaceous segnosaurids of Mongolia and China. Unlike *Deinonychus* and *Adasaurus,* however, they had four toes on their hind feet and not three. Also unlike *Deinonychus,* there was no enlarged, scimitar-shaped claw. In addition, segnosaurids lacked anterior teeth in the skull but had a beak instead.

Struthiomimus, of the North American Late Cretaceous, stood 8 to 9 feet (2.4 to 2.7 m.) high when erect and combined the proportions of an ostrich with such typically reptilian features as a saurischian pelvis, four legs, and a long tail. The small head was ostrichlike too, and its toothless jaws were covered with a horny beak.

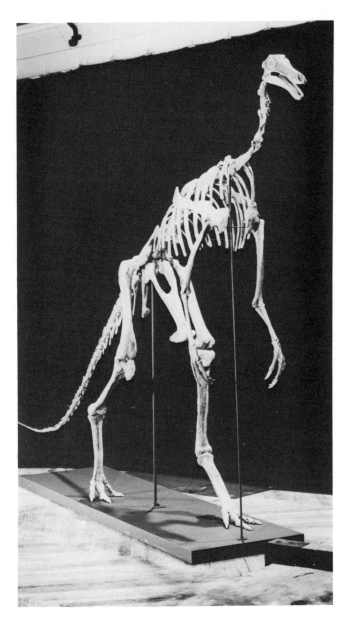

Skeleton of Gallimimus, *length 13 feet (4 m.), from the Late Cretaceous of the People's Republic of Mongolia. It was related to its North American contemporary* Struthiomimus. *(Photo by Frank Coffa, courtesy of Zofia Kielan-Jaworowska, Institute of Paleobiology (Warsaw) and the Museum of Victoria, Melbourne)*

Struthiomimus apparently lived on humid lowlands and sandy plains, where it walked or ran swiftly on its long hind legs. It also found safety in escape, not in self-defense. Its slim, three-toed hind feet could not be used to kick, like the heavy feet of ostriches.

Ornithomimids (the family name) probably were omnivores. They could easily pull fruit from low trees; their beaks could snap up small reptiles; their handlike forefeet could dig eggs from nests on the ground and hold them while their beaks broke the shells.

Oviraptorids, as the name ("egg thieves") implies, were also adept at feeding on eggs. Their skulls were shorter and more robust than those of ornithomimids, but, like them, they lacked teeth. Generally these thieves escaped, but one *Oviraptor* in Mongolia was killed while robbing the nest of another dinosaur. Its crushed skull was preserved among the petrified shells.

CHAPTER XXVIII

Bird-hipped Dinosaurs

 In 1822 the wife of Gideon Mantell, a British country doctor, found some petrified teeth in rocks of Early Cretaceous age. Her husband later secured additional teeth and a few bones which experts in England and France variously assigned to a rhinoceros, a hippopotamus, and a fish. Dr. Mantell himself thought the teeth belonged to a reptile resembling the modern lizards called iguanas, and therefore named them *Iguanodon.* Years passed before the teeth and bones were recognized as remains of an ornithischian, or bird-hipped, dinosaur.

ORNITHOPODS, OR "BIRD FEET"

Iguanodon is an advanced member of a suborder called ornithopods ("bird feet"), though their feet really are less birdlike than those of "beast-footed" theropods. A much more primitive type, *Camptosaurus,* appeared in North America and Europe during Late Jurassic times and survived into the Early Cretaceous, possibly reaching Australia. It was a rather clumsy biped 7 to 17 feet (2.1–5.2 m.) in length, with a low and rather heavy skull. The forefeet had five toes and the hind feet four, all tipped with hoof-like claws. The femur was curved, suggesting that *Camptosaurus* sometimes stooped over to walk on all fours. Like all ornithischians, it had an extra bone, the predentary, at the front of each lower jaw. Both upper and lower jaws were tipped by beaks, which were used to nip off leaves and fruits. Flattened, bladelike teeth were found in the hinder two thirds of the mouth. The jaw hinge was lower than the teeth, not on a level with or even above them, as in the carnosaurs, whose jaws closed with a shearing motion, but those of *Camptosaurus* came together with a "nutcracker" action that crushed pulpy food.

First discovered in Europe, *Iguanodon* is also known from North America, Asia, and North Africa. The varied species were 15 to 30 feet (4.6–9.1 m.) in length and reached 15 feet (4.6 m.) in height. All had narrow bodies and compressed tails, walked on hind feet bearing three large toes and a very

Camptosaurus, 17 feet (5.2 m.) long. A Jurassic ornithischian of Europe and North America. It may have reached Australia in the Early Cretaceous

Skull fragment of a small ornithopod dinosaur, closely related to Camptosaurus, *from the Early Cretaceous rocks of southern Victoria, Australia. Length 2 inches (5 cm.). (Photo by Frank Coffa, courtesy of the Museum of Victoria, Melbourne)*

small one, and had five-toed forefeet on which the "thumb" had become a bony spike. Before well-preserved skulls were found, some people thought this spike belonged on the animal's nose.

In the coal-mining district near Mons, Belgium, Early Cretaceous streams eroded gorges as much as 600 feet (180 m.) deep in Carboniferous strata. Streams filled the gorges with mud, dead plants, and reptile carcasses brought from swampy lands nearby. In 1878, miners tunneled into an ancient gorge and there found the remains of twenty-three large iguanodonts, as well as crocodiles, turtles, and fish. The iguanodonts seem to represent both sexes of one species, and reveal their anatomy in unusual detail.

Another notable discovery was made in a coal mine near Cedaredge, Colorado. There a Late Cretaceous iguanodont walked on muck that now is coal, and its footprints were filled by sand that hardened into gray sandstone. These footprints measure 34 inches (86 cm.) in width and length, indicating that their owner was much larger than any other known iguanodont.

Hypsilophodon, a primitive bird-hipped dinosaur from the Early Cretaceous of Europe and North America, was 5 to 6 feet (1.5–1.8 m.) long and had a 6-inch (15-cm.) skull. Its forelegs were short, and its back and side may have borne thin armor. *Hypsilophodon* is one of the better-known representatives of a primitive stock of relatively small ornithopods that persisted little changed from the Late Triassic to the Late Cretaceous. But there were early evolutionary "experiments" within this group. One such was the Late Triassic or Early Jurassic *Heterodontosaurus* (the name means "the lizard with different teeth"), from South Africa. In addition to cheek teeth, it had prominent tusks. Though basically a conservative group, out of it evolved not only the iguanodontids but, ultimately, all the other ornithischians as well.

Iguanodon, *about 11 feet (3.4 m.) high, and the bones of its right forefoot.* Iguanodon *lived in Europe, North America, Asia, and North Africa during the Early Cretaceous*

Duckbills, or Hadrosaurs. These reptiles are distinguished by very long skulls that end in broad, toothless expansions. During life these were covered with horny beaks that may have been flexible and probably were used to pull off soft plants, grub in the mud for roots, and shovel loose food into the mouth. Food was crushed by teeth arranged in overlapping banks which

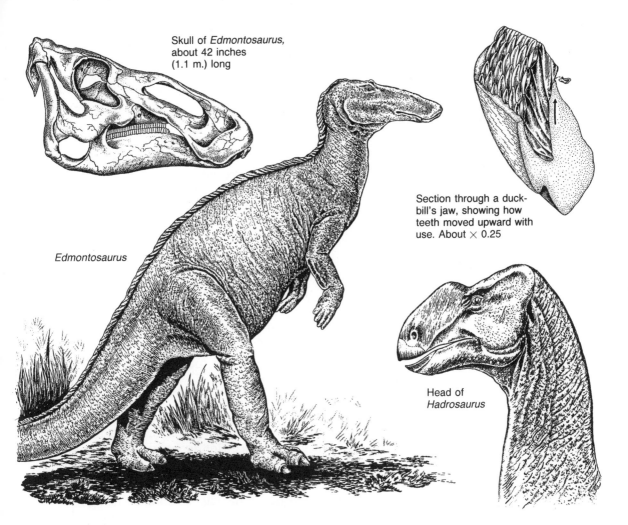

Skull of *Edmontosaurus*, about 42 inches (1.1 m.) long

Edmontosaurus

Section through a duck-bill's jaw, showing how teeth moved upward with use. About × 0.25

Head of *Hadrosaurus*

Some Cretaceous duck-billed dinosaurs of North America: **Edmontosaurus** and **Hadrosaurus**, *both 15 to 18 feet (4.6–5.5 m.) high, ranged from New Jersey to northwestern Canada*

pushed new teeth upward as old ones became worn and fell out. Though confined to the hinder part of the mouth, they numbered two hundred to five hundred per jaw, or eight hundred to two thousand in all when both right and left sides are included. About one third of these were in actual use, the remainder being reserves.

Hadrosaurs ranged from 12 to 40 feet (3.7–12.2 m.) in length, the average being about 30 feet (9.1 m.). The creatures walked in a stooping position and frequently dropped to all fours. The body was deep but not very wide, the tail was deep and narrow, and the thin, wrinkled skin was covered with platelike scales that did not overlap. There were four toes in front and three behind; the claws were blunt and shaped like hoofs; there were webs between the toes of the forefeet and probably between those of the hind.

There is no doubt that duckbills swam as well as waded, and walked on dry land. This is shown by their webbed feet and deep, narrow tails, which could be used as sculling oars. The backbone also was strengthened by heavily calcified tendons, which still allowed the muscles to swing both body and tail from side to side. These tendons are preserved in many petrified duckbills.

Remains of fruits, twigs, seeds, and pine needles in the body cavities of some hadrosaurs indicate that though they were good swimmers, some of them, at least, preferred a diet of land plants. Perhaps the ability to swim well was primarily an adaptation allowing escape from predators, rather than making it possible to live on water plants.

From the neck downward, the bodies of hadrosaurs are almost identical, but the skull is quite a different story. In general, the skull was moderately long and deep, sloped gently from back to front, and had very large openings for the nostrils. The bones surrounding these openings were thin.

Within this general pattern there was a wide variety of forms. Basically, there are two skull types: those with no crest or a solid one, and those with a hollow crest. The differences in the form of the heads were probably useful to the hadrosaurs in recognizing members of their own species, particularly during mating. A similar situation prevails in Africa today, where antelopes recognize their own kind by the form of the horns.

Hadrosaurs such as *Edmontosaurus,* from North America, had no crest at all, and *Tsintaosaurus,* from China may have had flaps of skin along the side of the face. They could be blown up like balloons, much like the inflated throat of the living boomslang lizard. Perhaps brightly colored, this made these dinosaurs look larger and more ferocious. They may have also used these flaps of skin to make a noise, much as the vocal sacs of frogs are used.

In the hollow-crested hadrosaurs, the nasal passages looped through the crest. This added volume to the nasal passages, acting as a resonating chamber when these hadrosaurs called to one another.

Hadrosaurs evolved from iguanodontids in Late Cretaceous times, when they ranged into Europe, across Asia, and through North America to South America. Their fossils are most abundant in stream-channel deposits that accumulated in eastern Asia and along the western shore of a sea that invaded North America from Texas to northern Canada.

In the badlands of the Red Deer River, near Drumheller, Alberta, Canada, part of the area where hadrosaur fossils are plentiful has been set aside as a provincial park. Many almost complete skeletons have been found, some with outlines of the flesh and impressions of the skin. These animals evidently died in the water, floated downstream, and came to rest beyond the reach of carnivores. There also are scattered bones from bodies that were pulled to pieces, probably by tyrannosaurids.

At a remarkable fossil locality in central Montana, a veritable hadrosaur nursery has been found. There the remains of eggs, juveniles, and adults of *Maiasaura* have been found clustered together. From the manner in which the fossils are arranged, it is clear that the adults provided care for the young after they hatched.

Skeleton of Tsintaosaurus, *a hadrosaur from the Late Cretaceous of the People's Republic of China. Length about 33 feet (10 m.). (Photo by Frank Coffa, courtesy of the Museum of Victoria and the Institute of Vertebrate Paleontology and Paleoanthropology, Academia Sinica, Beijing)*

Restoration of the skeleton of Tsintaosaurus, *a hadrosaur from the Late Cretaceous of the People's Republic of China. Length about 33 feet (10 m.). (Drawing by Peter Trusler, courtesy of the Museum of Victoria, Melbourne)*

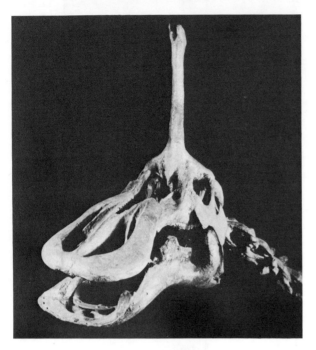

Skull of Tsintaosaurus. *Length about 50 inches (1.3 m.) (Photo by Frank Coffa, courtesy of the Institute of Vertebrate Paleontology and Paleoanthropology, Academia Sinica, Beijing, and the Museum of Victoria, Melbourne)*

Three duck-billed dinosaurs with hollow, bony crests

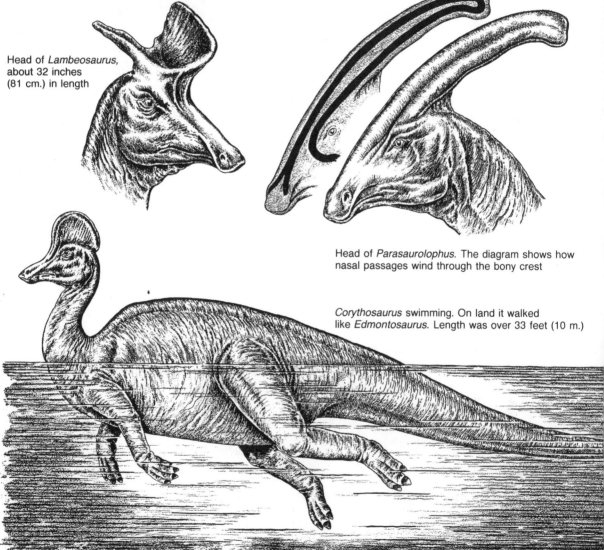

Head of *Lambeosaurus*, about 32 inches (81 cm.) in length

Head of *Parasaurolophus.* The diagram shows how nasal passages wind through the bony crest

Corythosaurus swimming. On land it walked like *Edmontosaurus.* Length was over 33 feet (10 m.)

Bone-headed Dinosaurs. These reptiles first appear in Early Cretaceous deposits of England. However, they are better known from the Late Cretaceous of western North America and eastern Asia. *Majungatholus* is known from Madagascar, which demonstrates that these dinosaurs also reached Gondwana.

Stegoceras is one of the better known boneheads. It was a harmless herbivore 5 to 6 feet (1.5–1.8 m.) long, with five short toes on each forefoot and four longer toes behind. It nipped off plants with sharp-edged teeth that came to the front of the mouth, since there was no beak. The premaxillary bones were small, but those forming the roof of the skull were solid and 3 inches (7.6 cm.) thick. There were several small spikes at the back of the head.

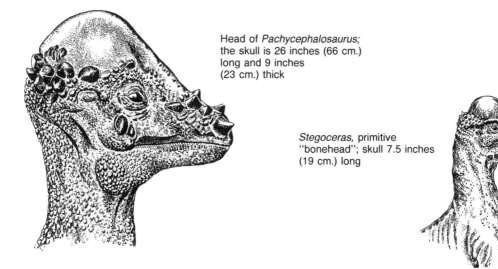

Head of *Pachycephalosaurus;* the skull is 26 inches (66 cm.) long and 9 inches (23 cm.) thick

Stegoceras, primitive "bonehead"; skull 7.5 inches (19 cm.) long

Pachycephalosaurus (the "thick-headed reptile") lived during the latest Cretaceous, when tyrannosaurids were at their zenith. Its dome-shaped skull was 26 inches (66 cm.) long and 9 inches (22.9 cm.) thick over the brain and was trimmed with both knobs and spines. Because the rest of the body was not protected, this massive skull was of no value as armor. Rather, it was probably used as a battering ram between rival males in much the same fashion that modern mountain sheep compete for females in the rutting season.

Smallest of the bone-headed dinosaurs was *Micropachycephalosaurus* (the "tiny thick-headed reptile"), which lived in China during the Late Cretaceous. It was only 20 inches (51 cm.) in length.

All of the bone-headed dinosaurs mentioned so far had dome-shaped skulls. However, *Wannanosaurus, Homalocephale,* and *Goyocephale,* from the Late Cretaceous of eastern Asia, had flat heads. Whether this was a superior kind of battering ram or just a different one is unclear.

Armor-plated and Dreadnought Dinosaurs. Two groups of ornithischians developed armor. The plate bearers (Stegosauria) appeared in the Middle Jurassic of Europe and China. They culminated in the Late Cretaceous of India with the "miniature" stegosaur *Dravidosaurus,* length only 10 feet (3 m.). When alive, *Dravidosaurus* was a "living fossil" isolated on the island continent which India was at the time. Elsewhere, the stegosaurs had become extinct by the end of the Early Cretaceous.

The best-known member of the group and one of the most familiar of all dinosaurs is *Stegosaurus,* from the Late Jurassic of North America. Full-grown specimens were 18 to 25 feet (5.5–7.6 m.) long, stood 12 to 13 feet (3.7–4.0 m.) high, and weighed 7 to 10 tons (6.4–9.1 t.). The 16-inch (41-cm.) skull was low and flat-roofed, with a well-developed beak and 90 to 100 small teeth. The body was deep but narrow; the hind legs were long, while the forelegs were short; and three of the toes on each foot ended in hoof-like appendages. The broad sides were covered with leathery skin, but two rows of bony plates ran along the neck, back, and tail, which also carried two to eight long spikes.

We picture *Stegosaurus* as a peaceful and very sluggish land dweller, too low at the shoulders to wade in deep swamps, and too lightly armored to risk encounters with carnivores such as *Allosaurus.* For those plates protected only its back, its tail made only a fair war club, and its sides were wide open to attack. In fact, the plates may not even have been for protection. Instead, they may have been used to allow *Stegosaurus* to cool off or warm up quickly by shunting its blood through a network of vessels that

Sacral (or hip) ganglion

Brain drawn on same scale as ganglion

Stegosaurus, *a Jurassic armored dinosaur of western United States; 18 to 25 feet (5.5–7.6 m.) long. This reptile is famous for its sacral ganglion, or "second brain"*

crisscrossed these plates. It probably remained among trees, whose trunks stopped the rush and deflected the jaws of predators.

Next to the sauropods, *Stegosaurus,* with a brain weighing only 2.5 ounces (70 gm.) was one of the mental lightweights of the Mesozoic. Like them, *Stegosaurus* probably carried out much of its mental activities in large ganglia between the shoulders and another one above the hips that weighed 50 ounces (1.4 kg.). This arrangement inspired Bert Leston Taylor's humorous poem *The Dinosaur,* which has become one of the classics of popular paleontology:

> Behold the mighty dinosaur,
>   Famous in prehistoric lore,
> Not only for his power and strength
>   But for his intellectual length.
> You will observe by these remains
>   The creature had two sets of brains—
> One in his head (the usual place),
>   The other at his spinal base.
> Thus he could reason "A priori"
>   As well as "A posteriori."
> No problem bothered him a bit
>   He made both head and tail of it.
> So wise was he, so wise and solemn,
>   Each thought filled just a spinal column.
> If one brain found the pressure strong
>   It passed a few ideas along.
> If something slipped his forward mind
>   'Twas rescued by the one behind.
> And if in error he was caught
>   He had a saving afterthought.
> As he thought twice before he spoke
>   He had no judgment to revoke.
> Thus he could think without congestion
>   Upon both sides of every question.
> Oh, gaze upon this model beast,
>   Defunct ten million years at least.

The Well-protected Ankylosaurs. Technically, "dreadnought" dinosaurs form the suborder Ankylosauria. Appearing in the Late Jurassic of Europe, they became broad, low-set herbivores with short, massive legs and stubby, hoof-bearing feet. One of the best-known types, *Ankylosaurus,* was 17 feet (5.2 m.) long, 6 feet (1.8 m.) wide, and a little more than 4 feet (1.2 m.) high. The 27-inch (69 cm.) skull was massive, without temporal openings; thick plates of bone overhung both eyes and nostrils and extended outward like ears. Ribs were fused tightly to the vertebrae, and the back and sides were sheathed in thick plates. Other plates covered the tail, which ended in a bony club firmly fastened to the vertebrae. The jaws were heavy, but the teeth were so small as to be almost useless.

Euoplocephalus reached a length of 18 feet (5.3 m.) and a width of 8 feet (2.4 m.); its feet were so far apart that it must have taken short, waddling steps. Its body was covered with bone-studded skin that bore bosses and spines ranging from 4 to 6 inches (10–15 cm.) in length. The tail ended in a bony knob and carried two large spines that were sheathed with horn.

Unlike *Ankylosaurus* and *Euoplocephalus, Panoplosaurus* lacked a bony club on the end of its tail. However, it made up for this by having sharp spikes along its sides. These were largest over the shoulder and curved forward upon the neck.

Some ankylosaurs have been found in windblown sand, which suggests that the animals lived among sand dunes, feeding on plants that grew in hollows or in areas marginal to the dunes. It seems more likely, however, that they spent most of their time in moist forests and swamps, where they could crawl about like enormous, rough turtles or slip and scramble over the mud. When enemies found them, they lay flat on the ground with legs tucked close to their sides and tail ready to batter any creature that touched it. Even *Tyrannosaurus* could not pierce their armor or turn them over to expose their defenseless bellies. Like modern porcupines, ankylosaurs found safety merely by keeping still. That they may have actually defended themselves in this manner is suggested by the number of tyrannosaurids that suffered broken ankles during life, possibly from a swipe by an ankylosaur's tail.

Excavation of the ankylosaur Saichania *from Late Cretaceous deposits in the People's Republic of Mongolia. Note the skull on the opposite side of the picture from the person excavating the fossil. (Photo by W. Skarzynski, courtesy of Zofia Kielan-Jaworowska, Institute of Paleobiology, Warsaw)*

Skull of Ankylosaurus, 27 inches (69 cm.) long

Panoplosaurus, with spikes on its sides. 23 feet (7 m.) long

Euoplocephalus, 18 feet (5.5 m.) long

Three armored dinosaurs of Cretaceous age, from western United States and Canada

EGGS, FRILLS, AND HORNS

In 1887, Professor O. C. Marsh of Yale described petrified horns found near Denver, Colorado, calling them *Bison alticornis.* Two years later, similar horns were found on reptile skulls. Thus, the supposed bison became a ceratopsian, or horned dinosaur.

Though these creatures were first found in North America, they probably evolved in Asia. There at least one primitive species lingered on into Late Cretaceous times in what now is the Gobi Desert. The fossils have been named *Protoceratops*—literally, "first horn-face," or "first ceratopsian."

This name is inappropriate, since *Protoceratops* rarely had a horn and was not the earliest ceratopsian. Its ancestry goes back to *Psittacosaurus* ("parrot saurian"), of the Early Cretaceous, a biped related to *Hypsilophodon.* As millions of years went by, descendants of this pioneer became quadrupeds with short tail and legs, stocky body, and a bony frill at the back of the head. The teeth were set side by side in a groove, and the upper beak became attached to a new and separate bone at the front of the upper jaw.

(Left) Psittacosaurus, *4 feet (1.2 m.) long, was a very primitive frilled dinosaur.*
(Right) Protoceratops, *5 to 6 feet (1.5–1.8 m.) long, had a frill but almost no horn*

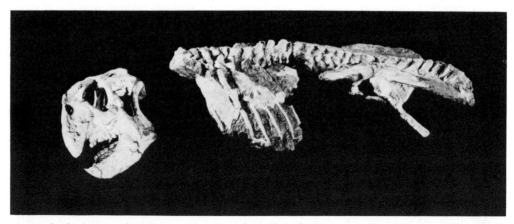

Partial skeleton of Psittacosaurus, *a bipedal dinosaur with a parrot-type beak from the Early Cretaceous of eastern Asia. Length of complete skeleton would have been about 3 feet (90 cm.). (Photo by Frank Coffa, courtesy of the Institute of Vertebrate Paleontology and Paleoanthropology, Academia Sinica, Beijing, and the Museum of Victoria, Melbourne)*

These traits survived in *Protoceratops,* a creature 5 to 6 feet (1.5–1.8 m.) in length. Its hind legs still were longer than its forelegs; it had five toes in front and behind, the frill at the back of its skull contained two very large openings, the nose was hornless, and the jaws bore hooked beaks. Two cylindrical teeth remained on each premaxillary bone.

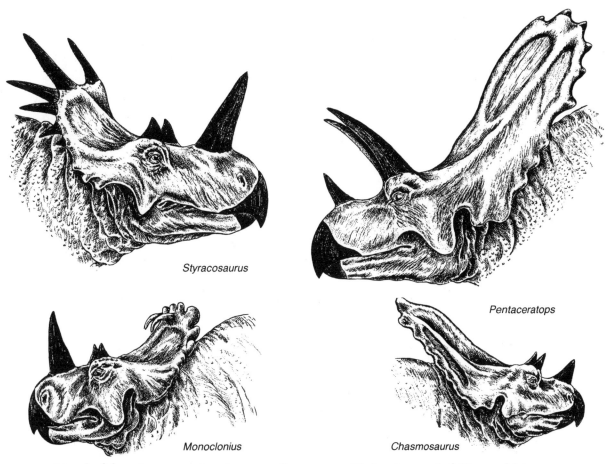

Head of four large ceratopsians, or dinosaurs with beaks, neck frills, and horns. Late Cretaceous of North America. All about × 1/30

At breeding time, the female *Protoceratops* dug a nest in loose sand and laid a dozen or more eggs about 6 inches (15 cm.) long. Sand around the eggs sometimes was soaked by heavy rains, smothering the embryos. They then were petrified, as were skeletons ranging from newly hatched youngsters to full-grown dinosaurs. They show, in unequaled detail, the development of animals that lived and died some 80 million years ago.

Ceratopsians reached North America long before *Protoceratops* laid its eggs in Mongolian sand. They also became large animals with thick bodies, drooping tails, and legs that formed upright columns. The forefeet had five toes, the hind feet four and a remnant of the fifth, and all fully developed toes bore hoofs. Horns grew on the nose and above the eyes, and the skull, with its frill, became very large. Vertebrae fused in the neck, and massive muscles attached to the base of the skull supported the heavy head. As in the "dreadnought" ankylosaurs, the ilium spread and bent outward, forming a plate above the hip joint, but the skin remained without armor.

Such was the general plan; we must now consider variations. Early in

Dinosaur egg from Cretaceous floodplain deposits in South China northwest of Canton (Guangdong Province)

their American career, the ceratopsians divided into two groups, the long-frilled and the relatively short-frilled. The former began with types that had short horns on the nose, long ones above the eyes, and openings in the frills. These characters continued to develop, reaching their zenith in such forms as *Pentaceratops* and *Torosaurus,* whose skulls were 7 feet to 8 feet 6 inches (2.1–2.6 m.) long, with 2-foot (60-cm.) horns above the eyes. The overall length of these reptiles was about 20 feet (6.1 m.).

Changes were less consistent in the short-frilled group. It began with *Monoclonius,* a deep-skulled form with a long, straight horn on its nose, shorter horns above its eyes, and knobs along its border. *Styracosaurus* turned the knobs into horn-covered spikes, but *Triceratops* reversed the trend. Its frill became solid and smooth, and the horns above its eyes were larger than the narrow one on its nose.

Triceratops marked the high point in ceratopsian progress, as well as its end. Varied species were 20 to 25 feet (6.1–7.6 m.) long and 8 to 10 feet (2.4–3.0 m.) high, and weighed 8 to perhaps 12 tons (7.3–10.9 t.). The skull was about 8 feet (2.4 m.) in length, carried 40-inch (1-m.) horns above the eyes, and sheltered a brain weighing almost 2 pounds (900 gm.), or a dozen times as much as that of *Stegosaurus.* As dinosaurs went, these creatures were abundant; one collector saw remains of about five hundred skulls during seven summers on horseback and foot in the Hell Creek Formation, of central Montana. These numbers probably are explained by a rare combination

Triceratops, *a Late Cretaceous horned dinosaur, 20 to 25 feet (6.1–7.6 m.) long. It was sometimes attacked by* **Tyrannosaurus**

of strength, armament, pugnacity, and agility. Scarred frills show that *Triceratops* often fought with its own kind, perhaps in defense of home territory and for females in the breeding season. With its sturdy legs, strong neck, and dangerous horns, *Triceratops* also could ward off attacks by carnivores or rush under the guard of their jaws and pierce their unprotected bellies. Though tyrannosaurids may not have been mental giants, they doubtless knew enough to avoid such an enemy unless they could deliver a surprise attack from the rear.

A DINOSAUR STAMPEDE

Some dinosaurs look, to our eyes, as if they were built for speed. That they could move rapidly when the occasion demanded has also been suggested by analysis of fossil footprints.

In the Middle Cretaceous, in what is now central Queensland, Australia, a mixed group of ornithopods and small theropods were drinking at the edge of a lake. There were at least 130 of them, ranging in size from a bantam chicken to an emu. Suddenly, a large theropod perhaps 8 meters (26 feet) long appeared and slowly strode toward them at about 7 kilometers per hour (4 m.p.h.). It turned to the right, and there our record of its movements ceases, as it walked out of the area where the footprints are preserved.

But, only moments later, the ornithopods and small theropods ran by, all going in the direction from which the large theropod had come. The ornithopods averaged 16 kilometers per hour (10 m.p.h.), and the small theropods 12 kilometers per hour (7 m.p.h.). Slowest were the young ones, whose tracks

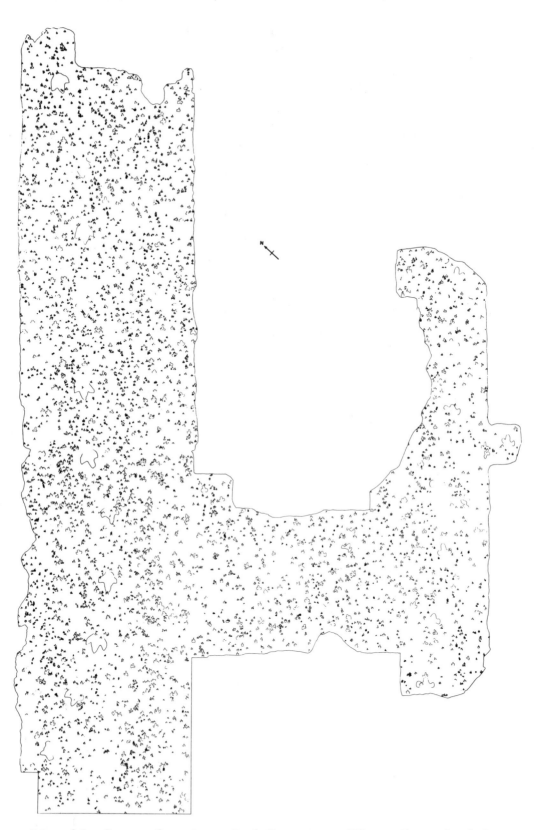

Map of the dinosaur footprints at Lark Quarry, near Winton, Queensland, Australia. These occur in the Late Cretaceous Winton Formation and were probably made by a large theropod (Tyrannosauropus), *smaller ornithopods* (Wintonopus), *and small theropods* (Skartopus). *(Courtesy of Mary Wade, Anthony Thulborn, and the Queensland Museum, Brisbane)*

were therefore the last to be laid down and are often on top of those of their elders. Apparently, in the panic of the moment, it was every dinosaur for itself. Even if adults normally protected the younger ones, in this situation it did not happen. The same thing occurs today when a herd of zebra is surprised by a lioness.

PATTERNS OF ADAPTIVE RADIATION

Dinosaurs present good examples of adaptive radiation, the process by which related animals or plants change in order to be able to live in various ways and under varied conditions. Thus, early saurischians, which were primarily meat-eating bipeds of modest size, evolved into bipedal dwarfs and gigantic hunters, four-footed plant eaters that were the largest animals to ever walk the face of the earth, and ostrichlike animals that lost their teeth and adopted an omnivorous diet. In these various ways they lived and prospered for at least 130 million years.

The ornithischians also sprang from carnivorous bipeds but became confirmed plant eaters. During the Late Jurassic and the Cretaceous periods they developed five adaptive patterns:

1. Bipedal life among forests. The forefeet generally were used to grasp food, though they could be employed in walking. These forms had no defense except to run away. *(Camptosaurus, Hypsilophodon,* iguanodontids, pachycephalosaurids, and other small, two-legged herbivores)

2. Life in forests that provided a firm footing for large, slow quadrupeds. Defense was accomplished by armor and by swinging the tail, on which spikes developed. (Stegosaurs)

3. Life in swamps, both fresh and salt water, but with frequent trips on land. Food was pulled or shoveled into the mouth by means of a beak like a duck's. Walking was done mostly on the hind legs, but a tail was used for occasional swimming. Since weapons and armor were lacking, safety was found in escape by running or swimming. (Duckbills, or hadrosaurs)

4. Life on uplands and in swamps, where broad-bodied reptiles waddled about or crept over mud. Food was cropped with horny jaws; defense was achieved with bony armor and massive, clublike tails, though broad, heavily armored creatures that merely lay still also were safe from enemies. ("Dreadnought" ankylosaurs)

5. Active life on openly wooded lowlands amid deltas and swamp habitats much like the lifestyle of the living rhinoceros. For defense there was armor (the frill) and horns, behind which was the power of an 8-to-12-ton (7.3–10.9 t.) body. The horns also were used in fights between the dinosaurs themselves. (Large ceratopsians)

WERE THE DINOSAURS WARM-BLOODED?

For many years it was customary to regard the dinosaurs as large, slow, dull-witted reptiles that were finally displaced by the small, quick, intelligent mammals. Then a group of scientists began to question this picture. Eventually, some began to think of dinosaurs as having been large, agile reptiles, perhaps warm-blooded. Maybe they would still dominate the earth if it were not for some fortuitous event that caused their extinction and allowed the mammals to evolve and take their place.

As a result of this debate, many serious attempts were made to reconstruct what dinosaurs were like as once-living animals. It has become apparent that dinosaurs had a whole range of adaptations and that it is no more possible to generalize about their mode of life than it is about all mammals or all reptiles.

Some dinosaurs were probably not very intelligent. Sauropods, for example, have a brain only about one fifth as big as would be expected for reptiles of their size. On the other hand, the brain of the small theropod *Stenonychosaurus* was almost six times as big as to be expected of a reptile its size and just large enough to be within the range of a bird or mammal its size.

To be warm-blooded, an animal requires about ten times as much food per day as a cold-blooded one. So, though increased activity is a benefit of being warm-blooded, there is a price to be paid. In the case of sauropods, with their small heads and relatively weak teeth, there probably would not have been enough hours in the day to eat enough to keep themselves going as warm-blooded animals. Another difficulty for the largest sauropods, paradoxically, would have been getting rid of the excess heat. Whales the same size are able to do this, but whales live in water, which is much more efficient than air in transferring heat. Actually, sauropods are almost ideally suited to be cold-blooded. As large as they were, they would not have cooled down significantly during the day/night temperature cycle. So, if by basking in the sun over several days they managed to raise their temperature to a level at which they could be active, this level could be maintained without the input of such large quantities of food.

If the circumstantial evidence strongly suggests that sauropods were cold-blooded, an equally convincing case can be made that at least some of the small carnivorous dinosaurs were warm-blooded. We know today that birds are warm-blooded. It seems likely that the earliest flying birds must have been warm-blooded, for flight requires a high metabolism. Birds arose from small theropods, so unless it just happened that in the generation in which the two groups split, warm-bloodedness was acquired by birds, it seems likely that some small theropods, too, were warm-blooded.

GIANTS VERSUS DWARFS

We have traced the history of the dinosaurs during the Late Triassic, Jurassic, and Cretaceous periods, which totaled about 165 million years. During those ages, several families and larger groups evolved into giants while others remained modest in size or even became dwarfs. What advantages did good-sized reptiles gain by growing larger, and what penalties did they incur? How did their little relatives profit, and what did they lose as their size decreased?

The penalties of giantism have been stressed in articles, books, and even animated cartoons. One of these is size itself; the big animal must constantly struggle against its own bulk and the downward pull of gravity. We have seen how these factors forced the great sauropods to develop complex vertebrae and massive limbs to support their weight. On dry land, such monsters as *Albertosaurus* and *Tyrannosaurus* may have approached the limits to which ligaments could keep the body together and muscles could propel tons of blood, flesh, and bone fast enough to capture food.

Food—enough food—posed another problem. A big animal eats more than a small one, be it herbivore or carnivore, fish, mammal, or reptile. Today such large creatures as elephants and tigers cannot dwell on small islands: they contain too little food to support a breeding population. Similarly, great sauropods could not inhabit small forests, nor could hordes of them exist in large ones. Large theropods always were fewer than their prey, and each one probably had a home range which it defended against invaders. Instinct prompted it to do so, but the basis of that instinct was the need for nourishment.

Such were the penalties for size, but it also brought advantages, especially to herbivores. The really big animal is always relatively free from attack, no matter how dull it is or how poor its defenses. No large theropod would have been so stupidly overconfident as to attack a full-grown *Apatosaurus* or *Diplodocus,* and even as allosaur probably looked twice before attacking one of those creatures. The allosaur itself had no known enemies, except possibly fellow allosaurs, once it had reached its full growth, and the tyrannosaurids were equally secure.

Even the need for food had its favorable side. True, a 30-ton (25-t.) dinosaur needed more food than one weighing 55 pounds (25 kg.), but not a thousand times as much. The cost of living for a great sauropod, therefore, was much less than that for an equal weight of Triassic dinosaurs. At the same time, the sauropod gained the advantages of size and a long lifespan, which probably exceeded that of any modern reptile.

Finally, as explained above, comes the matter of heat. By their great size, large dinosaurs could maintain a nearly even temperature. For them, there probably was no slowing down at night, no stiffening in cool air, no retirement during chilly periods. However sluggish their ways may have been, they could live at an almost uniform rate.

This advantage also worked in reverse. Accustomed to stress, the effects of cold, we forget that modern reptiles are equally sensitive to heat. They estivate in summer months, hide from the hot midday sun, and may die after surprisingly short exposure to it. But the great dinosaurs, with small surface area in proportion to their bulk, absorbed a minimum of sunshine and thus reduced its effects.

The gains and losses of dwarfism are those of large size reversed. The dwarf is not burdened by weight; it lives actively with a modest framework and prospers in places out of bounds for big animals. It also thrives on very little food relative to its larger kin, which means that it does not need an extensive home range and is seldom beyond reach of a mate. On the other hand, it may be killed by all except mature giants, whose very size makes them indifferent to small fry. Its consumption of food is relatively high, which forces it to compete with creatures of similar needs. Its lifespan is almost sure to be short: a few years against decades or even centuries. Finally, no dwarf can keep a uniform temperature or live at a uniform rate. It may live rapidly—for a reptile—when conditions are right, but it must slow down when the weather grows cool, and take shelter from too much heat and sunshine.

We need not and cannot weigh these advantages and penalties. All we can say with assurance is that one set let certain dinosaurs prosper as giants, while the other allowed some of their kin to remain small or evolve into dwarfs. It means nothing that giants are common and small forms scarce, for the former stood a much better chance of becoming fossils. It also is not significant that the giants died out and were replaced by smaller reptiles, for some of those forthwith became large. The process did not stop until the Cretaceous Period ended—and then the dinosaurs vanished, with only the birds as their descendants.

THE PUZZLE OF EXTINCTION

For over a century, paleontologists have been aware that dinosaurs became extinct relatively quickly at the end of the Mesozoic. Many ideas have been advanced to explain this. Some thought that the climate became too hot, others that it became too cold. Still other ideas were that the brainier mammals living alongside the dinosaurs somehow were able to slay their large but stupid contemporaries.

It should first be remembered that the dinosaurs were not the only group to become extinct at the end of the Mesozoic. Pterosaurs disappeared from the skies, plesiosaurs and mosasaurs vanished from the sea. In addition, among invertebrates, the ammonites, and inoceramid and rudist bivalves became extinct, as did the bulk of genera and species in several groups such as brachiopods, bryozoans, coccoliths, and pelagic foraminiferans. Thus the extinction of the dinosaurs was not an isolated event but part of a more widespread phenomenon.

To explain why all of these extinctions occurred at the same time is a challenge. Toward the end of the Cretaceous, the climate did become somewhat cooler, though you and I would have considered places like Alberta, Canada, as an outdoor greenhouse even in winter. In addition, the sea level dropped, causing a decrease in the amount of area of shallow seas over the world. Out of these facts, one theory has been proposed that the chemistry of the ocean changed as greater amounts of sediment washed into the sea. A change in the amount of trace elements, some of them biological poisons, may have been responsible for the decline of many different marine organisms, particularly the smaller ones that form plankton. With their extinction, the animals that fed upon them soon suffered, and in turn the animals that preyed upon the animals that preyed upon the plankton became extinct as well.

Another theory is that with the decrease in temperature, land near the north pole became unsuitable for the dinosaurs. There, unencumbered by dinosaur predation, the mammals were able to evolve and become larger. As the climate cooled, this community of mammals began to spread toward the equator, displacing the dinosaurs.

With the use of very sensitive chemical techniques, it is clear that in many places where sedimentary rocks were deposited during latest Cretaceous and earliest Tertiary times, there is an unusually high concentration of iridium at the boundary between the two periods. Rare on earth, iridium, one of the platinum metals, is found in much higher concentrations in meteorites. To explain this unusually high level of iridium, it has been suggested that a large meteor, perhaps 10 kilometers (6 mi.) in diameter, struck the earth at the very end of the Cretaceous.

Exactly how this would have caused extinctions except for the unfortunate individuals near the site of impact is uncertain, but it may have been because dust thrown up would have obscured the sun. This would mean that photosynthesis would have ceased for a few months to a few years, killing adult plants but not necessarily their seeds. Without a luxuriant growth of plant life for a few years, only those herbivores capable of surviving by hunting out scattered individual seeds or leaves would be able to survive. This would rule out the large herbivores, for only smaller ones can gain enough nourishment by locating food in this way to make it worthwhile in terms of the energy required for the search. (An elephant would starve if it tried to live like a mouse, by finding seeds.) In addition, the temperature would have become much lower.

Another effect of such an impact may have been a momentary heating of the atmosphere that made conditions unsuitable for organisms unable to find temporary refuge.

Comets have been described as "dirty snowballs," because they are formed of frozen water, carbon dioxide, ammonia, and methane. As the sun is approached, these substances melt and vaporize, forming the spectacular tail of the comet. Impacting on earth, all the substances in a comet would vaporize, including any poisons such as ammonia. The instantaneous release of a large quantity of poisonous compounds could have brought about extinctions.

"What if?" can often lead to interesting speculations about alternative history or prehistory. What if Kaiser Wilhelm II had had a normal birth and grown up without his withered arm? Would World War I had been avoided? What would our world be like today? Similarly, what if the dinosaurs had survived the events at the end of the Cretaceous? One scientist has speculated that out of the small carnivorous dinosaurs might have arisen an intelligent biped. We shall never know, but it is fun to think about.

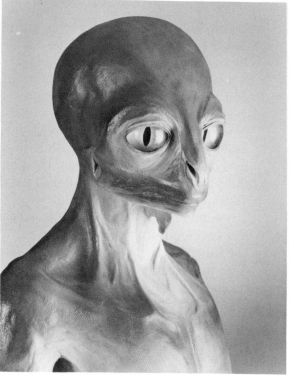

An intriguing hypothesis, based on an idea of Dale Russell, as to what a small, highly intelligent dinosaur might have looked like had these reptiles not become extinct at the end of the Mesozoic Era. Here, the dinosauroid is in the foreground, with Stenonychosaurus inequalis, *a man-sized theropod dinosaur, alongside (Courtesy of D. Russell)*

Close-up of the head of dinosauroid (Courtesy of D. Russell)

CHAPTER XXIX

Flying and Gliding Reptiles

While Late Triassic and Jurassic dinosaurs were becoming giants, two other innovations appeared in the reptilian world. Certain archosaurs developed warm blood and wings, and took to the air. On some, feathers appeared; these became the birds. On others, hair developed; these became the pterosaurs.

THE WINGED PTEROSAURS

The first fossil of a flying reptile was found in the same Jurassic limestones that contain insects, prawns, and well-preserved jellyfish. In 1784, a specimen was described briefly as "one of those vertebrated animals which in olden times inhabited the sea." In 1809 it was restudied by the great French anatomist Cuvier, who probably knew more about bones than any other man then living. He realized that the fossil was a winged reptile and called it *Pterodactylus,* or "wing finger." The group to which it belonged is now termed the Pterosauria.

We compare pterosaurs with birds; yet they really looked and acted like no other vertebrates. All had short bodies and large, bony heads, with brains expanded in the region devoted to sight, and sclerotic plates in the eyes. Tails were either long or short; the wings were skin on a framework of bone. Large wing bones were hollow and filled with air, and a wide breastbone (sternum) furnished attachment for the muscles used in flight. Although long suspected, good evidence for the presence of hair on the bodies of pterosaurs had to await the discovery of *Sordes,* a rhamphorhynchoid the size of a pigeon, from Late Jurassic deposits in Kazakhstan, U.S.S.R.

Like bones in the wings of bats and birds, those of the pterosaurs had once been forelegs and "hands." We can trace humerus, radius, and ulna; shoulder, elbow, and wrist. Old books even describe five digits: a greatly elongated "little finger" supporting most of the wing, three short fingers tipped with claws, and a rudimentary thumb. It now seems that this "thumb" was only a hardened tendon, that the "little finger" was the fourth, and that the fifth finger had been lost as pterosaurs evolved.

Long-tailed Pterosaurs.   Tails, toes, and teeth divide flying reptiles into two contrasting groups. The older of these was characterized by a long tail, five-toed feet, and teeth that generally were well developed though they might not be numerous. Fossils have been found in Late Triassic and Jurassic rocks.

Dimorphodon lived during the Early Jurassic. As might be expected in one of the earliest long-tailed pterosaurs, it was quite primitive. Though the skull was light, with three large openings on each side, the snout was not elongated as typical of all later pterosaurs. In addition, the teeth were quite similar to those of an unspecialized thecodont, rather than specialized in any one of the several ways common among pterosaurs.

Rhamphorhynchus, one of the last and more advanced long-tailed pterosaurs, lived during the Late Jurassic. With an elongated snout and large, sharp, curved teeth, it was well adapted to catching fish. The slender tail ended in an upright flap of skin that probably served as a rudder during flight.

Rhamphorhynchus *(left) was an advanced long-tailed pterosaur about 24 inches (61 cm.) long.* Dimorphodon *(right) had a deep but very light skull and reached a length of 42 inches (107 cm.). Both lived in Europe during the Jurassic Period*

Short-tailed Pterosaurs.   These reptiles apparently descended from long-tails, though their exact ancestor is unknown. In their evolution, progress meant reduction of the tail to a stub, shrinking or loss of the fifth hind toe, and teeth that first became slender and numerous but finally gave way to beaks. The group appeared during the Late Jurassic and died out before the Cretaceous Period closed.

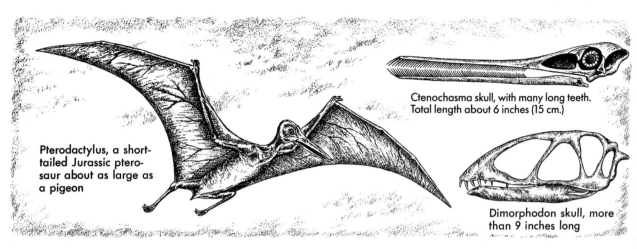

Ctenochasma skull, with many long teeth. Total length about 6 inches (15 cm.)

Pterodactylus, a short-tailed Jurassic ptero-saur about as large as a pigeon

Dimorphodon skull, more than 9 inches long

Flying reptiles with a variety of tooth types

Ctenochasma, from the German Jurassic, was a primitive and beakless short-tail with a head about 6 inches (15 cm.) long. The teeth were almost as slender as bristles, and the hinder part of the skull had lost several bones. In *Pterodactylus* this loss was obscured; though bones that had vanished did not reappear, those that remained expanded over the missing portions. Teeth were lacking from the back of the jaws, and a beak apparently was present.

About two dozen species of *Pterodactylus* ranged from Africa to northern Europe during the Late Jurassic and Early Cretaceous. Though some species weighed as much as a goose, others were not much larger than an English sparrow.

As short-tailed pterosaurs evolved, they increased the spread of their wings. The Late Cretaceous *Nyctosaurus,* for example, combined a body about as large as a pigeon's with wings broader than those of an eagle. Even it was outdone by *Pteranodon,* which ranged from Kansas to Europe and probably around the world. *Pteranodon's* wings, which spread 22 to 27 feet (6.7–8.2 m.), supported a body 20 inches (51 cm.) long (excluding head and tail) that weighed 20 to 25 pounds (9-11 kg.). The neck was longer than the body, and the skull measured 45 to 75 inches (114–191 cm.), depending on

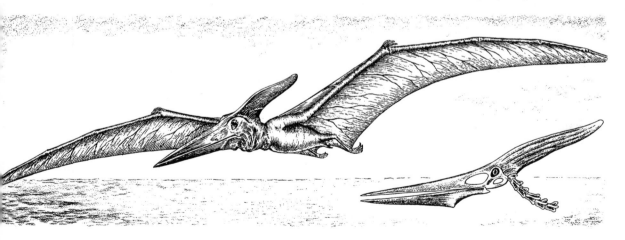

Pteranodon *and its skull. This short-tailed, toothless Cretaceous pterosaur from Kansas had a wingspread of 22 to 27 feet (6.7–8.2 m.)*

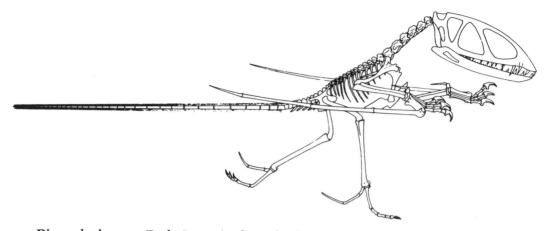

Dimorphodon, *an Early Jurassic rhamphorhynchoid from Europe. Skull length 20 centimeters (8 in.). (Photograph by Steven Morton, from Kevin Padian)*

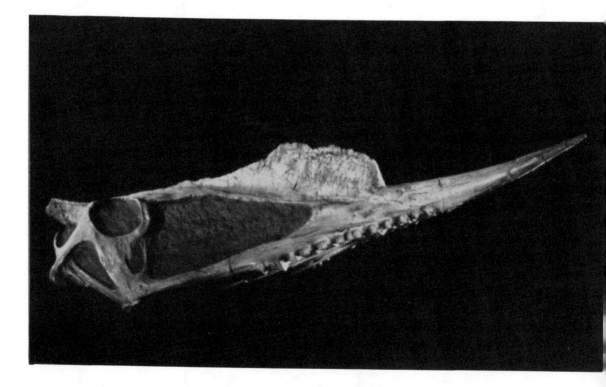

Skull of Dzungaripterus, *a primitive pterodactyloid retaining teeth at the rear of the jaws. Skull length 41 centimeters (16 in.) and wing span 3.5 meters (11 ft. 6 in.). Found in Late Jurassic or Early Cretaceous deposits of Xinjiang, China. (Photographed by Frank Coffa, courtesy of the Institute of Vertebrate Paleontology and Paleoanthropology, Beijing, China, and the Museum of Victoria, Australia)*

whether or not a bony crest balanced the 3-foot (0.9-m.) beak. The lower jaw was deeply indented, making room for a large pouch in which food was stored until it could be swallowed and digested.

As might be expected, *Quetzalcoatlus,* the largest known pterosaur, or, for that matter, the largest organism yet discovered that ever flew, was found in Texas. Unfortunately it is known only from fragments of the head, wing, and vertebral column. However, enough has been found to strongly suggest that the wingspan was 11 to 12 meters (36–39 ft.) and, when alive, the animal weighed 86 kilograms (189 lbs.).

Among the more peculiar pterosaurs was *Dsungaripterus,* from the Early Cretaceous of Xinjiang, China. It had a crest not at the back of its head, as in *Pteranodon,* but, rather, above its eyes. In addition, the snout and lower jaw both turned upward.

Even more unusual was *Pterodaustro,* from the Late Jurassic or Early Cretaceous of San Luis Province, Argentina. In the lower jaw were long, needle-like teeth. So fine were these teeth that there were about twenty-four of them per centimeter (60 per in.), and they were probably flexible as well. Perhaps *Pterodaustro* used these unusual teeth much as a black skimmer does today, flying along just above the surface of shallow water, dipping its lower jaw into the water and scooping up small fish. Though the black skimmer does not have true teeth, it does have a comblike structure, in each of its lower jaws, which functions to hold the prey it catches.

Habits of Winged Reptiles. Old books show pterosaurs as living much like bats, being hardly able to walk and almost helpless when on the ground, unable to fly until they managed to scramble up a tree to launch themselves into the air. Frequently, they were shown as hanging upside down from beneath tree limbs or in caves, as bats often do today.

More recently, however, it has been realized that pterosaurs were more birdlike than batlike in their habits. Unlike bats', their hind legs were not joined to the wing membrane. Rather, unencumbered by such wing attachments, pterosaurs were quite capable of walking about on their hind legs. Some even had webbed feet. The arrangement of the flight muscles was similar to that of birds, rather than bats, and pterosaurs probably could launch themselves into the air without difficulty from either land or water.

Pterosaurs hunted by sight, not by smell, for brain casts show that the centers of sight, the optic lobes of the brain, were greatly enlarged, while those of smell had dwindled. Small species may have eaten insects, snapping them up in flight or as they alighted on trees. Large pterosaurs ate both fish and aquatic invertebrates. Remains of food not yet damaged by digestion have been found near the throat of *Pteranodon,* where its capacious pouch once dangled. Others may even have been scavengers, taking advantage of a large quantity of protein available in rotting dinosaur carcasses.

Pterosaurs of Jurassic Germany lived on islands and wooded shores, within easy reach of the sea. *Pteranodon* also roosted close to the sea, and strong winds sometimes drove it as much as a hundred miles from shore. Other winged reptiles probably lived near and hunted over lakes in which fish were plentiful.

Two dangers confronted pterosaurs, little as well as big. First came the threat of being eaten by larger winged reptiles as they soared and by mosasaurs or plesiosaurs as they swooped to catch fish or invertebrates. Next came the menace of torn wings. To strengthen and stiffen the wing membrane, there was a meshwork of fibers within the skin that also prevented the spreading of any tear that got started.

GLIDING LIZARDS

Twenty to thirty million years before the first pterosaurs flew, another group of reptiles, the lizards, took to the air. However, they did so in a much more modest way. Rather than developing wings by modifying the forelimbs, the ribs on these lizards expanded to support a membrane that enabled them to glide from tree to tree.

These lizards are known only from the Triassic of New Jersey *(Icarosaurus)* and the Permian to Jurassic of England *(Kuehneosaurus, Kuehneosuchus)*. Apparently only a few different flying lizards evolved, and they disappeared without descendants. One hundred ninety million years later, another lizard has developed that is also capable of doing much the same thing. This is the living *Draco,* or gliding lizard, of eastern Asia.

CHAPTER XXX

Birds, Inventors of the Feather

Only birds have feathers, and this is the single feature that all creatures classified as birds possess. Feathers are remarkable structures that were probably derived from highly modified reptilian scales. They are good insulators, which help the bird retain body heat. When lubricated with oil from the gland at the base of the bird's tail, they provide shelter from wetting. Perhaps most important, they provide lightweight structures that form the main part of a bird's wing and tail, necessary for flight. Flight, of course, is the hallmark of birds, despite the fact that a few have become flightless after having gone through a flying phase.

THE BEGINNING OF BIRDS

The Late Jurassic limestone in which the flying reptile *Pterodactylus* was discovered also contains another vertebrate called *Archaeopteryx.* The first specimen of this interesting vertebrate, a single feather, was found in August of 1861. A feathered, but headless, skeleton appeared one month later, and yet another, complete with skull, was dug up in 1877. Though the first was named *Archaeopteryx* and the second *Archaeornis,* both apparently belong to the same genus.

Archaeopteryx, meaning "ancient wing," is the oldest known creature that had feathers. Six specimens are now known, including the original feather. The other five fossils are partial skeletons, some of which preserve the impressions of feathers. *Archaeopteryx* is known *only* from the 150-million-year-old lagoonal sediments in southern Germany. It has taken more than one hundred years to find even these few, prized specimens. Had it not been for the feathers, however, *Archaeopteryx* might well have been classified as a reptile, and not a bird, especially at the time it was first discovered.

In *Archaeopteryx* the braincase is enlarged (thus indicating that its brain, too, was much enlarged over its reptilian ancestors'), and the sutures between individual bones in the skull are nearly fused. But, in most other features, this crow-sized extinct animal is much more like a small running

491

Archaeopteryx *preparing to flap its wings and glide from a cycad. Length about 18 inches (46 cm.)*

Archaeopteryx lithographica. *Late Jurassic, Eichstätt, West Germany. (Photo by Frank Coffa, courtesy of the Museum of Victoria, Melbourne, and Dr. P. Wohl)*

dinosaur. For instance, the bony axis of the tail was long like small theropod dinosaurs', not extremely reduced with several vertebrae fused together like the bones in the tails of modern birds.

The bones of *Archaeopteryx* were solid, not hollow as in most birds. The jaws had many small conical teeth set in sockets, and the sternum, or breast-bone, was not enlarged as it is in birds, in which it serves as an attachment for the supracoracoidius muscles, which pull the wing upward after the power stroke. In modern birds, only a small area on the sternum actually serves as an attachment for the pectoralis muscles, which provide the power stroke of the wing. Additionally, the general shapes and proportions of the limb bones resemble much more those of tiny theropod dinosaurs than anything else.

John Ostrom, a dinosaur specialist at Yale University, has studied *Archaeopteryx* quite thoroughly and concluded that its ancestors must have been theropod dinosaurs. Not every paleontologist would agree, some claiming the ancestors were closer to crocodiles or bird-hipped, rather than lizard-hipped, dinosaurs. Still, the evidence that Ostrom presents in favor of a theropod ancestry is very compelling.

Whether *Archaeopteryx* flew, glided, or simply ran is yet a controversial subject. The asymmetry of its primary wing feathers suggests that it may have been an active flier. In living birds that fly, primary feathers are definitely asymmetric; that is, the vanes on either side of the main shaft of the feather are not of equal area. This gives the wing better aerodynamic qualities and helps increase lift when the bird is flying. Alan Feduccia and Storrs Olson, both paleontologists who study birds in the United States, have further pointed out that the structure of the shoulder girdle (the scapula and the wishbone, or furcula, which is unique to birds) provides all the elements that are needed for powered flight.

TOOTHED CRETACEOUS BIRDS

Archaeopteryx was an experiment that was successful for a time and then was replaced by vertebrates more similar to living birds. By the middle of the Cretaceous Period, birds with many of the skeletal specializations of modern birds were present. *Hesperornis* ("western bird"), known best from the rocks left behind by the great inland sea that cut North America in half during the Cretaceous, is a good example. The Niobrara Chalk, of Kansas and surrounding states, has produced a number of partial skeletons of *Hesperornis,* and bones have been found as far north as the Canadian Arctic. The shapes of the bones closely resemble those of modern birds. But *Hesperornis* still had teeth, and its bones were thick-walled, because it was a diving bird. Just as a human diver needs weights on his belt to allow him to sink through the water, so did *Hesperornis*. Flight being unnecessary, its wings

Toothed birds of the Late Cretaceous. (Left) Icthyornis; *(right)* Hesperornis. *Other restorations of* Hesperornis *depict it as a noncrested form with webbed, rather than lobed, toes*

An Early Cretaceous feather from Koonwarra, Victoria, Australia. Length about one-half inch (1 cm.). The feather occurs in 110-million-year-old rocks, demonstrating that birds were widespread early in their recorded history. (Photo by Frank Coffa, courtesy of the Museum of Victoria, Melbourne)

were greatly reduced. Some forms reached more than 5 feet (1.5 m.) in length, and were among the larger carnivores in the shallow inland seas of the time.

Hesperornis is only one of as many as thirteen kinds of hesperornithiform birds, which were distributed worldwide. One freshwater form has even been recovered from the Late Cretaceous of South Dakota, though most were restricted to a marine environment. They paralleled loons and grebes in their body form and lifestyle but may not have been related at all.

The same rocks that produced *Hesperornis* yielded a small, flying toothed bird, *Icthyornis* ("fish bird"). *Icthyornis* had a large keel on its sternum, unlike *Hesperornis,* and probably led a successful life as an airborne carnivore over the Cretaceous seas, at least in North America.

Cave deposits in France of Eocene and Oligocene age have produced a rich collection of fossil birds. This locality in Quercy is one of the best known. (Photo courtesy of Bernard Sigé and Cécile Mourer-Chauvire)

One of the Plotopteridae, penguinlike birds related to the pelicans. Penguins are known from the Southern Hemisphere. The plotopterids occurred only in the Northern Hemisphere, developed from a different bird group from the penguins, but had a similar lifestyle. This specimen is from marine sediments of middle Tertiary age in Japan. Fossils in this family are known from the North Pacific and represent medium-to-large-penguin-sized birds. (Photo courtesy of Y. Hasagawa)

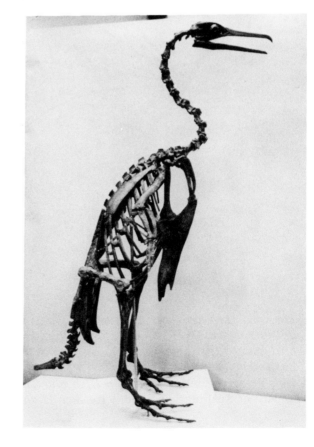

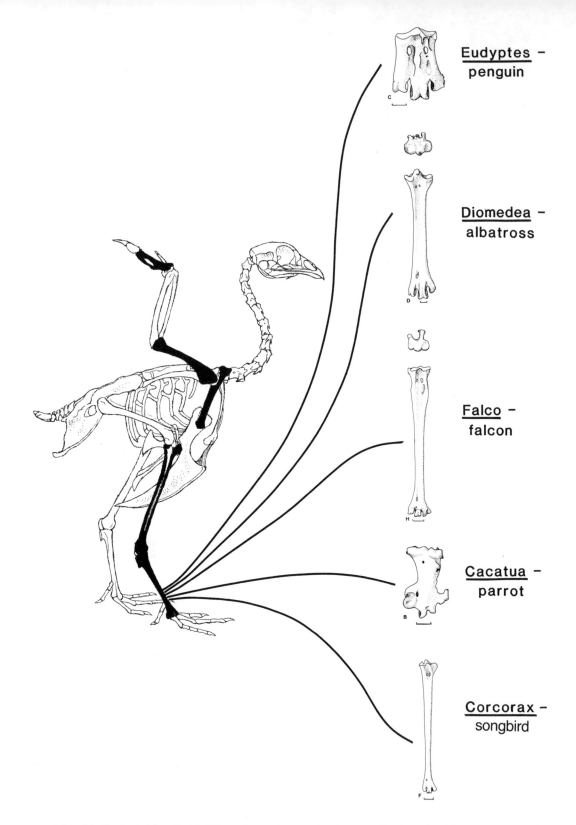

Eudyptes –
penguin

Diomedea –
albatross

Falco –
falcon

Cacatua –
parrot

Corcorax –
songbird

The bird skeleton (left) illustrates the main bones (in black) important to the paleontologist. A variety of tarsometatarsi show some of the differences between bird groups. The tarsometatarsus is frequently preserved as a fossil and often can be used to determine the family, or identify even more precisely if the specimen is well preserved. (Modified from Rich and Thompson, 1982, The Fossil Vertebrate Record of Australasia.) *Scale = 0.4 inch (1 cm.)*

CENOZOIC "FLYING MACHINES"

By the end of the Cretaceous, toothed birds had disappeared. The birds that characterize the Cenozoic Period share many similarities that are correlated with their flying lifestyle, even though some may have become secondarily flightless. In order to be an efficient flier, it is important to have a lightweight, but sturdy, skeleton. So the skeleton of birds has become lighter by the loss of teeth, the hollowing out of bones, the shortening of the tail from several elongate vertebrae to a few very short ones, and the fusion of many vertebrae into the pygostyle, onto which the tail feathers attach. The tail feathers, themselves very lightweight structures, serve for balance and maneuvering in flight, just as a long, bony tail does in flying reptiles—but is, of course, much lighter. Several other bones in the wing and hind leg have been fused to reduce weight yet retain strength.

Further strength is afforded the bird skeleton, especially in the chest region, by bone fusion and the development of the little uncinate processes on the ribs. The process of one rib touches the rib behind and prevents the chest cavity from collapsing during flight. This protects the vital organs of the bird such as the heart and lungs, when the powerful forces produced by flight are exerted on this area. The fusion of certain bones in the wing and the construction of the joints ensure the efficiency of movement, thus cutting down on the energy loss during the extremely vigorous exercise of flight.

All these characteristics of birds make them unique. Thus, the paleontologist studying even single bones can often identify them as birds and even what kind of bird, and often what sort of lifestyle that bird led. Some bones are more useful than others. One bone in the leg is especially useful, the tarsometatarsus, generally missing in the skeleton of a chicken bought at the butcher's. It is the bone "bodyward," or proximal, of the foot. It is a fusion of a part of the tarsals and metatarsals of the foot, though from the outside it looks like a part of the leg. It is most important as a fossil, because it is a very solid bone and thus often preserved. It is also a very complex bone with many recognizable features, which makes identification even of a fragment of this bone often possible.

Based mostly on bone fragments, the record of birds during the Early Cenozoic is one reflecting evolutionary experiments and continued modernization. The birds of this time are generally intermediate in structure between the families of birds we know today. If you could go bird watching in the Paleocene or Eocene, you might not be able, for instance, to easily place the birds you saw in a modern family.

One such bird known from Eocene deposits in southern Wyoming and Utah is *Presbyornis*. *Presbyornis* was a mosaic, a jigsaw, of characters now possessed by shorebirds (such as sandpipers), ducks, and flamingoes. *Presbyornis* was a long-limbed wading bird whose skull was very ducklike;

its wing was shorebirdlike, its hind limb was intermediate between those of shorebirds and of flamingoes; and it had a specialized hinge between two bones of the skull that was very flamingolike. So, where could you place *Presbyornis* in your bird book of the Eocene? Intermediate between many of the groups we know today, of course. It is intermediate forms like *Presbyornis* that allow some insight into the family trees of birds and give us some idea of what major groups of birds are related.

Birds of the Early Cenozoic differed from modern ones in other ways too. Certain groups of birds that are unimportant in numbers today, such as the crane-like birds (Gruiformes), were much more diverse in the Paleocene and Eocene. Some of these birds terrorized the mammals of the time. *Diatryma*, in North America, and its counterpart in Europe, *Gastornis,* were swift-running, large, carnivorous birds. Their wings were reduced to small stumps, and their huge legs bore terrible claws that could easily grasp the small horses *(Hyracotherium)* of the time. Both birds had a large, narrow, deep beak with a sizable hook on the end of it, such as eagles possess; the head was nearly as large as that of a modern horse.

Skull of *Phororhacos longissimus,* from the Early Miocene (Santacruzean) of Argentina, about 27 inches (70 cm.) long. (Photograph courtesy of Rosendo Pascual, La Plata Museum Argentina)

Diatryma, a flightless Eocene bird from Wyoming, about 7 feet (2.1 m.) in height

Restoration of the head of *Argentavis magnificeus,* from the Late Miocene (Huayquerian) of Argentina, about 27 inches (70 cm.) in length. (Photograph courtesy of Rosendo Pascual)

Gruiform birds from the Cenozoic of the New World

Footprints of birds from the Eocene Green River Formation, of Utah, about 1 to 1.5 inches (2.5–3.8 cm.) across. Many water birds, including Presbyornis, *lived in and around the large lakes that spread across Wyoming, Utah, and Colorado at this time*

Protoplotus beauforti, *a Tertiary bird related to pelicans, cormorants, and anhingas, from lake deposits in southern Sumatra. (Reconstruction by Peter Trusler)*

Restoration of one of the bony-toothed or false-toothed birds, Pseudodontornis, *which had an estimated 15-foot (4.5-m.) wingspread. Relatives of this form first appeared during the Eocene and survived until the Pliocene. This form is from New Zealand. (Courtesy of Shell New Zealand)*

In South America, a related group, the phororhacids, radiated widely in the Cenozoic, remaining among the prime carnivores during all that time. When terrestrial vertebrates crossed the Middle American land bridge, one of these forms, *Titanus,* evidently made the trip north, for a gigantic toe bone of a phororhacoid has been found in Pleistocene deposits of Florida.

In addition to the crane-like birds and their relatives, the shorebirds (Charadriiformes) were diverse, especially flamingolike forms such as *Presbyornis.* Fowl-like birds (Galliformes) and owls (Strigiformes) were more diverse than they are today.

Some groups that existed at this time left no living kin. One such is the bony-toothed, or false-toothed, birds (the pseudodontorns) known from several parts of the world including North America and New Zealand. Though these giant relatives of pelicans and cormorants had no true teeth, they developed a series of bony outgrowths of the jaws that functioned as teeth, probably making them excellent surface fishers. Among the largest flying birds ever known, they survived from the Eocene into the Pliocene.

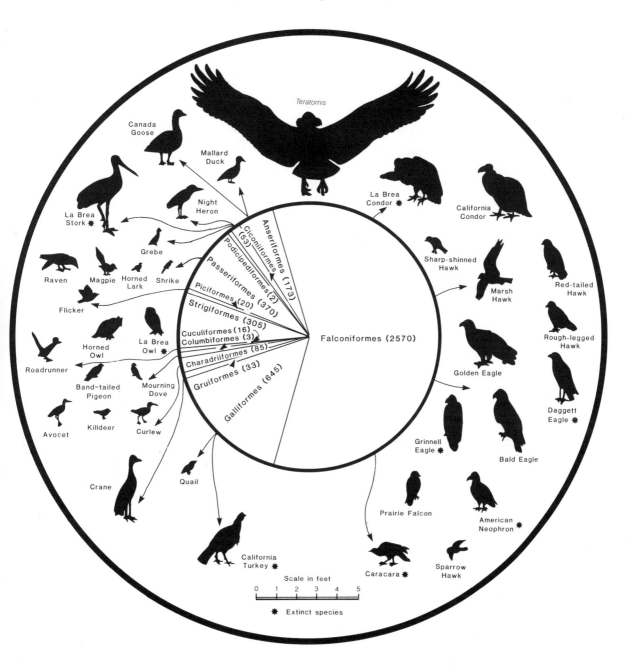

Relative abundances of different groups of birds collected from the Rancho La Brea tar pits, of Pleistocene age. Carnivorous birds and scavengers have a much greater abundance as fossils in these ancient tar seep deposits than they do in natural populations, because they were trapped as they preyed on other animals. This clearly shows how the fossil record is biased, not always a clear reflection of the true abundance of the animals that existed at the time the fossil animals lived. (Based on work of Hildegarde Howard; drawn by Draga Gelt)

A WORLD WITHOUT SONG

Some groups of birds that are so noticeable and numerous today didn't even exist in the early part of the Cenozoic. There were no songbirds (Passeriformes) before the Oligocene. So, there would have been no caw of the crow or morning chorus of the meadowlark in the Eocene. Instead, a whole variety of little perching birds, among them the primobucconids, distant relatives of the woodpeckers and puffbirds, occupied the space now held by the songbirds. When the songbirds did finally appear, they were tremendously successful, radiating into hundreds of forms. Today they make up more than half of the nine thousand species of birds known.

VERY MODERN BIRDS

By the beginning of the Miocene, about 22 million years ago, birds very like the ones of today began to appear in the fossil record. These fossils still did not belong to living species, but were closely related. Some of the archaic birds of the Early Cenozoic were still present, such as the false-toothed birds and the flamingolike palaelodids. But, for the most part, the birds were primitive types in modern families and genera.

Modern *species* of birds began to appear in the Late Pliocene. By the beginning of the Pleistocene, some 1.8 million years ago, many living species existed. The Ice Age birds were a mixture of living and extinct species. Our fossil record of birds for this time period is better than for any previous time —and so the number of kinds of birds is much higher than for any previous time. This is probably just a result of the good record, however, and not a true reflection of how many more species existed in the Pleistocene than in the past, or, for that matter, the present.

By the end of the Pleistocene, some ten thousand years ago, a number of groups that had survived from the earlier Cenozoic into the Pleistocene had become extinct—such as the giant mihirungs (Dromornithidae), of Australia; most of the moas (Dinornithiformes), of New Zealand; and most of the elephant birds (Aepyornithiformes), of Madagascar. Many avian groups had produced truly gigantic forms in the Pleistocene, such as the giant megapodes *(Progura),* of Australia, and the gargantuan vulturelike *Teratornis,* of the New World. By the end of the Pleistocene these giants, too, were gone. The question is still open concerning what or who caused their extinction—climate and/or mankind?

MOAS, MIHIRUNGS, AND OTHER FLIGHTLESS BIRDS

Ostriches, cassowaries, rheas, and kiwis belong to a varied group of birds called ratites, though paleognaths is a preferable name. Some of its members

Raphus, *a restoration of the extinct dodo, from Mauritius. Related to the pigeons, the dodo had reduced wing bones, enlarged leg bones, a greatly reduced keel of the breastbone—all correlated with its loss of flight. (Courtesy of the American Museum of Natural History, New York)*

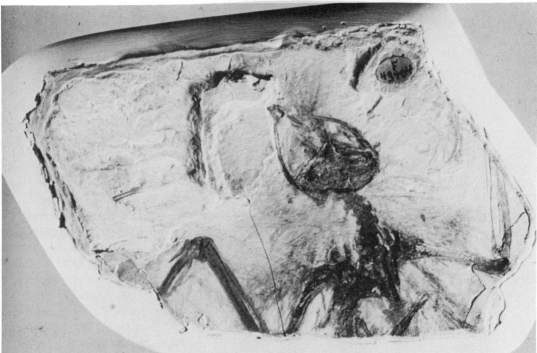

Skeleton of Quipollornis, *the oldest owlet-nightjar, from Miocene lake deposits in New South Wales, Australia. It is unusual in being so complete, even preserving feather impressions, and in being well dated. Soon after the bird died, a lava flow covered the lake; these volcanic rocks have now been dated using a radioactive-decay technique (13.7–17 million years). Skull length is about 1.6 inches (4 cm.). Typical of birds that lived in Miocene times, it belonged to a modern family but was primitive within that group. (Photo by Frank Coffa, courtesy of the Museum of Victoria, Melbourne)*

Neophrontops americanus, *from the Quaternary tar seeps of Rancho La Brea, California. This vulturine bird belongs in a group quite distinct from the true New World vultures, such as the turkey vulture (Cathartes aura),* which is similar in size to N. americanus, *the American Neophron. (Courtesy of the Los Angeles County Museum of Natural History)*

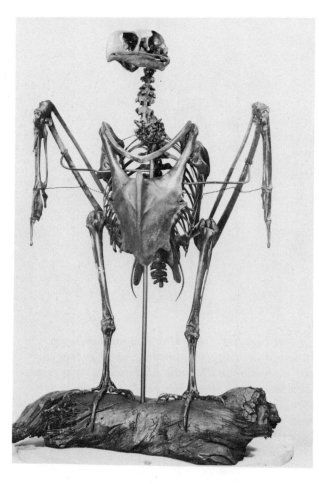

Teratornis merriami, *from the Quaternary tar seeps of Rancho La Brea. This bird weighed about 31 pounds (14 kg.) and had a wingspan reaching nearly 13 feet (4 m.). Its near relative Argentavis, from South America, may have reached 176 pound (80 kg.) and had a wingspan of 20 to 26 feet (6–8 m.), truly the largest flying bird ever known. (Courtesy of the Los Angeles County Museum of Natural History)*

Shandongornis shanwanensis, a quail-like bird skeleton from Miocene deposits in Shandong Province, central China. Thousands of skeletons of vertebrates and plants were preserved in the fine lake deposits laid down in a volcanic caldera. (Courtesy of the Institute of Vertebrate Paleontology and Paleoanthropology, Academia Sinica, Beijing)

The Cuban Pleistocene owls in the genus Ornimegalonyx *are the largest owls known. Classified as a typical, or strigid, owl,* Ornimegalonyx *had small wings and a reduced sternum, or breastbone—all signs of reduced flying power. Here the owl is shown attacking a 2-foot (60-cm.) long* Solenodon, *a Cuban insectivore. (Reconstruction by Peter Trusler)*

were and are small, such as the kiwi, but others became some of the largest birds that ever lived. Interesting too, these birds seem to have a distribution on fragments of old Gondwana. The kiwis and moas live in New Zealand, the rheas in South America, the ostriches in Africa, Europe, and Asia, and the cassowaries and emus in Australia. Another possible ratite group is the elephant birds, of Madagascar. The disjointed distribution of the ratites could be explained by an ancestral form, which perhaps resembled the South and Central American tinamous, once living over much of Gondwana. As the supercontinent began to break up, parts of this ancestral population may have been isolated in South America, Africa, Madagascar, Australia, and New Zealand. These populations then could have followed their own evolutionary pathway to produce the several kinds of ratites that we know today, both living and extinct.

All of the ratites have greatly reduced their wings, as compared to their flying ancestors, in response to a life on the land, not in the air. Most are omnivores, and their foods vary widely. The kiwi, however, has specialized by feeding on worms and insects. It, like the unrelated woodcock (a shorebird), has a long bill able to flex delicately at the tip, so that it can grasp food underground. It also has a very keen sense of smell, which, together with its good hearing, is used in finding food.

Not all scientists agree that ratites are closely related. The mihirungs, for

Two species of Aepyornis, *9 to 10 feet (2.7–3 m.) or more high. At the left are foot bones and eggs of the larger species. The black dot is a hen's egg on the same scale.*

example, may be more closely related to fowl-like birds. It will be some time before the relationships of these birds are clearly understood.

Aepyornis and Its Kin. *Aepyornis* gives its name to an order, the "elephant birds," of Madagascar. Though a few bone fragments from North Africa have been called elephant birds, as have eggshell fragments from the Canary Islands, in the Atlantic Ocean, only the fossils from Madagascar are unquestionably part of this group.

Aepyornis ("lofty bird") reached a height of about 8 feet (2.4 m.), which means that the largest species was no taller than the modern ostrich. "Heavy bird" would have been a better name, for a broad body and massive legs brought the weight to about 1,000 pounds (450 kg.), in contrast to 350 pounds (160 kg.) for an ostrich. In one species, the drumstick was 25 inches (64 cm.) long, 18 inches (46 cm.) around at its broad, upper end, and 6 inches (15 cm.) wide near its middle. The thighbone was shorter, but thicker; its girth was made possible, perhaps, by the fact that it was somewhat hollow. Eggs were in keeping with the leg bones; they reached 12 to 13 inches (30 to 33 cm.) in length, and their capacity was about two American gallons (7.3 l.). Long after the last *Aepyornis* died, people dug eggshells from swamps and used them for bowls or jugs. The first ones to be seen by Europeans were brought to a trading post as receptcles for rum. Later, they were trade items sometimes carried to the far corners of the world by sea captains.

Moas, the "Terrible Birds." While *Aepyornis* prospered and died in Madagascar, another group of feathered giants went through a similar history in New Zealand.

This second group was made up of the moas, whose technical name (Di-

Pyramid Valley Swamp, on South Island, New Zealand. The remains of literally thousands of moas still lie buried here, and many hundreds have been recovered.

Long-legged and short-legged moas of postglacial New Zealand. The tallest may have stood more than 12 feet (3.6 m.)

nornithiformes) may be roughly translated as "terrible birds." Actually they were herbivores, probably eating a variety of plants. They had little means of offense or defense except to use their powerful legs either to kick or to run.

The oldest moa remains lie in clays on South Island. The age of the clays has been estimated at about 3–4 million years, sometime in the Pliocene. These oldest moas were not giants, unlike many of the younger Pleistocene forms such as *Dinornis*. Though the entire record of the moas is restricted to this short time span, it was probably very much longer, perhaps as long as 80 million years. New Zealand broke away from the rest of Gondwana about that time, and it is likely that it took the ancestors of the moas with it. Eighty million years of isolation could have produced the variety of forms known. But also adding to this diversity were the several sea-level rises and falls in the Cenozoic. These resulted in New Zealand being divided into a series of several islands with changing sizes, shapes, and numbers through time.

Remains of moas preserved in dry caves show that the head and most of the neck of some moas were nearly naked, like those of the emu. The scythe-edged beaks and stomach contents of several moas suggest that many of the birds were browsers, though some may have grazed as well. Heights ranged from 7 to more than 10 feet (2.1–3.0 m.), weights to more than 500 pounds (225 kg.), and shapes from graceful, long-legged creatures to barrel-bodied birds whose short legs were thickly encased in flesh. Feathers were thin and silky, very like those of the down on young birds. Like those of the emu and the cassowary, and the kiwi, each feather had two shafts, not one main shaft as have the rhea and the ostrich. Colors of feathers ranged from brown or chestnut tipped with white to black and white, like the plumage of a Plymouth Rock hen.

Moas are very often found as fossils in swamps, such as that in Pyramid Valley, North Canterbury, on the South Island of New Zealand, estimated to contain at least eight hundred skeletons per acre. Skeletons are found often with the limbs oriented vertically in the black, greasy muds, evidently in the position they died in after becoming bogged in ancient swamps. Often associated with the skeletons are piles of stones—gastroliths, or gizzard stones—that moas had picked up and stored in their "upper stomach" to help grind the leaves and twigs that made up a large part of their diet. Some of the best specimens, however, come from the dry caves that have over the years produced three specimens worthy of dissection (the skin, muscles, and feathers have been preserved). Further study will perhaps give some clues as to just

Skeleton showing gastroliths (stomach stones) found inside the skeleton. The tarsometatarsi, the leg bones in the bottom of the figure, are about 1.2 inches (3 cm.) long

how closely related this extinct group is to other living and fossil groups. Studies also underway on the basic building block of bones, collagen, in moas and other ratites, may also allow comparisons of members of this group to one another and to other birds.

Mihirungs, Probably Not Ratites. Moas and elephant birds were large, but probably the largest of all birds, certainly by weight, was *Dromornis stirtoni,* from Late Miocene sediments of central Australia. *D. stirtoni* probably stood more than 10 feet (3.0 m.) tall and weighed more than 1,000 pounds (450 kg.). It was one of at least eight species of mihirungs (Dromornithidae), which came in a variety of sizes ranging from about emu-sized to the largest of birds.

The mihirungs were unique in having little, hoof-like terminal toe bones and in having a highly reduced inner toe, approaching the condition in ostriches, in which that toe has been completely lost. The quadrate, a small bone that connects the upper and lower jaws in birds, however, tells the most interesting tale. It is not like that of the rest of the ratites at all. It, instead, is similar to that of fowl-like birds such as the pheasants, turkeys, and megapodes. It may be that an ancestral fowl-like bird was also isolated in Australia, just as was the ancestor of the Australian ratites, the cassowaries and emus.

The mihirungs remained varied through the Miocene and then dwindled to

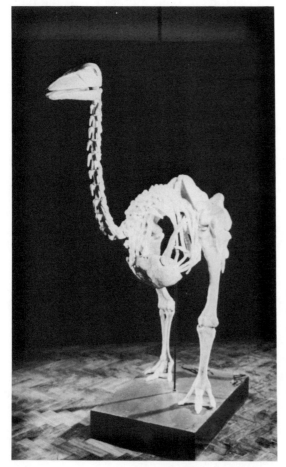

Genyornis newtoni, *a cast of a dromornithid bird, a mihirung, from Pleistocene lake muds of Lake Callabonna, South Australia. The bird stood about 6 feet (1.8 m.) high (Courtesy of the Museum of Victoria, Melbourne)*

Reconstruction of Genyornis newtoni. *A relative of this bird,* Dromornis stirtoni, *from the Miocene of Australia, was probably the largest bird that ever lived, standing more than 12 feet (3.6 m.) high. (Drawing by F. Knight, courtesy of the Museum of Victoria and Pioneer Design Studio)*

The lower and upper jaws of Genyornis newtoni, *showing the depth of the lower element so typical of mihirungs*

511

The base of this Pleistocene sinkhole has been breached by the sea on the Isle of Pines, New Caledonia. The limestone being chipped away contained the remains of a giant mound builder, several rails, some now extinct, and a variety of other birds unknown in New Caledonia today

Ancient dune deposits on Norfolk Island, in the southwestern Pacific Ocean, have produced large collections of seabirds that lived on that island before and after the arrival of Polynesian man. Fires lighted by man probably led to the extinction of some birds on Norfolk, and Europeans later caused the extinction of others

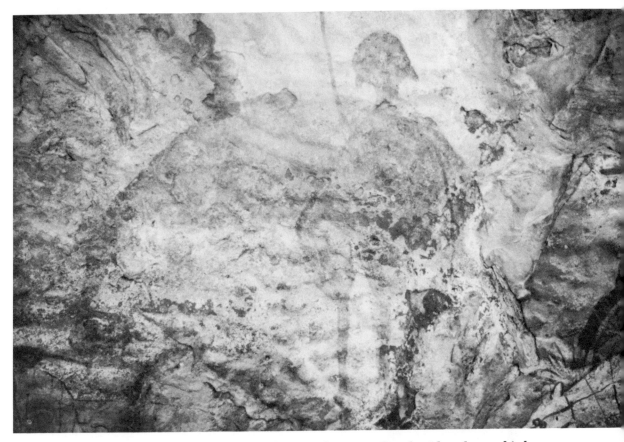

Rock painting of a mythical humanlike Quinkan standing beside a larger bird from the Cape York Peninsula, Queensland, Australia. It is decidedly larger than the living emu and may represent an extinct mihirung, Genyornis. *(Photo by Xenia Dennett, courtesy of Percy Trezise)*

one species by the Pleistocene. The youngest dated member of this group comes from a twenty-six-thousand-year-old swamp deposit at Lancefield, in southeastern Australia. Here it overlaps in time with man for at least ten thousand years. Perhaps man and climatic change together brought about the demise of this group. Many species were probably confined to the forested environments that characterized much of Australia until the Pliocene. As these were reduced when Australia began drying out, and as grasslands spread, some species of mihirungs evidently moved into the grassland environs, such as *Ilbandornis,* which had elongate hind legs and gracile proportions that typify open-grassland cursorial (running) animals. But on those grasslands there already lived a variety of kangaroos. The mihirungs may have lost the competitive battle when they met these "bounders," which led to extinction.

Paleontologist bird. The nest of a Kittlitz's sand plover (Charadrius pecuarius) *in the floor of the Chemfos Phosphate Mine, Langebaanweg, South Africa, is built of fossil bones (of birds, reptiles, and mammals). Usually this bird uses twigs, pebbles, and dung for its nest. Vertebrate fossils are so abundant here (more than ten thousand bird bones alone have been identified), in the Early Pliocene Varswater Formation, that they form a very convenient nesting material. Man may not have been the first fossil collector! (Photograph courtesy of Brett Hendey, South African Museum, Cape Town)*

An unusual "fossil." Recent spring deposits hardened this bird's nest and eggs, a rare chance of preserving such remains. This specimen is in the American Museum of Natural History, New York. Scale is in 0.4-inch (1-cm.) divisions

Fossils sometimes serve as items of interest for stamp collectors. Ornimegalonyx *appears in this stamp from Cuba. (Courtesy of Óscar Arredondo)*

A SUMMATION

Birds are a very distinct group of vertebrates in possessing feathers. Though probably first favored because they provided insulation for a warm-blooded animal, feathers proved to be lightweight, strong structures that were ideally preadapted for flight. Birds took to the air and utilized space that had previously been successfully invaded only by the insects and the pterosaurs in large numbers. Some birds returned to the ground, such as the ostrich and the emu, and some to the water, such as the penguins. The real success of the group, however, is still tied to the air, where birds reign supreme among the vertebrate animals.

CHAPTER XXXI

Hairy Reptiles with Complex Ears: the Early Mammals

 While winged saurians flew and flightless birds swam, members of another group remained small and obscure. They had done so, indeed, since the Late Triassic, hiding in trees and thickets to escape carnivorous reptiles and feeding mainly at night. So they occupied a niche not used by most other animals and slowly evolved as minor members of the land community of vertebrates.

FROM REPTILE TO MAMMAL

We sometimes call these creatures "beasts"; more often we say "animals" in a tone that tries to set them aside from the rest of the animal kingdom. The correct term, however, is *mammals.* It is the only word in English that fits all creatures having hair, warm blood, and glands that secrete milk as food for young ones. With a few exceptions, the young are born instead of emerging from eggs.

Changes in Bones and Teeth. These special characters are found in soft parts and generally cannot be traced in fossils. But some mammalian hard parts, such as bones and teeth, also differ from those of typical reptiles. The braincase, for example, is much larger than in reptiles, accommodating a brain whose "thought centers," or cerebral hemispheres, were steadily increasing in size. The old bar or plate behind each eye opening (orbit) was lost, though mammals such as monkeys and horses have replaced it with a new one.

The external nostrils occupy a single opening (naris) in the skull. The internal nares moved to the back of the mouth, and a new, or secondary, palate was developed. Though this arrangement reminds us of the palate in crocodiles, the mammalian structure has a different origin and allows breathing while the animal eats. Each side of the lower jaw contains only one bone, the dentary, and the teeth are of several sorts, adapted to such varied tasks as nipping, slashing, cutting, and grinding. The molar teeth at

516

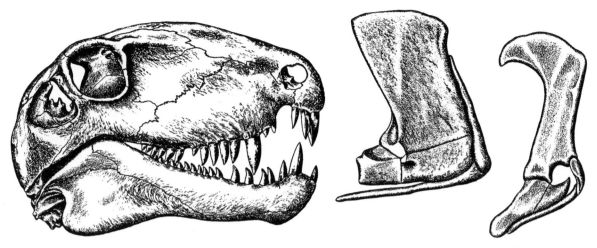

(Left) skull of the pelycosaur **Dimetrodon,** *with the varied teeth that show relationship to mammals; length 13 inches (33 cm.). (Center) shoulder girdle of a mammal-like reptile; and shoulder girdle of a mammal (right)*

the rear of the tooth row develop two or more roots. The single ball-and-socket joint, the occipital condyle, connecting skull with backbone in reptiles, is, in mammals, divided into two parts, or condyles, one of which lies on each side of the spinal nerve cord.

Other new features are typical of the mammal skeleton. The shoulder girdle is much narrower than it is in reptiles and commonly loses two bones. The uppermost bone in the hip girdle slants forward, and a large opening occurs below the hip joint. Both the thigh bone (femur) and upper "arm" bone (humerus) are longer and more slender than those of typical reptiles, and the head of the femur is at one side, rather than at the end of the shaft. This, as well as new locations for attachment of muscles, is related to changes in the way the legs move. Those of mammals are held close to the body and are pulled backward and forward instead of sprawling sidewise in typical reptilian style.

Links between Reptiles and Mammals. In Chapter XXV we traced the history of the synapsid reptiles. The oldest synapsids are among the earliest reptiles, appearing in the Late Carboniferous along with the cotylosaurs, the generalized group out of which all other reptiles were derived. Most primitive of the synapsids were the pelycosaurs. During the course of their history, some groups became decidedly mammal-like. In the Middle and Late Permian, pelycosaurs were displaced by therapsids. Within therapsids were groups that continued to develop features increasingly like those of mammals until, in the Late Triassic, the earliest true mammals first appeared.

THE EARLIEST MAMMALS

Mammals may have evolved only once, from a single reptilian ancestor. However, the relationships of the several primitive mammalian groups to

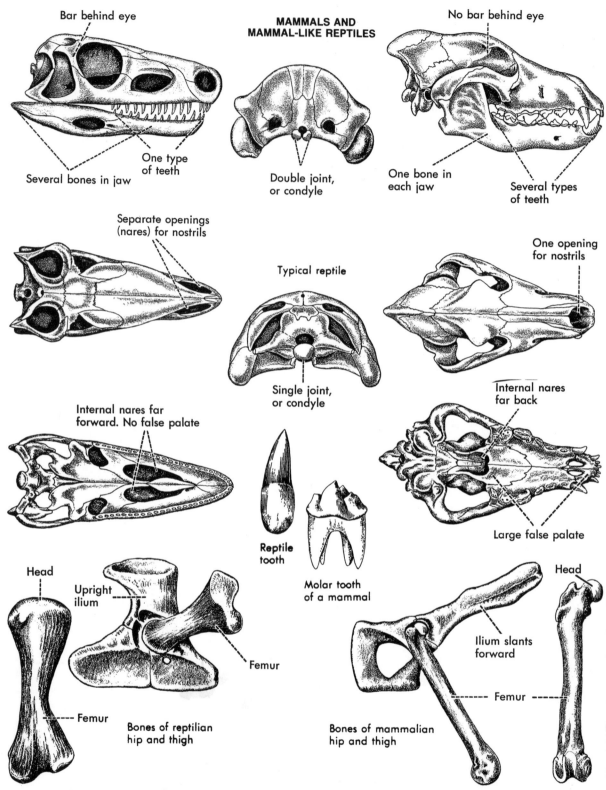

STRUCTURES IN TYPICAL REPTILES

Bar behind eye

One type of teeth

Several bones in jaw

Separate openings (nares) for nostrils

Internal nares far forward. No false palate

Head

Upright ilium

Femur

Femur

Bones of reptilian hip and thigh

MAMMALS AND MAMMAL-LIKE REPTILES

Double joint, or condyle

Typical reptile

Single joint, or condyle

Reptile tooth

Molar tooth of a mammal

STRUCTURES IN TYPICAL MAMMALS

No bar behind eye

One bone in each jaw

Several types of teeth

One opening for nostrils

Internal nares far back

Large false palate

Head

Ilium slants forward

Femur

Bones of mammalian hip and thigh

A comparison of skulls, bones, and teeth in typical reptiles, mammal-like reptiles, and mammals

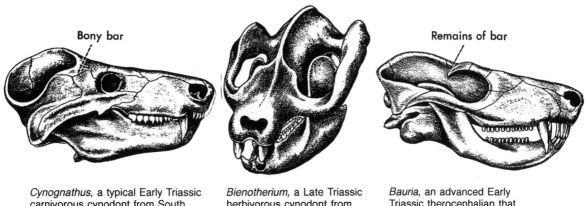

Cynognathus, a typical Early Triassic carnivorous cynodont from South Africa, which had a broad bar of bone behind the eye. Length 30 centimeters (12 in.)

Bienotherium, a Late Triassic herbivorous cynodont from China, with no trace of a bar behind the eye. Length 13 centimeters (5 in.)

Bauria, an advanced Early Triassic therocephalian that had lost part of the bar behind the eye. Length 5 inches (13 cm.)

Three therapsids with varying development of a bar of bone behind the eye

one another are uncertain, and there is the possibility that various reptilian groups gave rise to various mammalian groups.

The most primitive mammals.   In the Late Triassic of Lesotho, in southern Africa; Western Europe; Arizona; and Yunnan Province, China, the morganucodontids appeared. These, the most primitive known mammals, had evolved to the point where the major contact between the lower jaw and the skull was between the dentary and the squamosal bones. Other small bones still remained in the lower jaw, but they were no longer of great importance in the chewing process. Because several bones were still involved in the jaw, however, this meant that the specialized middle ear of mammals had not yet developed. The articular and the quadrate bones, which in morganucodontids were involved in jaw articulation, later became the malleus and incus bones, in the ear, important in refined hearing ability.

These early mammals resembled living shrews. Like the shrews, they were small, active predators searching at night through the leaf litter for insects and grubs, the mainstay of their diet. Active hunting for their food was necessary, because, being warm-blooded, they probably required about their own weight in food two or three times a day.

Despite their superficial shrewlike appearance, the morganucodontids retained many primitive features besides those of the jaws. For example, the acetabulum, in the pelvis of morganucodontids, into which the head of the femur, or thighbone, fits, has a broad notch, just like in therapsid reptiles. In more advanced mammals, the notch is closed with a wall of bone. Also, the brain of morganucodontids was smaller, and the area devoted to the sense of smell was less developed than in similar-sized modern shrews.

Morganucodontids are the oldest and most primitive of the triconodontans. During the Jurassic and Cretaceous, this group became more advanced, reducing the bones in the lower jaw to only the dentary. The name "triconodont" means "three-cusped tooth" and refers to the fact that, typi-

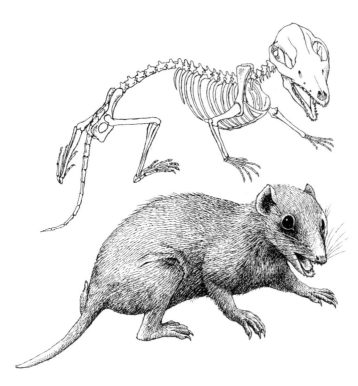

Megazostrodon, *a Late Triassic triconodont from Lesotho, southern Africa. Length about 6 inches (15 cm.) (Drawing by Frank Knight modified from one by F. Jenkins and F. R. Parrington)*

cally, the cheek teeth of these animals have three prominent cusps in a line from front to back. Most triconodontans were small, shrew-sized animals. One of the largest Mesozoic mammals, however, was a Cretaceous triconodontan about the size of a house cat.

Out of the triconodontans or forms close to them evolved a number of other mammalian groups during the Jurassic and Cretaceous. Some of these became extinct before the end of the Mesozoic, while others evolved into mammals that live today, including ourselves.

Docodonts were a group of rat-sized, omnivorous mammals known only from Middle and Late Jurassic rocks. Though there are not many kinds of docodonts, they were successful enough to have spread between the western United States and Western Europe. As the best records of Middle and Late Jurassic mammals are confined to those two areas, we cannot safely assume that docodonts were not more widespread or, for that matter, more varied. We need much more fossil material before we can say such with any conviction.

Multituberculates, another early mammal group, arose in the Late Jurassic and lived on into the Early Oligocene. During that time, they became widespread over the entire Northern Hemisphere and evolved into a great variety of forms. Some were the size of mice, while others grew to be as large as a modern beaver.

The name of the group refers to the many cusps arranged in rows on the molar teeth, a condition very similar to that of the tritylodont cynodonts, to

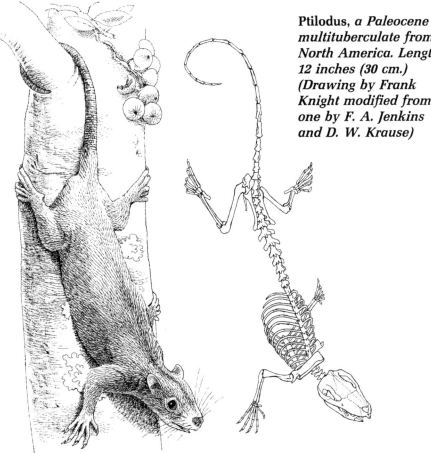

Ptilodus, *a Paleocene multituberculate from North America. Length 12 inches (30 cm.) (Drawing by Frank Knight modified from one by F. A. Jenkins and D. W. Krause)*

which they were once thought to be closely related. The skulls of multituberculates were flattened and wide. With powerful incisors, their diet and mode of life was probably quite similar to that of rodents. Their extinction occurred shortly after the appearance and early radiation of the rodents and may have been caused by competition between the two groups.

The egg-laying monotremes of Australia are the most primitive living mammals. There are only two types, the water-dwelling duck-billed platypus and the ant-eating echidna. These are about as different from one another as an otter and a hedgehog, which suggests that there must have been a large number of intermediate forms that are now extinct. Prior to the Pleistocene, however, the record of monotremes is extremely meager: only a few bones and teeth from the Miocene and a single jaw from the Early Cretaceous. The Miocene monotreme, *Obdurodon,* is clearly a platypus but differs from the living ones in having well-developed teeth, rather than being essentially toothless like a modern adult. *Steropodon,* an Early Cretaceous monotreme from Australia, has teeth much like those of *Obdurodon* but with much simpler roots. It might be a platypus or something intermediate between this group and the echidnas.

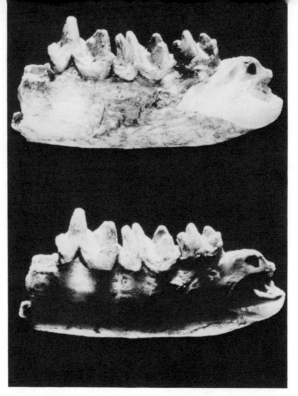

The opalized jaw of Steropodon, *from the Early Cretaceous opal field at Lightning Ridge, New South Wales, Australia. The bottom picture was taken using reflected light; in the top picture, the light is shining through the specimen from behind. (Photo by John Fields and courtesy of the Australian Museum, Sydney)*

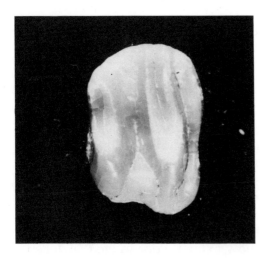

An enameled upper tooth of **Obdurodon,** *the second-oldest known platypus, from Middle Miocene rocks of northern South Australia. Today adult platypuses have no teeth, and in juveniles only dentine forms their short-lived teeth. Horizontal length 0.25 inch (6.5 mm.). (Photo by Frank Coffa, courtesy of the Museum of Victoria, Melbourne)*

When the Mesozoic fossil record of Australia becomes better known, it is quite likely that there will be a wide variety of these primitive mammals. Similarities in the form of the braincase and microstructure of the teeth of multituberculates and monotremes suggest the two groups may be closely related. Primitive, unspecialized therians first appeared in the Late Triassic in some of the same deposits in the Mendip Hills, near Bristol, England, where morganucodontids have been found. It is this group which gave rise to the marsupials and placental mammals sometime during the Cretaceous.

Though they remained small in size during the Mesozoic, this is not to say that they did not evolve. As in the tricondodontans, all but one of the bones were eliminated from the lower jaw. Two of these former bones of the jaw became incorporated into the chain of three little bones that link the eardrum to the nerves for hearing. The articular and the quadrate of the reptile became the malleus and the incus, respectively, of mammals, and both were linked to the old reptilian ear bone, the columella—or stapes in mammals.

This new development in the mammals was presumably related to increased hearing acuity. And since most early mammals were small, nocturnal animals, better hearing would have been an advantage in both avoiding predators and finding prey.

Unlike the triconodontans, however, the teeth allowed much more efficient chewing of food by means of a complex pattern of interlocking cusps on the upper and lower molars. These changes did not occur in a single direction, however. There was much "experimentation" during Mesozoic times.

The most primitive therian lower cheek teeth were essentially simple triangular pillars (the trigonids) that had slicing edges. As the group evolved, a basin (the talonid) developed on the lower molars, into which a new cusp (the protocone), on the upper molars, pounded, pulverizing and crushing food. Among therians that evolved into marsupials and placentals, the crushing basin was added behind the slicing pillar during the Late Jurassic and Early Cretaceous. But a Middle or Late Jurassic jaw of *Shuotherium* found in Sichuan, China, has the basin in front of the pillar. All therians with talonids behind the trigonids are put in the yangotheres, and *Shuotherium* has been placed in a group called the yinotheres (reflection beasts), as their teeth are the mirror image. The names derive from the Chinese concept of yin and yang, the idea of the inevitability of the interlocking and reflection of opposites.

With the development of teeth efficient at both cutting and pounding food, therians were able to radiate into the myriad of forms known to us as marsupials and placentals, with a broad range of diets.

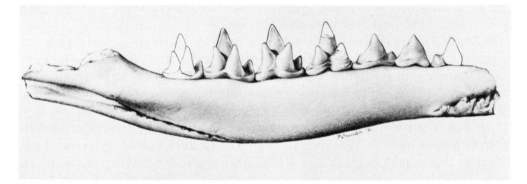

Lower jaw of **Shuotherium,** *a shrew-sized mammal with "backward" lower molars, from the Middle to Late Jurassic of Sichuan, People's Republic of China. Length of jaw 0.5 inch (12 mm.). (Drawing by Peter Trusler)*

The Rise of Marsupials. Generalized therians evolved into marsupials somewhere on the four continents of Australia, Antarctica, and South and North America. Later, they spread to the other continents. The oldest records of marsupials are Late Cretaceous fossils from both of the Americas. But their absence from the Antarctic and Australian records of that age may be related to the lack of discovery rather than that they were not originally there. Some advanced features common to all Australian marsupials and unknown in almost all American ones imply that marsupials migrated from South America across Antarctica to Australia, rather than in the reverse direction. This would have occurred by the end of the Cretaceous or in the earliest Cenozoic, before Australia separated from Antarctica (and therefore South America) and began moving northward toward Asia.

Though we generally think of Australia as the home of marsupials, with its kangaroos and wombats, the plodding American opposum is probably closer to what the most primitive marsupials looked like. It also belongs to an old American stock, for small opossums left bones and teeth in Cretaceous deposits in the western United States that also contain remains of beaked, frill-bearing dinosaurs. Like most modern marsupials, these pioneers apparently had no effective means of nourishing embryonic offspring within the mother. The young, therefore, were born as tiny, extremely immature creatures that crawled into a pouch (the marsupium) on the underside of the mother. There they attached firmly to a teat and sucked milk as they continued development.

Though the history of marsupials in North America is a long one, there was never a great variety of these animals on that continent. Many became extinct at the end of the Cretaceous, and during the Cenozoic only a single family, the Didelphidae, was known. Didelphids became extinct in North America during the Miocene, and a single species, *Didelphis marsupialis,* reappeared there in the Pleistocene, having immigrated from South America.

The robust didelphids were the only marsupial family that ever reached Europe, but that was not until the Paleocene. They were never diverse there and became extinct in the Miocene. Marsupials have only a short record, in the Eocene and Oligocene of Africa, and the Oligocene of Asia.

It is in Australia and South America that the great variety of marsupials are known, both past and present.

In South America, marsupials were the principal terrestrial vertebrate carnivores from the beginning of the Tertiary until the Pliocene, when the phororhacoid birds displaced the larger carnivorous marsupials, the borhyaenids. *Thylacosmilus* was a close relative of the borhyaenids, and at first or even second glance, it can be mistaken for the saber-toothed tiger *Smilodon.* Their similarities are an excellent example of convergent evolution: two species arise that evolve from totally different ancestors and yet, because the selection pressures are similar, a similar-looking organism results. Besides being the principal carnivores during much of the South American Cenozoic, some marsupials did evolve into small herbivores.

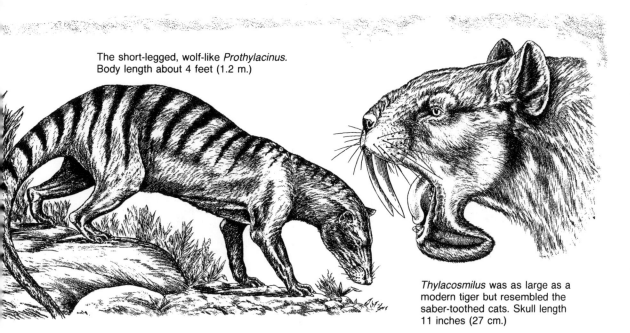

The short-legged, wolf-like *Prothylacinus*.
Body length about 4 feet (1.2 m.)

Thylacosmilus was as large as a
modern tiger but resembled the
saber-toothed cats. Skull length
11 inches (27 cm.)

Two South American marsupials that resembled carnivores

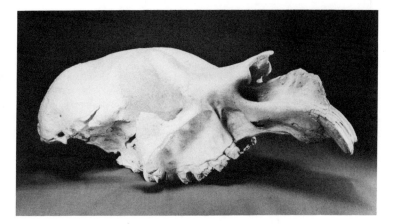

Skull of **Diprotodon**, *the
largest marsupial that
ever lived, from
southeastern Australia.
This skull is only 26
inches (66 cm.) in length,
but the largest were half
again as long. (Photo by
Frank Coffa, courtesy of
the Museum of Victoria,
Melbourne)*

Presumably, at some stage marsupials passed between South America and Australia via Antarctica. The only fossil evidence that they did so is a few jaws and teeth from Seymour Island near the Antarctic Peninsula, which juts northward toward South America.

But it was in Australia that the marsupials underwent their broadest adaptive radiation. During the 60 million or so years that Australia was isolated from the rest of the world by ocean barriers, opposumlike marsupials produced descendants that took on the forms and habits of many other animals as well as new ones of their own.

In the Middle Miocene, the largest known Australian land mammals were about the size of sheep. These were the diprotodontids, four-footed browsers. As the Cenozoic drew to a close, diprotodontids gradually became larger and larger. Finally, in the Pleistocene, *Diprotodon* appeared. It was an animal the size of a rhinoceros and looked much like one except that it

525

Palorchestes, *a close relative of* Diprotodon, *but quite different in habits. With their large claws, these animals may have been the marsupial equivalent of the ground sloths. They lived during the Pliocene and Pleistocene in Australia; the largest species may have been about 7 to 8 feet (2–2.5 m.) long. (Painting by Frank Knight, courtesy of the Museum of Victoria, Melbourne, and Pioneer Design Studio)*

An adult female Diprotodon (length 8 ft., or 2.5 m.) stands by helpless as her young struggles in a swamp in which it became trapped while searching for water twenty-six thousand years ago near Lake Callabonna, South Australia. (Painting by Frank Knight, courtesy of the Museum of Victoria, Melbourne and Pioneer Design Studio)

Sthenurus *(length 7 ft., or 2 m.), a browsing kangaroo from the Pliocene and Pleistocene of Australia. One toe of the hind foot was predominant; the others were reduced to tiny splints if present at all. Horses are similarly modified, but in them the reduction occurred on both the front and the hind feet. (Painting by Frank Knight, courtesy of the Museum of Victoria, Melbourne, and Pioneer Design Studio)*

Thylacoleo (length 5 ft., or 1.5 m.), from the Pliocene and Pleistocene of Australia, used its greatly expanded last premolars as a deadly slicing blade. The thylacoleonids are one of the few mammalian carnivores to have evolved from omnivorous or herbivorous ancestors. (Painting by Frank Knight, courtesy of the Museum of Victoria, Melbourne, and Pioneer Design Studio)

Propleopus, *the extinct giant rat kangaroo known from Pleistocene rocks of Australia, shown here eating emu eggs. Kangaroos are today plant eaters, but* **Propleopus** *may have been a carnivore. (Painting by Frank Knight, courtesy of the Museum of Victoria Melbourne and Pioneer Design Studio)*

lacked a horn. *Diprotodon,* though large, was no mental giant, for most of its head was filled with air pockets, rather than brain.

Another group that grew much larger in the Late Cenozoic were the kangaroos. The largest Middle Miocene ones were about the size of small rabbits. As the continent became more arid, there was an evolutionary explosion as many new, larger species evolved. By the end of the Pleistocene, the largest stood about 2.6 meters (9 ft.) high.

Not all Australian marsupials that showed a marked increase in size during the Late Cenozoic were placid herbivores. Though the thylacoleonids were descended from herbivorous or omnivorous stock, their last premolars were modified into fierce slicing blades one fourth as long as the entire jaw. The largest of these animals was the size of a leopard, and the smallest that of a house cat. Along with many other large marsupials, they became extinct near the end of the Pleistocene.

Other Australian marsupials with a fossil record are wombats, together with koalas, possums, and omnivorous bandicoots. Of these, only the wombats include forms strikingly different from the living species. Some in the Pliocene and Pleistocene were 80 centimeters (2 ft. 7 in.) high and 2 meters (7 ft.) long, twice as high and long as any alive today. If these built underground tunnels as their modern relatives do, they must have been the largest burrowing mammals that ever lived.

A peculiar offshoot of the possums were the ektopodontids. With numerous cusps on their teeth, they were first thought to be related to multituberculates. These Miocene and Pliocene animals probably lived on a diet of hard nuts, like squirrels, and may have looked much like them as well.

THE MAMMALS WITH A PLACENTA

Though marsupials did not lay eggs, few of them found an effective way to nourish young ones inside maternal bodies. That change was made in Cretaceous times by a mammal that joined an egg membrane to the lining of its uterus, or womb. The result was a new organ, the placenta, through which

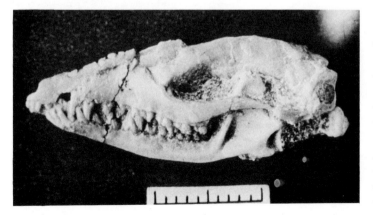

Skull of Asioryctes, *an insectivore with a skull about 1.2 inches (30 mm.) long. Cretaceous of the Mongolian People's Republic. (Photo by W. Skarzynski and courtesy of Zofia Kielan-Jaworowska and the Institute of Paleobiology, Polish Academy of Science)*

food and oxygen could reach the young ones while waste material was removed. Both processes allowed the embryos to develop fully, producing in
general a more complex brain than that of any marsupial. Interestingly,
some marsupials, the bandicoots, have developed a structure quite similar to
the placenta.

Early Insectivores. Much of this is conjecture based mainly on existing
animals. Late Cretaceous fossils from Mongolia continue the story, for they
are remains of placental mammals. Some were specialized beasts, but others

Asioryctes *looked and probably lived
like a modern shrew. Skull about 2
inches (5 cm.) long*

*Collecting Cretaceous mammals at Bayn Dzak, the Mongolian People's Republic.
(Photo courtesy of Zofia Kielan-Jaworowska and the Institute of Paleobiology,
Polish Academy of Sciences)*

were very primitive insectivores. Out of them arose the diverse placental mammals we see today.

These primitive insectivores were inconspicuous creatures that probably fed at night or in twilight on a diet of insects mixed with grubs and worms. Their heads were long in proportion to their bodies, their legs were short, and their tails were long. Some species, at least, had as many as forty-four teeth, or eleven on each side of each jaw. These teeth were arranged according to a definite order, or formula: three incisors at the front and then one canine, followed by four premolars and three molars. Many later mammals would lose some of these teeth and change the shapes of others, but only a few specialized groups such as whales and edentates would greatly increase their number. In dentition as well as in other features, Cretaceous insectivores were ready to produce more modern orders, which they did, and which we shall look at in Chapter XXXIII.

CHAPTER XXXII

The World Blossoms

The road from Bernalillo to Aztec, New Mexico, skirts the Nacimiento Mountains and swings westward into the San Juan Basin. It is a dry region of varicolored shales and sandstones exposed in canyons, arroyos, and badlands. Indians live in isolated hogans, though the ruins of prehistoric towns still stand in several canyons. The largest town, Pueblo Bonito, once sheltered more than a thousand people.

THE LARAMIDE REVOLUTION

Archaeologists detour to these ruins, but fossil hunters seek arroyos in which a long succession of strata tell how the Age of Reptiles ended and the Age of Mammals began. The story opens with coarse yellow sandstones of Late Cretaceous age, in the Ojo Alamo Sandstone. It contains bones and skulls of frill-bearing dinosaurs, as well as petrified logs and ganoid fish scales. Both rocks and fossils tell of a well-watered lowland where dead reptiles were washed into streams and buried in rapidly growing sandbars. Trees met a similar fate when they toppled from undercut banks.

We do not know how long deposition continued, for the latest Cretaceous deposits were removed by erosion, which also wore pits and channels in the Ojo Alamo Formation. These are local evidence of the great mountain-building event, the Laramide revolution, which closed the Mesozoic Era and continued into the Cenozoic. Actually, the revolution was only the culmination of changes that had begun in latest Jurassic or Early Cretaceous times and continued intermittently through 65–75 million years. In many places, such as the San Juan Basin, it produced only moderate uplift followed by millions of years of erosion. Elsewhere great belts of rock were forced sidewise until they bent, crumpled, or broke, forming mountain ranges that extended from Cape Horn to the Caribbean Sea and from Mexico to Alaska. The molten granite forced upward during this long phase of orogenic activity forms the thousands of square miles of spectacular scenery so characteristic of the North American West, and of the Andes, of South America.

The Appearance of Flowers

Land plants responded to these events, at first by chance and then explosively as they adapted to new conditions. Jurassic dinosaurs lived among forests of ginkgos, or maidenhair trees; cycads; and *Williamsonia*—plants belonging to a cycadlike group that is extinct today—and also a variety of cone-bearing gymnosperms. The once dominant seed ferns and club mosses by this time were inconspicuous. Despite this variety, however, the fragrance of flowers we know so well today did not scent the air.

Before the dinosaurs were extinct, however, at the close of the Cretaceous, a myriad of flowering plants dominated the world. They underwent a veritable explosion of diversification after they first appeared, in the Early Cretaceous. Leaves, pollen, and flowers are all preserved in rocks of this age, as are undoubted monocots (flowering plants with one embryonic "leaf" and parallel-veined leaves), dicots (two embryonic "leaves" and branching

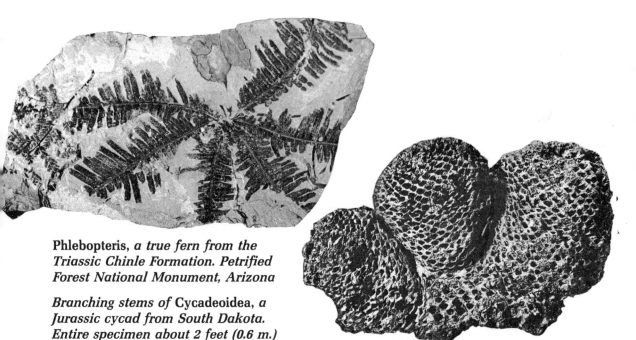

Phlebopteris, a true fern from the Triassic Chinle Formation. Petrified Forest National Monument, Arizona

Branching stems of Cycadeoidea, a Jurassic cycad from South Dakota. Entire specimen about 2 feet (0.6 m.) wide

Spore of Cyathidites australis, a fern, from the Mesozoic of Australia. The species is known worldwide at this time. Magnification is × 1000 through an optical microscope. (Courtesy of B. Wagstaff)

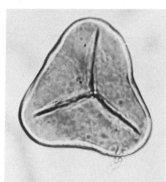

Populus (a poplar). Eocene–Recent, North America

Zelkova (a keati tree). Cretaceous–Recent. Northern Hemisphere

Alnus (an alder). Cretaceous–Recent, Northern Hemisphere

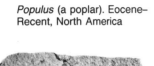

Platanus (a sycamore). Cretaceous–Recent, Northern Hemisphere

Porana, a flower. Oligocene (John Day), central Oregon

Juglans (a walnut). Paleocene–Recent, Northern Hemisphere

Clathropteris, a fern. Triassic, Petrified Forest, Arizona

Metasequoia (a dawn redwood). Cretaceous–Recent, Northern Hemisphere

Some typical Tertiary plants and a Triassic fern

veins), and both wind- and insect-pollinated flowers. The variety of types of flowering plants suggests that the history of the angiosperms must have begun at least in the earliest Cretaceous—we probably haven't yet found the oldest fossils of this group.

The oldest records of angiosperms are small, pinnately veined, simple leaves from the Early Cretaceous (Neocomian) of Siberia, in rocks about 120 million years old. Slightly younger (Barremian–Aptian) are a number of different leaves, both monocots and dicots, from the Potomac Group, of eastern North America. From here and elsewhere in North America, fossils resembling modern proteas, aralias, birches, figs, and poplars are known. By Late Cretaceous times, relatives of oaks, walnuts, sycamores, magnolias, laurels, and many others were present. They are the dominant forms in sites in many parts of North America as far north as Alaska, as well as in Greenland, Europe, and Asia. They are also known, by Albian times, in Australia.

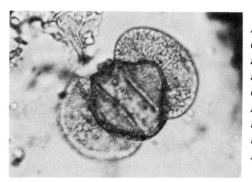

Pollen grain of **Podocarpidites ostentatus,** *common in Oligocene and Miocene rocks of southeastern Australia;* × *500. Minute fossils such as these can be recovered in large quantities from well cores and are very important in determining the age of both terrestrial and marine rocks, often being tested for oil and gas content. (Courtesy of J. McEwen Mason)*

Pollen, the microscopic male reproductive cells of plants that gives many of us "hay fever," also first occurs in the Early Cretaceous of England and in slightly younger rocks in West Africa and North America, some grains *(Clavatipollenites* and *Liliacidites)* closely resembling those of magnoliaceous plants. The development of variety in pollen types is similar to the variety in leaf types.

Wood of early flowering plants, however, is rare, one exception being vessel-less material from the Aptian of Japan.

Fruits of flowering plants first appear in the Early Cretaceous (Barremian), the oldest resembling the ribbed fruit of the tupelo *(Nyssa)*. Flowers also come from this time, but some of the best, older flowers come from the early part (Cenomanian) of the Late Cretaceous of North America. Seed heads of plants in the plane family and catkinlike collections of flowers are also known from these rocks. Many of the flowers are quite primitive and seem to resemble members of the rose (Rosaceae) and witch-hazel (Hamamelidaceae) families most closely.

In rocks of nearly the same age at Rose Creek, Nebraska, many beautiful fossil flowers have been collected over the past few years. One of the best is medium-sized, about 1.5 inches (about 3.5 cm.) in diameter. It had five petals, five stamens bearing pollen (also preserved), five sepals, and five carpals. At the base of the carpals were some swollen areas that most likely produced nectar. Flowers of roses and grapes resemble this generalized fossil flower. The facts that the pollen of this flower was exceedingly small and that the plant had the swollen nectar-producing organs suggest it was insect-, rather than wind-, pollinated.

In the Late Cretaceous many of the fossil plant assemblages indicate more even, and often more humid, conditions than we have today. The Medicine Bow flora of south-central Wyoming, now a high-altitude desert, contains a variety of broad-leaved angiosperms such as figs *(Ficus)*, *Magnolia*, laurels *(Laurus)*, as well as palms *(Sabal)* and dawn redwoods *(Metasequoia)*.

Tertiary Floras

With the beginning of the Cenozoic Era (consisting of the Tertiary and Quaternary periods), some 65 million years ago, plants did not at first change dramatically. The Paleocene Fort Union Formation, in Montana, eastern Wyoming, and western North and South Dakota, contains a varied collection of plants, including concentrations of vegetal material forming minable coal. Algae, mushrooms, mosses, ferns, conifers including *Araucaria* (the Norfolk Island pine), and ginkgos are all there, as are a great variety of angiosperms such as palms, maples, ash, and even breadfruit *(Artocarpus)*. These indicate that a warm, even (equable), subtropical climate still remained and continued even into the Eocene, while the London Clay flora, of England, is reminiscent of a mixture of upland and lowland plants of tropical Southeast Asia today. Why these plants occurred together in one place at one time has not been satisfactorily explained.

But throughout the remainder of the Tertiary and Quaternary three trends dominated: A general cooling occurred that was sometimes interrupted by warmer periods. Interiors of continents dried out, especially from Miocene times onward. In some cases this occurred because mountain ranges were uplifted, for example in western North America. In other cases, such as in Australia, this was a result of its movement northward and the global contraction of tropical belts. Thirdly, there was an alternation of glacial and nonglacial conditions toward the end of the Cenozoic. All these changes caused plant assemblages to change and "migrate" or be restricted to certain areas, dependent on the prevailing climate.

Grasslands were favored in North America, South America, and Australia, for instance in Middle Cenozoic times, because of the drying out of these continents. Tropical vegetation invaded northern Australia or evolved there as a result of its moving into a tropical climatic regime. Coniferous forests

Stump, cone, and vegetation of Sequoia *(above); Oligocene near Florissant, Colorado. The stump has been called* Sequoioxylon. *The pine stumps* (Pityoxylon) *(below, right) stand on Specimen Ridge, a cliff of Oligocene volcanic agglomerate in Yellowstone National Park, Wyoming. At the left is a piece of* Pityoxylon *wood (about × 1)*

moved north and south in North America and Europe as the giant ice sheets advanced and retreated several times in the past 1.8 million years.

One of the most famous of the Tertiary floras comes from Oligocene rocks in the Florissant beds, near Colorado Springs, Colorado. Hundreds of thousands of plant fragments are embedded in finely banded layers of volcanic pumice and dust that were deposited in an ancient lake. Palms and many deciduous trees make up the assemblage, including many species that no longer occur in North America *(Zelkova,* the keaki tree; *Ailanthus,* the tree of heaven). Using the known habits of living plant relatives, paleobotanists have estimated that the climate supporting such a flora was warm temperate to subtropical, with enough rainfall to encourage large forests along streams. Pines and oaks dominated the uplands, and the Florissant locality then lay at about 1,000 to 3,000 feet elevation.

One very interesting tree in the Florissant flora was *Sequoia,* the redwood, which still lives in very restricted patches of California today. The coast redwoods and giant sequoias reach more than 300 feet (about 95 m.). *Sequoia* is a conifer, not a flowering plant, and is interesting because it has a long history and a much wider distribution in the past than it does at present. The history of *Sequoia* stretches back into the Cretaceous of the Northern Hemisphere, with a much wider geographic distribution in North America than at present.

A related tree, often found in association with *Sequoia* in the fossil record, also has a striking tale to tell. *Metasequoia,* which has foliage resembling *Sequoia's,* differs in having pairs of "needles" opposite one another, rather than alternating as they branch off the main stem. *Metasequoia* likewise spans more than 70 million years of time. It was known as a fossil before it was discovered as a living tree—a true "living fossil." In 1948, among the rice fields of Sichuan Province, of west-central China, a large, previously unknown conifer was found. It was unusual in that during the winter it shed its leaves, much as an elm or maple—a deciduous conifer! This tree turned out, upon further comparison, to be *Metasequoia,* in recent times restricted to this small patch of China. It had once ranged over North America, Europe, Asia including the Arctic, and Greenland. While mild, equable climates prevailed, these trees prospered. As temperatures cooled in the Tertiary, their northern ranges were restricted farther south. As aridity encroached too, *Metasequoia* became extinct in many areas, finally to become a relict in the forests of western China. It has been reintroduced to many areas of the world.

Triumph of the Flowers

Today, the flowering plants, which began when the dinosaurs flourished, dominate the world. During their history, more than a quarter of a million species have existed, a number decidedly greater than that of all other plant groups combined. They have prospered at the expense of the other plant groups, and only the ferns, among the plants, have expanded as the flowering plants have thrived.

With this expansion of the flowering plants came related trends in insects, birds, and mammals, for the livelihoods of many of these animals are directly tied to these most amazing fragrant plants. They eat their nectar, and inadvertently pollinate them; they eat their foliage or fruits and help disperse their seeds. And so they are adapted to each other.

CHAPTER XXXIII

The Great Placental Radiation

 As we learned in Chapter XXXI, placentals are mammals that bear their young at a relatively advanced stage. Among marsupials, on the other hand, the young are born soon after conception and undergo much of their development firmly attached to a teat outside the mother's body.

THE NOT QUITE TOOTHLESS EDENTATES

Armadillos. The modern armadillo has a pointed nose, a body covered with jointed armor made of bony plates set in skin, and a number of peg-shaped molar teeth, all others having been lost. Food consists chiefly of spiders, centipedes, scorpions, adult insects, grubs, and worms. Most of these are caught with the long, sticky tongue.

Armadillos are edentates (literally "toothless ones"), a group that in many respects comprises the most primitive of all placental mammals. Edentates first appear in the South American fossil record in Paleocene rocks; they certainly diversified only on that continent during most of the Tertiary. However, the presence of a convincing edentate from the Late Paleocene of China, *Ernanodon,* and the less certain record of an edentate, *Eurotamandua,* from the Middle Eocene of Europe, cast some slight doubt on South America as the continent of origin for the group.

Be that as it may, early edentates were small, long-tailed beasts that lacked armor; they reached lengths of 15 to 18 inches (38 to 46 cm.). Their descendants evolved into five distinct types divided among armored and "naked" suborders. The former includes armadillos and glyptodonts. The latter contains anteaters and tree and ground sloths.

Armadillos' shells never become rigid, but include several bony rings that allow the body to bend. The largest living species is about 3 feet (91 cm.) long, but the Pleistocene *Chlamydotherium* became as large as a rhinoceros and weighed about 4,000 pounds (1.8 t.).

Glyptodonts. Glyptodonts are named for their teeth, which show patterns that look as if they were carved. The really distinctive features of the group, however, are very deep heads, solid "shells" made of bony plates cemented together, and tails encased in rings or solid sheaths of bone. Miocene genera were barely 36 inches (91 cm.) long, but those of Pleistocene age measured up to 12 feet (3.7 m.). *Glyptodon* itself had a tail surrounded by movable, overlapping rings set with spikes. In *Sclerocalyptus* the hinder rings were fused, and in *Doedicurus* the tail ended in a club set with massive spikes. Powerful muscles swung the tail from side to side, delivering blows that could crush the bones of any carnivore. Glyptodonts were especially common on the Argentinian pampas during the Pleistocene.

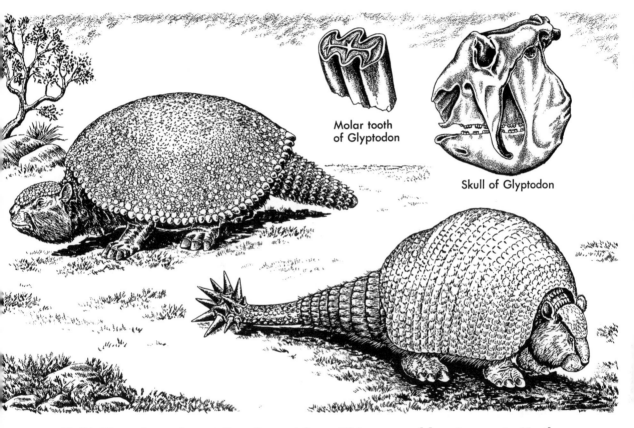

Molar tooth of Glyptodon

Skull of Glyptodon

(Left) Glyptodon, *about 9 feet (2.7 m.) long. This armored beast came to North America during the Pleistocene Epoch. (Right) the club-tailed* Doedicurus *did not leave South America. Length 12 to 15 feet (3.7–4.6 m.)*

Sloths. Tree sloths today are sluggish animals that hang upside down from branches; their remains have not been found as fossils, and fossils of anteaters are rare. Ground sloths were plentiful, however, and became quite specialized. Beginning with Oligocene beasts barely 3 feet (91 cm.) long, they evolved into a variety of browsers and grazers. Though none became completely toothless, their teeth degenerated into pegs that were supplemented by bony cropping plates.

Oligocene ground sloths are not well known, but the Miocene *Hapalops* was a primitive genus about 4 feet (1.2 m.) long, including the tail. There were five toes on each foot, all bearing claws; wrists and ankles were twisted so much that the beast walked on the outer knuckles of its forefeet and on outer sides of the hind. The skull was low and relatively long, with a spoutlike projection at the front of the lower jaws. This projection bore plates with which the beast pulled leaves from bushes.

Nothrotherium was a Pleistocene descendant of *Hapalops* about 7 feet 6 inches (2.3 m.) long. The hind legs and feet were massive; one toe had disappeared, and two were clawless rudiments. The forefeet still had five toes, but the first and fifth were too small to bear claws. Though *Nothrotherium* evolved in Argentina, it later crossed the Isthmus of Panama and ranged northward to Shasta County, California. It apparently preferred dry, mountainous regions, where it fed on the leaves of yucca and other hardy plants, many of the lily family. A skeleton preserving dry skin and tendons was found near Aden, New Mexico, and dung, hair, claws, and bones—some scraped by stone knives—were discovered in Gypsum Cave, east of Las Vegas, Nevada. These remains, which are eighty-five hundred to about eleven thousand years old, show that *Nothrotherium* lived into the present geologic epoch and was eaten by ancient Americans.

Megatherium also evolved in South America but ranged northward to Ohio and the Carolinas in the United States during the Pleistocene. When fully grown, this animal reached a length of 20 feet (6.1 m.) and a weight exceeding 10,000 pounds (4.5 t.). The skull was relatively small, with deep lower jaws that ended in a spoutlike projection that was used in pulling leaves from trees. A broad flange projected below each eye, which was completely encircled by bone. The neck was short, but the body was long and thick, and so was the tail. The hip girdle had two bones that extended forward and spread out like shovels, an adaptation that supported the internal organs when *Megatherium* sat upright. Bones of the hind legs and feet were massive, but the forelegs were not so heavy. Each forefoot had four claws, but the hind foot bore only one. The first two toes had disappeared, and the last two were degenerate. The heel bone was very large, because it and the stubby toes bore most of the animal's weight.

Mylodon and its close relatives were grazers 10 to 13 feet (3–4 m.) long and probably weighed a little more than a ton (0.9 t.). They had short, wide heads with broad muzzles and shallow lower jaws. All four legs were massive; the forefeet had five toes, with claws on the first three, but the four-toed hind foot bore claws only on toes two and three. As in *Megatherium,* the heel bone was very large.

We often picture ground sloths as timid, awkward creatures that were defenseless victims of sabertooths, lions, jaguars, and cave bears. But this conception overlooks their claws and the evidence of powerful muscles in their forelegs. Those muscles may have been used chiefly to pull down trees

Skull of Mylodon

Bones of Mylodon's right hind foot

Megatherium, *the largest ground sloth, about 20 feet (6.1 m.) long, and the skull and hind foot of* Mylodon, *an animal 10 feet 3 inches (3.1 m.) in length*

or break off branches, but it is hard to believe that they did not also batter enemies. Sitting up and swinging its forelimbs freely, *Megatherium* and *Mylodon* must have been far more formidable than any living bear.

MACROSCELIDS, THE ELEPHANT SHREWS

With a long, narrow muzzle, even the largest macroscelids, with a length of 31 centimeters (12 in.), are rather shrewlike in appearance. Ranging from the Oligocene to the Recent in Africa, this small group may be the closest living relative of the rabbits. If this is so, their common ancestor may have been the anagalids, which lived in eastern Asia during the Paleocene.

LAGOMORPHS, A NARROW SUCCESS STORY

Rabbits, hares, and pikas first appear in the Eocene and Oligocene of Asia, Europe, and North America. By the Pliocene, rabbits and hares had reached Africa, and in the Late Pleistocene, South America.

Had you been alive when the earliest lagomorphs were, they would not have appeared much different from their living descendants. Even the pikas, despite their short ears, do not look markedly different from other lagomorphs. This similarity of external appearance belies their adaptability. With this common body form, they have managed to be a success in a variety of environments. On every landmass they reached, they prospered. Introduced by Europeans into Australia and New Zealand, they quickly assumed the status of a major pest by their successful colonization of these areas, displacing many former residents.

PRIMITIVE CARNIVORES, THE CREODONTS

Known from the Late Paleocene and Early Eocene of North America and Europe, *Oxyaena* was one of the earlier creodonts. It was a short-legged carnivore more than 3 feet (91 cm.) long whose general form reminds us of the modern wolverine. Some authorities think *Oxyaena* swam like an otter, catching fish and soft-shelled turtles. Others suggest that it stayed on land and ate carrion or prey that could be killed from ambush. All agree that the beast's brain was incapable of the cunning that is routine to the living wolverine, a much more advanced carnivore in a different family.

The "father of cats," *Patriofelis,* was a Middle Eocene relative of *Oxyaena* confined to North America. Though not a giant, it was a good-sized creodont. It weighed no more than a black bear but had a skull almost as large as that of a lion. The lower jaws were heavy and deep, with powerful muscles that

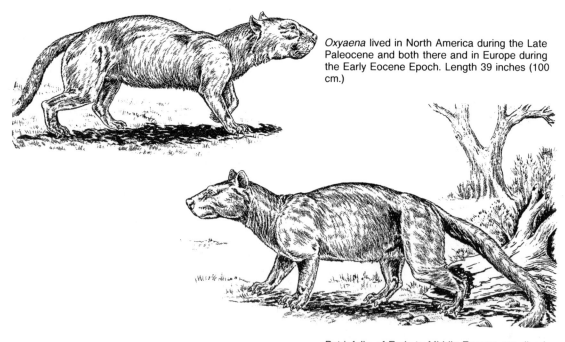

Oxyaena lived in North America during the Late Paleocene and both there and in Europe during the Early Eocene Epoch. Length 39 inches (100 cm.)

Patriofelis, of Early to Middle Eocene age, lived only in North America and was some 5 feet (1.5 m.) long, with a skull as large as a lion's

Two Eocene creodonts

must have given great crushing power. The teeth were those of a meat eater, but the legs were too short for active hunting. This contrast has led some paleontologists to suggest that *Patriofelis* also had otterlike habits. Other paleontologists think this animal sometimes lay in wait for prey on land but fed largely on carrion, in the manner of modern hyenas, which are known to take live prey occasionally.

Hyaenodon was one of the most successful creodonts. It appeared in the Late Eocene of Europe, North America, and Asia and persisted on all three of these continents through the Oligocene. It also reached Africa during that epoch, finally becoming extinct there in the Early Miocene. Several species of *Hyaenodon* are known. From the Early Oligocene of the western United States there are at least four species that range in size from that of a small coyote to a large grizzly bear.

The creodonts became extinct by the end of the Miocene and gave rise to no other groups of mammals. The mammals we call carnivores living today are another group, the true carnivores.

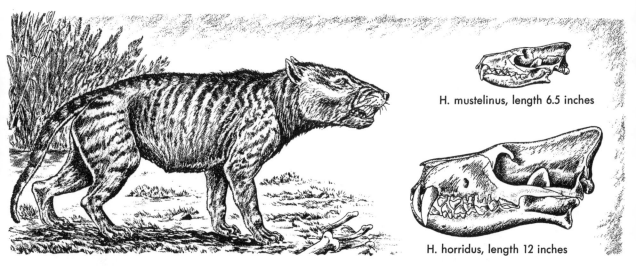

H. mustelinus, length 6.5 inches

H. horridus, length 12 inches

Hyaenodon horridus, *a creodont; its skull, which was 12 inches (30.5 cm.) long; and the skull, length 6.5 inches (16.3 cm.), of a smaller species,* H. mustelinus. *Both lived in North America during the Oligocene Epoch.*

Carnivora: the True Carnivores. True carnivores, that is, members of the order Carnivora, appear in the Paleocene. Until the Oligocene, all carnivores were so much alike that they have been put in a single family, Miacidae. All were rather small, the largest being about the size of a collie.

With the extinction of the mesonychid condylarths, by the end of the Early Oligocene, and the decline of the creodonts, the stage was set for the rise of the true carnivores. Or perhaps it was competition between these groups that resulted in the triumph of the true carnivores. They divided into two major groups: The "Dog Group" includes, besides dogs, the bears, racoons, skunks, and weasels. Besides cats, the "Cat Group" includes hyaenas and civets. Among other features, most members of the "Dog Group" cannot retract their claws, while most of the "Cat Group" can.

Two families of cats developed saber teeth. The false saber-toothed cats appeared in the Early Oligocene and died out at the end of the Miocene. Two members of this group were *Dinictis* and *Hoplophoneus.* The true saber-toothed cats are a part of the living cat family, the Felidae, which includes not only the familiar domestic cat but also the lion and the tiger. Included too were animals such as *Smilodon californicus,* well known from thousands of specimens found in the tar pits at Rancho La Brea, in Los Angeles. They appeared at the beginning of the Miocene and thus overlapped for the length of that epoch with the false sabertooths.

The development of saber teeth in mammalian predators, however, was not restricted to true carnivores. *Thylacosmilus,* a carnivorous marsupial from the Pleistocene of South America, which we met in Chapter XXXI, was well endowed with saber teeth, the roots of which extended above its eyes. Also, several of the creodonts had prominent saber teeth. Independently developed at least four times in mammals, obviously it was a quite success-

Dinictis *(left), a false sabertooth, 40 inches (102 cm.) long from nose to base of tail.* **Hoplophoneus** *(below) was a true sabertooth of slightly larger size and heavier build. Both are found in the Oligocene White River Group of the central United States*

ful way for a meat eater to get its food. The puzzle is why none of them survived to the present day.

By the beginning of the Miocene, some true carnivores started to live in the sea. These are called pinnipeds ("fan-footed ones") in reference to their limbs being paddles. Actually two different sea-dwelling groups separately evolved from land carnivores.

The sea lions and walruses are one of these. They apparently evolved from animals similar to bears, and their history seems to have been centered around the Pacific Basin. However, sea lions did enter the Atlantic through the seaway that existed between North and South America prior to the formation of the Panamanian isthmus.

Seals, on the other hand, are virtually worldwide in their distribution. They probably evolved from relatives of the skunks and weasels.

Ancestral Carnivores and Their Noncarnivorous Descendants. As we learned in Chapter XXXI, some of the earliest placentals are found in the Late Cretaceous deposits of Mongolia. Among them were generalized carnivorous mammals from which the creodonts and true carnivores arose. But also from them came many noncarnivorous descendants.

One of the best known of these is the Late Paleocene and Early Eocene pantodont *Coryphodon,* because its thick bones resisted destruction and therefore became good and common fossils. Though some species were no larger than tapirs, others weighed as much as an ox, 1,600 to 1,800 pounds (725–820 kg.), and were more heavily built. *Coryphodon* had a long body, short legs, and five-toed feet that resembled those of an elephant. The skull was large, broad, and blunt, and the canine teeth had become tusks, which

Skull of
Coryphodon

Coryphodon, an early Eocene
amblypod about 8 feet long. It
may have been a swamp-dweller.

Coryphodon, *a Late Paleocene and Early Eocene pantodont found in Europe, Asia, and North America. It was about 8 feet (2.4 m.) long and may well have been a swamp dweller.*

Barylambda, *another pantodont. Found in the Late Paleocene of North America, it was about 8 feet (2.4 m.) long. Near it are the skull and the bones of the left forefoot*

the males used in fighting. The general form was that of a pigmy hippopotamus, suggesting that the animal spent much of its time in swamps.

Coryphodon was a traveler, being known from North America, Asia, and Europe. Another pantodont, *Barylambda,* never left North America and lived only during the Late Paleocene.

INSECTIVORES, PRIMITIVE AND SPECIALIZED

For a long time, paleontologists have thought of living insectivores as "living fossils," virtually unchanged from the Late Cretaceous ancestors of all the other placental mammals. However, the hedgehogs, shrews, and moles of today have had their Cenozoic histories too, and are certainly more advanced than those of the Late Cretaceous and Early Cenozoic, so much so that they are often put in a separate order, the Lipotyphla.

Alongside the Late Cretaceous insectivores that showed carnivorous specializations were others with a more generalized dentition. It was out of these that the remaining placental mammals arose.

We tend to think of hedgehogs as small, harmless animals. For the most part this is true. However, with a head the size of a wolf and a body the size of a coyote, *Deinogalerix* was certainly an exception. This animal lived on what is today the Gargano Peninsula, which juts into the Adriatic Sea about halfway up the northeastern coast of Italy. In the Late Miocene, however, this area was an island. Missing from the fauna that lived on the island were carnivores the size of *Deinogalerix.* Though not as efficient as a similar-sized true carnivore, because its limbs were not suitable for running, *Deinogalerix* was able, just the same, to function in this role, because there was no competition.

550

BATS: THE ONLY FLYING MAMMALS

Except for their adaptations for flight, bats are not as markedly changed from their generalized insectivore ancestors of the Late Cretaceous as most other placental mammals. We often compare them with pterosaurs, because both developed broad wings covered with very thin skin. But the pterosaur wing ran from body and legs to the fourth "finger," with no support between. Bats avoided this defect by lengthening bones in the "arm" and using four of the five fingers to strengthen and stretch the wing. They also developed strong breast muscles and enlarged the auditory regions of the brain. Ancient bats apparently guided their flight by squeaking and listening to echoes, as many of their descendants use such echolocation today.

The oldest known bats were small creatures that had lost a few ancestral teeth and possessed well-developed wings. Some species lived among groves, but others pursued insects over the Green River (Eocene) lakes of southwestern Wyoming. Now and then a bat swooped so low that it struck the water. There it soon drowned and sank to the bottom, where its bones and sometimes even its skin were preserved in fine-grained sediment.

By Oligocene times the group had split into two, one group remaining small insect eaters, while the other began to eat fruit. The fruit eaters increased in size and added length to their skulls, becoming the "flying foxes" that now range from islands near Africa to India, Australia, and Japan.

Since the Oligocene, most other living mammalian orders with many spe-

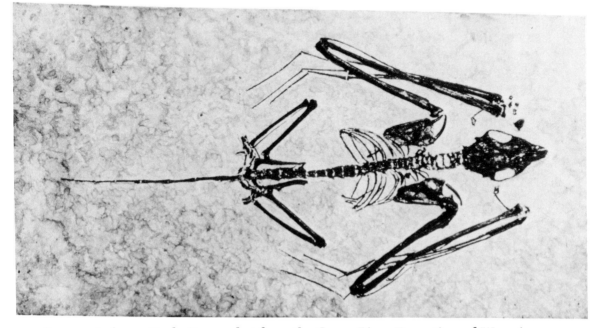

Icaronycteris, *an Early Eocene bat from the Green River Formation, of Wyoming, North America. Length 5 inches (12 cm.). (Photo courtesy of Don Baird)*

cies have changed a great deal. Not so the bats. Many living then differ only in minor details from bats flying about today.

FLYING LEMURS—SOME PECULIAR GAPS

Flying lemurs don't fly, they glide, and they are not really lemurs, either. But that is not all that is odd about them. Today they live in Southeast Asia and the Philippines. Their only fossil record, however, is from a few Paleocene and Eocene specimens found in North America. Together with the bats and the primates (which includes monkeys and humans), they appear to form one branch of the mammalian family tree, the archotans. Common to all the archotans is that at least their primitive members were specialized for living in trees.

PEOPLE AND OTHER PRIMATES

Perhaps because we are primates ourselves, much effort has been expended to unravel the evolutionary history of this group. However, even if we belonged to some other order of mammals, the primates would be fascinating to study, because over and over again different groups became adapted to similar environments. Thus they provide a fertile ground to study the various ways in which animals may become modified to live in the same manner.

Primitive Primates.   The first eutherians to take to the trees were probably Paleocene primates. There they found the multituberculates well established. These earliest known primates, the plesiadapids, were a specialized side branch that have a gap in the tooth row and large, forward-pointing lower incisors. In these features, they are more reminiscent of living squirrels or the arboreal possums of Australia than of other primates. No later primates have such a large gap in the tooth row between the incisors and the premolars.

Primitive primates climbed in trees much as squirrels do today. That is, they dug into the bark with sharp claws. As primates evolved, their claws were reduced to nails, and climbing was then accomplished by grasping the limbs with fingers and toes.

The eyes of ancient primates did not have the overlapping field of vision that makes it possible for most living primates to see in three dimensions. Rather, the field of vision of each eye was directed more to the side. As, with the passage of time, the primates became more visually oriented, their sense of smell was correspondingly reduced.

The known Paleocene primates are from North America and Europe. It is quite likely that the direct ancestors of modern primates lived elsewhere, perhaps in the equatorial regions, where lush tropical forests provided the habitat they liked.

By the Eocene, animals that can be recognized as belonging to the most primitive groups of living primates, the lemurs and tarsioids, had appeared.

One of the best known of these primitive primates is *Notharctus.* Quite lemurlike in appearance with its relatively long snout, during the Middle Eocene it was probably an active leaper in the forest canopy of what is now southwestern Wyoming. To do that successfully, the eyes were situated so that the fields of vision overlapped, giving the animal the ability to see in three dimensions.

Tarsiers. The living *Tarsius,* of Southeast Asia, is a lone leftover of a once diverse group of small primates, the tarsioids, which flourished during the Eocene in Europe, Asia, and North America. *Tetonius,* from the Early Eocene of North America, is one of the few members of these earlier tarsiers in which the skull is known. The tiny skull, only 3 centimeters (1.2 in.) long, had an enlarged brain and large eyes. Presumably, such eyes would have been quite useful even at night.

New World Monkeys. South American, or New World, monkeys first appeared in the Early Oligocene. Much ink has been spilled over the question as to whether they came from North America or Africa, and still scientists have not come to an agreement. The technical name for them is the platyrrhines, meaning "flat noses." The name refers to the fact that their two nostrils are far apart and open sidewise instead of lying close to one another and opening forward, as in Old World monkeys. Most South American monkeys have thirty-six teeth and prehensile tails, which are endlessly useful in climbing. Marmosets, which have thirty-two teeth, are unique. They have

Notharctus, *a primitive Eocene lemur, and its skull, 3 inches (8 cm.) long. At the* **right is the head of** Tetonius, *a tiny Eocene tarsioid from Wyoming, skull length 1.2* **inches (3 cm.)**

lost the last four molars ("wisdom teeth") but retain four premolars that have been lost by Old World primates.

A few monkeys have been found in Oligocene and Miocene deposits of South America, but many more come from Pleistocene cave deposits of Brazil. Though spider monkeys now range northward to Mexico, no fossil monkey is known from Central or North America, but they have been found in very young deposits in Jamaica and the Dominican Republic.

Apes and Old World Monkeys.　In the Late Eocene of Burma and the Early Oligocene of Africa occur the earliest representatives of the anthropoids, which include apes, humans, and the Old World monkeys. These earliest known anthropoids are about the size of small living monkeys but are so primitive that they are not true Old World monkeys. Rather, they could be the common ancestor of all later anthropoids. In fact, undoubted Old World monkeys are the last of the anthropoids to arise, not appearing until the Early Miocene and not becoming diverse until later. Rather, 20 million years ago the roles now played by monkeys in Africa were for the most part occupied by similar-sized apes. It was only later that the Old World monkeys evolved to displace the smaller apes.

The apes themselves appeared by the Middle Oligocene. The ancestors of the living apes remained forest dwellers. In contrast, our ancestors became adapted to life in the savannas and grasslands that were spreading at the expense of the forests across the Old World during the Miocene and Pliocene as climates became drier. With this change, posture became more erect, and eventually they walked only on their hind limbs, freeing the hands for carrying tools and for other activities.

A PLETHORA OF UNGULATES

All the remaining placental mammals can be grouped together as ungulates, literally "hoofed." Actually, not all ungulates have hoofs, but many do, and for the most part they are terrestrial herbivores.

The most primitive ungulates are the arctocyonid condylarths, which appeared in the earliest Paleocene. In the form of the body and the feet, these small four-footed beasts make almost perfect structural ancestors for the later ungulates. Within a very short time geologically, a few million years at most, arctocyonids gave rise to many groups.

Tillodonts.　Many of these descendants were small or short-lived groups. One such was the tillodonts, a Northern Hemisphere Eocene group. With large, chisel-like incisors, these animals had an appearance somewhat like that of a rodent, to which they were once thought to be related. However, they are a quite separate group. *Trogosus,* a Middle Eocene tillodont, was the giant of the group, being as large as a brown bear.

Aardvarks.　The living aardvark, of Africa, is the sole surviving species in its order, the Tubulidentata. The teeth have a characteristic pattern of minute tubes within them, hence the name for the order. They first appear in the Early Miocene of Africa and spread to Europe and Asia. However, after the Pliocene, they were once again restricted to Africa. Four genera of tubulidentates evolved which differ from one another mainly in the degree to which their skeletons were modified for eating termites and ants as well as digging and climbing.

Uintatheres.   Another arctocyonid descendant combined bulk and essentially primitive bodies with a veneer of specialization. *Uintatherium*, of Middle Eocene age, stood 5 feet (1.5 m.) high at the shoulder and weighed as much as a modern rhinoceros, which it somewhat resembled. The long, low head bore three pairs of blunt bony "horns" that were covered with skin and were 2 to 10 inches (5 to 25 cm.) high. Males had daggerlike canine tusks on the upper jaws—tusks that could be used against large carnivores or other males during fights for mates. A successor, *Eobasileus*, was even larger, for its skull was 40 inches (1 m.) long, whereas that of *Uintatherium* was only 30 inches (76 cm.). *Eobasileus* was almost 7 feet (2.1 m.) tall at the back, and its tusks extended 9 inches (23 cm.) below the upper jaws.

With these gains in size and armament went obvious weaknesses. A big beast needed much food, yet *Eobasileus* had teeth that were neither larger nor better than those of *Uintatherium*. The brain also was small, at least by modern standards. Not only was the uintathere brain much smaller than that

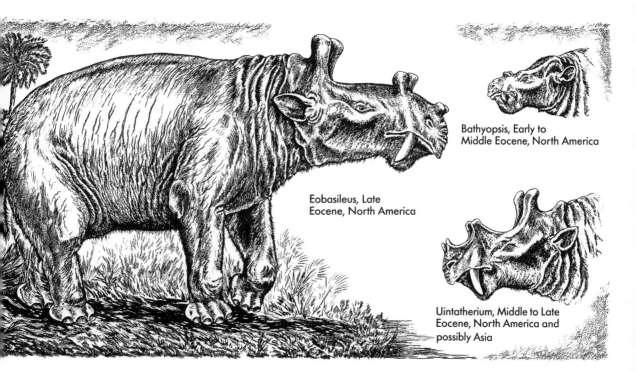

Bathyopsis, Early to
Middle Eocene, North America

Eobasileus, Late
Eocene, North America

Uintatherium, Middle to Late
Eocene, North America and
possibly Asia

Three kinds of uintatheres: Bathyopsis, *which stood 3 feet (90 cm.) high,* Uintatherium, *which stood 5 feet (1.5 m.) high at the shoulder, skull 30 inches (76 cm.), and* Eobasileus, *whose height was about 5 feet (1.5 m.) and whose skull was 40 inches (102 cm.) long*

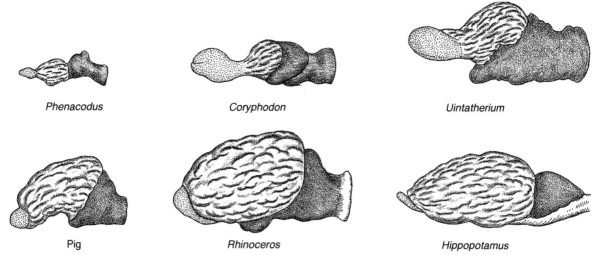

Phenacodus   *Coryphodon*   *Uintatherium*

Pig   Rhinoceros   *Hippopotamus*

Brains of archaic mammals (upper row) had much smaller cerebral hemispheres than those of modern mammals (below) and were from much less intelligent animals. One-fourth natural size

of a hippo or rhino of equal size, it also had diminutive cerebral hemispheres and probably very limited intelligence. Uintatheres were able to think, but so dimly that instinct and reflex must have governed their lives almost as fully as they governed the lives of big dinosaurs.

This statement, in fact, applies to all "archaic" mammals—condylarths, creodonts, as well as the primitive ungulates. With clumsy bodies controlled by small brains, they were ill prepared to meet competition as new and more intelligent beasts evolved.

EVEN-TOED UNGULATES, THE ARTIODACTYLS

Among these more intelligent beasts were the artiodactyls, the cloven-hoofed mammals. They are characterized by having the main axis of the support for the foot passing between the second and third toes. Thus, support for the foot was equally shared between the two toes and both are equally developed. This contrasts with the perissodactyls, in which the main axis of support passes though the third toe. In that order, the third toe is the largest on the foot and may be the only one of any consequence, as in the living horse.

Though artiodactyls appeared in the Early Eocene, it was at the end of that epoch that they underwent a virtual evolutionary explosion. Most of the modern families appeared then or soon after, along with some that flourished for a time, only to become extinct. Included among these were piglike and deerlike beasts of several types, primitive camels, and many species of oreodonts, a group confined entirely to North and Central America.

Oreodonts. Those variously called *Oreodon* or *Merycoidodon* were short-legged, blunt-headed herbivores that still had five toes on each front

556

Three oreodonts common in the Late Oligocene deposits of South Dakota. (Left)
Agriochoerus, *a climber 4 to 5 feet (1.2–1.5 m.) long.* Merycoidodon *(right), an abundant fossil, 16 inches (41 cm.) high at the shoulder. In the water is* Leptauchenia, *swimming with its body concealed*

foot. The first toe was very small, however, and the hind foot had an even number: four. *Merycoidodon* probably lived in great herds, for its bones, teeth, and well-preserved skulls are among the commonest mammalian fossils in the Badlands of South Dakota and Nebraska. One skeleton is that of a female with the bones of unborn twins near what was her abdomen.

Leptauchenia had still shorter legs, a stubby tail, and tiny hoofs. These hoofs, plus elevated eyes and nostrils, on top of the muzzle, indicate that this mammal spent much of its time in the water, where it could swim with its body concealed. *Agriochoerus,* on the other hand, had a very long tail and clawed feet, and looked like some creodonts. It probably could climb trees to escape enemies but may have used its claws chiefly to dig roots and bulbs, because its teeth were those of a plant eater.

Oreodonts thrived in the Oligocene and Early Miocene. They tapered off in importance through the remainder of the Miocene and were extinct by the end of the epoch. Completely restricted to North and Central America, they have been found as far south as the Panama Canal. Why such an abundant group on one continent was unable to migrate is a bit of a mystery when other families managed to pass across the Bering land bridge. Perhaps they were unable to withstand the relatively cooler climates of the area near the land bridge.

The Story of Camels. Today we think of camels as inhabitants of the deserts of the Old World. With a little further reflection, we remember that the llamas of South America are also members of the camel family. Thus it is strange to realize that most of their history took place in North America and it was only toward the end of the Cenozoic that they emigrated to other continents.

Protylopus, a Primitive Camel. The first known member of the camel family appeared late in the Eocene Epoch. This patriarch, *Protylopus,* was a short-legged beast not much larger than a jackrabbit, with an elongated skull and eye sockets partly closed by bony projections instead of continuous bars. The jaws contained forty-four teeth, of which the canines resembled incisors, while the grinders (molars) had very low crowns. There were four toes in front and two behind, with splint bones as vestiges of two additional toes. The hoofs were pointed like those of a deer, showing that the toes were not padded as are those of modern camels. Because hind legs were longer than forelegs, the animals most likely leaped as they ran.

Poëbrotherium. Descendants of *Protylopus* ranged the North American West in abundant herds during the Oligocene Epoch. Most characteristic was *Poëbrotherium,* whose bones are found in the South Dakota Badlands and other regions underlain by the White River Group. *Poëbrotherium* looked like a llama, was about 26 inches (66 cm.) high at the back, and weighed less than most sheep. Its teeth resembled those of *Protylopus,* but the forefeet had only two toes, and splints had disappeared from the hind feet. The tail, though short, was longer than that of the living llama.

We sometimes assume that all ancient animals with one generic name looked alike, so that a description fitting one applies to all related species.

Skull of the larger species

Two species of **Poëbrotherium,** *the large one 26 inches (66 cm.) high at the shoulder. Both are from the Oligocene of the North American Great Plains. In the center is the skull of the larger species*

Actually our description of *Poëbrotherium* fits only the species *P. labiatum;* another, *P. wilsoni,* had longer and much more slender legs, a shorter head, and a strongly arched back. Curvature did not come after death, for the vertebrae could not have straightened out when the animal was alive.

The Delicate Gazelle Camels.   Three groups of Miocene camels evolved in separate ways. One led to the pad-footed, humpbacked beasts of today and may be regarded as the trunk of the family tree. The other two groups were branches that prospered briefly and died out.

Stenomylus typifies the branch whose small bodies and slender legs account for the descriptive name "gazelle camel." *Stenomylus* was just over 2 feet (60 cm.) high at the shoulder, with a thin neck, and lower jaws that seem to have had twelve incisor teeth. There actually were six—three on each side—but the canines and two premolars had assumed the shape of incisors and were also used to nip off food.

Most fossils of *Stenomylus* have come from the Early Miocene of Agate Springs Ranch, in western Nebraska. The quarry seems to be part of an ancient "bed ground," where a huge herd of gazelle camels spent the night, as herds of modern guanacos sleep on the plains of Patagonia. Before morning the sick and the aged had died and were covered by windblown sand. One night's death might account for the hundred or more bodies whose bones have been found.

Camels as Tall as Giraffes.   Though *Stenomylus* resembled a gazelle, its neighbor *Oxydactylus*—the name means "long toe"—belonged to a branch whose lengthening legs and necks remind us of giraffes. *Oxydactylus* itself was a rather small browser that stood 4 feet 6 inches (137 cm.) high at the shoulder, though by stretching its neck it could reach leaves 8 feet (2.4 m.)

(Left) head of Protylopus, *Late Eocene of North America, the oldest known member of the camel family; length of skull 4.7 inches (12 cm.). (Right)* Stenomylus, *an Early Miocene camel from North America, stood 27 inches (69 cm.) high at the shoulder*

Head and skull of Procamelus, a Miocene ancestor of modern camels and guanacos

Three North American camels. (Left) Oxydactylus, *a long-necked Miocene camel 4 feet 6 inches (137 cm.) at the shoulder. (Right)* Aepycamelus, *a Miocene beast with such long legs and neck that it has been nicknamed the "giraffe camel." (Top left) head and skull of* Procamelus, *length of skull 12 inches (30 cm.)*

above the ground. Each foot had two toes with pointed hoofs but no trace of pads.

This group culminated in *Aepycamelus* ("tall camel"), of the Middle to Late Miocene. Large species were 12 feet (3.7 m.) tall, rivaling modern giraffes in height, but their bodies did not slope toward the tail. The low-crowned, short teeth still were adapted to browsing, and the feet had nail-shaped hoofs as well as pads that carried them over sandy ground.

From Procamelus to Modern Camels. During the Middle and Late Miocene, the main line of camel development was typified by *Procamelus,* which looked like *Poëbrotherium* but had a longer neck and was 4 feet (1.2

560

(Left) **Camelops,** *an American camel 7 feet (2.1 m.) high at the shoulder. An Ice Age animal, it survived into Recent times. (Right) the guanaco, a humpless camel of modern South America; it lives on both mountains and plains*

m.) high at the shoulder. The head was long and low; teeth had vanished from the front of the upper jaw, forcing the beast to graze by catching grass between its hard upper gums and the lower incisors. The bony arch behind each orbit was complete, and the feet (like those of *Aepycamelus)* had both pads and hoofs.

Descendants of *Procamelus* were great travelers. Some went to Mexico and southeastward, crossing to South America as soon as marine barriers were removed, late in the Pliocene Epoch. These migrants gave rise to several forms with well-developed pads on the toes, including the modern guanaco and vicuña. The former, a humpless beast fitted to life among mountains as well as on plains, was tamed by prehistoric Indians. Its domestic descendants are the llama, a beast of burden, and the alpaca, which is bred for its wool.

Camels also reached Asia in Pliocene times, evolving into two genera, *Camelus* and *Paracamelus,* which ranged from China to Europe and northern Africa during the Pleistocene. The latter is now extinct, but the former survives in two fully domesticated species. The one-humped dromedary, which may be native to Africa, is a big animal, 10 to 11 feet (3–3.3 m.) long and 6 to 7 feet (1.8–2.1 m.) high at the shoulder. Two-humped, Bactrian camels, of central Asia, are not so large, have longer hair, and can endure colder climates than their one-humped relatives.

No one knows when or where humps evolved, for these fat-filled structures leave no mark on the skeleton. Many authorities assume that humps appeared in the Old World; others put them on Pleistocene camels of North America. Some of the latter camels were as large as dromedaries, but others were 15 feet (4.6 m.) tall and were much more heavily built than the earlier giraffe camels. At least one genus, *Camelops,* survived into the Recent Epoch, for its skull, with shreds of dry flesh, has been found in a cave near Fillmore, Utah.

Mesonychids, Carnivorous Ungulates. Less closely related to the arctocyonids were a number of other ungulate groups. Among the most unusual of these were the mesonychids. For many years they were considered to be creodonts, but while obviously carnivorous, they had nothing to do with the

Synoplotherium, *a doglike mesonychid of Middle Eocene age. Length about 4 feet (1.2 m.)*

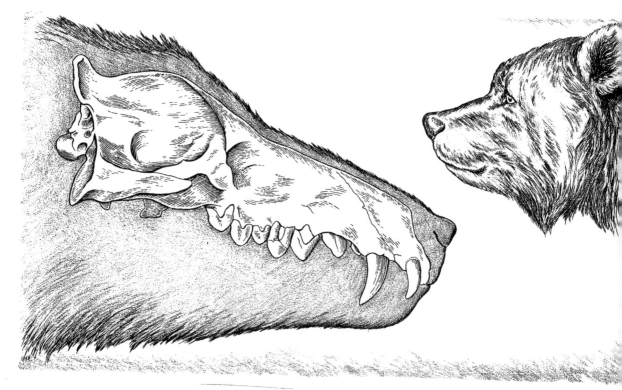

Head of an Alaska brown bear (right), the largest living carnivore, and the giant mesonychid Andrewsarchus, *from Mongolia, drawn to the same scale. The bear's skull is 18 to 19 inches (46–48 cm.) long; that of the mesonychid measures 34 inches (86 cm.) in length*

true carnivores. More recently, however, it has been found that mesonychids were part of the great radiation of placental ungulates.

Synoplotherium lived during the Middle Eocene in North America; apparently it was an active hunter and resembled a short-legged wolf with an oversized head. *Andrewsarchus,* from the Late Eocene of Asia, had a skull 34 inches (86 cm.) long—that of the Alaska brown bear is only 18 to 19 inches (46–48 cm.). If other dimensions were in proportion, that creodont would have been 12 feet 6 inches (3.8 m.) long and more than 6 feet (1.8 m.) high when it stood on all fours.

Though we do not see mesonychids today, they gave rise to one very successful modern group, the whales.

MAMMALS TO THE SEA

We have found that reptiles, which evolved on land, soon sent invaders into the water. Early mammals did the same, in the form of whale-like beasts known as archaeocetes, zeuglodonts, or yoke-toothed whales.

The oldest known archaeocete whale comes from Early Eocene rocks of Pakistan. Its skull and teeth suggest that its ancestor was a mesonychid creodont that presumably fed upon fish and spent more and more time in the water. Other than the skull, the skeleton of this earliest archaeocete is unknown. It is likely, however, that it could come out on land from time to time.

However, by the Middle Eocene, archaeocetes were fully aquatic. We see this in the pointed muzzle, elongate body, flipperlike forelegs, and hind legs so tiny that they were hidden under flesh. The serrate cheek teeth had double roots, but teeth at the front of the mouth were pointed or peglike. Nostrils had moved to the top of the head, about halfway between the muzzle and the eyes.

Archaeocetes culminated in *Basilosaurus,* also known as *Zeuglodon* ("yoke tooth"), whose remains are found in Late Eocene deposits near the southern Atlantic coast of North America. *Basilosaurus* reached lengths of 55 to 70 feet (16.8–21.3 m.), with a relatively short head and a very long tail whose vertebrae were larger than those of its short, slim body. Tail vertebrae of this and other archaeocetes are frequently found in eastern North America, Africa, Europe, and New Zealand.

A few small, short-bodied archaeocetes survived into the Oligocene. Their place in the sea was taken by true whales, which probably were descended from unspecialized archaeocetes. Early whales had short, stocky bodies, and their nostrils formed a single blowhole that lay between or even behind the eyes. Some genera possessed triangular teeth much like those of sharks, though their bodies resembled porpoises'. During Miocene and later times, however, the group divided into true porpoises, beaked whales, sperm whales, and whalebone whales. The first three of these retained their teeth

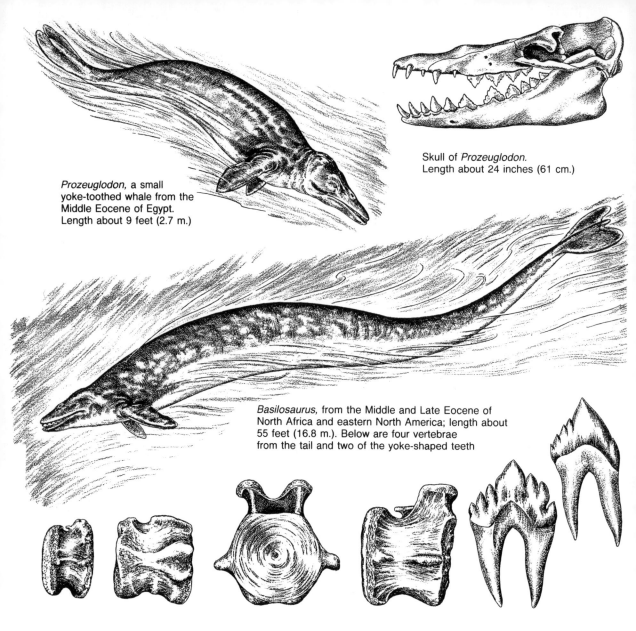

Prozeuglodon, a small yoke-toothed whale from the Middle Eocene of Egypt. Length about 9 feet (2.7 m.)

Skull of Prozeuglodon. Length about 24 inches (61 cm.)

Basilosaurus, from the Middle and Late Eocene of North Africa and eastern North America; length about 55 feet (16.8 m.). Below are four vertebrae from the tail and two of the yoke-shaped teeth

A primitive and an advanced archaeocete, or yoke-toothed whale

and even increased their number to several times the original forty-four. Whalebone whales, however, became toothless and began to capture small animals in plates of "whalebone"—really specialized skin—hanging down from the roof of the mouth. Whalebone whales also have become the largest of all living animals. The modern blue whale, for example, reaches lengths 30 meters (98 ft.) and weights of 112.5 tonnes (123.8 T.). No dinosaur is known for sure to have been as large as this, though some incomplete skeletons suggest that there may have been (see Chapter XXVII).

Condylarths. *Phenacodus*, known from the Late Paleocene to the Early Eocene of North America and the Early Eocene of Europe, is almost exactly what one would predict for the ancestor of the horses and other perissodactyls before the unique structure of the ankle of the hind foot evolved. Though some species were as small as a fox, others reached the height of a sheep but were not so heavy. All had long heads with eyes that were placed far forward, long tails, and five-toed feet that bore small hoofs.

Condylarths also reached South America. The Early Eocene *Didolodus,* from Argentina, was quite similar to *Phenacodus.* While condylarths became extinct in the Northern Hemisphere at the end of the Eocene, they carried on in South America until at least the Middle Miocene, when *Megadolodus* lived in what is now Colombia.

Phenacodus, *a condylarth found in the Late Paleocene to Early Eocene of North America and the Early Eocene of Europe. The largest species were about 5 feet 6 inches (1.7 m.) in length*

PERISSODACTYLS, THE ODD-TOED UNGULATES

At the end of the Paleocene, a group of ungulates arose that had the axis of force on the feet pass through the single, central toe. As this group of ungulates, the perissodactyls, evolved, side toes were often reduced and the central one became more and more emphasized until, in some groups like the modern horse, there was only one functional toe. All that remained of the other toes were mere splints of bone.

In addition to this, the ankle of the hind foot developed in such a manner as to reduce the amount of side-to-side motion of the foot. This made the perissodactyls better runners, just as did the modifications to the ankles of artiodactyls.

The Massive Titanotheres. Titanotheres are the only major group of perissodactyls that are now extinct. The largest denizens of the Early Oligocene of Asia and North America were the titanotheres, or brontotheres, which reached lengths of 12 to 14 feet (3.7–4.3 m.), heights of 7 feet to 8 feet 4 inches (2.1–2.5 m.), and weights of 4 to 5 tons (3.6–4.5 t.). In shape they resembled modern rhinos, with broad, deep bodies and massive legs. Like the rhinos, titanotheres were perissodactyls. Their stubby feet had three hoof-bearing toes behind and four in front. The head was long, low, and concave. Two broad, blunt, bony "horns" grew side by side on the nose and were larger in males than in females. They were dangerous weapons when backed by their owners' weight. The bulls used them to batter predators and rivals, some of which carried away broken ribs as souvenirs of battle.

Early Eocene titanotheres are known from Asia and were plump beasts 12 to 20 inches (30 to 51 cm.) in height, with skulls that bore no trace of horns. By the Middle Eocene, when they had reached North America, titanotheres had evolved larger bodies, some 40 inches (1 m.) tall, and horns had begun to develop as low knobs above the eyes. Horns, as well as overall body size, continued to become larger in the Late Eocene. One of the earliest Oligocene species was 10 feet (3 m.) long and 5 feet (1.5 m.) tall, or as large as a good-sized rhinoceros. The real giants, which appeared somewhat later, were massive beasts with big horns and low, broad skulls that matched the bulk of their bodies.

All titanotheres seem to have been browsers, though the smallest species fed on plants that were little more than herbs. Giants, such as *Brontops* and *Brontotherium,* pulled leaves from tall shrubs and low trees with their lips, because their incisor teeth were too small for use or had disappeared. Molars, however, had grown into large crushing and grinding teeth which were twice as wide in the upper jaw as they were below. Their size shows that they could dispose of coarse food, though they were neither long enough nor hard enough to cope with gritty, siliceous grasses.

The brain of the brontothere increased in size until it rivaled that of the modern rhinoceros. Brontotheres seem to have been less intelligent, however, for they had fewer folds in the cerebellum, whose forward parts were not much swollen. The brain also was still *relatively* small; in a 4-ton (3.6-t.) titanothere, it was little larger than a man's clenched fists. A rhinoceros with a brain of similar size weighs little more than 2 tons (1.8 t.). Some theorists have suggested that poor brains plus teeth that could not cope with a steady diet of grass explain why titanotheres died out at the end of the Early Oligocene.

Rhinos, the horned and the hornless.   Today we think of rhinoceroses as large, ponderous animals with prominent horns. But, in the Early Eocene, their ancestors were quite small and agile and lacked horns.

Some rhinos such as *Hyracodon* persisted into the Middle Oligocene of North America as small, hornless animals with slender legs, which suggests that they ran upon dry uplands. *Metamynodon,* however, was a barrel-bodied beast 8 to 14 feet (2.4–4.3 m.) long that suggests an overgrown version of the modern pigmy hippopotamus. *Metamynodon* undoubtedly spent most of its time in rivers and swampy lakes, where its large size protected at least the adults from prowling crocodiles.

A quite different rhinoceros was one that lived in the Oligocene and Miocene of Asia. In 1911 a British scientist working in the hills of Baluchistan, in

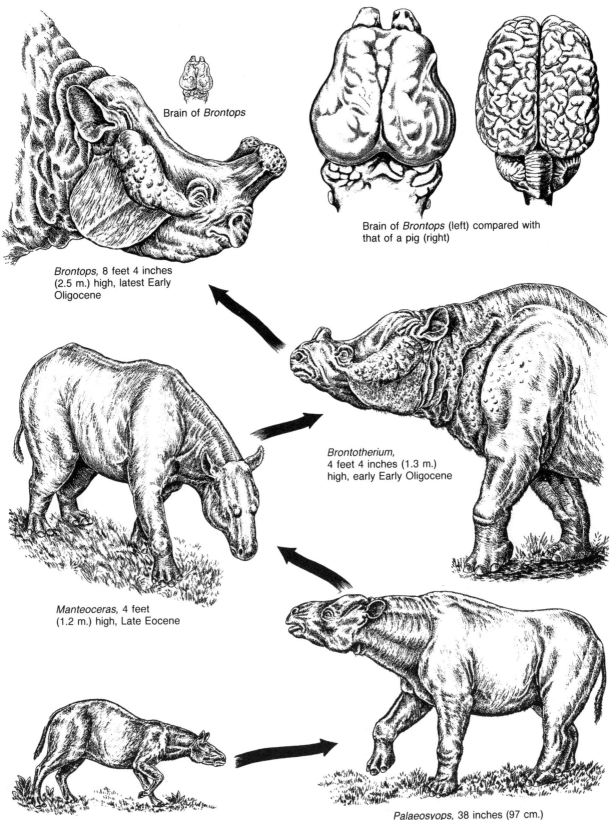

Brain of *Brontops*

Brain of *Brontops* (left) compared with that of a pig (right)

Brontops, 8 feet 4 inches (2.5 m.) high, latest Early Oligocene

Brontotherium, 4 feet 4 inches (1.3 m.) high, early Early Oligocene

Manteoceras, 4 feet (1.2 m.) high, Late Eocene

Palaeosyops, 38 inches (97 cm.) high, Middle Eocene

Eotitanops, 20 inches (51 cm.) high, Early Eocene

Evolution of the North American titanotheres

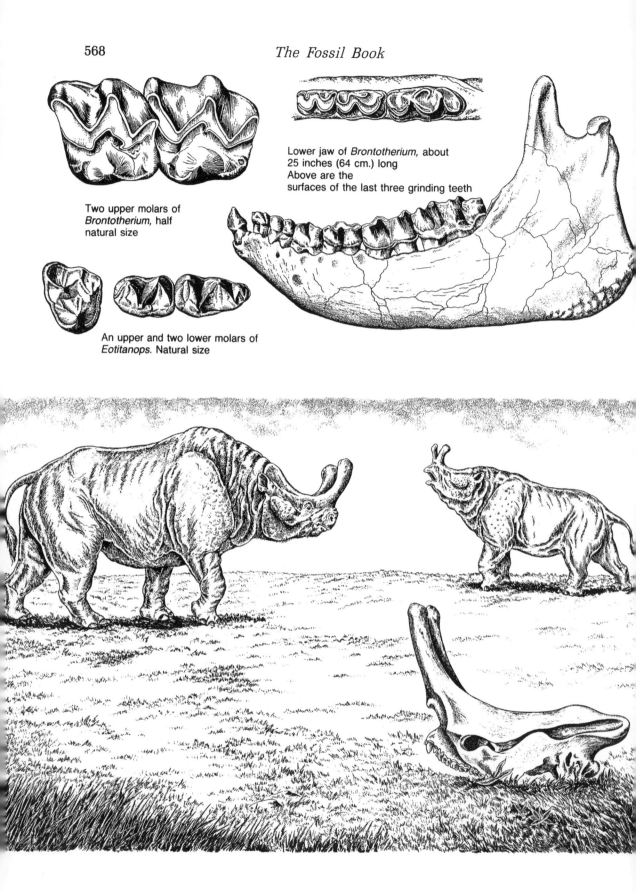

Two upper molars of
Brontotherium, half
natural size

Lower jaw of *Brontotherium,* about
25 inches (64 cm.) long
Above are the
surfaces of the last three grinding teeth

An upper and two lower molars of
Eotitanops. Natural size

what was then northwestern India, found a few bones of a creature that seemed to be a rhinoceros but was larger than any known elephant. He called it *Baluchitherium* ("beast of Baluchistan") and hoped that more adequate fossils would be discovered.

That hope was fulfilled in 1922 by Walter Granger, from the American Museum of Natural History, working in Mongolia. There he found three partial skeletons of *Baluchitherium,* one of which included the skull. Its 365 fragments were removed and shipped to New York, where a skilled preparator and his assistants spent three months putting the pieces together. In the end they had the world's biggest rhinoceros and the largest mammal known to have lived on land.

In an age when a hippopotamus is big and the elephant a giant, *Baluchitherium* seems almost unreal. Its head was about 5 feet (1.5 m.) long, yet it was absurdly small upon the gigantic body, which stood 18 feet (5.5 m.) high at the shoulder and was very deep. *Baluchitherium* was a browser that lived in small herds; by raising its head and neck it could easily nibble twigs and leaves 20 feet (6.1 m.) above the ground.

Brontotherium platyceras, *one of the largest titanotheres. The female is smaller than the male and has shorter horns. The male skull lying on the ground is about 45 inches (114 cm.) long*

Metamynodon *(top), a swamp-dwelling rhinoceros of the Late Eocene to Late Oligocene of North America and Early to Late Oligocene of Asia; length 8 to 14 feet (2.4–4.3 m.). At bottom right is* Hyracodon, *a swift-running rhinoceros about 5 feet (1.5 m.) long. Best known from the Late Eocene to Late Oligocene of North America, it may also have reached Europe in the Early Oligocene. It must have lived on dry uplands*

Baluchitherium, *an Oligocene rhinoceros from Asia, was 18 feet (5.5 m.) high at the shoulder. At the left, its femur is compared with a 6-foot (1.8-m.) man*

A slab from the Miocene bone bed at Agate Springs, Nebraska. It contains about forty-three hundred bones and skulls. (Photo courtesy of the American Museum of Natural History, New York)

Most fossil rhinos occur singly or in small numbers. However, in 1877 Captain James Cook, a pioneer scout and ranchman, discovered near the postoffice at Agate, Nebraska, a great fossil deposit crowded with the remains of thousands of individuals. In the Early Miocene, dry plains were often swept by dust storms that smothered piglike oreodonts that had huddled together for shelter. Streams turned into floods after sudden rains, drowning many animals and sweeping away the carcasses of others that had died and lay on the ground. These remains were then deposited in sandbanks that became veritable bone beds, crowded from top to bottom with remains of mammals.

The concentration that James Cook found lies in two flat-topped hills and was the sand, gravel, and bones that filled the channel of an ancient Miocene stream that roughly paralleled the present Niobrara River. No one knows how many bones the deposit once contained, because all except the two small hills has been worn away. But there are forty-three hundred skulls and separate bones in one slab of gray-buff sandstone with an area of 44 square feet (4.1 sq. m.); at that rate, one of the two hills must contain thirty-four hundred skulls and bones belonging to seventeen thousand skeletons. Enough to meet the needs of museums for all time to come!

Of those seventeen thousand skeletons, at least sixteen thousand represent a rhinoceros named *Diceratherium* (see Chapter I, where there is pictured a mold of this animal preserved in a lava flow). It weighed no more than a smallish hog, though its legs were longer and thicker. Males had two small horns side by side on the nose, but the female was hornless. *Diceratherium* must have ranged the Early Miocene plains in the western United States in herds as great as those of the modern bison, which numbered about 60 million before the Europeans came.

Rhinos remained prominent in North America through the Miocene, but by the Middle Pliocene they had become extinct. They continued to thrive in Africa, Asia, and Europe through the Pleistocene.

Diceratherium *(left), the Miocene rhinoceros whose remains are abundant in the Agate bone beds. Height at the shoulder, about 3 feet 4 inches (102 cm.). The two small horns were side by side.* **Promerycochoerus** *(right), a piglike oreodont of Miocene age about 5 feet 6 inches (168 cm.) long*

Chalicotheres, the clawed perissodactyls.   When we think of perissodactyls, we tend to think of hoofed animals, as the living horses, tapirs, and rhinos all have them. However, one branch of the family tree was noted for the prominent claws developed on its feet. These are the chalicotheres. When first found, the skulls were correctly recognized as belonging to the perissodactyls, but the feet were regarded as either giant pangolins' or edentates'. More than sixty years were required to realize that these various parts of the skeleton belonged together. So much for the popular view that a paleontologist can reconstruct an entire skeleton from a single bone or tooth with unerring accuracy!

(Left) Dinohyus, *a "giant pig" of the Agate Springs bone bed. Height at shoulder 7 feet (2.1 m.). (Right)* Moropus, *the herbivore whose hoofs had become claws*

One of the largest chalicotheres was *Moropus,* skeletons of which are known from the Agate bone bed. This creature had a head like a horse, the thick body and stubby tail of a tapir, the stocky forelegs of a rhino, hind legs suggesting those of a bear, and the heavy claws that are the hallmark of the group. Both canines and upper incisors were missing. The cheek teeth were broad and low. Because they must have chewed soft food, one theory makes *Moropus* a browser that sat up and pulled down branches with its powerful forelegs. Another theory, which is more convincing, says that *Moropus* fed largely on roots and bulbs and therefore used its claws for digging. They may also have become weapons when it was attacked.

Horses of Many Kinds. The most familiar perissodactyl to most of us is the horse. The earliest ancestral horse was discovered twice, with attendant complication in names. The first discovery, made in Europe, was called *Hyracotherium,* because of a superficial resemblance to the Old World cony, or hyrax. American fossils were better interpreted and became *Eohippus,* or "dawn horse"—a name that must be abandoned in technical works, for *Hyracotherium* was named first and so has priority. Because eohippus is familiar and well established, however, we may keep it in nontechnical usage without the capital *E.*

The Ancestral Dawn Horse. Like most really promising ancestors, eohippus was small and unspecialized. Some species were 10 inches (25 cm.) high at the shoulder, weighed 8 or 9 pounds (3.6–4.1 kg.), comparable to an alley cat in bulk. Others ranged up to 20 inches (51 cm.) high and weighed about four times as much. All had arched, flexible backs and high hindquar-

573

ters, which gave the beasts an almost rabbitlike appearance. We are tempted to say they would have made fine pets.

This idea vanishes when we examine eohippus' brain. It was small, primitive, and probably not much more developed than that of *Phenacodus.* The skull resembled that of a condylarth too, with eyes placed near the middle and sockets, or orbits, that were open behind. There were forty-four teeth—the primitive number—with small gaps between incisors and canines, and then between canines and premolars. The grinding teeth, which had low crowns, were fit only for eating soft leaves and pulpy fruits. The front feet had four toes, each with a tiny hoof; the hind feet possessed only three and so showed eohippus to be a perissodactyl. Most of the weight was carried by pads like dogs' on the soles of the feet, not by the hoofs.

Hind foot

Forefoot

Hyracotherium, or eohippus, the oldest known ancestor of horses

The "dawn horse," eohippus, of Early Eocene age in Europe and North America. This particular species was about 18 inches (46 cm.) long and 9 inches (23 cm.) high at the shoulder

Branching of the Family Tree. Eohippus disappeared from Europe during the Middle Eocene. Before doing so, however, it produced descendants called palaeotheres, which had large bodies, short legs, long necks, and large heads with snouts like tapirs'. Hoofs were well developed, and some species acquired high grinding teeth with cement on the crowns. Palaeotheres once ranged into western Asia, and they survived until Early Oligocene times. The latest species were as large as some modern rhinoceroses and twice as heavy as any modern horse.

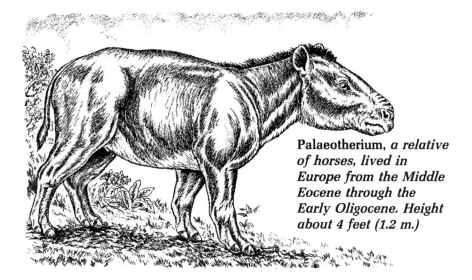

Palaeotherium, *a relative of horses, lived in Europe from the Middle Eocene through the Early Oligocene. Height about 4 feet (1.2 m.)*

In North America, eohippus survived to the end of the Eocene. Some of its Middle and Late Eocene descendants lost the splint bones from their hind feet, while their premolar teeth began to resemble molars. These variants have been dignified by two names, *Orohippus* and *Epihippus,* but only experts can distinguish them from the original genus.

Two Primitive Three-toed Horses. Greater change was made by *Mesohippus,* of the Oligocene. Though species varied in size, the typical *Mesohippus* was about 20 inches (51 cm.) high and 40 inches (1 m.) long, or about as large as a collie dog. The skull was slender and rather deep, with a horse-type muzzle but shallow lower jaws. The eyes were farther back than those of eohippus, the orbits were still open behind, and the brain was surprisingly large for that of an Oligocene mammal. The gap between canines and premolars, or diastema, was much larger than it had been in eohippus. The grinders still had low crowns, showing that *Mesohippus* browsed on leaves and perhaps ate pulpy fruits.

Progressive and old-fashioned characters also mingled in the feet of *Mesohippus.* Each forefoot had lost one toe, whose only remnant was a splint hidden under the skin. The middle toe of each foot was the largest, but all three had usable hoofs. Still, most of the weight rested on dog-type pads, much as it did in eohippus. The back also was arched, and the hind legs still were longer than the forelegs. *Mesohippus* apparently ran with deerlike leaps.

Mesohippus was followed by *Miohippus,* a larger and somewhat more horselike beast, whose descendants split into four principal groups. Two of these kept low browsing teeth and three usable toes on which some species crossed the land bridge to Asia and finally wandered into Europe. Back in

Mesohippus, *a three-toed horse of Oligocene age, from the White River Badlands of South Dakota. Length about 40 inches (102 cm.)*

Forefoot

Hind foot

North America, other species apparently became as large as the African rhinoceros, which is 5 feet (1.5 m.) tall and 11 to 12 feet (3.4–3.7 m.) long, and weighs about 4,000 pounds (1.8 t.). Appropriately named *Megahippus* ("big horse"), these giants contrast with a third American group, *Archaeohippus*. Its members evolved into pigmies no larger than a good-sized eohippus.

Progressive Merychippus. Fourth among the descendants of *Miohippus* was a group we call progressive merely because it led toward modern horses. Its most important member, *Merychippus,* appeared in the Early Miocene and lived on through to Late Miocene times. Contrasting *Merychippus* with earlier genera, we notice these horselike traits:

SIZE. About as large as a Shetland pony. Height at the shoulders 40 inches (1 m.), which a horseman would call 10 "hands."

BUILD. Horselike, with an almost straight back. Some stocky species were slow runners; others were slender and swift.

EYES. Far back on the head, as in modern horses. Each orbit was closed behind the eye by a bar of bone.

LEGS. Bones of the foreleg were fused. Part of one bone (fibula) in the hind leg had disappeared, leaving only a spike.

FEET. The middle toe of each foot was large, with a broad hoof that carried the weight. The second and fourth toes were very short.

TEETH. Though *Merychippus* was born with low-crowned teeth, they were replaced by high-crowned premolars and molars whose enamel was deeply folded and crumpled and was set in bone-like cement. These teeth grew throughout most of the animal's life, presenting rough grinding surfaces as they were worn down. Roots finally formed and growth was halted at the onset of old age. The jaws worked with a side-to-side, grinding motion as well as up and down.

High-crowned teeth that kept growing while they were used enabled *Mer-*

Equus, 5 feet (1.5 m.) high at the shoulder. This horse originated in North America during the Pliocene and became extinct there near the end of the Pleistocene. In Asia, Africa, and Europe it persists to the present day and has been introduced by Europeans to all continents except Antarctica

Pliohippus, the first one-toed horse. Middle to Late Miocene of North America

Mesohippus, a primitive three-toed horse. Early to Middle Oligocene of North America

Merychippus, an advanced three-toed horse about 40 inches (102 cm.) high. Only one toe on each foot touched the ground. Early to Middle Miocene of North America

Hyracotherium, or eohippus, the oldest known horse. Early Eocene, Europe, Asia, and North America

The "dawn horse" and some of its descendants

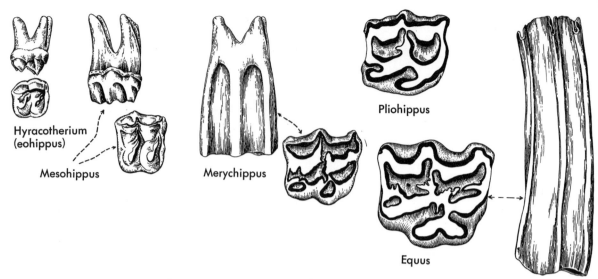

As horses evolved, their molars, or grinding teeth, grew larger and the enamel (shown in black) was folded into more and more complex patterns

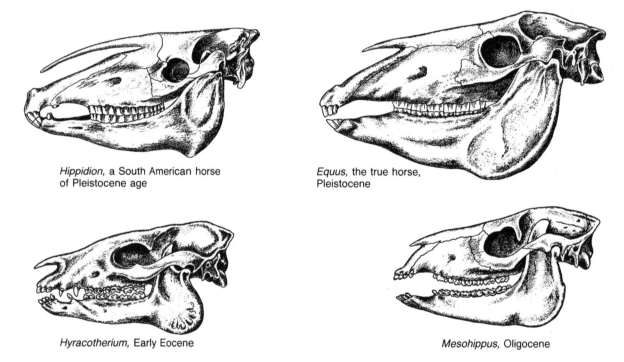

Hippidion, a South American horse of Pleistocene age

Equus, the true horse, Pleistocene

Hyracotherium, Early Eocene

Mesohippus, Oligocene

How skulls changed in the horse family

ychippus to give up browsing and feed upon grass, which contains abrasive silica. Grass spread widely during Miocene times, allowing the new three-toed grazers to take up life on prairies and plains, where their long legs and running feet provided escape from carnivores. Descendants of *Merychippus* ranged through North and South America, Asia, Europe, and Africa during the latest Miocene and Pliocene epochs. One African form lived on through much of the Pleistocene.

From Three Toes to One. Further advances were made by *Pliohippus,* of Middle to Late Miocene age. In some of its species the small toes became vestigial; in others they were reduced to tiny *splint bones* below the hock and "knee." *Pliohippus* also developed a deep body and grinding teeth that grew higher and higher, while canines became small and the gap behind them widened. As the Pliocene closed, these changes turned certain North American descendants of *Pliohippus* into *Equus,* the modern horse. In South America, another branch of *Pliohippus* gave rise to short-legged horses of the genus *Hippidion,* whose skull had amazingly long nasal bones supported by a ridge of cartilage that is not preserved in fossils. Some of these beasts ranged the open, level pampas, but others apparently lived on eastern slopes of the Andes.

Equus, The Modern Horse. Though *Equus* arose in North America during the Pleistocene, it soon spread to other continents and evolved into varied subgenera and a large number of species. Those that remained in their homeland included animals 40 inches (102 cm.) in height and others as large as the modern Belgian draft horse, which stands 5 feet 5 inches (165 cm.) high at the shoulder and weighs as much as a ton (0.9 t.). An abundant species of the Great Plains of central North America was not quite as large as the modern quarter horse, now ridden by many ranchers. Another Pleistocene species was about the size of a zebra but was less gracefully built. It became extinct in North America near the end of the Pleistocene. Entering Asia in the Early Pliocene, it quickly spread to Africa and Europe, where it persists to the present day. Reintroduced into North America by Europeans, it has also been taken by them to all other continents.

The Decline of Wild Horses. Enormous herds of horses lived in Europe, Asia, and Africa during the Pleistocene. In the Americas they ranged from Alaska to the Straits of Magellan. Horses died out in the New World, became scarce, and finally vanished from Europe, remaining abundant only on the plains of Africa and, for a while, in Asia. Survivors include the Africa ass, three species of zebras, the Asiatic onager, and another Asiatic species that may survive only in zoos. Domestic breeds are descended from extinct Asiatic horses and the ass of Africa.

This widespread extinction of horses is a puzzle. True, humans have destroyed some modern species and others have suffered from crossing with domestic breeds. But these factors seem inadequate to explain the decline that took place during Late Pleistocene and early Recent times. We also find no evidence that glaciation, disappearance of pastures, predatory carnivores, epidemics, or competition with other grazers was responsible. The mystery is deepened by the fact that domestic horses from the Old World ran wild and became plentiful in both North and South America after they were reintroduced by Europeans.

PRODUCTS OF ISOLATION: THE SOUTH AMERICAN UNGULATES

For much of the Cenozoic, South America was much as Australia is today, completely surrounded by water. Apparently a few ungulates managed to reach the continent in the Paleocene before connections with the outside world were almost completely severed. Alternatively, they may have evolved there from nonungulate stock. In any case, from these pioneers, several orders unique to South America evolved.

The vast majority of South American ungulates are included in the notoungulates. They are not restricted to that continent, but certainly their history is centered there. Two specimens are known from North America, and three genera occur in Asia in the Paleocene. But after that they are an exclusively South American group. Common throughout the Cenozoic, one of the last notoungulates was *Toxodon,* a Pliocene and Pleistocene form with a deep head, thick body, and three-toed feet that seem too small to have been able to support their great bulk. *Toxodon* may have been semiaquatic, or it may have been a browser in the manner of titanotheres. Other notoungulates lived like, and even resembled, creodonts and modern rabbits.

The Litopterns. The second-most-abundant ungulate group in South America were the Litopterns. They probably began as descendants of primitive hoofed mammals much like *Phenacodus.* In later times some became queer, long-snouted creatures, while others were more horselike than contemporary horses.

Macrauchenia *(left) and* Toxodon *(right), two Pleistocene ungulates of South America. The former stood 5 feet (1.5 m.) high at the shoulder;* Toxodon *was more than 4 feet (1.2 m.)*

Thoatherium, *a "false horse" 17 inches (43 cm.) high, from the Miocene of South America; and the bones of one hind foot*

That statement sounds like a paradox, but it makes anatomical sense. To us the word *horse* means a mammal that has one large toe on each foot, covered by a hoof. Miocene and Pliocene horses had three toes; though the beasts might walk on only one, the other two were there and bore hoofs. But such litopterns as *Thoatherium* had one-toed feet with only two very small splint bones to show where other toes had been. With a light body and long, slender legs, this animal probably ran as swiftly as the modern antelope.

The second family of litopterns reached its zenith in *Macrauchenia,* of Pliocene and Pleistocene age. The best-known species had a broad body about 5 feet (1.5 m.) high, with thick legs and three-toed, hoofed feet. The neck and the head resembled those of the camel, or would have done so except for the short, muscular trunk.

Other South American ungulates. Four other South American ungulate orders are known. All are rather large animals and show some convergence on unrelated forms elsewhere in the world. Pyrotheres have been compared to elephants, astrapotheres and trigonostylopids to amynodont rhinoceroses, and xenungulates to pantodonts and dinoceratans. Compared to the notoungulates and litopterns, none of these four orders had many species, the xenungulates only two. All appeared in the Paleocene or Eocene, and the last of them became extinct before the end of the Miocene. In contrast, the notoungulates and the litopterns persisted until the Pleistocene.

PROBOSCIDEANS: LONG NOSES AND TUSKS

The story of proboscideans is one of repeated migrations, with evolutionary changes that turned small, undistinguished beasts into tusked, trunk-bearing giants that weighed 5 to perhaps 7 tons (4.5–6.4 t.).

Ancestors and Aberrant Tuskers. *Moeritherium* could be a proboscidean, a sirenian, or a desmostylan. Whichever group it belongs to, it is the oldest known member. Perhaps it is closely related to all three. The name *Moeritherium* was given because fossils of this animal were first found near ancient Lake Moeris, whose bed is now a fertile valley in the Egyptian province of Fayum. *Moeritherium* was about 5 feet (1.5 m.) long and 25 inches (64 cm.) high at the shoulder, with a long, thick, round body, sturdy legs, and short, five-toed feet. The skull was low, wide, and blunt, the eyes were far forward, and the high-placed nostrils suggest a snout like a tapir's. The grinding teeth were low-crowned, but four incisors were large enough to show that the growth of tusks had begun. It probably was at least partially aquatic, for the body shape is similar to that of the hippopotamus, and it has always been found in marine deltaic deposits.

Moeritherium was no wanderer, but remained in the lowlands of northern Africa during the Late Eocene and Early Oligocene epochs. At least three divergent groups of proboscideans evolved there from *Moeritherium* or close relatives.

Moeritherium, *about 2 feet (60 cm.) high at the shoulder. The oldest known close relative of elephants, it lived in swampy regions of northern Africa during Late Eocene and Early Oligocene times*

Deinotherium was the most aberrant of these: a beast of elephantine build and bulk that was still not a true elephant. One Miocene species had a low-browed skull about 48 inches (122 cm.) long, with a square jaw and projecting bones in the nose, which certainly was a trunk. Grinding teeth were low-crowned and primitive. The upper jaw was short and lacked incisors, but the chin extended outward and downward and carried two short, curved tusks. *Deinotherium* became common in Africa, Asia, and Eastern Europe during the Miocene. It then died out in Europe and Asia but survived well into the Pleistocene of tropical Africa. There is no hint that it ever reached the Americas.

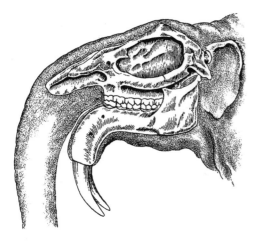

Skull of Deinotherium, *with downcurved jaw. Length 48 inches (122 cm.). Widespread in the Old World during the Miocene, it persisted into the Pleistocene in Africa*

A Variety of Mastodonts. A second group that sprang from a stock close to *Moeritherium* began with *Palaeomastodon*, found in Early Oligocene rocks of North Africa. Some species were tapirlike beasts 3 to 4 feet (0.9–1.2 m.) high, but others reached a height of 6 feet (1.8 m.) and weighed a couple of tons (1.8 t.). All had thick legs, blunt feet, skulls that were high at the back, and short trunks instead of snouts. Both upper and lower jaws bore tusks, but those of the upper jaw were longer and curved downward. The grinding teeth had low crowns with blunt-tipped crests and ended in several roots.

During the next 5 million years, descendants of *Palaeomastodon* reached Europe and crossed Asia to North America but left few if any fossils along their routes of travel. As the animals wandered, they also evolved, becoming elephantine in bulk and shape but retaining their low-crowned, crested teeth. Some also kept four tusks, but others lost those of the lower jaw.

The term *Mastodon* was once applied to a long series of these animals that lived during the Miocene and later epochs. The Miocene and Pliocene beasts then received other names, restricting *Mastodon* to two species of Pleistocene and Early Recent age. Then an older name, *Mammut,* was found,

Palaeomastodon from North Africa, Late Eocene to Middle Oligocene age, ranged from 3 to 6 feet (0.9–1.8 m.) in height. It had developed a short trunk and tusks, and its grinding teeth were becoming large

The American mastodon, 7 feet to 9 feet 6 inches (2.1–2.9 m.) in height; and one of its molar teeth

and rules required that it be used for technical purposes. Mastodon thus became a general word, like eohippus, and is not to be capitalized.

So much for names and their changes. *Mammut* itself, which knew nothing of nomenclature, was an elephantine beast whose teeth (which are often found as fossils) still had separate roots and blunt crests. There were two good-sized tusks on the upper jaw, but the lower tusks had disappeared or were vestigial. The body was covered with rusty brown hair, and though each foot had five toes, most of the weight was carried by a springy pad. Heights ranged from 7 feet (2.1 m.) in females to 9 feet 6 inches (2.9 m.) in big bulls.

This description fits *Mammut americanum.* Another species found only in the American West differed in details. The American mastodon ranged from New England and Florida to Mexico, California, and Alaska. Fossil teeth indicate that it also crossed northern Asia and reached the plains of Eastern Europe. In North America, *M. americanum* lived beyond the end of the Ice Age and was hunted by early man. An animal whose remains were found in Ohio died eight to nine thousand years ago.

The Rise of Gomphotheres. Though mastodons had tusks and long trunks, they did not give rise to true elephants. The latter beasts are descendants of gomphotheres, a complex family whose teeth are so much like those of mastodonts that the two are sometimes confused.

The founder of this family was *Phiomia,* another descendant of the *Moeritherium* stock. *Phiomia,* which lived in Egypt during the Oligocene Epoch, was 4 feet 5 inches (135 cm.) in height, with a snoutlike trunk, long lower jaws, and very short tusks. Its grinding teeth were distinctive, for they had

Skull of Gomphotherium, or Trilophodon, about 36 inches long

Phiomia (right), about 4 feet 5 inches (135 cm.) high, was an Oligocene relative of mastodons. It lived in Egypt, but its descendant Gomphotherium (left) wandered into Europe, Asia, and North America; it reached 8 feet (2.4 m.) in height and had a very long lower jaw, and its skull was about 36 inches (91.5 cm.) long

divided crests and additional cusps, or blunt points. Except for their size, they resemble the molars of a pig.

Phiomia remained in Egypt, producing offspring that are variously known as *Gomphotherium* and *Trilophodon*. Again, names are not very important. What counts are changes in teeth and lower jaws. The former were increasingly complex; the latter became longer and longer, until some measured as much as 6 feet (1.8 m.). The upper jaws were relatively short, but the tusks they bore were longer than those of *Phiomia*. Some species were only 6 feet (1.8 m.) high, but others reached 8 feet (2.4 m.) and so equaled many circus elephants in size.

Aberrant Mud Grubbers. *Gomphotherium* apparently evolved in Africa but soon spread to Europe, Asia, and North America. With it came a related genus called *Platybelodon,* which had lost its upper tusks. The lower jaws narrowed in front of the cheek teeth but then flared out to accommodate two wide, flat tusks that formed a broad scoop with which *Platybelodon* dug roots from swamps. A short trunk kept the roots on the shovel, while a striplike tongue separated food from muck and passed the former back for chewing.

585

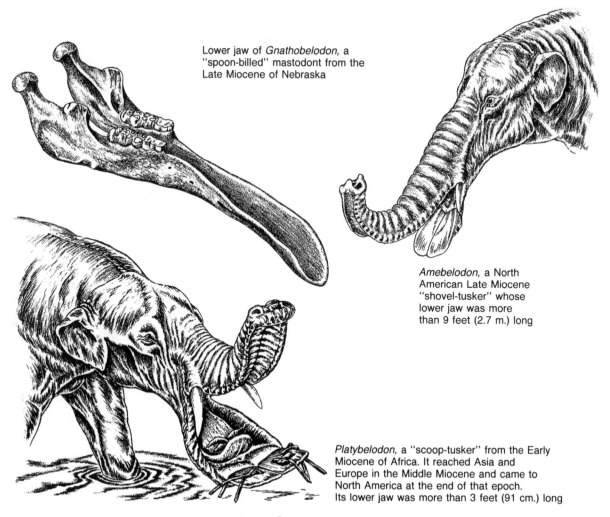

Lower jaw of *Gnathobelodon*, a "spoon-billed" mastodont from the Late Miocene of Nebraska

Amebelodon, a North American Late Miocene "shovel-tusker" whose lower jaw was more than 9 feet (2.7 m.) long

Platybelodon, a "scoop-tusker" from the Early Miocene of Africa. It reached Asia and Europe in the Middle Miocene and came to North America at the end of that epoch. Its lower jaw was more than 3 feet (91 cm.) long

Various aberrant mud grubbers

Scoop-tuskers were discovered in the Caucasus and made news in the early 1920s, when they were found in Mongolia. Then both jaws and skulls came to light in northwestern Nebraska, along with other mastodonts termed shovel-tuskers and spoon-bills. The former had tremendously long lower jaws bearing flat tusks that were longer but narrower than those of *Platybelodon*. Spoon-bills had lost their lower tusks, but their lower jaws formed concave, thin-edged "spoons" that were excellent for grubbing.

Stegodon and True Elephants. The ancestor of true elephants probably was an early *Gomphotherium*. Somewhere—perhaps in central Asia—it produced descendants whose skulls became short but high and whose lower jaws also were shortened. Their premolars became small too, but the molars increased in size and developed ridgelike crosswise crests of enamel partly covered by cement. New teeth began to advance obliquely instead of growing straight upward or downward, and only eight could be used at one time.

The first result of these changes was *Stegodon*, a very primitive elephant that evolved in the Late Miocene in Asia but reached Africa during the

Elephas, the modern elephant of Asia, and one of its complex molar teeth; the tusks are relatively small. Height 8 to 10 feet (2.4–3.0 m.) at the shoulder

Molar tooth of *Loxodonta*

Loxodonta, the modern African elephant. This genus also lived in Europe during the Pleistocene. Height 3 to 14 feet (0.9–4.3 m.) at the shoulder

Stegodon and one of its molars. This very primitive elephant appeared in Asia during the Pliocene Epoch

Three stages in the evolution of elephants, showing the increasing size and complexity of molar teeth and the reduction of tusks in the modern Elephas

Reconstruction of fossils of pygmy elephants from a Pleistocene island in the Mediterranean. (Photo courtesy of the Basel Natural History Museum, Switzerland)

Pliocene. Meanwhile it gave rise to three other groups, which ranged through Asia, Europe, Africa, and North America. Including species that survive today, we divide these true elephants as follows:

Loxodonts.   This group, which appeared in the Pliocene, includes modern African elephants *(Loxodonta)* and their fossil relatives, one species of which lived in Europe after man reached that continent. The loxodont skull is not much higher than that of *Stegodon,* and its grinding teeth are relatively low, with irregular, lozenge-shaped cross plates that rarely number more than ten. In *Loxodonta* itself the tusks are long but not deeply curved, the back is depressed behind the shoulders and slopes abruptly to the tail, and the ears are very large. The forelegs are longer than the hind, and there are four toes on each forefoot but only three behind.

Some loxodonts are very large; the big African species reaches a height of 11 feet 6 inches (3.5 m.) at the shoulder, and *Loxodonta antiqua,* of the Ice Age, is said to have reached 14 feet (4.3 m.). On the other hand, species that inhabited Malta and other Mediterranean islands were pygmies, the smallest being a little more than 3 feet (90 cm.) high and weighing no more than a good-sized pig. They were much smaller than the forest-dwelling pygmy elephant, of modern Africa, which reaches a height of about 6 feet (1.8 m.).

Mammoths.   These extinct elephants of the Pleistocene, or Ice Age, and early postglacial times have been given several names but now are placed in the genus *Mammuthus,* which must not be confused with *Mammut.* The skull is pointed at the back and was carried higher than that of *Loxodonta.* The tusks grew downward at first and then arched forward, becoming very large. In old males they often curved so far that they crossed and turned back toward the body. In some primitive European and Asiatic species, such as the southern mammoth *(Mammuthus meridionalis),* the molars contain only ten to twelve plates, but in progressive American types, plates of the third molars number twenty-six to thirty. There were four hoofs on each hind foot, but it is not clear whether the forefoot had four hoofs or five. If the number was five, one hoof was very small.

The largest North American mammoth, appropriately called *Mammuthus imperator,* lived in the South and Southwest of the United States and is one of the two tar-pit species described in Chapter XXXV. The other, generally called *M. columbi,* ranged northward through temperate regions. With allied species or subspecies, it reached a height of 10 feet 6 inches (3.2 m.) at the shoulder, in contrast to 13 feet 6 inches (4.1 m.) for big bulls of *M. imperator.*

Though fossils of the Columbia mammoth and its kin outnumber those of other American species, the animals are less widely known than *Mammuthus primigenius.* This is the woolly mammoth, which ranged from Western Europe across Asia and North America. In spite of its name, it was not very large; a big bull stood 9 feet (2.7 m.) high at the shoulder, though its head was 8 to 12 inches (20 to 30 cm.) higher. The tusks were large and

A woolly mammoth (Mammuthus primigenius). *This species ranged across Europe, Asia, and North America, and stood 12 feet (3.7 m.) at the shoulder*

deeply curved; those of one specimen measured 16 feet (4.9 m.) in length. The forelegs were long and the hind legs short, making the back slope steeply toward the tail. The skin bore a coat of gray wool covered by long, coarse, reddish-brown hair. This protection against rain, snow, and cold explains why the mammoth was able to live in comfort only a few miles from a glacier.

The woolly mammoth is one of those rare fossils whose soft parts are known, because frozen bodies complete with hair, skin, and dried blood have been found in Alaska and Siberia. It also appears in paintings and statuettes made by cave dwellers of Europe, who trapped the beast in pits and killed it with stone mauls attached to rawhide ropes that were thrown across overhanging branches, allowing the hammers to be pulled up and then dropped on the victims' backs or heads.

Asiatic Elephants (Elephas). These presumably are descendants of early mammoths; today, as in Pleistocene times, they inhabit southeastern Asia and the East Indies but are familiar in zoos and circuses. The skull is very short and deep and is rounded on top, often with a bulging "forehead." The tusks are directed downward and seem to be disappearing, because they never are very large. Many females, indeed, lack them, and so do some males. The molars are high and broad, and the last ones to appear have twenty-four closely folded cross plates. The back is arched behind the shoul-

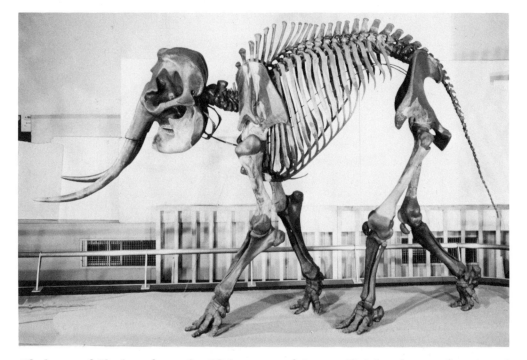

Skeleton of Elephas *from the Pleistocene of Japan. Height about 7 feet (2 m.). (Photograph provided by Yoshikazu Hasegawa, courtesy of the National Science Museum, Tokyo)*

ders; the feet are short and blunt, with five toes and pads of elastic tissue that receive most of the weight because they touch the ground before the toes do. There are five hoofs on each forefoot and four behind, though the hoof on each fifth toe may be very small. The brain, which weighs 10 to 11 pounds (4.5–5.0 kg.), seems to be superior to that of *Loxodonta.* The height of full-grown males reaches 8 to 10 feet (2.4–3.0 m.) at the shoulder, and the weight is 8,000 to 10,000 pounds (3.6–4.5 t.).

AQUATIC RELATIVES OF THE MOERITHERES

As *Moeritherium* seems to have been amphibious, it is not surprising that, besides proboscideans, two fully aquatic groups may have descended from it or its near relatives.

Sirenians, Aquatic Herbivores. Along the shores of the Tethys Seaway in the Early Eocene appeared the first sirenians. They soon spread through the tropics from the Americas across Africa and Europe to Asia and Australia. During the Miocene they reached their peak abundance, when about a dozen genera lived. Today there are only two genera, *Dugong* and *Trichechus.* A third one, however, Steller's sea cow *(Hydrodamalis)* was hunted to extinction in the eighteenth century, just twenty-seven years after it was first discovered.

Sirenians are the only mammals that feed exclusively on water plants. Their flippers are modified forelimbs and lack nails. The hind limbs have been completely lost. Characteristically, the bones, particularly the ribs, are very dense. This enables the animal to submerge easily.

Desmostylans, "linked pillars." For many years desmostylans were known only from their most peculiar teeth. They resemble a series of short segments of pipe that have been welded alongside one another, hence the name. So odd were these teeth that one early worker thought they might be relatives of the primitive mammals, the multituberculates.

Some skeletal material was subsequently found in Japan and California. Desmostylans are now known to have been marine mammals with four well-developed limbs. Presumably, they paddled around in shallow water and lived by crushing shellfish between their heavy, columnar teeth.

Desmostylans are confined to the circum-Pacific area. They appeared there in the Early Miocene and became extinct by the end of that epoch.

PHOLIDOTA, THE SCALEY ANTEATERS

Pangolins today are scale-covered specialized anteaters living in Africa and southern Asia. In the Oligocene, however, they were also present in

Paleoparadoxia from the Early Miocene of California

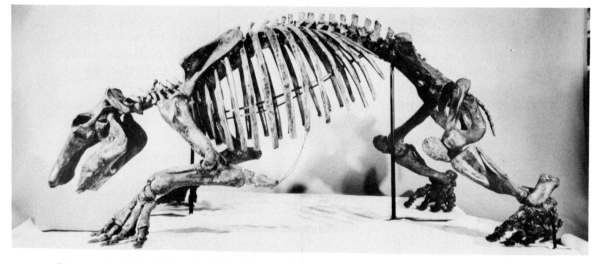

Paleoparadoxia tabatai, from the Middle Miocene of Japan

Two **Paleoparadoxia** *(desmostylans), from opposite sides of the Pacific. Lengths about 8 feet (2.4 m.). (Photos provided by Yoshikazu Hasegawa, courtesy of the National Science Museum, Tokyo; and Donald Savage, University of California, Berkeley)*

Middle Miocene marine outcrops in the Mizunami Basin, near Mizunami, Japan. From these deposits have come sharks and other fish; birds, deer, and porpoises; and two desmostylans: Desmostylus *and* Paleoparadoxia. *(Photograph provided by Keeichi Ono, courtesy of the National Science Museum, Tokyo)*

North America and Europe. Exactly where they arose in this area and out of which group is as yet unknown. During the 35 million years of their existence, they have not changed a great deal in their appearance.

RODENTS, A GREAT SUCCESS STORY

Most successful of all mammalian orders in terms of the number of genera and species are the rodents. There are more of them than all other mammals combined. It is, therefore, somewhat disquieting that their origins are the most obscure of any eutherian group and that their interrelations are still most uncertain as well.

Undoubtedly, rodents arose from some primitive insectivorous placental group during the Late Cretaceous or Paleocene. However, the oldest known, *Paramys* and *Franimys,* from the Late Paleocene of North America, are so markedly different from all other placentals that they provide no more clues than later rodents.

Once they appeared, rodents radiated rapidly and dispersed to all continents except Antarctica. Like primates, rodents reached South America in the Early Oligocene. Also like primates, these rodents, the caviomorphs, are almost restricted to that continent. Only the North American porcupine successfully emigrated from South America, after the Panamanian isthmus was established in the Pliocene. The most familiar example of this group is the guinea pig. While we tend to think of rodents as small to medium-sized mammals, one Pleistocene caviomorph from Argentina, *Telicomys,* was nearly the size of a rhinoceros.

North America, Europe, Asia, and Africa share the other major groups of rodents, though each continent was families unique to it. On each of these continents, the rodents are highly diversified. Australia, in contrast, has representatives of only one family, the murids, which includes the rats and mice. However, rodents only reached Australia in the Pliocene, and so they may not have had time to diversify there as much as elsewhere.

Beavers today all live in water, but in the Miocene of North America there were fully terrestrial forms. One of the oddest of these was *Ceratogaulus.* The name means "horned digger" and refers to the fact that there was a prominent pair of horns on the skull of these animals and that they excavated burrows in which to live. It is known that they did this, because fossil burrows have been discovered. Called *Daemonelix,* or the Devil's corkscrew, these spiraling burrows were filled with sediment that eventually became harder than the surrounding rock. Today they frequently can be seen in western Nebraska, where erosion has partially exposed them. Some of the burrows spiral downward for 5 feet (1.5 m.) and have a nearly horizontal chamber leading off from the bottom that is almost as long.

CHAPTER XXXIV

Moving Continents, Changing Climates, and Their Effects on Mammals

INTRODUCTION

 The history of mammals did not occur on a uniform, unchanging surface. Instead, during their nearly 200 million years of existence, the world has changed markedly. Continents have moved with respect to one another (see Chapter III). Some have split in two with an ocean forming between the pieces as they moved apart. Others have collided, with mountain ranges marking the area of impact.

In addition, the climate has changed rather drastically during the past 200 million years. Generally it was warm during the Mesozoic, and, with major exceptions, there was a general cooling trend during the Cenozoic, which led to the ice ages of the past one million years or so.

Correlated with increases and decreases of temperature were rising and falling sea levels. This relationship between temperature and sea level existed not only during the ice ages, when continental glaciers tied up large quantities of water on land that otherwise would have been in the sea; it also operated all through the Cenozoic, even when there was no significant glaciation.

When mammals first appeared, in the Late Triassic, 200 million years ago, the continents of the world were united into one large landmass, Pangaea. The climate was generally warmer and drier than at present. With no great oceanic, topographic, or climatic barriers between what are now the various continents on earth, the small, primitive mammals of that time were able to move much more freely from one region to another. This is reflected in the occurrence in many parts of the world of virtually identical mammals. *Morganucodon,* a primitive mammal often thought of as ancestral to the living monotremes, was first recognized in Great Britain in the 1940s. More recent work has shown that it also lived in Switzerland, China, and Arizona, with two closely related forms occurring in South Africa.

While *Morganucodon* was alive, Pangaea was starting to break up. Africa and South America began to split apart, and the first traces of the South Atlantic appeared. But another 100 million years was to pass before this ocean would be a serious barrier to the dispersal of mammals between the two continents.

After somewhat moister conditions in the Early Jurassic, the climate for the remainder of the period was on the average, drier. At the end of that period, mammals were still able to move across what are today major barriers to terrestrial animals. The Late Jurassic mammals of Como Bluff, Wyoming, show a striking resemblance to those from Durlston Head, England. The dinosaurs, too, that lived in western North America and Western Europe at that time are also similar. *Camptosaurus* and *Hypsilophodon* were just two found on both continents. As the Atlantic Ocean had started to form during the Late Jurassic, it is possible that the path of migration between North America and Europe may have been through Central and South America and Africa. Alternatively, it may have been through Greenland and Scandinavia.

By the end of the Cretaceous, both the mammalian and the dinosaur faunas of the world had begun to show the effects of separation of the continents. The ceratopsian dinosaurs, which include forms like *Triceratops* and the well-known egg-laying *Protoceratops,* were confined to western North America and eastern Asia. A seaway from the Gulf of Mexico to Hudson Bay divided what is today North America into eastern and western landmasses. Similarly eastern Asia was cut off from land farther west by seaways in the position of the modern Ural Mountains. In contrast, western North America and eastern Asia were close together, if not a single landmass. The mammal fossils suggest that there was dispersal from eastern Asia to western North America, but none or very little in the other direction. Forms common to the two areas appear earlier in eastern Asia. In addition, no unquestioned marsupials have been found in eastern Asia, while three families of this group occurred in North America during the Late Cretaceous.

Generalized marsupials similar to some of the North American forms have been found in the Late Cretaceous of South America. But at least one specialized form of the same age indicates that marsupials already had started on a separate evolutionary pathway in South America. There was no further interchange of marsupials between North and South America for another 60 million years, until the present Isthmus of Panama formed, a few million years ago.

During the Cretaceous, the climate over the entire planet was quite warm. Probably the highest average world temperatures in the Phanerozoic were reached in the early part of the Late Cretaceous. On average, these higher temperatures were probably about 10° C. (18° F.) above those now in tropical and temperate latitudes. There is no indication of continental glaciation even at high latitudes in either hemisphere. Varied temperate floras existed at what was 70° to 85° latitude south in southeastern Australia. Similarly, plants also indicating mild climatic conditions in the Northern Hemisphere have been found in western Alaska within a few degrees of where the north pole was at that time.

At the end of the Cretaceous, in the northern part of North America, placental mammals may have begun to diversify even before the dinosaurs became extinct. Once the dinosaurs did become extinct and the Paleocene Epoch had begun, the rate of development of new forms increased. Larger mammals appeared, and they began to take up new modes of life.

This change from a world dominated by dinosaurs to one dominated by mammals took place during a shift to cooler (but certainly not frigid) climates. Cooling of the climate coupled with increased yearly rainfall continued through the Paleocene.

At the beginning of the Eocene, there was a temperature increase, but precipitation still remained high. At the very end of the Eocene there was a sharp drop in temperature. Until this temperature drop occurred, terrestrial plants retained a tropical aspect into the high latitudes in both hemispheres.

During the Oligocene, there was a general decrease in temperature, with minor reversals toward warmer conditions at the beginning and at the end of that epoch. Precipitation generally decreased, and glaciation began in Antarctica.

In the Miocene, the contrast in average temperatures between the tropics and polar latitudes continued to increase as the overall temperature decreased. While glaciation affected much of Antarctica in the Miocene, there was none in the Northern Hemisphere. This was the first continental glaciation since the Permian. In the nonglaciated regions, the vegetation responded by the development of widespread grasslands at the expense of forests. This was in addition to the contraction of high-temperature-loving forests toward the equator and their replacement in the higher latitudes by the cold-temperate coniferous forests. Both trends had started in the Oligocene and were well underway by the Miocene.

In the Early Pliocene, glaciation in Antarctica was more extensive than today. Glaciers also developed in the Andes. By contrast, there is no evidence of a substantial amount of ice development in the Northern Hemisphere at this time.

After a warming period in the Middle Pliocene, glaciation once again expanded in the Southern Hemisphere and began in the Northern Hemisphere for the first time in the Cenozoic. In the Late Pliocene, glaciation in the Northern Hemisphere reached two thirds the extent it was to attain at its maximum, during the Pleistocene.

Glaciation became ever more extensive during the Pleistocene. By 780,000 years ago, a cyclic pattern had become established, with a major advance and retreat of continental glaciers about every 100,000 years. The advances were relatively slow and the retreats, rapid. The most recent glacial maximum was 18,000 years ago, and by 10,000 years ago, the subsequent major retreat of the glaciers worldwide had been completed.

SOUTH AMERICA AND ANTARCTICA

South America's mammalian fossil record begins in the Late Cretaceous with a few specimens from Peru and Bolivia. During the Tertiary, South America has the most complete mammalian fossil record of all the southern continents. Much of it comes from Patagonia, in southern Argentina, but important Tertiary sites also occur farther north in that country as well as in Colombia, Bolivia, and Brazil.

The terrestrial mammal fauna of South America shows three significant episodes of interchange with other continents. The first is in the Late Cretaceous and the Paleocene, the second is in the Oligocene, and the third is in the latest Miocene to the Pleistocene.

In the Late Cretaceous and the Paleocene, marsupicarnivorans, condylarths, edentates, notoungulates, and possibly Dinocerata occur in South America, and, except for edentates, in North America as well. An edentate does occur in the Paleocene of China, the genus *Ernanodon*. A less certain edentate record is of *Eurotamandua*, from the Middle Eocene of Europe. To date, North America's earliest record of an edentate is Late Miocene.

An interesting puzzle is why the notoungulates are represented by only two specimens in North America but by innumerable specimens belonging to four genera in Mongolia and China. Perhaps the environments sampled in the Paleocene deposits of eastern Asia and South America differ fundamentally from those in North America.

Only one mammalian order, the litopterns, occurs exclusively in South America during the Late Cretaceous and the Paleocene. However, only two mammalian families, both marsupials, the didelphids and the pediomyids, present there at that time also occur elsewhere. The great similarity between North and South American mammals at the ordinal level in the Late Cretaceous and the Paleocene suggests that a route across which animals could move existed between the two continents at that time. These orders had only just come into existence. But, because of familial dissimilarity on these two continents, the connection was probably not continuous dry land. Certainly, a Panamanian isthmus did not exist. Rather, a filtering effect took place such as might happen if the immigrants had to move from island to island across a water gap. Thus, only one or a few species of each order made the complete journey from one continent to the other, and had a separate history after their journey.

Once established on the new continent, the successful immigrant diversified and split into several species. Thus, all members of the new family would likely possess features unique to the founder species within the old family from which it evolved. This "founder effect" explains why new major groups often arise when new areas are invaded.

During the Eocene, there was, with one exception, no interchange of mammals with the outside world. South America was an isolated, island continent on which the mammals evolved without competition from new immigrant groups. However, South American mammals may have been dispersing to other continents. A Late Eocene polydolopid marsupial is known from Seymour Island, off the Antarctic Peninsula. This polydolopid is quite similar to some known from Early Eocene deposits in Patagonia, 2,000 kilometers (1,200 mi.) to the north.

In the Early Oligocene, platyrrhine primates and caviomorph rodents (today's guinea pig is an example) reached South America by rafting. Two schools of thought exist as to where the rafts came from. One group of paleontologists suggests that the rafting immigrants came across the Atlantic Ocean from Africa; the other, that they rafted from North America. In both Africa and North America there are groups that have some resemblance to the South American caviomorph rodents and primates. However, none of the similarities are so close as to be unquestionable.

After the arrival of primates and rodents, by the Early Oligocene, and bats, by the Late Oligocene, the South American mammalian fauna was not further added to by immigration until the Late Miocene, about 7 to 9 million years ago, when the Great American Faunal Interchange began. This event started with the entrance into South America of racoons through rafting from Central America. At about the same time, megalonychid and mylodontid ground sloths reached North America, where they diversified. The barrier to dispersal then was the Bolívar Trough, a narrow seaway, less than 400 kilometers (250 mi.) wide, at the southern end of Central America, in southern Panama and northwestern Colombia.

By the Late Pliocene, 3 million years ago, the Panamanian isthmus had formed. Once that happened, the floodgates were open and the exchange began in earnest. Savanna conditions prevailed in a significant area of Central America and northern South America, enabling forms adapted to latitudes as high as 45 degrees to cross the equator. At least twenty-two of the thirty-one genera that moved from one continent to the other in the Late Pliocene and Early Pleistocene were savanna-adapted forms. With the displacement of savannas by rain forest in these areas in the Late Pleistocene, the rate of interchange declined dramatically, as there were no longer favorable intermediate habitats for forms that might have moved from the center of one continent to that of the other.

The effect of the Great American Faunal Interchange was quite unequal on the two continents. About half the living genera of South American mammals were derived from North American groups that arrived as part of this episode. Many of these groups, once in South America, underwent considerable diversification, becoming new species and genera.

By contrast, only about 10 percent of the mammalian fauna of Central and North America is a result of this episode. As a whole, these southern immigrants have not been overly successful. However, there are notable exceptions such as the opossum *Didelphis virginiana,* the armadillo *Dasypus novemcinctus,* and the porcupine *Erethizon dorsatum.* All of these are quite successful at present, and the former two have extended their ranges northward significantly during the past century.

AFRICA

The Age of Mammals begins in Africa with at least a tenuous connection to the Eurasian landmass lying to the north across the great Tethys Seaway. The Tethys was an ocean belt that not only occupied the present Mediterranean, but extended eastward across what is now the Himalaya to Southeast Asia. The specific nature of the gradual contraction of that ocean during the Cenozoic affected the timing and amount of interchange between Africa and Eurasia.

Toward the end of the Cenozoic, the spreading of desert conditions across northern Africa and Arabia became a major barrier to the interchange of terrestrial mammals with Eurasia, in many ways just as effective as the Tethys Sea had been earlier.

For most of the Cenozoic, Arabia was an integral part of the African continent. Only late in that era was the Red Sea Basin formed and its flooding begun. Rifting and the downdropping of land, as can be seen today in the East African Rift Valley, was how the Red Sea Basin started. It was a part of the plate-tectonics episode that earlier had broken up Gondwanaland.

The few scraps of evidence concerning what African mammals were like at the beginning of the Cenozoic suggests that they came from Eurasia. How long they had been in Africa and precisely how distinct they were from Eurasian forms is unclear.

In the Eocene, much of northern Africa was covered by the Tethys Sea. The mammals known of this age are a mixture of aquatic and land-dwelling forms. They include primitive whales, elephants such as *Moeritherium,* and sea cows, plus large ground birds. Fossils of these animals have been collected right across northern Africa from Somalia to Senegal. The mammals may all be members of a single related group that evolved on the shores of the Tethys and have hence been dubbed "tethytheres" by some paleontologists. Members of this group are also known from rocks of similar age in what was the northern shore of the Tethys in India and Pakistan.

Not all the Eocene mammals of Africa were large aquatic or semiaquatic forms. The durable didelphid marsupials also were present, having entered Africa either from Europe or across the much narrower Atlantic from the New World.

Fossils from the Oligocene, however, provide the first varied faunas of terrestrial mammals of Africa. Though still a strictly North African record, the fossils occur in sediments deposited in swamps, lakes and streams, rather than the sea. These faunas were a mixture of groups restricted to Africa, as well as immigrants from Eurasia. Some of the groups, such as anthropoid apes, occurring for the first time in the Oligocene may have been in Africa during the Eocene and simply have not yet been found. This is not unlikely, since anthropoids do occur in the Eocene of Burma along with the more aquatic tethytheres.

Other groups seen for the first time in the Oligocene of Africa are known only from that continent and must have had a long previous history there. One of these is the genus *Arsinotherium.* With two forward-projecting, conical horns on their skulls just above their eyes, they are such peculiar hoofed animals that they have always been placed in their own order, the Embrithopoda. No known close ancestor has been suggested for them, though ultimately they were probably derived from arctocyonid stock. They disappeared without descendants before the beginning of the Miocene.

Most closely related to the Embrithopoda are the hyraxes, another solely African group with a first appearance in the Oligocene. Today they are small, rabbitlike animals that typically live among rocks. But the Oligocene *Megalohyrax* was as large as a tapir.

Among the Oligocene newcomers were rodents, artiodactyls, and bats. The phiomyid rodents are exclusively African, but as rodents have often evolved quickly, they may have immigrated from Eurasia only a short time before their first appearance in the African fossil record. Only a few Oligocene artiodactyls are known, hardly more than a hint of the dominant position they have come to occupy now, producing the vast antelope herds that dot the African savannas today. The anthracotheres were clearly immigrants from Eurasia, while *Mixtotherium,* the only other Oligocene artiodactyl, was an endemic genus, the sole member of its family, the Mixtotheridae.

Bats are known elsewhere in the Eocene and probably spread quickly to Africa. Small mammals are as yet scarcely known in the African Eocene, so it is likely that the absence of bats in that epoch is due to a poor record, rather than their not having been there.

At the end of the Oligocene and the beginning of the Miocene, the trickle of immigrants into Africa became a flood. Twenty-seven new families of terrestrial mammals appeared in the Early Miocene alone; seventeen of these are clearly immigrants from Asia and Europe. Only fourteen families carried over in Africa from the Oligocene. The cause of this great faunal turnover is not difficult to understand. Africa "docked" against Eurasia, as a ship against its wharf, severing the continuity of the Tethys Sea between the Atlantic and the Indian Oceans. The terrestrial exchange, however, was not just one way. A number of groups previously known in Africa, such as three families of elephants, entered Asia and Europe at the same time.

Langebaanweg, a Late Miocene and Early Pliocene locality near Cape Town, South Africa, was once the site of a large river. It is now a phosphate mine, and through the wholehearted cooperation of operating company Chemfos Ltd., tons of fossils have been recovered as a by-product of mining activity. (Above) Aerial view. (Below) Fossiliferous outcrop of the Varswater Formation (Courtesy of Q. B. Hendey, South African Museum, Cape Town)

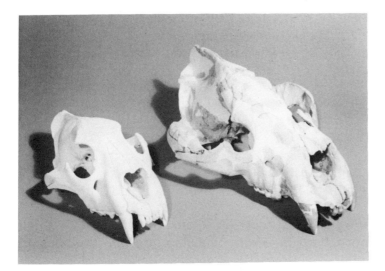

Skull of the bear **Agriotherium** *(length 17 in., or 42 cm.) compared to that of a smaller modern lion. This particular specimen was found in South Africa, but* Agriotherium *is also know from Late Miocene and Early Pliocene deposits of Asia and Europe, as well as North America. (Photo by C. Booth, courtesy of Q. B. Hendey and the South African Museum)*

In the late Miocene, the western end of what can be called the Proto-Mediterranean Sea became blocked for a brief period. In addition, the Proto-Black Sea was still connected to the Indian Ocean as part of the old Tethys Seaway. Thus, all the rivers draining eastward out of Europe today, such as the Danube, were cut off from the Mediterranean. With a diminished supply of fresh water and no source of seawater from the World Ocean, the Mediterranean began to dry up, as the evaporation rate was higher than the resupply rate. It became a massive salt lake similar to the modern Great Salt Lake, in Utah, and the Dead Sea, only much larger. Thick deposits of salts formed at the bottoms of shallow hypersaline water bodies 3,280 feet (1,000 m.) below sea level. The landscape was a harsh desert with deep canyons cut where rivers such as the Nile and the Rhône flowed into this landlocked basin. Salt creeks and springs surrounded the hypersaline lakes found in the deepest part of the Mediterranean. This drying up occurred at the end of the Miocene, during the Messinian Stage, and has therefore been called the "Messinian Hydrographic Crisis."

With the landlocked Messinian salt lake between Eurasia and Africa, further exchanges of mammals occurred. Yet Africa retained a very distinct fauna. Though a broad terrestrial connection did exist for the first time in the Cenozoic between Africa and the continents to the north, the harsh desert nature of this temporary bridge prevented many forms adapted to less rigorous environments from crossing.

After about 1 million years, the isthmus between Africa and Europe was breached, and water from the Atlantic poured into the Mediterranean, forming a mighty waterfall much larger than the modern Niagara or even the East African Victoria Falls.

During the Late Cenozoic, Africa continued to receive many different mammals from continents to the north as well as being the source of some that entered Eurasia. In the Late Pleistocene, interchange was reduced when the Sahara became a harsher barrier to cross for those forms not adapted to such a desert environment.

AUSTRALIA

At the beginning of the Cenozoic, Antarctica straddled the South Pole, much as it does today, and Australia lay alongside Antarctica, far to the south of its present location. Soon afterward, Australia began drifting northward.

Before separating, however, Australia had a tenuous contact with South America across Antarctica. Probably the trans-Antarctic connection was not continuously dry land. Rather, that part of Antarctica in the western longitudes was an archipelago of large and small islands. Thus, interchange of terrestrial vertebrates across West Antarctica was possible, but quite chancy. Much the same situation exists today, where elements of the faunas of Asia and Australia are now slowly mixing through movement along the islands of the Malay Archipelago: Java, Sumatra, Timor, and so on. Probably one or only a few species of marsupials made the crossing between South America and Australia. The direction of this migration is not certain, but it probably occurred around the middle of the Cretaceous, when marsupials had evolved and placentals probably had not. This would explain why marsupials made the trip and placentals did not utilize the same route to enter Australia. Another explanation is that marsupials happened by chance to cross this "sweepstakes route" through the Antarctic archipelago and the placentals did not.

By the beginning of the Miocene, Australia had moved about sixteen degrees of latitude northward from Antarctica, and the climate was mild and moist. Southern beech *(Nothofagus)* forests were widespread, and even in the most arid regions of the time, they at least lined stream banks. In the streams were freshwater dolphins as well as ancestral platypuses. On the banks of these streams were small diprotodontids, such as *Ngapakaldia,* that would give rise to truly giant forms by the Pleistocene, including *Diprotodon,* the largest marsupial ever to live. Along with them lived larger animals, bizarre relatives of the wombats that were soon to become extinct. Even the largest of these forms were no bigger than a modern tapir. Potoroos and other kangaroos were present, but all were quite small.

The various possums seen today had relatives that were not too different from those living in the Miocene. Unlike the carnivorous, sometimes omnivorous, American opossums, the Australian possums are a group of herbivorous and omnivorous marsupials. One group of possums existed in the Miocene and Pliocene that have no living descendants. These were the

Skull of a wynyardiid (length 5.5 in., or 14 cm.), a primitive family of diprotodontans from the Middle Miocene of South Australia. Older animals similiar to this one may have been members of primitive families of kangaroos and diprotodontids. That

probably happened during the Eocene or the Oligocene. (Photo courtesy of Neville Pledge and the South Australian Museum, Adelaide)

An evening scene in South Australia during the Middle Miocene. Three Ngapakaldia *(length 43 in., or 1.1 m.), distant relatives of* Diprotodon, *come down to a stream for a drink. From a branch overhead, they are watched by a curious squirrellike* Ektopodon *(length 2 ft., or 60 cm.) while a primitive rat kangaroo (2 ft., or 60 cm.), right rear, momentarily pauses among the ferns before deciding whether to bound away. (Restoration by Peter Trusler)*

Permanent lakes in Central Australia were inhabited by a number of water birds, some of which no longer occur on this continent. Palaelodids (lower right) are similar to those in middle Tertiary Europe and North America. Two kinds of flamingos, a more robust form, Phoeniconotius *(dark legs), and a more slender form,* Phoenicopterus novaehollandiae *(middle foreground), were both about the height of the largest living relatives. Cormorants lived in these lakes as well, along with a variety of pelicans, rails, and ducks. Freshwater dolphins (rhabdosteids) also occurred in some of the more southerly lakes near today's Lake Frome. (Restoration by Peter Trusler)*

Lake Palankarinna, northern South Australia, one of the richest Cenozoic localities for fossil mammals and birds in all of Australia. It is of further importance because Miocene, Pliocene, and Pleistocene mammal-bearing rocks are stacked one upon another at this locality

ektopodontids. With their peculiar, many-crested teeth, apparently adapted to crushing seeds, this group shows a vague resemblance to the quite distantly related multituberculates, of the Northern Hemisphere. They may have filled the same niche as squirrels do in the Northern Hemisphere.

Carnivorous marsupials, as well as herbivorous ones, were present in the Australian Miocene. The Tasmanian wolf, *Thylacinus*, was a predator first known in central Australia in the Late Miocene. The last known living member of this genus died in 1936. And not all possums remained herbivorous or omnivorous. One group, the Thylacoleonidae, or marsupial lions, definitely became carnivores, as their premolars evolved into elongate, shearing blades. One species reached the size of modern lions and indeed must have been Australia's top mammalian carnivore.

Not all of the large predators were mammals, however. Large lizards, such as *Megalania* and *Varanus*, and crocodiles, including the terrestrial ziphodont *Pallimnarchus*, also were fierce meat eaters both on land and in the water.

Bats occur in nearly the oldest fossil mammal assemblages known in Australia. They were the only "terrestrial" placental mammals we know of in Australia until the Pliocene. Then the murid rodents reached Australia, having migrated across the Malay Archipelago from southeastern Asia.

By the Pliocene, New Guinea and Australia were close to their present positions, having drifted northward, away from Antarctica. In the Pliocene, the face of Australia began to change. The forests of southern beech became gradually restricted to the highlands of New Guinea in the north and the extreme southeast of Australia, where they are today. With the spread of savannas and grasslands across Australia, the mammals responded by evolving rapidly in these new conditions. Most noticeable in their responses were the kangaroos, wombats, and diprotodontids. Many new, large forms developed in these groups, quite in contrast to their relatively modest sizes in the Middle Miocene.

As in the other southern continents, except Antarctica, glaciation was not extensive in Australia during the Pleistocene. However, the trend toward large size continued, and resulted, by the end of the Pleistocene, in the largest marsupials that ever lived. As elsewhere in the world, many of these large forms became extinct just before the end of the Pleistocene, leaving a fauna somewhat reduced in size and diversity. Some forms, such as *Macropus giganteus*, the eastern gray kangaroo, however, survived by becoming smaller.

EUROPE, NORTH AMERICA, AND ASIA

With the extinction of the dinosaurs at the beginning of the Paleocene, North American mammals suffered a slight setback, with the loss of three families. One of these was a multituberculate, but two new multituberculate families also appeared at this time. The two other families lost were both marsupials. From the beginning of the Paleocene onward in North America, the only marsupials to survive were the durable didelphid opossums.

The placental mammals suffered no setback but instead rapidly diversified. In the earliest Paleocene, families with only a few members, such as the generalized arctocyonid plant eaters, had quadrupled their number before five million years had passed. Other families, such as some condylarths, with no Mesozoic record at all, diversified into a variety of genera in the same period of time. The Early Paleocene was clearly the time of the highest rate of origination of mammalian families and genera.

These rapid changes occurred as the climate cooled from the subtropical conditions of the Cretaceous to warm-temperate ones. As the Paleocene progressed, the climate became warmer and reached subtropical conditions again in North America by the Early Eocene. Year round, the climate was warm and without pronounced seasons, much the same each day. No deserts are known to have existed. Broadleaf evergreen forests lived as far north as 60 degrees. Closer to the pole were deciduous broadleaf forests, which finally gave way to conifers at higher latitudes.

Mammalian carnivores were small and probably did not prey upon the larger adult herbivorous mammals at the beginning of the Paleocene. This condition soon changed with the evolution of the earliest members of the Carnivora, the miacids (doglike forms now extinct), by the end of the Early Paleocene. There is little evidence of other predators in the earliest Paleocene of North America: no carnivorous birds or lizards, and crocodiles are almost unknown in the same deposits as these miacids.

The groups that eventually gave rise to the modern mammals that we see today evolved slowly. Not so several orders of mammals that would appear most peculiar to modern eyes. Many of these forms quickly became the giants of the Paleocene and Eocene, only to soon become extinct.

One of the earliest of these groups to arise was Taeniodonta. Restricted to North America, the animals in this group appeared in the Early Paleocene and persisted until the Late Eocene, when they became extinct without leaving any descendants. In structure of the teeth and feet, they show some resemblance to ground sloths, but they were not closely related to them. Instead they were simply convergent in lifestyle.

Even larger were Dinocerata and Pantodonta. First appearing in the Middle Paleocene, these forms increased markedly in size by the Eocene. The largest species of the pantodont *Coryphodon* was as big as an ox, and the dinocerate *Uintatherium* as large as a rhinoceros. Both groups are also known in Asia, and the pantodonts reached Europe.

Elements of the North American Paleocene fauna are shared with both Asia and Europe, indicating that some degree of interchange was then possible. Presumably this was by two routes. One route, direct to Asia, was

Late Paleocene of eastern Asia. In the foreground, a small, carnivorous **Cimolesta** *watches three pika-like anagalids while, in the background, two edentates,* **Erna-nodon,** *come down for a drink. (Restoration by Peter Trusler)*

Late Cretaceous and early Tertiary sediments of southeastern China that have produced dinosaur eggs and mammalian remains

through the region of the modern Bering Strait. The second was across the North Atlantic land connection to Europe before a seaway had completely opened. Europe, however, may have been separated from Asia by a seaway, the Turgai Straits, at the present site of the Ural Mountains. Northwestern Europe was probably a series of islands until the Late Miocene.

Interchange "peaked" in the Early Eocene, when half the genera of mammals in Europe were also known in North America. Fully 85 percent of the European genera at that time appear to be forms that had immigrated into the area, rather than evolved in place from earlier stocks. Many of the same genera common to these two continents were also to be found in Asia. Among these travelers was the well-known *Hyracotherium,* or eohippus, the "dawn horse," which has been found on all three continents. It, along with many other typical Early Eocene mammals, occurs on Ellesmere Island, Canada, near northwestern Greenland, showing that the route across the North Atlantic would then have been equable enough for mammals to survive.

Within 3 million years, the route across the North Atlantic had been severed, and isolation of one continent from another had begun. The faunas of Europe and North America then evolved in different directions. There was no more significant interchange between the two areas until the beginning of the Oligocene. Europe was nearly as isolated from Asia for the balance of the Eocene as well.

Some of the most spectacular preservations of Early Cenozoic mammals anywhere give us a glimpse of life in the Middle Eocene of Europe. These are the oil-shale deposits of Geiseltal, East Germany, and Darmstadt, West Germany. Not only are the entire skeletons of the mammals preserved but, in some cases, the skin as well. In a few instances, the quality of preservation of the skin has been good enough to determine that some of the ungulates had spots on their coats, though what the actual colors were when the animal was alive remains unknown.

In the Middle Eocene, Asia had a mixture of forms related to those of

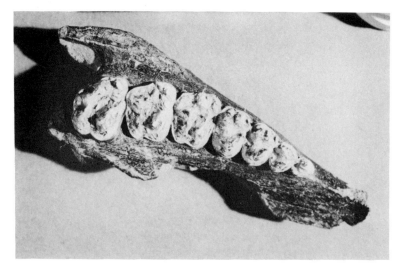

A skull fragment of a primitive Early Eocene rhinoceratoid, **Hyrachyus,** *from Ellesmere Island, Canada, near northwestern Greenland. Length of toothrow 3 inches (80 mm.).* **Hyrachyus** *also occurs in the Early and Middle Eocene of the United States, Europe, and Asia (Photo courtesy of M. Dawson, Carnegie Museum, Pittsburgh)*

Eocene outcrops of the Eureka Sound Formation, Ellesmere Island. Probably during the Early Eocene, land mammals moved through this area, crossing between North America and Europe over a land bridge across a much narrower Atlantic Ocean than today's. The mammals from these rocks show close affinities with those in Wyoming and the Paris Basin (Photo courtesy of M. Dawson, Carnegie Museum, Pittsburgh)

A Middle Eocene evening in West Germany. In the upper left-hand corner, one Messelobunodon (length 31 in., or 78 cm.), a primitive artiodactyl, forages among the leaf litter while, behind it, others have settled down for the night. In the upper right-hand corner, the possible edentate Eurotamandua (length 30 in., or 75 cm.) starts to break into a termite mound. Below it is an interested pangolin, Eomanis (length 19 in., or 48 cm.). In the lower left-hand corner, the primitive hedgehog Pholidocercus (length 12 in., or 30 cm.), with a curious armor on its skull, is consuming a beetle. (Restoration by Peter Trusler)

North America and Europe, as well as some unique to that continent. On the north shore of the Tethys Seaway were aquatic and amphibious forms similar to those in Africa such as sea cows, elephants, and primitive whales. At about this time, India, which had been drifting northward from Gondwanaland, crashed into Asia, throwing up the beginnings of the Himalaya.

During the Late Eocene and Early Oligocene, an explosive diversification of artiodactyls and rodents took place in Asia, Europe, and North America. Nearly 30 percent of all mammalian families made their first appearance during this interval, and many of the ancient groups such as the Dinocerata and the pantodonts became extinct. In North America, this may have been because the climate was becoming more severe (lower and less even temperatures). Europe continued to enjoy a more even climate during the Late Eocene. Paradoxically, despite the many first and last appearances of animal groups in North America and Europe over the last 12 million years of the Eocene, there seems to have been little change within groups.

In the Late Eocene, a contrast can be detected between an open-savanna fauna in northern Asia and a tropical-forest fauna in the southern part of that continent. The savanna grassland may have been the first such habitat developed in the Northern Hemisphere during the Cenozoic. As such, it may have provided the necessary conditions for the rise of such mammalian groups as the cats, the cricetid rodents (such as the pack rat), and rhinoceratids, or true rhinoceroses.

In the tropical forest of southern Asia during the Late Eocene, animals of the circum-Tethys region, shared with Africa, were still to be found. Prominent among these were the oldest known primates in the group to which people belong.

The beginning of the Oligocene in Europe was marked by a massive immigration of families new to the continent. Among these were the true rhinos, the weird clawed chalicotheres, the water-loving anthracotheres, the peccaries (tayassuids), and perhaps the massive titanotheres. Though some of these families originated in North America, all reached Europe via Asia, as the connection across the North Atlantic was broken for the last time at the end of the Early Eocene. This influx of new families to Europe occurred when the climatic conditions there began to decline, as they had earlier in North America. For the remainder of the Oligocene, Europe neither received major immigrant groups nor sent out emigrants. Rather, the mammals there at the beginning of the epoch evolved in place. As the epoch progressed, fewer families were present as fewer new ones evolved from the existing stock on the continent than became extinct.

In Asia, the Oligocene opened with an exchange of animals between North America and Europe. By the Middle Oligocene, exchange with Europe had ceased, but it did continue slowly with North America.

A major change in the North American fauna occurred at the beginning of the Oligocene. Only one quarter of the genera were holdovers from the Late

During the Miocene, this present-day diatomite mine in Shandong Province, People's Republic of China, was the bottom of a large lake. Fossil fish are very common in these rocks, but entire skeletons of birds and mammals are also found (Courtesy of M. Chow, Institute of Vertebrate Paleontology and Paleoanthropology, Beijing)

Eocene. As no immigrant genera are recognized in North America throughout that epoch, this suggests that a major diversification of groups was already underway in North America. During the remainder of the Oligocene, the pattern was similar to that in Europe: a slow evolution within groups already present and a decline in the number of families present.

A small spurt of immigration marked the beginning of the Miocene in North America. However, the level remained relatively low until the Late Miocene, when there was a major changeover in the fauna. Then widespread extinction of longtime North American resident groups occurred, including hedgehogs and amphicyonid carnivores. At the same time, there arrived immigrant carnivores from Asia among which were the bears *Agriotherium* and *Indarctos,* the cat *Machairodus,* skunks, and badgers, as well as two groups of ground sloths from South America *(Megalonyx* and *Thinobadistes).*

Europe began to receive new groups of mammals from Africa, as well as Asia and North America, at the start of the Miocene. Europe was still a series of islands. About 12 million years ago, the horse *Hipparion* entered the Old World from North America, where it had originated. *Hipparion* quickly spread through Asia to Europe and Africa. This was relatively unusual in Europe at the time, for there was still relatively little interchange of faunal elements at the end of the Middle Miocene, when this occurred.

In the Late Miocene, with the Alpine orogeny lifting the Alps skyward, Europe was no longer a cluster of islands. Finally, near the end of the Miocene there was the temporary isolation of the Mediterranean Basin and the consequent lowering of the water level because of evaporation, the Messinian Hydrographic Crisis. Contemporaneous with these drastic changes to the European landscape, the fauna of the continent underwent a crisis, with many groups becoming extinct: the oreopithecid primates, the swamp-dwelling anthracotheres, the tragulid artiodactyls (including the chevrotain), the clawed chalicotheres, and the deinotheres (elephants with their downcurved lower-jaw tusks). As well, there was immigration of new families and genera from Asia and North America, but particularly from Africa, for example the hyraxes and the Old World porcupines.

During the Miocene, Asia retained a distinctive fauna, but throughout the epoch, two to four times as many genera were shared with Europe as with North America.

In the Pliocene, savanna environments became widespread in Eurasia and North America. Contrary to popular opinion, it is these environments that support the greatest mass of mammals and not the lush rain forests, where they are actually quite rare. Ungulate groups became very prominent on all three continents. In Eurasia, dominant among these are the bovids, rhinos, giraffids and *Hipparion* horses. In North America, camels, American antilocaprids, and the *Equus* horses are most prominent.

Interchange between North America and Eurasia reached a peak in the Middle Pliocene. At this time, a variety of carnivores as well as deer and the elephant *Stegomastodon* entered North America from Eurasia. Moving in the other direction were the rabbit *Hypolagus;* the squirrel, *Citellus;* the beaver *Castor,* and the horse *Equus.*

With the onset of glaciation, in the Pleistocene, migration between North America and Eurasia increased in frequency. More forms were shared between Europe and North America then than at any time since the Early Eocene. However, it was the cold-adapted groups such as the musk-oxen and the coyotes that were able to cross the Bering land bridge, not the forms restricted to temperate climates.

The migration during the Pleistocene was possible because, with the glaciations, sea levels dropped significantly, making a broad, dry land connection between Alaska and Siberia. Though North America was mostly covered with thick glaciers from the Atlantic to the Pacific oceans at such times, much of Alaska and part of the Yukon Territory were glacier-free. When the glaciers retreated, as they did a number of times during the Pleistocene, the groups that had migrated from Eurasia as far as Alaska were then able to spread south into the rest of North America and in certain cases, such as with the common otter, on into South America.

So we see that, during the Cenozoic, there were episodes of interchange between Eurasia and North America followed by periods when the mammals in these areas evolved in isolation from one another. In the Early Eocene, there was evidently a broad connection between Europe and North America across the North Atlantic that permitted the mammals to move freely back and forth. When that route was suddenly cut off, the faunas of the two areas rapidly became distinct as they evolved in response to different conditions.

When contact was reestablished, at the beginning of the Oligocene, it was not as easy for mammals to move back and forth between the two areas. The route of interchange was now across Asia and through the Bering Strait area. For the most part, only mammals that were adapted to the cooler conditions of the time made the crossing. One exception may be the tapirs, now restricted to the tropics of Central America and Southeast Asia. However, rare fossils of *Tapirus* at higher latitudes suggest that their present-day restriction to tropical latitudes may not have always been the case. Though in the Northern Hemisphere it was colder in the north all during the Cenozoic, the difference between northern and southern parts of the continents becomes progressively greater as we near the present day. Therefore, as late as the Miocene, there does not seem to be a marked difference among the mammals found in northern and southern faunas except in extreme cases such as between the Eocene rain-forest fauna of Burma and the contemporaneous high-altitude-savanna fauna of Mongolia.

In the Early Eocene, most of the movement seems to have been from North America to Eurasia. However, after that time, though each episode of interchange involved movement in both directions, more forms entered North America from Eurasia than went the other way. As Eurasia was a large, varied landmass, the forms that survived there were those that were best able to adapt to a wide variety of competitors. Fewer competitors arose in a given time span in the smaller area of North America. In addition, Eurasia received more mammals from other areas, such as Africa. Similarly, North America had been subjected to the impact of new immigrants much more frequently during the Cenozoic than South America. Thus, when connection through the Panamanian Isthmus was established, at the end of the Cenozoic, there was a much greater displacement of the earlier South American fauna by immigrants from North America than the reverse.

CHAPTER XXXV

Beasts and Birds of the Ice Age: the Interplay of Climate and Man

"Near the Pueblo de los Ángeles there are more than twenty springs of liquid petroleum, pitch, etc. Farther to the west of the said town, in the middle of a great plain of more than fifteen leagues' circumference, there is a great lake of pitch, with many pools in which bubbles or blisters are continually forming and exploding. . . . In hot weather, animals have been seen to sink into it, and when they tried to escape they could not do so, because their feet were stuck, and the lake swallowed them. After many years their bones come through the holes, as if petrified. I brought away several specimens."

Thus a Spanish explorer, José Longinos Martínez, wrote of the Rancho La Brea tar pools, which he saw in 1792. But contemporaries ignored Martínez's bones that looked "as if petrified," and so did explorers, ranchmen, and geologists who saw the tar pools during the century that followed. Not till 1906 were excavations begun by paleontologists. Within ten years they took out hundreds of thousands of bones—the greatest and most comprehensive array of Pleistocene, or Ice Age, fossils found anywhere on the globe. Other thousands of bones remain in the tar under what is now Hancock Park, in western Los Angeles.

THE PLEISTOCENE ICE AGE

Before going further, we must clarify that deceptively simple term, Ice Age. The earth has passed through several "ages" during which climates grew cool and glaciers spread widely in one part of the world or another. The first of these epochs came during Huronian times, 2,300 million years ago. There were others near the end of the Proterozoic and during the Paleozoic eras, but the last one began about 1.5 million years ago and has not necessarily come to an end. This latest ice age has been occurring during the Quaternary Period. The Quaternary ice age is the one whose results are most often seen

616

Limestone karst country near Qi Xing Yan (Seven Star Cave), in South China, west of Canton, is one of many hundreds of caves developed in Paleozoic limestones that have produced abundant Pleistocene fossil vertebrates in China

and most easily recognized. We frequently call it *the* Ice Age, forgetting that others lasted longer and that their glaciers sometimes covered more ground, *and* that there was more than one ice age during the Quaternary itself!

Condensed summaries often make the Quaternary ice age seem like winter, followed by catastrophic floods as ice sheets melted. That picture, however, is too simple. Over much of North America, Asia, and Europe, there were four major glacial advances and a minor fifth. Between them came intervals of warmth and melting, in which climates sometimes were warmer than they are today. Interglacial deposits near Toronto, for example, contain trees that now grow in the central Mississippi Valley, Ohio, and Pennsylvania.

During the Quaternary, glaciations have tended to last about two to three hundred thousand years, and interglacials ten to sixteen thousand years. The onset of glaciation was gradual, while the retreat of the glaciers was rapid. The last glaciation began about three hundred thousand years ago and finally reached its height only eighteen thousand years ago. By ten thousand years ago, it was over. If the cyclic pattern between glacials and interglacials that has persisted through the Pleistocene continues, we may expect the next glaciation episode to slowly begin in the next few thousand years. Within major episodes of glaciation there were short warming phases, and conversely, cooling phases occurred within interglacials.

The cyclic nature of the Quaternary ice age seems to be related to regular, minor changes in the shape of the earth's orbit around the sun. These

A male southern, or Columbian, mammoth; height at shoulder about 10 feet 6 inches (3.2 m.). Found at many places in the Southwest, this one is shown east of San Gorgonio Pass, California

changes cause the amount and distribution of solar heat received by the earth to fluctuate. Such fluctuations are great enough to significantly affect the amount of ice that melts from year to year. A decrease in melting brings about a net accumulation of ice over a year. Repeated year after year, the ice builds up slowly until the weight is so great that it begins to flow outward because of the pressure built up within it.

Though these changes in the earth's orbit can explain why the glaciers have come and gone during the Quaternary, they do not explain why the glaciation started in the first place. The cyclic changes in the earth's orbit existed prior to the Quaternary, but an ice age did not occur. Evidently, as the temperature of the earth declined during the Cenozoic from the Cretaceous high, a threshold was crossed which allowed this slight change in the heat received by the earth to cause glaciation.

A number of ideas have been put forward to explain the decline of the earth's temperature during the Cenozoic. One is that there has been a reduction in the amount of heat produced by the sun. Unfortunately, no one has yet figured out how to test this idea.

Another is that the Cenozoic, and particularly the Late Cenozoic, has been a time of extensive mountain building. According to this theory, a significant area of land was thus raised into higher, cooler air, resulting in net global heat loss.

A final theory suggests that as the continents moved about as a result of plate tectonics, the circulation patterns of air currents, and particularly ocean currents changed. With heat flow from the tropics to the high latitudes reduced, global cooling might be expected. In addition, the changing relative amounts of land and sea at various latitudes would affect the net amount of heat immediately reflected back into space and thus lost, in comparison to that absorbed by the planet. Perhaps all of these changing factors brought about our latest glaciation.

During the Quaternary, there were four major centers of continental glaciation in the Northern Hemisphere; two in North America, one in Europe, and one in Asia. At the height of the glaciations, the two in North America combined to cover more than 6 million square miles (15.5 million sq. km.). This was all of the continent north of an east-west line drawn through the southern end of the Great Lakes with the exception of a large part of Alaska and the western Yukon Territory. Though cold enough for glaciers to form, this ice-free area of Alaska and the Yukon did not receive enough precipitation to develop glaciers.

For the same reason, apparently, northeastern Siberia was free of glaciers except in mountainous areas. Continental ice sheets developed in northwestern Siberia and the Finno-Scandinavian district. These two combined to cover a maximum area of about 3.7 million square miles (9.6 million sq. km.).

Continental ice sheets exist today only in Greenland and Antarctica. The Antarctic ice cap was the only extensive continental glaciation in the Southern Hemisphere during the Quaternary. It probably was about one-third larger than at present at the height of the last glaciation and may have been one-third less ten thousand years ago, during the warmest phase of the most recent interglacial.

When the tar-pool fossils were first studied, scientists thought they had been formed during the Early Pleistocene. That error has been corrected, and the remains are now considered to range in age from twelve thousand to forty thousand years; that is, toward the end of the last, or Wisconsin, glaciation.

LIFE ON THE ANCIENT LOS ANGELES PLAIN

So much for geologic background. Let us now examine the record of Ice Age life and conditions preserved in the tar pools.

The country itself provides no surprises, for the nearest glaciers were in the Sierra Nevada, 150 miles (240 km.) away. Then, as now, the region of Los Angeles was a plain rimmed by the Santa Monica, San Gabriel, and Santa

Scene at the Rancho La Brea tar pits in Late Pleistocene times, perhaps twenty thousand years ago, showing typical mammals and birds: **1.** *The great vulture* Teratornis, *with a wingspread of 10 to 13 feet (3.0–4.0 m.).* **2.** *Small prong-horned antelope* (Breameryx), *20 inches (51 cm.) high.* **3.** *Ground sloth* (Nothrotherium), *3 feet 3 inches (99 cm.) high at back.* **4.** *Stork, about 4 feet (1.2 m.) high as it stands here*

Ana mountains. Creeks flowed to an early version of the Los Angeles River that ran southward to what is now San Pedro Bay. Grassy flats were dotted with chaparral thickets and groves of live oak, juniper, cypress, and bishop pine. Small mammals were much like those of the present, for they included mice, ground squirrels, kangaroo rats, cottontails, and jackrabbits, but plants suggest that the climate was warm and less influenced by the ocean than it is today. Seasons of moderate rainfall alternated with summer and autumn droughts.

Hoofed and Clawed Herbivores. Though small mammals were familiar, most of the large ones seem strange. Bison were plentiful, for example; not the modern "buffalo," but a species more than 7 feet (2.1 m.) tall at its hump.

More mammals of the Brea tar pits, in what is now Hancock Park, Los Angeles, site of the George C. Page Museum: 5. Giant short-faced bear, 4 feet 2 inches (127 cm.) high. 6. The Brea lion, 4 feet 2 inches (127 cm.) at the shoulder. 7. Two imperial mammoths, 10 to 13 feet (3–4 m.) in height. 8. Camelops, 7 feet (2.1 m.) at shoulder. 9. Bison skull. 10. Horse skull

Big bulls had skulls 27 to 32 inches (69–81 cm.) wide between the horns, which curved less than those of the present-day bison.

Wild horses were less abundant than bison, but they roamed the plain in small bands or herds. All belonged to one species, *Equus occidentalis,* which stood 4 feet 10 inches (147 cm.) high between the shoulders, with a bulging forehead, a thick body, and relatively short legs. Though not so tall as the modern quarter horse (a favorite "cow pony" in the West), it was more heavily built.

Camels of the tar pits also were large, standing 7 feet (2.1 m.) at the highest part of the back. The skull suggests that of a llama, but bones of the body resemble those of the modern two-humped Asiatic species. There were great herds of *Breameryx,* a prong-horned "antelope" 19 inches (48 cm.) in height at the shoulder. Its horns were divided into two straight spikes, one of which was much larger than the other. Teeth indicate that it had a diet of grass, which the pronghorn eats today.

The largest mammals found in the tar pools were mastodons and mammoths. The former was *Mammut americanum;* the latter included two species, *Mammuthus imperator* and *M. columbi.* None of these were abundant, however.

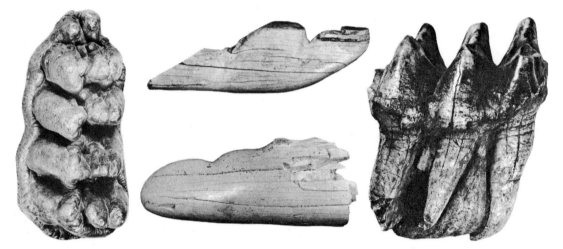

Upper molar of *Serridentinus,* a mastodont from Florida

Tips of two American mastodon tusks. They show grooves that were worn by roots which the animal dug from the ground

Second left lower molar of the American mastodon. It shows the high cusps, two of which are slightly worn

The commonest edentate of Rancho La Brea is the ground sloth called *Mylodon* or *Paramylodon,* which ranged from Patagonia to southern Oregon and eastward in North America as far as Nebraska. *Nothrotherium* wandered down from nearby mountains, where it probably was common. A third genus, *Megalonyx,* also lived among mountains but sometimes visited the plain and was trapped in tar. The La Brea fossils belong to a species that ranged eastward to the Atlantic coast. It was described in 1797 by Thomas Jefferson, who mistook its claw-bearing toe bones for those of an enormous lion. Jefferson carried the fossils with him when he rode to Philadelphia to become President. His description, published in 1799, was entitled *A Memoir on the Discovery of Certain Bones of a Quadruped of the Clawed Kind in the Western Parts of Virginia.*

Varied Carnivores. Where plant-eating animals were common, carnivores were sure to come. They included weasels, skunks, badgers, foxes, coyotes, bobcats, and bears, all belonging to modern species or closely related to them. With them was the now extinct dire wolf, *Canis dirus,* a heavy-headed beast not quite so large as the timber wolf of today. It was

Smilodon, *last of the sabertooths, about 40 inches (102 cm.) high. The skull shows how widely the beast could open its jaws, freeing the canine teeth for use as daggers*

common and probably hunted in packs, but ate carrion as well as freshly killed food.

Cats included the puma, or mountain lion, as well as *Felis* (or *Panthera) atrox.* This was a powerful lionlike creature that ranged from Alaska to Mississippi and the plateau on which Mexico City now stands. Males were one-fourth larger than the biggest tiger, though females were about the size of a jaguar. This "Brea lion" was an active hunter that preyed on horses, camels, bison, and other herbivores.

Smilodon, last of the saber-toothed cats, was a short-tailed beast, much more heavily built than the modern lion. Its body was massive, its legs were heavy, and its brain was smaller than that of the Brea lion and the puma. Its canine teeth, like those of all other sabertooths, were curved, knifelike weapons used for slashing or stabbing—not biting—large animals such as bison and ground sloths. *Smilodon* did not run its prey down, since its legs were not built for speed. We picture it as a beast that lay in wait near groves or water holes, pouncing upon ground sloths and other victims. Strong forelegs and claws gripped the victim's back, while the teeth slashed downward again and again, inflicting jagged wounds that deepened as the gaping jaws partly closed. High-placed nostrils enabled *Smilodon* to breathe even when his muzzle was buried in the long, coarse hair of a ground sloth.

Largest of all tar-pool carnivores was *Arctodus,* a gigantic short-faced bear that ranged from the Yukon to Pennsylvania and Texas. The California species stood 4 feet 2 inches (127 cm.) high at the curve of the back and was 7 feet 6 inches (229 cm.) long. Corresponding dimensions for a large grizzly are a height of 3 feet 4 inches (102 cm.) and a length of 5 feet 10 inches (178 cm.). If the Pleistocene giants had the habits of other bears, as they probably did, neither grizzlies nor black bears had much chance to succeed on the ancient Los Angeles plain. The remains of both are much less common than those of *Arctodus*.

Insects and Birds. Unlike many other fossil faunas, that of Rancho la Brea includes large numbers of insects and birds. Among the former are many carrion beetles, which fed upon and even lived in decaying carcasses. Birds ranged from geese and a stork more than 4 feet (1.2 m.) high to woodpeckers, waxwings, and tiny sparrows. More than half of them, however, represented the order of vultures, eagles, and hawks.

Many hawks belonged to modern species, and so did bald and golden eagles. Others were related to species now found in Central America. Eight or more species of vultures fed at and were trapped in the tar pools. One was much like the modern California condor but belonged to an extinct species that ranged from the Cascade Mountains to Florida and Mexico. Another was more closely related to condors of South America but had a longer beak. Both seemed small beside the vulturine *Teratornis,* which ranged from California to Texas, Florida, and northern Mexico. *Teratornis* stood 30 inches (76 cm.) high as it perched, weighed about 50 pounds (22.7 kg.), and had a wingspread of 12 feet (3.7 m.). The openings for its nostrils were very large, suggesting that it hunted by smell, rather than sight. Though perhaps vulturine in habits, it probably was not at all closely related to the other vultures.

WHY AND HOW DID THEY DIE?

Examining these varied creatures, we wonder why they are found in the tar pits. What brought them there in the first place? How did they get into a substance that they should have done their best to avoid?

The answers appear when we look at the fossiliferous tar pits as they were in Late Pleistocene time. Contrary to the commonly held view, the fossils at Rancho La Brea were not found in the small lakes there, which have a sheet of water over a deep basin of tar. Rather, they came from stream channels in which sticky tar, oozing out of the ground, became mixed with clay, sand, and gravel. In some places, asphalt-impregnated quicksand was the deadly result of this combination. Small pools within the stream channels provided homes for snails, water beetles, and water bugs, as well as feeding places for geese, ducks, and grebes. Herons, cranes, and shorebirds waded in the shallows, and toads came to lay their strings of gelatinous eggs. Now and then herds of bison, antelope, or horses paused at the pools to drink.

This picture fits the moist season: in the dry one, which lasted from late spring until autumn, the streams stopped flowing and shrank to a series of isolated pools. These became almost the only source of water. Herbivores traveled miles to reach them; most stood on the banks or the firm bottom to drink and were safe, but others waded into the sticky asphalt quicksand and were caught. So, too, were meat eaters that came to feed upon the trapped herbivores.

There was, in fact, an orderly sequence of mammals, birds, and insects. First came a thirsty herbivore, which might be anything from a rabbit to an imperial mammoth. Going too far in its haste to drink, it found itself mired in the tar. Struggling to escape, the beast sank more and more deeply, at the same time attracting attention from prowling carnivores. They made an easy kill—but unless they were both careful and lucky, they, too, were trapped in the tar. So were carrion-eating dire wolves, which snarled and snapped at each other on the torn carcasses.

Hawks, eagles, and vultures watched these struggles or caught the odor of dead meat. Some came down, ate their fill, and left, but when several attacked one body, fights were sure to result. The birds pushed and beat each other with their wings, and those that lost their balance often fell into the tar. The final stage came when blowflies laid eggs in the carrion and beetles fed upon it. Many of these insects either fell into the tar or were buried with carcasses as they sank.

Sinking took place more slowly than we might suppose. Many bones in the tar pools are deeply weathered; others were gnawed by mice after carnivores had finished with them. Such bones must have lain at the surface for weeks or months, perhaps in such large, tangled piles that they could not sink rapidly. Thus, they attracted still more mammals and served as perches for the small birds whose remains also are found in the tar.

As a result of such a sequence of events, there is a much higher proportion of carnivorous and carrion-eating birds and animals than one would expect, giving us a rare "glimpse" at these normally scarce forms.

ANIMALS OF THE ICE FRONT

Though the tar-pool animals lived in the Ice Age, none of them ever saw a glacier or experienced a snowstorm. However, other mammals lived within a few miles of the shifting ice, moving northward when the glaciers melted and southward when the ice advanced again.

One of these hardy beasts was the musk-ox. During the Pleistocene, this animal ranged from the Middle Atlantic States across Asia and Europe to England. A stocky animal 3 feet 6 inches to 4 feet (1.1–1.2 m.) high, its long hair stopped rain and snow, while a woolly undercoat kept it warm. The modern musk-ox actually seems to prefer cold, blustery weather. Related animals that lived in California may have chosen less rigorous climates, but others apparently lived near the edge of the ice.

Caribou also are animals of Arctic "barren grounds" that lived near the front of the ice during Pleistocene times. There they often met woolly mammoths and mastodons, though the latter also ranged far south of the ice front, even to Florida. They apparently preferred swampy woodlands, where they often waded in search of food and sometimes were mired in mud. Moose also were swamp feeders, but mountain goats (really antelopes) preferred dry barrens where the weather ranged from cool to cold. Except for the exclusively North American mastodon, all these forms that preferred the barren ground of the Arctic had a circumpolar distribution during the Pleistocene, occurring in Asia, Europe, and North America. Even the mastodon had originated in the Old World in the Late Miocene, but it had become extinct there by the Pleistocene.

The majority of Pleistocene mammals lived in less exposed regions. In North America, the Great Plains and plateaus swarmed with horses, which also ranged across prairies and among forests of the East. The commonest western species was about the size of a modern cow pony, but *Equus giganteus*, of Texas, was bigger than the largest draft horse, while *E. tau*, of Mexico, was as small as a Shetland pony.

Tapirs, which had lived in North America since Middle Oligocene times, were common east of the Mississippi River until glaciers made their last great advance. Rhinoceroses, however, had vanished from North America at the end of the Pliocene Epoch, though a species with two long horns survived until the close of the Ice Age in Europe and Asia, where it lived along with the woolly mammoth. Like that animal, it had a woolly undercoat covered with long, coarse hair that was yellowish red in color.

(Left) **Preptoceras,** *which resembled a musk-ox, lived in California. True musk-oxen ranged widely near the front of continental glaciers. (Right)* Cervalces, *the elk-moose, ranged from New Jersey to Iowa*

North American artiodactyls included most of the species now living there, as well as a bulbous-nosed saiga antelope and another large animal that closely resembled the African eland. *Cervalces,* the elk-moose, was a large beast with divided antlers and very large hoofs that lived in forests from Iowa to New Jersey. It was very different from the so-called Irish elk, of Europe. The latter species, which survived until about ten thousand years ago, really was a gigantic fallow deer whose antlers spread 7 to 10 feet (2.1–3 m.). Skeletons, which have been found in peat bogs, seem much too delicate to have supported those enormous antlers. Surprisingly, then, careful study has shown that the relative size of the antlers and skeleton in the Irish elk is just what is to be expected if modern deer were to grow as large.

The oldest bison occur in the Early Pleistocene of China and India. By the Middle Pleistocene, they had reached Europe, and by the Late Pleistocene, North America. In North America, several species of bison ranged the Great Plains and prairies but were less abundant in the well-wooded East. *Bison latifrons,* which apparently ranged from Florida to Oregon, was an enormous creature with spreading, slightly curved horns 5 to more than 6 feet (1.5–1.8 m.) in width. The animal commonly called *Bison taylori,* of the southwestern plains, apparently should be called Figgins' bison. It was closely related to the high-humped species *(B. antiquus)* of the tar pits and was about as large. Figgins' bison was one of those killed and eaten by prehistoric Americans some eleven thousand years ago. Flint spear points were found among the bones of this extinct "buffalo" in 1926, near the town of Folsom, New Mexico. The skeletons lacked tails, suggesting that they had

Figgins' bison (right) was killed by ancient men; it was closely related to the species found at Rancho Le Brea. **Bison latifrons** *(left) was a large species with a very high hump and horns that spread more than 6 feet (1.8 m.)*

(Left) Megaloceros, the giant deer, or Irish elk, of Europe, North Africa, and Asia. Height at shoulder about 6 feet (1.8 m.). (Right) the woolly rhinoceros (Coelodonta) lived in both Europe and northern Asia

been cut off when the animals were skinned. Similar finds have been made in other regions, where "Folsom men" killed camels, horses, and mammoths as well as bison. This critical find was the proof needed to show that ancient man had actually hunted and killed these animals, not simply lived alongside them.

Some Ice Age beavers belonged to the living species and ranged through a large part of Europe, Asia, the United States, and northern Mexico. Giant beavers *(Castoroides)* were northern animals that inhabited lakes from New York to Nebraska. They were slightly larger than a black bear and measured 8 feet (2.4 m.) from nose to tip of tail. Though their gnawing teeth were large, the animals may have fed on water plants in preference to bark. There is nothing to show whether or not they built houses and dams, as beavers do today.

Porcupines, which now are animals of mountains and northern forests, emigrated from South America and spread over the whole United States and into Canada. With these prickly rodents came the ground sloths *Mylodon, Nothrotherium,* and *Megatherium.* We have seen the first two among mammals of the tar pits, but *Megatherium* ranged eastward to Florida and South Carolina. It must have frequently encountered *Megalonyx,* which had arrived during the Pliocene.

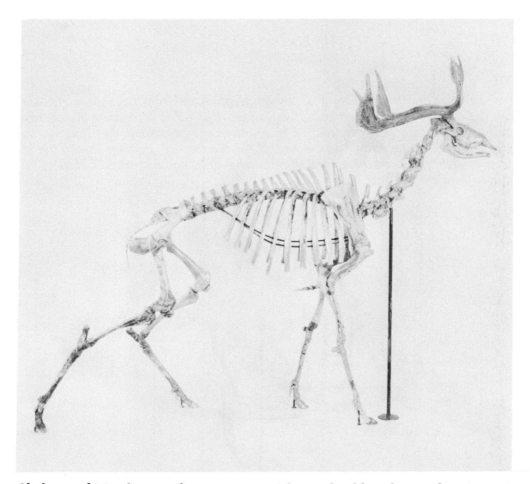

Skeleton of Megaloceros *from Japan. Height at shoulder about 6 feet (1.8 m.). (Photograph provided by Yoshikazu Hasegawa courtesy of the National Science Museum of Japan)*

THE SOUTHERN HEMISPHERE

On Antarctica, the ice sheet, which had formed by the Miocene, only waxed and waned slightly during the Pleistocene. Never during the Pleistocene was a significant area of land exposed where terrestrial mammals and birds were able to get a foothold.

Of the other three southern continents, only South America developed continental ice sheets, and these only at the southern tip, in Tierra del Fuego. However, mountain glaciers were present on South America, Australia, and Africa, plus New Zealand and New Guinea.

While the growth and decline of the continental ice sheet was the main result of the Pleistocene temperature fluctuations in Antarctica, on the other three southern continents there was only an alternation between wet and dry conditions. These seem to be correlated with the advances and retreats of the ice sheets in the Northern Hemisphere. Apparently, the dry periods correspond to the maximum advances of the glaciers and the wet ones to the retreats.

Just some of the many Late Pleistocene glyptodonts from Argentina. As with many groups of mammals, a host of variations evolved on a common theme. Like many groups that were successful in South America during the Tertiary, the glyptodonts became extinct at the end of the Pleistocene, perhaps due to the effects brought about by the arrival of numerous different mammals, including humans, from North America

Carapace and tail armor 1 m.

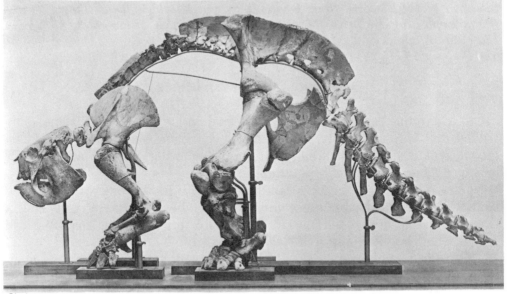

Skeleton

Glyptodon clavipes, a glyptodont edentate from the Late Pleistocene of Argentina. The carapace is about 5 feet (1.5 m.) long, and the skeleton is 9 feet (2.7 m.) long. (Photos courtesy of R. Pascual, La Plata Museum, La Plata, Argentina)

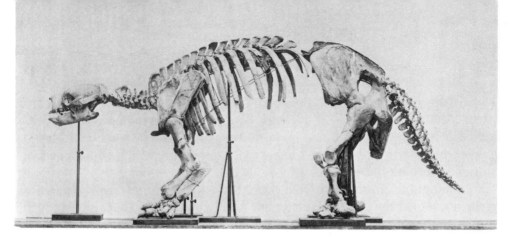

Skeleton, about 8 feet (2.3 m.) long

(Above and below) Glossotherium myloides, a mylodont ground sloth edentate from the Late Pleistocene of Argentina. (Photos courtesy of Rosendo Pascual)

Skull in front view, about 10 inches (25 cm.) wide   Skull in side view, about 18 inches (45 cm.) long

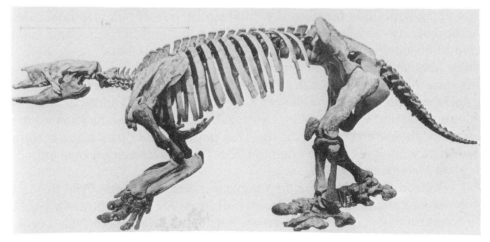

Skeleton, about 9 feet (2.7 m.) in length

Scelidotherium leptocephalum, a Late Pleistocene mylodont ground sloth edentate from Argentina. (Photographs courtesy of Rosendo Pascual)

Skull in front view, about 8 inches (20 cm.) wide   Skull in side view, about 20 inches (50 cm.) long

During the wet phases, the now mainly dry lake beds of the Sahara and central Australia became filled with water. In many cases, the water reached a level at which these lakes drained into the sea, whereas today what water gets into them, on the rare occasions on which rain does fall, simply evaporates there.

The mammalian fauna of Africa probably underwent the least change of any in the world during the Pleistocene to Recent times. Certainly, though, animals that were there would appear most odd to us today. One of the oddest was the deer-antlered giraffe *Sivatherium,* with its short neck and two sets of horns. In front was a pair of conical knobs like those on a living giraffe. Behind was a second pair of palmate horns reminiscent of a moose or a European elk. Yet even this odd beast was a member of a family still living in Africa. This reflects the general pattern for Africa, where even though many mammalian genera and species became extinct during the Pleistocene, only a few families did. Those families that did disappear tended to be like the chalicotheres, ones that had already become extinct or highly reduced elsewhere and were only relicts in Africa.

In South America, a much more dramatic decline of the mammals occurred. Many long-established families that had flourished through much of the Cenozoic became extinct. Among the more noticeable of these were the glyptodontids. As many as ten genera of these large, armadillolike mammals lived in the Middle Pleistocene of northern Argentina, and even in the Late Pleistocene there were still eight. Now the group has become completely extinct along with three families of ground sloths, two of notoungulates, and one litoptern. All had long Cenozoic histories in South America and even survived into the Pleistocene, many in considerable numbers.

Fewer families of mammals became extinct in Australia during the Pleistocene, but there were fewer to become extinct: diprotodontids, palorchestids, and thylacoleonids (see Chapter XXXI). These three families of Australian marsupials that became extinct during the Pleistocene all had something in common; they were large animals. This pattern holds true elsewhere in the world as well. It was more often the larger mammals that become extinct during the Pleistocene.

This was true not only on the continents but also on islands. And this not only applies to mammals, but birds as well. In Madagascar, however, both the elephant birds and the giant lemurs succumbed not in the Pleistocene, but during the past few thousand years. The same is true in New Zealand, where the extinction of the flightless moas occurred.

In both instances, the decline occurred only after humans arrived. In all land areas, humans had arrived before the most intense episode of Pleistocene extinction occurred. The adverse effect of humans on these larger animals may not have been simply due to hunting. Rather, it may have been caused by alteration of the landscape, such as the common practice of widespread burning.

Footprint of the extinct giant marsupial Diprotodon, *from Lake Callabonna, in South Australia. The footprint was originally pressed into mud, and sand and blew into the print, filling it. After that, both sand and impression were covered with more mud. Later, after the sand cast of the footprint had become hardened into stone, erosion exposed it as pictured here. (Photo by R. Tedford, American Museum of Natural History, New York)*

Hand (manus) of Diprotodon *being excavated at Lake Callabonna on an Australian Army-Museum of Victoria-Australian Museum expedition in 1983. (Photo by Robert Jones, Australian Museum, Sydney)*

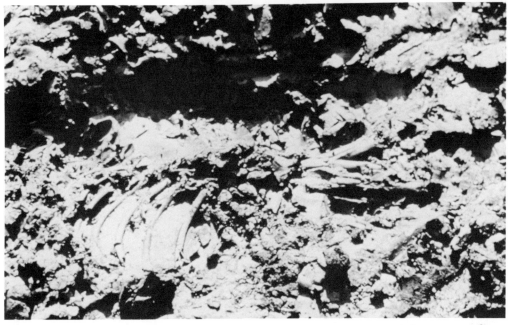

Skeleton of an extinct kangaroo preserved in lake sediments laid down in a "fire hole" burned into the Morewell coal seam, southern Australia. A "fire hole" is produced when a fire burns exposed coal, forming a depression in which a lake or a swamp develops. (Photograph courtesy of C. Tassell, Queen Victoria Museum and Art Gallery, Launceston, Tasmania)

One other factor could have played a part in this worldwide phenomenon of extinction of the larger mammals and birds toward the end of the Pleistocene, the rigorous climatic conditions. However, earlier glaciations were as severe as, if not more so than, the last one.

Extinction did occur all through the Pleistocene, so both factors probably played a role toward the end of the epoch. In combination, the effect may have been more severe than either would have been alone.

THE HUMAN RACE, A PRODUCT OF THE ICE AGE?

The hominids, the family that includes people, split from the chimpanzees (and the great apes) between 7 and 5.5 million years ago. This probably took place in Africa, though some scientists think that Asia may have been a more likely place.

The earliest known fossils of hominids are fragments dated at 5.5 million years. Specimens of *Australopithecus* 3.7 million years of age are the oldest hominids well enough preserved to allow a generic name to be given. To our eyes, with their small brains and heavy jaws, they probably would have looked more like somewhat unusual apes than humans. However, footprints preserved in a volcanic ash at Laetoli, in Tanzania, Africa, and skeletal remains from several sites in South and East Africa, show that they walked fully upright.

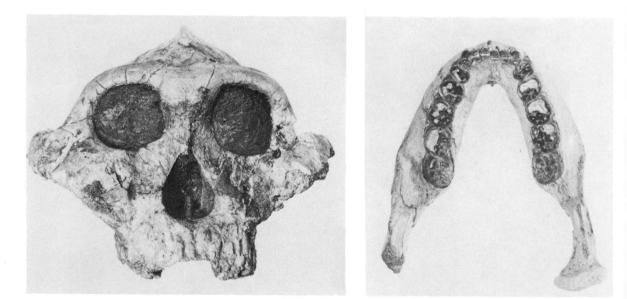

Skull, width 6.5 inches (16 cm.)   Jaw, length 6 inches (15 cm.)

Australopithecus robustus, *from the Late Pliocene of Africa. (Photos courtesy of M. G. Leakey and the National Museums of Kenya)*

Adults of *Australopithecus* ranged from 4 to 5 feet (1.3–1.5 m.) in height, somewhat smaller than most humans living today.

They lived not in the forests, but in the savannas, where instead of soft fruits their food was probably tough tubers and hard nuts. This is reflected in the structure of their teeth, in which the incisors are reduced and the enamel of the molars complicated and thickened. No longer did they have to bite through tough skins with their incisors to reach the soft pulp of fruits. Rather, their molars were used to crush and grind the harder food found on the savanna.

The genus *Homo,* to which we belong, probably arose from a species of *Australopithecus* about the beginning of the Pleistocene. However, *Australopithecus* did not become extinct then, but continued to live alongside *Homo* until about one million years ago.

Australopithecus never left Africa, but soon after *Homo* appeared on that continent, it reached and spread across Asia.

Though *Australopithecus* may have used primitive stone tools, *Homo,* as he evolved, developed more elaborate tools. More elaborate, too, was the social structure of *Homo.* Instead of foraging for food individually, members of a group shared their food with one another. With this development must have come language.

Though it can be truthfully said that the general trend of evolution of the

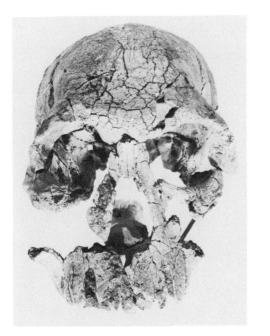

Skull, width 5 inches (13 cm.)

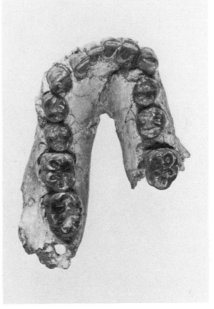

Jaw, length 3 inches (8 cm.)

Homo habilis, *from the Late Pliocene of Africa. (Courtesy of M. G. Leakey and the* *National Museums of Kenya)*

brain in hominids was toward larger size, it is a curious fact that the Neanderthals, the earliest members of our own species, *Homo sapiens,* had brains on average larger than ours. In addition, their skeletons show that they were stronger as well. Yet, modern *Homo sapiens* replaced them beginning about forty thousand years ago. Sheer size was probably not critical. Rather, the reasons for this may be related to subtle ways our brains work. Though Neanderthals looked much like us, they may have behaved quite differently, and quite clearly did not survive to the present day. What comes next is anyone's guess!

CHAPTER XXXVI

How to Care for a Fossil

Because the number of professional paleontologists in the world is small, amateurs, company geologists, landowners, or any lucky passerby will always play a significant part in the discovery of fossils, which may at any time be an important find. So it is likewise important that the person who finds fossils know what to do with them once found and how to gain an appreciation for what that fossil represents.

IN THE FIELD

It is important to remember that once a fossil is removed from the ground or rock, unless done so with a knowledgeable person in attendance, a great deal of irreplaceable information can be lost. Information about position in the rock sequence, orientation of the fossil, geographic location, association with other fossils—all need to be recorded in detail BEFORE a fossil is removed. And once the fossil is removed from the ground, it needs to be preserved, and packed, carefully enough to ensure that it arrives, at the institution where it will be permanently stored, in reasonably good order. Often, fragile fossils, if not preserved, will, upon drying out and with rough transport, change from beautiful works of art to piles of rubble; this benefits no one: amateur, professional paleontologist, and least of all the fossil!

Once a fossil has been found, the first step is to try to identify it, first using books and papers. If the specimen is unusually complete or if you have trouble identifying it from your search of the library and it appears to be something rare or unusual, try to contact a professional paleontologist. Several institutions, from all corners of the world are listed in the next chapter; a letter to the one nearest you could be very helpful in working out the identity of what you have found.

Paleontologists use may methods to ensure that fossils are properly collected, preserved, prepared, and stored. A number of excellent books are available that discuss the techniques used, including Kummel and Raup, 1965; Macdonald, 1983; and Rixon, 1976. These are good advisers to have on hand in your library for ready reference.

The foremost rule for proper care of a fossil is that it needs to be collected as complete as possible with as much field information as possible. Once the specimen has been collected, unless field data have been taken down in a notebook they may be lost forever—and so may much information about how, where, and when the animal lived and died and what happened to its remains as it settled into some sedimentary environment. One checklist that we have found useful to jog our memory in the field is reproduced from Ager (1963) later in this chapter. Answering the questions on that list will ensure that most of the necessary field information has been recorded.

PROSPECTING

The prospecting techniques that paleontologists use vary a great deal depending upon the kind of fossils they find and the kind of rocks these occur in. Once fossils are found, the first thing paleontologists usually do is to prospect all around the general area of that find. They need to decide where the most fossils are coming from and then concentrate their efforts at that spot. Then, after deciding where best to systematically excavate, they begin, preferably using a grid system that allows both lateral and vertical mapping of fossils relative to some datum point. All this information is duly recorded in a field notebook.

COLLECTING TECHNIQUES

Many fossils, expecially those of medium to large size, will appear as digging proceeds. But many small fossils will be missed unless they are recovered from the sediments in which they were buried by sieving. Large quantities of such sediment are wet-washed through flywire screen. The water generally decomposes the sediment, such as sand, clay, or silt, and washes it off the fossils. The sediment then passes through the screen and leaves behind a "concentrate" of stones, bones, teeth, shells, or whatever more resistant elements the soft rocks have contained. This is then dried and sorted by hand or with the help of mechanical sorters for the "goodies" that delight the heart of the determined fossil hunter.

Another procedure is used by paleontologists when faced with fragile fossils that need protection when moved from the field to the laboratory-plaster jacketing. The fossils to be plaster-jacketed are first exposed and a trench is dug around them. Then they are preserved with some penetrating, soluble wood glue such as Elmer's Glue (Aquadhere). Rixon (1976) suggests a variety of good alternative preservatives. Once preserved, a layer of wet toilet paper or newspaper is applied tightly to the bone. This acts as a separator between plaster and bone, which is essential for careful preparation later, when the cast is removed. Next, 2-to-4-inch (5–10-cm.) -wide strips of burlap (hessian) are cut into long lengths and dipped into a thin mixture of plaster and water and then applied to the fossil bone and surrounding matrix just as a doctor would apply a plaster cast to a patient's broken leg. Once the plaster becomes hard (and a fast-setting plaster is preferred), the cast is undercut, and the bone, matrix, and hardened plaster are rolled over. The same procedure is followed on this "underside" after some of the matrix is removed carefully, to cut down on the weight of the final cast. Sometimes, if the casts are large, lengths of wood or metal are strapped into the plaster block to give it strength. Then, after the plaster has hardened all around, the cast is ready for transport. The cast can be packed into a wooden crate or 55- (44- imperial) gallon drum. To prevent the cast from smashing into other blocks, it should be padded with straw, newspaper, foam, or whatever padding is at hand. Drums are good packing cases, as they are often available, and they can be rolled, which means they are easier to deal with when loading and unloading them onto and from trucks and trains.

USEFUL EQUIPMENT

Both the screen-washing and the plaster-jacketing techniques have revolutionized paleontology, especially vertebrate paleontology, in this century and have allowed finer and finer detail to be preserved on fossil material.

For collecting invertebrates and plants, the above techniques have some use, but in many cases the most helpful field equipment includes a geologic hammer, a number of different-sized rock chisels, plugs and feathers (used in an old rock-mining technique and illustrated in this chapter), newspaper and strapping tape for wrapping specimens, cardboard or wooden boxes to pack specimens in, collecting bags, and labels. A portable jackhammer and rock saws are of great use in collecting from hard rock. Dental tools, awls, and various sizes of paintbrushes and whisk brooms can be of use too, in excavating small specimens. And it's always important to have pens, including marking pens, with permanent ink that won't wash off in a rainstorm, to mark each parcel or specimen with some sort of field number. If the pen won't mark directly on the specimen, a spot of white paint can be added, then the number written on this when it dries. The paleontologist can then record in his or her field notebook that field number and all the information available for that specimen: who collected it, on whose property it was collected, what collecting conditions were like, what techniques were used to collect it. A map showing the geographic location of the collecting site, drawn as accurately as possible, or as accurately pinpointed on an existing map or aerial photograph, is also a help. If the fossil was collected in a stream bank or a cliff face, a columnar section (a drawing of the cliff face or bank) showing the different rock types present and where the fossil was found in that pile of rocks is also of help.

Specimens, once labeled, should be individually wrapped in paper or tis-

sue and labeled on the outside of the wrapping by marking on the tape used
to seal the package. These can, in turn, be packed into sturdy boxes. And
now they are ready to be moved.

BACK IN THE LABORATORY

Once the fossils are back in the museum, home, or institution where they
will remain permanently, a long procedure begins. This involves unpacking
the specimens, storing them until they can be prepared, preparing them,
numbering them, copying field data, and finally storing the fossils in some
logical manner that allows them to be retrieved for study at a moment's
notice. Some specimens also are needed for display, so that people can
observe the material and learn about how the fossils allow paleontologists
to reconstruct past climates, past arrangements of continents (which have
not always been where they are today), and the family histories of a vast
array of animals and plants.

To a large extent, this aspect of paleontology is the most difficult of all,
because it is often very difficult to acquire enough money and, in turn, staff
to allow speedy progress to be made once a collection arrives from the field.
The excitement attached to expeditions going to faraway places with
strange-sounding names (Lake Kittakittaooloo, Shandong Province, or the
Bridger Basin) often draws numerous volunteers and sometimes even funding. The day-to-day, sometimes monotonous collection-management and
preparation work are often not very appealing. But over the past few years
an encouraging increase in the number of public volunteer groups attached
to museums and universities, often calling themselves "Friends of the Museum," etc., is a heartening change. These groups are offering responsible,
long-term volunteer staff that can participate in preparation, collecting, curation, and even expeditions and research that otherwise might go undone for
years. Real problems still do exist in many major public fossil collections all
over the world. These collections still often lack the staffing and funding for
optimum efficiency.

In summary, keep in mind that fossils are a nonrenewable resource. They
tell us something of past history of the earth that can be told by nothing else.
Fossil finds by nonprofessional paleontologists have always been important
in paleontology. So if you think you have found something unusual, it is
always best to contact a paleontologist, usually first by letter, to allow a
professional evaluation of your find. It is also better NOT TO DISTURB a
fossil specimen beyond its first discovery unless you understand proper collecting techniques. Precious information can be lost forever and the fossil
destroyed if the right procedures are not used at this stage. It is best if you
can somehow associate yourself with a museum or institution with geologic
interests, and go from there to learn how to be a responsible collector who

can add both to your own knowledge about fossils and to that of the field of paleontology.

Field Questionnaire (modified from Ager, 1963)

These questions should be answered, as far as possible, for each separate rock unit.

DISTRIBUTION

1. Are the fossils evenly distributed throughout the rock unit?
2. Are they in pockets, lenses, bands, or nodules?
3. Are they more abundant at any particular level in the unit?
4. Do they occur in reefs or shell banks?
5. Are the various kinds of fossils distributed in the same way?
6. Are the same fossils present as are seen in the same bed elsewhere?
7. Are any of the species present unusual in the studied area but more common elsewhere?
8. Approximately how many species are present?

ASSOCIATIONS

1. What, very roughly, is the relative abundance of the different groups of fossils present?
2. Are there any obvious close associations; for example, crinoids with wood fragments?
3. Are there any obvious absentees; for example, no ammonoids in a Cretaceous marine shale?
4. Are there any obvious fossils that seem out of place with the rest of the fossil assemblage?
5. Are all growth stages present for each species? If not, which stages are present for each?
6. Are any of the fossils encrusted or bored? If so, how (for example, bryozoans inside and/or outside pelecypod shells)?
7. Are there any fossils attached to one another in any way?
8. Is there any evidence of the mixing of organisms from different environments; for example, land plants and echinoderms?

PRESERVATION

1. Are there any unusual features about the preservation, such as color banding on nautiloids?
2. Are all the fossils preserved in the same way?
3. Are there any traces of "soft" parts?

4. Are any delicate structures preserved; for example, spines on mollusc shells?

5. Are the fossils worn or broken, and are some species more so than others?

6. Are the valves of bivalves separated (molluscs, brachiopods, and/or arthropods such as ostracods)? If so, are both valves present in equal numbers?

7. If the valves of bivalves are still joined together, are they tightly closed, partly open, or wide open?

8. If there are crinoid or other pelmatozoan stems present, are the ossicles separated, preserved as short sections of the column in short lengths, or in complete columns?

9. If higher-plant remains are present, which parts of the plants are they (roots, stem, leaves, fruits)?

RELATION TO SEDIMENT

1. What is the nature of the enclosing sediment?

2. Are there any sedimentation structures, such as false bedding, slumps, ripple marks, and scour marks?

3. Is there any obvious relationship between the fossil and the nature and/or grade of the sediment (for example, larger foraminifera in coarser-grained sands)?

4. Are any of the fossils obviously out of place in the sediment, such as reef corals in shale?

5. Are the fossils in nodules, if any, preserved in the same way as those in the surrounding sediment?

6. What is the nature of the infilling of any closed shells?

7. Are there any signs of a general disturbance of the sediment by organisms?

8. Are any of the fossils in positions of life? If so, what percentage of each species?

9. Are any of the other fossils oriented in a particular way, such as belemnite rostra lying parallel to one another?

FORM

1. Are there any noteworthy growth forms, such as delicately branched corals?

2. Are there any possible peculiarities of adaptation (e.g., expanded glabella on trilobites)?

3. Are there any obviously pathological specimens or any that have been damaged during life?

4. Are there any cemented forms, for example oysters, or forms requiring a firm substratum for anchorage?

5. Are there any borings, burrows, tracks, or trails?
6. Are there any signs of organic activity, such as coprolites?
7. Are the fossils highly ornamented or smooth, or are there some of each?
8. Are there any signs of stunting or gigantism?
9. Are there any signs of unusual thickness of shell or excessive ornamentation?
10. Are there any signs of seasonal growth or of general change in growth rate or direction during life?

GENERAL

Are there any other phenomena of paleoecological interest in the assemblage?

HOW FOSSILS ARE COLLECTED

1. PLASTER JACKETING OF LARGER SPECIMENS.

Upon discovery, fossils often don't look particularly impressive. Here the forelimb of the giant marsupial Diprotodon *lies on the surface of windblown Lake Callabonna, South Australia. (Photograph by Robert Jones)*

Excavation exposes the extent of the skeleton, and once exposed the fossil is ready for plaster-jacketing, a technique used to protect the specimen being transported from the field to the laboratory. This is the specimen pictured above, after excavation. (Photograph by Robert Jones)

Fossils are first exposed and then trenched around, leaving them on a pedestal. Bones are then covered by a tightly adhering layer or two of wet toilet tissue and/or newspaper. After this, strips of burlap (hessian) are dipped into a soupy mixture of plaster of paris, and these strips are tightly bound around the fossil blocks just as surgical strips are bound around a broken limb. Here Robert Emry works on bones at Lake Callabonna, a Pleistocene site in South Australia. (Photo by Richard Tedford)

Big plaster jackets are often reinforced with timber or metal to be sure of stability before they are removed. Here Robert Emry completes a cast at Lake Callabonna. (Photo by Richard Tedford)

When one side of the cast is dry and the plaster hard, the fossil is undercut, below where bones occur, and the specimen is rolled over. Then plaster is applied to the exposed underside. Peta Knecht is finishing off the plaster jacket covering a dinosaur. (Photo by James Jensen)

The casts must then be transported to the laboratory, where they can be opened and prepared. Here Jim Jensen (with Rod and Mila Scheetz), using his Super Truck with its tripod, begins to remove several very large plaster jackets from Dry Mesa Quarry, Colorado. (Photo by James Jensen)

If fossils must be transported over long distances, often the plaster-jacketed specimens are crated up like these bones from Lake Callabonna. These had to travel nearly ten thousand miles, to the American Museum of Natural History, in New York. (Photo by Richard Tedford)

2. REMOVING SPECIMENS IN HARD ROCK.

When rock is hard, saws can be used to remove small blocks. Dennis Belnap removes a block with fossil eggshell in it. (Photo by James Jensen)

Another method for removing small blocks of hard rock is an old mining technique called "plugs and feathers." Here holes are being drilled into which the plugs (dull chisel-like bits of steel) and feathers are placed. This locality, Riversleigh, in the western part of Queensland, Australia, is in Miocene freshwater limestone, which has produced a vast array of vertebrates through the efforts of Michael Archer and his co-workers.

Once the holes are drilled, plugs and feathers are driven in with a sledge hammer

And, rather quickly, a block splits out that can be removed and either carefully wrapped or even plaster-jacketed to protect the fossils. Limestone blocks are often prepared by soaking in acetic acid to remove the carbonate and leave the fossils behind

If crates cannot be built, metal drums can be used to transport rocks or sediments. Frank Bussat bends down the top of a drum containing Miocene limestone blocks from Bullock Creek, Northern Territory, Australia. Drums are easy to move, because they roll and don't require lifting to move them from one point to another. (Photograph by Lucinda Hann)

Drums can be transported by trailer to the nearest railhead or trucking depot. (Photograph by Lucinada Hann)

3. SCREEN-WASHING SOFT SEDIMENTS FOR SMALL FOSSILS

Excavation of the sands and clays representing ancient streams is carried out by hand or with heavy equipment. This site in northern South Australia has yielded a variety of small to medium-sized marsupials that lived in the more forested Miocene times

Once sediments are excavated, they are bagged for transport to a source of water, where they can be processed

The bags are then emptied, small bits at a time, into screen boxes that can then be placed in the water to be soaked and agitated. In central and northern South Australia, stock dams are ideal spots for such processing. Elsewhere, streams, ponds, or watering troughs can serve the same purpose

When the sediments are soaked in water (and sometimes kerosene), most tend to break down and pass through the screens, leaving behind a "matrix" of bone and other insoluble residue. This is dried, either in the screens or on plastic sheets, bagged again for transport, and carefully labeled as to locality, age, date when collected, and collector

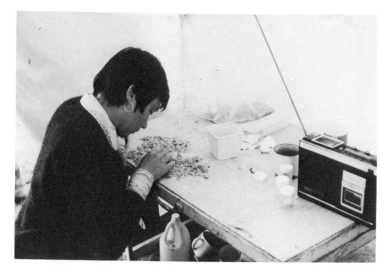

The concentrate must be carefully picked by hand, sometimes using a binocular microscope, to recover the tiny teeth and bones that have been preserved in such ancient stream beds

4. MUSEUM CURATION AND STORAGE.

When fossils have been prepared, they must be carefully stored in collections so that they are protected from breakage and yet available for study. These drawers of Pleistocene mammals from West Texas in the Texas Tech Museum, Lubbock, show how proper storage boxes and padding can achieve this goal. Each specimen, in addition, has a museum number that is recorded in a permanent catalogue that contains all the information on that specimen: identification, age, locality where found, collector, date. (Photo by Daniel Womochel)

5. FIELD NOTES.

27 June 1971 Sunday

Flies bad as usual beginning to congregate by 8AM. In the afternoon visited the locality that Tom and I had found last night (to be called South Prospect A) and made a section of the sediments there. Did the same for Eric mas Quarry earlier in the day. Continued to actual surface prospect and found part of an edentulous mammal jaw – probably phascolarctid. Dick and Rod worked on south along the scarp as Tom and I continued to surface prospect at South Prospect A. I dug into the gray clays at the place I had found the fragmentary mandible but found nothing more.

Tom and I then drove on south along the scarp past Rod and Dick and then began working back towards them. We happened onto a spot (South Prospect B) that produced a cetacean ear region and a partial tooth which Dick thinks may be a bandicoot (tho it's higher crowned than most) somewhat like Choeropus (sp?). The roots are quite small for a mammalian tooth. Two phalanges of mammals and an ulna representing a very large mammal (+ a frag of a large mammal tooth) were found in or near this prospect.

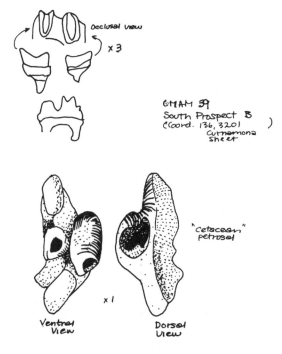

Occlusal View

x3

QMAM 39
South Prospect B
(Coord. 136, 3201
Curnamona
sheet

)

"cetacean"
petrosal

Ventral
View

x1

Dorsal
View

Journal entry in field notes, arranged much as in a diary, telling about field conditions, collecting techniques, and so on. Drawings, such as those of the fossil platypus tooth and dolphin ear bone, help describe what is contained in the field packages. A field notebook should contain as much information as possible about where the fossil was found. Information not recorded there can be lost forever.

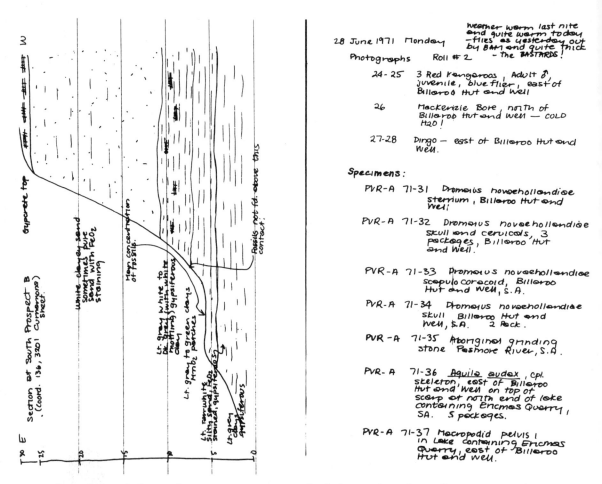

Drawings of the rock outcrops can contain information that allows comparison with rocks at other localities. They can also be useful in recording paleoenvironmental data and the exact point where fossils were located. Lists of photographs taken help identify them later. A list of wrapped specimens with their field numbers (e.g., PVR-A 71-31) is useful in determining the contents of each field package without opening it

6. MOLDING AND CASTING OF SPECIMENS.

Preparation of molds and casts of specimens. *Preparation of molds and casts of fossils is an important procedure. This allows copies of important fossils to be exchanged between paleontologists who are studying them without risk to the original specimens. It also allows material to be placed on display without preventing the study of it. The following illustrations show how molds are made using a silicon rubber and then how casts of a lightweight plastic material are made, in this instance of large fossils, dinosaurs. This work was carried out at the Museum of Victoria, Melbourne, and photographed by Frank Coffa. The photographs were provided courtesy of that museum; the text is modified after a paper written by Mike Traynor.*

Planning the Mold and Building the Dividing Wall. *Before making the mold, it is important to study shapes and irregularities of the fossils. This allows you to decide what is the most efficient way to make the mold, which is basically made in two or more pieces. The first step in making the mold is to make a plasticine or modeling-clay wall around the bone to stop the flow of the liquid silicone rubber that will form the mold.*

Application of Silicone. *Once the modeling-clay walls are built, the silicone rubber is mixed and poured over the bone. The bone is usually prepared with hardeners, which protect it, before application of the molding material. Silicone can be dried more quickly by using a hair blower. Silicone is a quick-setting, strong, and durable material, which will permit a number of casts to be poured without disintegration of the mold*

Application of Gauze—Final Silicone Coat. *To strengthen the mold, layers of gauze are applied and more liquid silicone rubber is added. Then a final coat is applied, and small prefabricated silicone keys are pressed into the walls of the mold. These keys will serve to restrict movement of the various parts of the mold during its casting*

Application of plaster. *A hard plaster jacket is next formed over the silicone-rubber mold. First a thin coat of plaster is applied, then it is reinforced with fabric and metal. Once the plaster has hardened, the plaster jacket, mold, and fossil are turned over. Then work can begin on the unmolded side of the fossil*

653

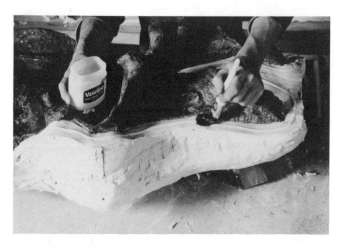

Use of a separator. *In order to keep the two molds from sticking together, petroleum jelly (Vaseline) is applied to all of the exposed surfaces of the silicone rubber. This will allow the pieces of the mold to separate easily*

Completing the mold. *The same procedure as that shown in the preceding photographs is repeated until the bone is entirely encased in a silicone mold and a protective plaster jacket*

Removing the fossil. *The sections of the mold are now taken apart, and the fossil is removed*

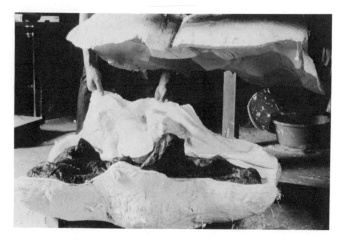

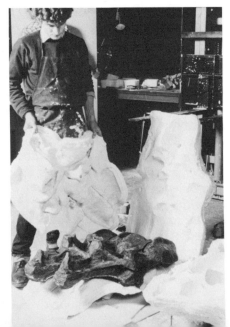

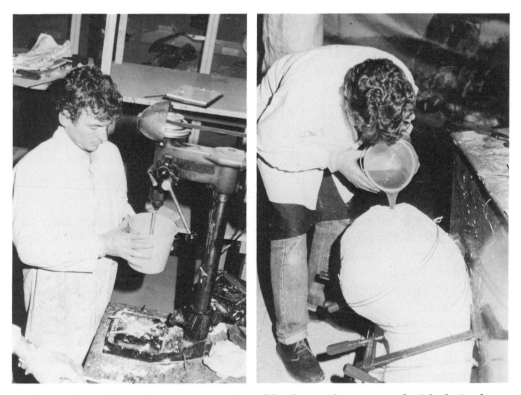

Casting. *The mold sections are now placed back together, covered with their plas-ter-jacket cradles, and firmly wired together. Then the casting material is mixed up. Many kinds of plastics are available; consulting the book written by Rixon (1976) or a plastics firm such as Dow Corning can help you select what is best for your purposes. In this case, a polyurethane foam was used. This gives a light-weight cast, ideal for mounting in a public display*

Removal of the cast. *After the casting material has hardened, the cast is ready for removal. Here the cast, on the right, is compared with the original, on the left. The cast can be trimmed of any excess material and colored to match the original—often to the extent that it is difficult to distinguish the cast from the original*

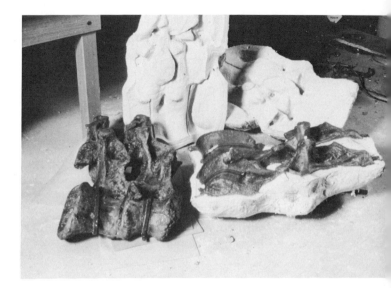

CHAPTER XXXVII

How to Learn More About Fossils

Fossils tell many stories, and in order to squeeze the most information out of such ancient remains, a fossil enthusiast can use several avenues. Most important is to read as much as time allows about the subject. Another avenue is to make contact with someone who is also interested in paleontology, be he or she amateur or professional. Also important is learning how to properly collect fossils and record information about them, as well as learning when NOT to collect. Then, too, one needs to know how to prepare and store collections of fossils properly. This chapter tells where to begin to get this type of information, so that anyone seriously considering doing something about a paleontological interest will know where to start.

MUSEUMS, UNIVERSITIES, AND OTHER INSTITUTIONS

Information about fossils comes mainly from museums, universities, state or national geological surveys, and, most important, books. Museums such as the American Museum of Natural History (New York); the National Museum of Natural History, Smithsonian Institution (Washington, D.C.); the Los Angeles County Museum (Los Angeles), and the British Museum (Natural History) (London) all have large collections of fossils held both as research collections behind the scenes and as public display specimens on view for everyday examination. Museums can be used in a number of ways. Firstly, the public displays can provide much information about identification of individual specimens, but also a great deal of information about reconstruction of the fossil, what kind of environment it lived in, what other living things it coexisted with, and so on. Professional paleontologists who work for museums can also be directly contacted, often first by letter and perhaps later by a personal appointment. They can help a great deal in identifying and interpreting fossils that cannot easily be identified by using the public displays. Such professionals can also determine the importance of certain fossils and suggest further reading for information also not readily available in the public displays.

Often museums have an education department, which can provide much information about their collections, and they sometimes offer courses dealing with museum material. More and more today there are volunteer groups associated with natural-history museums, often called "Friends of the Museum," that provide help in the way of preparing, preserving, and sometimes even helping in the study and collection of fossils. Being involved in one of these groups can be a great deal of fun and can provide an in-depth education on many of the techniques associated with paleontology. Information about all of these museum services and activities can be obtained by either visiting or writing to the museum nearest you. Later in this chapter we have provided a list, with addresses, of some of the major museums in the world. For an even greater variety, you can use the following book, which lists most of the museums in the world: J. Benson and others, 1981, *Museums of the World,* 3rd edition (K. G. Saur, Munich, Germany). Both museums and universities are listed in another publication, *The World of Learning 1979–1980* (Europa Publications, London). You should be able to find these books in, or have them ordered through, your local library. Failing that, a letter to the publisher is a way of purchasing the book.

Universities quite often have scientists on their staff who know something about fossils. These people most often work in geology or earth-sciences departments, or in biology, zoology, or botany departments. So, if there is no museum near you, a college or university may well be another good place to start. It is always courteous, just as with museums, to write a letter to the institution first with your inquiry so that an appointment for you to visit can be made that is convenient for both you and the paleontologist you will visit. Often there are good libraries associated with universities, as with many museums, and these can be a rich source of information.

State and national geological surveys and institutes are another source of information; their addresses and phone numbers are available in telephone directories. Museums and universities are also listed in such directories.

The following list gives a selection of institutions around the world that are interested in paleontology.

MUSEUMS

Africa

ALGERIA

Institut de Biologie
Université d'Oran
ES Senia
Oran

EGYPT

Geological Museum
15 Sheik Rihan St.
P.O. Box Dawawin
Cairo

LIBYA

Faculty of Science
P.O. Box 9480
Garyounis University
Benghazi

SOUTH AFRICA

Bernard Price Institute for
  Paleontological Research
University of Witwatersrand
Johannesburg

SOUTH AFRICA

South African Museum
P.O. Box 61
Cape Town
8000

SOUTH AFRICA

Transvaal Museum
Box 413
Pretoria 0001

ZIMBABWE

National Museum
P.O. Box 240
Bulawayo

Asia

CHINA (PRC)

Institute of Vertebrate
  Paleontology and
  Paleoanthropology
Academia Sinica
P.O. Box 643
142 Xi Zhi Men Wai St.
Beijing (2)

CHINA (PRC)

Shanghai Museum of Natural
  History
The East Avenue of Yenan
Shanghai.

INDIA

Geology Department,
Punjab University
Chandigarh, 160014

INDIA

Geological Studies Unit,
Indian Statistical Institute
203 Barrackpore Trunk Rd.,
Calcutta

INDIA

Geological Survey of India
12A&B Russel St.
Calcutta, 700071

INDIA

S-S-449 Mukkaramjahi Rd.
Manoranjan
Hyderabad, 500001

INDONESIA

Geological Survey of Indonesia
Jalan Diponogoro
Bandung

JAPAN

National Science Museum,
3-23-1 Hyakunin-cho
Shinjuku
Tokyo, 160

PAKISTAN

Pakistan Museum of Natural
　History
Block 2
F 7/2
Main Markaz
Islamabad
Pakistan

Australia

Australian Museum
6–8 College St.
Sydney, New South Wales 2001

Bureau of Mineral Resources,
P.O. Box 378
Canberra, A.C.T. 2601

Institute of Aboriginal Studies
P.O. Box 553
Canberra, A.C.T. 2601

Museum of Victoria
285–321 Russell St.
Melbourne, Victoria 3000

Northern Territory Museum
Darwin, Northern Territory

Queensland Museum
Fortitude Valley
Brisbane, Queensland 4006

Queen Victoria
Museum and Art Galley
Wellington Street
Launceston, Tasmania 7250

South Australian Museum
North Terrace
Adelaide, South Australia 5000

Tasmanian Museum
4 Argyle St.
Hobart, Tasmania

Western Australian Museum
Perth, Western Australia

Europe

AUSTRIA

Paläontologisches Institut der
　Universität Wien
Universitätsstrasse 7
1010 Wien 1 (Vienna)

BELGIUM

L'institut Royal des Sciences
　Naturelles de Belgique
31 Rue Vautier, B-1040
Bruxelles (Brussels)

DENMARK

Universitetets Mineralogisk-
　Geologiske Museum
Ostervoldgade 5–7
1350 Köbenhavn (Copenhagen)

ENGLAND

British Museum (Natural History)
Cromwell Road
London SW7 5BD

ENGLAND

Institute of Geological Science
Exhibition Road
London SW7

FINLAND

Museum of Zoology
SF00100 Helsinki, 100

FRANCE

Department des Sciences de la
  Terre
Université Claude-Bernard
27-43 boulevard du 11 Novembre
Lyon
69622 Villeurbanne Cedex

FRANCE

Laboratoire de Paléontologie,
Place Eugène-Bataillon, 34
Montpellier

FRANCE

Laboratoire de Paléontologie des
  Vertèbres et de Paléontologie
  Humaine
4 Place Jussieu
75230 Paris Cedex 05

FRANCE

Museum National d'Histoire
  Naturelle
38 rue Geoffroy-Saint Hilaire
Paris 5

GERMANY

Institut für Geologie und
  Paläontologie der Technischen
  Universität Berlin (1)
Hardenbergstrasse 42
Berlin 12

GERMANY

Institut für Paläontologie und
  historische Geologie
Richard Wagnerstrasse 10
D-8000
München, 2 (Munich)

GERMANY

Senckenberg Museum
D-6000
Frankfurt am Main
Senckenberg Anlage, 25

GERMANY

Staatliches Museum für
  Naturkunde Stuttgart
Zweigstelle Ludwigsburg
Arsenalplatz 3D-714
Ludwigsburg

HOLLAND (THE NETHERLANDS)

Rijksmuseum voor Geologie en
  Mineralogie
Hooglandse Kerkgracht
17 Leiden

ITALY

Museo di Geologia e Paleontologia
  dell' Università di Firenze
Via La Pira 4
(gia Via Lamermora)
50121 Firenze (Florence)

NORWAY

Paleontologisk Museum
Sarsgate 1
Oslo, 5

ROMANIA

Laboratory of Paleontology
Faculty of Geology-Geography
University of Bucharest
Blvd. N.
Balescu No. 1
Bucharest

SPAIN

Instituto de Geología (C.S.I.C.)
José Gutiérrez Abascal 2
Madrid, 6

SPAIN

Instituto de Paleontología
Escola Industrial
23 Sabadell

SWEDEN

Naturhistoriska Riksmuseum
Stockholm, 50

SWEDEN

Swedish Museum of Natural
  History
S-104 05
Stockholm

SWITZERLAND

Naturhistorisches Museum
Augustinergasse 2
Basel

SWITZERLAND

Paläontologisches Institut und
  Museum der Universität
Kinstlergasse 16
CH-8006
Zürich

U.S.S.R.

Paleontological Institute of
  U.S.S.R. Academy of Sciences
Profsojiznaja Ulitza 113
117321 Moskva (Moscow)

U.S.S.R.

Paleontological Museum
Academy of Science of the
  U.S.S.R.
Leninsky Prospect 16
Moskva V-71 (Moscow)

Middle East

ISRAEL

Geology Department
Ben Gurion University
Box 2053
Beer Sheva, 84120

ISRAEL

Department of Zoology
Hebrew University
Jerusalem

SAUDI ARABIA

Directorate General
Mineral Resources
P.O. Box 345
Jidda

SAUDIA ARABIA

Department of Geology
Riyadh University
Riyadh

North America

CANADA

Geological Survey of Canada
601 Booth St.
Ottawa, Ontario
K1A 0C8

CANADA

Laboratory for Vertebrate
Paleontology
Departments of Geology and
Zoology
The University of Alberta
Edmonton, Alberta T6G 2E9

CANADA

Manitoba Museum of Man and
Nature
190 Rupert Ave.
Winnipeg
Manitoba R3B 0N2

CANADA

Paleontology Division
National Museum of Natural
Sciences
Ottawa K1A 0M8

CANADA

Provincial Museum (Natural
History) of Alberta
12845-102 Avenue
Edmonton
Alberta T5N 0M6

CANADA

Redpath Museum
McGill University
859 Sherbrooke St. West
Montreal
Quebec
H3A 2K6

CANADA

Royal Ontario Museum
100 Queen's Park
Toronto
Ontario M5S 2C6

CANADA

Tyrrell Museum of Palaeontology
Box 7500
Drumheller, Alberta T0J 0Y0

CUBA

Departamento de Antropología
Universidad de Habana
La Habana

MEXICO

Instituto de Geología
Apartado Postal 70-296
Ciudad Universitaria
Mexico 20, D.F.

U.S.A.—ALASKA

The Museum
University of Alaska
Fairbanks 99701

U.S.A.—ALASKA

Department of Geology
University of Alaska
Fairbanks 99701

U.S.A.—ALASKA

U.S. Geological Survey
101-12th Avenue
Box 11
Fairbanks 99701

U.S.A.—ARIZONA

Department of Geosciences
University of Arizona
Tucson 85721

U.S.A.—ARIZONA

Museum of Northern Arizona
Rt. 4, Box 720
Flagstaff 86001

U.S.A.—CALIFORNIA

California Academy of Sciences
Golden Gate Park
San Francisco 94118

U.S.A.—CALIFORNIA

George Page Museum
5801 Wilshire Blvd.
Los Angeles 90036

U.S.A.—CALIFORNIA

Los Angeles County Museum of
  Natural History
900 Exposition Blvd.
Los Angeles 90007

U.S.A.—CALIFORNIA

Raymond M. Alf Museum
1175 West Base Line Road
Claremont 91711

U.S.A.—CALIFORNIA

San Diego Natural History
  Museum
P.O. Box 1390
San Diego 92112

U.S.A.—CALIFORNIA

Scripps Institution of
  Oceanography
University of California
P.O. Box 109
La Jolla 92037

U.S.A.—COLORADO

The Geological Society of America
3300 Penrose Place
Boulder 80301

U.S.A.—COLORADO

University of Colorado Museum
Department of Ecological Sciences
University of Colorado
Boulder 80302

U.S.A.—CONNECTICUT

Dinosaur State Park
West Street
Rocky Hill 06067

U.S.A.—CONNECTICUT

Peabody Museum
Yale University
New Haven 06520

U.S.A.—FLORIDA

Department of Natural Sciences
Florida State Museum
University of Florida
Gainesville 32611

U.S.A.—IDAHO

The Museum
Idaho State University
Box 240
Pocatello 83201

U.S.A.—ILLINOIS

Department of Zoology
Augustana College
Rock Island 61201

U.S.A.—ILLINOIS

Field Museum of Natural History
Roosevelt Road at Lake Shore
  Drive
Chicago 60605

U.S.A.—ILLINOIS

Illinois State Museum
Corner of Spring and Edwards
  Streets
Springfield 62706

U.S.A.—INDIANA

Dept. of Earth and Space Sciences
Indiana University - Purdue
  University at Fort Wayne
2101 Coliseum Boulevard
Fort Wayne 46805

U.S.A.—IOWA

Department of Geology
University of Iowa
Iowa City 52242

U.S.A.—KANSAS

Museum of Natural History
University of Kansas
Lawrence 66045

U.S.A.—KANSAS

Sternberg Memorial Museum
Kansas State University
Fort Hays 67601

U.S.A.—KENTUCKY

Museum of History and Science
727 W. Main St.
Louisville 40202

U.S.A.—LOUISIANA

Department of Geology
Louisiana State University
Baton Rouge 70803

U.S.A.—MARYLAND

Calvert Marine Museum
Solomons 20688

U.S.A.—MASSACHUSETTS

Museum of Comparative Zoology
Harvard University
Cambridge 02138

U.S.A.—MASSACHUSETTS

Pratt Museum
Amherst College
Amherst 01002

U.S.A.—MASSACHUSETTS

Woods Hole Oceanographic
  Institution
Woods Hole 02543

U.S.A.—MICHIGAN

Museum of Paleontology
University of Michigan
Ann Arbor 48109

U.S.A.—MINNESOTA

Science Museum
30 East 10th Street
St. Paul 55101

U.S.A.—MISSISSIPPI

Museum of Natural Science
111 N. Jefferson Street
Jackson 39202

U.S.A.—MICHIGAN

Cranbrook Institute of Science
500 Lone Pine Road
Box 801
Bloomfield Hills 48103

U.S.A.—MONTANA

Carter County Museum
Ekalaka 59324

U.S.A.—MONTANA

Museum of the Rockies
Montana State University
Bozeman 59715

U.S.A.—NEBRASKA

University of Nebraska State
  Museum
W-435 Nebraska Hall
Lincoln 68508

U.S.A.—NEW JERSEY

Department of Geology
Princeton University
Princeton 08540

U.S.A.—NEW JERSEY

Geology Museum
Rutgers University
New Brunswick 08903

U.S.A.—NEW JERSEY

Newark Museum
49 Washington Street
Newark 07102

U.S.A.—NEW JERSEY

New Jersey State Museum
205 West State Street
Trenton 08608

U.S.A.—NEW MEXICO

Department of Geology
University of New Mexico
Albuquerque 87131

U.S.A.—NEW MEXICO

New Mexico Bureau of Mines and
  Mineral Resources
Socorro 87001

U.S.A.—NEW YORK

American Museum of Natural
  History
Central Park West at 79th St.
New York 10024

U.S.A.—NEW YORK

Lamont Doherty Geological
  Observatory
Palisades 10964

U.S.A.—NORTH CAROLINA

North Carolina State Museum of
  Natural History
P.O. Box 27647
Raleigh 20560

U.S.A.—OHIO

Cleveland Museum of Natural
  History
Wade Oval
University Circle
Cleveland 44106

U.S.A.—OHIO

Geology Museum
Miami University
Oxford 45056

U.S.A.—OREGON

Department of Geology
University of Oregon
Eugene 97403

U.S.A.—PENNSYLVANIA

Academy of Natural Sciences
19th St. and the Parkway
Philadelphia 19103

U.S.A.—PENNSYLVANIA

Carnegie Museum of Natural
  History
4400 Forbes Ave.
Pittsburgh 15213

U.S.A.—SOUTH CAROLINA

The Charleston Museum
360 Meeting St.
Charleston 29403

U.S.A.—SOUTH DAKOTA

Museum of Geology
South Dakota School of Mines
Rapid City 57701

U.S.A.—TEXAS

Connor Museum
Texas A and I University
Kingsville 78363

U.S.A.—TEXAS

Dallas Museum of Natural History
P.O. Box 26193
Fair Park Station
Dallas 75226

U.S.A.—TEXAS

The Museum
Texas Tech University
Lubbock 79409

U.S.A.—TEXAS

Vertebrate Paleontology
  Laboratory
Balcones Research Center
10100 Burnet Rd.
Austin 78758

U.S.A.—TEXAS

Shuler Museum of Paleontology
Department of Geological Sciences
Southern Methodist University
Dallas 75275

U.S.A.—UTAH

Dinosaur National Monument
Vernal 84078

U.S.A.—UTAH

Earth Sciences Museum
Brigham Young University
Provo 84602

U.S.A.—WASHINGTON

Burke Museum
DB-10
University of Washington
Seattle 98125

U.S.A.—WASHINGTON, D.C.

National Museum of Natural
  History
Smithsonian Institution
Washington 20560

U.S.A.—WISCONSIN

Milwaukee Public Museum
Geology Department
800 West Wells
Milwaukee 53233

U.S.A.—WYOMING

The Geological Museum
Department of Geology
University of Wyoming
Laramie 82071

U.S.A.—WYOMING

Wyoming State Museum
Cheyenne 82002

New Zealand

SOUTH ISLAND

Canterbury Museum
Rolleston Avenue
Christchurch

NORTH ISLAND

Auckland Institute and Museum
Private Bag
Auckland

NORTH ISLAND

National Museum of New Zealand
Wellington

South America

ARGENTINA

Museo Argentino de Ciencias
   Naturales
Av. Ángel Gallardo No. 470
1405 Buenos Aires

ARGENTINA

Museo de La Plata
Paseo del Bosque
1900 La Plata

BRAZIL

Museu Nacional
Quinta da Boa Vista
Dept. Geologia e Paleontologia
S. Cristovão
Rio de Janeiro 20940

URUGUAY

Museo Nacional de Historia
   Natural
CC 399
Montevideo

VENEZUELA

Museo del Hombre
Calle Zamora
Casa del Balcón de Los Arcaya
Coro, Edo. Falcón

LIBRARIES AND THEIR USE

Keep in mind, however, that the best place to *start* learning about fossils is by reading—*before* you begin contacting professional scientists. And the best place to begin reading is at your local library. The librarian can direct you to the paleontology, geology, and biology sections, all of which are related to the study of fossils. Use the books that are in the library not only by reading them but by looking at their bibliographies to give yourself additional titles of interest. There are also a number of geological and biological bibliographies and abstracts that you can browse through to look for books and papers of interest; many of these will be listed a bit later in this chapter. Through the librarian in a larger library you can even use computer search facilities to help find literature on the topics you are interested in.

Just because a book or a magazine is not in your local library needn't discourage you from asking the librarian if he or she can obtain the book from another place on interlibrary loan. This may take a while, but if it is difficult for you to go to a larger library, it is usually possible to do this, even if it means borrowing from overseas.

Libraries are, of course, not the only places where books can be had. Newsstands, drugstores (chemists), and bookshops are only a few of the places worth visiting and looking through the shelves. Magazines, such as *Scientific American* and *National Geographic,* appear monthly on commercial shelves or can be received on subscription, as is true of a number of other, related publications. These not only carry occasional articles related to paleontology but can offer further references and the names of people working on certain groups of animals or plants who can be contacted.

A Library Search: Where to Start

When using a library, it is best to first consult the person in charge so as to understand organization within that library. Once this is done, many appropriate papers and books can be found by checking the subject index under your area of interest, such as *Fossils, Dinosaurs, Trilobites,* and so on, in the library catalogue.

The keywords used in most English-speaking countries are those listed in the *Library of Congress Subject Headings.* So it is helpful to check these first in your local public library to be sure what the proper heading will be. Once an interesting reference has been found, be sure to check the literature cited at the end of that article for further interesting papers to read.

Reference publications and bibliographies held in the library can also be of great help in locating technical (and popular) papers. Two particularly good guidebooks to literature on the earth sciences, especially for older literature, are as follows:

PEARL, R. M., 1951. *Guide to Geologic Literature.* McGraw-Hill, New York.
WOOD, D. N. (ed.), 1973. *Use of Earth Science Literature.* Butterworth, London.

Bibliographies are also a rich source for further reading. They vary in coverage and comprehensiveness, and subject area; so you should choose which is at the right level. Not all are the same, by any means. The following are a few where you can start:

Biographisch-Literarisches Handwörterbuch zur Geschichte der Exacten Wissenschaften, by J. C. Poggendorf, 1953. A multivolume bibliographic-biographic account from early times to 1953. Mainly for university-level students, scholarly and comprehensive. (In German)
Bibliography and Catalogue of Fossil Vertebrata of North America, 1902, by O. P. Hay. Bulletin of the United States Geological Survey, Washington, D.C., 1929–30.

Second Bibliography and Catalogue of the Fossil Vertebrata of North America. Carnegie Institution of Washington.

Bibliography and Index of Geology Exclusive of North America, 1933–1968. Geological Society of America. Several volumes covering the period 1785–1970.

Bibliography of Fossil Vertebrates, 1928–1973, by C. L. Camp et al. Special issues of the Geological Society of America Special Paper and Memoir Series. Taken over by J. W. Gregory et al. in 1978 with annual volumes published by the American Geological Institute and the Society of Vertebrate Paleontology. One single volume by this group covers 1973–77.

Bibliography of North America Geology. United States Geological Survey, Washington, D.C. Covers literature from 1785 to 1970.

Bibliography of Fossil Vertebrates Exclusive of North America, 1509–1927, by A. S. Romer. Geological Society of America, New York. Author and subject listing of world literature on fossil vertebrates.

Catalogue of Scientific Papers, 1800–1900. Royal Society of London, London. Published between 1867 and 1925. Author index to mainly European literature in the nineteenth century.

Dictionary of Scientific Biography, 1974. Scribner's, New York. 16 vols. Sponsored by American Council of Learned Societies.

Geologists and the History of Geology: An International Bibliography from Origins to 1978. W. A. S. Sarjeant, 1978. Arno Press, New York. 5 volumes, dealing with the development of geology, including paleontology, in general and in specific countries.

International Catalogue of Scientific Literature, 1900–1914. Royal Society of London, London. Section K is paleontology. Catalogue is arranged under broad subjects.

Zoological Record, 1865 to the present. Zoological Society of London, London. Contains subject, author, and systematic arrangement of zoological literature, including paleontology.

Besides these bibliographies that cover recent and older literature, there are a number of sources that are excellent for recent literature but don't go too far back in time. Some of these give a brief abstract or summary of articles and often have a subject index, which can be organized much as a card catalogue.

Australian Earth Sciences Information System (AESIS), 1976–to present. Australian Mineral Foundation, Glenside, South Australia.

Bibliography and Index of Geology, 1969–to present. Geological Society of America (1969–78). American Geological Institute (1979–to present).

Bibliography and Index of Micropaleontology, 1972–to present. American Museum of Natural History, New York.

Books in Print, published each year. Bowker Company, New York and London. A listing of books still in print, and thus those that can be purchased.

Bulletin Signalétique-Bibliographie des Sciences de la Terre: Section 227. Cahier H. Paléontologie. Bureau des Recherches Géologiques at Minières et Centre National de la Recherche Scientifique, Paris. (In French)

Current Contents: Physical, Chemical, and Earth Sciences, 1957–to present. Institute of Scientific Information, Philadelphia. An extremely useful weekly magazine, reproducing contents pages of major international journals.

Geotitles Weekly, 1969–to present. Geosystems, London. A listing weekly by author, title, and source of current titles.

Dissertation abstracts. International, 1969–00. University Microfilm Corporation, Ann Arbor, Michigan. Summaries of doctoral theses. Section C is paleontology. Much unpublished information is contained in papers submitted at various universities as a part of a degree program. Often these can be purchased for a small sum either in microfilm or paper copy form.

Mulvihill, J. (ed.), 1982. User Guide to the Bibliography and Index of Geology. American Geological Institute, Washington.

Zentralblatt für Geologie Teil 2: Palaeontologie. Schweizerbartsche Verlagsbuchhandlung, Stuttgart. (In German)

Encyclopaedias dealing with paleontology and related subjects can be useful in addition to those that are much more general. They orient, introduce, and explain a topic, and frequently give a brief bibliography, a place to start learning about a new topic. R. W. Fairbridge and D. Jablonski's The Encyclopaedia of Palaeontology (Dowden, Hutchinson, and Ross, Stroudsburg, Pennsylvania, 1979) is one detailed account on paleontology only. Another, more general book of this sort is the McGraw-Hill Encyclopaedia of the Geological Sciences (McGraw-Hill, New York and Sydney, 1978).

Computerized Information Services

Use of computers to retrieve information developed in the 1970s as an aid for abstracting and indexing journals. For people wanting to use such services, several are available, generally through a larger library. GEOREF is a databank of the American Geological Institute and covers international literature, including that on paleontology, since 1967. GEOARCHIVE is produced by Geosystems, London, covering literature from 1974 to present. AESIS is the data base of the Australian Earth Sciences Information System covering 1976 to the present. Many more exist; a check with the information desk at the library will quickly tell what is available.

Books, Magazines, and Journals

The books and articles that have been written on paleontological subjects are too numerous to even begin to summarize in this book. In the past few decades alone, new publications have appeared in such large numbers, so quickly, that it is impossible for even the professional paleontologists to keep up with them except in their own specialities.

So it is difficult to choose from the massive amount of literature. We have given a number of suggestions, nonetheless. Included with these references are several that themselves contain large lists of other books, magazines, and papers, so they can be used to explore the literature even further.

GEOLOGIC BACKGROUND

BEERBOWER, J. R., 1968. *Search for the Past: An Introduction to Paleontology.* Second Edition. Prentice Hall, Englewood Cliffs, N.J. As the title suggests, an introduction to paleontology, in Beerbower's very readable style.

DOTT, R. H., JR.; and R. L. BATTEN, 1971. *Evolution of the Earth.* McGraw-Hill, New York. An excellent overview of the historic geology of North America, including much information on fossils. A university-level text. Revised editions have been published after 1971, but we like the original best.

EICHER, D. L., 1976. *Geologic Time.* Second Edition. Prentice Hall, Englewood Cliffs, N.J. An introduction to the concept of geologic time and how it is measured.

—— and A. L. McALESTER, 1980. *History of the Earth.* Prentice Hall, Englewood Cliffs, N.J. A good, compact introduction to geology.

——; A. L. McALESTER, and M. ROTTMAN, 1984. *History of the Earth's Crust.* Prentice Hall, Englewood Cliffs, N.J. A brief, informative look at those rocks of the earth that hold fossils.

FENTON, C. L.; and M. A. FENTON, 1940. *The Rock Book.* Doubleday, New York. About the various types of rocks found on earth, with many illustrations, including nearly one hundred pages of those rocks that most commonly hold fossils: sedimentary rocks.

HAY, E. A.; and A. L. McALESTER, 1984. *Physical Geology: Principles and Perspectives.* Prentice Hall, Englewood Cliffs, N.J. An up-to-date, succinct introduction to physical geology.

HOLMES, A., 1965. *Principles of Physical Geology.* Second Edition. Nelson, London. Ronald Press, New York. An authoritative and all-time-great general geology text. Slightly out of date with regard to plate tectonics, but an outstanding and enduring, well-written book.

LAPORTE, L. F., 1968. *Ancient Environments.* Prentice-Hall, Englewood Cliffs, N.J. An introductory book on the kinds of rocks deposited in various kinds of environments, and how these rocks can be interpreted.

STOKES, W. L., 1982. *Essentials of Earth History: An Introduction to Historical Geology.* Fourth Edition. Prentice Hall, Englewood Cliffs, N.J. A classic introductory text to the history of the earth.

WYLLIE, P. J., 1976. *The Way the Earth Works: An Introduction to the New Global Geology and Its Revolutionary Development.* John Wiley & Sons, New York. A university-level book.

HISTORY OF PALEONTOLOGY

ANDREWS, H. N., 1980. *The Fossil Hunters: In Search of Ancient Plants.* Cornell University Press, Ithaca, N.Y. A history of paleobotanists and paleobotany mainly in the Northern Hemisphere.

BERRY, W. B. N., 1968. *Growth of a Prehistoric Time Scale.* W. H. Freeman, San Francisco. A detailed summary of how the geologic time scale was developed.

BRONOWSKI, J., 1978. *The Ascent of Man.* British Broadcasting Corporation, London. A well-illustrated adult-level book on the history of western science. Based on a BBC television series by the same name.

COLBERT, E. H., 1980. *A Fossil Hunter's Notebook: My Life with Dinosaurs and Other Friends.* E. P. Dutton, New York. An autobiographical account of Colbert's life as a practicing vertebrate paleontologist.

———, 1968. *Men and Dinosaurs: The Search in Field and Laboratory.* E. P. Dutton, New York. The great dinosaur hunters and their discovery of the world of prehistoric reptiles.

DESMOND, A. J., 1977. *The Hot-Blooded Dinosaurs.* Futura Publications Ltd., London. A popular account of the debate, both historical and current, of whether dinosaurs were "warm-blooded" or "cold-blooded."

ELDREDGE, N., 1982. *The Monkey Business: A Scientist Looks at Creationism.* Washington Square Press, New York. A look at a topic of heated debate—that between evolutionists and creationists—including discussion of how fossils are interpreted by each debater.

FENTON, C. L., and M. A., FENTON, 1952. *Giants of Geology.* Doubleday, New York. A survey of the development of geology and related sciences through biographies of their leaders.

HOWARD, R. W., 1975. *The Dawnseekers: The First History of American Paleontology.* Harcourt Brace Jovanovich, New York. A popular account of the history of vertebrate paleontology in North America.

HUXLEY, T. H., 1967. *On a Piece of Chalk.* Charles Scribner's Sons, New York. 90 pp. This book presents a lecture given by the great evolutionist T. H. Huxley to the working men of Norwich. It beautifully explains what can be told about earth history based on clues given by a piece of chalk.

LANHAM, V., 1973. *The Bone Hunters.* Columbia University Press, New York. A look at those vertebrate paleontologists who pioneered their science in North America, such men as O. C. Marsh, E. D. Cope, and J. B. Hatcher.

LEY, W., 1968. *Dawn of Zoology.* Prentice Hall, Englewood Cliffs, N.J. Though a history of zoology, this very readable text contains a great deal of historical information on paleontology, especially Chapter 8, titled "Man the Digger."

MILLER, H. *The Old Red Sandstone* (various editions and dates). Hugh Miller's most famous book, it deals primarily with the Old Red Sandstone and its fossil fish. It shows how much an amateur can accomplish in paleontology.

MOORE, R., 1953. *Man, Time, and Fossils.* A. A. Knopf, New York. A look at the development of evolutionary theory traced through the lives and work of outstanding paleontologists.

RUDWICK, M. J. S., 1972. *The Meaning of Fossils: Episodes in the History of Palaeontology.* Macdonald, London; and American Elsevier, New York. An excellent account of paleontology from its beginnings to modern times, discussing people and their ideas. Contains valuable references and a detailed historic overview.

SMITH, G. G. R., 1972. *Science and Society in the Sixteenth and Seventeenth Centuries.* Science History Publications, New York. Contains an interesting account of developments in Western science during the late Middle Ages and the Renaissance, and its effect on society, showing origins of the modern scientific method.

WILSON, D. B. (ed.), 1983. *Did the Devil Make Darwin Do It?* Iowa State University Press, Ames, Iowa. An excellent account of the evolution-creationist debate.

TEXTBOOKS, REFERENCE WORKS, AND TECHNICAL ARTICLES ON PALEONTOLOGY

ANDREWS, N. H., JR., 1961. *Studies in Paleobotany.* John Wiley & Sons, New York. A textbook on fossil plants. Though somewhat out-of-date, it contains abundant, good illustrations and much still useful information.

BEERBOWER, J. R., 1968. *Search for the Past: An Introduction to Paleontology.* Second Edition. Prentice Hall, Englewood Cliffs, N.J. As the title suggests, an introduction to paleontology, in Beerbower's very readable style.

BEHRENSMEYER, A. K.; and A. P. HILL, 1980. *Fossils in the Making.* The University of Chicago Press, Chicago. An excellent series of papers on taphonomy: what happens to fossils between death and discovery.

BELL, P.; and C. WOODCOCK, 1968. *The Diversity of Green Plants.* Edward Arnold, London. A university-level text on both present-day and fossil plants.

BOUREAU E. (ed.), 1964. *Traité de Paléobotanique.* Masson, Paris. A technical, detailed account of fossil plants. (In French).

BRASIER, M. D., 1981. Microfossils. George Allen & Unwin, Boston, London, Sydney. A readable, university-level text on fossil microorganisms including both plants and animals. Well illustrated and relatively low-cost.

BUCHSBAUM, R., 1948. *Animals Without Backbones.* University of Chicago Press, Chicago. An excellent account of the living invertebrates.

CLARKSON, E. N. K., 1979. *Invertebrate Paleontology and Evolution.* George Allen & Unwin, Boston, London, Sydney. An easily read, university-level text on fossil invertebrates, excluding microorganisms. A companion volume to Brasier, 1981.

COHEE, G. V.; M. F. GLAESSNER, and H. D. HEDBERG (eds.), 1978. *Contributions to the Geologic Time Scale.* American Association of Petroleum Geologists, Tulsa, Okla. An authoritative collection of papers concerning the basis of the geologic time scale. Good source of further references.

COLBERT, E. H., 1969. *Evolution of the Vertebrates.* John Wiley & Sons, New York. A readable beginning book on fossil backboned animals.

DAVIES, A. M.; F. E. Eames; and R. J. G. Savage. *Tertiary Faunas: A Textbook for Oilfield Paleontologists and Students of Geology.* George Allen & Unwin, London. Vol. 1 (1971), Vol. 2 (1975). A detailed account of the fossil record of animals that lived during the past 65 million years.

FAEGRI, K.; and J. IVERSEN, 1975. *Textbook of Pollen Analysis.* Hafner Press, New York. A text on how to process and analyze pollen.

HAQ, B. U.; and A. BOERSMA, 1978. *Introduction to Marine Micropaleontology.* Elsevier, New York. A detailed, well-written survey of fossil marine microorganisms useful in telling time and interpreting past environments. Contains good bibliographies for further reading.

HALSTEAD, L. B., 1969. *The Pattern of Vertebrate Evolution.* Oliver and Boyd, Edinburgh. An account of the history of vertebrate animals and their evolutionary patterns.

HILDEBRAND, M., 1974. *Analysis of Vertebrate Structure.* John Wiley & Sons, New York. Besides a good overview of vertebrate anatomy, this book provides several chapters on form and function.

LEVI-SETTI, R., 1975. *Trilobites: A Photographic Atlas.* University of Chicago Press, Chicago. As the name implies, contains many illustrations of trilobites.

LURIA, S. E.; S. J. GOULD, and S. SINGER, 1981. *A View of Life*. Benjamin/Cummings Publishing Company, Menlo Park, California. A modern college-level text on biology, with paleontological sections.

MCALESTER, A. L., 1977. *The History of Life*. Prentice Hall, Englewood Cliffs, N.J. An excellent introduction to paleontology and the fossil history of plants and animals.

MOORE, R. C. (ed.) *Treatise on Invertebrate Paleontology*. Geological Society of America. Boulder, Colo. Moore began as editor, and currently C. Teichert and others have taken over his job. A detailed account of most invertebrate groups, illustrating them and discussing their classification. Several volumes exist, each on a different major group of invertebrates.

MOORE, R. C.; C. G. LALICKER, and A. G. FISHER, 1952. *Invertebrate Fossils*. McGraw-Hill, New York. Though somewhat out-of-date, this detailed account of classification and biology of invertebrates is still excellent. It is primarily limited to North American forms and is richly illustrated.

MOSSMAN, D. J.; and W. A. S. SARJEANT, 1983. "The Footprints of Extinct Animals," *Scientific American* 248 (1):64–74. A good introduction to ichnology, the study of fossil footprints, with a bibliography for further reading.

PETERSEN, M. S.; J. K. RIGBY, and L. F. HINTZE, 1973. *Historical Geology of North America*. W. C. Brown, Dubuque, Iowa. A paperback of moderate length on North American fossils and geologic history.

PIVETEAU, J. (ed.), 1952–69. *Traité de Paléontologie*. Masson, Paris. Multivolume, detailed account on fossil animals, fossilization, and history of paleontology. (In French).

RANSOM, J. E., 1964. *Fossils in America: Their Nature, Origin, Identification and Classification, and a Range Guide to Collecting Sites*. Harper & Row, New York. Contents, as title suggests, contains listing of some libraries and museums. Though several collecting spots are noted in this book, such collecting is best done together with a trained paleontologist as an adviser.

RAUP, D. M.; and S. M. STANLEY, 1978. *Principles of Paleontology*. Second Edition. W. H. Freeman, San Francisco. Excellent higher-level text on underlying theory and techniques of paleontology.

RENSCH, B., 1972. *Homo Sapiens: From Man to Demigod*. Columbia University Press, New York. A look into the mental and physical evolution of man, from his earliest ancestors to the present, including his cultural development.

ROMER, A. S., 1959. *Osteology of the Reptiles*. University of Chicago Press, Chicago. A detailed account, well illustrated, of the bones of reptiles living and extinct.
——, 1966. *Vertebrate Paleontology*. University of Chicago Press, Chicago. A comprehensive textbook; technical but with abundant illustrations. The book is currently being revised by R. Carroll.

SAVAGE, D. E.; and D. E. RUSSELL, 1983. *Mammalian Paleofaunas of the World*. Addison-Wesley, Reading, England. The only comprehensive compilation of fossil mammal faunas of the world.

SHRIMER, H. W.; and R. R. SHROCK, 1944 (and later reprintings). *Index Fossils of North America*. John Wiley & Sons, New York. Describes and illustrates a vast number of typical invertebrate fossils. A very good single volume for identification, though some of the names may be out of date.

SILVER, L. T.; and P. H. SCHULTZ (eds.), 1982. *Geological Implications of Impacts of*

Large Asteroids and Comets on the Earth. Geological Society of America, Special Paper 190, Boulder, Colo. An authoritative collection of papers looking at what effect the impact of extraterrestrial bodies might have had on extinctions of animals and plants through time.

SPOCZYNSKA, J. O. I., 1976. *An Age of Fishes: The Development of the Most Successful Vertebrate.* David & Charles, London. Presents an introduction to a variety of fossil fishes and provides many reconstructions.

STEBBINS, G. L., 1982. *Darwin to DNA, Molecules to Humanity.* W. H. Freeman, San Francisco. A lucid look at modern evolutionary theory.

STRAHL, B., 1974. *Vertebrate History: Problems in Evolution.* McGraw-Hill, New York. A readable text on the history of backboned animals.

SWINTON, W. E., 1973. *Fossil Amphibians and Reptiles.* British Museum of Natural History, London. A detailed account of the record of these two groups, with numerous illustrations of both bones and "fleshed" restorations.

TARLING, D. H.; and S. K. RUNCORN (eds.), 1973. *Implications of Continental Drift to the Earth Sciences.* Academic Press, New York, 2 vols. A technical but very interesting collection of papers, many paleontological, on how the concept of moving continents has affected previous ideas.

TASCH, P., 1973. *Paleobiology of the Invertebrates.* John Wiley & Sons, New York. A lengthy, detailed account of invertebrate fossils.

TSCHUDY, R. H.; and R. A. SCOTT, 1969. *Aspects of Palynology.* John Wiley & Sons, New York. An authoritative text on spore and pollen analysis and the geologic history of these plant remains.

WHITMORE, T. C. (ed.), 1981. *Wallace's Line and Plate Tectonics.* Clarendon Press, Oxford, England. A recent look at how Wallace's Line, which divides the Australasian and Oriental realms, has been explained in light of moving continents.

WHITE, M. E., 1986. *The Greening of Gondwana.* Reed Books, Frenchs Forest (NSW). An up-to-date and wonderfully illustrated account of development of plants on the southern continents, most illustrations in color.

COLLECTION, PREPARATION, AND CURATION TECHNIQUES

BASSETT, M. G., 1979. "Curation of Palaeontological Collections." Special Paper, *Palaeontology* 22:1–280.

COMPTON, R. R., 1962. *Manual of Field Geology.* John Wiley & Sons, New York. A thorough, detailed guide to techniques used in field geology; for the practicing student or geologist.

HAMILTON, R., 1978. *Fossils and Fossil Collecting.* Hamlyn, New York. A pocket-sized publication covering major fossil groups, general geology, and some collecting, preparation, and curation techniques used in paleontology.

KIELAN-JAWOROWSKA, Z., 1969. *Hunting for Dinosaurs.* MIT Press, Cambridge, Mass. Concerns what it is like to hunt for dinosaurs; by the leader of the Polish-Mongolian expedition to the Gobi Desert.

KUMMEL, B.; and D. RAUP, 1965. *Handbook of Paleontological Techniques.* W. H. Freeman, San Francisco and New York. A detailed account of most of the techniques used in field and laboratory by paleontologists.

MACDONALD, J. R., 1983. *The Fossil Collector's Handbook: A Paleontology Field Guide.* A Spectrum Book. Prentice-Hall, Englewood Cliffs, N.J. A good guide about how to organize everything for a fossil-collecting trip, how to collect and prepare fossils, as well as a guide to geologic principles, major fossil groups, and places to collect.

MOSELEY, F., 1981. *Methods of Field Geology.* W. H. Freeman, Oxford and San Francisco.

RIXON, A. E., 1976. *Fossil Animal Remains: Their Preparation and Conservation.* Athlone Press, University of London, London. An excellent summary of techniques and materials used in preservation and preparation of fossils.

Also such journals as *Curator,* published by the American Museum of Natural History (New York), and the section titled "Preparators Corner" in the *News Bulletin of the Society of Vertebrate Paleontology* can offer helpful hints.

GUIDES FOR COLLECTING AND MUSEUM VISITORS

Since the original edition of this book, such a variety of museum and collection guides have been published, it is beyond us to begin listing them. Most museums have guides to their exhibits, which can be purchased in the museum when you visit it. State and federal geological surveys as well as private publishers produce guidebooks, geologic maps, and informative brochures on many areas. Such guides can often be obtained by writing to the publications department of the survey or museum, and sometimes from local state and national parks, where literature is also available. Examples of such publications are P. J. Fleisher's (1975) *Geology of Selected National Parks and Monuments* (Kendall/Hunt, Dubuque, Iowa) and R. C. Rowe's (1974) *Geology of Our Western National Parks and Monuments* (Binfords & Mort, Portland, Ore.). Both contain listings of numerous more specific guides.

In addition to guidebooks, the state and federal geological surveys also produce detailed geological maps and aerial photographs, which are useful in determining where rocks of certain ages are exposed and thus where various types of fossils are likely to be found (or not found). The American Association of Petroleum Geologists also has prepared a series of geologic maps of the United States with major highways and fossil localities clearly indicated.

CHILDREN'S BOOKS

Children's literature is also vast on prehistoric animals. We have tried to list some of the better books available.

ANDREWS, R. C., 1953. *All About Dinosaurs.* Random House, New York. Much, but by no means all, about these reptiles.

BRISTOW, P., 1980. *All Colour World of Prehistoric Animals.* Octopus Books, London. A reference book for late primary school and high school, covering animal fossils of the past 600 million years.

CHARIG, A. J.; and C. M. B. HORSFIELD, 1975. *Before the Ark.* British Broadcasting Corporation, London. Aimed at high school and above, a serious and authoritative book on a series of problems that are still lively topics of debate in vertebrate paleontology.

COHEN, D., 1977. *What Really Happened to the Dinosaurs?* E. P. Dutton, New York. A book, for later primary school children, that examines the theories for dinosaur extinction.

COLE, J., 1974. *Dinosaur Story.* William Morrow, New York. Very simple book on dinosaurs for young children, with pencil illustrations.

CUISIN, M., 1980. *Nature's Hidden World—Prehistoric Life.* Ward Lock, London. Accurate, advanced text covering fossils known throughout geologic time; well illustrated.

DICKINSON, A., 1966. *Prehistoric Animals.* Franklin Watts, London. An advanced primary school book discussing in detail the history of the invertebrates and vertebrates.

DIMENT, J., 1976. *Fact Finders—Animals of Long Ago.* Macmillan Education, London. Well-written text on a number of different fossils, including good illustrations and a glossary. Mid-primary school level.

FENTON, C. L., 1966. *Tales Told by Fossils.* Doubleday, Garden City, N.Y.

―――― and M. A. FENTON, 1959. *Prehistoric Zoo.* Doubleday, Garden City, N.Y.

―――― and M. A. FENTON, 1962. *In Prehistoric Seas.* Doubleday, Garden City, N.Y. Richly illustrated accounts of many prehistoric vertebrates; written for the primary school level.

GLUT, D. F., 1972. *Dinosaur Dictionary.* Citadel Press, Secaucus, N.J. Covers all known genera of dinosaurs, illustrates them, and gives useful bibliography. Can be used as a reference book for adults involved with children on this subject.

HAMILTON, W. R., 1975. *The Life of Prehistoric Animals.* Macdonald Education, London. An advanced, high school level introduction to the life habits of many kinds of fossils. A good reference for parents and teachers.

KAUFMANN, J., 1977. *Little Dinosaurs and Early Birds.* Thomas Y. Crowell, New York. Excellent account of where birds originated and their early evolution. Well illustrated and written for mid-primary school level.

KNIGHT, C. R., 1935. *Before the Dawn of History.* McGraw-Hill, New York. Many large illustrations, mainly paintings by C. R. Knight in the Chicago Field Museum of Natural History. Knight is one of the better-known painters of fossil vertebrates.

KNIGHT, D. C., 1977. *Dinosaur Days.* McGraw-Hill, London. Accurate and concise book about dinosaurs for primary school children.

LAMBERT, D., 1983. *Collins Guide to Dinosaurs.* Collins, Sydney. An excellent, popular book using many professional paleontologists as consultants. Covers much about the biology of dinosaurs as well as discussing most dinosaurs known. Good for children and adults alike.

―――― , 1978. *Dinosaurs.* Rigby, Adelaide, South Australia. An excellent reference for children twelve years or older. Accurate and readable text with excellent color illustrations and photographs.

McGOWEN, T., 1974. *Dinosaurs and Other Prehistoric Animals.* Rand McNally, New York. A well-illustrated, accurate look at a number of dinosaurs and their associated plants and animals. Pronunciation guide provided.

PRINGLE, L., 1978. *Dinosaurs and People—Fossils, Facts, and Fantasies.* Harcourt Brace Jovanovich, New York. Suitable for high school level. An excellent account of the history of dinosaur collection and people's fascination with them. Also discussed are why dinosaurs became extinct and what they were like as living animals.

RICH, P. V., 1987. *Australian Dinosaurs and Their Mesozoic World.* A Golden Project Book, Golden Press, Drummoyne, N.S.W. Australia. An activity book about dinosaurs, collecting them, and interpreting their environments.

RICH, P. V.; and B. SCOTT, 1987. *Kadimakara* (An Australian Bunyip's Colouring Book), Monash University, Clayton. A young child's coloring book of Australia's prehistoric vertebrates.

SALSAM, M. E., 1978. *Tyrannosaurus rex.* Harper & Row, London. An excellent mid-primary school book on how this giant dinosaur was collected and reconstructed. Includes history with old photos.

——, 1977. *Sea Monsters of Long Ago.* Four Winds Press, New York. Discusses marine reptiles, their life, and why they became extinct. Aimed at mid- to late-primary ages.

—— and J. HUNT, 1982. *A First Look at Dinosaurs.* Scholastic Inc., New York, Toronto, London, Auckland, Sydney, Tokyo. An early-primary school, short introduction to major groups of dinosaurs.

SEYMOUR, D., 1975. *Prehistoric Animals.* A. & C. Black, London. Informative book about dinosaurs for mid-primary school level. List of various museums worth visiting is included.

SHAPP, M.; and C. SHAPP, 1970. *Animals of Long Ago.* Franklin Watts, New York. Simple introduction for primary school children to fossils and the work of paleontologists.

SHEEHAN, A., 1978. Dinosaur Library. Franklin Watts, London. This series has three books: *Triceratops, Brontosaurus,* and *Tryannosaurus.* Books for primary school children that trace a period of time in a particular dinosaur's life. Details are accurate, and a "things to do" section is included for further work.

STRAHLER, A. N., 1967. *The Story of Our Earth.* Parent's Magazine Press, New York. A primary school child's introduction to general geology.

WELLFARE, G., 1978. *Dinosaurs and Prehistoric Animals.* Ladybird Books, Leicestershire, England. Crammed with information about many prehistoric animals, aimed at ten- to twelve-year-olds.

ZIM, H. S., 1963. *Dinosaurs.* World's Work, London. Accurate book that covers how fossils are used to interpret the dinosaurs. Pronunciation guide included; suitable for ten-year-olds and up.

POPULAR WORKS ON PALEONTOLOGY

ATTENBOROUGH, D., 1979. *Life on Earth.* Collins, London. A beautifully illustrated book patterned after the British Broadcasting Corporation's series on the evolution of life over the past three billion years plus.

——, 1980. *Life on Earth: A Natural History.* The augmented and enlarged edition. Reader's Digest Services, Surrey Hills, England.

AUGUSTA, J.; and Z. BURIAN. Together published several books with beautiful color restorations of many prehistoric organisms. Titles include: 1956, *Prehistoric An-*

imals; 1961, *Prehistoric Reptiles and Birds;* 1964, *Prehistoric Sea Monsters.* Paul Hamlyn, London.

BRADBURY, R., 1983. *Dinosaur Tales.* Bantam, New York. The result of a well-known science fiction author writing on an already fascinating group of animals, the dinosaurs. An imaginary and imaginative collection of short stories.

CAMPBELL, B. G., 1974. *Human Evolution: An Introduction to Man's Adaptations.* Aldine Publishing Company, Chicago.

DARLINGTON, P. J., 1980. *Evolution for Naturalists: The Simple Principles and Complex Realities.* John Wiley & Sons, New York. A summary of evolutionary principles written for beginning university-level students. For the general reader it is also a palatable introduction to modern evolutionary thinking.

DIXON, D., 1981. *After Man: A Zoology of the Future.* Granada, London. An imaginatively illustrated book and accompanying text on the animals that might evolve if man were to go extinct. A look into the future.

FEDUCCIA, A., 1980. *The Age of Birds.* Harvard University Press, Cambridge, Mass. An enjoyable, informative book on the history of birds over the past 140 million years; richly illustrated.

SIMPSON, G. G., 1951. *Horses: The Story of the Horse Family in the Modern World and Through Sixty Million Years of History.* Oxford University Press, New York. A comprehensive but readable account of the evolution of horses as of 1951. Well illustrated.

TWEEDIE, M., 1977. *The World of Dinosaurs.* Weidenfeld & Nicholson, London. A richly illustrated, in both color and black and white, popular source book on all aspects of dinosaurs, including the history of collection and how they are prepared and preserved.

POPULAR AND INFORMATIVE (OR SEMITECHNICAL) MAGAZINES

Articles on fossils occasionally appear in a variety of nontechnical magazines; these can often be very good introductions to certain fossil groups. Only a few examples are given, as there are hundreds that appear on the market.

American Scientist (Sigma Xi, The Scientific Research Society of North America, New Haven, Conn.)

Australian Natural History (Australian Museum, Sydney)

Discovery (Yale University, Peabody Museum, New Haven, Conn.)

Geology (Geological Society of America, Boulder, Colo.)

Hemisphere. An Asian-Australian magazine. (Australian Government Publishing Service, Woden, A.C.T., Australia)

National Geographic (National Geographic Society, Washington, D.C.)

Natural History (American Museum of Natural History, New York)

Pacific Discovery (California Academy of Sciences, Golden Gate Park, San Francisco)

Scientific American (Scientific American Inc., New York)

Smithsonian (Smithsonian Institution, Washington, D.C.)

SCHOLARLY (OR TECHNICAL) JOURNALS

Scholarly or technical books and articles are published by geological surveys, museums, universities, scientific societies, and research institutions. Results of scientific meetings that often are the most up-to-date printed information on a topic are published by these same institutions as well as a number of commercial publishers such as Elsevier and Academic Press.

University and museum libraries generally have big collections of these publications, and so do some public libraries. Small libraries may own a few specialist journals that deal with subjects of general interest or with fossils of the area in which the library is situated. Often, understanding of such literature depends on a prior knowledge of the field and a familiarity with the scientific words used by researchers.

Major technical journals that are related to paleontology are those such as: *Alcheringa* (Australia), *Ameghiniana* (Argentina), *Evolution* (U.S.A.), *Journal of Paleontology* (U.S.A.), *Journal of Vertebrate Paleontology* (U.S.A.), Lethaia (Norway), Palaeontographica (West Germany), Paleontologicheskii Zhurnal (U.S.S.R.) Palaeontology (U.K.), Paleobiology (U.S.A.), *Vertebrata Palasiatica* (China). *Science* (U.S.A.) and *Nature* (U.K.) are also important journals that carry some articles on fossils, along with scientific results of current international research. A detailed list of publications often carrying paleontological information can be found at the beginning of the Bibliography of Fossil Vertebrates, cited earlier in this chapter.

Clubs and Societies

Yet another way to make contact with people interested in fossils is to join a club or society that has interests in this area. There are many amateur rock clubs and others whose members are a mixture of amateurs and professionals (for example, The Society of Vertebrate Paleontology, c/o Florida State Museum, University of Florida, Gainesville, Fla. 32611), while others are primarily made up of professionals (for example, The Society of Economic Paleontologists and Mineralogists). Many of these groups put out a bulletin or journal at regular intervals that will give information on activities in the area of interest as well as articles and bibliographies that are related to fossils. Again, a trip to the library, especially a university or museum library or a larger municipal or state library, and a quick look through the periodical section, will provide a number of society names and addresses inside the journals or other publications such societies produce.

APPENDIX 1

References for Further Reading

CHAPTER 1   Tales Told by the Dead

AGER, D. V., 1963. *Principles of Paleoecology.* McGraw-Hill, New York, San Francisco, Toronto, London.

BEHRENSMEYER, A. K.; and A. P. HILL, 1980. *Fossils in the Making.* The University of Chicago Press, Chicago and London.

CHAPPELL, W. M.; J. W. DURHAM; and D. E. SAVAGE, 1948. "Mold of a rhinoceros in basalt, Lower Grand Coulee, Washington, *Bulletin of the Geological Society of America* 62:907–18.

RAUP, D. M.; and S. M. STANLEY, 1978. "Paleoecology." In: *Principles of Paleontology.* W. H. Freeman, San Francisco.

Voorhies, M., 1969. "Taphonomy and population dynamics of an Early Pliocene vertebrate fauna," Knox County, Neb. *Contributions to Geology,* Special Paper No. 1, University of Wyoming Press, Laramie, Wyo.

CHAPTER 2   Rocks, Fossils, and Ages

BERRY, W. B. N., 1968. *Growth of a Prehistoric Time Scale.* W. H. Freeman, San Francisco.

EICHER, D. L., 1976. *Geologic time.* 2nd Ed. Prentice-Hall, Englewood Cliffs, N. J.

―――― and A. L. McALESTER, 1980. "Earth chronology." *In: History of the Earth.* Prentice-Hall, Englewood Cliffs, N. J.

FAUL, H., 1966. *Ages of rocks, planets, and stars.* McGraw-Hill, New York.

HARLAND, W. B.; and others, 1982. *A Geologic Time Scale.* Cambridge University Press, Cambridge, England.

McALESTER, A. L., 1977. *The history of life.* Prentice-Hall, Englewood Cliffs, N. J.

ODIN, G. S., 1982. "The Phanerozoic time scale revisited," *Episodes* 3:3–9.

CHAPTER 3   Continents Have Moved and Climates Have Changed

DIETZ, R. S.; and J. C. HOLDEN, 1970. "The Break-up of Pangaea," *Scientific American* 223(4):30–41.

FRAKES, L. A., 1979. *Climates Through Geologic Time.* Elsevier, Amsterdam.

GRAY, J.; and A. J. BOUCOT, 1979. *Historical Biogeography, Plate Tectonics and the Changing Environment.* Oregon State University Press, Eugene, Ore.

MIDDLEMISS, F. A.; P. F. RAWSON; and G. NEWALL, 1971. *Faunal Provinces in Space and Time.* Seel House Press, Liverpool.

SMITH, A. G.; A. M. HURLEY; and J. C. BRIDEN, 1981. Phanerozoic Paleocontinental World Maps. Cambridge University Press, Cambridge, England.

TARLING, D. H.; and M. P. TARLING, 1975. *Continental Drift.* Pelican, Aylesbury, England.

CHAPTER 4 Groups, Names, and Relationships

BROWN, R. W., 1956. *Composition of Scientific Words.* Reese Press, Baltimore, Md.

GOULD, S. J., 1977. *Ever Since Darwin.* W. W. Norton, New York, London.

———— 1980. *The Panda's Thumb.* W. W. Norton, New York, London.

———— and N. ELDREDGE, 1977. "Punctuated equilibria: the tempo, and mode of evolution reconsidered," *Paleobiology* 3(2):115–51.

RIDLEY, M., 1983. "Can classification do without evolution?" *New Scientist* 647–51.

WILEY, E. O. *Phylogenetics. The Theory and Practice of Phylogenetic Systematics.* John Wiley, New York, Brisbane, Chichester, Toronto, Singapore.

CHAPTER 5 Earth's Oldest Remains

CLOUD, P.; and M. F. GLAESSNER, 1982. "The Ediacaran Period and System: Metazoa inherit the earth," *Science* 217 (4562):783–92.

COOK, P. J.; and J. H. SHERGOLD, 1984. "Phosphorous, phosphorites and skeletal evolution at the Precambian-Cambian boundary, *Nature* 308:231–36.

GLAESSNER, M. F., 1961. "Pre-Cambrian animals," *Scientific American* 204(3):72–78.

————1984. *The Dawn of animal life.* Cambridge University Press, Cambridge, England.

GOULD, S. J., 1984. The Ediacaran experiment," *Natural History* 84(2):15–23.

PLAYFORD, P. E., 1980. "Australia's stromatolite stronghold," *Natural History* 89(10):58–61.

WALTER, M. R., 1977. "Interpreting stromatolites," *American Scientist* 65(5):563–71.

WETHERILL, G. W., 1981. "The formation of the earth from planetesimals," *Scientific American* 244(6):131–40.

————1982. "Dating very old objects," *Natural History,* Vol. 91, no. 9, pp. 14–20.

WOESE, C. R., 1981. "Archaebacteria," *Scientific American* 244(6):94–106.

CHAPTER 6 A Variety of Protists

BRASIER, M. D., 1981. *Microfossils.* George Allen & Unwin, Boston and Sydney.

FUNNELL, B. M.; and W. R. RIEDEL (eds.), 1971. *The Micropalaeontology of Oceans.* Cambridge University Press, Cambridge, England.

HAQ, B. V.; and A. BOERSMA (eds.), 1978. *Introduction to Marine Micropaleontology.* Elsevier, Amsterdam.

LIPPS, J. H., 1981. "What, if anything, is micropaleontology?" *Paleobiology* 7(2):167–99.

MOORE, R. C. (ed.), 1954. *Treatise on invertebrate paleontology. Protista* 2. Part D.

Radiolaria, Tintinnina. Geological Society of America, University of Kansas Press, Lawrence, Kan.

————, 1964. *Treatise on invertebrate paleontology. Protista* 2. Part C. Vol. 1–2. *Foraminiferida, etc.* Geological Society of America, University of Kansas Press, Lawrence, Kan.

MURRAY, J. W., 1973. *Distribution and Ecology of Living Benthic Foraminiferids.* Heinemann, London.

CHAPTER 7 Sponges, True and Problematical

GUO, S. Z., 1983. "The receptaculitid *Soanites* from the Early Ordovician of China," *Memoirs of the Association of Australian Palaeontologists* 1:75–84.

HARTMAN, W. D.; J. W. WENDT; and F. WIEDENMAYER, 1980. "Living and fossil sponges" (notes for a short course): Sedimenta VIII. Rosenstiel School of Marine and Atmospheric Science, University of Miami, Miami, Fla.

MOORE, R.C. (ed.), 1955. *Treatise on invertebrate paleontology.* Part E. *Archaeocyatha and Porifera.* Geological Society of America, University of Kansas Press, Lawrence, Kan.

————, 1972. *Treatise on invertebrate paleontology.* Part E. *Archaeocyatha* (rev.). Vol. 1. Geological Society of America, University of Kansas Press, Lawrence, Kan.

MORRIS, S. C. (ed.), 1982. *Atlas of the Burgess Shale.* Palaeontological Association, London.

————; and H. B. WHITTINGTON, 1979. "The animals of the Burgess Shale," *Scientific American* 241(1):110–20.

NITECKI, M. H.; and F. DEBRENNE, 1979. "The nature of radiocyathids and their relationship to receptaculitids and archaeocyathids," *Geobios* 12:5–27.

RIGBY, J. K.; and C. W. STEAM, 1983. "Sponges and spongimorphs" (notes for a short course). University of Tennessee, Department of Geology.

CHAPTER 8 Simple Coelenterates: The Cnidarians

GOULD, S. J., 1984. "The Ediacaran experiment," *Natural History,* 84(2):15–23.

MOORE, R. C. (ed.), 1956. *Treatise on invertebrate paleontology.* Part F. *Coelenterata.* The Geological Society of America, University of Kansas Press, Lawrence, Kan.

————, 1981. *Treatise on invertebrate paleontology.* Part F. Supplement. *Coelenterata (Anthozoa: Rugosa and Tabulata).* Geological Society of America, University of Kansas Press, Lawrence, Kan.

NEWELL, N. D., 1963. "Crises in the history of life," *Scientific American* 208:76–92.

————, 1971. "An outline history of tropical organic reefs," *American Museum Novitates* 2465:37.

OLIVER, W. A., 1980. "The relationship of the scleractinian corals to the rugose corals," *Paleobiology* 6(2):146–60.

SCRUTTON, C. T., 1979. "Early fossil cnidarians." *In:* M. R. House (ed.), *The Origin of Major Invertebrate Groups.* Academic Press, London, New York, pp. 161–207.

TYNAN, M. C., 1983. "Coral-like microfossils from the Lower Cambrian of California," *Journal of Paleontology* 57(6):1188–1211.

CHAPTER 9 "Moss Animals," or Bryozoans

BROOD, K., 1978. "Bryozoa." *In:* B. U. Haq and A. Boersma. *Introduction to Marine Micropaleontology.* Elsevier, New York and Oxford, pp. 189–201.

FARMER, J. D., 1977. "An adaptive model for the evolution of the ectoproct Life Cycle." *In:* R. L. Zimmer and R. M. Woollacott (eds.). *Biology of the Bryozoans.* Academic Press, New York, pp. 487–517.

McLEOD, J. D., 1978. "The oldest bryozoans: New evidence from the Early Ordovician," *Science* 200:771–73.

MOORE, R. C. (ed.). 1953. *Treatise on invertebrate paleontology.* Part G. *Bryozoa.* Geological Society of America, University of Kansas Press, Lawrence, Kan.

ROBISON, R. A. (ed.). 1983. *Treatise on invertebrate paleontology.* Part G. *Revised-Bryozoa.* "Introduction, Order Cystoporata, Order Cryptostomata." Geological Society of America, University of Kansas Press, Lawrence, Kan.

TAYLOR, P. D.' and G. B. CURRY, 1985. "The earliest known fenestrate bryozoan, with a short review of lower Ordovician Bryozoa," *Palaeontology* 28(1):147–58.

VALENTINE, J. W.; and E. M. MOORES, 1970. "Plate-tectonic regulation of faunal diversity and sea-level: A Model," *Nature* 228:657–59.

CHAPTER 10 The Sturdy Brachiopods

CLARKSON, E. N. K., 1979. "Brachiopods." *In: Invertebrate Paleontology and Evolution.* George Allen & Unwin, Sydney. pp. 103–36.

GRANT, R. E., 1966. "A Permian productoid brachiopod: life history," *Science* 152:660–62.

HALL, J.; and J. M. CLARKE, 1892, 1894. *An introduction to the study of the Brachiopoda, intended for a handbook for the use of students. New York State Geological Survey,* Ann. Rep. 11: 133–223; pt II Ann. Rep. 13: 345–1137.

———, 1892, 1893. *An introduction to the study of genera of Paleozoic Brachiopoda.* New York State Geology and Paloeontology, pt. 1:1–367; pt. 2, 1–394.

MOORE, R. D. (ed.), 1965 *Treatise on Invertebrate Paleontology.* Part H. *Brachiopods.* 2 vols. Geological Society of America, University of Kansas Press, Lawrence, Kan.

RUDWICK, M. J. S., 1970. *Living and Fossil Brachiopods.* Hutchinson University Library, London.

TASCH, P., 1973. "Moored to the sea bottom: pump-filter modules in space and time." *In:* P. Tasch. *Paleobiology of the Invertebrates.* John Wiley, New York, London, Sydney, pp. 251–311.

WRIGHT, A. D., 1979. "Brachiopod radiation." *In:* M. R. House. *The Origin of Major Invertebrate Groups.* Academic Press, London, New York, pp. 235–52.

CHAPTER 11 Worms, Burrows, Trails, and Other Problematica

BASAN, P. B. (ed.), 1978. *Trace fossil concepts.* Society of Economic Paleontologists and Mineralogists, Short Course No. 5, Oklahoma City, Okla.

CARNEY, R. S., 1981. "Bioturbation and biodeposition." In: A. J. Boucot. *Principles of Benthic Marine Paleoecology.* Academic Press, New York, London, Sydney, pp. 357–99.

MOORE, R. C., 1966. *Treatise on invertebrate paleontology.* Part W. *Miscellanea. Conodonts, Conoidal Shells of Uncertain Affinities, Worms, Trace Fossils, and Problematica.* Geological Society of America, University of Kansas Press, Lawrence, Kan.

RICHARDSON, E. S., JR., 1965. "Wormlike fossils from the Pennsylvanian of Illinois," *Science* 151:75–76.

SASS, D. B.; and D. C. MEISSNER, 1983. "Electrography of trace fossils," *Journal of Paleontology* 57(5):1047–49.

SIMPSON, S., 1975. "Classification of trace fossils." *In:* W. Frey (ed.). *The Study of Trace Fossils.* Springer-Verlag, New York, pp. 39–54.

TASCH, P., 1973. Chapter 9. "Worm's eye view: the world of polychaetes and other worms." *In:* P. Tasch. *Paleobiology of the Intertebrates.* John Wiley, New York, London, Sydney, pp. 443–73.

—— and J. R. STUDE, 1966. "Permian scolecodonts from the Ft. Riley limestone of southeastern Kansas," *Wichita State University Bulletin,* University Studies no. 68, 43(3):3–35.

CHAPTER 12   Animals in Three Parts: The Trilobites

CLARKSON, E. N. K., 1979. "Arthropods." *In:* E. N. K. Clarkson. *Invertebrate Palaeontology and Evolution.* George Allen & Unwin, London, Boston, Sydney. pp. 258–302.

ELDREDGE, N., 1977. "Trilobites and evolutionary patterns." *In:* A. Hallam (ed.). *Patterns in Evolution.* Elsevier, Amsterdam.

FORTEY, R. A., 1975. "Early Ordovician trilobite communities," *Fossils and Strata* 4:331–52.

LEVI-SETTI, R., 1975. *Trilobites: A Photographic Atlas.* University of Chicago Press, Chicago.

MOORE, R. C. (ed.), 1959. *Treatise on invertebrate paleontology.* Part O. *Arthropoda 1. Arthropoda—general features. Protarthropoda. Euarthropoda—general features. Trilobitomorpha.* Geological Society of America, University of Kansas Press, Lawrence, Kan.

RAYMOND, P. E., 1922. "A trilobite retaining color markings," *American Journal of Science* 4:461–64.

SINCLAIR, G. W., 1947. "Two examples of injury in Ordovician trilobites," *American Journal of Science* 245(4):250–57.

TASCH, P., 1973. "The skeleton shedders (Arthropods-II)." *In:* P. Tasch. *Paleobiology of the Invertebrates.* John Wiley, New York, London, Sydney, Toronto, pp. 504–44.

CHAPTER 13   Crustaceans

BRASIER, M. D., 1980. "Phylum Crustacea—ostracods." *In:* M. D. Brasier, *Microfossils.* George Allen & Unwin, Boston, Sydney, pp. 122–49.

DARWIN, C., 1851. *A monograph on the fossil Lepadidae, or, pedunculated cirripedes of Great Britain.* Palaeontolographical Society Monograph 88.

HAZEL, J. E., 1971. *Ostracod biostratigraphy of the Yorktown Formation (Upper Mio-*

cene and Lower Pliocene) of Virginia and North Carolina. United States Geological Survey Professional Paper 704. 13 pp.

MOORE, R. C. (ed.), 1955. *Treatise on invertebrate paleontology.* Part P. *Arthropoda 2. Chelicerata with Sections on Pycnogonida and* Palaeoisopus. Geological Society of America, University of Kansas Press, Lawrence, Kan.

———, 1961. *Treatise on invertebrate paleontology.* Part Q. *Arthropoda 3. Crustacea, Ostracoda.* Geological Society of America, University of Kansas Press, Lawrence, Kan.

——— and C. Teichert (eds.). 1969. *Treatise on invertebrate paleontology.* Part R. *Arthropoda 4,* Vols. 1–2. Geological Society of America, University of Kansas Press, Lawrence, Kan.

POKORNY, V., 1978. "Ostracodes." *In:* B. U. Haq and A. Boersma. *Introduction to Marine Micropaleontology.* Elsevier, New York, Oxford, pp. 109–49.

SWAIN, F. M. (ed.), 1975. "Biology and paleobiology of Ostracoda. A symposium." *Bulletin of American Paleontology* 65, University of Delaware, 1972.

CHAPTER 14   Arthropods from Shoals to Air

BERGSTROM, J., 1975. "Functional morphology and evolution of xiphosurids," *Fossils and Strata* 4:291–305.

BORROR, D. J.; D. M. DELONG; and C. A. TRIPLEHORN, 1981. *An introduction to the study of insects.* 5th ed. Saunders College Publishing Company, Philadelphia.

BOUDREAUX, H. B., 1979. "Evolution in the Class Insecta. In: A. P. Gupta (ed.). *Arthropod Phylogeny.* John Wiley, New York, Brisbane, Toronto. pp. 139–261.

BRIGGS, D. E. G., 1977. "Bivalved arthropods from the Cambrian Burgess Shale of British Columbia," *Palaeontology* 20:595–621.

BRITTON, E. B.; and others, 1970. *Insects of Australia.* Melbourne University Press, Carlton.

DALY, H. V.; J. T. DOGEN; and P. R. EHRLICH, 1978. *Introduction to insect biology and diversity.* McGraw-Hill, New York.

GUPTA, A. P. (ed.), 1979. *Arthropod phylogeny.* Van Nostrand-Reinhold, New York, London, Toronto, Melbourne.

KUKALOVA, J., 1978. "Origin and evolution of insect wings and their relation to metamorphosis, as documented by the fossil record," *Journal of Morphology* 156:53–126.

MANTON, S. M., 1977. *The arthropods: habits, functional morphology and evolution.* Oxford University Press, Oxford.

——— and D. T. ANDERSON, 1979. "Polyphyly and the evolution of arthropods." In: M. R. House. *The Origin of Major Invertebrate Groups.* Academic Press, London, New York, pp. 269–321.

MOORE, R. C. (ed.), 1955. *Treatise on invertebrate paleontology.* Part P. *Arthropoda Chelicerata.* Geological Society of America, University of Kansas Press, Lawrence, Kan.

——— and C. TEICHERT (ed.), 1969. *Treatise on invertebrate paleontology.* Part R. *Arthropoda 4.* 2 vols. *Crustacea (except Ostracoda), Myriapoda—Hexapoda.* Geological Society of America, University of Kansas Press, Lawrence, Kan.

PETRUNKEVITCH, A., 1949. "A study of Paleozoic Arachnida," *Connecticut Academy of Arts and Science* 37:69–315.

TASCH, P., 1973. *Phylum beyond census: The jointed-leg animals (Arthropods-1).* In: P. Tasch. *Paleobiology of the Invertebrates.* John Wiley, New York, London, Sydney, Toronto, pp. 475–504.

TEICHERT, C.; and R. ROBISON (eds.), 1985. *Treatise on invertebrate paleontology.* Part R. *Arthropoda* 4. *Hexapoda (Collembola, Protura, Diplura, Insecta),* Geological Society of America. University of Kansas Press, Lawrence, Kan.

CHAPTER 15   Snails and Their Kin

GOULD, S. J., 1969. "An evolutionary microcosm: Pleistocene and Recent history of the land snail *Poecilozonites* in Bermuda," *Bulletin of the Museum of Comparative Zoology* (Harvard University) 138:407–532.

HERMAN, Y., 1978. "Pteropods." *In:* B. V. Haq and A. Boersma. *Introduction to marine micropaleontology.* Elsevier, New York, Oxford.

MOORE, R. C. (ed.)., 1969. *Treatise on invertebrate paleontology,* Part I. *Mollusca 1. (Principles, gastropods).* Geological Society of America, University of Kansas Press, Lawrence, Kan.

RUNNEGAR, B., 1980. "Hyolitha: status of the phylum," *Lethaia* 13:21–25.

———, 1983. "Molluscan phylogeny revisited," *Memoirs of the Association of Australasian Palaeontologists* 1:121–44.

SOLEM, G. A., 1974. *The Shell Makers; introducing mollusks.* John Wiley, New York and Toronto.

STANLEY, S. M., 1970. *Relation of shell to life habits in the Bivalvia.* Geological Society of America Memoir 125, Boulder, Colo.

YOCHELSON, E. L., 1979. Early radiation of Mollusca and mollusc-like groups. *In:* M. R. House (ed.). *The Origin of Major Invertebrate Groups.* Academic Press, London and New York, pp. 323–58.

CHAPTER 16   Bivalves—Clams, Mussels, and Oysters

MOORE, R. C. (ed.), 1969–71. *Treatise on invertebrate paleontology.* Part N. Vols. 1–3 (1969–71) *(Bivalves).* Geological Society of America, University of Kansas Press, Lawrence, Kan.

MORRIS, N. J., 1979. "On the origin of the Bivalvia." *In:* M. R. House. *The Origin of Major Invertebrate Groups.* Academic Press, London and New York, pp. 381–413.

POJETA, J.; and B. RUNNEGAR, 1974. *"Fordilla troyensis* and the early history of pelecypod mollusks," *American Scientist* 62:706–11.

———, 1976. *The palaeontology of rostronconch mollusks and the early history of the Phylum Mollusca.* United States Geological Survey Professional Paper 968. pp. 1–88.

——— and J. KRIZ, 1973. *"Fordilla troyensis* Barrande: the oldest known pelecypod," *Science* 180:866–68.

RUNNEGAR, B., 1983. *Molluscan phylogeny revisited.* Memoir of the Association of Australasian Palaeontologists 1:121–44.

——— and C. BENTLEY, 1983. "Anatomy, ecology and affinities of the Australian Early Cambrian bivalve *Pojetaia runnegari* Jell," *Journal of Paleontology* 57 (1):73–92.

———; and P. A. JELL, 1976. "Australian Middle Cambrian molluscs and their bearing on early molluscan evolution," *Alcheringa* 1:109–38.

STANLEY, S. M., 1970. "Relation of shell form to life habits in the Bivalvia (Mollusca)." Geological Society of America Memoir 125, Boulder, Colorado.

YOUNGE, C. M.; and T. E. THOMPSON, 1976. *Living marine molluscs.* Collins, London.

CHAPTER 17   Feet Before Heads: The Nautiloids and Their Relatives

FLOWER, R. H., 1957. "Nautiloids of the Paleozoic." *In:* H. S. Ladd (ed.). *Treatise on marine ecology and palaeoecology* 2. Geological Society of America. Boulder, Colo.

HOLLAND, C. H., 1979. "Early Cephalopoda." *In:* M. R. House, *The Origin of Major Invertebrate Groups.* Academic Press, London and New York, pp. 367–78.

MOORE, R. C. (ed.), 1964. *Treatise on Invertebrate Paleontology.* Part K. *Mollusca* 3 *(Nautiloids).* Geological Society of America, Boulder, Colo.

YOCHELSON, E. L., 1977. "Agmata, a proposed extinct phylum of Early Cambrian age," *Journal of Paleontology* 51:437–54.

———, R. H. FLOWER, and G. F. WEBERS, 1963. "The bearing of the new Late Cambrian monoplacophoran genus *Knightoconus* upon the origin of the Cephalopoda," *Lethaia* 6:275–309.

CHAPTER 18   "Ammon's Stones" and Naked Cephalopods

LEHMANN, V., 1981. *The Ammonites: Their Life and Their World.* Cambridge University Press, Cambridge, London, New York, Sydney.

MOORE, R. C. (ed.), 1957. *Treatise on invertebrate paleontology.* Part L. *Mollusca* 4. *Cephalopoda Ammonoidea.* Geological Society of America, University of Kansas Press, Lawrence, Kan.

MUTVEI, H.; and R. A. REYMENT, 1973. "Buoyancy control and siphuncle function in ammonoids," *Palaeontology* 16:623–36.

PACKARD, A., 1972. "Cephalopods and fish: The limits of convergence," *Biological Reviews* 47:241–307.

STANLEY, S. M., 1984. "Mass extinctions in the ocean," *Scientific American* 250(6):46–54.

TRUEMAN, A. E., 1941. "The ammonite body chamber, with special reference to the buoyancy and mode of life of the living ammonite," *Quarterly Journal of the Geological Society of London* 96:339–83.

CHAPTER 19   Mostly Stemmed Echinoderms

BRETT, C. E.; and others, 1983. "Coronoidea: A new class of blastozoan echinoderms based on taxonomic reevaluation of *Stephanocrinus*," *Journal of Paleontology* 57(4):627–51.

CLARKSON, E. N. K., 1979. "Echinoderms." In: *Invertebrate palaeontology and evolution.* George Allen & Unwin, Boston and Sydney, pp. 189–237.

JEFFERIES, R. P. S., 1979. "The origin of chordates—a methodological essay." *In:* M. R. House. *The origin of major invertebrate groups.* Academic Press, London and New York.

MACURDA, D. B., JR.; and D. L. MEYER, 1983. "Sea lilies and feather stars," *American Scientist* 71:354–64.

MOORE, R. C.; and C. TEICHERT (eds.), 1978. *Treatise on invertebrate paleontology. Part T. Echinodermata 2.* Vols. 1–3. *Crinoidea.* Geological Society of America, University of Kansas Press, Lawerence, Kan.

PAUL, C. R. C., 1979. "Early Echinoderm Radiation." In: M. R. House. *The origin of major invertebrate groups.* Academic Press, London and New York, pp. 415–34.

PHILIP, G. M., 1979. "Carpoids—echinoderms or chordates?" *Biological Review* 54:439–71.

SPRINKLE, J., 1976. "Classification and phylogeny of 'pelmatozoan' echinoderms," *Systematic Zoology* 25:83–91.

CHAPTER 20   Stars, Urchins, and Cucumbers of the Sea

CLARK, W. B., and M. W. TWITCHELL, 1915. *The Mesozoic and Cenozoic echinodermata of the United States.* U.S. Geological Survey Monograph 54:1–341.

DURHAM, J. W., 1966. "Evolution among the Echinoidea," *Biological Reviews* 41:368–91.

KERMACK, K. A., 1954. "A biometrical study of *Micraster coranguinum* and *M. (Isomicraster) senonensis,*" *Philosophical Transactions of the Royal Society of London,* B, 237:375–428.

MOORE, R. C. (ed.), 1966. *Treatise on invertebrate paleontology.* Part V. Vols. 1–2. *Echinodermata 3. Asterozoa-Echinozoa.* Geological Society of America, The University of Kansas Press, Lawrence, Kan.

———, 1967. *Treatise on invertebrate Paleontology.* Part S. *Echinodermata 1.* Vols. 1–2. *General characteristics. Homalozoa-Crinozoa (except Crinoidea).* Geological Society of America, The University of Kansas Press, Lawrence, Kan.

NICHOLS, D., 1959. "Changes in the chalk heart urchin *Micraster* interpreted in relation to living forms," *Philosophical Transactions of the Royal Society of London,* B, 242:347–437.

———, 1974. *Echinoderms.* Hutchison, London.

SMITH, A., 1984. *Echinoid Palaeobiology.* George Allen & Unwin, London.

STOKES, R. B., 1977. "The echinoids *Micraster* and *Epiaster* from the Turonian and Santonian chalk of England," *Palaeontology* 20:805–21.

CHAPTER 21   Nets, Wrigglers, and "Teeth" Without Jaws

BARNES, C. R. (ed.), 1976. *Conodont paleoecology.* Geological Association of Canada, Special Paper Number 15, University of Waterloo, Waterloo, Ont.

BENGSTON, S., 1983. "A functional model for the conodont apparatus," *Lethaia* 16:38.

BRASIER, M. D., 1981. "Group Conodontophorida." In: *Microfossils.* George Allen & Unwin. London, Boston, and Sydney, pp. 149–61.

GOULD, S. J., 1983. "Nature's great era of experiments," *Natural History* 7:12–20.

MOORE, R. C. (ed.), 1966. *Treatise on invertebrate paleontology.* Part W. *Miscellanea. Conodonts, conoidal shells of uncertain affinities, worms, trace fossils and problematica.* Geological Society of America, University of Kansas Press, Lawrence, Kan.

————, 1970. *Treatise on invertebrate paleontology*. Part V. *Graptolithina* (revised). Geological Society of America, University of Kansas Press, Lawrence, Kan.

MULLER, K. K., 1978. "Conodonts and other phosphatic microfossils." *In:* B. U. Haq and A. Boersma. *Introduction to Marine Micropaleontology*. Elsevier, New York and Oxford, pp. 276–91.

CHAPTER 22   From Starfish to Fish, Lords of the Water

BOUCOT, A. J.; and C. JANIS, 1983. "Environment of the early Paleozoic vertebrates," *Palaeogeography, Palaeoclimatology, and Palaeoecology* 41:251–87.

HALSTEAD, L. B.; Y. H. LIU; and K. PAN, 1979. "Agnathans from the Devonian of China," *Nature* 282:831–33.

JEFFERIES, R. P. S., 1979. "The origin of chordates—a methodological essay." *In:* M. R. House. *The Origin of Major Invertebrate Groups*. Academic Press, London, pp. 443–77.

MOY-THOMAS, J. A.; and R. S. MILES, 1971. *Palaeozoic Fishes*. 2nd ed. Chapman & Hall, London.

NITECKI, M. H., 1979. *Mazon Creek Fossils*. Academic Press, New York.

PHILIP, G. M., 1979. "Carpoids—echinoderms or chordates?" *Biological Reviews* 54:439–71.

RITCHIE, A.; and J. GILBERT-TOMLINSON, 1977. "First Ordovician vertebrates from the southern hemisphere," *Alcheringa* 1:351–68.

ROBER, A. S., 1962. *The Vertebrate Body*. W. B. Saunders, Philadelphia and London.

SCHAEFFER, B., 1967. "Comments on elasmobranch evolution." *In:* P. W. Gilbert, R. F. Mathewson, and D. P. Rall. *Sharks, Skates and Rays*. Johns Hopkins Press, Baltimore, pp. 3–35.

————; and D. E. ROSEN, 1961. "Major adaptive levels in the evolution of the actinopterygian feeding mechanism," *American Zoologist* 1:187–204.

SCHULTZE, H. P. (ed.), various years. *Handbook of Paleoichthyology*. Gustav-Fischer Verlag. Stuttgart, New York. Several volumes.

SCHWARZHANS, W., 1984. "Fish otoliths from the New Zealand Tertiary." New Zealand Geographical Survey, Report 113, Lower Hutt, a translation of "Die Tertiäre Teleosteer-fauna Neuseelands Reconstruiert Anhaud von Otolithen," 1980, Paläontologisches Institut Freie Universität Berlin, Berlin.

THOMPSON, K. S., 1969. "The biology of the lobe-finned fishes," *Biological Reviews* 46:9–154.

CHAPTER 23   The Greening of the Land

DOUGLAS, J. G., 1983. *What fossil plant is that? A guide to the ancient floras of Victoria*. Field Naturalists Club of Victoria. Jenkin Buxton Printers, West Melbourne.

EDWARDS, D., 1980. "Early Land Floras." *In:* A. L. Panchen (ed.). *The Terrestrial Environment and the Origins of Land Vertebrates*. Academic Press, London, pp. 55–85.

KNOLL, A. H.; and G. W. ROTHWELL, 1981. "Paleobotany: Perspectives in 1980; *Paleobiology* 7(1):7–35.

PRATT, L. M.; T. L. PHILLIPS; and J. M. DENNISON, 1977. "Evidence of Non-Vascular land plants from the early Silurian (Llandoverian) of Virginia, U.S.A." *Review of Palaeobotany and Palynology* 25:121–49.

RETALLACK, G., 1975. "The life and times of a triassic lycopod," *Alcheringa* 1:3–29.

TAYLOR, T. N., 1982. "The origin of land plants: A Paleobotanical Perspective," *Taxon* 31:155–77.

TIDWELL, W. D., 1975. *Common Fossil Plants of Western North America.* Brigham Young University Press, Provo, Utah.

WHITE, M. E., 1984. *Australia's Prehistoric Plants and their Environment.* Methuen, Australia, North Ryde.

———, 1986. *The Greening of Gondwana.* Reed, Australia, Frenchs Forest (NSW).

CHAPTER 24 Amphibians, Ancient and Modern

CARROLL, R. L., 1977. "Patterns of amphibian evolution: an extended example of the incompleteness of the fossil record." In: A. Hallam (ed.). *Patterns of evolution, as illustrated by the fossil record. Developments in Palaeontology and Stratigraphy* 5. Elsevier: Amsterdam, Oxford, New York. pp. 405–37.

WARREN, A. A.; and M. N. HUTCHINSON, 1983. "The last labyrinthodont? A new brachyopoid (Amphibia, Temnospondyli) from the Early Jurassic Evergreen formation of Queensland, Australia, *Philosophical Transactions Royal Society London* Series B, *Biological Sciences,* Vol. 303, (1113), pp. 1–62.

CHAPTER 25 A Myriad of Reptiles on Land

CARROLL, R. L., 1970. "The earliest known reptiles," *Yale Scientific Magazine,* October, pp. 16–21.

KEMP, T. S., 1982. *Mammal-like reptiles and the origins of mammals.* Academic Press: London.

CHAPTER 26 Farewells to Land

AUGUSTA, J.; and Z. BURIAN, 1964. *Prehistoric sea monsters.* Paul Hamlyn, London.

BUFFETAUT, ERIC, 1979. "The evolution of the crocodilians," *Scientific American,* Vol. 241, (4), pp. 124–32, 9 figs.

ROMER, ALFRED S., 1956. *Osteology of the Reptiles.* University of Chicago Press, Chicago.

CHAPTERS 27 and 28 Scale Bearers and Lizard-hipped Dinosaurs, and Bird-hipped Dinosaurs

ALVAREZ, L. W.; W. ALVAREZ; F. ASARO, and H. V. MICHEL, 1980. "Extraterrestrial cause for the Cretaceous–Tertiary extinction," *Science,* Vol. 208, pp. 1095–98.

ALVAREZ, W.; E. G. KAUFFMAN; F. SURLYK; L. W. ALVAREZ; F. ASARO, and H. V. MICHEL, 1984. "Impact theory of mass extinctions and the invertebrate fossil record," *Science,* Vol. 223, pp. 1131–35.

DODSON, P.; A. K. BEHRENSMEYER, R. T. BAKKER, and J. S. McINTOSH, 1980. "Taphonomy and paleoecology of the dinosaur beds of the Jurassic Morrison Formation," *Paleobiology,* Vol. 6, pp. 208–32.

LAMBERT, D., 1983. *Collins Guide to Dinosaurs*. Collins, London.

MOODY, R., 1977. *A Natural History of the Dinosaurs*. Hamlyn, London.

NORMAN, D., 1985. The Illustrated Encyclopedia of Dinosaurs. Salamander Books, London.

NITECKI, M. H. (ed.), 1981. *Biotic Crises in Ecological and Evolutionary Time*. Academic Press, New York.

RUSSELL, D. A., 1984. "The gradual decline of the dinosaurs—fact or fallacy?" *Nature,* Vol. 307, pp. 360–61.

THOMAS, R. D. K.; and E. C. OLSON (eds.), 1980. *A Cold Look at the Warm-Blooded Dinosaurs*. Westview Press, Boulder, Colo.

WADE, M., 1979. "Tracking dinosaurs: the Winton excavation," *Australian Natural History,* Vol. 19, pp. 286–91.

CHAPTER 29 Flying and Gliding Reptiles

AUGUSTA, J.; and Z. BURIAN, 1961. *Prehistoric reptiles and birds*. Paul Hamlyn, London.

BRAMWELL, C. D.; and G. R. WHITFIELD, 1974. "Biomechanics of *Pteranodon*," *Philosophical Transactions Royal Society London* Series B, Vol. 267, pp. 503–81.

LANGSTON, W., 1981. *"Pterosaurs," Scientific American,* February, pp. 92–102.

PADIAN, K., 1983. "A functional analysis of flying and walking in pterosaurs," *Paleobiology,* Vol. 9, no. 3, pp. 218–39.

SEELEY, H. G., 1901. *Dragons of the Air*. Methuen, London.

STEIN, R. S., 1975. "A reptilian adaptation to flight: dynamic analysis of *Pteranodon ingens," Journal Paleontology,* Vol. 49, (3), pp. 534–48.

CHAPTER 30 Birds, Inventors of the Feather

FEDUCCIA, A., 1978. *"Presbyornis* and the evolution of ducks and flamingos," *American Scientist* 66:298–304.

———, 1980. *The age of birds*. Harvard University Press, Cambridge, Mass., London.

FISHER, J.; and R. T. PETERSON, 1964. *The world of birds*. Doubleday, Garden City, N.Y.

OLIVER, W. R. B., 1949. "The moas of New Zealand and Australia," *Dominion Museum Bulletin* 15:1–206.

OLSON, S. L.; and Y. HASAGAWA, 1979. "Fossil counterparts of giant penguins from the North Pacific," *Science* 206:688–89.

OSTROM, J. H., 1974. *"Archaeopteryx* and the origin of flight," *Quarterly Review of Biology* 49:27–47.

———, 1975. *"Archaeopteryx," Discovery* 11(1):15–23.

RICH, P. V., 1981. "Feathered leviathans (Dromornithidae)," *Hemisphere* 25(5):298–302.

RICH, P. V.; and R. BERRA, 1979. "Bird-history—the first one hundred million years," *Australian Natural History* 19(12):392–97.

SIMPSON, G. G., 1976. *Penguins: past and present, here and there*. Yale University Press, New Haven, Conn.

TROTTER, M. M.; and B. McCULLOCH, 1984. "Moas, men, and middens." In: P. S. Martin and R. G. Klein (eds.). *Quaternary extinctions. A prehistoric revolution*. University of Arizona Press, Tucson. pp. 708–67.

CHAPTER 31 Hairy Reptiles with Complex Ears: the Early Mammals

ARCHER, M.; and G. CLAYTON (eds.), 1984. *Vertebrate zoogeography and evolution in Australasia.* Hesperian Press, Carlisle, Western Australia.

CROMPTON, A. A.; and P. PARKER, 1978. "Evolution of the mammalian masticatory apparatus," *American Scientist,* Vol. 66, pp. 192–201.

KEMP, T. S., 1982. *Mammal-like reptiles and the origin of mammals.* Academic Press, New York.

KIELAN-JAWOROWSKA, Z., 1975. "Late Cretaceous mammals and dinosaurs from the Gobi Desert," *American Scientist,* Vol. 63, pp. 150–59.

LILLEGRAVEN, J. A.; Z. KIELAN-JAWOROWSKA, AND W. A. CLEMENS, 1979. *Mesozoic Mammals, the First Two-Thirds of Mammalian History.* University of California Press, Berkeley.

RICH, P. V.; and E. M. THOMPSON (eds.), 1982. *The fossil vertebrate record of Australasia.* Monash University Offset Printing Unit, Clayton, Victoria.

CHAPTER 32 The World Blossoms

BECK, C. G., 1976. *Origin and early evolution of angiosperms.* Columbia University Press, London, New York.

DILCHER, D.; and P. R. CRANE, 1984. "In pursuit of the first flower," *Natural History* 3:57–61.

DOUGLAS, J. G., 1983. *What fossil plant is that? A guide to the ancient floras of Victoria.* Field Naturalists Club of Victoria. J. Buxton Printers, West Melbourne.

STEWART, W. N., 1983. *Paleobotany and the evolution of plants.* Cambridge University Press, London, New York.

TIDWELL, W. D., 1975. *Common fossil plants of western North America.* Brigham Young University Press, Provo, Utah.

CHAPTER 33 The Great Placental Radiation

HALSTEAD, L. B., 1978. *The Evolution of the Mammals.* Peter Lowe, London.

KURTEN, B., 1971. *The Age of Mammals.* Columbia University Press, New York.

MAGLIO, V. J.; and H. B. S. COOKE (eds.), 1978. *Evolution of African Mammals.* Harvard University Press, Cambridge, Mass.

SCOTT, W. B., 1937. *A History of the Land Mammals in the Western Hemisphere.* (Reprinted in 1962 by Hafner Publishing Company, New York)

SZALAY, F. S.; and E. DELSON, 1979. *Evolutionary History of the Primates.* Academic Press, New York.

CHAPTER 34 Moving Continents, Changing Climates, and their Effects on Mammals

KEAST, A.; F. C. ERK, and B. GLASS, 1972. *Evolution, Mammals, and Southern Continents.* State University of New York Press, Albany, N.Y.

McKENNA, M. C., 1972. "Possible biological consequences of plate tectonics," *BioScience,* Vol. 22, (9), pp. 519–25.

MURRAY, P., 1984. *Australia's prehistoric animals.* Methuen, Australia, North Ryde.

RICH, P. V.; and G. F. VAN TETS (eds.), 1985. *Kadimakara. The history of Australia's backboned animals.* Pioneer Design Studio, Lilydale, Victoria.

SAVAGE, D. E.; and D. E. RUSSELL, 1983. *Mammalian paleofaunas of the world.* Addison-Wesley Publishing Company, Reading, Mass.

SIMPSON, G. G., 1980. *Splendid Isolation, the curious history of South American mammals.* Yale University Press, New Haven, Conn., London.

CHAPTER 35   Beasts and Birds of the Ice Age: The Interplay of Climate and Man

BEATY, C. B., 1978. "The causes of glaciation," *American Scientist,* Vol. 66, (4), pp. 452–59.

FLOOD, J., 1983. *Archaeology of the dreamtime. The story of prehistoric Australia and her people.* William Collins Pty., Melbourne, Victoria.

KURTEN, B., 1968. *Pleistocene Mammals of Europe.* Weidenfeld & Nicolson, London.

KURTEN, B., 1972. *The Ice Age.* Rupert Hart-Davis, London.

————; and E. ANDERSON, 1980. *Pleistocene Mammals of North America.* Columbia University Press, New York.

MARTIN, P. S.; and R. G. KLEIN (eds.), 1984. *Quaternary Extinctions. A prehistoric revolution.* University of Arizona Press, Tucson.

NILSSON, T., 1983. *The Pleistocene. geology and life in the Quaternary Ice Age.* D. Reidel, Dordrecht, South Holland, the Netherlands.

PILBEAM, D., 1984. "The descent of hominoids and hominids," *Scientific American,* Vol. 250, (3), pp. 60–69 (March).

TRINKAUS, E.; and W. W. HOWELLS, 1979. "The Neanderthals," *Scientific American,* Vol. 241, (6), pp. 94–105 (December).

WU RUKANG and LIN SHENGLONG, 1983. "Peking Man," *Scientific American,* Vol. 248, (6), pp. 78–86 (June).

CHAPTER 36   How to Care for a Fossil

AGER, D. V., 1963. *Principles of Paleoecology.* McGraw-Hill, New York.

BEHRENSMEYER, A. K.; and A. P. HILL (eds.), 1980. *Fossils in the Making.* University of Chicago Press, Chicago.

KUMMEL, B.; and D. RAUP (eds.), 1965. *Handbook of Paleontological Techniques.* W. H. Freeman, San Francisco.

MACDONALD, J. R., 1983. *The Fossil Collectors Handbook. A paleontology field guide.* Prentice-Hall, Englewood Cliffs, N.J.

RIXON, A. E., 1976. *Fossil Animal Remains. Their preparation and conservation.* Athlone Press, University of London, London.

APPENDIX 2

Classification

● **Kingdom: Monera:** monerans (Precambrian – Recent)
  ● Phylum (Division): Cyanophyta: blue-green algae (Precambrian–Recent)
  ● Phylum: Schizomycota: bacteria (Precambrian – Recent)

● **Kingdom: Fungi:** fungi (Precambrian – Recent)
  ● Phylum: Eumycota: true fungi (Precambrian – Recent)

● **Kingdom: Protista:** protists (Precambrian – Recent)
  ● Phylum: Chrysophyta: diatoms, silicoflagellates, and coccolithophores (Jurassic – Recent)

  ◆ Group: Acritarcha: acritarchs (Precambrian – Recent)

  ◆ Phylum: Pyrrophyta: dinoflagellates and ebridians (Ordovician – Recent)

  ◆ Phylum: Sarcodina: sarcodines (Precambrian – Recent)
    ◆ Subclass: Radiolaria: radiolarians (Cambrian – Recent)
   ◆ Class: Rhizopoda: rhizopods (Precambrian – Recent)
      ◆ Order: Foraminiferida: foraminiferans (Cambrian – Recent)

● Suborder: Allogromiina: allogromiines (Cambrian –
     Recent)

◆ Suborder: Textulariina: textulariines (Cambrian –
     Recent)

◆ Suborder: Fusulinina: fusulinines (Ordovician – Tri-
     assic)

◆ Suborder: Miliolina: miliolines (Carboniferous – Re-
     cent)

◆ Suborder: Rotaliina: rotaliines (Permian – Recent)

◆ Group: Chitinozoa: chitinozoans (Precambrian – Permian)

■ **Kingdom: Plantae:** plants (Precambrian – Recent)

  ◆ Phylum: Rhodophyta: red algae (Precambrian – Recent)

  ● Phylum: Chlorophyta: grass-green algae and charophytes (Precam-
     brian – Recent)

  ■ Phylum: Bryophyta: mosses, liverworts (Carboniferous – Recent)

  ■ Phylum: Tracheophyta: vascular plants (Silurian – Recent)

    ■ Class: Rhyniopsida: primitive vascular plants (Silurian – Devo-
         nian)

    ■ Class: Psilopsida: whisk ferns (Recent)

    ■ Class: Zosterophyllopsida: primitive microphyllous plants (Silu-
         rian – Devonian)

      ■ Order: Asteroxylales: asteroxylalians (Silurian – Devo-
             nian)

    ■ Class: Lycopsida: club mosses (Silurian – Recent)

    ■ Class: Sphenopsida: horsetails (Devonian – Recent)

    ■ Class: Filicopsida: ferns (Devonian – Recent)

    ■ Class: Progymnospermopsida: progymnosperms (Devonian –
         Carboniferous)

    ■ Class: Gymnospermopsida: gymnosperms (Devonian – Recent)

      ■ Order: Pteridospermales: seed ferns (Devonian – Juras-
             sic)

      ■ Order: Cycadales: cycads (Permian – Recent)

      ■ Order: Cycadeoidales: cycadeoids (Triassic – Creta-
             ceous)

      ■ Order Caytoniales: caytoniales (Triassic – Cretaceous)

      ■ Order: Glossopteridales: glossopterids (Carboniferous –
             ?Jurassic)

      ■ Order: Ginkgoales: ginkgoes (?Permian, Triassic – Re-
             cent)

      ■ Order: Cordaitales: cordaites (Carboniferous – Per-
             mian)

      ■ Order: Voltziales: voltziales (Carboniferous – Triassic)

■ Order: Coniferales: conifers (Triassic – Recent)
■ Order: Taxales: yews (Jurassic – Recent)
■ Class: Angiospermopsida: flowering plants (Cretaceous – Recent)
   ■ Subclass: Monocotyledonae: monocots, grass, etc. (Cretaceous – Recent)
   ■ Subclass: Dicotyledonae: dicots, higher flowering plants (Cretaceous – Recent)

● **Kingdom: Animalia:** animals (Precambrian – Recent)
  ◆ Phylum: Porifera: sponges (Cambrian – Recent)
    ◆ Class: Demospongea: spongin sponges (Cambrian – Recent)
    ◆ Class: Calcarea: calcareous sponges (Calcispongea) (Cambrian – Recent)
    ◆ Class: Hexactinellida: glass sponges (Hyalospongea) (Cambrian – Recent)
  ◆ Phylum: Stromatoporoidea: stromatoporoids (Cambrian – Cretaceous)
  ◆ Phylum: Archaeocyathida: archaeocyathids (Early – Middle Cambrian)
  ◆ Phylum: Cnidaria: jellyfishes and corals (Precambrian – Recent)
    ◆ Class: Hydrozoa: hydrozoans (Cambrian – Recent)
      ◇ Order: Hydroida: hydroids (Cambrian – Recent)
      ◆ Order: Milleporina: stinging "corals" (Tertiary – Recent)
      ◆ Order: Stylasterina: stylasterines (Tertiary – Recent)
      ◆ Order: Spongiomorphida: spongiomorphids (Triassic – Jurassic)
    ◆ Class: Scyphozoa: jellyfishes (Precambrian – Recent)
    ◆ Class: Anthozoa: corals (Cambrian – Recent)
     ◆ Subclass: Octocorallia: octocorals (Cretaceous – Recent)
     ◆ Subclass: Zoantharia: corals (Cambrian – Recent)
      ◆ Order: Rugosa: rugose corals or tetracorals (?Cambrian – Triassic)
      ◆ Order: Tabulata: tabulate corals (?Cambrian – Permian)
      ◆ Order: Scleractinia: hexacorals (Triassic – Recent)
  ◆ Phylum: Bryozoa (Polyzoa): bryozoans (Ordovician – Recent)
    ◇ Class: Phylactolaemata: phylactolaemates (Mesozoic – Recent)
    ◆ Class: Stenolaemata: stenolaemates (Ordovician – Recent)
      ◆ Order: Cyclostomata: cyclostomes (Ordovician – Recent)

- ◆ Order: Cystoporata: cystopores (Ordovician – Permian)
- ◆ Order: Trepostomata: trepostomes (Ordovician – Permian)
- ◆ Order: Cryptostomata: cryptostomes (Ordovician – Permian)
- ◆ Class: Gymnolaemata: gymnolaemates (Ordovician – Recent)
  - ◆ Order: Ctenostomata: ctenostomes (Ordovician – Recent)
  - ◆ Order: Cheilostomata: cheilostomes (Jurassic – Recent)
- ◆ Phylum: Brachiopoda: brachiopods (Cambrian – Recent)
  - ◆ Class: Inarticulata: inarticulate brachiopods (Cambrian – Recent)
    - ◆ Order: Lingulida: lingulids (Cambrian – Recent)
    - ◆ Order: Acrotretida: acrotretids (Cambrian – Recent)
    - ◆ Order: Paterinida: paterinids (Cambrian – Ordovician)
    - ◆ Order: Obolellida: obolellids (Early – Middle Cambrian)
    - ◆ Order: Kutorginida: kutorginids (Early – Middle Cambrian)
  - ◆ Class: Articulata: articulate brachiopods (Cambrian – Recent)
    - ◆ Order: Orthida: orthids (Cambrian – Permian)
    - ◆ Order: Strophomenida: strophomenids (Ordovician – Jurassic)
    - ◆ Order: Pentamerida: pentamerids (Cambrian – Devonian)
    - ◆ Order: Rhynchonellida: rhynchonellids (Ordovician – Recent)
    - ◆ Order: Spiriferida: spiriferids (Ordovician – Jurassic)
    - ◆ Order: Terebratulida: terebratulids (Silurian – Recent)
    - ◆ Order: Terebratulida: terebratulids (Devonian – Recent)
- ● Phylum: Mollusca: molluscs (Cambrian – Recent)
  - ◆ Class: Monoplacophora: monoplacophorans (Cambrian – Recent)
  - ◆ Class: Amphineura: chitons (Cambrian – Recent)
  - ◆ Class: Scaphopoda: tooth shells, tusk shells (Ordovician – Recent)
  - ◆ Class: Bivalvia (Lamellibranchia, Pelecypoda): clams (Cambrian – Recent)
    - ◆ Subclass: Palaeotaxodonta: palaeotaxodonts (Ordovician – Recent)

◆ Subclass: Cryptodonta: cryptodonts (Ordovician – Recent)

◆ Subclass: Pteriomorpha: pteriomorphs (Ordovician – Recent)

● Subclass: Palaeoheterodonta: palaeoheterodonts   (Ordovician – Recent)

◆ Subclass: Heterodonta: heterdonts (Triassic – Recent)

◆ Subclass: Anomalodesmata: anomalodesmates   (Triassic – Recent)

◆ Class: Rostroconchia: rostroconchs (Cambrian – Permian)

● Class: Gastropoda: snails (Cambrian – Recent)

  ● Subclass: Prosobranchiata (Cambrian – Recent)

    ◆ Order: Archaeogastropoda: archaeogastropods (Cambrian – Recent)

    ◆ Order: Mesogastropoda: mainly mesogastropods (Ordovician – Recent)

    ◆ Order: Neogastropoda: neogastropods   (Cretaceous – Recent)

  ◆ Subclass: Opisthobranchiata: opisthobranchs   (?Carboniferous – Recent)

  ○ Subclass: Pulmonata: pulmonates (Mesozoic – Recent)

◆ Class: Cephalopoda: cephalopods (Cambrian – Recent)

  ◆ Subclass: Endoceratoidea: endoceratoids   (Ordovician – ?Silurian)

  ◆ Subclass: Actinoceratoidea: actinoceratoids   (Ordovician – Carboniferous)

  ◆ Subclass: Nautiloidea: nautiloids (Cambrian – Recent)

  ◆ Subclass: Bactritoidea: bactritoids (Ordovician – Permian)

  ◆ Subclass: Ammonoidea: ammonites (Devonian – Cretaceous)

  ◆ Subclass: Coleoidea: octopuses,   etc.   (Carboniferous – Recent)

● Phylum: Platyhelminthes: flatworms (?Carboniferous – Recent)

● Phylum: Nemathelminthes, or Nematoda: roundworms (Carboniferous – Recent)

● Phylum: Nematomorpha: horsehair worms (Eocene – Recent)

◆ Phylum: Chaetognatha: arrow worms (Cambrian – Recent)

◆ Phylum: Nemertea: proboscis worms, priapulid worms (Cambrian – Recent)

◆ Phylum: Sipunculoida: peanut worms (Cambrian – Recent)

◆ Phylum: Annelida: segmented worms (Precambrian – Recent)

● Phylum: Arthropoda: arthropods (Precambrian – Recent)

  ◆ Superclass: Trilobitomorpha: trilobitomorphs   (Cambrian – Permian)

    ◆ Class: Trilobitoidea: trilobitoids (Cambrian – Devonian)

- ◆ Class: Trilobita: trilobites (Cambrian – Permian)
  - ◆ Order: Agnostida: agnostids (Cambrian – Ordovician)
  - ◆ Order: Redlichiida: redlichiids (Early – Middle Cambrian)
  - ◆ Order: Corynexochida: corynexochids (Early – Middle Cambrian)
  - ◆ Order: Ptychopariida: ptychopariids (Cambrian – Devonian)
  - ◆ Order: Proetida: proetids (Ordovician – Permian)
  - ◆ Order: Phacopida: phacopids (Ordovician – Devonian)
  - ◆ Order: Lichida: lichids (Ordovician – Devonian)
  - ◆ Order: Odontopleurida: odontopleurids (?Cambrian – Devonian)
- ● Superclass: Chelicerata: chelicerates (Cambrian – Recent)
  - ● Class: Merostomata: merostomates (Cambrian – Recent)
    - ◆ Subclass: Xiphosura: horseshoe crabs (Cambrian – Recent)
    - ● Subclass: Eurypterida: water scorpions (Ordovician – Permian)
  - ■ Class: Arachnida: spiders (Silurian – Recent)
- ● Superclass: Crustacea: crustaceans (Cambrian – Recent)
  - ◆ Class: Branchiopoda: branchiopods (Devonian – Recent)
    - ◆ Order: Notostraca: notostracans (Carboniferous – Recent)
    - ● Order: Conchostraca: conchostracans (Devonian – Recent)
  - ● Class: Ostracoda: ostracods (Cambrian – Recent)
  - ◇ Class: Euthycarcinoidea: euthycarcinoids (Triassic)
  - ● Class: Copepoda: copepods (Miocene – Recent)
  - ◆ Class: Cirripedia: barnacles (Silurian – Recent)
  - ● Class: Malacostraca: malacostracans (Cambrian – Recent)
    - ◆ Subclass: Phyllocarida: phyllocarids (Cambrian – Recent)
    - ● Subclass: Eumalacostraca: eumalacostracans (Devonian – Recent)
      - ■ Order: Isopoda: isopods (Triassic – Recent)
      - ● Order: Decapoda: crabs, shrimps (Permian – Recent)
- ■ Superclass: Onychophora: onychophorans (?Precambrian, Cambrian – Recent)
- ■ Superclass: Myriapoda: centipedes, millipedes (Silurian – Recent)
- ■ Superclass: Hexapoda: hexapods (Pennsylvanian – Recent)
  - ■ Class: Insecta: insects (Pennsylvanian – Recent)

- ◆ Phylum: Echinodermata: echinoderms (Cambrian – Recent)
  - ◆ Subphylum: Homalozoa: carpoids (Cambrian – Devonian)
  - ◆ Subphylum: Blastozoa: blastozoans (Cambrian – Permian)
    - ◆ Class: Eocrinoidea: eocrinoids (Cambrian – Silurian)

- ◆ Class: Diploporita and Rhombifera: cystoids (?Cambrian, Ordovician – Devonian)
- ◆ Class: Parablastoidea: parablastoids (Early – Middle Ordovician)
- ◆ Class: Blastoidea: blastoids (Silurian – Permian)
- ◆ Class: Coronoidea: coronoids (Ordovician – Silurian)
- ◆ Class: Paracrinoidea: paracrinoids (Middle Ordovician)
- ◆ Class: Edrioblastoidea: edrioblastoids (Middle Ordovician)
- ◆ Subphylum: Crinozoa: crinozoans (Ordovician – Recent)
  - ◆ Class: Crinoidea: crinoids (Ordovician – Recent)
- ◆ Subphylum: Asterozoa: asterozoans (Ordovician – Recent)
  - ◆ Class: Somasteroidea: somasteroids (Ordovician – Recent)
  - ◆ Class: Asteroidea: starfish (Ordovician – Recent)
  - ◆ Class: Ophiuroidea: brittle stars (Ordovician – Recent)
- ◆ Subphylum: Echinozoa: echinozoans (Cambrian – Recent)
  - ◆ Class: Echinoidea: echinoids (Ordovician – Recent)
  - ◆ Class: Edrioasteroidea: edrioasteroids (Cambrian – Carboniferous)
  - ◆ Class: Camptostromatoidea: camptostromatoids (Early Cambrian)
  - ◆ Class: Ophiocystoidea: ophiocystoids (Ordovician – Devonian)
  - ◆ Class: Helicoplacoidea: helicoplacoids (Early Cambrian)
  - ◆ Class: Cyclocystoidea: cyclocystoids (Ordovician – Devonian)
  - ◆ Class: Holothuroidea: sea cucumbers (Ordovician – Recent)

- ◆ Phylum: Hemichordata: hemichordates (Cambrian – Recent)
  - ◆ Class: Enteropneusta: acorn worms (Recent)
  - ◆ Class: Pterobranchia: pterobranchs (Ordovician – Recent)
  - ◆ Class: Graptolithina: graptolites (Cambrian – Carboniferous)
    - ◆ Order: Dendroidea: dendroids (Cambrian – Carboniferous)
    - ◆ Order: Tuboidea: tuboids (Cambrian – Silurian)
    - ◆ Order: Camaroidea: camaroids (Ordovician)
    - ◆ Order: Crustoidea: crustoids (Ordovician)
    - ◆ Order: Stolonoidea: stolonoids (Ordovician)
    - ◆ Order: Graptoloidea: graptoloids (Ordovician – Devonian)

- ◆ Phylum: uncertain
  - ◆ Class: uncertain
    - ◆ Order: Conodontophorida: conodonts (?Precambian – Triassic)

● Phylum: Chordata: chordates (Cambrian – Recent)
   ● Superclass: Agnatha: jawless fish (Cambrian – Recent)
      ◆ Class: Pteraspidomorphi: pteraspidomorphs (Cambrian – Devonian)
        ◆ Subclass: Heterostraci: heterostracans   (Cambrian – Devonian)
          ◆ Order: Arandaspidiformes: arandaspidiforms (Middle Ordovician)
        ◆ Subclass: Thelodonti: thelodonts (Ordovician – Devonian)
      ◆ Class: Cephalaspidomorphi: cephalaspidomorphs   (Silurian – Recent)
   ● Superclass: Gnathostomata: jawed vertebrates (Silurian – Recent)
      ● Class: Placodermi: placoderms (Silurian – Devonian)
      ◆ Class: Chondrichthyes: sharks and kin (Silurian – Recent)
      ● Class: Acanthodii: "spiny sharks" (Silurian – Permian)
      ● Class: Osteichthyes: bony fish (Devonian – Recent)
      ● Subclass: Sarcopterygii (lobe-finned fishes.)
        ● Infraclass: Dipnoi: lungfish (Devonian – Recent)
        ● Infraclass: "Crossopterygii": fringe-finned fish (Devonian – Recent)
          ● Superorder: Actinistia: actinistians (Devonian – Recent)
            ● Order: Coelacanthida: coelacanths   (Devonian – Recent)
          ◇ Superorder: Rhipidistia: rhipidistians   (Devonian – Permian)
      ● Subclass: Actinopterygii: ray-finned fish (Devonian – Recent)
   ○ Class: Amphibia: amphibians (Devonian – Recent)
      ○ Subclass: Labyrinthodontia: labyrinthodonts   (Devonian – Cretaceous)
        ○ Order: Ichthyostegalia: ichthyostegalians   (Devonian – Carboniferous)
        ○ Order: Temnospondyli: temnospondyls   (Carboniferous – Jurassic)
        ○ Order: Anthracosauria: anthracosaurs   (Carboniferous – Permian)
      ○ Subclass: Lepospondyli: lepospondyls   (Carboniferous – Permian)
        ○ Order: Aistopoda: aistopods   (Carboniferous – Permian)
        ◇ Order: Nectridia: nectridians   (Carboniferous – Permian)
      ○ Subclass: Lissamphibia: lissamphibians (Triassic – Recent)
        ○ Order: Urodela: salamanders (Jurassic – Recent)

○ Order: Anura: frogs (Triassic – Recent)

■ Order: Apoda: caecilians (Recent)

○ Subclass: uncertain

  ○ Microsauria: microsaurs (Carboniferous – Permian)

● Class: Reptilia: reptiles (Carboniferous – Recent)

  ● Subclass: Anapsida: anapsids (Carboniferous – Recent)

    ■ Order: Captorhinomorpha: captorhinomorphs (Carboniferous – Triassic)

    ◇ Order: Mesosauria: mesosaurs (Permian)

    ● Order: Testudinata: turtles (Triassic – Recent)

  ■ Subclass: Synapsida: synapsids (Carboniferous – Jurassic)

    ■ Order: Pelycosauria: pelycosaurs (Carboniferous – Permian)

    ■ Order: Therapsida: therapsids (Permian – Jurassic)

  ● Subclass: Archosauria: archosaurs (Permian – Recent)

    ■ Order: Thecodontia: thecodonts (Permian – Triassic)

    ● Order: Crocodilia: crocodiles (Triassic – Recent)

    ■ Order: Ornithischia: bird-hipped dinosaurs (Triassic – Cretaceous)

    ■ Order: Saurischia: lizard-hipped dinosaurs (Triassic – Cretaceous)

    ○ Order: Phytosauria: phytosaurs (Triassic)

    ■ Order: Pterosauria: pterosaurs (Triassic – Cretaceous)

  ● Subclass: Lepidosauria: lepidosaurs (Permian – Recent)

    ■ Order: Eosuchia: eosuchians (Permian – Recent)

    ○ Order: Choristodera: champsosaurs (Triassic – Eocene)

    ■ Order: Rhynchosauria: rhynchosaurs (Triassic)

    ● Order: Squamata: snakes and lizards (Triassic –Recent)

  ◆ Subclass: Euryapsida: euryapsids (Permian – Cretaceous)

    ◆ Order: Ichthyosauria: ichthyosaurs (Triassic – Cretaceous)

    ◆ Order: Nothosauria: nothosaurs (Permian – Triassic)

    ◆ Order: Plesiosauria: Plesiosaurs (Triassic – Cretaceous)

    ◆ Order: Placodonta: placodonts (Triassic)

● Class: Aves: birds (Jurassic – Recent)

    ■ Order: Archaeopterygiformes: archaeopterygiforms (Late Jurassic)

    ■ Order: Ambiortiformes: ambiortiforms (Cretaceous)

    ◆ Order: Hesperornithiformes: hesperornithiforms (Cretaceous)

- ◆ Order: Ichthyornithiformes: ichthyornithiforms (Cretaceous)
- ■ Order: Gobipterygiformes: gobipterygiforms (Cretaceous)
- ■ Order: Alexornithiformes: alexornithiforms (Cretaceous)
- ■ Order: Tinamiformes: tinamous (Pliocene – Recent)
- ■ Order: Struthioniformes: ostriches (Miocene – Recent)
- ■ Order: Rheiformes: rheas (?Miocene, Pliocene – Recent)
- ■ Order: Aepyornithiformes: elephant birds (Pleistocene)
- ■ Order: Dinornithiformes: moas (Pliocene – Recent)
- ■ Order: Apterygiformes: kiwis (Pleistocene – Recent)
- ■ Order: Dromornithiformes: mihirungs (Miocene – Pleistocene)
- ■ Order: Galliformes: fowl-like birds (Eocene – Recent)
- ■ Order: Cuculiformes: cuckoos (Paleocene – Recent)
- ■ Order: Columbiformes: pigeons (?Eocene, Oligocene – Recent)
- ■ Order: Psittaciformes: parrots (Eocene – Recent)
- ■ Order: Coliiformes: colies (Miocene – Recent)
- ■ Order: Coraciiformes: rollers, kingfishers, etc. (?Cretaceous, Eocene – Recent)
- ■ Order: Strigiformes: owls (Paleocene – Recent)
- ■ Order: Caprimulgiformes: nightjars, etc. (Eocene – Recent)
- ■ Order: Apodiformes: swifts (Eocene – Recent)
- ■ Order: Piciformes: woodpeckers and related forms (Miocene – Recent)
- ■ Order: Passeriformes: songbirds (?Oligocene, Miocene – Recent)
- ■ Order: Accipitriformes: birds of prey (Eocene – Recent)
- ■ Order: Gruiformes: cranes, rails, and related forms (Tertiary – Recent)
- ○ Order: Podicipediformes: grebes (Miocene – Recent)
- ■ Order: Diatrymiformes: diatrymiforms (Paleocene – Eocene)
- ○ Order: Charadriiformes: wading birds (Cretaceous – Recent)
    - ◆ Family: Phoenicopteridae (Eocene – Recent)
- ● Order: Anseriformes: ducks, geese, swans (Eocene – Recent)
- ○ Order: Ciconiiformes: herons and allies (Eocene – Recent)

● Order: Pelecaniformes: pelicans and related forms (Eocene – Recent)

◆ Family: Pelagornithidae: pseudodontorns, or
"false-toothed" birds (Eocene – Miocene, ?Pliocene)

◆ Family: Plotopteridae: plotopterids (Oligocene –
Miocene)

◆ Order: Procellariiformes: petrels and related forms
(Miocene – Recent)

◇ Order: Gaviiformes: loons (Eocene – Recent)

◆ Order: Sphenisciformes: penguins (Eocene – Recent)

● Class: Mammalia: mammals (Triassic – Recent)

■ Subclass: Prototheria: prototheres (Triassic – Recent)

■ Order: Triconodonta: triconodonts (Triassic – Cretaceous)

■ Order: Docodonta: docodonts (Jurassic)

■ Order: Multituberculata: multituberculates (Jurassic –
Oligocene)

■ Order: Monotremata: monotremes (Cretaceous – Recent)

● Subclass: Theria: therians (Triassic – Recent)

■ Infraclass: Trituberculata: trituberculates (Triassic – Cretaceous)

■ Order: Symmetrodonta: symmetrodonts (Triassic – Cretaceous)

■ Order: Pantotheria: pantotheres (Jurassic – Cretaceous)

■ Order: Shuotheridia: shuotheres (Jurassic)

■ Infraclass: Metatheria: marsupials (Cretaceous – Recent)

■ Order: Didelphiformes: opossums and relatives (Cretaceous – Recent)

■ Order: Paucituberculata: paucituberculates (Paleocene – Recent)

■ Order: Dasyuroidea: marsupial carnivores, native cats
(Oligocene – Recent)

■ Order: Peramelina: bandicoots (Miocene – Recent)

■ Order: Diprotodonta: diprotodontans—kangaroos,
wombats, possums, etc. (Oligocene – Recent)

● Infraclass: Eutheria: placentals (Cretaceous – Recent)

■ Order: Edentata: edentates (Paleocene – Recent)

■ Order: Macroscelidea: golden moles (Oligocene – Recent)

■ Order: Lagomorpha: rabbits (Eocene – Recent)

■ Order: Cimolesta: cimolestans (Cretaceous – Miocene)

- Order: Creodonta: creodonts (Paleocene – Miocene)
- Order: Carnivora: carnivores (Paleocene – Recent)
- Order: Lipotyphla: lipotyphlans (Paleocene – Recent)
- Order: Dermoptera: flying lemurs (Paleocene – Recent)
- Order: Chiroptera: bats (Eocene – Recent)
- Order: Primates: primates (Cretaceous – Recent)
- Order: Arctocyonia: arctocyonids (Paleocene)
- Order: Tillodontia: tillodonts (Eocene)
- Order: Taeniodontia: taeniodonts (Paleocene – Eocene)
- Order: Tubulidentata: anteaters (Miocene – Recent)
- Order: Dinocerata: uintatheres (Paleocene – Eocene)
- Order: Pantodonta: Pantodonts (Paleocene – Eocene)
- Order: Embrithopoda: arsinoitheres (Oligocene)
- Order: Artiodactyla: artiodactyls (Eocene – Recent)
- ◆ Order: Cetacea: whales (Eocene – Recent)
- Order: Litopterna: litopterns (Paleocene – Pleistocene)
- Order: Notoungulata: notoungulates (Paleocene – Pleistocene)
- Order: Astrapotheria: astrapotheres (Eocene – Miocene)
- Order: Trigonostylopoidea: trigonostylopoids (Paleocene – Eocene)
- Order: Xenungulata: xenungulates (Paleocene)
- Order: Pyrotheria: pyrotheres (Eocene – Oligocene)
- Order: Condylarthra: condylarths (Paleocene – Miocene)
- Order: Perissodactyla: horses, tapirs, and rhinos (Eocene – Recent)
- Order: Hyracoidea: hyrax (Oligocene – Recent)
- Order: Proboscidea: elephants (Eocene – Recent)
- Order: Sirenia: sea cows (Eocene – Recent)
- ◆ Order: Desmostylia: desmostylians (Miocene)
- Order: Pholidota: pangolins (Eocene – Recent)
- Order: Rodentia: rodents (Eocene – Recent)

APPENDIX 3

Identification Key

Sometimes it is difficult to know where to begin when identifying a fossil. The three keys on pages 708–10 offer some help in solving this problem. The key is based on overall shape of the fossil, which generally falls into three basic types: radial, bilateral (one side is a mirror image of the other), or no apparent symmetry.

SYMMETRY

I RADIAL

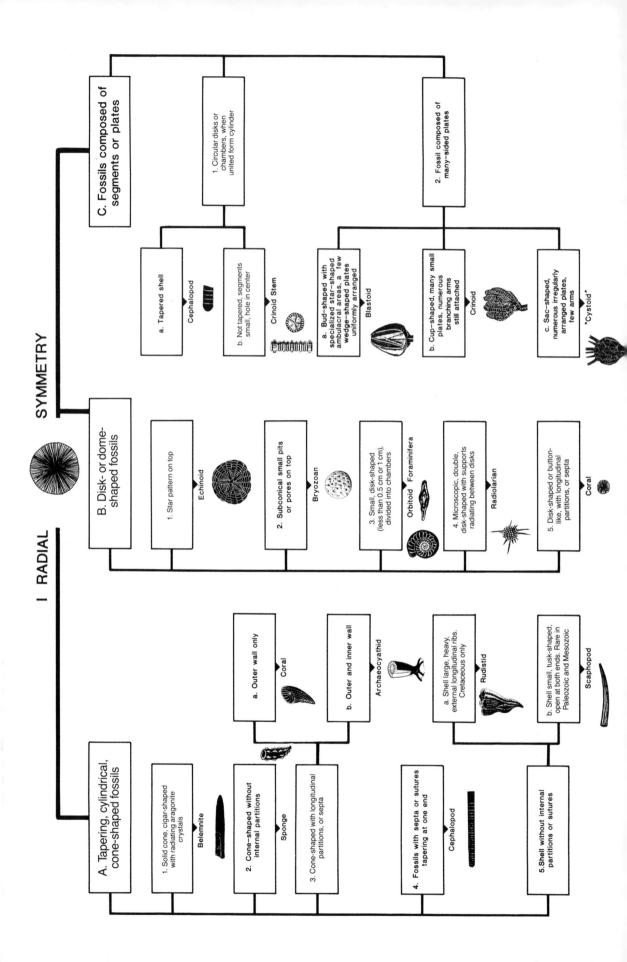

A. Tapering, cylindrical, cone-shaped fossils

1. Solid cone, cigar-shaped with radiating aragonite crystals — **Belemnite**

2. Cone-shaped without internal partitions
   - a. Outer wall only — **Coral**
   - b. Outer and inner wall — **Archaeocyathid**

3. Cone-shaped with longitudinal partitions, or septa — **Sponge**

4. Fossils with septa or sutures tapering at one end — **Cephalopod**
   - a. Shell large, heavy, external longitudinal ribs. Cretaceous only — **Rudistid**
   - b. Shell small, tusk-shaped, open at both ends. Rare in Paleozoic and Mesozoic — **Scaphopod**

5. Shell without internal partitions or sutures

B. Disk- or dome-shaped fossils

1. Star pattern on top — **Echinoid**

2. Subconical small pits or pores on top — **Bryozoan**

3. Small, disk-shaped (less than 0.5 cm or 1 cm), divided into chambers — **Orbitoid Foraminifera**

4. Microscopic, double, disk-shaped with supports radiating between disks — **Radiolarian**

5. Disk-shaped or button-like, with longitudinal partitions, or septa — **Coral**

C. Fossils composed of segments or plates

1. Circular disks or chambers, when united form cylinder
   - a. Tapered shell — **Cephalopod**
   - b. Not tapered, segments small, hole in center — **Crinoid Stem**

2. Fossil composed of many-sided plates
   - a. Bud-shaped with specialized star-shaped ambulacral areas, a few wedge-shaped plates uniformly arranged — **Blastoid**
   - b. Cup-shaped, many small plates, numerous branching arms still attached — **Crinoid**
   - c. Sac-shaped, numerous irregularly arranged plates, few arms — **"Cystoid"**

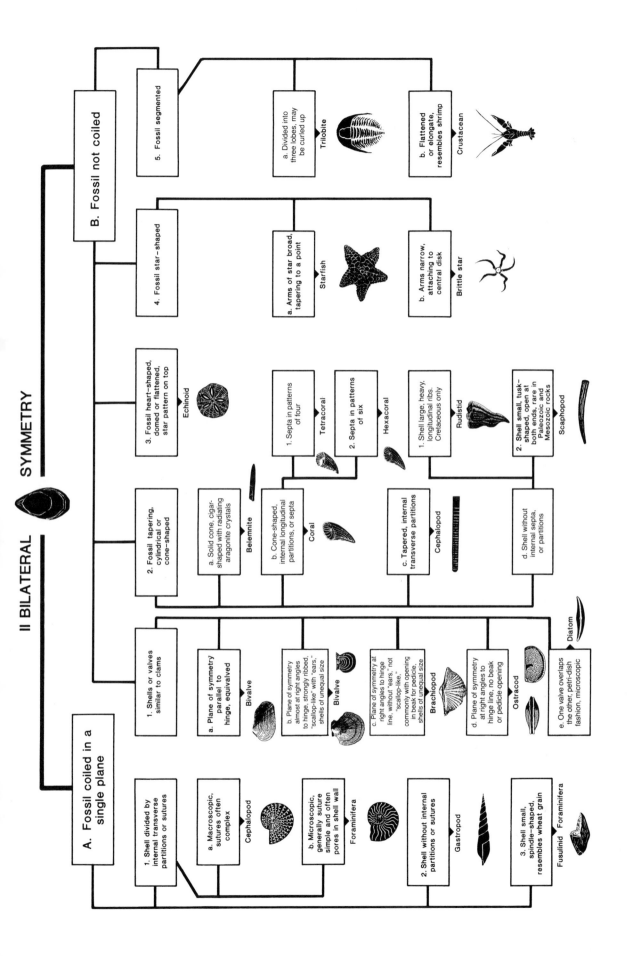

SYMMETRY

II BILATERAL

A. Fossil coiled in a single plane

1. Shell divided by internal transverse partitions or sutures

   a. Macroscopic, sutures often complex — **Cephalopod**

   b. Microscopic, generally suture simple and often pores in shell wall — **Foraminifera**

2. Shell without internal partitions or sutures — **Gastropod**

3. Shell small, spindle-shaped, resembles wheat grain — **Fusulinid Foraminifera**

B. Fossil not coiled

1. Shells or valves similar to clams

   a. Plane of symmetry parallel to hinge, equivalved — **Bivalve**

   b. Plane of symmetry almost at right angles to hinge, strongly ribbed, "scallop-like" with "ears," shells of unequal size — **Bivalve**

   c. Plane of symmetry at right angles to hinge line, without "ears," not "scallop-like," commonly with opening in beak for pedicle, shells of unequal size — **Brachiopod**

   d. Plane of symmetry at right angles to hinge line, no beak or pedicle opening — **Ostracod**

   e. One valve overlaps the other, petri-dish fashion, microscopic — **Diatom**

2. Fossil tapering, cylindrical or cone-shaped

   a. Solid cone, cigar-shaped with radiating aragonite crystals — **Belemnite**

   b. Cone-shaped, internal longitudinal partitions, or septa — **Coral**

      1. Septa in patterns of four — **Tetracoral**

      2. Septa in patterns of six — **Hexacoral**

   c. Tapered, internal transverse partitions — **Cephalopod**

      1. Shell large, heavy, longitudinal ribs. Cretaceous only — **Rudistid**

      2. Shell small, tusk-shaped, open at both ends, rare in Paleozoic and Mesozoic rocks — **Scaphopod**

   d. Shell without internal septa, or partitions

3. Fossil heart-shaped, domed or flattened, star pattern on top — **Echinoid**

4. Fossil star-shaped

   a. Arms of star broad, tapering to a point — **Starfish**

   b. Arms narrow, attaching to central disk — **Brittle star**

5. Fossil segmented

   a. Divided into three lobes, may be curled up — **Trilobite**

   b. Flattened or elongate, resembles shrimp — **Crustacean**

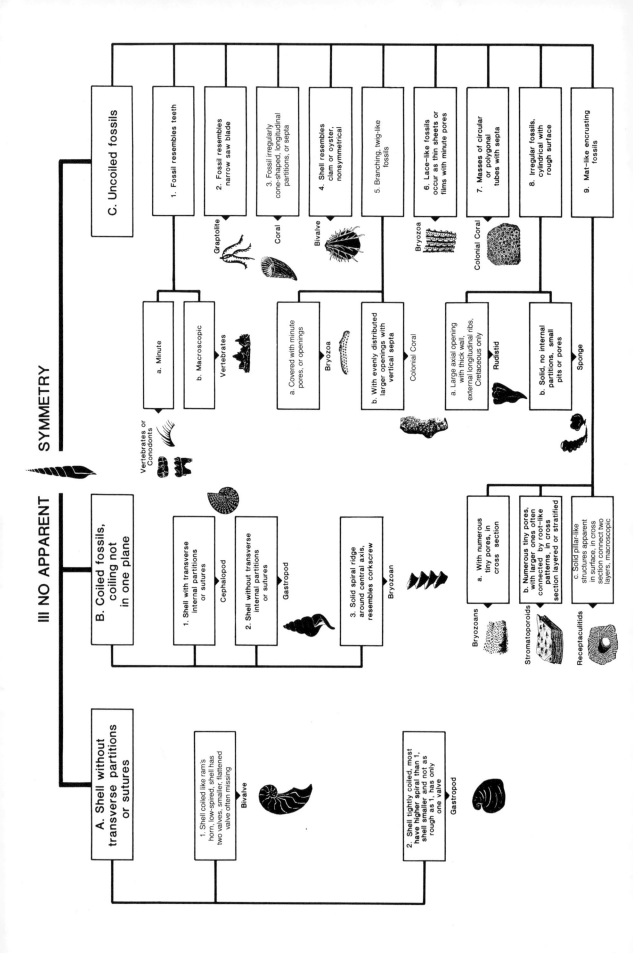

III NO APPARENT SYMMETRY

A. Shell without transverse partitions or sutures

1. Shell coiled like ram's horn, low-spired, shell has two valves, smaller, flattened valve often missing

Bivalve

2. Shell tightly coiled, most have higher spiral than 1, shell smaller and not as rough as 1, has only one valve

Gastropod

B. Coiled fossils, coiling not in one plane

1. Shell with transverse internal partitions or sutures

Cephalopod

2. Shell without transverse internal partitions or sutures

Gastropod

3. Solid spiral ridge around central axis, resembles corkscrew

Bryozoan

a. With numerous tiny pores, in cross section

Bryozoans

b. Numerous tiny pores, with larger ones often connected by root-like patterns, in cross section layered or stratified

Stromatoporoids

c. Solid pillar-like structures apparent in surface, in cross section connect two layers, macroscopic

Receptaculitids

C. Uncoiled fossils

1. Fossil resembles teeth

a. Minute

b. Macroscopic

Vertebrates

Vertebrates or Conodonts

2. Fossil resembles narrow saw blade

Graptolite

3. Fossil irregularly cone-shaped, longitudinal partitions, or septa

Coral

4. Shell resembles clam or oyster, nonsymmetrical

Bivalve

5. Branching, twig-like fossils

a. Covered with minute pores, or openings

Bryozoa

b. With evenly distributed larger openings with vertical septa

Colonial Coral

6. Lace-like fossils occur as thin sheets or films with minute pores

Bryozoa

7. Masses of circular or polygonal tubes with septa

Colonial Coral

8. Irregular fossils, cylindrical with rough surface

a. Large axial opening with thick wall, external longitudinal ribs, Cretaceous only

Rudistid

b. Solid, no internal partitions, small pits or pores

Sponge

9. Mat-like encrusting fossils

APPENDIX 4

Glossary

This glossary includes terms that are repeatedly used but, with a few exceptions, are not the names of groups. The latter can be found in Appendix 2, and terms that apply to limited groups of organisms may be found by means of the Index. The plurals of a few words are given in parentheses.

Abdomen. In arthropods, the main division of the body behind the thorax; in crayfish and lobsters, it is often miscalled the tail. The mammalian abdomen lies behind the diaphragm and contains the liver, stomach, and intestines.

Abdominal ribs. Bony supports developed in the flesh that encloses the thorax and abdomen, especially of reptiles.

Adaptation. Any structure or function, including instinct, that fits an organism to its surroundings and way of living.

Agnaths. Jawless vertebrates that do not have true paired limbs.

Ambulacral areas. Double rows of ambulacral plates found in echinoids. Some ambulacral areas are narrow and almost straight; others are petal-shaped.

Ambulacrum (ambulacra). A radial band of porous plates in the test, or shell, of echinoderms. During life, the ambulacra contain tube feet. In crinoids and other relatively primitive echinoderms, the ambulacra are grooves along which cilia take food to the mouth.

Antenna. A sensory organ extending from the head, especially in arthropods. It is not concerned with sight or the perception of light.

Appendage. A movable, projecting part of the animal body—leg, antenna, and so on.

Archosaurs. The group of reptiles that includes thecodonts, crocodilians, flying reptiles, and dinosaurs.

Artiodactyls. Hoofed mammals that typically have two or four toes on each foot. The first toe is almost always absent.

Asexual reproduction. Reproduction by budding or any other method that does not depend on the union of male and female cells.

Auricle. The outer part of the ear in mammals; also any earlike projection, even on shells.

Beak. The rounded or pointed extremity of a pelecypod or brachiopod shell, at which it began to grow. Horny growth on the jaws of birds and some reptiles. The horny jaws of cephalopods also are sometimes called beaks.

Body cavity. The open space between the body wall and the internal organs of an animal. It is lined with mesoderm and is often called the coelom.

Bone. One of the parts in the vertebrate skeleton. Also a hard material containing irregular, branched cells and relatively large blood vessels.

Brachia. The organs of a brachiopod that bear cilia, which set up currents of water that carry food to the mouth. In brachiopods, same as lophophore.

Brachial valve. In brachiopods, the valve to which the brachia, or lophophore, is attached. Also called the dorsal valve.

Braincase. A boxlike structure of cartilage or bone that encloses the brain and is attached to the backbone. It forms the essential part of the skull.

Byssus. A cluster of threads that some pelecypods (bivalves) secrete, attaching themselves to other shells or to rocks.

Calcite. Limy material that is found in corals, shells, etc. It can be grooved with a knife and bubbles when weak acid is dropped on it. Calcite also forms beds of limestone.

Calyx. The depression, or cup, at the top of a coral skeleton. Also the structure of plates enclosing the body of a crinoid or similar echinoderm.

Canine teeth. Teeth between the incisors and premolars of mammals. The canines generally are sharp and may be very long.

Carapace. The hard shell that covers the head and part or all of the abdominal region of an arthropod. Also the bony shell of a tortoise, turtle, or glyptodont.

Carbonization. A process of incomplete decay that destroys volatile substances but leaves carbon. Carbonization has been especially important in the preservation of ancient plants.

Cardinal area. A flat or curved surface between the beak and hinge line of a pelecypod or brachiopod. The cardinal area of brachiopods is also termed the interarea.

Cartilage. Relatively soft, translucent material containing rounded cells; it is found in the vertebrate skeleton. Cartilage may be strengthened by limy material, or it may be replaced by bone.

Cell. A small lump or mass of living material; one of the units of which living things are composed.

Cell wall. A covering, generally hard or woody, which a cell forms around itself. Wood is made up of cell walls.

Cement. A layer of bony material that covers the roots and often the crowns of teeth. Most conspicuous in the teeth of horses and proboscideans.

Cephalothorax. A body division that combines head and thorax. Best seen in arthropods (crustaceans, merostomes, arachnids).

Character. Any distinguishing feature or trait of an organism. Most characters are inherited, but some are determined by environmental factors such as foods, temperature, or chemicals in water.

Cheek teeth. The molars and premolars.

Chelicerae. The first, or front, pair of appendages in spiders eurypterids, etc.; one is a chelicera. These organs generally are used to cut or tear food.

Chitin. Stiff material forming the outer skeletons of arthropods and some other animals. There are many types of chitin, which differ in chemical composition.

Chordate. Any animal that has a notochord at some stage in its life history. Many books put all chordates in one phylum.

Cilia. Soft, hairlike structures developed by many cells. They are shorter and more numerous than flagella.

Coelom. Same as body cavity.

Colonial. Living together. Most colonial organisms build up complex exoskeletons that support many individuals.

Column. The jointed stalklike structure to which the bodies of crinoids and many other echinoderms are attached. Each section of a column is a columnal.

Condyle. An enlarged, rounded surface of bone forming part of a movable joint; especially the occipital condyle.

Conifers. Cone-bearing shrubs and trees that produce sexual cells, not spores. The leaves generally are needles or scales. Lycopods have cones but bear spores.

Corallite. The skeleton built up by one coral animal, or polyp, whether solitary or part of a colony.

Correlation. In geology, the process of linking beds and formations of similar age.

Costa (costae). A ridge on the surface of a coral or shell. The costae of shells are radial ridges produced by thickening.

Craniate. An animal with a braincase of bone or cartilage. Same as vertebrate.

Cranium. Same as braincase. This term is also used for the whole skull.

Cycads. Palmlike trees and shrubs that became very abundant during the Mesozoic Era. The modern sago "palm" is a cycad.

Dentary. A tooth-bearing bone that forms the whole lower jaw of mammals.

Diaphragm. A membrane, especially the muscular one that divides the thoracic and abdominal regions of mammals.

Dolomite. A rock resembling limestone but consisting largely of another mineral less readily attacked by acids. Many stromatolite deposits are dolomite.

Dorsal valve. The brachial valve of a brachiopod.

Ectoderm. The outer body-layer of animals.

Egg. The female sex cell. It often contains a supply of food for the organism that is to develop.

Embryo. A newly forming organism. The embryo exists before hatching or birth, at which time the organism becomes a juvenile.

Enamel. Dense material covering the scales of some fish and the teeth of vertebrates in general. It is the hardest substance produced by animal bodies.

Endoderm. The inner body layer of animals.

Environment. The surroundings of any organism, including other living things.

Exoskeleton. An outer skeleton; an external structure that supports the body. Commonly called a shell.

Femur. The upper bone of the hind limb or leg. Commonly called the thighbone.

Finfold. A lengthwise fold of skin which, in theory, divided into fins.

Flagellum. A long lashlike or threadlike extension of a cell, able to beat to and fro.

Flora. The group of plants living in one region or at a particular time. Thus we speak of the John Day flora, or the flora of the Painted Desert in Triassic times.

Foramen. An opening through a bone or shell. A round opening at or near the beak of a brachiopod, accommodating the pedicle. Other types of openings have other names.

Formation. A series of beds that are essentially uniform in character and formed during a limited part of geologic times.

Fossils. In everyday terms, "prehistoric" organisms. Technically, the remains or traces of organisms that lived during ancient geologic times and were buried in rocks of the earth's crust.

Ganglion. A group or cluster of nerve cells that acts as a center of nervous influence.

Ganoine. Enamellike material on the scales of fish. Ganoid scales have thick layers of ganoine forming their outer surface.

Gastrolith. A stone swallowed by a bird or reptile and used to help grind food in the stomach. Popularly called gizzard stone.

Genus (genera). A group of related species.

Gills. Organs for breathing in water. They developed in various ways in the various phyla of animals.

Grinding teeth. Broad, rough-crowned molars and premolars adapted to grinding food.

Habitat. The kind of place in which an organism lives. Swamps were the habitat of large herbivorous dinosaurs.

Hinge line. The edge of any bivalve shell along which its two parts are held together.

Humerus. The upper bone of the forelimb, often called the upper arm bone.

Ice Age. When capitalized, this term refers to the last, or Quaternary , glacial period. It involved several glacial advances and retreats in the Northern Hemisphere. There were several earlier ice ages.

Igneous rocks. Rocks that once were hot and molten. Some cooled and hardened underground, others at the earth's surface. Few contain fossils.

Ilium. The uppermost of the three bones on each side of the pelvic girdle.

Incisors. Teeth at the front of the mammalian jaw. They generally are adapted to biting, but those of elephants are tusks.

Index fossil. A fossil that indicates the geologic age of the rocks in which it is found.

Instinct. An inherited pattern of action. Nest building and digging are instincts.

Interarea. See cardinal area.

Invertebrate. An animal without a skull or braincase. The term is generally applied to any creature that lacks a backbone.

Ischium. The dorsal and posterior of the three bones on each side of the pelvic girdle.

Jaw. One of the structures forming the framework of the mouth in vertebrates, or a similar structure among invertebrates. Vertebrate paleontologists often use the term for one half of the lower jaw. Each half consists of one or several bones and is joined to its counterpart at the midline.

Laminae. Thin layers of solid material—bone, enamel, or sediment.

Larva. An early stage of an animal, between embryo and adult or fully formed juvenile. Larvae generally move about freely and feed but differ anatomically from adults.

Ligament. A band or sheet of compact tissue that fastens one vertebrate structure to another. Ligaments that bound the vertebrae of bird-hipped dinosaurs together were often stiffened with limy material and are found in fossils.

Lophophore. A ring or similar structure bearing tentacles and cilia. See brachia.

Mantle. In brachiopods and molluscs, a sheet of flesh that secretes the shell.

Mesoderm. The middle body layer in animals. It becomes thicker than the other layers, forming muscles, bones, and other organs.

Metamorphic rocks. Rocks that have been greatly modified by heat, pressure, and water, or all three in combination. Seldom contain fossils.

Metamorphosis. A pronounced change in form from one growth stage to another, as the metamorphosis of a soft larval mollusc into one with a shell.

Micropaleontology. The study of microscopic fossils, especially Foraminifera.

Molars. The rear teeth of mammals. Most molars are adapted to grinding or crushing.

Muscle. An organ made up of fibers that contract and produce movements. The muscles of most fossils are traced by impressions made upon bones or shells.

Muzzle. The projecting jaws and nose of an animal, especially a mammal.

Naris (nares). An opening in the skull that contains one or both nostrils. The external nares are at the surface; the internal nares are in the hard palate.

Nostrils. Openings in the top of the head, the muzzle, or the nose. In most fish they let water into the organs of smell, but in some fish and in higher vertebrates they are used in breathing. See naris.

Notochord. An elastic, rodlike structure running lengthwise of the body and supporting it. Found in at least the embryonic stage of all animal phyla that are sometimes grouped together as chordates.

Nucleus (nuclei). A special structure within the cell of all organisms except monerans. It seems to control the life of the cell and determines heredity.

Occipital condyle. The rounded knob of bone by which the skull is attached to the first vertebra.

Orbit. The bony socket of the eye.

Organ. A group of cells or tissues that function as a unit—the eye, heart, etc.

Organism. A living thing; one cell or a complex of many cells that exist and function as one complete unit.

Palate. In fossils, the bony roof of the mouth.

Pectoral. Pertaining to the anterior or upper thoracic region, as the pectoral fins of a fish.

Pelvis. The bony girdle to which the hind limbs are attached. Often called the hip girdle.

Perissodactyls. Hoofed mammals that have an odd number of toes on the hind feet and generally on the forefeet.

Pineal body. A small, conical organ above or between the opposite halves of the brain. Some pineal bodies apparently served as crude eyes.

Placenta. A soft organ that develops in the uterus of most mammals. In it the mothers blood comes so close to that of the young that food and wastes can be exchanged.

Plication. A small fold or corrugation that affects the whole shell and is not a thickening of it. Contrast with costa.

Polyp. A soft-bodied animal, especially a hydroid, coral, or sea anemone.

Precambrian. Before the Cambrian Period, or older than the Cambrian system of formations.

Premolars. Teeth between the canines and molars of mammals. Premolars may be adapted to grinding, shearing, or crushing.

Protoplasm. Living material; the semifluid material of cells.

Pseudopod. An extension of the cell's protoplasm, used in moving or feeding.

Pubis, or pubic bone. The anterior of the three bones in each side of the pelvic girdle. In "bird-hipped" dinosaurs, the pubis also has a long backward projection or becomes almost vestigial.

Radula. A rasplike organ, or "tongue," in the mouth of a snail.

Reflex. An automatic action in response to some stimulus.

Sclerotic plates. Bony plates in the eyes of certain reptiles and birds. The plates in each eye form a ring.

Scute. A thin plate or large scale.

Sedimentary rocks. Rocks formed of sand, mud, and other materials that settled in layers or beds. Often called "stratified rocks." Most fossils are found in sedimentary rocks.

Segment. A part of the body that is marked off or separated from other parts, especially if they are in series. Segments of the eurypterid body are good examples.

Septum. A dividing wall or partition between two cavities or structures.

Shell. Any hard covering of an animal body. Shells develop in various ways.

Silica. Glassy material found in many sponges. It also replaces wood, shells, and other material in many petrified fossils.

Siphon. A tubelike organ that takes water into the body or carries it out. Found in molluscs.

Siphuncle. A tube that leads from the living chamber of a cephalopod to the tip of the shell.

Sperms. Male sex cells. Also called spermatozoa.

Spiracle. In blastoids, one of five openings that allow water to flow out of the body. In insects, an opening that lets air into tubes that run through the body. In fish, the first gill slit, modified into a tube. In amphibians, the spiracle becomes the eustachian tube of the ear. This is kept by reptiles, birds, and mammals.

Spore. A special reproductive cell that can develop into a new organism without being fertilized.

Suture. The line along which two hard structures join. Cephalopod sutures are formed where septa meet the cell wall. Sutures between bones of the skull close with age.

Tabula (tabulae). In corals, an almost horizontal plate across the center of the corallite.

Temporal opening. An opening between bones of the skull. Temporal openings determine the classification of reptiles.

Tentacle. An elongate flexible (not jointed) appendage, usually near the mouth. Corals capture food with their tentacles.

Test. A hard covering or supporting structure; a shell.

Thorax. The main division of the body behind the head. In amphibians and most higher animals, it is the part enclosed by ribs.

Tuff. A rock formed of cemented volcanic dust and ash.

Tusk. A long pointed tooth that protrudes from the mouth. A boar's tusk is a long canine; the elephant's tusk is an incisor.

Umbo. The strongly convex part of a brachiopod or pelecypod shell, next to the beak.

Valve. One half of a bivalve shell, either brachiopod or molluscan. Also any fleshy structure that closes or partly closes an opening.

Ventral valve (of a brachiopod). Same as pedicle valve.

Vertebra. One of the bones or sets of bones forming the vertebral column, or backbone.

Vestigial organ or structure. One that has been greatly reduced during the course of evolution. The side toes of horses became vestigial.

Index